INTRODUCTION TO
Social Problems

ABOUT THE AUTHOR

Thomas J. Sullivan earned his Ph.D. at the University of California at Santa Barbara. He is Professor of Sociology at Northern Michigan University, specializing in social psychology, applied sociology, research methods, and medical sociology. He is the author of *Sociology: Concepts and Applications in a Diverse World* 3d ed. (Allyn and Bacon, 1995) and *Applied Sociology: Research and Critical Thinking* (Allyn and Bacon, 1992); he is the co-author of *Applied Social Research: Tool for the Human Services,* 3d ed. (Harcourt Brace, 1994). He has published articles in *Social Science and Medicine* and *Humboldt Journal of Social Relations.* He has served in various committee positions for the American Sociological Association, the Society for Applied Sociology, and the Midwest Sociological Society. He holds an elected position on the Council of the Section on Sociological Practice of the American Sociological Association.

INTRODUCTION TO
Social Problems

F O U R T H   E D I T I O N

Thomas J. Sullivan
NORTHERN MICHIGAN UNIVERSITY

ALLYN AND BACON

Boston ■ London ■ Toronto ■ Sydney ■ Tokyo ■ Singapore

Editor-in-Chief, Social Sciences: Karen Hanson
Editorial Assistant: Jennifer Jacobson
Marketing Manager: Karon Bowers
Composition and Prepress Buyer: Linda Cox
Manufacturing Buyer: Megan Cochran
Cover Administrator: Linda Knowles
Cover Designer: Studio Nine
Photo Researcher: Laurie Frankenthaler
Production Administrator: Deborah Brown
Text Designer: Melinda Grosser for *Silk*
Editorial-Production Service: P. M. Gordon Associates

Library of Congress Cataloging-in-Publication Data

Sullivan, Thomas J., 1944–
    Introduction to social problems / Thomas J. Sullivan.—4th ed.
      p.   cm.
    Includes bibliographical references and indexes.
    ISBN 0-205-19148-7
    1. Social problems.   2. United States—Social conditions.
  3. United States—Social policy.   I. Title.
  HN28.S92 1996   96-21523
  361.1—dc20   CIP

Printed in the United States of America
10 9 8 7 6 5 4 3 2 1   01 00 99 98 97 96

FOR NANCY

CONTENTS

CHAPTER THREE

Family-Related Problems   78

CHAPTER FOUR

Health and Illness   118

CHAPTER FIVE

CHAPTER SIX

CHAPTER SEVEN

Gender and Social Inequality   240

CHAPTER EIGHT

Age and Social Inequality   278

CHAPTER ELEVEN

Sexual Behavior   394

CHAPTER TWELVE

Population Growth and Urbanization   432

CHAPTER THIRTEEN

Environmental Problems   472

CHAPTER FOURTEEN

*Violence, War,
and Terrorism*   508

CHAPTER FIFTEEN

Emerging Issues: Science and Technology   546

PREFACE

As the twentieth century draws to a close, the study of social problems continues to be one of the most demanding, exciting, and fast paced fields in sociology and the other social sciences—in part because the world changes so fast. Old problems evolve and new ones are continually emerging. To name just a few examples, some significant advances have been made on environmental issues, such as substantial reductions in the amount of lead released into the atmosphere; at the same time, evidence is growing that global warming is a problem produced by human activities (see Chapter 13). In response to recent changes in the world political scene, the world economy continues to change, with global corporations becoming larger and more concentrated. This has resulted in well-paying jobs in the United States disappearing as employers seek cheaper labor in Mexico, Indonesia, or other third-world nations (see Chapter 2). Terrorism continues to stalk the globe, with Arab terrorists killing civilians in Israel and terrorists in the United States bombing a federal office building in Oklahoma City (see Chapter 14). The scourge of drugs continues to exacerbate health and crime problems, despite millions of dollars spent on the "War on Drugs" (see Chapter 10).

I could mention many other examples, but the point is that much has changed in the world in the past few years—some changes, thankfully, have been for the good, but too many changes have intensified the social problems that confront the United States and the world. This fourth edition incorporates these and other developments to provide students with the most current assessment of social problems and their solutions.

Sociology and the other social sciences provide a set of unique and important tools in the analysis of social problems. In particular, they use scientific research to assess the nature and extent of social problems and the effectiveness of solutions to them. Just as society has changed, the social sciences have also changed in the past two decades: With their theoretical foundations solidly established, they have begun to develop in a more applied direction. Increasingly, social scientists have shaped their research tools toward evaluating solutions to social problems rather than limiting their focus to understanding the nature of those problems. Now social research often focuses on questions such as: Does it work? Who benefits? What are the negative consequences of the program? Is there a way that we can achieve the same gain for less expense? In fact, over the past few decades, the study of social problems has become, in my view, one of the most exciting and innovative wings of the social sciences because it involves the application of social science research and knowledge to the solutions of some of the most difficult, agonizing, and controversial problems confronting the United States and the world today.

Organization

Many serious social problems confront the United States and the world, too many to cover in a single book. From among these social issues I have chosen to discuss problems that are particularly serious, affect many people, and expose students to a broad array of concerns in varied sectors of life in the United States. By studying these problems, students will gain the tools and the insight that will enable them to analyze other problems and solutions not explicitly covered in this book. Thus, this book is more than a catalog of particular problems and their solutions; it is also a training manual for the study of social problems.

Chapter 1 introduces students to the sociological analysis of social problems, including a discussion of the theoretical perspectives that will be used throughout the book and of the importance of the scientific approach and applied research in the analysis of social problems and their solutions. Chapters 2–4 cover social problems that relate directly to some of the major social institutions in society: government, the economy, the family, and health care systems. Chapters 5–8 focus on problems that are linked by the common theme of social inequality: poverty, racial and ethnic discrimination, and inequality based on gender and age. Chapters 9–11 analyze problems surrounding behavior that some people consider unconventional or deviant: crime and delinquency, alcohol and drug abuse, and some forms of sexual behavior. Finally, Chapters 12–15 focus on problems involving changes or disruptions in the physical and social world: urban problems, population growth, environmental pollution, violence and war, and new developments in science and technology.

Features

To reflect the trends of the past few decades, this book includes a number of creative elements:

1. *Policy Issues inserts:* An important theme of this book is that finding solutions to social problems is a political process in which groups differ with one another over which solutions are preferred. One's choice of solutions is influenced in part by one's cultural and subcultural values. Therefore, every chapter includes inserts titled "Policy Issues" in which contemporary debates on social policy related to that problem are discussed.

2. *Applied Research inserts:* Another theme in this book is that the application of social science research is central to solving problems and evaluating how well solutions work. Therefore, I have included inserts titled "Applied Research" that illustrate how and why this is the case. In this way, I emphasize the point that the choice of solutions to problems, although shaped by personal values and the public policy debate, should be constrained by the assessment of those solutions through systematic and scientific observation. In other words, the choice of solutions to problems should involve an interplay between human values and social research.

3. *Laissez-Faire versus Interventionist Debate:* The debate over social policy and social problems is centered in part on the role of the government in such issues. This debate is incorporated into the text in the form of two opposing positions. The laissez-faire stance posits that the government is, in most cases, either inefficient at finding or unable to find such solutions and should stand aside and let private enterprise and impersonal economic forces produce solutions. The interventionist position gives the government prime, although not sole, responsibility for finding and initiating solutions to problems. This debate is addressed periodically in the text where it is relevant.

4. *Myth versus Fact:* To emphasize further the role of research in understanding social problems, I point out some ways in which people's commonsense beliefs about social problems are proved incorrect by research data. This encourages the student to distinguish beliefs that have no scientific foundation and may be myths from

facts that have been substantiated by observational testing.

5. *Theoretical Perspectives:* I have organized the analysis of social problems and their solutions around the three core theoretical perspectives in sociology: functionalism, conflict theory, and interactionism. These perspectives offer tremendous insight into the sources of problems, the effectiveness of solutions, and the ramifications—both obvious and hidden—of adopting particular solutions. These perspectives are used in every chapter of the book to provide the student with a set of tools to analyze any social problem, including problems not directly discussed in this book.

6. *International Perspectives:* The intent of this feature is to provide students with a more global picture of particular social problems and their solutions. One reason this is important is the growing interdependence among the world's peoples and nations. Another reason is that we can gain insight into problems and their solutions when we observe them in societies and cultures that are different from our own. In addition, some social problems are inherently global rather than national or regional.

7. *Linkages:* To encourage the student to see the interconnections between social problems, a brief insert at the end of each chapter points out how a problem discussed in that chapter is linked to problems discussed in other chapters. This encourages the student to recognize that the worsening of one problem can mean that other, seemingly unconnected, conditions may also deteriorate, and that alleviating one problem can result in improvements in others.

8. *Study and Review:* At the end of each chapter, a new "Study and Review" section has been added to give students an opportunity to test how well they have grasped the material. Each section contains a list of key terms, multiple-choice questions, true-false questions, fill-in questions, matching questions, and essay questions. Correct answers are also provided. These various testing formats offer an assessment of the different kinds of information found in each chapter and will assist students in organizing their study. Students, thereby, will have a good measure of how much they have learned and a comprehensive review of the content in the chapter, as well as help in preparing for exams.

New to the Fourth Edition

Although the book's basic organization remains the same in the fourth edition, it has been thoroughly revised and updated to reflect contemporary developments in sociology as well as new social, political, and economic developments relating to particular social problems. Special attention has been given to ensuring that the data presented on the various social problems is the most current available.

One significant change in organization involves Chapters 12 and 13, and was in response to the suggestions of professors who had used the book. They observed that many issues discussed as a part of urban problems in Chapter 12 are also discussed in other chapters; they also suggested that more attention be devoted to environmental problems in Chapter 13 than was done in the third edition. In response to these suggestions, Chapter 12, which had focused solely on urban problems, now combines urban and population problems. Chapter 13 is now devoted solely to environmental problems, permitting a much more extensive review of these problems.

Four new "International Perspectives" inserts have been added to the text, so that almost all chapters have one such insert. This is supplemented with more in-text discussion of social problems from a global perspective to provide students with a broader perspective on social problems. The "Policy Issues" and "Applied Research" inserts have remained much the same as in the previous edition because, with some updating, they continue to work well. The "For Further Readings" sections at the end of each chapter have also been thoroughly updated with challenging books for the student who wishes to pursue a topic in greater depth. Totally new to this edition are the "Study and Review" sections found at the end of each chapter.

Regarding the text material itself, I have made many revisions throughout that update discussions, present new research, and address issues that have come to prominence or have changed in some fashion since the previous edition was completed. A detailed listing of the revisions in each chapter can be found in the Instructor's Manual that accompanies this book. These revisions are partially reflected by the following:

- More material on global corporations and the global concentration of power, using world systems theory as an explanatory framework (Chapter 2)
- A Policy Issues section on the position of gay families in society and the problems they confront (Chapter 3)
- Expanded discussion of health maintenance organizations (HMOs) and managed care as means of organizing and financing health care (Chapter 4)
- A comparison of the extent of poverty and the concentration of wealth in the United States and in other nations (Chapter 5)
- A discussion of innovative political structures in Switzerland that might encourage multiethnic cooperation (Chapter 6)
- More material on gender inequality and the women's movement around the world (Chapter 7)
- Additional material on the problems that confront children and youth in modern societies and place them at risk of difficulties in social development (Chapter 8)
- A discussion of urban problems with a global perspective as the world economy affects cities in the United States and the Third World (Chapter 12)
- Extensive new material on environmental problems, including the social sources of environmental problems in economic and

social practices and the social construction of environmental problems (Chapter 13)
- New technologies and their effect on the concentration of the global communications network (Chapter 15)

These additions and revisions are called for by world developments in the past few years and will make the fourth edition of *Introduction to Social Problems* an even better vehicle for use with students in the study of social problems.

Acknowledgments

Many people have contributed to the completion of this new edition. Karen Hanson served ably as the editor of this new edition, suggesting timely and sound revisions to make the book even more valuable to students. I am especially thankful for the research assistance that I received from some students at Northern Michigan University, especially Jason Maki, who made some very positive contributions to the book. I also received some excellent advice and assistance from a number of colleagues: Carole A. Campbell, California State University, Long Beach; Chris Girard, Florida International University; George R. Gross, Northern Michigan University; Gary Hodge, Collin County Community College; Christine Johnson, Quinsigamond Community College; Kirk A. Johnson, Washburn University; Anthony W. Zumpetta, West Chester University.

Of all the people who have had an impact on this work, the students in my various classes have probably been most significant. They have questioned and challenged me, agreed and disagreed with me, and generally forced me to be more careful, analytical, and critical in my teaching and writing than I might otherwise have been. Their collective imprint on this book is greater than they probably imagine.

Thomas J. Sullivan

INTRODUCTION TO
Social Problems

CHAPTER ONE

Approaches to the Study of Social Problems

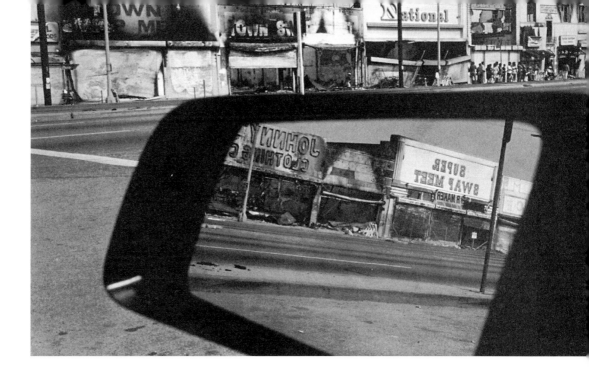

English novelist Charles Dickens characterized life in England and France in the late 1700s with these words: "It was the best of times, it was the worst of times. . . . It was the spring of hope, it was the winter of despair" (1859:1). Dickens was expressing a deep-felt ambivalence held by many people of that era regarding life in their time. England was undergoing industrialization, which promised greater levels of economic productivity, wonderful inventions, and new heights of affluence. For many, however, it also meant agonizing poverty, horrid crowding in filthy cities, and virulent disease. For the entrepreneur, it was a time to dream of riches yet to be made. For the pauper, it was a time to wonder where one's next meal might be found.

The United States at the end of the twentieth century can be viewed through an equally ambivalent lens. We, too, can find promise of a better life in emerging technologies such as computers, telecommunications, and nuclear power. We, too, have seen remarkable inventions that provide a level of comfort and security thought impossible by our ancestors. Imagine, for example, how you would be limited by the absence of but one amenity of modern living that you probably take for granted: electricity. Yet not much more than one hundred years ago most people lived without it.

But there is a dark side to all this promise— a "winter of despair"—that is the topic of this book. There remain poverty, violence, drug addiction, alcoholism, and a host of other social problems. Some people are alienated from their dull and demeaning jobs, and others have no jobs at all. Lakes are polluted and dying because of acid rain, and chemical dumps make useless the water supplies of many communities. In our cities, which are technological wonders in themselves, many people are frightened by crime and a few respond by turning their homes into armed camps. Perhaps nuclear power provides the best symbol for the contradictions of our time: We use it to produce our electricity, but no one wants its deadly wastes stored near them. And we stand terrified at the specter of death and destruction that would surely accompany a nuclear war.

One can understand, then, how life in today's world might be thought of as "the best of times . . . the worst of times." A principal challenge that we face is to conquer these social problems or at least to alleviate their impact on people's lives. In this book, I take a sociological approach to understanding these social problems. **Sociology** is *the scientific study of societies and human social behavior,* and it provides one of the most useful approaches for understanding social problems and a most effective tool for finding solutions to them. In fact, modern sociology might be considered an offspring of industrialization, because it emerged in Europe and the United States in the nineteenth century shortly after the era of which Dickens had written. A major motivation of many early sociologists was to develop a "science of society" to deal with the dislocations, disruptions, poverty, and violence that accompanied industrialization. The same purpose underlies this book: to remove, as best we can, the poverty, crime, violence, and other problems that persist as the United States and the world move into an advanced industrial era. Along with these early sociologists, we assume that we *can* do something to improve social conditions and to attack social problems. Furthermore, our actions regarding social problems need to be grounded in *scientific research* on the problems and in *scientific assessments* of the effectiveness of solutions. Uninformed or casual meddling in social problems can create more difficulties than it solves.

This chapter will serve as a framework for the study of specific problems in later chapters. First, what makes a social condition a social problem and why sociology is an essential tool in understanding and solving problems will be discussed. Then consideration will be given to the three major theoretical perspectives in sociology and how they are important in the study of social problems. Finally, it will be shown how scientific research provides the most useful information about problems and their solutions.

What Is a Social Problem?

There are some issues that practically everyone today agrees are social problems, such as crime or racial discrimination. About other issues, however, there is more disagreement. There is great debate, for example, over whether water pollution, pornography, or the use of marijuana are social problems. A commonsense approach might define a condition as a social problem if it "harms people" or is "detrimental to society." But this is far too imprecise for our purposes. To develop a more rigorous definition of what is a social problem, it is helpful to distinguish problems that affect individuals from those that involve an entire society.

Personal Troubles, Public Issues, and Social Problems

A distinction made by sociologist C. Wright Mills (1959) between personal troubles and public issues may be the best place to begin. Personal troubles are things that affect individuals and those immediately around them. When parents discover that their daughter has a serious drug problem, theirs is a personal trouble because the values and goals of only that family are threatened. The trouble is seen as being primarily that family's difficulty. Public issues, on the other hand, have an impact on large numbers of people and are matters of public debate; collective solutions, rather than individual or familial ones, are considered. When statistics reveal that our nation loses millions of dollars every year because of accidents, suicide, and worker absenteeism due to drug abuse, we are dealing with a public issue because the values and goals of a large group are threatened. The issue is debated in public forums, and collective solutions are usually proposed. So every condition that adversely affects some individuals is not necessarily an issue of great public concern toward which we should, or could, direct societal resources. Of course, public issues may translate into personal troubles in the lives of some people, but every personal trouble is not a public issue. Mills's distinction between personal troubles and public issues make us aware that problems need to be viewed in the broad context of their impact on society.

How do we place these issues in a broader societal context? We propose the following definition: A **social problem** exists when *an influential group defines a social condition as threatening its values; when the condition affects a large number of people; and when the condition can be remedied by collective action* (Spector and Kitsuse, 1987; Miller and Holstein, 1993). Let's look briefly at each element in this definition. An *influential group* is one that can have a significant impact on public debate and social policy. For example, groups opposing discrimination against women in employment and other areas have been able to mount a campaign that has forced politicians and the public nationwide to listen to their demands. Groups such as People for the Ethical Treatment of Animals, on the other hand, have not been able to generate significant debate about experimentation with animals or cruelty

to animals, and relatively few people consider these to be social problems. Personal troubles do not become public issues, then, unless an influential group so defines them. The mere existence of a social condition does not make it problematic, no matter how harmful it may be. For example, smoking tobacco has been a contributing factor in lung cancer for as long as humans have used the substance, but it was not defined as a social problem until biomedical research made people aware of the link between smoking and lung cancer.

Conditions are viewed as social problems when they threaten a *group's values*. **Values** are *people's ideas about what is good or bad, right or wrong.* We use these values as guidelines for choosing goals and judging behaviors. Because values are necessarily ranked in terms of priority in any group or society, there is disagreement over which conditions will be viewed as social problems. Some Americans, for example, place great value on work and industriousness. Because of this, they may view people who receive welfare with considerable disdain and even consider them threatening to their own way of life. Other Americans, emphasizing religious or humanitarian values, might argue that poverty— not poor people—is the real threat and that the poor should be helped, not castigated.

Conditions do not typically become social problems unless they affect *a large number of people.* When they affect relatively few people, they are private issues and there is little public debate over them or search for collective solutions. The more people they affect, the more likely they are to be publicly debated and defined as a problem that society should address. When the unemployment rate is low, for example, relatively few people are adversely affected. It may be a terrible personal hardship for those few who are unemployed, but it does not threaten large or influential groups and there will likely be little societal pressure directed toward alleviating the problem.

Finally, a social condition may satisfy the previous criteria but not be regarded as a social problem because the condition does not have social causes and cannot be *remedied by collective human action.* Earthquakes, tornadoes, and other vagaries of nature, for example, are harmful and frightening natural disasters, but they would not be considered *social* problems because they are not produced by social conditions and cannot be prevented by collective action or changes in social policy.

The Social Context of Social Problems

Social problems differ from personal troubles because the former are public issues rather than personal ones. In addition, social problems are fundamentally social rather than personal in nature because their causes and their solutions have something to do with the workings of society. Social problems may have an impact on individuals, but their roots are found in social life. We will illustrate the social basis of social problems here by briefly describing four distinct social conditions that can play a role in the emergence of social problems: deviation from group values and norms, a decline in the effectiveness of social institutions, extensive social and cultural diversity, and the exercise of power. The importance of these social conditions will be further elaborated in the next section on theoretical perspectives in sociology and throughout this book.

Societies are generally stable and orderly, although change and disruption do occur. This social stability arises in part because societies pass on to their members values and norms that serve to guide people in their behavior. Values have already been defined in the United States, for example; the values of most people hold that it is preferable to be materially comfortable than to be poor or that the private ownership of goods is preferred over public or communal ownership. **Norms** are much more specific and concrete than values; they are *rules of conduct that guide people's behavior.* They are expectations that people in society share about how they ought to behave. Values are general preferences, whereas norms are specific guidelines

for behavior. Norms dictate, for example, that men should wear pants, not dresses, and that motor vehicles are to be driven on the right side of the road rather than the left. Note how norms, like values, can vary from one culture to another and from one group to another. In some societies, men wear dresses and in others people drive on the left side of the road.

Values and norms, then, serve as a script for how to behave, and they enable us, to an extent, to predict how others will behave and to coordinate our behavior with theirs. Thus, values and norms lend stability and orderliness to society. A basic tenet of the sociological view of society is that people live in a socially created reality in which their behavior is shaped by social objects, such as values and norms, as much as by physical objects. However, people do not always behave in conformity with accepted values and norms. *Behaviors or characteristics that violate important group norms and as a consequence are reacted to with social disapproval* are called **deviance.** Laypeople often approach deviant or unconventional behaviors in an absolute way, judging them to be good or bad, right or wrong, by comparing them with some fixed standards, such as some religious teachings. Sociologists view deviance as relative, or based on the social definitions of some group. For sociologists, it is not behaviors or characteristics in themselves that are deviant. Rather, it is the judgments of some group whose norms have been violated that make a behavior unconventional or deviant. This makes deviance relative in the sense that a behavior is deviant only when so defined by some group. So, deviance can be understood only within the context of the norms and values of a particular culture, subculture, or group. As one sociologist put it: "Deviance, like beauty, is in the eyes of the beholder" (Simmons, 1969: 4). Deviance does not refer only to the violation of group norms; some stigma, or mark of disgrace, must also be attached to the violation that sets the deviant apart from others (Goffman, 1963). When people violate the values and norms of the influential or powerful, the reaction against the deviant can be very strong. So, some social problems—prostitution, alcoholism, and drug abuse, to name a few—arise in part because they are defined as deviant and stigmatized. Some people are unwilling or unable to conform their behavior to the dictates of influential groups.

Beyond values and norms, another important element of society is **social institutions:** *relatively stable clusters of social relationships that involve people working together to meet some basic needs of society.* The family, for example, is a social institution ensuring that children will be born and raised properly to be contributing members of society. These institutions—the family, religion, politics, education, and others—serve as further guides for people's behavior and also involve social relationships that offer people a sense of community involvement and self-worth. In fact, many behaviors and personal qualities—happiness, mental stability, morality, respect for the law, and others—arise out of such social relationships, out of a sense of community and personal involvement with others. A person who is fired from his job, for example, experiences a social loss that can result in psychological problems as well as physical ailments. Industrialization has threatened such traditional sources of support and authority as the family and religion. Unless their decline is replaced by other sources of support, crime, substance abuse, and other problems may increase. In other words, many social problems arise from the ineffectiveness of social institutions in guiding behavior and offering people a sense of community and self-worth.

Social and cultural diversity is another important element of societies. The United States, for example, is extremely diverse. The norms of the inner-city slum are light-years away from those of the middle-class suburb; the values of the young have little meaning for the elderly; and many beliefs of the affluent are foreign to the poor. One result of all this diversity is that many groups in the United States inhabit their own social worlds, called "subcultures." A **subculture** is *a group within a culture that shares some of the beliefs, values, and norms of the larger culture but also has some that are distinctly its own.* Each of the following could be considered a subculture: teenagers, Cubans in Miami, gays in most large cities, skinheads, the drug set, prison inmates, hip-hop youth of the 1990s, even the few hippies left over from the 1960s. In fact, everyone in the United States belongs to a wide array of subcultures based on age, sex,

As the clothing and hairstyles of these U.S. teenagers suggest, there is much social and cultural diversity in most societies. Subcultural diversity is an important element in the study of social problems because differing subcultures create the potential for conflicts over values and lifestyles.

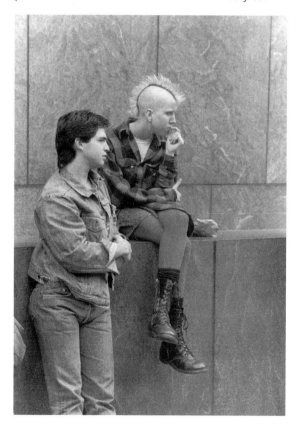

social standing, religion, leisure pastimes, or other characteristics.

Subcultural diversity is an important element in the study of social problems because it points to the potential for conflict between groups in our society. The values of one group are likely to clash with the values of another. One group, for example, may find the widespread availability of abortion offensive to its religious tenets, whereas another views restrictions on abortion as a threat to women's reproductive choices. Such conflicts are enhanced by **ethnocentrism,** *the tendency to view one's own culture or subculture as the best and to judge other cultures or subcultures in comparison to it.* Because of ethnocentrism, people may view the practices of another subculture as a social problem because they differ from their own practices. For example, are prostitution or the use of marijuana truly problems for society, or are they just offensive to the values of some particular subcultures?

A final element of society to be mentioned here is the exercise of power. **Power** is *the ability of one group to realize its will, even in the face of resistance from other groups* (Weber, 1958, originally published 1919; Boulding, 1989). Power can arise from many sources: the strength of numbers, efficient organization, access to wealth or status, or control of the political and economic institutions that dominate society. Whatever its source, power enables its possessor to compel others to act in a particular fashion. Ultimately, societies can use force or coercion to induce conformity to values and norms or to reduce conflicts or threats to a way of life. **Authority** refers to *legitimate power that is obeyed because people believe it is right and proper that they obey.* Most Americans, for example, believe that the Congress and the president, working together, have the legitimate authority to declare war on another country and to compel military service on the part of the citizenry. Many people may prefer not to fight in a war, but they would go because they believe the government has the authority to require that of

them. Most social problems are related to the exercise of power and the use of authority, either as forces that intensify problems or as crucial elements in their solution. After all, a group needs some power in order to have a condition defined as a social problem to begin with. Then, which solutions are settled on often depends on which groups can most effectively utilize the power and authority available to them.

This brief description of four elements of society suggests the ways in which social problems are "social" in nature: They are both created and alleviated by social mechanisms. To understand and solve social problems, then, we need to know something about how society works.

The Sociological Imagination

Before going on to a more detailed analysis of the sociological perspective and social problems, it is valuable to step back and consider the implications of this perspective for your own life. The sociological perspective on human beings is a unique and remarkable one, recognizing as it does that human behavior consists of far more than individuals acting independently of one another. It emphasizes the powerful role that group membership and social forces play in shaping behavior. Sociologists focus on social interaction and social relationships rather than on individuals. The sociological perspective offers a special awareness of the world that enables people to approach their own lives with introspection and insight. Peter Berger (1963) referred to the sociological perspective as an "emancipated vista" that can free people from blind submission to social forces that they do not understand. C. Wright Mills (1959) coined the term **sociological imagination** to refer to *the ability to understand the relationship between what is happening in people's personal lives and the social forces that surround them.* For both Berger and Mills, the more people learn about society and social problems, the better equipped they will be to understand their own lives and the impact—both desired and intrusive—of society and social problems on them. To be emancipated, of course, is not always pleasant because we often learn that social problems hinder us from achieving sought-after goals. Poverty-stricken parents, for example, may not welcome the realization that their children will be penalized by the inequities of the school system in the United States, which has adverse effects on the poor. Nevertheless, it is precisely a better understanding of the role of such inequities that can open the door to making improvements in the educational process. So the sociological imagination involves the insight into how social forces can bring problems into our own lives and how other social forces might alleviate the problems.

Theoretical Perspectives on Social Problems

Every science, including sociology, accumulates knowledge through an interplay between theory and research. In the previous section, we described the sociological perspective in very general terms. Now we need to provide a more detailed account of the theories commonly used in the sociological analysis of social problems. A **theory** is *a set of statements that explains the relationship between phenomena.* The key role of theories is to tell us why something occurred. They help us organize the data from research into a meaningful whole. In this section, we will discuss the most general and important theoretical approaches in sociology. In the next section, we will return to the importance of research.

Some sociological theories focus on specific social problems, such as the causes of juvenile delinquency, or the explanations for divorce. We will discuss quite a few of these theories in this book. In addition to these highly specialized theories, however, there are a num-

ber of broader explanations of social reality that are called **theoretical perspectives.** These perspectives *provide some fundamental assumptions about the nature and operation of society and commonly serve as sources of the more specific theories* mentioned previously. Most sociologists today are guided by one or more of the following theoretical perspectives: functionalism, conflict theory, or interactionism. The functionalist and conflict approaches are frequently referred to as *macrosociology* because they focus on large groups and social institutions and on society as a whole. The interactionist perspective falls under the category of *microsociology* because it concentrates on the intimate level of everyday interactions between people. We will first summarize the perspectives and then suggest how you should use them in analyzing social problems.

The Functionalist Perspective

The functionalist perspective grew out of the similarities early sociologists observed between society and biological organisms. The human body, for example, is composed of many different parts—the heart, the eyes, and the kidneys, to name but three—each of which performs a particular function. The heart pumps blood to the other organs of the body, the eyes transmit information about the external world to the brain, and the kidneys remove waste materials from the blood. These parts of the body do not exist in isolation, however; rather, they are interrelated and interdependent. If one of them ceases to perform its function—if the heart stops, the eyes go blind, or the kidneys fail—the effective operation of the whole body is threatened and survival itself may be in doubt.

Society, functionalists argue, operates in a way somewhat analogous to that of a biological organism. According to the **functionalist perspective,** *society is a system made up of a number of interrelated elements, each performing a function that contributes to the operation of the whole* (Parsons,

1951; Turner and Maryanski, 1979). The elements of society include, for example, institutions such as the family, education, and the economy. The family provides for the bearing and rearing of children until they can live on their own. Educational institutions provide training in the various skills needed to fill jobs in society. The economy is responsible for producing food, clothing, and other necessities needed by families to survive, as well as for providing the books and other supplies needed for education. The family and the schools could not survive without the goods provided by the economy, and economic organizations need workers who have been socialized by the family and trained by the schools to work industriously. In addition to institutions, society is also made up of many social roles, social groups, and subcultures, and all these parts fit together into a reasonably well-integrated whole. For functionalists, then, all parts of society are interdependent and function together to provide the things that are essential to maintain society. In addition, there needs to be considerable agreement among the members of society regarding the content of important values and norms.

In a system with all the parts so tightly interdependent, a change in one element of society will probably lead to changes in other parts. For example, the establishment of compulsory education in the United States caused significant alterations in the economic sphere by removing children and eventually adolescents from the labor force, which made more jobs available for adults. Compulsory education also affected the family; with young people no longer working, the financial burden on parents was increased. When children could no longer help support the family financially, a gradual shift to smaller families began. Thus, changes in the educational sphere had important ramifications for family and economic structures. Small changes can usually be absorbed with relative ease, but large or sudden changes can cause major social disruption and

lead to problems. Because of this, functionalists argue, social systems are characterized by stability and a tendency toward equilibrium—a state of balance in which the relationships among the various parts of the system remain the same.

A central concern of the functionalist approach is the determination of just what functions each part of society performs. This is not always easy to do because some functions are not as obvious as those in our previous example. In fact, sociologist Robert K. Merton (1968) suggests that there are two different types of functions: manifest and latent. *Manifest functions* are the intended consequences of some action or social process and refer to what most people expect to result. *Latent functions* are consequences that are unexpected or unintended. For example, one of the manifest functions of colleges and universities is to provide people with specialized training. However, institutions of higher education perform a number of latent functions. For instance, they serve as a marriage market, and they reduce unemployment by keeping some adults out of the job market. These latent functions are just as much a part of the system of higher education as its manifest purposes. In addition, some social practices may be *dysfunctional;* that is, they may disrupt social equilibrium rather than contribute to it. For example, encouraging large families, as some religious teachings do, would be dysfunctional in a society that is already overpopulated.

According to the functionalist perspective, a social problem exists when some element in society becomes dysfunctional and interferes with the efficient operation or stability of the system or the achievement of societal goals. In other words, social problems arise from social disorganization, in which the parts of society work at cross-purposes rather than together. One sign of this disorganization is the decline in the effectiveness of social institutions, discussed in the preceding section. Functionalists search for the sources of this societal breakdown. Consider how divorce might be viewed by functionalists: Marital dissolution involves the breaking up of what is perhaps society's most basic institution, the family. Divorce could be seen as a social problem if those functions that are typically served by the family were to go unperformed, such as children not being raised properly to become contributing members of society (see Chapter 3).

The functionalist perspective is a very useful one, but it does tend to overemphasize the extent of stability and order in society and to downplay the fact that social practices that are beneficial to one group in society may be dysfunctional to another. These cautions should be kept in mind when using this perspective.

The Conflict Perspective

Conflict theorists emphasize the inevitability of coercion, domination, conflict, and change in society. The **conflict perspective** is based on *the idea that society consists of different groups who struggle with one another to attain the scarce societal resources that are considered valuable, be they money, power, prestige, or the authority to impose one's values on society.* Karl Marx provided the foundation for the conflict perspective when he

The conflict perspective makes us aware that people vary substantially in terms of the social and economic resources available to them. The social programs and policies that would benefit the business people in this photo are, undoubtedly, quite different from those that would benefit the homeless person.

viewed society as consisting of different social classes (1967, originally published 1867–1895). The two central classes of his era were the proletariat, or the workers, and the bourgeoisie, or those who owned the businesses, factories, and textile mills in which the proletariat toiled. Marx saw these classes as being in constant struggle with one another to improve their respective positions in society. The workers tried to gain more income and control over their work; the owners tried to make more profits by lowering labor costs and getting workers to work more. For Marx, this conflict was irreconcilable, because what benefits one group necessarily works to the disadvantage of the other. Furthermore, if those in one group can gain an advantage in this struggle, they will use it to dominate and oppress the other group and enhance their own position. They might, for example, gain control of the government and pass legislation that limits the ways the subordinate groups could otherwise compete. A century ago in the United States, for example, it was illegal for workers to organize for the purposes of collective bargaining. This benefited the factory owners because workers were unable to use their strength of numbers to gain higher wages or better working conditions.

Although Marx limited his focus to class conflict, modern versions of conflict theory in sociology hold that domination, coercion, and the exercise of power occur to some degree in all groups and societies because they are the basic social mechanisms for regulating behavior and allocating resources (Dahrendorf, 1959; Duke, 1976; Collins, 1990). In addition to class conflict, groups and subcultures can engage in conflict over contrasting values. For example, some religious groups, such as the Mormons, place great value in family life, whereas many nonreligious people view the traditional family as only one of a number of ways people can organize their personal lives. These two groups are likely to view social problems such as divorce and childbirth outside marriage in quite different ways. In fact, as we have seen, whether these conditions are even viewed as social problems depends on one's values. Another source of conflict in society is the gap that can arise between values and social practices. The United States, for example, professes to value equality for all. Yet at one time or another, African Americans, Italian Americans, Irish Americans, women, and Jewish Americans, to name but a few, have suffered severe discrimination.

In the conflict view, then, groups exert what power they possess over others when this serves their interests, and society consists of a wide array of such interest groups struggling to acquire a share of societal resources. An **interest group** is *a group whose members share distinct and common concerns and who benefit from similar social policies and practices.* Things that benefit one interest group may work to the disadvantage of others. Some interest groups are formally organized, such as the National Rifle Association, the Sierra Club, the National Manufacturers Association, or the American Civil Liberties Union. Other interest groups are informal, and people may not fully recognize that they are members of them. For example, college students constitute an informal interest group because all college students benefit from such things as lower tuition and increased government funding of student loans. Taxpayers without children of college age, however, might oppose such policies because their taxes would increase.

In the conflict view, social change involves redistributing scarce resources among various interest groups. A *vested interest group* is an interest group that benefits from existing policies, practices, and social arrangements, and generally resists social changes that might threaten their privileges. However, the inevitable clash of interests ensures that any existing social arrangements eventually will be rearranged. Out of the resulting struggle, new winners will emerge and uneasy truces will be established. These truces, however, will be temporary, because new conflicts will develop that will lead to further struggle and change.

For the conflict theorist, a social problem exists when a group of people, believing that its interests are not being met or that it is not receiving a sufficient share of resources, works to overcome what it perceives as a disadvantage. Unlike functionalists, conflict theorists view a phenomenon such as divorce as normal because it represents one way of dealing with marital discord. This does not mean that the disruptive effects of divorce are ignored or that divorce is not a social problem. Rather, it means that divorce becomes a social problem when particular groups that have power regard their interests as being threatened by the extent of divorce in society.

Some caution is also called for in using the conflict perspective, especially the tendency to overemphasize the importance of conflict and inequality and to disregard the prevalence of stability and consensus in society. This can lead one to overlook factors important to social problems.

The Interactionist Perspective

Although the functionalist and conflict perspectives offer competing views of social life, the interactionist perspective is more of a supplement to the first two, showing how the social processes described in those perspectives enter into people's daily lives and shape their behavior. The **interactionist perspective** *focuses on everyday social interaction among individuals rather than on large societal structures such as politics, education, and the like* (Blumer, 1962; Hewitt, 1994). For interactionists, society consists of people interacting with one another; to understand society we must understand social interaction. It is through such interactions that groups, organizations, and society as a whole are created, maintained, and changed. The operation of educational institutions can be observed, for example, through students interacting with teachers and through school ad-

ministrators making decisions. It is these day-to-day interactions that give education its shape and substance.

A central assumption of the interactionist perspective can be summarized in a paraphrase of a statement by sociologists William and Dorothy Thomas (1928): If people define situations as real, they are real in their consequences. In other words, people act on the basis of their beliefs and perceptions about situations. The term **definition of the situation** refers to *people's perceptions and interpretations of what is important in a situation and what actions are appropriate*. A central part of social interaction, then, is people's interpretations or definitions of others' behavior.

This process of definition and interpretation rests on the ability of human beings to use symbols. It is our symbol-using capabilities that enable us to attach complex social meanings to objects, events, or people. A *symbol* is something that stands for, represents, or takes the place of something else. Anything—any object, event, or word—can serve as a symbol. A crucifix, for example, symbolizes the beliefs of Roman Catholicism, whether it is made from wood, metal, or plastic; the Star of David likewise symbolizes Judaism. The meaning attached to a symbol is derived from social consensus. We simply agree that a particular object will represent something. During World War II, for example, Winston Churchill used two fingers extended into the air and spread apart to symbolize victory in battle, and others agreed on the meaning of this gesture. In the 1960s, the same gesture came to mean opposition to war as people used the gesture to indicate support for the peace movement.

Because of our ability to use symbols, we live in a world that we create ourselves, through the meanings we attach to phenomena. In other words, we respond to symbolic or social meanings rather than to actual physical objects or actions, and what we do is the result of how we define and interpret those meanings. For example, we attach meanings to people

Central to the interactionist perspective is the importance of symbolic meanings. Any gesture has the meanings that people invest it with. Two fingers raised in the air and spread apart has meant "peace" to some groups and "victory in battle" to others.

through the use of labels, including deviant labels that carry some stigma with them. We call people "whores," "queers," "crooks," and "crazies." These labels influence how we relate to these people. And when people have been labeled, we come to expect them to behave in certain ways. A central tenet of the interactionist approach is that such social expectations, or norms, tend to influence the behavior of people who have been labeled, especially when the people themselves accept the meaning of the label attached to them. The prostitute, for example, who internalizes the social meaning implied by the label "cheap whore" may not aspire toward any other way of life. Her world and behavior are shaped by the fact that she accepts the stigmatizing label, whether it is true or not. This fact points to another important assertion of the interactionist perspective: What is important is not whether a particular definition of the situation is actually true but rather whether people believe the definition to be true.

Social life rests on the development of consensus about expected behavior. Such shared expectations guide our activities and make cooperative action possible. If this consensus breaks down, some sort of change must occur. Thus, for interactionists, social change involves developing some new consensus with different meanings and expectations.

From the interactionist perspective, a social problem exists when some social condition is defined by an influential group as stigmatizing or threatening to their values and disruptive of normal social expectations. For example, the interactionist would observe that there have been important changes in attitudes toward divorce in industrial societies. In addition to being more common today, divorce has less stigma attached to it than it did around the turn of this century. At the same time, however, divorce is viewed by many groups as a social problem because they see marital dissolution as posing a threat to family stability. If the family is such a basic social institution, divorce may challenge shared meanings and definitions that these groups hold about this institution.

Once again caution is called for in using the perspectives. Because of the emphasis on face-to-face interaction in shaping social reality, the interactionist approach can lead one to deemphasize the part that social institutions, such as religion and politics, and large-scale social forces, such as industrialization, play in molding human behavior.

Using the Theoretical Perspectives

The preceding discussion of the sociological perspectives is brief and simplified, and more detail will be provided in later chapters. The major elements of each perspective and its view on social problems have been outlined in Table 1.1. The three perspectives should not be viewed as either right or wrong, nor should one select a favorite and ignore the others. In-

TABLE 1.1 An Outline of the Sociological Perspectives

	Functionalism	Conflict Theory	Interactionism
View of Society	A system of interrelated and interdependent parts	Made up of groups struggling with one another over scarce resources.	Individuals in face-to-face interaction create social consensus.
View of the Individual	People are shaped by society to perform important functions for society.	People are shaped by the position of their groups in society.	People are symbol manipulators who create their social world through social interaction and consensus.
View of Social Change	The social system tends to resist change as disruptive.	Change is inevitable and continuous.	Change occurs when there is no shared consensus about expected behavior and a newly found consensus develops.
View of Social Problems	Caused by dysfunctional activities or disorganization in the social system.	Arise when a group believes its interests are not being served and works to overcome perceived disadvantage.	Arise when a condition is defined as stigmatizing or disruptive of normal social expectations.
Key Concepts	integration, interdependence, stability, equilibrium	interest, power, dominance, conflict, coercion	interpretation, consensus, shared expectations, socially created reality

stead, the perspectives should be seen as three different "tools," each of which is useful in analyzing particular social problems. The three perspectives are not equally useful for examining every social problem, nor can any single perspective explain all aspects of human behavior and society. Furthermore, to gain a full understanding of any particular problem, the use of more than one approach may be required. In a sense, the perspectives are similar to a physician's instruments. Because of the body's complexity, a doctor needs many devices to keep tabs on people's health. Social problems are also very complex, and the theoretical perspectives are the "instruments" that sociologists have developed over the years to help them understand these problems in conjunction with human behavior and society.

Research on Social Problems

Theories by themselves are not of great utility in understanding social problems, especially when they are untested. Until research has been done to test a theory, it is merely speculative. **Research** refers to *the systematic examination of empirical data.* Research can provide the most coherent and objective information about the causes of social problems, their extent, and the effectiveness of solutions. Without a foundation in research, our approach to problems is likely to be surrounded by speculation, misunderstanding, and bias, and we may expend resources in the pursuit of ineffective solutions. If this occurs, we have not only wasted resources but also left the real source of the problem to grow more serious. For these reasons, we must understand what good research is and how we can use its principles in our everyday assessment of social problems.

The Scientific Method

Research conducted by sociologists is based on the scientific method. **Science** is *a method of ob-*

taining objective and systematic knowledge through observation. The foundation of the scientific approach is the belief that claims about what is correct or incorrect must be demonstrated to be true through some observations in the world (Sullivan, 1992). Intuition, speculation, or common sense can never replace the empirical test of one's claims. Scientific theories are linked to scientific research through **hypotheses,** which are *tentative statements that can be tested regarding relationships between two or more factors.* Hypotheses are statements whose accuracy can be assessed through observation. If hypotheses are verified through observation, this provides support for the theory; if they are not, our confidence in the theory is reduced. The more empirical support there is for a theory, the more useful it is in attacking social problems.

Science is not foolproof, but it is the most effective means available for acquiring systematic, verifiable knowledge about the world and about social problems and their solutions. In the Applied Research insert (see pp. 18–19), science is compared with some other ways of gaining knowledge, showing what makes the scientific approach superior in this realm. Science does have its limitations, however, and it is crucial to understand which issues it cannot resolve. Science is the preferred source of knowledge on issues that can be resolved *through observation.* Some issues are not amenable to such resolution. For example, science cannot verify the existence of a supreme deity or say which religious beliefs are correct because these are not issues that can be settled through observation. They are matters of faith, choice, or revelation but not of science. Likewise, science cannot tell us which personal values are right and preferable because these are again matters of personal choice or judgment. As we have already seen, social problems and their solutions involve questions of personal and cultural values. In analyzing social problems, we need to be sensitive to the interplay between values and science, probing the extent to which values and science will play a part in the solution of problems. Science may help show us how to live up to our values, but it cannot tell us which values to live by.

Values, Interest Groups, and Objectivity

An issue that is especially important and quite controversial regarding research on social problems is that of scientific objectivity, or the attempt by scientists to prevent their personal values from affecting the outcome of their research. This does not mean that scientists are without values or passions. Many are intensely concerned about social problems such as crime, divorce, family violence, and nuclear war. At the same time, scientists realize that their personal values can, and probably will, bias their research. Early in the twentieth century, sociologist Max Weber laid out one position on this issue when he argued that sociology should remain as *value free* as possible because human values can distort sound scientific investigation (1958, originally published 1919). Weber argued that sociologists should suspend their personal and political values when engaging in scientific research. Contemporary advocates of Weber's position would concede that such suspension is difficult to accomplish but that abandoning the effort would be disastrous: There would be no means of acquiring an accurate body of knowledge about human social behavior to guide our consideration of ways of alleviating social problems (Gordon, 1988). Karl Marx (1964, originally published 1848) eloquently stated a position opposite to that of Weber's on this controversy. Marx was a strong champion of the cause of the poor and the downtrodden, and he wanted to use science to improve their plight. He argued that social scientists should bring strong moral commitments to their work and use science to change inequitable or immoral social conditions. Likewise, there are sociologists today who believe that social research should be guided by personal and political values and directed toward alleviating social ills (Harding, 1986; Fay, 1987).

Sociologist Alvin Gouldner (1976) has suggested a reasonable middle ground between these two positions. He agreed that scientists have values and that the influence of those values on research, which is often very subtle, can never be totally eliminated. But Gouldner proposed that we should deny neither our values nor the negative impact they can have on research. He urged that scientists should be explicit about what their values are. In this way, other scientists are forewarned and are thus better able to spot ways in which research findings may be influenced by personal bias.

The problem of enhancing scientific objectivity can be especially difficult for scientists who are closely associated with some interest group. Close involvement with an interest group can lead, often unknowingly, to distortions and misperceptions that throw into question the scientist's research on topics of interest to that group. For example, sociologists who are actively involved in such environmental groups as Greenpeace or Campaign for the Earth may have difficulty in recognizing ways in which the outcome of their research might be influenced by their personal position on the issues. Any research on environmental issues conducted by these people should be reviewed carefully for such sources of bias. Furthermore, scientists should cautiously review their own research plans to detect ways in which their own values might be influencing the outcome.

One final point needs to be made regarding interest groups and scientific research. In the public debate over social problems, the findings of science are often used by interest groups to further their own ends, and such groups may, wittingly or unwittingly, distort research findings to support their own position. This manipulation of scientific data can leave the public with misleading impressions. The purpose of these uses of science is to persuade people to support particular programs or

APPLIED RESEARCH
Untangling Myths and Facts About Social Problems

Sociologists take the position that scientific research provides the most accurate and useful knowledge with which to cope with social problems. Science, of course, is not the only way to gain an understanding of the world. For example, people often use tradition as a source of guidance. This might take the form of religious teachings about sex and marriage or proverbs such as "Birds of a feather flock together" and "Two heads are better than one." People also turn to their own personal experience for direction. If we visit a prison and see that most inmates are nonwhite, this can lead us to believe that crime rates are much higher among nonwhites than whites. Knowledge from tradition and experience often accumulates and blends together to form what people call "common sense": practical wisdom that encourages people to make decisions that they believe are sound without having any special training or expertise.

In fact, sociology has been called "the science of common sense" by critics who assume that it merely "proves" what everybody else already knows. In fact, sociology sometimes does confirm what many people already accept. We should not be surprised that scientific research shows that some commonsense beliefs are true, because people need some accurate commonsense knowledge of human behavior to interact with others and function in society. However, research shows that other commonsense beliefs about social problems are false, or at least oversimplified. Consider these statements:

1. If poor people were willing to work, there would be little need for welfare in the United States.
2. The crime rate is much higher in the lower class than it is in the middle class.
3. Reading pornography increases the likelihood that men will commit acts of sexual violence against women.

4. Because of the civil rights movement and affirmative action legislation, the gap in income between blacks and whites has narrowed substantially in the past three decades.
5. A person who does not engage in homosexual activities or use drugs intravenously has very little risk of becoming infected with the virus for Acquired Immune Deficiency Syndrome (AIDS).

At one time or another, each of us has probably believed that at least some of these statements are true. Yet social science research has shown each one to be false, or at least to be far too simple.

1. Most people receiving public assistance are children, single mothers who cannot afford the day care that would free them for work, the aged, and the disabled. Very few adult males who could work receive welfare (see Chapter 5).
2. If we use arrest statistics as our data, then this statement is supported, but most people who commit crimes are not arrested. A growing body of evidence based on self-reports of criminal activity suggests that what distinguishes the social classes is not the amount of crime but rather the types of crimes and the likelihood of being arrested. The poor are more likely to commit highly visible crimes, such as homicide or assault, that are likely to be reported to the police and result in arrests. Middle-class people commit crimes such as embezzlement, fraud, or tax evasion that often go unreported (see Chapter 9).
3. There is no convincing evidence that pornography predisposes a person to commit sexual violence, although people who commit such crimes may also read pornography. Much

pornography portrays violence against women, and it may well be the violence rather than the sexual content of pornography that encourages violence against women (see Chapter 11).

4. Unfortunately, research shows that the gap has hardly changed over the past three decades. Although many blacks have benefited from such legislation, the gap between the incomes of blacks and whites has been especially impervious to change (see Chapter 6).

5. Although it is true in the United States that 85 percent of those who contract AIDS are men who have sex with other men or people who engage in intravenous drug use, heterosexual transmission of AIDS has been growing rapidly, up 500 percent between 1985 and 1990. And worldwide, 60 percent of HIV infections result from heterosexual intercourse (see Chapter 4).

What is wrong with common sense in these realms? Basically, common sense does not normally involve an empirical and systematic effort to distinguish fact from fiction. Rather, it tends to accept untested and unquestioned assumptions because "everyone knows" they are true, and to reject contradictory information. In other words, some commonsense knowledge is a "myth" in that there is little evidence of its truth, although some people still accept it as true. Commonsense knowledge is also very slow to change—even when change seems called for—because the change may threaten cherished values or social patterns.

Scientific research does far more than merely document what we already know. Sometimes it does just that, but at other times it directly contradicts common sense. Most of the time, however, the truth is vastly more complicated than common sense suggests. Sociological research incorporates procedures that advance our knowledge by establishing facts through observation and by using procedures that reduce bias. Common sense is important and should not be ignored, but an unthinking and unverified acceptance of commonsense beliefs can blind people to social realities. This has important implications for social policy. The recognition, for example, that most people receiving welfare need it desperately just to survive is a strong argument against cutting back on public assistance programs. It is only through the development of an accurate, scientifically verified understanding of such social problems that we can hope to overcome them—even if it means relinquishing some of our most cherished commonsense preconceptions.

Each of the remaining chapters includes two features that emphasize these points. At the beginning of each chapter, a Myths and Facts section will contrast some inaccurate or misleading commonsense beliefs about some problem with the facts as they have been established through research. This comparison encourages students to distinguish between beliefs that have no empirical foundation and may in fact be myths from facts that have been substantiated through observation. Somewhere in most chapters, an Applied Research section is also included which illustrates the use of sociological research in solving problems or evaluating how well solutions work. This emphasizes the theme that the development of social policies about social problems should be influenced by systematic and scientific assessment of their impact as well as by our own personal values.

policies rather than to advance our knowledge of social problems. Because science enjoys a great deal of legitimacy in the United States, such appeals to "scientific proof" can be very persuasive. Because of this, people, especially in a democracy in which the citizenry participates in making public policy, need to be skilled at assessing the data and information with which they are barraged.

Assessing Data: Problems and Pitfalls

How can we detect error or bias in what we read? There are, of course, no foolproof guidelines, but we can draw some lessons from scientific research to become better-informed consumers of information. The following are a few such guidelines.

Sampling Problems   A basic question to ask about any set of data is: Upon whom or what were the observations made? In scientific research, collecting data on all the people or events about whom you are interested is normally impossible. In a study of divorce in the United States, for example, interviewing all couples who have divorced would be too expensive and time consuming, because more than a million do so every year. Instead, researchers typically study a **sample,** which consists of *elements that are taken from a group or population and that serve as a source of data.* To be useful, samples should be *representative,* or reflect the group or population that is under study in ways that are considered important.

The sampling problems that can arise when unrepresentative samples are used in the analysis of social problems—and the misleading conclusions that can result—are well illustrated by investigations of homosexuality. In the 1940s and 1950s, studies of gay men by psychologists and psychiatrists typically came to the conclusion that homosexuality is the result of a personality disturbance stemming from dis-

ordered relationships with parents during childhood. They also concluded that, as a group, gay men were unhappy and maladjusted individuals. The samples used in these studies consisted of gay men who were the patients of psychologists or psychiatrists. Virtually all the gay men in these samples were unhappy, maladjusted, and had disordered relationships with their parents—a strong association indeed. Yet the problem with the sampling in these studies should be fairly obvious: Gay men who seek psychological counseling are probably not representative of all gay men. People who seek counseling, irrespective of their sexual orientation, do so because they already have personal problems. Gay men who do not have such problems do not seek counseling, and they do not appear in samples of gays collected in this fashion. These early studies, then, contained a built-in bias, caused by poor sampling procedures, toward the conclusion that gay men are psychologically disturbed. Studies using more representative samples have concluded that sexual orientation, by itself, probably does not lead to personality disturbances or unhappiness (Ross et al., 1988; Savin-Williams, 1990).

A basic question to ask regarding any data or information, then, is whether it is based on a representative sample. Not that it is always easy to tell whether a sample is truly representative. But one should always ask: Are there people about whom conclusions are being made who are not represented in a particular sample?

Assessing Causality   One of the major goals in the study of social problems is to find their causes. By **causality,** we mean that *one factor has an effect on or produces a change in some other factor.* Establishing causality is one way of determining why something happened. Once we have established the causes of a social problem, we are in a better position to determine what programs or policies might alleviate it. However, discovering causal relationships can be a difficult task because causality cannot be directly observed. Rather, we infer causality from the observation of *associations* or *correlations* between things in the world. If changes in one factor are regularly associated with changes in the other factor, then the first factor may be causing those changes (Hirschi and Selvin, 1967).

The early studies of gay men mentioned previously had established an association between sexual orientation and psychological maladjustment, but a little thought will show that this association alone is not sufficient to infer that psychological disturbance causes homosexuality. It is equally logical to infer that being gay, especially in a society in which homosexuality is highly stigmatized, produces psychological disturbance and unhappiness. Thus, in addition to establishing an association, a second criterion to be satisfied before inferring causality is that the *time sequence* be correct: The causal factor must occur before whatever it is presumed to cause. The psychological disturbance would have to exist before people became homosexual in order to infer that the former causes the latter.

A third criterion to be satisfied in assessing causality is that the association not be spurious. A *spurious relationship* is one in which the association between two factors occurs because each is independently associated with some third factor. For example, there is a strong association between rates of ice cream consumption and juvenile delinquency, but few people would argue that eating ice cream causes delinquency or vice versa. Obviously, the relationship is a spurious one in which both ice cream consumption and delinquency are related to a third factor, the summer season. School vacations and warm weather offer greater opportunity to eat ice cream and to engage in delinquent acts.

Once we have satisfied the three criteria, we can feel reasonably confident that we have discovered a causal relationship. Unfortunately, much research on social problems can satisfy only one or two of the criteria, and this leaves us less confident regarding causality. The central point here is to be cautious and critical about any claims regarding causal relationships.

Measuring Social Problems All scientific research involves *measurement,* which refers to making observations that are presumed to be evidence that something exists or that something has a certain value. The observations that are made are referred to as "indicators." An indicator of juvenile delinquency, for example, might be vandalism at a school gymnasium. Likewise, severe bruises on a child's forearm might be considered indicators of child abuse.

A central concern in the study of social problems is that the indicators of variables have *validity,* or that they accurately measure what they are intended to measure. A thermometer, for example, is a valid measure of temperature but not of volume. The study of child abuse provides illustrations of some of the difficulties of finding valid measures of social problems. If we define child abuse as injuring a child not by accident but in anger or with deliberate intent, then most would agree that a cigarette burn on a child's buttocks is a valid indicator of child abuse; there is no other imaginable reason why such burns should occur (Gelles, 1987). But what about a bruise on the arm? Some groups in our society approve of physically striking a child for disciplinary reasons, even if some bruising results. Other groups define any physical punishment as unacceptable. As another example, invalid measures of crime are often used in assessing the crime problem. The most common source of crime statistics is the reports by the Federal Bureau of Investigation, but these statistics are based on crimes for which an arrest has been made or, in some cases, crimes known to the police (see Chapter 9). Yet there are many crimes that the police do not know about or do not make an arrest for, which means that these crime statistics are not totally accurate indicators of all crime.

In assessing data relating to social problems, we must consider issues of validity because these measurement problems can drastically influence the interpretation of data. Policy based on conclusions drawn from invalid measures can be very harmful. It may lead us to think we are moving toward alleviating a problem when in fact we are not. Meanwhile, the problem may become more serious as we experiment with untested and ineffective solutions.

Assessing Claims   In many cases, we are not in a position to apply the above criteria to claims about social problems. You may not have any information, for example, about the validity of a measuring device or any basis for judging a sample. What, then, can you do to reduce the chance of deception or distortion? There are a number of additional guidelines that should be kept in mind:

1. Is the claim made by a person or group of people with a strong self-interest in a particular interpretation or conclusion? Their personal interest may be biasing their presentation or interpretation of the data.

2. Can the claim be verified by yourself or others? Even reputable newspapers and magazines sometimes report data, in good faith, that cannot later be verified. In 1977, for example, *Newsweek* reported that "officials reckon" that 28 percent of the voters in San Francisco were gay. Diligent search by others failed to locate these alleged officials. Yet the *Newsweek* report became a major source of verification for data on the size of the gay population in San Francisco (Plissner, 1978).

3. Are the claims presented in a propagandistic fashion? There are a number of propaganda techniques that are used to persuade the public (Jowett and O'Donnell, 1986). For example, "glittering generalities" involve the use of highly attractive but vague and meaningless words and phrases such as "restoring law and order" or "communism." "Testimonial" is the

technique of using famous and respected people to support a program or policy as a means of engendering public support.

Future Prospects: Solving Social Problems
The Interplay of Policy and Research

Our goal is not only to understand problems but also to solve them or at least to alleviate some of their more undesirable consequences. Solutions to problems, however, never magically appear. Some action must be taken if solutions are to be effected. These actions develop into what is called **social policy:** *laws, administrative procedures, and other formal and informal social practices that are intended to promote social changes focused on alleviating particular social problems* (Gil, 1990; Jencks, 1992). Social policies are inherently controversial because they are based, in part, on human values. Groups with differing values will often push for very different solutions to the same problem. Or they may, as we have seen, disagree over which social conditions are social problems. This controversy and disagreement is an inevitable feature of the debate over social problems and their solutions.

Within the confines of this debate, however, sociological theory and research can be applied as tools for assessing the validity and effectiveness of particular positions and solutions. The power of scientific observation can be trained on problems and solutions to help resolve some of the controversy. Science, as we have seen, cannot tell us what values to hold, but it can help us assess whether the factors we believe underlie a problem are the actual sources of the problem. Scientific observation can also assess whether particular solutions to problems actually work. Is the problem alleviated once the solution is put into effect? Did the solution bring about the improvement, or was it something else? Does the solution have any side effects, detrimental or beneficial? The Policy Issues insert describes a successful attempt to use research as a basis for social policy. This attempt focused on a particularly disturbing problem—spouse abuse—and the effectiveness of various ways of dealing with it. Some further linkages between research and social policy are outlined in Table 1.2. In fact, there is a specialty area in the social sciences— variously called applied sociology, applied social research, or evaluation research—that is devoted precisely to this endeavor (Nathan, 1988; Sullivan, 1992). It uses modern social science research tools to assess the extent of social problems, to plan and monitor programs intended to alleviate those problems, and to determine how effectively the programs achieve their goals. The most effective approach to finding and implementing solutions to social problems, then, involves an interplay between social policy and social research. This recognizes the role of human values in the process, but it also tempers their enthusiasm and potential bias with systematic observation and assessment.

Who Provides Solutions?

Social problems, as we have seen, are conditions that can be remedied through some form of collective action. "Collective action" merely means that people work together toward a solution. In some cases, this takes the form of interest groups working through the normal political process. In the United States, this could occur at the federal, state, or local level. Politicians who are aware of a problem pass legislation to alleviate it, judges make rulings that have an impact on a problem, or private corporations and foundations develop programs to solve a problem. The solution to a problem may even be developed in good part by people who are unaffected, or at best indirectly affected, by the problem. Corporate executives, for example, may not experience poverty themselves but may feel a moral obligation to contribute some of their earnings to charity. Or they may be motivated by a fear that poverty generates an unsettled political and economic environment that adversely affects corporate profits.

Organized protest and social action outside the normal political process represent another way that solutions to social problems can emerge. Groups affected by a problem can strike, riot, or march in the streets to force government or private organizations to change their practices. In some cases, a **social movement** may emerge, *a collective, organized effort to promote or resist social change through some noninstitutionalized or unconventional means.* The civil

TABLE 1.2 Linkage Between Social Policy and Social Science Research

Stages in the Policy Process	Possible Research Contribution
Problem Formulation	Assess extent of problem, who is affected, and costs of doing nothing
Policy Formulation	Assess positive or negative impact of various policy alternatives
Policy Implementation	Assess whether a program achieves policy goals in an efficient and effective manner
Evaluation	Assess whether and how a solution has an impact on a problem or on other groups in society; determine whether any new problems are created
Closure	Assess whether any further policy application would be warranted

Domestic violence is a particularly tragic social problem with its jarring intrusion of injury and cruelty into the intimacy of the family. It is also a difficult problem for police officers who are often first on the scene of such violence and whose job it is to make complex and troubling decisions about how to handle the alleged perpetrator of the violence. Should the officer make an arrest? Would it be better to just order the alleged abuser out of the house to cool off? Or would mediation and counseling from the officer be more effective at preventing future abuse?

In the past, such decisions have been left to the discretion and judgment of the officer in the field. Using applied social research, criminologist Lawrence Sherman and sociologist Richard Berk have offered a basis for developing social policies regarding this issue (Sherman and Berk, 1984). Working with the Police Foundation, a research organization in Washington, D.C., Sherman and Berk designed a study to assess which actions by police officers could be shown to reduce the likelihood that a spouse abuser would be involved in future domestic violence incidents. When police officers respond to a domestic violence call, they have basically three alternatives: They can arrest the person accused of spouse abuse; they can separate the couple for a time by ordering the alleged abuser to leave the premises; or they can attempt to serve as mediators between the parties.

Sherman and Berk asked police officers in Minneapolis to randomly apply one of these three intervention strategies—arrest, separation, or mediation—to each domestic violence call of which they were a part. For ethical and practical reasons, they limited the study to simple, or misdemeanor, assault where there was no severe injury or life-threatening situation. Their measure of the effectiveness of these interventions was whether an alleged abuser was involved in another domestic violence incident in the six months following the original police intervention.

Somewhat surprisingly, their basic finding was that arrest is the most effective of the three types of police intervention. Those arrested were significantly less likely to be involved in a repeat episode of domestic violence. This was not, however, a result of the fact that being jailed left them with less opportunity than others to commit acts of domestic violence, because those arrested were released very quickly and were thus equally able to engage in such acts as were those who experienced separation or mediation.

After Sherman and Berk reached their conclusions, the Minneapolis police department established administrative policies encouraging officers

rights movement and the environmental movement are examples of social movements that have used demonstration and protest to force recalcitrant politicians and corporations to change their practices related to social problems.

In recent years, there has been vigorous debate over the role of the government in identifying and solving social problems. Beginning with the New Deal of the 1930s and continuing through the 1960s, there was considerable support for the government to take responsibility for trying to solve social problems such as crime, poverty, and environmental pollution. In particular, the government used its ability to raise revenue through taxation—its fiscal policy—to attack social problems. For example, it raised money to support such programs as Medicare and Social Security. In addition, in times of economic downturn, the government went into debt, creating a budget deficit, to provide support for the unemployed, stimulate business activity, and create jobs to put people to work temporarily.

to use the arrest strategy when responding to spouse abuse calls. Many other police departments developed similar policies after learning of the Sherman-Berk results, and a number of states *required* that arrests of abusers be made if there is probable cause to suspect abuse. Thus, many law enforcement agencies have begun to take a stronger stand in protecting women from domestic assault, a stand that was shown empirically by Sherman and Berk to have a better chance of reducing the problem. Because social problems are complicated, sociologists recognize that one research study is not likely to tell us all we need to know. And this is true with domestic violence. To see if the results would hold up in other places and at other times, variations on the Sherman-Berk study have been done in a number of cities, including Omaha, Milwaukee, Atlanta, and Charlotte, North Carolina (Dunford, Huizinga, and Elliott, 1990; Hirschel, Hutchison, and Dean, 1992; Pate and Hamilton, 1992). Generally, the results have not been as supportive of the efficacy of arrest over other approaches in reducing repeats of spouse abuse. Why the difference in findings? It may be that Sherman and Berk, given the way they designed their study, inadvertently studied a select group of abusers on whom arrest was particularly effective. This illustrates the concern with

sampling problems affecting research, mentioned previously in this chapter. The later studies, looking at a broader sampling of abusers, found that arrest may work well with people whose reputations would be more negatively affected by an arrest, such as the affluent or those with middle-class jobs. On the other hand, for those who are unemployed or irregularly employed, arrest may not be as significant a threat to their reputations or as disruptive to their lifestyles. Thus, research on this topic continues in an effort to understand with which offenders and under what circumstances arrest is an effective deterrent to spouse abuse.

These studies on domestic violence illustrate the continuous interplay between research and policy, showing how social policy emerges in part from scientifically supported recommendations about how to handle social problems. Although personal and cultural values play a part in determining which solutions we choose, scientific research helps us to assess better the consequences of particular alternatives. In each of the following chapters, a Policy Issues section will analyze similar issues related to a particular social problem.

The size of the government grew substantially, and many social programs were established. At the risk of oversimplification, we can call this approach to the role of the government in social problems the "interventionist" approach.

With Ronald Reagan's election as president of the United States in 1980, pressure from another direction regarding social problems mounted. This pressure was based on the belief that government itself is a hindrance to the solution of many problems and should play only a limited role in attacking them. Rather, the government's primary role should be to create a climate that promotes business expansion. Then, the prosperity associated with such expansion will alleviate many, although certainly not all, social problems. Furthermore, appropriate government intervention in solving social problems should come predominantly from local and state rather than federal levels. Finally, some proponents of this approach argue for reemphasizing the importance of individualism, of people using their

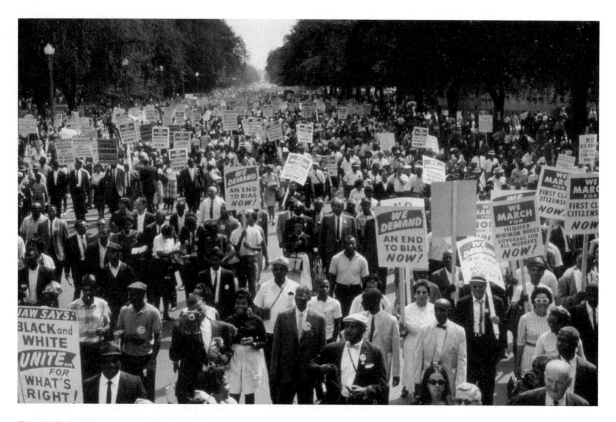

The civil rights movement in the United States is one of the most influential social movements of recent times. Through such mass demonstrations and other tactics, the movement serves as a key vehicle in alleviating problems of racial discrimination and social inequality.

own efforts to improve their lot in life. These individual efforts should be sustained more by family and friends than by the federal government. Social policy, in short, should be less related to government intervention and more dependent on the actions of individuals or private groups and the working of impersonal, economic forces. Again, at the risk of oversimplification, we can label this approach the "laissez-faire" approach. The French term *laissez-faire*, meaning "to let do" or to leave people alone, refers to the belief that government should intervene as little as possible in eco-

nomic affairs. This laissez-faire approach has remained fairly prominent in public policy debates in the 1980s and 1990s, supported by George Bush's control of the presidency (1989–1992) and the Republican's capturing of both houses of Congress in 1994.

Historian Arthur Schlesinger, Jr. (1986) argues that the United States experiences a cyclical shift in national involvement between these extremes, changing from an emphasis on public action to that of private interest and self-fulfillment and back again every twenty-five years or so. Whether it is cyclical or not, these contrasting views of the government's role in solving social problems certainly have been joined in debate in the 1990s as never before. The outcome of this debate shapes which policies will be developed to attack the problems that we will address in later chapters. We will, therefore, discuss the interventionist and laissez-faire positions at greater length when they are relevant to particular social problems.

Should We Solve the Problem?

Once a social condition has been judged to be a social problem, the search for solutions begins. At this point, there may be widespread agreement, at least in the abstract, that the problem should be solved. There are still, however, some final issues that need to be weighed.

1. Can we accept the costs of a solution? Because economic resources are limited, money used to clean up the environment is not available to fight crime or build defense weapons. Any effort to solve social ills will mean that fewer resources are available to solve other problems. There are also noneconomic costs to solving problems. If televised violence has adverse effects on children, then we could ban violent programs from television. But many Americans enjoy those television shows, whereas others would see this as an unacceptable imposition of government censorship.

2. Does a solution to one problem create yet other problems? As we emphasized in discussing the sociological perspectives, a society is a complex intertwining of many parts, and changing one part may have consequences for other parts. If, for example, we could effectively eliminate prostitution and drug dealing, what would happen to the people who earn a living that way? Would they turn to other crimes to support themselves? Or might they become a further welfare burden? The point is that we need to look at all the outcomes of particular solutions in order to plan very carefully. There

may be times when we decide that the "cure" is worse than the "disease."

3. Is a particular solution feasible? Given the political and social climate and the cultural values in the United States, are there some solutions to problems that would be impossible to accomplish because of resistance from some groups? Coping with alcoholism, for example, by banning all use of alcohol is simply not feasible, as the experiment with Prohibition in the 1920s showed. We currently use the prohibition approach to deal with drug abuse, which is equally difficult to eradicate. The point is that particular social policies may not be feasible if they go against the strongly held values and ingrained social practices of large or important groups in society.

International Perspectives: Social Problems in Other Societies

People in the United States, of course, tend to be most concerned about social problems in their own country. And sociologists in the United States have tended to devote most of their attention to American social problems. However, there are three reasons why we should focus some of our attention on social problems in other societies and cultures. First of all, we can gain additional insight into problems and their solutions when we observe them in cultures different from our own. Is the nature and extent of some social problem in the United States different from other countries? If so, then we can look for the factors unique to the American experience that produce this difference. We can also examine which solutions have worked elsewhere. This does not mean that they will automatically work here, but it does give us some insight into which solutions to consider.

A second reason for taking an international perspective is that nations today are intertwined in complex relationships in which we all depend on one another to an extent.

International trade agreements affect the jobs available to people in Portland, Maine, and Albuquerque, New Mexico; Bolivian farmers survive by growing coca plants, which produce illegal drugs available in the United States; political instability in Southeast Asia sends immigrants to the United States, increasing cultural diversity here and contributing to racial and ethnic conflict. Therefore, to find the causes of and solutions for social problems affecting the United States, it is sometimes necessary to explore social and economic developments in other parts of the world.

A third reason for a more global perspective is that some social problems are inherently global rather than national or regional in nature. This is true of many environmental problems. The sources of acid rain and global warming, for example, are found in many nations, and these problems will affect all the peoples of the world. By their very nature, the spread of such problems will not be stopped by national boundaries.

We do not have the space to cover all of the global dimensions of social problems. However, where most appropriate, illustrations of the nature and extent of social problems in other societies and cultures are included in the discussion of problems in the United States. To focus attention on this issue, most chapters contain a boxed section titled "International Perspectives," which elaborates on some of the

LINKAGES

The discussion of whether we should solve particular problems points to a final issue: Social problems do not exist in isolation from other social problems. Rather, problems tend to be linked together such that the worsening of one problem can contribute to the worsening of other problems. For example, an epidemic disease such as Acquired Immune Deficiency Syndrome is a health problem discussed in Chapter 4, whereas the use of crack cocaine is related to drug abuse discussed in Chapter 10. Yet, these two problems are linked because crack addicts who use needles tend to use dirty needles and share equipment. This is fertile ground for the spread of the AIDS virus. So, as intravenous drug use becomes more prevalent, the AIDS virus has a better chance of spreading. Alleviate one problem, and we will have made some progress toward alleviating the other. Many of these linkages will be made in the following chapters, and the student will learn to draw linkages that are not explicitly mentioned in this book. To encourage this consideration of linkages, we will include a brief insert at the end of the text material in each chapter that suggests one or two of the less obvious ways in which the problem focused on in that chapter is linked to problems discussed in other chapters.

global connections and issues relevant to the problem discussed in the particular chapter. Global issues are further explored in the text itself.

Summary

1. Sociology offers one of the most useful approaches to understanding social problems and finding solutions to them. Social problems involve public issues and are not merely personal troubles. They are fundamentally social in nature because their causes and solutions have to do with the workings of society. Four social conditions that can play a part in the emergence of social problems are: deviation from group values and norms, a decline in the effectiveness of social institutions, extensive social and cultural diversity, and the exercise of power.

2. The sociological imagination is the ability to recognize the relationship between what is happening in your own personal life and the social forces that surround you.

3. Sociological insights are formulated into theories. Very general explanations of social reality are called theoretical perspectives. The three major theoretical perspectives in sociology today are functionalism, conflict theory, and interactionism.

4. From the functionalist perspective, society is viewed as a system made up of a number of interrelated and interdependent parts, each performing a function that contributes to the operation of the whole society. Social problems arise, according to this perspective, when some element of society becomes dysfunctional and interferes with the efficient operation or stability of the system or the achievement of societal goals.

5. From the conflict perspective, society is viewed as consisting of a variety of groups who struggle with one another to attain scarce societal resources that are considered valuable. Social problems arise when a group, believing that its interests are not being met or that it is not receiving sufficient scarce resources, works to overcome what it perceives as a disadvantage.

6. The interactionist perspective shows how the social processes described by the first two perspectives enter into people's daily lives, focusing on everyday social interaction among people rather than on larger societal structures. It emphasizes the importance of definition and interpretation and the role of shared expectations in shaping behavior. Social problems arise, according to this perspective, when a condition is defined by an influential group as stigmatizing or threatening to its values and disruptive of normal social expectations.

7. Theories must be tested through research, which for sociologists is based on the scientific method. Science emphasizes objective and systematic observation as a source of knowledge. Theories are linked to research through hypotheses, which are tentative statements that can be tested about the relationship between two or more factors.

8. Although the subject is controversial, most scientists emphasize the importance of objectivity, or the attempt to prevent personal values from affecting the outcome of research. There are a number of things to watch for in assessing research data, including sampling problems, the assessment of causality, measurement problems, and assessing the claims people make.

9. The best means for finding effective solutions to social problems is through an interplay between the development of social policy and its assessment through scientific research. However, not all problems can or should be solved because the costs may be too high or there may be profound disagreement over how to solve them.

STAND Review

Key Terms

authority

causality

conflict perspective

definition of the
situation

deviance

ethnocentrism

functionalist
perspective

hypotheses

interactionist
perspective

interest group

norms

power

research

sample

science

social institution

social movement

social policy

social problem

sociological
imagination

sociology

subculture

theoretical perspective

theory

values

Multiple-Choice Questions

1. Public issues are different from personal troubles in that public issues:
   a. Affect large numbers of people.
   b. Affect mostly the elite.
   c. Lead to the disintegration of family life.
   d. Involve the violation of societal values and norms.
   e. Involve personal rather than collective solutions.

2. Sociologists refer to rules of conduct that guide people's behavior as:
   a. Values.
   b. Deviance.
   c. Authority.
   d. Subcultures.
   e. Norms.

3. Ethnocentrism can play a role in the emergence of social problems because ethnocentrism:
   a. Reduces group cohesion.
   b. Works at counterpurposes to social institutions.

c. Can enhance conflicts between subcultures.
   d. Involves criminal behavior.

4. The term "macrosociology" refers to theoretical perspectives in sociology that:
   a. Focus on large groups and social institutions and on society as a whole.
   b. Derive from the functionalist perspective.
   c. Focus on the intimate level of everyday interactions between people.
   d. Focus on people's ability to use symbols and to interpret social meanings in social interaction.

5. Which sociological perspective posits that social problems arise from social disorganization in society?
   a. Conflict perspective.
   b. Functionalist perspective.
   c. Sociological imagination.
   d. Interactionist perspective.
   e. Evaluation research.

6. Which sociological perspective has at its core the idea that coercion and the exercise of power are basic social mechanisms for regulating behavior and allocating resources?
   a. The functionalist perspective.
   b. The conflict perspective.
   c. The sociological imagination.
   d. The interactionist perspective.

7. Which of the following statements would be most consistent with the interactionist perspective?
   a. Society is made up of groups struggling with one another over scarce resources.
   b. People are symbol manipulators who create their own world.
   c. Social problems arise when some element in society becomes dysfunctional.
   d. Society is a system made up of interrelated and interdependent parts.

8. In conducting research on social problems, the best kind of sample to use is one that:
   a. Focuses only on people who are suffering from the problem being studied.

b. Will confirm the hypotheses of the research.
c. Is consistent with the values of the researcher.
d. Represents the population under study.

9. According to the text, commonsense knowledge:
   a. Is often superior to scientific knowledge.
   b. Is based on systematic observation.
   c. Usually involves representative samples.
   d. Tends to accept untested and unquestioned assumptions.

10. The laissez-faire approach to social problems is based on the idea that:
   a. The government should take prime responsibility for solving social problems.
   b. The conflict perspective is most useful in understanding social problems.
   c. The government should play a limited role in seeking solutions to social problems.
   d. Most social problems are global in nature rather than national in scope.

True/False Questions

1. The definition of a social problem given in the text includes both conditions that can be remedied through collective action as well as those that cannot.
2. In comparison to values, norms are much more specific and concrete rules of conduct that guide people's behavior.
3. Authority can also be referred to as "legitimate power."
4. Conflict theory is the sociological perspective that grew out of the similarities sociologists observed between society and biological organisms.
5. One of the core ideas of the interactionist perspective is that society consists of parts that are interrelated and interdependent.
6. The functionalist perspective views social problems as being caused by dysfunctional activities or disorganization in the social system.
7. Max Weber is the sociologist who argued that sociology should remain as value free as possible.

8. Sociologists do not conduct research on commonsense beliefs because they mostly turn out to be true.
9. Social policy is influenced by both scientific research and social and cultural values.
10. The interventionist approach is the approach arguing that government is generally a hindrance to the solution of many social problems.

Fill-In Questions

1. According to the text, a social problem exists when _____ defines a social condition as threatening its values.
2. Teenagers, skinheads, the elderly, and prison inmates are all examples of _____ .
3. The ability to understand the relationship between what is happening in people's personal lives and the social forces that surround them is what C. Wright Mills called _____ .
4. According to the functionalist perspective, social practices that disrupt social equilibrium rather than contribute to it are called _____ .
5. Two key concepts of the conflict perspective are _____ and _____ .
6. The concept of _____ is attributed to sociologists William and Dorothy Thomas and is a key concept of the interactionist perspective.
7. Scientific theories are linked to scientific research through _____ , which are tentative statements that can be tested regarding relationships between factors.
8. The three criteria used to assess whether there is a causal relationship between two phenomena are (1) a correlation be found between the two, (2) the correlation not be spurious, and (3) _____ .

9. When we consider issues of measurement, a central concern is that the indicators of social problems have _____ .

10. The specialty area in the social sciences that is devoted to assessing the effectiveness of solutions to social problems is _____ .

Matching Questions

_____ 1. authority

_____ 2. Karl Marx

_____ 3. definition of the situation

_____ 4. value-free sociology

_____ 5. social movement

_____ 6. deviance

_____ 7. functionalist perspective

_____ 8. samples

_____ 9. social institution

_____ 10. norms

    A. legitimate power
    B. interactionist perspective
    C. Max Weber
    D. civil rights movement
    E. conflict perspective
    F. representative
    G. macrosociology
    H. rules of conduct
    I. the family
    J. stigma

Essay Questions

1. Give the text's definition of what a social problem is. Draw out the implications of each element in that definition.

2. How do social institutions and subcultures play a role in the emergence of social problems?

3. What are the basic assumptions of the functionalist perspective regarding the nature and operation of society?

4. Describe how the conflict and interactionist theories would define whether a social problem exists.

5. Describe the various positions that sociologists have taken on the issue of scientific objectivity. Include in your answer a discussion of values and interest groups.

6. What is commonsense knowledge? What are its weaknesses? How does scientific knowledge differ from common sense? How does science overcome the weaknesses associated with commonsense knowledge?

7. Describe some of the difficulties that sociologists confront in measuring social problems. Include in your answer a discussion of the concepts of "measurement" and "validity."

8. Describe the contributions that social science research makes to the social policy process and the search for solutions to social problems.

9. Compare and contrast the interventionist and laissez-faire approaches to understanding and solving social problems.

10. What are some of the considerations to be taken into account when deciding whether solutions to social problems should be sought at all?

Answers

Multiple-Choice
1. A; 2. E; 3. C; 4. A; 5. B; 6. B; 7. B; 8. D; 9. D; 10. C

True/False
1. F; 2. T; 3. T; 4. F; 5. F; 6. T; 7. T; 8. F; 9. T; 10. F

Fill-In
1. an influential group
2. subcultures
3. sociological imagination
4. dysfunctional
5. interest, power, dominance, conflict, coercion
6. the definition of the situation

7. hypotheses
8. the time sequence be correct
9. validity
10. applied sociology; applied social research; or evaluation research

Matching

1. A; **2.** E; **3.** B; **4.** C; **5.** D; **6.** J; **7.** G; **8.** F; **9.** I; **10.** H

For Further Reading

Robert N. Bellah, Richard Madsen, William M. Sullivan, Ann Swidler, and Steven M. Tipton. *The Good Society.* New York: Knopf, 1991. This is a thought-provoking book about the extent to which the confidence of people in the United States about their society has been shaken. It suggests ways to transform such institutions as the family, politics, and the economy. As you will see, such transformations may well be an integral part of the attack on social problems.

Joel Best, ed. *Images of Issues: Typifying Contemporary Social Problems,* 2nd ed. New York: Aldine de Gruyter, 1995. This book contains some excellent articles that elaborate the social constructionist view of social problems. Building off the interactionist perspective, this viewpoint focuses on the ways in which social conditions come to public attention and are defined as a social problem.

Randall Collins. *Sociological Insight,* 2nd ed. New York: Oxford University Press, 1992. This book, in the vein of Mills' sociological imagination, tries to impart the power and insight of the general perspective of sociology.

Randall Collins. *Three Sociological Traditions.* New York: Oxford University Press, 1985. A short book that covers the functionalist, conflict, and "micro-interactionist" traditions in sociology. This is a complex book including considerable historical material, but it is well worth the time for the student willing to expend the energy.

Howard E. Freeman, Russell R. Dynes, Peter H. Rossi, and William Foote Whyte, eds. *Applied Sociology: Roles and Activities of Sociologists in Diverse Settings.* San Francisco: Jossey-Bass, 1983. This book contains twenty-seven articles covering the complete range of applied research methods and applied settings in which sociologists can be found working on various social problems.

Willard Gaylin, Ruth Macklin, and Tabitha Powledge, eds. *Violence and the Politics of Research.* New York: Plenum, 1981. This book raises issues regarding whether researchers should be bound by moral or ethical considerations when they conduct research on social problems and whether they should be responsible for making decisions about these problems. The particular problem focused on in this volume is violence and how to control it.

William Hastings. *How to Think About Social Problems.* New York: Oxford University Press, 1979. A readable book that can help guide you through the maze of possible deceit and trickery that surrounds much debate on social policy and social problems. Hastings shows you how to assimilate and reflect on sociological information and how to analyze issues clearly and in an unbiased way.

Howard M. Rebach and John G. Bruhn, eds. *Handbook of Clinical Sociology.* New York and London: Plenum, 1991. A detailed overview of consulting and clinical sociology, the book provides many illustrations of the specific kinds of work that applied sociologists do.

Lawrence W. Sherman. *Policing Domestic Violence: Experiments and Dilemmas.* New York: The Free Press, 1992. This book is about the research on domestic violence discussed in the Policy Issues insert in this chapter. It provides an interesting analysis of the role of social research in the development of public policy.

Sam D. Sieber. *Fatal Remedies: The Ironies of Social Intervention.* New York: Plenum, 1981. An excellent book on the many efforts at social intervention that become self-defeating when their outcomes run counter to their intentions. This book preaches a healthy dose of caution when considering social intervention.

Thomas J. Sullivan. *Applied Sociology: Research and Critical Thinking.* New York: Macmillan, 1992. This book provides a brief introduction, easily understandable by the undergraduate, to applied social science research. It presents the many ways in which social science research can be used to shape social policy and alleviate social problems.

TWO *CHAPTER*
Growth of Corporate and Government Power

The culture of the United States places substantial value on the sanctity of the individual and the importance of democratic decision making. In fact, the U.S. political and legal system goes to great lengths—much further than most nations—to protect the rights of people from being intruded upon by the government or other large organizations. In the legal realm, for example, the judicial system is based on the presumption that a person is innocent until proven guilty. It is the government's burden to prove that one is guilty rather than the individual's burden to establish innocence. So people are released on bail before trial on the grounds that the government has no authority to incarcerate people until after guilt has been established. Also, the court system makes it possible for individuals—even those with few economic or other resources—to take on large corporations or the government in the courts. For example, lawyers take some cases on a "contingency fee" basis, which means that they receive payment only if their client wins the case. This means that anyone, even poor people, can hire a lawyer with no financial risk to themselves. With such a system, powerless individuals frequently fight—and sometimes win—battles against corporations with enormous economic clout.

All too often, however, these cultural ideals are threatened by the extreme concentration of power in the hands of a few people in the political and economic realms. The result is often an abuse of power that works to the detriment of many citizens. Consider the following episodes:

- The savings and loan fiasco of the 1980s, the most expensive financial debacle in U.S. history, in which hundreds of savings and loan banks across the country had to be bailed out by the government in a program that will eventually cost the public as much as $500 billion. Contributing to this debacle was the deregulation of the Reagan years, which enabled speculators and corrupt business people to engage in highly questionable business practices and investments that put their depositors' funds at great risk. The result was to gut once-sound savings and loans while regulatory agencies looked the other way. Also playing a part was a Congress that was willing to ignore all this because senators and representatives were getting hefty political contributions from the very people who were plundering the institutions (Lowy, 1991).

- The defense fraud scandal of the late 1980s, in which corporations engaged in bribery and theft to get lucrative defense contracts from the government. In 1988, major corporations, such as Emerson Electric and Teledyne Electronics, were indicted for bribing consultants in exchange for information about U.S. defense contracts. By 1991, forty-one

corporate and government officials, along with five corporations, had pled guilty to charges that included bribery and theft of information. Among these, the highest ranking government official was an assistant secretary of the navy who was accused of taking bribes from such major American corporations as Pratt & Whitney (owned by United Technologies Corporation) and Martin Marietta (Lewis, 1991).

- The 1995 episode in which 70 illegal immigrants from Thailand, mostly women, were freed from a prison-like California garment factory where they worked and lived in virtual slavery. Some had worked there for as long as seven years. The workers received very low wages, toiled under violation of health and safety laws, and were not free to leave the factories at any time. However, some corporate giants benefited from this involuntary servitude. Some large clothing manufacturers in the United States ordered their clothing stock from such factories, and many major department and clothing stores in the United States sold products from the factories.

There is substantial concern that such abuses of power may threaten national goals. They may, for example, foster a cynicism in the average citizen that may reduce support for our political and economic institutions. To understand this problem, we need to know something about how our political and economic institutions work. **Politics** refers to *the agreements in society over who has the right to exercise control over others, who can establish laws to regulate social life, and how conflicting interests in society will be resolved.* By establishing laws and exercising control, political institutions, in effect, determine whose values will predominate and how rewards and resources will be allocated in society. **Economics** refers to *the processes through which goods and services are produced and distributed.* Al-

Myths & FACTS

ABOUT BUSINESS AND GOVERNMENT

Myth: The economy of the United States represents a pure form of capitalism.

FACT: There are no pure forms of capitalism in the world today. Even in the United States, the government is involved in controlling and regulating the economy in many different ways.

Myth: The people who hold stock in a corporation own the corporation and can control the policies of the corporation.

FACT: In reality, a corporate board of directors and the professional managers they hire run the daily affairs of the corporation. The vast majority of the stockholders own such a small share of the company that they have neither the time, the expertise, nor the inclination to pay much attention to how the corporation is run. In addition, stockholder meetings are held very infrequently, and thus stockholders have few opportunities for input.

Myth: Finally, in the 1980s, the growth in the size of government in the United States was halted.

FACT: The federal budget continues to grow larger each year and to constitute close to one-quarter of our gross national product. However, the number of full-time government employees has actually been dropping since 1970.

Myth: The United States' corporate economy works toward the common good.

FACT: The primary motivation of corporations is to turn a profit and to ensure corporate growth. Corporations have been known to market shoddy, even dangerous, products to the public because a quick profit could be made.

Myth: The economy of the United States has become uncompetitive in world markets because so many workers in the United States are members of powerful unions that force employers to pay unjustifiably high wages.

FACT: At the unions' peak in the 1950s, only one of every four workers in the United States was a member of a union, and that number has dwindled to one out of six today. The other five workers have no organized body speaking for them and are on their own when demanding a living wage from their employers.

though politics and economics are distinct institutions, they are closely intertwined. Both focus on a central issue in society: the exercise of power in the allocation of scarce resources. In fact, a classic description of politics could be aptly applied to *both* political and economic institutions: They determine "who gets what, when, and how" (Lasswell, 1936).

The problem associated with these institutions is not the use of power—because this is precisely their purpose in society—but rather the abuse of power: the exercise of power in ways that work against the interests of substantial numbers of less powerful people and result in their exploitation. Abuse of power is often linked with the size and complexity of businesses and government, along with the concentration of power in the hands of a small number of people or organizations.

As we will see, political and economic concentration of power creates many problems. In addition, political and economic institutions are often closely linked with many of the other social problems discussed in this book. Levels of poverty, for example, are clearly linked to the workings of the economy and to political decisions about whether and how to attack unemployment. Some crime, as we will see, has its foundation in economic problems. Government and corporate policies regarding such things as day care and maternity leave influence the shape of the family. So the analysis of political and economic institutions in this chapter will serve as a helpful foundation to the remaining chapters in the book.

We begin our investigation of social problems associated with government and the economy by looking at the types of economic systems that exist in modern societies.

Types of Economic Systems

To survive, every society must ensure that food, clothing, shelter, and other materials are produced and distributed to the members of society who need them. The rules and social practices governing this production and distribution make up the economic institution of a society. The economies of most nations today are *market economies,* which are based on the exchange of money for goods and services in the marketplace. People sell their labor for a certain amount of money and then the money is used to purchase goods and services. Although modern economies share this market foundation, they differ from one another in significant ways. We will look at three main types of modern economic systems: capitalism, socialism, and mixed economics.

Capitalism

Capitalism contains three features that, taken together, distinguish it from other economic systems: *The means of economic production and distribution are privately held; the profit motive is the primary force guiding people's economic behavior; and there is free competition among both producers and consumers of goods* (Gottlieb, 1988). The proponents of capitalism argue that these features provide for consumer control over the quantity, quality, and price of goods. In its pure form, capitalism works like this. Seeking profits is, in a sense, merely unleashing personal greed. But this is quite appropriate, argue proponents of capitalism, because this gives capitalists the motivation to provide more and better goods and services. If there is a demand for some product, someone will come along and provide it if they can profit from doing so. Furthermore, the profit motive encourages innovation and creativity because there will be entrepreneurs looking for novel goods and services—some that the consumer has not even thought of— that they can sell for a profit. Capitalists must be constantly on the lookout for new products lest someone else beat them to the punch and corner a market. Thus, from this profit-seeking motive, consumers benefit from having more and better goods available. Open competition among capitalists also benefits consumers by enabling them to choose among a number of items, comparing price against quality. If the quality of products is too low or the price too high, people will not buy them and the capitalists will be out of business unless they change. Adam Smith referred to the conjunction of profit seeking with competition as the "invisible hand" of market forces that would ensure that the supply of goods is roughly equivalent to the demand for them and that the public has available the goods that it wants with the highest quality possible.

The role of government in this process, argue those who favor pure capitalism, should be to stand aside and let market forces operate unhindered. The government is necessary to maintain public order and protect against foreign threats, but any effort by the government to regulate the market is regarded as disastrous. Government regulation of prices or wages, for example, would interfere with both the profit motive and the competitive element and thus reduce the incentive to develop new and better products. In short, government policy under capitalism should be one of laissez-faire: The government should leave the market alone.

There are no pure forms of capitalism in the world today. Even in America, the government has always been involved to a degree in controlling and regulating the economy. Despite this, the American economy is still one of the most capitalistic in the world. There is strong resistance to government interference in the economy and little support for government ownership of utilities, railroads, or other industries that are often government owned in other capitalist societies.

Socialism

Socialism refers to *economics in which the means of production and distribution are collectively held so that the goods and services that people need are provided and equitably distributed.* In capitalism, production is based on economic demand: Goods and services are provided if people can afford to purchase them. With socialism, production is based on human need: Goods and services are produced because people need them, irrespective of whether they can afford them (Harrington, 1989; Le Grand and Estrin, 1989). Pure socialist economies reject the profit motive, recognizing that one person's profit is another's loss. In addition, socialists argue, the profit motive provides a built-in incentive for one person to exploit another, for example, by keeping wages low in order to increase profits. In other words, it is inherent in capitalism that one person is set in competition with another—either capitalist against capitalist or capitalist against consumer—and the inevitable outcome is a highly unjust and inequitable distribution of resources.

In socialist economies, the primary motivation for economic activity is to achieve collective goals, such as a higher standard of living for all citizens. To do this, the economy is highly centralized, with decisions about what to produce and how to distribute these products being made for the whole nation by national authorities. Because profit and consumer demands are not key elements in these decisions, the decisions can presumably be made with the collective interests of society as a whole in mind.

As with capitalism, pure socialism is rare. Most socialist economies do allow for the private ownership of some goods, such as personal or household items. In addition, some people are allowed to engage in capitalist activity. In China, for example, farmers are allowed to sell some of their produce in a competitive marketplace. China is also experimenting with programs in some industries in which consumer demand, rather than central authorities, determines how much is produced. In these programs, factory managers can, within limits, manipulate wages and other costs in order to break even or make a profit. Most means of economic production, however, are still collectively rather than privately owned.

At this point, a word needs to be said about *communism,* a term that is routinely misused by many people. **Communism** is the term used by Karl Marx to describe the utopian end stage of the struggle over capitalism. In a communist society, *all goods would be communally owned; people would not work for wages but rather would give according to their abilities; and there would be no scarcity of goods and services, allowing people to receive whatever they needed. In addition, the state would become less important and its role would dwindle.* According to these criteria, there are no communist societies in the world today. Nations that are commonly referred to as communist are actually socialist.

Mixed Economies

The economies discussed thus far tend toward pure capitalism or pure socialism, although each includes some elements of the other. Another type of economy, found in England and much of Western Europe, is the **mixed economy,** *in which there are strong elements of both capitalism and socialism* (Brus and Laski, 1989). In mixed economies, most industry is privately owned and oriented toward profit making. In addition, despite considerable government regulation, there is a competitive market economy, and consumer demand determines much of what is produced. However, in mixed economies, many important industries, such as banks, railroads, the communications industry, the media, and hospitals, might be state owned. Mixed economies provide for strong regulation of the private sector by the state. High taxes and an elaborate welfare system are established in hopes of achieving the national goal of a fair and equitable distribution of resources. Through such mechanisms, proponents of mixed economies hope to avoid the extensive social inequality that can accompany capitalism and the economic inefficiency that sometimes afflicts socialist economies.

Understanding these basic economic arrangements is important because the social policy debates relating to social problems often involve the question of which economic arrangements are most likely to achieve specified goals. We introduced this debate in Chapter 1, in which we discussed the interventionist and laissez-faire approaches. Although we need to be careful about oversimplifying positions, many interventionists argue that we should learn from mixed economies about how government policy can help us achieve goals of fairness and equity. Laissez-faire advocates, on the other hand, argue that an approach closer to that of pure capitalism would lead to greater economic growth and affluence, which would help solve many of the problems that we face. As we will see, proposals for solving problems of corporate and government growth tend to follow one of these two approaches.

The Concentration of Economic and Political Power

The Corporate Economy

Capitalism in the United States has undergone considerable change in the past two centuries. Our economy once consisted of small, local businesses and many competitors. Consequently, power in the economic sector was decentralized, diffused, and limited to local or regional levels. It was almost impossible for businesses to accumulate substantial power at the national level. Today, our economy is very different: It is highly centralized and international in scope, and a small number of people can gain enormous control over wealth and power.

Furthermore, capitalism in the United States is no longer based on the individual ownership of businesses. Rather, the dominant form of business today is the **corporation,** *a business enterprise that is owned by stockholders, most of whom are not involved in running the daily affairs of the business.* There are three key things that distinguish corporations from individually owned businesses. First, corporations have access to a much broader source of capital than do individuals because the former can sell stock to thousands of stockholders. Second, stockholders, who own the corporation, have only a limited liability should the corporation be sued or go bankrupt. Stockholders lose only the funds they have invested. Third, the ownership of corporations is separate from the control of its policies and daily affairs. The stockholders own a part of the corporation, but most stockholders are not involved in the actual running of the company. The corporation is run by professional managers who are ultimately appointed by a board of directors that is elected by the stockholders. These managers typically own little or no stock in the company. Legally, the stockholders run the corporation, but for all practical purposes the board and the managers do. Most shareholders own only a small number of shares in the company, and they have neither the time, the expertise, nor the inclination to pay much attention to how the company is run. The board and the managers are in a position to make recommendations that most shareholders will accept with little thought. So the board and corporate managers control the corporation without being substantial owners of it. Unlike individually owned businesses, the ownership of corporations is easily transferable, and should a major stockholder die, the corporation continues to function as usual. Because of these characteristics, the corporate economic structure is extremely attractive to investors. Large amounts of capital can be accumulated with minimum risk to individuals.

Because of the advantages that stem from corporate organization, corporations now dominate our economy, with a relatively small number of corporations accounting for most business activity. There are over three million corporations in the United States, but most are small and have a minor impact on society. Economic resources, and thus influence and power, tend to be concentrated in the larger corporations. For example, the largest two hundred corporations employ 80 percent of all people who work for corporations. Of all the assets held by the largest five hundred industrial corporations in the United States, 75 percent of those assets are held by the largest one hundred of those corporations (U.S. Bureau of the Census, 1994: 558–559). As these large corporations have come to dominate the economy, it has become possible for some to control substantial segments of economic life to the point of restricting competition in the marketplace. One form of restrictive growth is called a *monopoly*—the control of a product or service by one company. For example, in the early 1990s, Nintendo controlled about 80 percent of the $5 billion video-game market in the United States. Related to the monopoly is the *oligopoly*, in which a few corporations control a market. Some sectors of the U.S. economy are highly

oligopolistic, in some cases approaching a monopoly. In the cigarette industry, for example, the four largest corporations control close to 90 percent of production. In a 1980s court case, the American Telephone and Telegraph Company was forced to divest those companies that were providing local telephone service. The government has also filed suit against IBM and against the four largest producers of breakfast cereals for monopolizing their markets.

Another form of corporate growth representing a concentration of economic power is the *conglomerate*, which is a corporation that owns other companies in fields quite different from that of the parent company. For example, through a merger in 1993, Paramount Viacom International Inc. became the owner of the following: four cable television channels (USA Network, Showtime, MTV, and Nickelodeon), two book publishers (Simon & Schuster and Prentice Hall), Paramount Movie Studios, Madison Square Garden, the New York Knicks basketball team, the New York Rangers hockey team, and assorted other corporations. In fact, some corporations, such as Transamerica, are in large part "holding companies" whose major purpose is to coordinate the activities and profits of all the corporations they own. Conglomerates are advantageous in that they provide stability through diversity: losses in one industry can be counterbalanced by the parent company through profits made in an unrelated business.

As corporations have grown over the decades, the larger ones have extended their activities into a number of different countries (Barnet and Cavanagh, 1994). By the 1970s, multinational corporations had emerged, which made a large commitment of resources in international business and engaged in manufacturing, production, and sales in a number of countries. But these overseas corporate activities tended to involve separate operations in the various countries, often tailored to local social and economic conditions. By the 1990s, global corporations had become the prominent actors on the world scene: a few hundred corporations whose economic activities span the globe, using modern financial, industrial, and telecommunications technology to mount a world-wide, integrated system of production and distribution. Corporations have gone multinational, and then global, because enormous profits can be made with such an organization. There are lucrative markets for their goods outside the United States. In addition, the cost of labor, land, and taxes is considerably lower in places such as Mexico, Taiwan, and Korea than in the United States. In 1988, 8 percent of all money spent for plants and equipment by corporations headquartered in the United States was spent outside the United States; this percentage has been growing steadily for a number of years (Uchitelle, 1989). This fact reflects the extent to which U.S. corporations now participate in a "global economy," in which national boundaries have become less important as determinants of or restraints on economic competition. This means that labor and capital in the United States now compete with labor and capital in many countries around the world.

Unionization

Although conglomerates and multinationals, along with capitalists and entrepreneurs, play important roles in creating and running large business concerns, they are far overshadowed in number by the masses of working people who staff these organizations. And workers have made significant efforts to concentrate economic power in their own hands. The rudiments of labor organizing in the United States can be traced to the colonial period, when impressment, or enforced labor, led to rioting among sailors and longshoremen. It was not until the late nineteenth century, however, and the emergence of business firms employing thousands of workers, that the labor movement emerged as a significant political force in the U.S. economy. Capitalists, pursuing the profit motive, were inclined to pay workers as little as possible. The capitalists' ability to do this was made easier because large numbers of people had immigrated to the United States in the late 1800s, creating a labor surplus in some industries. In response, working people organized to pursue their own interests. Capitalists staunchly opposed the labor movement, believing that higher wages would generate laziness among workers and threaten the "American way of life." The owners' resistance and the workers' determination made U.S. labor history one of the bloodiest and most violent of any industrial nation. In Lattimer, Pennsylvania, in 1897, for example, thirteen striking coal miners were shot to death and another thirty-nine were wounded by a sheriff's posse who stopped their march. In 1913, seventy-four people, including eleven children and two women, were killed in a clash between National Guard troops and strikers in Colorado (Novak, 1978; Taft and Ross, 1969). There were hundreds of other such incidents. However, the workers eventually prevailed, and by the 1930s legislation gave them the right to organize and to bargain collectively with employers.

The number of U.S. workers belonging to labor unions continued to grow, reaching over twenty-two million people in the 1970s. With the right to strike firmly established for most workers, unions have been in a strong position to gain even higher wages and more benefits for their members. Just as businesses formed conglomerates and oligopolies, labor unions from many industries have combined their forces. The American Federation of Labor and Congress of Industrial Organizations (AFL–CIO) is over thirteen million strong, for example, and almost two thirds of all U.S. labor unions are affiliated with it. This enables unions to pool resources and information and to provide mutual support through the refusal of members of one union to cross the picket lines of another. In recent decades, public employees such as teachers and fire fighters have proved to be a significant source of recruitment to the ranks of unionization, although it is illegal in many states for public employees to strike. In fact, some teachers have been fired for joining illegal strikes.

Although unions have gained considerable power in the United States, their future is somewhat uncertain (Craypo and Nissen, 1993). Union membership as a proportion of the work force has been declining since the mid-1950s and is presently at its lowest point since 1940 (see Figure 2.1). The number of people belonging to unions has declined to less than seventeen million. The primary reason for this is that occupations traditionally unionized—blue-collar industrial jobs—have been declining in numbers, whereas the number of white-collar employees, who have traditionally not unionized, is growing. In fact, the United States is called a "postindustrial" society because a shrinking proportion of its work force labors in industrial occupations. Because of automation, robotization, and other technological developments, fewer workers are needed to make the products necessary for our lifestyle (see Chapter 15). The largest growth in the work force has been in white-collar jobs such as sales, management, teaching, or clerical work (see Figure 2.2). A second reason for the decline in unions is that many corporations over the past four decades have relocated in states having weak union organizations. Third, unions have been facing increased hostility from the American public, especially when they demand sizable pay increases in times of high unemployment. In 1981, for example, air traffic controllers demanded what the Reagan administration considered an excessive wage hike; the controllers went on strike to push their demands, even though this action was illegal. Rather than concede, President Reagan fired the controllers for striking.

FIGURE 2.1 Union Membership in the United States as a Percentage of Total People Employed, 1950–1994. *Sources:* U.S. Bureau of the Census, *Statistical Abstract of the United States, 1984* (Washington, D.C.: U.S. Government Printing Office, 1983), p. 439; U.S. Department of Labor, Bureau of Labor Statistics, *Employment and Earnings,* January, various years.

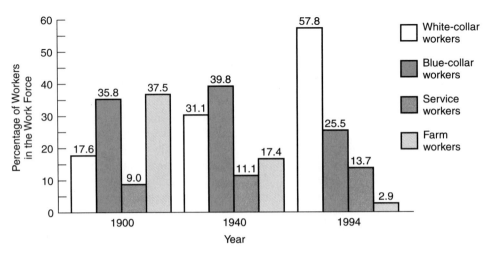

FIGURE 2.2 Changing Occupational Structure in the United States, 1900–1994. *Sources:* U.S. Bureau of the Census, *Historical Statistics of the United States, Colonial Times to 1970, Bicentennial Edition, Part 2* (Washington, D.C.: U.S. Government Printing Office, 1970), p. 139; U.S. Department of Labor, Bureau of Labor Statistics, *Employment and Earnings,* Vol. 42, No. 1, January 1995, p. 174.

There was considerable public support for his decision, even among many union members. This reflects a growing concern that unions have concentrated so much power in their organizations that they can raise wages, and therefore prices, to levels having little relationship to actual worker productivity. Other episodes during the 1980s, such as the machinists' strike against Eastern Airlines in 1989, provided further evidence that the public climate in the United States had become less favorable for labor unions. Possibly in response to this, labor unions have been noticeably less inclined to use the strike in their struggle with corporations than they were in earlier decades (see Figure 2.3).

Big Government

The founding fathers of the United States intended for the federal government to be small and not extremely powerful. After all, the American Revolution was fueled by hatred for British tyranny over the colonies. After winning independence, the revolutionaries wanted to avoid a domineering federal government. So the role of the central government under the new Constitution was to be limited: to raise an army, to establish a national currency, and to provide an environment in which states and individuals could pursue the common good. And the U.S. government did remain rather small throughout the nineteenth century.

The twentieth century, however, has been witness to a massive growth of government in the United States and other industrial nations. Since 1950, the expenditures for all levels of government—federal, state, and local—in the United States have exploded from $70 billion to over $2.4 trillion (U.S. Bureau of the Census, 1994: 297). This reflects a twentyfold increase during a period when our population did not even double in size. These expenditures have increased from $460 per person in 1950 to $7,000 today. Sixty-one percent of these expenditures involve the federal government. The federal budget has grown from 10 percent of the gross domestic product just prior to World War II to 22 percent today (see Figure 2.4 on p. 46). However, despite what many people believe, the number of people employed by the federal government has remained about the same since 1970 (U.S. Bureau of the Census, 1994: 347).

Several factors explain this growth in government. A major one is that industrial societies for centuries have been shifting responsibility for regulating social and economic policy to the central government. This shift has occurred because nations have grown so complex and interdependent that some central authority becomes increasingly necessary to regulate economic and social life. In the realm of social policy, for example, the government is now seen as having final responsibility for the sick, the poor, and others who are unable to take care of themselves and do not have families or other support networks to help them.

Responsibility for economic policy has also been shifted to the central government, and this has become a larger and more complex task as our corporate economy has grown. The freewheeling economic environment of the last century worked reasonably well until business empires became so large that they could monopolize large parts of the economy. Then government had to step in to regulate industry with the interests of the whole society in mind. Also, as technology produced increasingly complex and sometimes dangerous products, it grew beyond the ability of the average citizen to evaluate these products, and the government stepped in to offer control and regulation.

A second reason for the growth of government in the United States has been the emergence of the philosophy that social ills can be cured through aggressive spending policies and elaborate government-sponsored programs. This view came to dominate American politics with Franklin D. Roosevelt's New Deal during the Great Depression of the 1930s. In an effort to combat the Depression, Roosevelt used government spending policies extensively to spread money and expand the federal government into many new areas. Out of the New

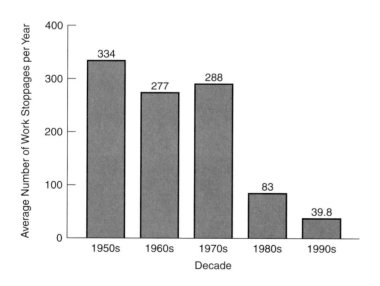

FIGURE 2.3 Average Number of Work Stoppages per Year Involving 1,000 or More People, 1950s–1990s. *Source:* U.S. Bureau of the Census, *Statistical Abstract of the United States, 1989* (Washington, D.C.: U.S. Government Printing Office, 1989), p. 413; U.S. Bureau of the Census, *Statistical Abstract of the United States, 1995* (Washington, D.C.: U.S. Government Printing Office, 1995), p. 442.

FIGURE 2.4 Federal Expenditures as a Percentage of the Gross Domestic Product, 1940–1995. *Source:* U.S. Bureau of the Census, *Statistical Abstract of the United States, 1995* (Washington, D.C.: U.S. Government Printing Office, 1995), p. 333.

Deal emerged such diverse programs as Social Security, the Tennessee Valley Authority, and the Civilian Conservation Corps. Massive government spending during World War II continued this infusion of government funds into the economy. This monumental military endeavor called for highly centralized decision making and control over resources, and this further enhanced the size and impact of the federal bureaucracy. As can be seen in Figure 2.4, government expenditures increased dramatically during World War II and have never dropped to prewar levels.

A final reason why government has grown is that people demand many more services from it today than in the past. People rail against the costs of welfare, but they want the government to maintain the national park system, build monuments to Vietnam veterans, and keep our public libraries open and current. Few would want the government to stop providing insurance for individual citizens' deposits in banks and savings and loan institutions, and pleasure

boaters whose engines die ten miles from shore are unlikely to rant about excess government expenses when a Coast Guard vessel rescues them. People in the United States have come to expect the government to provide many services that are not provided by private industry, and this has been a major pressure contributing to the growth of big government.

This discussion of political and economic concentration focuses on the United States, but similar issues of the concentration of resources can be addressed on a global scale. The International Perspectives insert does this.

Perspectives on the Concentration of Power

The recent historical trend, then, has been toward the concentration of power in the hands of large political and economic organizations. Is this inevitable? Is it necessarily bad? This section will analyze these issues using the socio-logical perspectives.

The Functionalist Perspective

According to the functionalist perspective, societies are made up of interrelated and interdependent parts, including economic and political institutions and practices as well as cultural values. These various parts should be sufficiently integrated that people can use them to work together toward common goals. As we have seen, American cultural values place emphasis on the sanctity of individuals and their right to control their destiny, the importance of democratic decision making, and the value of free enterprise and private property. Yet mammoth corporations and big government threaten these values. When corporate managers in New York make a decision to close a factory in Pennsylvania and move the work to Malaysia, what should the thousands of displaced workers in Pennsylvania make of the value of individual autonomy and control? What control do they have over their fate? If economic power is concentrated in the hands of a few monopolies or oligopolies, then is free enterprise and competition able to provide the most benefit for the greatest number of people? For functionalists, one of the key elements in the problem of the concentration of power is the inconsistency between cultural values and political and economic reality.

Some inconsistency between values and reality is an expected part of the social disorganization that results from rapid social change. There are good reasons why economic and political organizations have become so large: Large size is functional in providing large numbers of complicated goods and services to many people. For example, producing and distributing the vast array of goods that are a part of our lifestyle would be impossible without organizing ourselves into large nationwide business enterprises. The disorganization results because this bigness can develop in ways that conflict with cherished cultural values and threaten common goals. For functionalists, further change is needed whereby some adaptation and accommodation is made. Cultural values may have to change to recognize the reality and centrality of these mammoth structures in our lives. At the same time, new methods of exercising social control over corporations and government may need to develop to counterbalance their concentration of power.

The Conflict Perspective

From the conflict perspective, there is no necessary harmony among corporations, the government, and the various groups of citizens in society. Rather, society is made up of a variety of different interest groups that come into conflict with one another over the resources available in society. This conflict of interests is an inherent feature of economic and political life. The accumulation of power in the hands of a few is the outcome of the struggle for advantage in society. Large corporations and big government become the mechanisms in modern society through which powerful groups maintain their control over resources. From the conflict perspective, a conflict of interests and maldistribution of resources reflect a normal state of affairs.

Concentration of power is not by itself a social problem. It becomes a social problem, from the conflict perspective, when some influential group of people believes that it is not receiving its fair share of resources and strives to do something about it. These groups sometimes combine their forces and form social movements to improve their lot. Through collective action, they can sometimes redress their grievances. Yet this does not mean that inequalities in power can be, or ever will be, eliminated. From the conflict perspective, collective action leads to a rearrangement of inequalities, not to their elimination. Furthermore, powerful economic interests are most often at a substantial advantage in this struggle.

Just as political and economic power is concentrated in the United States, such concentration can be found in other nations, especially the concentration of power and resources in large corporations. When one looks at the world economy, however, some additional aspects of economic concentration are found. For example, the world's corporate resources are concentrated in the hands of a very few nations—the highly industrialized, capitalist nations of North America, Europe, and Asia which now dominate the world economy. Figure 2.5 suggests the extent of that domination by showing that most of the large corporations in the world are headquartered in a small number of nations. The United States, Japan, and three European nations account for four hundred seventeen of the largest five hundred corporations in the world. Even more astonishing, 60 percent of those five hundred corporations are found in just *two* of the world's more than two hundred nations: the United States and Japan. So, when we talk of global corporations dominating world trade, we really mean that a relatively few nations of the world dominate that trade.

This concentration of corporate wealth has been assisted by some global financial institutions that have emerged during the twentieth century (George and Sabelli, 1994; Rich, 1994). Among such institutions are the International Bank for Reconstruction and Development (or World Bank) and the International Monetary Fund (IMF). These global financial institutions lend money, guarantee private investments, help stabilize prices and currencies, and encourage private investment in development. They receive their funding from their member nations (most nations belong), but their decision making and voting power tends to be dominated by the wealthy industrial nations of Europe and North America. In short, they function much as a central bank for the world, lending money and expertise to support economic development in developing nations. However, the support is not free: They demand that nations organize their economies in ways that support corporate growth. Often this means reducing domestic spending on things like schools, health, and social services. It can also require that nations stress export industries rather than production for domestic consumption.

The global concentration of power has also been enhanced by global trade agreements that encourage free trade among nations and discourage hindrances to trade, such as tariffs or restrictive labor policies. The most recent such trade agreements are the North American Free Trade Agreement (NAFTA) of 1994 and the World Trade Organization (WTO) of 1995. This global free-for-all in trade benefits the large, established corporations because they have the resources with which to compete in this environment. Small or new corporations, or noncorporate forms of organization, are no match for these established concentrations of power.

These global corporations and their supporting organizations generally subscribe to the ideology that levels of world prosperity are unlimited, that such prosperity can extend to all people, and that economic development and capitalist expansion, largely unfettered by government intervention, is the best means to achieve such global prosperity.

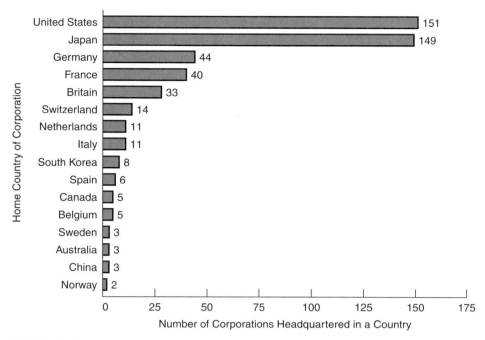

FIGURE 2.5 The Nations with the Greatest Share of the World's Largest Corporations, 1994. *Source: Fortune,* August 7, 1995, pp. F30–F40.

In fact, many supporters of these organizations claim that they will eventually eradicate poverty around the world. To support such economic development, world economies have become organized around market-oriented production and continual mass consumption. This has been called the "commodification of the globe," according to which everything is a commodity to be sold and market value determines all (Rich, 1994: 6). In such a global economic environment, political boundaries and national allegiances are becoming less important determinants of economic activity. Such global concentration has many ramifications for all nations, including its effects on opportunities for people in the United States. One focus of this chapter and the remainder of this book will be the extent to which people in the United States are affected—sometimes positively but often in a negative way—by this global concentration of power. We will see that the emerging global economy plays a part in many of the social problems investigated.

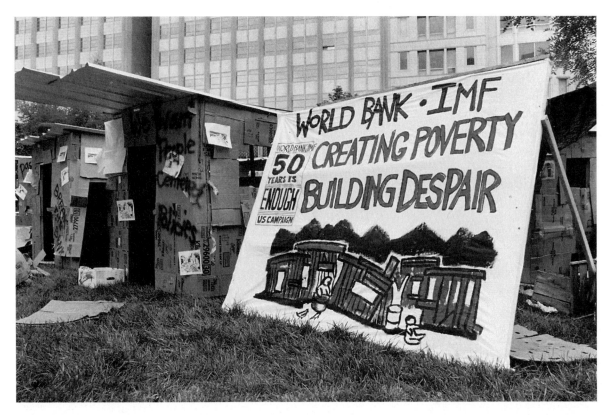

Global financial institutions, such as the International Monetary Fund and the World Bank, are controversial elements of the global economic system. Proponents argue that they help spread prosperity around the world while opponents claim that their policies perpetuate poverty and enhance environmental degradation.

Economic advantage is routinely translated into political advantage, and control of the government can lead to the passage and enforcement of laws that benefit the powerful. The government becomes, in effect, a tool used by the powerful to protect their position.

The Iron Law of Oligarchy

Is the concentration of power inevitable? Although it may not be, there are factors that are very favorable toward its development in organizations. In 1915, Robert Michels used the term **oligarchy** to refer to *the concentration of power in the hands of a few people at the top of an organization*. From his study of political and economic organizations, he concluded that the pressures toward oligarchy were so strong that he coined the phrase "the iron law of oligarchy." Michels described the likelihood of this occurring very succinctly: "Who says organization, says oligarchy" (Michels, 1966, originally published 1915: 256). For Michels, the tendency toward oligarchy arises when groups reach a size where consensus-oriented decision making is no longer feasible, and it derives from the very nature of organizations. First, to operate effectively, any organization must develop mechanisms for coping with administrative and decision-making problems, and it is more efficient if only a few people are responsible. Spreading authority among a large number of people can create conflicting decisions and uncertainty over who has authority to do what. Second, those who emerge as leaders in organizations tend to be adept at influencing and controlling members, and they can utilize the resources of the organization to maintain their position. They can, for example, place loyal followers into strategic positions in the organizational administration. Finally, most rank-and-file members of organizations are apathetic: They do not have the time, energy, resources, or desire to contest the power of the leadership. This often leaves those at the top of organizations with considerable freedom and power to run the bureaucracy as they wish.

Given these oligarchical tendencies, it is hardly surprising that the concentration of power is a potential problem in political and economic institutions. The reasons for and extent of such concentration can be explored in more detail by looking at these issues first in regard to the United States and then with a more global focus.

Is There a Power Elite in the United States?

Researchers of both functionalist and conflict persuasions have conducted research that attempts to assess exactly how concentrated power and decision making actually are in the United States. Out of these efforts, two major models of power in society have been developed: the power elite model and the pluralist model.

The Power Elite Model   In the 1950s, the sociologist C. Wright Mills (1956) proposed what has come to be called the **power elite model** to explain the exercise of power in the United

States. Deriving his approach from the conflict perspective, Mills argued that *there exists a small group of very powerful people who make just about all the important decisions in the United States.* This power elite consists of the people who hold top positions in the government, business, and the military. Included in this group are the president and his cabinet, the executives who run the large corporations, and the generals and admirals who run the Pentagon. According to the power elite model, the government, corporations, and the military dominate our lives today, and it is from controlling these spheres that power is derived.

According to Mills, the power elite is a cohesive group, and the interests of its various members in the government, military, and corporate sectors tend to coincide. There are elaborate social networks that link the members of the elite to one another. For example, they attend a small number of private schools and universities, vacation in the same spots, and go to the same parties. All of this social contact helps them to maintain a consensus about what is in their interests and to develop strategies for ensuring their success. Below the elite, there is a middle level of diverse interest groups including most members of Congress, professional organizations, many lobbyists, and most unions. They participate in making decisions about issues of secondary importance that have little effect on the elite. At the bottom of America's political structure is the great mass of citizens who have virtually no power because they do not belong to those organizations wielding power. These people may vote, but Mills viewed this privilege as meaningless because most elected officials are in middle-level positions, while real decision-making power rests with the elite. In addition, the power elite is highly influential in determining which candidates the political parties will place before the electorate. One source of such influence is the mass media. The Applied Research insert (see pp. 52–53) analyzes how the media, especially

APPLIED RESEARCH
The Media and the Power Elite

That the media is powerful is no secret. The press in the United States, in fact, is intended to be powerful and to serve a free society as an alternative source of power to the government and large corporations. Yet the media are themselves private companies and usually corporate in structure. They pursue greater profits and larger amounts of power in the same fashion as other corporations discussed in this chapter. And as has occurred in other corporate sectors, there has been concentration of power among the media:

> Sooner or later a handful of corporations [will] control most of what the average American reads, sees, and hears . . . the same few corporations will control all the important mass media not just in the United States but globally. Nevertheless, there is close to total silence in the mainstream news on the social consequences of this concentration. (Bagdikian, 1990: x)

Historically, all newspapers in the United States were local affairs—small businesses whose main concerns focused on the town or county in which their readers lived. To be sure, newspaper owners, executives, and editors were often heavily involved in local issues, such as who was elected mayor or which new employers moved to town, but their influence only rarely extended beyond the local region.

Today, the press is big—and concentrated—business. Sociologist Peter Dreier (1982) found that the twenty-five largest newspaper companies accounted for 53 percent of the daily newspapers sold in the United States. In fact, many newspapers have achieved legal monopolies as cities both small and large have become "one-newspaper towns." In addition, the parent corporations of newspapers are often members of the power elite, with influence that stretches far beyond the local level. The newspaper companies are linked to other corporate members of the power elite through the membership of newspaper executives on the boards of business corporations, banks, and financial institutions. The Times Mirror Company, for example, which publishes the *Los Angeles Times,* had twenty-four such linkages with the thirteen hundred largest corporations listed by *Fortune* magazine. Newspaper executives are also involved in the "revolving door" through which members of the economic elite serve for a time in high-level government positions and then return to their corporate jobs. At the time of Dreier's research, thirty-six executives from the twenty-four largest newspaper companies had been or were then serving in one of these government positions.

So, especially if you live in an urban area, some of the men and women who own and operate your daily newspaper are, in all likelihood, members of the power elite. What is the impact of this on the role of the media in the analysis of social problems? The simple conclusion is that most newspapers become mere apologists for the power elite and corporate capitalism. Dreier found, however, that the impact was much more subtle. As newspaper companies become larger, form monopolies, and establish links with the power elite, Dreier found, they often develop a viewpoint that has been labeled "corporate liberalism," which tends to look positively on unions, social welfare programs, and government regulation. However, it is not a socialist position, as discussed in this chapter, because corporate liberalism retains the belief that a corporate economy based on private enterprise is the most efficient economic system. In this view, government programs and regulations are intended to protect people against the few weaknesses or excesses that can be found in capitalism. In fact, newspapers following this corporate liberal ideology may sometimes be very critical of big government and corporate capitalism, but this criticism stems not from an opposition to capitalism but from a desire to promote responsible capitalism. One latent function of such criticism is to protect capitalism from challenges and discourage interest in more radical changes that would significantly threaten corporate control by the power elite.

Much has occurred since Dreier published the results of his research in 1982. In particular, control over the media has become much more concentrated and global in scope. By the 1990s, over 70 percent of the daily newspapers in the United States were owned by outside corporations and fourteen of these corporations had most of the business. Despite the existence of more than twenty-five thousand media outlets in the United States, a mere "*twenty-three corporations* control most of the business in daily newspapers, magazines, television, books, and motion pictures" (Bagdikian, 1990: 4, italics added). What is emerging as the twentieth century draws to a close is a race by a few megacorporations to control the print and electronic media around the globe. One of the more ambitious efforts has been that of the Australian Rupert Murdoch and his News Corporation. The Corporation owns, in whole or in part, the Fox TV network with 158 affiliate stations in the United States; a number of publishing companies, including HarperCollins and Basic Books; Star TV of Hong Kong, which beams its programs through satellite to thirty-nine countries from the Middle East to Asia; the 20th Century-Fox movie studio; British Sky Broadcasting, a satellite-TV service for Britain and Europe; and many newspapers and magazines around the globe. Other giant corporations are working hard to compete with Murdoch,

and the concentration of media resources he has managed to achieve may be a portent of the future.

Executives in these corporate media empires, of course, insist that such concentration will *improve* the media. Less partial observers are more pessimistic. Reviewing all of these trends, Edward Herman concludes that, on the big and important issues, the media

> serve mainly as a supportive arm of the state and dominant elites, focusing heavily on themes serviceable to them, and debating and exposing within accepted frames of reference. (1993: 25)

Applied social researchers like Peter Dreier and Ben Bagdikian agree in their concern that concentrated power over public information is inherently antidemocratic:

> When the central interests of the controlling corporations are at stake, mainstream American news becomes heavily weighted by whatever serves the economic and political interests of the corporations that own the media. The voice of the giants become ever more loud and drown out with greater success the small media voices of dissent. Now that media owners are so large that they are part of the highest levels of the world economy, the news and other public information become heavily weighted in favor of all corporate values. (Bagdikian, 1990: x–xi)

The additionally disturbing aspect of such a trend is that, as the dissenting voices are silenced, people become less and less aware that they are being presented a distorted view because they have fewer guideposts with which to measure the accuracy or completeness of what they see, read, and hear.

newspapers, can help support the powerful in society.

The Pluralist Model   Some sociologists argue that Mills's view of the United States is distorted and overly conspiratorial because there is actually little concentration of power and coincidence of interests among the elite (Kornhauser, 1966; Rose, 1967). Instead, the **pluralist model** views power as *pluralistic,* or *spread over a large number of groups with divergent values, interests, and goals.* According to sociologist David Riesman (1961), there are veto groups in society with the ability to block decisions that might adversely affect their positions. For example, labor unions can exert considerable influence on issues affecting their members, such as raising unemployment benefits or minimum-wage laws. Similarly, farmers may fight to stop the lowering of price supports for farm products. To be sure, pluralists recognize that some groups have far more power and other resources than other groups, and there is considerable inequity in society. However, they argue, there is no single, cohesive, dominant elite, and power is not centralized in the hands of a few.

Below the elite, according to the pluralists, is the unorganized, but not entirely powerless, public. With the vote, the public can exercise some constraint over the behavior of those in power. In addition, there are other ways for the public to exert influence on more powerful groups. Cesar Chavez, for example, harnessed this power in the 1960s in his attempt to improve the plight of migrant farm workers. He organized a consumer boycott of the lettuce and grapes grown by those farm owners who refused to negotiate with farm workers. This boycott was effective, and the sales of lettuce and grapes dwindled. In part because of this effort, the farmers ultimately negotiated. The environmental movement has also used its ability to organize large numbers of people for public protest as a tool in struggling against corporate

power. Especially in the areas of air pollution and the use of pesticides, these groups have organized seemingly powerless people to successfully shape public policy (Hoberg, 1992). Given these examples, pluralists dispute the power elite view and argue that the mass of the citizenry can effectively exert an influence, even against what seem to be formidable corporate foes.

Assessment of the Models   What is one to conclude regarding who rules in the United States? Clearly, the realities of holding power in this society are more complex than either the power elite or the pluralist models alone suggest. Some research that points to this conclusion will be summarized. For example, political scientist Thomas R. Dye (1995) reviewed the corporate and governmental sectors in the United States and located approximately seven thousand positions in corporations, the government, and the military that direct most of the nation's economic and social policy. According to Dye, it is this very small group of people who represent Mills's power elite. Sociologist G. William Domhoff (1967, 1983) went a step further by studying the social backgrounds of the people who occupy these elite positions. He discovered that members of the upper class participate in an elaborate network of informal social contacts, just as Mills suggested. However, Domhoff did not find the cohesiveness or coincidence of interests among these people that Mills implied. Nevertheless, there are significant linkages and influence peddling among the various sectors of the power elite. Members of the corporate elite, for example, make sizable contributions to both the Republican and Democratic parties in hopes of influencing the decisions of the President, congressional representatives, and other politicians. In fact, some would argue that, because of political contributions, corporate lobbying, and other forms of influence, the corporate elite exercises overwhelming control over politicians, regulatory agencies, and government bureaucrats. In this view, the average citizen has little influence and is largely at the mercy of corporate goals (Greider, 1992).

Research on the power elite has also focused on links between business and the military. In his final speech before leaving office in 1961, former President Dwight D. Eisenhower, himself a five-star general during World War II, spoke of the **military–industrial complex,** referring to *the relationship between the military that wants to purchase weapons and the corporations that produce the weapons.* Both the military and the corporations benefit from a large military budget and from policies favoring military solutions to international problems (Brunton, 1991). The potential danger of a powerful military–industrial complex is that defense decisions and the development of weapons systems may be influenced by what is beneficial to the military and defense industries rather than by what is necessary for national security. One way in which the coincidence of interests among members of the military–industrial complex might occur is if there were a periodic interchange of top-level personnel between the military and defense industries. And, as Mills and others have shown, such interchanges do occur. A study by the government found that six thousand of the thirty thousand people with the rank of army major or higher who left the Pentagon in 1983 and 1984 worked for companies doing business with the Pentagon. Many worked on the same military projects in private industry that they had worked on at the Pentagon (Cushman, 1986). When corporations hire former government officials, they hope that their contacts and knowledge of government and the policy process will work to the benefit of the corporation.

Although there clearly are important links between the military and corporations suggesting a "military–industrial complex," the picture is considerably more complex than this. Many corporations actually oppose increases in defense spending, fearing that these will adversely affect the economy and result in higher taxes. One study, for example, found active opposition to increases in defense spending between 1948 and 1953—a period including the Korean War—among executives of some of the largest business, industrial, and financial corporations in the country, even among some firms with defense contracts (Lo, 1982). So the military–industrial complex, although important, does not exist in a vacuum. There are other powerful groups, even among the power elite, with competing interests, and there are less powerful groups that still wield considerable power, especially on domestic issues.

In short, both the power elite and pluralist models offer significant insight into the question of who rules the United States. As the power elite model suggests, a relatively small group of people hold enormous power. It controls much of foreign policy and makes decisions that shape the direction of economic development. This ruling group, although possibly not conspiratorial or completely cohesive, ranks far above most other citizens in political, economic, and social clout. Yet as the pluralist position suggests, many groups that are not a part of this elite can occasionally wield power, especially on domestic social policy and local and regional issues. This is the realm in which many of the battles over solutions to social problems discussed in this book are likely to be fought. And most people in the United States have an opportunity to play a part in these less powerful, but still quite important, groups.

The World Economic System

The power elite and pluralist models can be applied to other nations around the world, and each nation would have its own mosaic of power elitist and pluralist tendencies. Some nations would show more elitist concentration than the United States, while others would show less. To understand the emerging world economic system, however, we need to look at some considerations that transcend national boundaries. While there are a number of reasons for the dramatic concentration of economic resources on a global scale, one important explanation is that it results from the centuries-long historical expansion of capitalist economic systems around the world. **World system theory,** pioneered by the sociologist Immanuel Wallerstein (1979), posits that *the world's nations have become increasingly interdependent, both economically and politically, and are now linked in a worldwide system, with some nations having more power and resources than others.* The major force in this world system is capitalism and its emphasis on market forces, profit making, and surplus accumulation. Capitalism's drive to expand and find new markets creates a pressure to seek out new territories in which to invest. In fact, one of the unique characteristics of capitalism is its commitment to economic growth and expansion. The world expansion of capitalism began in the fifteenth century with the European voyages to the new world to find natural resources and trade that would be profitable for the European colonial nations, and it continues today as corporations seek new markets in a global economy.

Today, corporations' search for new markets has created a global economy with an international stratification system. According to world-system theory, a hierarchy of nations has emerged, divided roughly into *core nations* (capitalist, technologically advanced nations searching for opportunities to expand investment) and *peripheral nations* (less developed nations that provide cheap labor, produce food, and serve as a source of raw materials). There are also *semi-peripheral nations* that are large or have some special resources, and because of this they fall somewhere between the two classifications—less dependent on the core nations, and sometimes acting as core nations themselves (Apter, 1986; Chase-Dunn and Hall, 1993). The

peripheral and semi-peripheral countries are also sometimes called Third-World or less developed countries.

In this international stratification system, the core nations dominate and exploit peripheral nations. The key to the system is trade, with some nations being goods exporters while others serve primarily as a labor pool and source of natural resources. In fact, some world-system theorists argue that the nature of capitalism is such that it creates social inequalities through its tendency to distribute resources unequally. Such inequalities occur within nations, which have both rich and poor people, and at the international level, where the policies of core nations help keep peripheral nations less developed. The core nations extract natural resources from the peripheral nations and use them as cheap labor pools to produce agricultural and industrial goods that are then exported for profit. Through political, economic, and sometimes military intervention, the core nations encourage the emergence of political and economic elites in the peripheral nations that will support and assist in economic expansion of the core. This elite in the peripheral nations benefits from the world system and supports policies that will maintain their role in the world capitalist system. For example, the political elites in some less developed nations in Latin America have discouraged labor unions that would work to increase the pay and improve the working conditions of citizens of those nations because unions might discourage investment by corporations from core nations that are looking for a cheap and passive labor force. While elites in the peripheral nations may benefit from this, it tends overall to result in a shift of wealth from the periphery to the core as the corporations of the core nations drain profits from the periphery.

The world economic system, then, divides people into three groups. An international elite of well-to-do people is quite comfortable materially, and some of its members can become very wealthy. An international working class struggles to survive, with its fate determined mostly by decisions made by multinational corporations in core nations; even in this group, people can be thrown out of work and suffer serious economic declines because multinationals shift work to areas with lower labor costs. Finally, an international lower class lives in abject poverty with little hope of their circumstances improving. It was mentioned earlier that global corporations and their affiliated financial organizations hold the ideology that world capitalism will eliminate poverty. World-system theorists are more skeptical regarding whether this can happen. Looking at the historical record, they see world capitalism benefiting the elites and some others while exploiting many less powerful groups around the world. To this point, poverty has not been eliminated, and the inequitable distribution of wealth and power around the world has persisted.

Problems Created by the Concentration of Power

Societies today, much more so than in the past, live in an interdependent global community that is characterized by a significant concentration of economic and political power. Somebody in practically every nation benefits from such a system; but people in all nations, including the United States, suffer disadvantages because of it. This section will explore some of the problems created by the concentration of political and economic power, both in the United States and around the world.

Effects on Competition

One of the major problems is that corporate growth can restrict competition, which we have seen is one of the core characteristics of capitalist economies. When economic power becomes concentrated in an oligopolistic or monopolistic fashion, the individual consumer can become a relatively powerless force in the marketplace in comparison to corporations. As has been seen, in an economy based on competition, companies that are inefficient or produce inferior merchandise are likely to be driven out of business because consumers will purchase the less expensive and higher quality products of more efficient competitors. In this kind of economy, consumers have a degree of control over businesses through their discretionary buying power in the marketplace. In a less competitive environment, however, the consumer is at a substantial disadvantage because corporations are able to manipulate prices, quality, and product availability in ways that benefit them and without the controlling force of competition. As these processes continue, power and wealth continue to be concentrated in the hands of a small number of gigantic business enterprises. The larger corporations can offer poorer quality merchandise to enhance their profit structure, and consumers suffer.

The growth of conglomerates can also lead to a dwindling of the competitive marketplace. For example, a particular corporation could lower the prices on videocassette recorders until they sold at well below production costs. The losses incurred could be absorbed by the profits earned in different sectors of the conglomerate. Smaller competitors in the VCR business, without the support of a conglomerate, would be unable to sell their units at less than production price. Once the competition from these less powerful companies is reduced, the corporation in control would be free to raise its prices on VCRs.

In the long run, this lack of competition could smother the economy of a nation because it would mean less innovation and little technological development. Advances occur, according to the capitalist argument, because one fears being bested by one's competitor. Without competition, there is little motivation for innovation, reducing the ability to compete with foreign companies. So excessive concentration of economic power might make the economy of any nation less competitive in world markets.

Conflict Between Societal and Corporate Goals

The concentration of economic power in corporate structures also raises the issue of whether corporations pursue goals that are broadly beneficial to society or that enhance the narrow interests of particular groups. Large corporations control such vast resources that their activities shape in very substantial ways the lives of average people. With the primary goal of corporations being to make and increase profits and to ensure corporate growth, corporations may not necessarily act in the best interests of other groups or of society as a whole. For example, when a corporation leaves the United States for a Third-World country that has lower taxes and labor costs, the United States loses jobs and tax revenue, and this loss can bring about increases in unemployment, poverty, and related social problems such as crime and alcoholism. Economic decisions based solely on the criterion of corporate profit, therefore, may create or intensify social problems that have negative effects on other groups in society.

This conflict between societal and corporate goals has become especially noticeable and clearcut with the spread of the global economic system in the last few decades. For example, the president of NCR Corporation, when asked about the competitiveness of the United States, responded, "I don't think about it at all. We at NCR think of ourselves as a globally competitive company that happens to be headquartered in the United States" (quoted in Uchitelle, 1989: 13). The chairman of President Reagan's Council of Economic Advisors, reacting to comments such as these, saw a "growing tension between the global nature of American business and the goals of the territorial United States" (quoted in Uchitelle, 1989: 13). In fact, a major element of

the economic stagnation of the 1980s and the 1990s has been the transfer of U.S. jobs to other countries. However, others argue that at least some of this drain of U.S. productive dollars is offset by foreign corporations that pump money into their U.S. operations, thus creating jobs in the United States.

On a global scale, there is considerable controversy over whether the policies of organizations such as the World Bank or the IMF benefit all, or even most, citizens of the nations in which they operate (George and Sabelli, 1994; Rich, 1994). While many people do benefit, the policies have also meant drastic reductions in wages for some, lowered expenditures for health, education, and other social services, and devastating degradation of the environment. In some cases, tens of thousands of poor people have been displaced from their homes and re-settled, often in less desirable areas, in order to make way for dams, logging activities, or large-scale agricultural and industrial developments. In fact, some dispute whether these organizations have been very successful in their stated goal of promoting development through large loans to governments. Critics of these organizations argue that their practices have dislocated people, exacerbated economic inequality and ethnic tensions, and promoted environmental degradation while benefiting corporations, elites, and a small segment of the work force.

Threats to Democratic Institutions

The globalization of corporate control in the past century has created new or enhanced threats to democratic practices and institutions around the world. These large corporations are sometimes wealthier than the nations in which they operate, giving the corporations enormous power from which to demand that a country adopt policies that are beneficial to the corporation. In fact, governments in smaller nations may deliberately avoid political and economic policies inconsistent with the goals of the corporations. In these ways, social policies in some nations, even in the United States, may result not from the democratic wishes of the populace but from implied or explicit demands from powerful corporations. In many cases, corporations intervene in the democratic process of a nation by supplying campaign funds to particular political candidates or in a few cases by attempting to overthrow elected officials (Barnet and Cavanagh, 1994).

Global economic institutions, such as the International Monetary Fund and the World Bank, represent very organized threats to the democratic process in some nations. Since these world institutions often operate in secret, ordinary citizens and their governments may have little knowledge of or input into what these international organizations do. Dispensing large amounts of money and making policies at the international level, these organizations have become almost quasi-governments themselves, whose policies affect the lives of people around the world. For example, as a condition of supporting a nation, these organizations often require the establishment of an administrative structure within the government, partly under World Bank or IMF control, that may circumvent or ignore the policies of elected or appointed officials in government. Corporations and their world financial institutions are private or semi-private organizations and as such are largely beyond democratic control. The result is that the important economic and political decisions that shape the lives and opportunities of people around the world are in the hands of these powerful private and semi-private entities. Their decisions often change traditional cultures and ways of life as they push social and political changes that further economic development.

The Dwindling of Unions

Traditionally, unions have enabled employees, who have relatively little power unless they organize, to combine their efforts and counter the substantial resources available to their cor-

porate employers. Unions remain powerful in America, but the social and economic environment in which they function is shifting. Although predicting an outcome is difficult, many people believe it unlikely that unions will play the same role in a postindustrial society that they did during the industrial period. This may mean that corporations will have a freer hand in establishing wages and working conditions. Especially if unemployment levels rise, as they did in the 1980s, workers will be competing with one another for a limited number of jobs, and union employees willing to strike over labor issues may find themselves replaced by other workers for whom a lower paying job is better than no job at all. This happened in 1989 during the Eastern Airlines labor dispute, where nonunion mechanics were hired to replace those who were on strike. It happened again in 1992 when thirteen thousand workers struck the Caterpillar Corporation. Tens of thousands of people applied for jobs to replace the strikers, showing that they would be content to work for wages and benefits the strikers were refusing. The strikers caved in and went back to work out of the fear, probably realistic, that they would be replaced if they pushed their demands. Some companies have been accused of using high unemployment rates as a tool to attack unions and diminish their strength. As this occurs, many workers, especially those with few skills, may find it more difficult to locate jobs that pay what they consider a decent wage. These same trends are found in other industrial nations, and research shows that, as the extent and power of unions has dwindled in industrial nations, greater levels of social inequality have resulted (Freeman, 1993). This may mean that some people will confront a way of life that is little better than, and possibly worse than, that of previous generations.

Worker Discontent and Alienation

Industrialization has led to many changes that are regarded as positive by most people, such as a higher standard of living and a shorter work week. At the same time, the nature of work for many has changed—they work in large bureaucratic settings such as factories, schools, or corporations. Their work is often boring, repetitive, and unfulfilling. They have little control over the pace of their work, what they produce, or what happens to it once it is produced. The assembly line is the epitome of this kind of work, but increasingly office and clerical work has these characteristics. This type of work organization may be beneficial to employers in terms of efficiency and profitability, but it can result in considerable discontent among employees. Lack of control, monotony, and depersonalization often result in **alienation,** *a feeling of powerlessness in controlling one's surroundings and a sense that what one does has little meaning or purpose* (Vallas, 1988; Greenberger et al., 1989). Workers who are alienated are less productive workers; they may also express their discontent through drug or alcohol abuse or political discontent (Seeman, Seeman, and Budros, 1988).

Worker Dislocation and Unemployment

Over the past 40 years, the percentage of people in the United States who are unemployed has been gradually increasing (see Figure 2.6). Teenagers, African Americans, and other minority groups are most heavily affected by this problem. However, these official unemployment statistics do not include people who are unemployed but have quit looking for a job— so-called discouraged workers. It also does not include those who are underemployed, working part-time, or working at a temporary job that does not pay enough to support a family. When these people are counted, the unemployment problem in the United States is even more grave.

A part of this unemployment problem is directly related to trends in the world economic system described previously. Since the 1960s,

many traditional industries, such as steel and automobile manufacturing, have declined in the United States in the face of foreign competition, throwing many people out of work. Sometimes called "displaced workers," these unemployed persons numbered over 5 million workers between 1987 and 1992 (Aronowitz and DiFazio, 1994; U.S. Bureau of the Census, 1994: 415). These workers are often better educated and more highly skilled, and belong to groups with traditionally low levels of unemployment, factors that led some to assume that these same unemployed persons would quickly find jobs comparable to the ones they had lost. Research investigations have shown otherwise, suggesting that these unemployed are clear victims of the world economic system (Devins, 1986; Zippay, 1991). Some of these displaced workers never return to the labor force. Those who do often find themselves unemployed for some time—one and a half years, on average— and almost all experience a permanent decline in family income because of their job loss. Many are forced to accept irregular work at low-paying jobs with few fringe benefits. In addition, African Americans and Hispanic Americans are hit much harder by job displacement than whites: These groups are more likely to be displaced, are jobless longer, and are much less likely to be reemployed (Kletzer, 1991; Boisjoly and Duncan, 1994).

One disturbing trend during recent economic downturns has been a shift in the characteristics of the long-term unemployed in the United States: they are considerably more likely to be between the ages of 30 and 55 than in the past (Ilg, 1994). These workers are in the middle of their working lives and often have considerable work experience and workplace skills. Still, they find themselves out of work and facing substantial difficulties finding another job. In the past, these long-term unemployed were more likely to be younger people who had fewer job skills and less experience. This trend shows that today's unemployment problem is

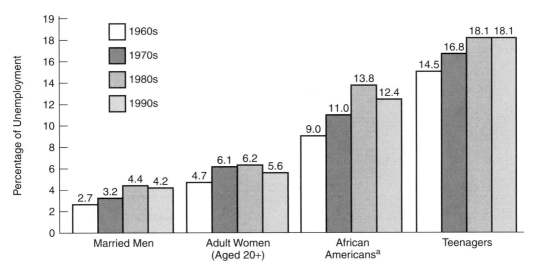

FIGURE 2.6 Unemployment Rates Among Selected Groups in the United States, 1960s–1990s.
[a]Before 1983, percentages include Native Americans, Alaskan Natives, Asians, and Pacific Islanders.
Source: U.S. Congressional Budget Office, *The Outlook for Economic Recovery, Part I* (Washington, D.C.:
U.S. Government Printing Office, 1983), p. 91; *Monthly Labor Review,* various years.

due more to the unavailability of jobs than to a dearth of job skills among those seeking work.

One of the reasons for this persistent unemployment in the United States has been increased competition for jobs in the world economic system. Factories in the United States have closed and moved overseas or contracted with manufacturers in other countries. Countries in Latin America and Asia have been especially receptive to U.S. businesses. The minimum wage in the United States is more than $4 per hour, while well-paid workers on automobile assembly lines can earn $24 per hour. By contrast, global sportswear companies headquartered in the United States pay young girls and women in Indonesia *$1.35 per day* to assemble sports shoes for export to the United States (Barnet and Cavanagh, 1994). Hundreds of U.S. companies have left the United States and opened up shop in *maquiladoras,* factories in northern Mexico that take advantage of the cheap labor, weak unions, and lax environ-

mental regulations to assemble products and export them to the U.S. Many thousands of U.S. jobs have been lost to these *maquiladoras* that have the best of both worlds—cheap labor and easy access to U.S. markets to sell their products.

While world competition is probably the major factor in the growth in unemployment in the United States, other factors contribute. There has been considerable growth in the teenage labor market, and the number of women joining the work force has grown over the decades. Still another dimension of the problem is automation, which is discussed in more detail in Chapter 15. Some casual observers are fond of pointing to such things as laziness, too much emphasis on welfare, too high wages, and illegal aliens as explanations for our nation's unemployment ills. Data do not back up these claims, however, and changes in the world economy, like the ones just described, are responsible.

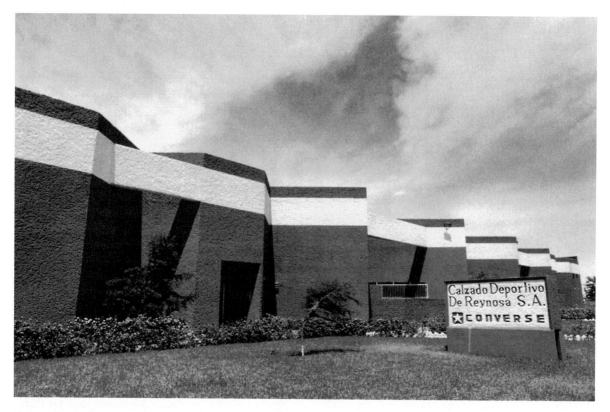

This *maquiladora* in Reynosa, Mexico, produces athletic shoes for import into the United States. Such foreign factories, with low labor and production costs, compete with workers in the United States and contribute to the problem of displaced U.S. workers.

Unemployment, as tragic as it may be, is not the only form in which difficulties confront workers in the United States. A related problem is that the jobs available to them may not pay as well as they did in the past. In fact, by 1990, more full-time workers had low-paying jobs than was the case in earlier decades (U.S. Bureau of the Census, 1992a). In 1964, 24 percent of full-time workers had poverty-level incomes. By 1979, this had dropped to 12 percent. However, it climbed steadily through the 1980s until, by 1990, 18 percent of full-time workers had incomes that would not bring

their families out of poverty. Apparently, although new jobs were created during the 1980s, the jobs tended to be at the low end of the pay scale. So, even when the U.S. economy provides work for people, that work is less likely to pay enough to support a family. The Policy Issues section analyzes various competing social policy positions that have been advanced to tackle some of these problems in the United States.

However, the problems of unemployment and underemployment are not limited to the United States or to industrial nations. A United

Nations report published in 1994 characterized the current situation as "the worst global employment crisis since the Great Depression of the 1930s" (Hartman, 1994: 5A). Around the world, 120 million people are officially registered as unemployed—a figure that everyone agrees is conservative—and at least another 700 million are underemployed, which means that they do not earn enough to support themselves and their families. As with unemployment in the United States, the world situation is due in part to the nature of the global economy that is emerging as industrialism and capitalism advance around the world. This world economy is characterized by a relative dearth of entry-level jobs that pay a decent wage. There is also a shortage of jobs for people with low levels of education or few skills. The modern work place is increasingly a high technology environment, calling for considerable education and training. Those who, because of poverty or lack of access, do not receive such training and education find few places where they can earn a living wage. These trends have resulted in a polarization of the work force: an increasing chasm between high-wage and low-wage workers. This means that people who get the good jobs do fairly well for themselves and their families, but those without the necessary education and skills live increasingly marginal and precarious lives. Added to this is the increasing use of a geographically mobile labor force—immigrants, both legal and illegal, who are forced to travel where the jobs, typically low-paying, are. It does not matter whether it is Mexican peasants coming to the United States, Palestinians going to Kuwait, or Turks going to Germany. Corporations depend on this flexible, low-paid pool of labor to help keep costs down and profits up.

Abuse of Government Authority

Is big government a problem? This depends, of course, on one's perspective, but there do seem to be a number of reasons why massive government bureaucracies can create potential problems. One reason is the opportunity for the abuse of power by government officials. When government is large and distant from its constituency, isolated bureaucrats are freer to make decisions that benefit themselves and their associates but not necessarily other groups in society. In fact, the growth of big government can become problematic through collusion between government and big business. The Department of Defense, for example, may look the other way when industries with defense contracts have enormous cost overruns. This problem goes to the very heart of freedom in a democratic society: Are people able to control the actions of elected or appointed officials? If anything, many people in the United States now assume that their government will keep secrets and hide misdeeds from the citizenry. Beginning with Watergate in the 1970s, the exposure of government misdeeds and coverups seems to have become routine. In the 1980s, the Iran-Contra scandal was revealed, in which government officials were said to have diverted funds to support the Nicaraguan contra fighters even though Congress, which represents the people, had voted against this policy. President Clinton was confronted with the Whitewater scandal, with charges that he covered up some of his financial dealings. The raid by agents of the Bureau of Alcohol, Tobacco, and Firearms on David Koresh and his Branch Davidian group in Waco, Texas, in 1993, seemed to be a symbol for many people of a government out of control in the abuse of its authority. In a free society, such abusive and sometimes secret exercises of government power are highly detrimental to the democratic process; in a democratic society, the belief that the government is deceiving the people is an insidious cancer that threatens important group values.

A second reason why big government is a problem, according to those who take a laissez-

POLICY ISSUES

The Deindustrialization and Reindustrialization of the United States Economy

The text describes shifts in the United States economy as a consequence of the emerging world economic system. These shifts, often referred to as the **deindustrialization** of the United States economy, are characterized by *high rates of unemployment in the industrial sector, an aging and deterioration of factories and other productive resources, and an inability to compete with other industrial nations, especially those in Asia* (Graham, 1992; Danziger and Gottschalk, 1993). Many fear that deindustrialization will produce a permanently weakened economy in which businesses struggle for marginal profitability, jobs are exported overseas, and the lifestyles of many people decline. What can be done about this seeming decline? In the debate over what to do, one of the major controversies has been the role of the government in attempting to reindustrialize the economy. While the debate is complex, it tends to revolve around the laissez-faire and interventionist positions outlined in Chapter 1.

The laissez-faire position on this issue arises from the belief that a free and competitive economic marketplace is the most efficient and effective system for allocating resources. Deindustrialization, to the extent that it exists, arises because of government interference with the free enterprise system and because our national tax and spending policies have encouraged noncompetitive elements to determine the allocation of resources (McKenzie, 1984). Government efforts to save certain companies or prevent factory closings, for example, foster the continuation of inefficient

businesses, making the overall costs of products more expensive and less competitive. In addition, laissez-faire advocates argue, the federally set minimum wage and government support of unions over the years has resulted in artificially high incomes for workers and made U.S. industry less competitive in world markets.

According to this "hands off" policy, the solution to these problems—the way to "reindustrialize"—is to shift power from the hands of the government to the corporate boardroom. The continued expansion of government programs funnels resources away from private enterprise and encourages the allocation of resources based on factors other than the economic marketplace. Less government spending will result in tax cuts that in turn will serve as an incentive for people to work harder, save more, and invest some of their earnings. Savings and investment will provide more capital for industry to expand, and this expansion will produce more jobs for people and reduce poverty and unemployment. For laissez-faire proponents, then, the solution to problems with the U.S. economy is a shift toward a purer form of capitalism.

Few people in the 1990s would take a strict laissez-faire position that gives the government absolutely no role in industrial policy. Even the Bush administration supported some government programs to encourage industrial development in certain areas. However, interventionists see the government playing a much more central role in reindustrializing the United States. Interventionists begin with some very different assumptions (Harri-

faire stance, is that big government is inherently detrimental to society: It funnels resources away from the private sector where they could be put to better use. Because the government is not constrained by competition and demands to make a profit, it can "afford" to be

highly wasteful. Government can lose money and still maintain existing programs if politicians continue to provide tax revenues. If tax money is not available, the government can borrow money and create a deficit. In fact, budget deficits played an important part in the ecoson and Bluestone, 1988; Aronowitz and DiFazio, 1994). Some assume, for example, that the U.S. government has always had an industrial policy of some sort, and the debate is really over how much and what kind of government intervention is called for. Others assume that national goals may differ from, and even conflict with, the goals pursued by private industry. In fact, they argue, many of the problems that we face today arise from excessive corporate greed and the search for unreasonably high profit margins. Plants are closed and people thrown out of work not because industries are unprofitable but because profit margins are judged by corporate managers to be too low. Seymour Melman (1983) argues that high labor costs are not really the culprit either. Rather, as labor costs rose, business managers sought cheaper labor overseas rather than developing more efficient means of producing goods in the United States.

Some economists and policy analysts argue that the unbridled emphasis on individualism, dog-eat-dog competition, and laissez-faire government in the United States places the United States in a very disadvantageous position in relation to major competitors on the world scene, especially Germany and Japan, where cooperation among business, workers, and government is extensive, harmonious, and long-standing (Thurow, 1992; Fallows, 1994). While German and Japanese governments nurture important industries with a variety of help, the United States lets new industries flounder on their own, and too often it loses the competitive edge in these industries to some foreign country.

Interventionists have many and varied proposals for what the government can do to reindustrialize the United States. Thurow and many others argue for heavy government investment in the economic infrastructure, such as roads, airports, and other things that businesses need to be competitive. They also propose much more government funding for job training and education in general so that the U.S. work force has the same skill and knowledge levels that are found among workers in other industrial countries. In their view, labor is an essential resource that needs to be nurtured rather than an expensive and balky cost of doing business. They also propose cooperation between government and industry, with the former providing funding and some leadership in promising economic arenas. This could take the form of significant public funding for some industries, as is now done in both Japan and Europe.

Other interventionists argue for legislation to restrict the ability of companies to move from one locale to another, thus dislocating workers. They also call for giving workers a larger voice in the running of the businesses in which they are employed. A few interventionists even insist that we need to replace private corporate decisions with public democratic planning, possibly through community ownership of certain industries. For the interventionists, then, the solution to the problems confronting the U.S. economy calls for more government direction and possibly a move toward a more mixed economy

nomic and political life of the 1980s and 1990s. Many economists have argued that a major culprit in generating inflation are the budget deficits of the federal government. These deficits reflect the excess of annual government expenditures over revenues. With the excep-

tion of 1960 and 1969, the federal government has spent more than it has taken in every year since 1940. The major concern with budget deficits is that the government must borrow money to operate and thus competes with corporate and other borrowers for the finite amount of loan money available. This competition increases the cost of loan money, which might lead some businesses to forego business expansion or capital improvements. When businesses forego expansion and improvement, there is less economic growth and fewer jobs.

A final reason why large government can create problems involves whether individuals can play significant roles in the decisions shaping their lives. As government grows, most people find themselves further and further removed from those who actually make the decisions. As C. Wright Mills (1959) pointed out, the key decision makers are usually those people who control the large economic and government bureaucracies in modern societies. The "faceless bureaucrats" in Washington take accumulated tax revenues and then tell most Americans what they can or cannot do. You cannot dump your garbage here, you need a wheelchair accessible ramp for your store, and your school can (or cannot) allow children to pray in school. As the government grows, the values of individualism and autonomy may become increasingly remote and irrelevant. Many groups feel powerless, and there is real danger that their interests will not receive a fair hearing in the halls of political power.

Future Prospects

What—if anything—should be done about big business and big government is highly controversial. We will analyze the major programs and policies that have been discussed or implemented.

Reducing Government and Deficits

Every president since 1980 has been a strong supporter of reducing the size of government and also reducing, if not eliminating, the deficit. Yet, the size of the federal budget grows every year, even though the number of government employees has not grown. This persistent growth in the government suggests that the reasons presented earlier in this chapter to explain why government has grown so large during this century remain powerful forces in keeping government large. It is easy to propose reducing government by cutting welfare, but all of the public assistance provided by the federal government amounts to only about one-half of the annual deficit and only 8 percent of the total budget. Defense spending, on the other hand, consumes 19 percent of the budget, and the two major programs for the elderly (Social Security and Medicare) consume almost one-third of the budget. This does not mean that cuts cannot be made in both the deficit and the size of government, but reducing them is much more difficult and complicated than is often imagined. In addition, serious efforts at it would significantly affect all people in the United States, not just the poor or some other powerless group.

Efforts have been made to reduce the budget deficit. The Gramm-Rudman-Hollings Act of 1986 and the Budget Enforcement Act of 1990 required substantial reductions in the federal budget over a period of years, but neither law had provisions that required such cuts. Without such requirements, Congress has found it impossible to cut government spending. The pursuit of deficit reduction continues in the 1990s, with the most recent hope being an amendment to the United States Constitution that would require a balanced budget. At this writing, the proposed amendment has not gotten very far. The whole battle over the budget deficit and the size of government shows the extent to which virtually every interest group benefits from some aspect of government spending, and no one wants to see their ox gored.

Government Reorganization

Whether the size of government is reduced or not, things can and have been done to moderate the negative effects of big government.

Politicians and government officials can be made more responsive to the demands of the citizenry. Because of the Watergate scandal and similar political episodes during the 1970s and 1980s, politicians are now required to disclose a great deal more about their personal finances, and this offers the public greater scrutiny over possible conflicts of interest. There is still, however, much more that can be done. Sociologist Herbert J. Gans (1988), concerned that most people in the United States will not become more politically active, has suggested some creative ways of increasing the responsiveness of elected government officials. One is to increase the staff available to them for providing constituency services. Each official would thus have more workers available to find out what their constituents want and to provide the services. A second suggestion is for more, and more diverse, public opinion polling organizations. After all, most such organizations today are very close to the political and economic elites and tend to gather information that those elites find useful. According to Gans, polls should tell elites what the public has on its mind about the issues that are important to it. Polls should tell us what should be on a politician's agenda, not what we think about a politician's already-established agenda. All of this would give citizens more input into the workings of government.

Government agencies and officials can be regulated much more closely than at present. This, of course, might mean that we would need more agencies to do the regulating, but not in all cases. Sometimes, bureaucrats in a government agency can do the regulating themselves if they are protected against reprisals should they uncover something detrimental to those heading the agency. In many cases, such whistleblowers are fired by the agency, but when their cases come to public view, they often find considerable support among the public. Further protections for, and even rewards given to, such internal auditors could make government bu-

reaus more sensitive to decisions that are viewed unfavorably by the public (Glazer and Glazer, 1989).

Government programs can be made more accountable. Policy analysts David Osborne and Ted Gaebler (1992) suggest a shift in focus from government services based on civil service regulations, which try to specify in detail *how* government services should be provided, to an "entrepreneurial government" that focuses on *results.* The idea is to establish measurable performance goals or outcomes as a part of government programs, and then use competition and decentralized authority to achieve the goals. This might call for privatizing some government services if private industry can do the job better than government bureaus can. But Osborne and Gaebler recognize that government is better than private industry at doing some things, especially when issues of fairness and equity come into play. Some programs, such as Head Start (see Chapter 5), currently do focus on results, and privatizing these services has so far not shown any advantages. The problem in the past, they argue, has not been government per se but the inefficient bureaucracy that government had become.

Collective Action by Citizens

In a democracy, one important way of controlling the actions of business and government is through collective, organized actions by citizens' groups to change the law or redirect social policy. In the past few decades, many such groups have emerged as watchdogs over whether government and business are acting in the public interest.

Among the most effective citizens' groups over the years have been those originated by consumer advocate Ralph Nader and his associates. Nader first came to public attention in the 1960s when he published *Unsafe at Any Speed,* a scathing critique of the auto industry. He revealed the extent to which General

Motors was willing to make unsafe automobiles in order to increase profits. His campaign resulted in legislation that corrected many of the abuses in the auto industry and also pushed the government into the role of watchdog over automobile safety. Eventually, a whole variety of consumer protection groups—often referred to as "Nader's Raiders"—grew up around Nader's efforts, including the Public Safety Research Institute, the Public Interest Research Group, the Corporate Accountability Research Group, and the Center for the Study of Responsive Law. These collective efforts contributed to the passage of consumer protection legislation in many areas: to ensure quality meats, to ban cyclamates and other harmful substances, and to enhance safety procedures in mining and other occupations, to name just a few. Currently, Nader's consumer advocacy organizations are working toward restrictions in the use of chlorinated fluorocarbons, the establishment of national health insurance, and a rollback in the cost of automobile insurance (Brimelow and Spencer, 1990).

Concerns about environmental pollution and degradation have also spawned a great deal of collective action by the citizenry (see Chapter 13). Beginning in the late nineteenth century with the Audubon Society and the Sierra Club, such interest groups have lobbied for social policies to protect and preserve our natural environment. These older environmental groups have been joined by newer ones such as the National Wildlife Federation, Campaign for the Earth, and Greenpeace. In the 1990s, Greenpeace, for example, has taken the lead in challenging corporations that dump nuclear wastes at sea, build energy plants that destroy rainforests and dislocate people, and release chemicals into the atmosphere that destroy the ozone layer. Greenpeace has focused some of its attention on the more environmentally damaging activities of the World Bank, which was discussed earlier in this chapter.

Some public interest groups, such as Common Cause, are not limited to any particular realm, such as environmental problems or oc-

cupational safety, but focus rather on any area where government or business appears to be ignoring public interests. Common Cause opposes waste and corruption through the legislature or the courts. The group has been especially active on issues of election campaign financing. Its major concern has been that interest groups with substantial economic resources, such as large corporations or wealthy individuals, could "bribe" public officials by making large donations to their campaigns. In part due to Common Cause's efforts, the Federal Election Campaign Act was amended in 1975 to place limitations on the amounts that businesses and individuals can contribute to a candidate. There are still ways to get around these limitations, however. For example, the law limits contributions to candidates but not to political parties. People can still give unlimited amounts to the Republican or Democratic parties even if the party will spend the money to promote a particular candidate. In addition, people can donate unlimited amounts to tax-exempt "educational" organizations that may work very hard for particular candidates or positions on issues. The only restriction is that these organizations not be used for political purposes. Acting as "think tanks," these concerns disseminate information that supports the position of particular candidates, and they analyze issues in ways that encourage people to vote for those candidates. So, although the campaign financing law helps to moderate the influence of the wealthy and powerful, these limitations in the law show that wealth still can have a powerful advantage.

On a global scale, collective action is also an important deterrent to government actions, international corporations, and international financial organizations. The term "nongovernmental organizations," or NGOs, is now used to refer to grassroots citizen organizations that have emerged to fight the intrusive and destructive policies of governments or groups like the World Bank and the International Monetary Fund (Rich, 1994). These NGOs use resources they have available, including education, boycotts, and demonstrations, to stop or change activities with detrimental social or environmental consequences. The NGOs are usually small and focus on specific problems that a village or a people confront. International networks of NGOs have emerged to provide mutual help through the exchange of information, resources, and personnel. These NGOs have had some success in alleviating the negative impacts of the actions of corporations or organizations such as the World Bank and the IMF.

Collective action, then, has served as a valuable constraint on the excesses of big business and big government. These efforts have offered ordinary citizens a valuable weapon in pursuing their own interests. The success of these groups depends on:

1. Their ability to appeal to large numbers of people and the financial resources those people provide.
2. Their strategic use of legislative and litigative tactics.
3. Their effective use of the media for public relations and communication.

Many of the existing public interest groups will undoubtedly continue to function, and more groups will likely emerge in the future as new issues develop and old ones evolve.

The Globalization of Labor

The global economy described earlier in this chapter points to an important world trend: the

These demonstrators are using collective action to oppose NAFTA, which they perceive as a policy that will work against their interests. Many corporations, on the other hand, support NAFTA. This illustrates how the resolution of social problems arises in part from the clash of competing interest groups.

globalization of labor as labor markets become world rather than simply national phenomena. Although global labor has existed for centuries (consider the Europeans bringing Africans to the Americas as slave laborers), today it is a much more extensive and complete world phenomenon. More so than in the past, corporations roam the globe looking for cheap sources of labor. This means that every worker is potentially competing with the lowest paid workers in the world. The recent trade agreements, NAFTA and WTO, work toward reducing barriers to free trade—including tariffs and other barriers that help support high wages for workers in places like the United States.

In response to this trend, some labor unions have recognized that the labor movement must also become transnational: if wages and working conditions are improved for workers around the world, then workers in high-wage nations benefit because there is less incentive for corporations to relocate. So, some unions in the United States have provided support for unions in less developed nations to help them organize workers and fight against low wages and poor or dangerous working conditions. It also opens the door to transnational labor action in which a multinational corporation might find itself facing simultaneous labor actions, possibly even strikes, in the many nations in which it does business. In this way, the plight of workers in one nation is linked to the plight of workers in other nations. Through such strategies, international labor organizations may be able to regain some of their strength relative to the concentration of power in corporations.

Economic Reorganization

Some policy analysts suggest that the problems identified in this chapter, such as alienation and the inequitable distribution of power, can be alleviated only by some fundamental reorganization of economic relations. Some of these proposals for reorganization are modest, while others are more radical. To deal with problems of alienation and loss of control in the workplace, some industrial relations experts and social scientists have proposed the elimination of the traditional assembly line to allow a group of workers to build a product, such as an automobile, from start to finish and to control the pace of their own work. Volvo and Saab in Sweden and Chrysler and General Electric in the United States have experimented with such programs (Gyllenhammar, 1977). Other companies have turned to *flextime,* a system of work scheduling that allows employees to start and stop work earlier or later than traditional working hours (Vanderkolk and Young, 1991). The goal of all these reorganizations of the traditional workplace is to offer employees more control over their working conditions and thus reduce discontent and alienation.

A more extreme and innovative approach to the problem of alienation and the inequitable distribution of power is *worker empowerment,* involving an attempt to provide workers with management authority and responsibility. In some cases, this has involved workers gaining partial ownership in a company and having a stake in how it is run and in the consequences of their own work performance. In 1992, ten thousand U.S. firms with eleven million employees had some form of employee ownership (U.S. Bureau of the Census, 1994). In other cases, worker empowerment has involved changes in the structure of companies so that employees have more of a say in company decision making, more opportunities for advancement, and increased access to powerful people and resources in the organization (Stein and Kanter, 1980). Whatever form it takes, worker empowerment has focused on reducing the sense of powerlessness and lack of control that many workers experience. And research shows that worker participation and employee ownership can increase a company's productivity (Blinder, 1990; Rosen and Youngs, 1991).

Another, more radical proposal for attacking the increasing dominance of corporations over workers and communities is to broaden our conception of who has a stake, and thus should have some say, in the decisions and activities of corporations (Craypo and Nissen, 1993). Traditionally, only the stockholders, along with the corporate directors and managers, have been seen as stakeholders. However, workers and communities make a long-term commitment to corporations and invest much energy and many resources in the corporation. And both workers and communities often suffer dire consequences from corporate decisions to downsize or relocate a production facility. If such commitment and involvement justify viewing workers and communities as stakeholders in the corporation, then they deserve some input into corporate policies and decisions. This could take the form of worker and community representation on the boards of directors of corporations. This approach is still largely unknown in the United States, although it is found in some European corporations. It requires a radical revision in our view of corporations from private domains to public and community assets.

Whether these changes will reduce alienation among workers or protect them from exploitation remains to be seen, but it is clear that U.S. business institutions are neither perfect nor stagnant. As the United States becomes an advanced industrial economy, the problems it faces are changing, and it is clear that economic arrangements must adapt. In fact, some have suggested that these issues of concentration of power and lack of control will not be ultimately resolved without some fundamental change in the economy. Some argue that it should become more of a mixed economy, with the government taking more control of some economic realms in order to pursue collective goals. Proponents of an extreme power elite position would argue that inequality and exploitation are inherent elements of capitalism because capitalism is ultimately fueled by personal greed and acquisition. As such, capitalism can only work to benefit the powerful. Some form of a mixed economy would balance the avarice inherent in capitalism by injecting an element of the public good into economic activities and decisions. Others, including some pluralists, would argue that capitalism can benefit most citizens through the checks and balances of competing interest groups. This is not to say that capitalism can achieve equality or that everyone will benefit. But if the government encourages the development of diverse interest groups, large numbers of citizens will be able to pursue their goals.

Economic concentration and more low-paying jobs mean that it is harder for families to avoid poverty (Chapter 5). This situation also puts more stress on families, possibly increasing divorce (Chapter 3). It also means that more women are forced to take jobs where they earn less than men, which increases the feminization of poverty (Chapter 7).

L I N K A G E S

Summary

1. Political and economic institutions focus on a central issue in society: the exercise of power in the allocation of scarce resources. The social problem associated with these institutions is the abuse of power.

2. The economies of most nations today are market economies, which are based on the exchange of money for goods and services in the marketplace. The three main types of modern economic systems are capitalism, socialism, and mixed economies.

3. The dominant form of business in modern economies is the corporation, which has many advantages over individually owned businesses. Economic resources have become highly concentrated in a small number of very large corporations. Such concentration can take the form of monopolies, oligopolies, conglomerates, and multinational or global corporations.

4. The number and size of unions in the United States has grown substantially over the past century, but they have declined some in the past few decades.

5. Government has also grown substantially in the past two centuries because it has taken on the responsibility for social and economic policy and because people demand so much more of it. Globally, immense political and economic power is concentrated in a few large corporations and global financial institutions.

6. From the functionalist perspective, big government and big business are problems because they can lead to policies and practices that are inconsistent with cultural values and political and economic reality. From the conflict perspective, concentration of power becomes a social problem when some influential group believes that it is not receiving its fair share of resources and strives to do something about it.

7. Oligarchy refers to the concentration of power in the hands of a few people at the top of an organization. Organizations have a strong tendency to become oligarchical.

8. There are two major models of power distribution in the United States: the power elite model and the pluralist model. The realities of holding power are more complex than either model suggests. Globally, world-system theory describes how and why political and economic power is concentrated among a small number of nations.

9. The concentration of power creates many problems for society, including a reduction in economic competition, the dominance of corporate profit-making goals over societal goals, threats to democratic institutions, the dwindling of unions, worker discontent and alienation, worker dislocation and unemployment, and abuse of government authority.

10. Efforts to alleviate problems stemming from the concentration and abuse of power have focused on a number of policies: shrinking the size of the government and budget deficits, reorganizing government so that abuses are less likely, encouraging collective action by citizens that serves as a counterbalance to government and corporate power, globalizing the labor force, and reorganizing the economy in ways that reduce worker exploitation, discontent, and unemployment.

STUDY AND Review

Key Terms

alienation
capitalism
communism
corporation
deindustrialization
economics
military-industrial complex

mixed economies
oligarchy
pluralist model
politics
power elite model
socialism
world-system theory

Multiple-Choice Questions

1. Which of the following is the central issue in society that both political and economic institutions focus on?
   a. The exercise of power in the allocation of scarce resources.
   b. The transition from socialist to capitalist economies.
   c. The emergence of market economies in advanced industrial societies.
   d. The globalization of labor.

2. According to proponents of a pure capitalist economy, the government should do all of the following *except:*
   a. Maintain public order.
   b. Protect against foreign threats.
   c. Regulate prices and wages.
   d. Government should do all of these.
   e. Government should do none of this.

3. As used by Karl Marx, the term "communism" refers to:
   a. Socialist economies in advanced industrial societies.
   b. The utopian end stage of the struggle with capitalism.
   c. Oligarchical political structures as they exist in Russia and China.
   d. The process of bringing corporations under state ownership and control.

4. Global corporations are different from multinational corporations in that:
   a. Global corporations emerged first.
   b. Multinational corporations represent more integrated world-wide systems.
   c. Multinational corporations emerged first.
   d. Global corporations represent the power elite while multinational corporations reflect pluralism.

5. Which of the following is *not* one of the reasons for the decline in the proportion of workers in the United States who are unionized?
   a. Traditionally unionized occupations have declined in number.
   b. Multinational corporations have declined in significance.
   c. Corporations have relocated to states with weak union organizations.
   d. The number of white-collar occupations has been growing.
   e. Unions have faced increasing hostility from the public in the United States.

6. Which of the following is true regarding changes in the occupational structure in the United States in the twentieth century?
   a. The proportion of farm workers has increased.
   b. The proportion of blue-collar workers has increased.
   c. The proportion of service workers has declined.
   d. The proportion of white-collar workers has increased.

7. "Concentration of power becomes a social problem when some influential group believes that it is not receiving its fair share of resources and strives to do something about it." This statement most clearly derives from which sociological perspective?
   a. Functionalist.
   b. Conflict.
   c. Interactionist.
   d. Pluralist.
   e. Capitalist.

8. Which of the following statements is consistent with the power elite model?
   a. A small group of powerful people makes most important decisions.
   b. Power is spread over a large number of groups.
   c. There is no significant military-industrial complex in the United States.
   d. Veto groups have the ability to block decisions that adversely affect them.
   e. The unorganized public can exercise constraint over those in power through use of the vote.
9. The problem of unemployment in the United States has grown worse over the decades because:
   a. There is increased competition from foreign workers.
   b. The proportion of blue-collar jobs has grown and the proportion of white-collar jobs declined.
   c. The number of women entering the work force has declined.
   d. U.S. corporations have avoided competing in global markets.
10. The text suggests that some problems of corporate concentration of power can be alleviated if the notion of "stakeholders" in the corporation is expanded to include:
   a. Corporate managers.
   b. Corporate stock owners.
   c. Oligopolies.
   d. Corporate workers.

True/False Questions

1. Political institutions are the ones through which goods and services are produced and distributed.
2. The primary motivation for economic activities in socialist economies is to earn a profit.
3. Laissez-faire advocates would say that we could learn more about how best to solve social problems from mixed economies than from pure capitalism.
4. In the United States, union membership as a proportion of the work force has been declining since the 1950s.
5. The number of people employed by the government has doubled in the past thirty years.
6. Michels' concept of oligarchy would be more consistent with the pluralist model of power than with the power elite model.
7. In assessing the power elite model, the text concludes that a small group of people in the United States holds enormous power, controls foreign policy, and shapes the direction of our economic development.
8. When economic power is concentrated in a monopolistic fashion, it can result in a less competitive marketplace.
9. Worker dislocation has affected white workers more severely than black workers in the 1980s and 1990s.
10. "Flextime" is a new way of scheduling work in corporations that tends to increase alienation among workers.

Fill-In Questions

1. In capitalist economic systems,

   _____ is the primary motive guiding people's economic behavior.
2. Economic systems in which there are strong elements of both capitalism and socialism are

   called _____ .
3. If the Ajax Company produces 95 percent of the widgets sold in the world, then this com-

   pany would be called _____ .

4. A _____ is a corporation that owns other companies in economic spheres quite different from that of the parent company.

5. In describing the tendency for power in organizations to concentrate in the hands of a few people at the top, Robert Michels described the likelihood of this as "who says organization, says _____ ."

6. Sociologist _____ originally proposed what has come to be called the power elite model of the exercise of power in the United States.

7. When workers lack control over their work and feel depersonalized by their work, feelings of powerlessness can arise that are called

_____ .

8. _____ are workers who have lost their jobs because manufacturing plants in the United States have closed in the face of foreign competition.

9. The _____ approach would argue for "reindustrializing" the United States economy through less government spending which would make more capital available for industry to expand.

10. _____ are those who are affected by corporate activities, and thus should have some say in how the corporations are run.

Matching Questions

_____ 1. capitalism

_____ 2. monopoly

_____ 3. power elite model

_____ 4. *maquiladoras*

_____ 5. nongovernmental organizations

_____ 6. mixed economy

_____ 7. Robert Michels

_____ 8. Dwight D. Eisenhower

_____ 9. deindustrialization

_____ 10. worker empowerment

A. conflict perspective
B. economic production and distribution privately held
C. collective action
D. a company that controls 90 percent of sales in a particular market
E. factories in Mexico producing goods for export to the United States
F. spoke of the "military-industrial complex"
G. aging and deteriorating factories and other productive resources
H. approach to the problem of alienation
I. oligarchy
J. England

Essay Questions

1. Define capitalism and socialism. Show how each economic system clearly differs from the other in terms of organization and motivation for economic activity.
2. What is a corporation? What are the benefits and disadvantages of corporate organization?
3. What are the major international organizations that work to support the spread of capitalism around the world? How do these organizations achieve their goals?
4. What are the trends in the unionization of workers in the United States? What accounts for these trends?
5. What would the functionalist and conflict perspectives have to say about the concentration of power in societies?
6. Assess how well the power elite and pluralist models describe the exercise of power in the United States. What evidence is presented on this issue in the text?

7. What are "displaced workers"? Who is most likely to be affected by this, and what particular problems do they confront?

8. What does the term "deindustrialization" refer to? Describe the laissez-faire and interventionist stances on how best to tackle this problem.

9. What sort of government reorganizations are suggested in the text to alleviate the problems posed by the concentration of power in the United States?

10. What sort of economic reorganizations are suggested in the text to alleviate the problems posed by the concentration of power in the United States?

Answers

Multiple-Choice

1. A; 2. C; 3. B; 4. C; 5. B; 6. D; 7. B; 8. A; 9. A; 10. D

True/False

1. F; 2. F; 3. F; 4. T; 5. F; 6. F; 7. T; 8. T; 9. F; 10. F

Fill-In

1. profit
2. mixed economies
3. a monopoly
4. conglomerate
5. oligarchy
6. C. Wright Mills
7. alienation
8. displaced workers
9. laissez-faire
10. stakeholders

Matching

1. B; 2. D; 3. A; 4. E; 5. C; 6. J; 7. I; 8. F; 9. G; 10. H

For Further Reading

Barry Bluestone and Irving Bluestone. *Negotiating the Future: A Labor Perspective on American Business.* New York: BasicBooks, 1992. Approaching workplace issues from the perspective of labor, these authors argue strongly for labor-management cooperation in the United States as the best way to advance the interests of both. They provide case studies to advance their point.

Jeremy Brecher and Tim Costello. *Global Village or Global Pillage: Economic Reconstruction from the Bottom Up.* Boston: South End Press, 1994. These authors have many constructive suggestions for how to alleviate the more damaging consequences of the actions of global corporations and institutions. But, they argue, labor, nongovernmental, and other grassroots organizations will have to make a concerted, global effort or the corporations and their supporting governments will gain the upper hand.

Paul Brodeur. *Outrageous Misconduct: The Asbestos Industry on Trial.* New York: Pantheon Books, 1985. This is an angry book about how widespread corporate malfeasance in the asbestos industry produced much pain and suffering for its workers. It documents how corporations often pursue corporate profits even when they know their actions are hurting people.

Dan Clawson, Alan Neustadtl, and Denise Scott. *Money Talks: Corporate PACs and Political Influence.* New York: Basic Books, 1992. Political action committees (PACs) have become very influential in the American political process as a means for elites to control politicians and elections. These authors show that it is a more subtle and complex influence than merely buying politicians' votes on issues.

William S. Dietrich. *In the Shadow of the Rising Sun: The Political Roots of American Economic Decline.* University Park, Penn.: Penn State Press, 1992. The author of this book, a corporate executive as well as a social scientist, argues strongly that our economic problems are partly political and cultural in nature. He particularly accuses our unrepentant individualism along with a lack of a strong industrial policy as contributing to our economic malaise.

G. William Domhoff. *The Power Elite and the State: How Policy Is Made in America.* New York: Aldine de Gruyter, 1990. Domhoff presents many case studies of social policy development that show how and why coalitions of the power elite get involved in various policy issues. It extends the power elite theory into the Reagan-Bush years.

Robert Heilbroner. *21st Century Capitalism.* New York: W. W. Norton, 1993. These brief but thoughtful essays explore what capitalism, which seems likely to be the dominant economic system of the next century, could be like in the future. The author argues that both capitalism and socialism contain strengths that should be incorporated into a "21st century capitalism."

Lewis H. Lapham. *The Wish For Kings: Democracy at Bay.* New York: Grove Press, 1993. This is a slashing criticism of politics in the United States in the 1990s. The author argues that our political system is oligarchical, with a few people put into power by a small part of the electorate that is frightened and willing to concede control.

Laton McCartney. *Friends in High Places: The Bechtel Story: The Most Secret Corporation and How It Engineered the World.* New York: Simon and Schuster, 1988. This is a fascinating case study of a very powerful corporation in the United States and its influence in the U.S. and around the world. It shows interlinkages between government and business and how, as the power elite view suggests, government can become a tool of corporate policy.

Robert B. Reich. *The Work of Nations: Preparing Ourselves for 21st Century Capitalism.* New York: Knopf, 1991. The author, President Clinton's Secretary of Labor, provides a good analysis of what the postindustrial economy of the United States will be like, including the kinds of jobs that will gain prominence. It is an optimistic view in that Reich feels that most people can prosper in this new work force.

Jeremy Rifkin. *The End of Work: The Decline of the Global Labor Force and the Dawn of the Post-Market Era.* New York: Putnam, 1994. This is a more pessimistic view of future changes in the world economy. This author sees automation and other changes in technology dislodging millions of workers from their jobs around the world.

THREE CHAPTER *Family-Related Problems*

Some of the problems that we examine in this book may not seem of immediate concern to many of you because you do not believe they affect your life in a direct and personal way. Problems involving the family, however, interest virtually everyone because we all spend much of our lives in some kind of family unit. And the family, it would seem, is an institution under considerable stress these days. Most of us know someone—a parent, a close friend, possibly ourselves—who has been divorced. Stories of parents beating their children and spouses assaulting one another abound in daily newspapers. Some employers today even extend health and life insurance benefits to the unmarried domestic partners of their employees, including gay and lesbian couples. So, what had been defined as "family" benefits in the past are now sometimes extended to those in living arrangements that some would not consider "families" at all. In fact, some people view such developments as a virtual assault on the sanctity of the conventional family in society. What is happening to the family in modern societies?

The family is the oldest and most fundamental of all social institutions. In fact, the family has been the center of political, economic, educational, and religious activities in most human societies throughout history. The position of the family in society today, however, has changed considerably, and there are many controversial issues and problems involved. Before addressing these concerns, we need to know what the family is and how it functions in society. The **family** is *a social institution based on kinship that functions to replace members of society and to nurture them.* This seemingly straightforward definition hides considerable complexity and controversy. In fact, there is a great deal of ethnocentrism associated with the family. Most people have strong feelings regarding what "the family" is and how family members should behave. This has a direct impact on social policy when people's conceptions of what the family should be like distort their analysis of family problems and restrict their consideration of ways to solve these problems.

To understand what is happening to the family and assess competing views of family problems, we need to evaluate the role of the family as an institution in society. We will do this before analyzing the scope and extent of these problems.

The Family in Society

Families can take on many different forms. In some cultures, males wield most power and authority in the family, whereas in other cultures females do. In some cases, a person can have only one marriage partner at a time, whereas other societies permit and even encourage a person to have many spouses simultaneously. In the United States today cultural norms call for people to practice **monogamy**, *to have only one spouse at a time;* our culture also encourages an **egalitarian family,** in which *power and authority are shared somewhat equally by husband and wife,* although male dominance may persist in some families. But the family of the past was different. In assessing problems in today's family, we must recognize the changes that have taken place in the family as a consequence of industrialization. At center stage in these changes is the transition from an extended family to a nuclear family.

An **extended family** consists of *three or more generations of people who live together or in close proximity and whose lives and livelihoods are closely intertwined* (Nimkoff, 1965). Such families are often large and involve strong kinship obligations. Family members are expected to help other family members and to remain loyal to the family. In cultures where extended families are common, prevailing norms stress the importance of the family over that of the individual and his or her goals. Extended families are also often dominated by males, and tasks are divided along age and sex lines. Extended families are more common in preindustrial than in industrial societies.

A **nuclear family** consists of *a married couple and their children.* In contrast to extended families, nuclear families are small and less likely to be male dominated. Furthermore, cultures in which nuclear families predominate emphasize values of individualism to a greater extent. Nuclear families are the most common family type in industrial societies. Actually, many families found in modern societies are, strictly speaking, neither extended nor nuclear. Rather, they are **modified extended families,** in which *elaborate networks of visitation and support are found even though each nuclear unit lives separately* (Reiss, 1962).

Why does such variation in family types occur from one culture to another or from one

Myths & FACTS

ABOUT THE FAMILY

Myth: Unhappy marriages should be maintained when children are involved—"for the sake of the children."

FACT: Repeated investigations of divorce and its effects on children have failed to demonstrate the psychological benefits to children of maintaining an unhappy marriage. It may, in fact, be more damaging than divorce itself.

Myth: Divorce is a modern phenomenon and was relatively unheard of in premodern societies.

FACT: Not only did divorce exist in primitive societies, but it was sometimes easier to obtain and more common than in America today.

Myth: Teenage pregnancies are on the rise in all modern societies because of the decline in traditional values and the rise in sexual promiscuity.

FACT: The United States has many more teenage pregnancies than does any other industrial nation. In societies where effective sex education programs and contraceptives are available to teens, the rate of such pregnancies is two to three times lower than in the United States.

Myth: High rates of childbearing outside marriage along with a decline in family size are unique to the wealthy industrial nations and come from the affluent lifestyle found in those nations.

FACT: The same trends are found in many nations around the world, including Third-World countries, and are an outgrowth of industrialization and modernization rather than affluence.

time period to another? The answer to this is provided by the three sociological perspectives.

The Functionalist Perspective

Functionalists argue that some form of the family exists in all societies because the family performs certain basic functions that are essential to human survival and the maintenance of society (Ogburn, 1938; Eshleman, 1991). Six major contributions that the family makes to society have been identified.

1. *Regulation of sexual behavior and reproduction.* All societies have rules governing who can engage in sexual activities with whom and under what conditions children should be conceived and born. In most societies, childbearing is lim-

ited to marriage and family contexts, which provide a stable setting for having and nurturing children. In this way, the family contributes to the process of replacing people from one generation to the next.

2. *Socialization and education.* All human beings must learn the values, norms, and language of their culture and develop the skills that are necessary to be useful in society. Parents and other family members usually have primary responsibility for ensuring that children are properly socialized. Thus, the family is the major agency of socialization.

3. *Status conferral.* Families confer upon their children a place in society—a position or status relative to other people. By virtue of being born into a particular family, we have certain resources or opportunities available to us. Our racial or ethnic heritage, religion, and social class are determined by the family into which we are born, although some of these characteristics may change later in life. At a minimum, our family confers upon us some initial status in society.

4. *Economic activity.* The family often serves as the basic unit for economic production, with kinship ties defining who is obliged to work together in order to catch game, grow food, or build shelters. Family members work together to accomplish the economic tasks necessary for survival. Kinship ties also determine the distribution and consumption of economic goods by establishing who has a right to a share of the goods produced by a family.

5. *Protection.* Families in all societies provide various forms of care and protection to their members, helping them when they are too young, weak, sick, or old to help themselves.

6. *Affection and companionship.* All human beings need love, affection, and psychological support, and for many people these needs are fulfilled by family members. Such support enables us to develop a positive self-concept and sense of self-worth and to dispel loneliness.

All these functions taken together contribute to the continuity of society by ensuring that new members are born and properly socialized.

Although these six functions are often performed by the family, they can be accomplished in other ways. In fact, the family has been undergoing a major transformation over the past few centuries as a consequence of industrialization, and alternative ways of fulfilling many of these functions are emerging. For example, although most childbearing still occurs in marriages, a growing number of women are having children without marrying. By the 1990s, 1.2 million births to unmarried women were recorded by the Census Bureau in the United States each year in comparison to about 400,000 in 1970 (U.S. Bureau of the Census,

1994: 80). This increase has occurred in part because women in industrial societies are better able to work and support their children without the assistance of a husband or other relatives. With regard to socialization and education, day-care centers, schools, and colleges are becoming increasingly important in transmitting culture and passing on skills and knowledge. Furthermore, people's positions in industrial societies are determined less by family position and more by their achievements than in the past, although family position does give a person a start in life. In terms of economic activity, most people work outside of the home, and the family no longer serves as the center of economic production. Finally, there are hospitals, nursing homes, retirement villages, and many other ways to offer the care and protection that people need.

In other words, the role of the family in performing these functions for society has become less central as other institutional means of accomplishing them have arisen through industrialization. As a consequence, the traditional roles of family and kinship in society have changed, because they are simply not as important as they once were. As this has occurred, the extended family that performed most of these functions in preindustrial societies has become less common. At the same time, the nuclear family has become more prominent because it is better suited to an urbanized industrial society. Industrialism calls for geographic mobility so that workers can go where the jobs are, and nuclear families with weaker kinship ties make this mobility possible. Industrial societies also emphasize achievement rather than ascription, and these modified kinship relations make it easier for people to be upwardly mobile. Furthermore, large extended families are dysfunctional in urban settings where children are not economic assets. In preindustrial societies, children could work in agricultural settings and therefore contribute economically to the family. Small families are better suited to industrial societies; in fact, the size of the average family in the United States has declined substantially throughout the twentieth century, and people are more likely to be living alone or in nonfamily households (see Figure 3.1).

The part that families play in society, then, has changed with industrialization, and this has contributed to such things as a rising divorce rate and the emergence of a number of alternatives to traditional family lifestyles. These

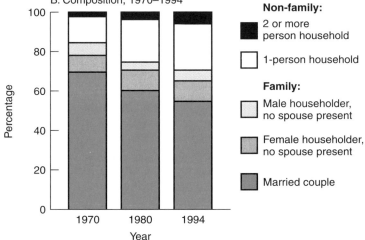

FIGURE 3.1 The Average Size and Composition of Households in the United States, 1930–1994. *Sources:* U.S. Bureau of the Census, *Statistical Abstract of the United States, 1982–83* (Washington, D.C.: U.S. Government Printing Office, 1982), p. 43; U.S. Bureau of the Census, *Statistical Abstract of the United States, 1995* (Washington, D.C.: U.S. Government Printing Office, 1995), p. 58.

social developments become a social problem when the changes in the family threaten society with disorganization or instability. One of the key debates regarding family problems centers on whether the traditional family functions can be adequately performed by other institutions. Can day care, for example, provide the same kind of socialization to cultural values and development of personality that occurs in the traditional family? This issue is analyzed in the Applied Research insert. Do divorced and one-parent families result in less effective socialization and more behavior problems for youth when compared with two-parent families? This question will be analyzed later in the chapter. The function of the family that has probably changed least during this process is the provision of affection and companionship, and nuclear families can probably perform this function as well as extended families did. But even this function might be fulfilled in other ways than by the traditional family.

The Conflict Perspective

According to the conflict perspective, the family, along with other social institutions, serves the interests of the dominant groups in society, and there is no reason to assume that a single form of the family would benefit everyone. Rather, the version of the family that is most prominent in society is likely to be the one that is consistent with the values and benefits of the dominant groups. For example, **patriarchy** refers to *a family in which males dominate in the regulation of political and economic decision making, whereas women and children are subordinate.* This is the most common type of authority structure in families, and it serves the interests of men by enabling them to be dominant. In some societies, in fact, women have been so powerless in the family that they were virtual slaves (Chagnon, 1968). In industrial societies, male domination is not this extreme, and fewer women today are willing to accept such a sub-

ordinate position; in general, women today demand more egalitarian family roles. However, this change is occurring because women have been accumulating resources that enable them to resist coercion by males. For example, male dominance can be expressed in the form of spouse abuse, which usually involves husbands assaulting their wives. However, research indicates that married women with greater economic, social, and educational resources are less likely to be abused and more likely to leave physically abusive husbands (Gelles and Cornell, 1990; Straus, 1991).

The dominant form of the family in society also benefits particular economic interests. For example, the nuclear family serves the interests of capitalist economic institutions because it maximizes the number of consumption-oriented units in society. Each nuclear family buys many consumer items even though some are used only infrequently. Most families, for example, own their own television, stove, food processor, and automobile. A washing machine is used for only a few hours a week, yet most families purchase their own rather than share one with others. In extended or communal families, fewer such consumer goods would be needed because they would be shared, and thus the market for these goods would be smaller, which would hurt the interests of capitalists. Communal families, which are based on the belief in common ownership of at least some material goods, also threaten the basic value of private property on which a capitalist economy rests.

Conflict theorists would also argue that family systems can contribute to the perpetuation of social and economic inequality because inheritance in many societies, especially capitalist ones, is based on kinship. Inheritance makes it possible for a family to accumulate and perpetuate its wealth over generations. Such families as the Carnegies, the Rockefellers, the Astors, the Kennedys, and the Gettys have amassed enormous fortunes. Anyone who can inherit wealth—of whatever amount—clearly has an advantage over those who come from modest or poor backgrounds. Thus, the family in such societies becomes a vehicle for perpetuating patterns of dominance and subordination.

Conflict theorists argue that the dominant groups protect against threats to their position by teaching people through the schools, the media, and other means that monogamy, nuclear families, family inheritance, and private property are best. Through socialization and education, people internalize these beliefs and they are unlikely, therefore, even to consider other forms of the family, such as communal arrangements. In addition, strong normative pressures motivate people to live in socially acceptable forms of the family. From the conflict perspective, family forms change when new groups acquire the power necessary to gain acceptance for a new form of family. The organization of family life becomes a social problem when groups with the power to make their concerns heard believe that the existing family structure is not serving their interests and they act to change it. The dispute over the proper family form, however, is not couched in the language of personal interests but rather in conflicting values.

The Interactionist Perspective

Given the many forms of the family, which one is "right"? That, according to the interactionist perspective, is a matter of social definition. Every society has rules and norms that shape family and kin relationships. Once the norms are established, people are socialized to accept their society's form of the family as "natural." In most societies, there is substantial social consensus regarding the proper form of the family and the appropriate way for family members to relate to one another. Most people in the United States, for example, probably consider monogamy to be the most "civilized" type of marriage. Few could accept for themselves the Tibetan practice in which a woman who mar-

ries a particular man is considered to be the wife of all of that man's brothers—even brothers yet to be born at the time of the marriage (Goldstein, 1971). Yet strict monogamy is one of the less common forms of the family, being practiced by only about one-quarter of all human societies.

What behavior is acceptable is interpreted in the light of cultural values and societal development. As society and its values change, the interpretations of behavior also change. In an earlier era, for example, when the traditional family was essential to accomplish such things as child rearing, family life was given a sacred or religious meaning, and divorce was highly stigmatized. By expressing shock or disgust at those who divorce, people in their daily lives helped to foster the "reality" that "marriage for life" was the right way to live. In a male-dominated society, the ritual by which women take on their husband's last name symbolized the distribution of power in the family and in society. Family violence was viewed as a "family affair" because it also reflected power relations in society, either the dominance of males over females or parents over children.

Today, the consensus regarding family and family-related behavior is much less widespread than it once was. People today are faced with issues that in the past were settled by strong social pressures: Should I get married? Should I stay married? Should I have sex, or even children, outside of marriage? Should I take my spouse's name or keep my own? There is a growing inconsistency regarding acceptable behavior in these realms. This creates tension for individuals who must make choices without the clear-cut guidance and support of society. According to the interactionist perspective, when people are not provided with clear expectations for how they should behave, the stability of society is threatened because people may make choices that are defined by others as detrimental to society. Whether such practices are in fact detrimental is, of course, another matter. What *is* essential is that some groups

APPLIED RESEARCH
Day Care: Problem or Solution?

In 1960, 18 percent of married women with children younger than six years were working; today 60 percent of such women work (U.S. Bureau of the Census, 1994: 402). Many of these women are single mothers and others have husbands who work, so someone must care for their children. Increasing numbers of such families turn to day care, often because relatives or friends are not available to assist. Day care has been controversial because it goes against the traditional notion that children should be raised by their parents. Some see day care as a symptom of the erosion of the family in modern society. Critics argue that children in day care do not get the love, attention, and intimate involvement they need to develop into emotionally healthy and competent adults. So, a key question regarding day care is whether it can do as good a job at socializing children as the parents do.

Child rearing is a sensitive topic because our attitudes about it are so strongly influenced by traditional values relating to the family. In the United States, we see the family as very important and also value the privacy of the family unit. Tradition places the family, and especially maternal care, as the primary and essential element of good child rearing. Given these strong values, opinions about child rearing may be subject to considerable ethnocentrism, in which traditional ways of raising children are seen as the only proper ways of doing so. In just such situations, social science research can help to alleviate the danger that one's values will lead to biased and inaccurate conclusions about which child-rearing approaches will be effective.

Decades of such research have now accumulated, comparing children in various types of day-care centers with children raised in the home by parents, relatives, or others. Virtually all this research shows that children exposed to day care do at least as well as, and often better than, children raised exclusively in the home by their parents (Clarke-Stewart, 1993). Day-care children do as well in verbal and cognitive abilities, creativity, cooperation, and social competence as do home-raised children. Children placed in day care do at least as well as children raised at home in intelligence and psychosocial development; they do at least as well in sociability and academic achievement; and economically disadvantaged children in day care show less decline in IQ scores than is typically found among such children (Ispa, Thornburg, and Gray, 1990; Wasik et al., 1990; Caughy, DiPietro, and Strobino, 1994). Day-care children are also as attached to their parents as are children cared for in the home.

Research does suggest a few situations in which day care may not be the best for children. For example, children enrolled in day care for extended periods or at a very young age may become more aggressive and less cooperative, and economically disadvantaged children are often sent to poor quality day-care centers, which may adversely affect their emotional development (Kahn and Kamerman, 1987; Mott, 1991; Honig and Park, 1993). But this mass of research leaves us fairly confident that good day care can do at least as good a job raising children as the parents can. Actually, this should not be surprising because day-care centers have the resources to offer children much more—in terms of people to interact with, adults trained in child development and education, and such physical resources as games and educational materials—than does the average home. The typical nuclear family offers a child a much more limited range of social contacts and educational experiences.

Recent research has shifted focus from the issue of whether day care can do a good job to that of the quality of day care in the United States. And that quality is disturbingly low. National surveys of day-care centers found that the care at many of them was barely adequate in terms of developmentally appropriate activities for the children, teacher–child ratios, and the training of teachers (Zaslow, 1991; Phillips et al., 1994). And quality of day care is related to children's development: Children in better quality day care exhibit more cognitive and social development compared with children in lower quality day care. This is a problem especially for less affluent families because the day care available to them tends to be of lower quality.

One of the reasons that the quality of day care is often lower than it should be is that we do not pay much for day care. Day-care workers are overwhelmingly female, young, and disproportionately minority. They are a well-educated, dedicated, and committed group of people. They are also paid, on average, poverty-level wages, receive few benefits such as health insurance or retirement, and do a very taxing and difficult job (Hofferth and Phillips, 1991; Phillips, Howes, and Whitebook, 1991). The picture one gets is that people in the United States are willing to pay autoworkers large salaries, but they scrimp when it comes to paying those who care for their children.

Higher quality day care is found where workers have higher wages, more extensive benefits, and better working conditions. Better quality day care is also found when there are low child-to-staff ratios (or more staff for a given number of children),

and stability of care, with low turnover among the staff. The average annual turnover among staff in day-care centers is 41 percent—almost one out of every two workers leaves each year! (Phillips, Howes, and Whitebook, 1991). The main reasons workers leave, of course, are low wages, poor benefits, and unsatisfactory working conditions.

What it comes down to is that good day care costs money. This creates a problem, however, because higher costs will price some parents out of the day-care market—they will not be able to afford it. In a sense, day-care workers have been subsidizing inexpensive day care for parents over the years by accepting poverty-level wages. So there is a tension between spending more money to improve the quality of day care and keeping day care affordable to parents, especially single parents or those with low incomes. This tension becomes especially noticeable when day-care centers are private, profit-making organizations, which is often the case in the United States. The pressure to increase profit margins can lead to cost-cutting measures that reduce the quality of care. Research shows that for-profit day-care centers, when compared with nonprofit centers, tend lo pay lower salaries, have fewer staff per child, provide a lower quality of service, and have more staff turnover (Culkin, Morris, and Helburn, 1991; Kagan, 1991).

Social science research of the sort described in this insert has dispelled the traditional notion that family and maternal care for children is inherently superior to care provided in day-care centers. This research is now serving as a foundation for developing social policy on the future of day care in the United States.

define these practices as threatening to their values and as a social problem.

The interactionist perspective, then, points to the fact that what is considered the family is a matter of social definition, becoming a part of the social reality that people create and live by. Variations in the family may come to be seen as deviant and may be highly stigmatized because they violate the shared expectations of some groups about how to lead one's life. If this occurs, these groups may view changes in the form of the family as a social problem.

Attitudes Toward Marriage and the Family

Given the changes that have occurred in the role of the family in industrial society, are marriage and family living still popular today? It would seem so: More people in the United States marry than ever before, well over 90 percent. In 1994, 63 percent of all adult men in the United States were married, as were 59 percent of all adult women. These figures are higher than they were in 1940 but somewhat lower than at any time since 1950 (see Figure 3.2). Surveys reveal that both young people and their parents have quite positive attitudes toward marriage and family (Martin and Martin, 1984; Thornton, 1989; Moore and Stief, 1991). In a national sample of high school seniors, three-quarters reported that marriage and family life were "extremely important" to them, and a survey of young adults aged eighteen to twenty-two found that most of them plan to marry before the age of thirty. The vast majority of them also believed that when people marry, it should be "for life." Despite these positive views of marriage, however, the surveys detected some important changes: Compared with attitudes of the 1960s, these young men and women have fewer negative attitudes toward staying single, see fewer advantages in getting married over remaining single, and are not as certain that having children is the best

thing to do. In fact, the people interviewed seemed reluctant to choose either marriage or being single as the preferred alternative. In short, marriage is viewed quite positively by many people in the United States today, but alternatives to marriage are also becoming more popular.

These attitudes may reflect the culmination of a long transition from "arranged marriages" to "participant-run" romances. In preindustrial societies, in which the extended family and kinship were core social institutions, parents played a key role in deciding when and who their children would marry. Because the family in these societies was the major institution performing the important functions described in the previous section, it is not surprising that marital decisions were not left to whim or fancy. In many of these societies, *arranged marriages* occurred in which parents would select marriage partners for their children, sometimes shortly after their birth. The selection was based on what was considered best for the family, and the prospective marriage partners had little other choice. Such arranged marriages are still common in India and some other societies, and their members generally accept this practice as the wisest way to make marital choices.

A modified form of arranged marriage existed in the preindustrial United States, with young people having some choice in selecting a marriage partner but with parents still retaining substantial control over the ultimate decision. Courtship was common, but it occurred under the ever-watchful eyes of parents and other elders in the community. It was a *parent-run* courtship process: Young men and women were allowed to choose from among a pool of partners who were considered acceptable by their parents but were strongly discouraged from going outside that pool (Gordon, 1978).

In modern industrial societies, the selection of a marital partner is based primarily on the individual desires of the prospective mates. Parents can and do play a role in this process,

FIGURE 3.2 Marital Status of Adults in the United States, 1940–1994. *Sources:* U.S. Bureau of the Census, *Statistical Abstract of the United States, 1982–83* (Washington, D.C.: U.S. Government Printing Office, 1982), p. 38; U.S. Bureau of the Census, *Statistical Abstract of the United States, 1995* (Washington, D.C.: U.S. Government Printing Office, 1995), p. 55.

but their influence is typically secondary and often no more important than the suggestions of a close friend. This courtship process, then, is more *participant-run,* with romantic love as a primary factor drawing couples toward marriage. One reason for this declining role of parents over the years is that kinship is less important in modern societies, and one's kin, including one's parents, have considerably less stake in who marries whom. A second reason is that children have a greater degree of eco-

nomic independence from their parents in industrial societies, and parents therefore have less leverage with which to demand a say in the choice of a marriage partner. In the past, parents could withhold economic support from a couple, which usually made it very difficult for them to establish a household. Today, young people are better able to get jobs independently of their families and to support themselves. As the position of the family in society has changed, then, people have gained more

This four-year-old bride in India is being paraded through a village with her husband. Such arranged marriages were common in some preindustrial societies but have been largely replaced by participant-run marriages in industrial societies.

freedom of choice regarding a marriage partner. Today, it seems, people are also gaining more freedom of choice regarding whether to marry at all. Although most people will continue to marry, there is no longer as strong a stigma attached to remaining single.

So, these changing attitudes toward marriage and children reflect the extent to which the family, at least in its more traditional forms, is less central in modern society. Some people see these changing attitudes as an indication that the family as an institution is in trouble. Other developments suggest trouble for the family, and three of these developments will be reviewed: divorce, lifestyle alternatives to the traditional family, and violence in the family.

Divorce

The Divorce Rate

People usually view the widespread incidence and easy availability of divorce as having arisen only recently. In fact, the option for a married couple to dissolve a marriage has existed in many premodern societies. In some hunting and gathering bands, for example, a marriage could be easily ended when a couple decided to stop living together (O'Kelly and Carney, 1986). Nevertheless, to those who believe that marriage should be a lifelong commitment involving a deep emotional sharing between the married couple, today's high divorce rate is viewed as a threat to the family as a social institution.

In calculating the incidence of divorce, most sociologists use a statistic called the **refined divorce rate,** *which is determined by dividing the number of divorces each year by the total number of existing marriages in that year.* This method provides a valid way of comparing the stability of marriages from one year to the next. As Table 3.1 illustrates, the divorce rate has more than doubled since 1940, going from 8.8 to 20.9. As a point of comparison, it has been estimated that there were only 1.2 divorces for every 1,000 marriages in 1869—reflecting a seventeenfold increase during the past century (Saxton, 1980: 380). Although the trend in divorce rates over the past fifty years has been up, the rate has fluctuated considerably. It rose to 17.9 in 1946, one year after the end of World War II, a rate that is close to the rates found in the past fifteen years. Since 1975, the divorce rate has pretty much leveled off.

If we want to know the probability that a given marriage will end in divorce, we need a different statistic. As Figure 3.3 illustrates, the likelihood that a marriage would end in divorce in 1870 was 8 percent. By the 1980s, this figure had risen to over 50 percent. So, though it may be disturbing to many, the statistical likelihood of marriages beginning today ending in divorce is about fifty-fifty. However, those people who divorce are apparently not totally disillusioned with marriage because 75 to 80 percent of them will eventually remarry. But a slightly greater number of these second marriages will end in divorce in comparison to first marriages (Collins and Coltrane, 1991). However, this percentage is a little deceiving because it includes a small number of people who divorce and remarry many times. When this group is removed, second marriages are reasonably successful, and many couples in their second marriage report that they are happy.

The divorce rate, however, is but one measure of marital dissolution. Approximately 3 percent of all marriages end in legal separation, where the partners decide to end their relationship but prefer, perhaps for religious reasons, not to divorce. Desertion is another way in which marriages are dissolved, although it is difficult to know the extent of these. In any

---

TABLE 3.1 The Rate of Marriage and Divorce in the United States, 1940–1993

	1940	1945	1950	1955	1960	1965	1970	1975	1980	1985	1990	1993[a]
Marriage Rate[b]	82.8	83.6	90.2	80.9	73.5	75	76.5	66.9	61.4	57	54.5	52.3
Divorce Rate[c]	8.8	14.4	10.3	9.3	9.2	10.6	14.9	20.3	22.6	21.7	20.9	
Remarriage Rate[d]						127.8	123.3	117.2	91.3	81.8	76.2	

[a]provisional
[b]marriages per 1,000 unmarried women older than 15
[c]divorce and annulments per 1,000 married women older than 15
[d]marriages per 1,000 divorced women older than 14

Sources: National Center for Health Statistics: Advance Report of Final Divorce Statistics, 1989 and 1990. *Monthly Vital Statistics Report,* Vol. 43, No. 9, DHHS Pub. No. (PHS) 95-1120, Hyattsville, Md., March 22, 1995, p. 9; National Center for Health Statistics: Advance Report of Final Marriage Statistics, 1989 and 1990. *Monthly Vital Statistics Report,* Vol 43, No. 12, Supplement, DHHS Pub. No. (PHS) 95-1120, Hyattsville, Md., July 14, 1995, pp. 7, 10.

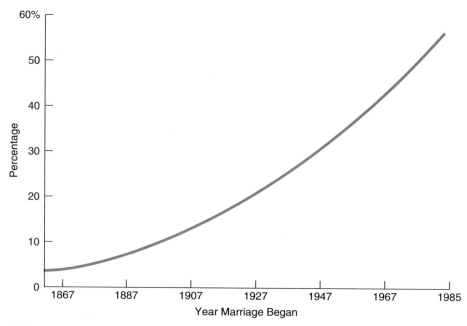

FIGURE 3.3 The Rising Percentage of Marriages Ending in Divorce, 1867–1985.
Source: Figure adapted from Marriage, Divorce, and Remarriage by Andrew J. Cherlin. Copyright © 1992 by the President and Fellows of Harvard College. Reprinted by permission of Harvard University Press.

event, we need to be aware that only a portion of all marital dissolutions is reflected in the divorce rate. In fact, given these marital practices, we might refer to our marriage system in the United States as one involving serial monogamy rather than monogamy or polygamy. **Polygamy** refers to *having more than one spouse at the same time.* **Serial monogamy** means that *a person is allowed to have more than one spouse, just not at the same time.*

People get divorces for many personal reasons—their spouse has become insensitive, they feel trapped by limited career opportunities, or their sex lives are no longer exciting. However, sociologists prefer to focus on the societal conditions that result in a high divorce rate rather than personal reasons for divorce. At least four such conditions account for the rising divorce rate over the past century.

First, we have seen that the family performs fewer functions today than in the past, which means there are fewer pressures on couples to stay together if they are unhappy. In the past, the same unhappy couple might have remained married because neither spouse felt he or she could raise the children alone or he or she needed the family for support in old age. Today, single parents are better prepared to raise a child, and most people are supported by retirement plans in their old age. In fact, the high levels of affluence afforded by industrialization have made people less dependent on kinship ties for support, with consequent changes in the family as an institution.

Second, the increasing equality between men and women has created both opportunities and tensions that contribute to the divorce rate (Brehm, 1985). In terms of opportunities, many women today are part of the labor force and thus have the economic ability to support themselves and their children without a husband. This reduces the likelihood of women being willing to remain in unsatisfying relationships. In terms of tensions, sexual equality has led to a redefining of the roles in the family, which can cause disagreements and stress that may precipitate divorce. A husband, for example, may feel that his wife should do most of the household chores, whereas she feels these tasks should be divided equally. Such conflicts are especially a problem for women who, after marrying, decide to pursue a career. This life change disrupts an established marital pattern and requires a renegotiation of male and female roles in the family, which is sometimes unsuccessful (Houseknecht, Vaughan, and Macke, 1984).

A third reason for the rising divorce rate is that there is considerably less stigma attached to divorce today than in the past (Thornton, 1985). Divorce in the past was often viewed as a serious failing in a person's life, with divorced people frequently labeled as morally inferior. Females in particular bore the stigma of the divorcee as a "fallen" woman. In precommunist China, for example, the divorce rate was extremely low, but the suicide rate for wives was very high. Wives were guided by a disturbing adage: "Good women should hang themselves; only bad women seek divorce" (Yang, 1965: 81). Today, with fifteen million divorced people in the United States, divorce is viewed by many as merely another lifestyle choice rather than a reflection of one's allegedly weak character.

Finally, as negative attitudes toward divorce have eased, pressures have surfaced to simplify the legal process for obtaining a divorce. These developments have encouraged more people to seek dissolution when they encounter marital difficulties.

Taking all of these factors together, we can make an important overriding observation about the reasons for divorce: People expect a great deal from the marriage relationship. We allow people to form families largely on the basis of romantic love, which can be fickle and unpredictable. Then we expect those relationships to afford a lifetime of emotional fulfillment, sexual gratification, companionship, and commitment. Is it so surprising, then, that many marriages fail to achieve these ideals? In the past, there were other, more pragmatic pressures for couples to stay together, such as economic constraints, reputation, religious ideals, and maintaining the marriage "for the sake of the children." Today, if the romantic ideal fails, other "barrier strengths" maintaining the marriage are less likely to prevent marital dissolution (Levinger and Moles, 1979).

Who Gets Divorced?

Some couples are at considerably greater risk of getting a divorce than are others (Bahr, 1989). Couples with an increased likelihood of divorcing have the following characteristics:

1. *Social differences between the couple, such as differences in religion, race, social class background, or values.* These differences can place substantial stress on a marriage.

2. *Low socioeconomic standing, such as low income or education.* Unemployment and other stresses that often accompany low social standing probably make it more difficult to achieve a successful marriage.

3. *Young age at marriage.* Very young couples seem especially ill equipped to make a go of marriage.

4. *Whirlwind romances.* People who have known one another for only a brief period are more likely to choose a partner with whom they will later prove to be incompatible.

The Effects of Divorce

As has been said, some fear that a high divorce rate will result in the collapse of the family as an institution. This implies that the family would fail to perform its functions, such as socializing children and providing emotional support. If this occurred on a widespread scale, the consequences could threaten society with severe stress and disorganization. Let us see what some of the effects of divorce are.

Widespread divorce has complicated kinship relationships and brought about what has been called a **blended family:** *a family based on kinship ties that accumulate as a consequence of divorces and remarriages* (Chilman, 1988; Cherlin and Furstenberg, 1994). These families involve relationships that are more complex than the standard nuclear family. For example, a child may live in a family with a full-blood sibling, a half-blood sibling, and a sibling with no blood and only marital ties. The same child may have a "real" mother and father as well as a stepfather or stepmother, and three sets of grandparents. Such arrangements, with their attendant complex kinship and legal linkages, can create complications and tensions that are less likely in traditional nuclear or extended family arrangements. In fact, sociologists now speak of "remarried couple households," defined as married couple households in which one or both spouses have been divorced. Forty-six percent of all marriages in the United States today involve a remarriage by at least one of the partners (U.S. Bureau of the Census, 1994: 102).

Divorce can be a disruptive and troubling experience, as those who have experienced it will attest. Marital dissolution often precipitates feelings of failure, loneliness, and rejection, along with intense anger and frustration. For many, it represents an assault on their sense of self-worth. Even when divorce is preferred by a person, an intimate bond is dashed nevertheless, and there is often nothing immediately to take its place. Symptoms of psychological distress, sometimes quite severe, are common among the newly divorced. Divorce is also sometimes associated with increased problems of physical health, with divorced people having more serious illnesses, more chronic disabling

conditions, and a higher suicide rate than do single or married people (Verbrugge, 1979; Kiecolt-Glaser et al., 1987). Men and women are affected by different elements of the divorce situation: Women's distress is more likely to arise from the fact that divorce leaves them with a lower standard of living and increased parental responsibilities; men's distress tends to arise from their difficulty in maintaining a close and supportive network of personal ties (Gerstel, Riessman, and Rosenfield, 1985).

There has been considerable debate regarding whether the husband or the wife is treated more unfairly in divorce proceedings. Husbands complain about being gouged for alimony or child-support payments, whereas wives protest over allegedly meager or missing payments from husbands. Social scientists have done considerable research on this issue, and the conclusions are remarkably consistent: Women are much more likely than men to suffer economic decline after divorce, and even when men suffer, their economic slide is much less severe and much more short-lived than is that of women (Holden and Smock, 1991; Seltzer, 1994).

One reason women end up worse off is that courts typically divide up only tangible property, such as a home, automobile, or belongings. Less tangible but often far more valuable property, such as a professional license that can translate into considerable income throughout a career, is usually not considered a part of the property settlement. It is the man who is far more likely to possess these less tangible forms of property. There are other reasons for the postdivorce economic decline of women: It is typically the woman who takes custody of children after divorce, and child support awarded by courts is usually meager compared to the father's income; only a minority of fathers comply fully with child-support awards; women earn substantially less than men (see Chapter 7); and women, having child-rearing responsibilities, suffer barriers in looking for jobs and finding child care. Women who are especially likely to suffer from divorce are the homemakers who devoted themselves to the housewife and mother roles and have few marketable skills.

Court rulings could create some change in these realms. For example, some courts have ruled that a spouse divorced after helping support a mate through medical or professional school might be entitled to a share of his or her mate's future earnings. Although these rulings have typically been overturned by a higher court, many experts are predicting that such rulings in the future may result in an expansion of the definition of "property" in divorce cases: Anything that might produce future income, such as a medical or law degree, could be considered property to be shared as a part of a financial settlement.

As far as the children of divorce are concerned, the jury is still out regarding whether they would be better off staying in a conflict-ridden, unhappy home rather than experiencing the divorce of their parents. Divorce is without question difficult for children, and living in a loving home is certainly preferable to experiencing an unhappy home or divorce. We simply lack the research to know all the effects if an unhappy family remains intact. There are some things that we do know, however (Wallerstein and Blakeslee, 1989; Furstenberg and Cherlin, 1991). First, the impact on children depends on their age. Children between five and ten, for example, often feel some responsibility for their parents' divorce, and this may lead to feelings of guilt and failure. Preteens often express tremendous anger at their parents. Teenagers, on the other hand, are often confronted with the matter of "parental loyalty," feelings that they must take sides in the conflict and form a coalition with one or the other parent. Furthermore, although adolescents are better able to understand the reasons for divorce, they are often very worried about the effects of separation on their future. A second thing we know about the impact of divorce is that children in divorced homes seem more prone to delinquency (Rankin, 1983; Wells and Rankin, 1991). Third, a common consequence of divorce for both boys and girls is a decline in school performance and a higher high school dropout rate. Finally, it is not the fact of the divorce itself that produces all of the negative consequences; the social and emotional conditions that often surround divorce are also a part of the problem (Amato, 1993; Amato and Rezac, 1994; Furstenberg and Teitler, 1994). The poor parenting, conflict between parents, and economic difficulties that often precede or follow divorce contribute to the negative consequences. In addition, divorce may reduce children's access to and ability to use various resources, such as the emotional support and role modeling of both parents.

The impact of divorce on children, however, is not all bad. Research shows that children living in one-parent families sometimes benefit from the experience (Amato, 1987; Goldscheider and Waite, 1991). For example, the single parent sometimes gives his or her teenage offspring more responsibility and a greater role in family decision making. Also, teenage boys in mother-only families tend to take on a considerably greater share of household chores than do boys *or* girls in two-parent homes. In fact, teenage boys living with their mothers develop more egalitarian attitudes toward men's and women's roles, and both boys and girls may become more independent and resourceful. In addition, the experience of divorce is less negative if a child continues to have contact with the parent with whom they no longer live, especially when the divorced parents have a low-conflict relationship.

So divorce does have some substantial negative consequences for society, and ways of alleviating their impact will be explored later in the chapter.

Emerging Family Lifestyles

People who divorce and those who never marry develop some type of lifestyle, including personal relationships and living arrangements, to replace the conventional family. These lifestyles are considered by many to be another dimension of the problems surrounding the family today. Figure 3.4 illustrates some of these changes in family structure over the past two decades. These alternative lifestyles did not emerge arbitrarily; they are a reflection of the diversified and to a degree fragmented society in which we live. Some of these lifestyles arise as people adapt to the void left by divorce, but some are chosen because elements of modern society make them more attractive options than in the past (Davidson and Moore, 1992). Following are three such elements of today's society:

1. There is an *increasing atmosphere of tolerance* about sexual and personal behavior that has re-duced the stigma that is attached to divorce, as well as enabled people to find sexual gratification without getting married.

2. There is *greater individualism and egalitarianism,* including increased geographic mobility and an emphasis on individual careers, that has produced an atmosphere of separation from the group, including the nuclear family. It also reduces barriers to sexual involvement during courtship and other expressions of sexuality.

3. There has been a *marketing of lifestyles and sexuality* in the mass media, providing role models for young people and making nontraditional lifestyles newsworthy and often presented by the media as "trendy" and "fashionable." This helps to spread their popularity.

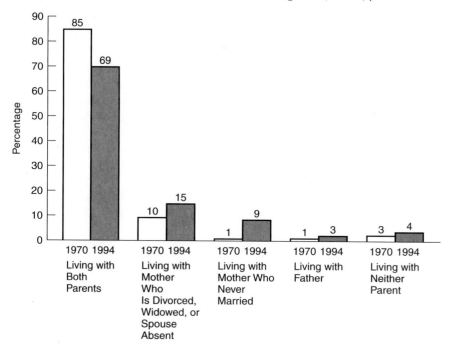

FIGURE 3.4 Living Arrangements of People Younger Than 18 Years of Age, 1970–1994. *Source:* U.S. Bureau of the Census, *Statistical Abstract of the United States, 1995* (Washington, D.C.: U.S. Government Printing Office, 1995), p. 66.

We now review some of the major alternatives to the conventional family with an eye on what future developments are likely.

Dual-Career Families

In the conventional nuclear family in the United States, women either did not work outside the home or their jobs were considered secondary to their husbands'. Today, in just over one-half of all two-spouse families, the wife works (see Figure 3.5). In addition, there is an increasing number of **dual-career families** *in which both wives and husbands are committed to career-oriented occupations that offer them fulfillment and opportunities for advancement.* Although it is difficult to estimate the number of dual-career families, census statistics suggest that the number of dual-career couples has grown from 900,000 in 1960 to 3.3 million by the mid-1980s (Sekaran, 1986).

One of the major tensions that people in dual-career families face is how to resolve disputes over whose career will take precedence. Such disputes can arise, for example, if either husband or wife wants to move to another city or state in order to advance a career, especially if such a transition would be detrimental to his or her spouse's career. On a routine basis, there may be disagreement over whose career must suffer in order to raise children or to accomplish household chores. Although these tensions suggest that dual-career marriages are more susceptible to divorce, there is little convincing evidence on this issue so far. Evidence does suggest that women who work out of choice are more satisfied with their marriages than women who work out of a sense of financial obligation, and the men in dual-career families seem to be happy with their marriages (Gilbert, 1985; Piotrkowski et al., 1987; Vannoy-Hiller and Philliber, 1989). In addition, dual-career couples are more likely to remain childless and childless couples tend to have higher levels of marital satisfaction than do

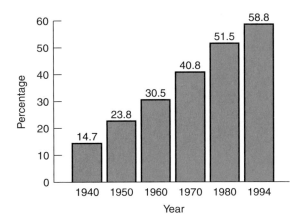

FIGURE 3.5 Percentage of Married Women with Spouse Present Who Are Employed, 1940–1994. *Source:* U.S. Bureau of the Census, *Statistical Abstract of the United States, 1978* (Washington, D.C.: U.S. Government Printing Office, 1978), p. 404; U.S. Bureau of the Census, *Statistical Abstract of the United States, 1995* (Washington, D.C.: U.S. Government Printing Office, 1995), p. 399.

couples with children (Houseknecht, 1987). An investigation of dual-career couples working in senior management positions described such marriages as "more equal than others" in that the couples share a more equal partnership, with a more egalitarian decision-making structure, than do couples in more traditional marriages (Hertz, 1986).

Careers are attractive to both men and women because their work offers financial rewards, status, and excitement. However, the time and commitment devoted to careers competes with the energy people devote to family life, creating tensions in the family. Higher rates of childlessness among dual-career families may be an effort to avoid such competing demands. This might create other problems, however. If more people choose careers in the future, it is possible that many will resolve competing demands by choosing not to have children, possibly even choosing not to get married. This may well create a substantial difference in the standard of living between those

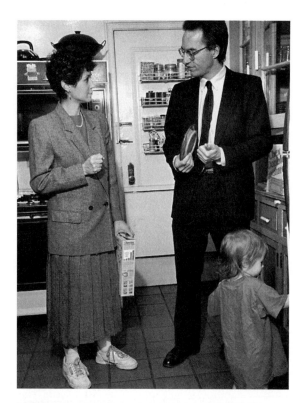

Marriages in which both parents work have become more common in the United States, creating tensions over whose career should take precedence and over the equitable allocation of childrearing duties.

who devote their energies to careers and those who feel family is important: Careerists will have a substantially more affluent lifestyle, which may make the decision to remain childless appealing to even more people. The outcome, potentially, might be the birth of even fewer children in society. This in turn could lead to a number of problems, such as an increasingly aged and dependent population that would be expensive to support (see Chapter 8).

Singlehood

Today, 42 million adults in the United States have never been married. This figure includes slightly more males than females. Many of these people, of course, will eventually marry, but some will choose singlehood over marriage as a lifelong lifestyle. In addition, although the proportion of our population that is single declined between 1940 and 1965, it has increased considerably since then (see Figure 3.2). Added to these never-married people are the many widowed and divorced who, at least temporarily, are living their lives as single men and women. For example, there are ten million widowed people over sixty-five years of age in the United States, 80 percent of whom are living alone (U.S. Bureau of the Census, 1994: 56).

Many people who elect to remain single do so because they believe this lifestyle affords them distinct advantages: freedom from unnecessary commitments, economic independence, opportunities to meet new people and develop new relationships, room for personal growth, or the ability to have a more varied sex life that is free of guilt (Cargan and Melko, 1982; Macklin, 1987). Remaining single does not mean of course that there is necessarily a lack of emotional involvement with a partner who is at least semipermanent. Many singles develop intimate relationships, but they refuse to allow these to become permanent bonds based on marital exclusivity. However, as with childlessness among dual-career couples, singlehood—especially if chosen permanently and in large numbers—may have a long-term effect of lowering the birthrate.

Cohabitation

Cohabitation, or what is commonly called "living together," refers to *relationships in which two people live in the same household and share sexual, emotional, and often economic ties without being legally married.* In 1988, a survey showed that 5 percent of women between the ages of fifteen and forty-four were in a cohabitation relationship, and fully one-third of all women had cohabited at some point in their lives (London, 1990). Most of the couples involved are young, with over 81 percent involving one partner under forty-five years of age. But a substantial number of the couples, as much as 5 percent, involve one partner over sixty-five, and two out of five people who cohabit were previously married (U.S. Bureau of the Census, 1994: 56).

People cohabit for many reasons (Loomis and Landale, 1994; Cherlin and Furstenberg, 1994). For some, it is a "trial marriage," a time for the couple to get to know one another and determine whether they are compatible before establishing the legal bond. For others, cohabitation may be viewed as a replacement for marriage, which some women and men may view as an unnecessary legal tie. In fact, one group among which cohabitation has increased considerably in the past 30 years is the divorced. People increasingly turn to cohabitation rather than remarriage as a vehicle for establishing an intimate relationship after a failed marriage. For these people, cohabitation has come to be seen as acceptable as marriage as a context for family-related activities such as having children. Finally, for some elderly couples, for whom marriage means a reduction in Social Security income, cohabitation may be a matter of economic convenience or necessity.

As the number of cohabiting couples has grown, the stigma associated with this lifestyle has declined. It is now widely accepted in cities and college communities, and it will probably become even more popular, especially among young and divorced people. As cohabitation has become more common, controversy has arisen about the legal status of the partners in the relationship. As was mentioned in the beginning of the chapter, some employers, including some city and county governments, have established "domestic partner" provisions that accord cohabitants much the same benefits and rights as married couples. This practice has become more common as employers adapt to the kinds of personal arrangements their employees seem to prefer for their personal lives (Wisensale and Heckart, 1993). As a significant number of employees choose not to marry, employers are taking this into consideration in their policies. In addition, a number of courts have ruled that the relationship between cohabitants is not unlike that of married couples. For example, cohabitants can make legal arrangements to share their property, and one partner can sue the other for a share of the property and for support payments, or "palimony," should the relationship dissolve. So, although some people continue to see marriage as the preferable route for organizing one's life, a growing number of people are choosing cohabitation, and the courts are establishing a legal framework that sees cohabitation as being very much like marriage.

Single Parenthood

A rapidly growing alternative to the conventional two-parent nuclear family is one in which there is only one parent. Today, almost 25 percent of all families with children under eighteen years of age are headed by only one parent, mostly by women (U.S. Bureau of the Census, 1994: 63). Furthermore, almost one out of every three children lives in a family in which one or both parents are absent (see Figure 3.4), and half of all children may spend at least part of their childhood in a single-parent home. Although some families have only one parent due to the death of a spouse, most are the result of divorce. Increasingly, however, children live with parents, usually mothers, who choose not to marry at all. In 1994, more than three million families were headed by a parent who had never been married. The number of children living with a mother who had never married increased to 9 percent in 1994 compared to 1 percent in 1970. Thirty percent of all births are to unmarried women today, in comparison with 4 percent in 1950 (U.S. Bureau of the Census, 1994: 80). Given these trends in divorce and single motherhood, the proportion of single-parent families is likely to grow considerably in the future. Needless to say, people who view marriage as the only acceptable context for raising children find such developments highly threatening to their values.

The issue of single parenthood has been controversial because suggestions that children raised by a single parent suffer more problems than children raised by both parents have been strongly attacked for implying that mothers are not adequate parents or that parents should not divorce. These suggestions have been interpreted as limiting women's choices in life, a stance that is not popular in this era of gender equality. Yet, the research on single-parent families does suggest, in a qualified way, that children are often worse off when raised by one parent than two, suffering consequences similar to those of children of divorce mentioned earlier. A recent summary of this research concluded:

> Growing up with only one biological parent frequently deprives children of important economic, parental, and community resources, and . . . these deprivations ultimately undermine their chances of future success. . . . While living with just one parent increases the risk of . . . negative outcomes, it is not the only, or even the major, cause of them. Growing up with a single parent is just one among many factors that put children at risk of failure. (McLanahan and Sandefur, 1994: 2–3)

Not all children in single-parent families will suffer the negative consequences because many factors influence a child's development. The researchers attribute the difficulties of children in single-parent families to three factors: low income, inadequate parental guidance, and less access to community resources. If a single parent can overcome these difficulties, then their children can do quite well. For example, when the decision to have a child is well considered by a woman with the social and economic resources to raise the child adequately, the outcome does not raise serious problems for society, although it might clash with the personal or religious values of some groups. So, the research does not lead neces-

sarily to the conclusion that divorce or single parenthood is bad. However, single parenthood is especially widespread among groups who are more likely to lack the financial resources to support the child, such as minorities and teenagers (Zill and Nord, 1994). For example, over half of all births to African American and Puerto Rican American women are to unmarried women, and both of these groups have some of the highest rates of poverty in the United States. For teenagers, in particular, becoming a mother is a difficult burden: They often lack the maturity and economic resources for good childrearing practices, and the burden often severely limits their educational and employment opportunities. Although the rate of teenage pregnancy is steady or falling in other industrial nations, it has risen over the last two decades in the United States. Teen pregnancy rates are now two-to-three times higher in the United States than in most industrial nations, and they are higher in the United States than in *any* other industrial nation (Moore and Stief, 1991). When single parents are unprepared for parenthood, society often ends up assuming some of the responsibility for the care and financial maintenance of their children, and problems such as poverty, child abuse, and delinquency are often exacerbated.

The Policy Issues insert (on pp. 102–103) explores some of the issues and controversies regarding whether gay unions should be considered an emerging family form.

A Global Perspective

Some of the trends in family life found in the United States are also occurring in other nations around the world (United Nations, 1991; Bruce, Lloyd, and Leonard, 1995). In the past few decades, for example, the proportion of births to unmarried women has increased in most nations, in some cases dramatically. The proportion has doubled in the United States to 30 percent, but in nations as diverse as Denmark, Norway, and Guam it has increased 300 to 400 percent. In the Seychelles, French Guiana, and Martinique, two out of every three births are to unmarried women. In addition, many households are headed by women: almost 50 percent in nations like Botswana and Barbados and 31 percent in the United States. Household size has also been decreasing in every part of the world, suggesting that the family is becoming a smaller kinship unit. The birth rate in most societies around the world has been declining, and the divorce rate has been increasing. All of these trends suggest the extent to which the form of the family is shaped by the needs of society. Earlier, this chapter pointed out that industrial societies generally tend to weaken kinship and family structures, in part because the family in such societies performs fewer functions and is thus less important. Industrial societies tend to encourage nuclear families and to be more permissive of divorce. Such societies also sometimes split families up as some members must migrate looking for work. In addition, greater gender equality and higher levels of education for women offer them more opportunities in terms of supporting their families. The result, in most nations, is that the family has declined in both size and significance and women have fewer supports with which to take care of themselves and their families. It is a worldwide trend—a byproduct of industrialization—although the pace and extent of the developments vary from one society to another.

Violence in the Family

The family is usually viewed as a place where love and affection abound, but one research team concluded that there is a darker side to family life: "Violence between family members is probably as common as love" (Straus, Gelles, and Steinmetz, 1980: 13). Part of the reason for the contrast between people's views of the family and the reality of violence relates to the so-

cial construction of reality. People are naturally reluctant to admit that such violence occurs in their own families for fear of being stigmatized. As a consequence, especially in the past, we would hear few if any reports of such violence, and the silence would lead us to assume that such behavior was in fact rare. Its occurrence in our own families, we would conclude, was isolated, odd, and best kept a secret. Thus, the social reality of the loving affectionate family was maintained despite the fact that family violence was common.

Given the widespread nature of family violence, let us examine the three major types: marital violence, child abuse, and abuse of the elderly.

Marital Violence

Family "violence" can be defined in a number of ways. For example, Murray Straus and Richard Gelles (Gelles and Cornell, 1990) employed an extremely general definition of violence, including everything from pushes and shoves to "throwing something" to "beating up their spouse" to "using a knife or a gun." On the basis of their national survey involving more than six thousand households, they determined that one-sixth of married people have engaged in at least one act of violence against a spouse each year, although these figures probably underestimate the total amount of violence between husbands and wives because people are often reluctant to admit such goings on in their family. They estimate that more than 50 percent of married couples have had violent exchanges with each other at some point during their marriages. Using these broad criteria, of course, some of the "violence" reported includes pushes and shoves from which no serious physical harm comes to victims. Even so, the numbers demonstrate that a serious problem exists. Of the 51 million married couples in the United States, at least 6 percent experience conjugal violence involving kicking, biting, punching, or more serious

POLICY ISSUES
Gay Families

As society changes, the family also changes, with new forms of the family emerging that may challenge traditional ways of thinking. The chapter points out how cohabitation was once viewed negatively by many but has now gained some respectability. The same thing may be happening with gay and lesbian couples, who for years have considered the same-sex unions they form to be "families" even though society has withheld such legitimation. Today, some ministers will perform marriage ceremonies to unite gay and lesbian couples, and more employers are beginning to provide benefits and rights to the domestic partners of their gay employees. To assess society's policy stance on this, it is worth exploring some of the sociological issues surrounding gay families.

From a sociological perspective, the domestic units formed by gay and lesbian couples resemble families because the units perform many of the functions that families perform in society, as described earlier in this chapter. These relationships are often monogamous, the norm for families in the United States, with some degree of permanence and an emphasis on sexual exclusivity (Berger, 1990; Lewin, 1993). In fact, lesbians value monogamy in relationships and are about as possessive of their partners as are men and women in heterosexual marriages. A smaller percentage of gay men put as much value on sexual exclusivity in a relationship. Gay and lesbian couples sometimes have children from previous marriages or they adopt or conceive through artificial insemination. Children in gay or lesbian families are much less common than in heterosexual families because the courts have been reluctant to give custody to an openly gay parent, and adoption agencies have viewed gay homes as inappropriate for child placement. Estimates are that one-third of lesbians are mothers and between one-quarter and one-half of all gay men are fathers, although many do not have custody of their

offspring (Green and Bozett, 1991). So, the socialization and educational functions of the family are performed by some gay couples, and research gives no evidence that the children are compromised in any significant way by being raised by a gay parent (Patterson, 1992; Golombok and Tasker, 1995).

Gay couples also often form an economic unit through the common ownership of property, such as a home, and the combining of financial resources. The courts have yet to give legal sanction to these economic ties, but some corporations are beginning to do so by extending benefits and rights to the unmarried domestic partners of their employees, whether they be a heterosexual couple or a gay couple. As evidence that the relationship is reasonably permanent, some employers look for signs of economic interdependence, such as joint bank accounts or co-owned property. Finally, many gay couples provide the protection and the personal gratification that are among the functions of the units typically called "families."

So, a significant number of gay men and lesbians form relationships that have many of the sociological attributes normally associated with families. To be sure, gay couples face significant stressors, especially when they insist on performing the parenting role (Levy, 1992). They may also suffer discrimination in both occupation and housing. They are also likely to be labeled deviant by many and cast into a marginal role. One way in which society marginalizes gays is by denying official legitimation to their bond in the form of marriage ceremonies or licenses that signify societal approval. Some gay couples have ceremonies to mark their commitment to each other; these rituals perform the same functions of public affirmation and legitimation that legally recognized marriage ceremonies do. In Denmark, same-sex couples were given the right to get married in a registry bureau in 1989. In the United States, however, many peo-

These marchers are using collective action to push for acceptance of gay and lesbian families. The domestic units formed by gay and lesbian couples have many of the sociological attributes normally associated with families; however, significant opposition persists to giving societal legitimation to such unions.

ple are still opposed to offering such societal approval to gay couples. Groups such as the Gay and Lesbian Parents Coalition International have formed to assist gay parents with these problems.

So, gay and lesbian organizations are lobbying for changes in policy that will permit them to live openly in same-sex relationships with all the same rights, privileges, and responsibilities of heterosexuals who live in families. Although there is more support for such a policy today than in the past, significant opposition persists, especially from conservative groups and some religions. How far such changes will proceed is uncertain at this point.

forms of violent behavior (Straus, 1991). Violence of this sort also occurs among dating couples and cohabitants. Estimates are that one out of every five college couples experiences kicking, biting, slapping, or more serious violence while courting (Murphy, 1988).

How are we to explain this high level of marital violence? One reason for it is that the use of violence to settle disputes is widely accepted in the United States, especially among males. Traditional norms in many subcultures support male domination in marriage. In fact, men with traditional, or nonegalitarian, views toward sex-role relationships are more likely to approve of using violence against a spouse and are more likely to have actually used severe violence against their own spouses. A second reason for marital violence is poverty: Serious violence within families is disproportionately a problem of the poor and economically disadvantaged. Families with low educational and occupational attainment are especially at risk of spouse abuse. A third reason for marital violence is sexual inequality (Kalmuss and Straus, 1982; Crossman, Stith, and Bender, 1990; Straus, 1991). Wife beating is much more likely to occur in families in which power over decision making is concentrated in the husband's hands—approximately twenty times the rate found in families in which egalitarian decision making occurs (Straus, Gelles, and Steinmetz, 1980). When women have more social and economic resources, such as a job with which to support themselves, they are less likely to be abused and more likely to leave an abusive husband. A fourth reason for marital violence is an inconsistency between the man's and woman's achievements. So, a high risk of marital violence is found when a man's occupation or educational attainment is significantly lower than his wife's. The husband may feel threatened by this and lash out with physical violence. A final reason for marital violence is social isolation: When a spouse has few contacts with people other than her husband, she is less likely to define the abuse as unjustified and to seek assistance (Stets, 1991).

Child Abuse

Equally if not more disturbing than the conclusions about marital violence are the findings concerning violence by parents against children; more than 60 percent of couples acknowledge performing at least one violent act against a child. One investigation reported that more than 10 of every 1,000 children younger than 18 years are victims of serious abuse or

Child abuse is a disturbingly common tragedy in the United States. Although it can be found among all social classes, child abuse, especially involving severe violence, is more common among the extremely poor.

neglect every year, and as Figure 3.6 disturbingly illustrates, child abuse and neglect are the leading causes of traumatic death for children aged four and younger (Straus and Gelles, 1986; U.S. Advisory Board . . . , 1995).

Researchers in this field regard these figures as conservative. Some research suggests that the rates of child abuse are increasing in the United States, but this conclusion is controversial and depends on how child abuse is measured. If we look at child abuse reported to police and health care workers, abuse appears to be up; but if we ask parents if they have shoved, hit, or in other ways hurt their children, rates appear to be down. A definitive conclusion on whether abuse is increasing is just not possible at this time (Gelles and Conte, 1990; Egley, 1991).

As with marital violence, there are economic correlates of child abuse. Investigations have shown that the maltreatment of children is concentrated not only among low-income families but also among the extremely poor. This is especially true for severe violence (Pelton, 1978; Gelles, 1992). For the poor, economic hardships interact with immediate situational stressors—disputes between parents, a burdensome number of children, a child who creates problems for parents—to bring about incidents of child abuse. Especially at risk of using the most abusive forms of violence against their children are poor and young parents, poor parents with young children, and poor single mothers (Gelles, 1992).

Irrespective of social class considerations, it appears that child abuse is a behavior pattern that is passed on from generation to generation in some families. For example, a review of studies on child abuse found that although between 2 percent and 4 percent of parents abuse their children, that rate is as high as 30 percent or more among parents who were

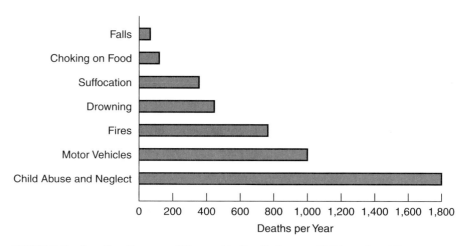

FIGURE 3.6 Leading Causes of Traumatic Death Among Children Aged Four or Younger in the United States. *Source:* U.S. Advisory Board on Child Abuse and Neglect, U.S. Department of Health and Human Services, *A Nation's Shame: Fatal Child Abuse and Neglect in the United States* (Washington, D.C.: U.S. Government Printing Office, 1995), p. xxiv.

themselves abused as children (Gelles and Conte, 1990).

Abuse of the Elderly

One form of violence in the family that has not received as much attention is abuse of the elderly by their spouses, offspring, or guardians. In 1985, the House Subcommittee on Health and Long-term Care uncovered episodes of abuse such as these: a seventy-five-year-old man was attacked with a hatchet by his son; a seventy-four-year-old woman was beaten and raped by her son-in-law and then threatened by her daughter not to squeal to anyone about it; a sixty-eight-year-old woman was neglected by the son with whom she lived and starved to death in a feces-fouled house while her son was well fed (Bruno, 1985).

The elderly can suffer the same kinds of abuses as do children and spouses: physical violence, psychological abuse such as insults and threats, and neglect of one's important and basic needs of daily living. Current estimates are that 32 of every 1,000 older people suffer some type of abuse, with well over half of that being physical violence (Pillemer and Finkelhor, 1988). This means that somewhere between 700,000 and 1.1 million elderly in the United States have suffered abuse. Surprising to some, men are more likely to be victims of elder abuse than are women, and women are more likely to abuse their elder husbands than men are to abuse their elder wives. However, women suffer more injuries and emotional distress when they are abused than do men. Finally, those who live alone or who are not married are less likely to suffer abuse than those who are married or live with others, and those who live with a spouse and an offspring are especially at risk of suffering abuse.

Some abuse of the elderly may arise from the stress of taking care of a dependent older parent or grandparent who is physically or mentally impaired (King, 1984; Steinmetz, 1987). To some extent, abuse of the elderly reflects one of the weaknesses of the modern nuclear family: It lacks the extensive support network and additional helping hands that are available in the extended family or even the modified extended family. As we have seen, we often expect each person in the nuclear family to be a breadwinner, a companion, and so on. When society burdens one person with a wide range of difficult tasks, including taking care of a child or an impaired older parent, the stresses will sometimes accumulate to the point where abuse is likely. Recent research, however, points to a different relationship between dependency and abuse: Abuse is more likely to occur when the caregiver is dependent on the elderly person under his or her care. This is especially true when the caregiver is financially dependent on the elderly person under his or her charge, is personally or emotionally troubled, or abuses alcohol or drugs (Pillemer and Finkelhor, 1989; Greenberg, McKibben, and Raymond, 1990). In these situations, caregivers may be responding to their feelings of powerlessness in the relationship and resorting to one of the few power resources they have available: force and violence.

So, research on abuse of the elderly provides further evidence for the part that inequitable distributions of power and resources play in family violence. Those who are dependent—whether they be children or frail elderly—are at risk of suffering violence at the hands of others. Those with access to economic and social resources, such as wives with careers or the elderly who can live on their own, are better equipped to avoid violence. And those who feel helpless and powerless—such as poor, single mothers or caregivers who are dependent on their elderly charges—may lash out in violence as a reaction to their circumstances.

Future Prospects

Most sociologists are confident that the family as a social institution will survive. The family performs important functions in society, and some type of family will undoubtedly continue to perform those functions in the future. But the family is changing, and the real issue is not whether the family will survive but what form it will take. New forms, such as single parenthood, cohabitation, and gay families, are emerging, and these perform the sociological functions of families discussed in this chapter. Given these trends, what seems to be emerging in modern industrial societies is a **pluralistic family** in which *a number of different types of family exists side by side, each having an attraction for some people.* So, in the United States today, some people live in extended families, some in traditional nuclear families, some in blended families, and still others in same-sex families. Given the vast diversity in the culture and the changing role of the family, such pluralistic family arrangements are probably more adaptive. They permit people of many occupations, religions, ethnic groups, and lifestyles to find a form of the family that best fits their values and needs. While some people are tolerant of this diversity, others find some of these alternatives to be morally unacceptable, and this conflict will probably persist in the future. Such conflict will be especially salient in the public policy arena in which groups do battle to gain acceptance for their values or way of life. The outcome of this conflict will determine which forms of the family find acceptance at any given moment, and that will likely change from time to time.

Some of these diverse forms of the family, however, can create serious problems for society, and many proposals and programs have been put forth to alleviate these problems.

The Future of Divorce

Despite the rapid rise in divorce in recent decades, the divorce rate will not necessarily continue to rise substantially in the future. In fact, since 1975, the increase in the divorce rate in the United States has been fairly stable. In part, this is due to a considerable decline in the marriage rate, which has dropped by about one-third over the past thirty years (see Table 3.1). However, it may also be that the divorce rate has risen as high as it is likely to in response to changing social conditions resulting from industrialization. On the other hand, there is no reason to believe that the divorce rate will decline significantly in the future. The current divorce rate may well be one that is commensurate with social conditions and the position of the family in a mature industrial society.

In the past, religious teachings, social norms, and practical considerations inhibited people from dissolving their marriages. Today, as we have seen, these factors are less prominent. Yet these traditional controls may be replaced with others. For example, our schools and colleges could offer more and better courses in marriage and family training so that young people would be prepared to make sounder marital choices and work more effectively at maintaining relationships. Such courses could help people identify the factors associated with successful and unsuccessful marriages so that they could use this information in making important life choices. In fact, the state of California, recognizing that people who marry at a young age are especially likely to divorce, requires people younger than eighteen to obtain a court order to marry and to submit to premarital counseling if directed. We might consider requiring all prospective marriage partners to take a course in premarital counseling. After all, we require people to pass a test of knowledge and skills related to driving laws before permitting them to drive an automobile. We might also encourage couples to seek periodically the advice of trained marriage counselors so that trouble spots in a relationship could be identified. By the time many couples seek such advice today, their difficulties are often beyond help. Steps such as these would not eliminate divorce, but they may help to reduce the divorce rate—and the agony of such dissolutions—to a degree, although probably not to preindustrial levels.

It might also be advantageous to assist people who are divorcing in order to avoid the more negative outcomes. Divorcing parents, for example, can be directed toward intervention programs that can help them make the transition a more positive one for their children. In some states, judges can order divorcing parents to attend parent education programs. These programs focus on such things as improvements in the parent-child relationship, contact with the noncustodial parent, development of effective discipline strategies, and development of a social network and problem-solving resources. These interventions focus on the factors, as noted earlier in the chapter, that cause problems for children in divorce, and they have been shown to make the postdivorce experience less negative for children who, as a result of these interventions, have a more positive psychological adjustment (Wolchik et al., 1993).

Reducing Family Violence

One of the most positive steps toward reducing family violence has been bringing the issue into the open. This has enabled us to concentrate resources on solving this problem. The Child Abuse Prevention and Treatment Act was passed in the mid 1970s and amended in 1988 to help states and communities develop programs for abusive or neglectful parents. The government has also funded research to find the causes of child abuse and the most effective ways of dealing with it. Programs have been established to train parents in "parenting skills" as a way of preventing future episodes of abuse. Prevention can also be enhanced when parents are connected to organizations and services in the community because this increases the chances of getting help before abuse recurs. Substance abuse treatment programs are made available to parents who might be at risk of abusing their children because of the known role of alcohol in child abuse. Self-help groups such as Parents Anonymous, in which a supportive personal relationship is used to help

parents stop mistreating their children, have also emerged. Finally, programs such as day care that ease the pressure and burden on parents may reduce the precipitating factors that can initiate episodes of violence.

Spouse abuse has also received much attention recently, and this has resulted in accelerated efforts toward pinning down its sources. As mentioned earlier, the improving economic and social position of women in society will likely make them less vulnerable targets of abuse in the future. Furthermore, spouse abuse centers can now be found in most communities, and these offer sanctuary and support to women who seek to change or leave an abusive relationship. Finally, the Policy Issues section of Chapter 1 pointed out that the criminal justice system today responds much more quickly and aggressively to cases in which spouse abuse is suspected. In many jurisdictions, police can arrest a suspected offender even if the victim declines to file a complaint. Convictions for spouse abuse are easier to obtain, and those convicted are often required to seek counseling to help them change their behavior. So, in comparison to earlier decades, people who abuse their spouses today are more likely to be caught and punished, and this should help alleviate the problem.

Efforts to control abuse of the elderly have not been as extensive as those focusing on other forms of family violence, but some progress has been made (Ross, 1991; Olinger, 1991). For example, many states have adopted laws that require reporting of abuse of the elderly to the police. They have also established many protective services for the elderly, increased penalties for abuse or neglect of the elderly, and created provisions for confidentiality in the reporting of cases of elder abuse. Yet there remain substantial restraints on what the authorities can do. Most states have no penalties for many forms of abuse or neglect of a parent. In the case of the sixty-eight-year-old woman who starved to death, criminal charges against her son were dropped because of a loophole in the law. According to a police

INTERNATIONAL PERSPECTIVES
Families and Children in Other Societies

Regarding families and children, social policy in the United States has historically been very laissez-faire, leaving people to get by on their own with little assistance from the government. This contrasts sharply with virtually all other advanced industrial nations, where social policies are based on a consensus that everyone benefits when families and their children are supported (Kamerman, 1991; Kamerman and Kahn, 1991). These nations take responsibility for protecting children, providing good early childhood education, serving children with special needs, supporting mothers' desires to continue working, maintaining family income during and after the birth of a child, and encouraging a birth rate that at least maintains current population size.

To achieve these goals, most industrial nations make publicly funded preschools universally available to children beginning at age three and continuing until the child enters school, irrespective of parents' income or work status. In France and Belgium, for example, the preschools are publicly financed and operated as an integral part of the educational system. All children are eligible, beginning some time after their second birthday, and the schools are free, with parents paying only for things like lunch or certain after-school programs. Similar programs are found in many other countries, including Israel and Hungary. In Sweden and Finland, preschools are separate from the school system and are heavily subsidized by the government, although parents do pay some fees if they can afford them. All children are eligible for these programs until compulsory school attendance begins at age 7, and the government enforces strict standards regarding such things as staff–child ratios and teacher qualifications. Such preschool education is coming to be viewed, by many of these European nations, as a "right" of citizenship, just as one has a right to a basic education.

Almost all advanced industrial nations also provide some level of maternity or parenting leave that enables one or both parents to stay home with their infant for a period after birth. These programs permit the parents to receive some level of their previous income while on leave and protect their job until they return to work. In France, for example, women are given a six-week leave before delivery and ten weeks after delivery, all with pay, and business leaders seem unconcerned about its effects on worker productivity or corporate profits. French parents can also take two years off after having a child without worrying about whether their job will be there when they return.

Given that maternity/parenting leaves enable parents to stay home with their infants, and preschool takes care of children aged three and older, the only children in need of child care in these industrial nations are those who are one and two years of age. While child-care programs are much more limited in these countries than are the infant and preschool programs, child care is increasingly being seen as a public responsibility and an entitlement for children. In addition to these programs, most industrial nations also provide publicly funded health care and housing allowances to families, paid leave to parents to care for sick children, and sometimes even direct subsidization of family incomes to reduce the economic disparity between those who choose to have children and those who choose to remain childless.

Despite the fact that United States policy leaves families very much on their own, the need for support seems greater in the United States than in these other countries (U.S. Bureau of the Census, 1994: 857). In the United States, 9 percent of all households have a single parent, compared to 2 percent in Japan and 3 percent in Sweden. In fact, just about all industrial nations have fewer single-parent households and a lower divorce rate than does the United States. So, the regulated capitalism of France and Sweden has produced family policies that protect and nurture children because children are seen as key resources for the future. The United States, on the other hand, leaves children to the largely unregulated free market which has so far meant that many children live in less affluent families and go without while others suffer low quality, inadequate, and possibly damaging preschool experiences.

sergeant working on the case: "You can't let your children, your wife, or your dog starve to death, but there's nothing in the penal code that says you've got to feed your mother" (Bruno, 1985). Even mandatory reporting has its weaknesses. Because the abused elderly are often dependent on their caregivers for support, they may choose not to seek needed medical care if they believe signs of abuse will be reported to the authorities by their doctor. What needs to be done is to establish a range of services that could defuse tensions in the family or help the elderly escape abusive settings. These services could take the form of shelters for abused elderly, counseling services, legal and nutritional services, and day-care programs for the elderly. Thus far, few funds have been directed toward these ends.

As family violence has commanded more attention in recent years, government agencies have started to "get tough." In the 1980s and 1990s, various government task forces investigating domestic violence have called for toughening the actions that could be taken to arrest, bring to trial, and imprison offenders (Brozan, 1984; U.S. Advisory Board . . . , 1995). Noting that domestic violence has often been ignored in the past, these task forces make some powerful recommendations, including:

1. Adopting the attitude that family violence in all forms should be regarded as criminal.

2. Establishing arrest as the preferred method of immediately dealing with such crimes.

3. Processing all complaints of family violence as reported criminal offenses.

4. Giving the victim and the suspect a statement of victim's rights.

5. Organizing special units to process family violence cases.

6. Eliminating the requirement that a victim sign a formal complaint before charges can be filed by the prosecutor, unless mandated by state law.

7. In the case of child abuse, relaxing the regulations governing the introduction of evidence into trials.

Although some may debate over the judiciousness of some of these steps, society clearly is taking a strong stand against family violence, and this posture will help to reduce the extent of such violence in the future.

Children and the Family

The changes that the modern family is undergoing create a number of problems beyond those of children in divorced families. There is concern, for example, that children born into single-parent families sometimes do not receive the best parenting. Social policies designed to deal with this problem, especially teenage pregnancies, have been highly controversial because they intrude into some very sensitive areas of family life (Zill and Nord, 1994). One way of reducing teen pregnancies is to make birth control information available to teens, and many family planning agencies have done so without informing the parents of the teens. In fact, countries with low rates of teen pregnancies also have liberal attitudes toward sex, make contraceptives easily available to teenagers, and provide effective sex education programs. Research in this country shows that teen pregnancy can be reduced by providing access to contraceptives, along with school counseling and job training (Plotnick, 1993). However, such programs are controversial because they rest in part on the assumption that many teenagers will continue to be sexually active. By contrast, recent social policies have emphasized sexual abstinence and parental involvement in their children's decision making. For example, the Adolescent Family Life Act of 1981, which is currently the only federal program designed to address teenage pregnancy, focuses on reducing teen pregnancies by preventing or postponing adolescent sexual activity, and encouraging adolescents to seek the guidance of their parents or other family members (White and White, 1991). Yet, research clearly shows that the most effective way to control teen pregnancies is through education in how to prevent conception and the provision of birth control devices.

We have discussed how some modern developments, such as dual-career families or singlehood, might lower the birth rate or lead to a two-tiered society in which those who have children will be substantially less well off than those who do not. In fact, some fear that our nation's children could become a permanent "underclass" (Weitzman, 1985). To ensure an adequate birthrate and sufficient resources for families to raise children, some have argued for a more explicit social policy on family issues (Ferber and O'Farrell, 1991). The International Perspectives insert describes the family policies currently being used in some other societies. As that insert points out, social policies in the United States tend to be laissez-faire, with comparatively little government direction regarding families and children. This situation changed somewhat in 1993 when President Clinton signed into law a family leave bill that requires large employers to give their employees unpaid leave to care for newly born children or ill family members. This protection, however, is still considerably more limited than that described in the insert in other industrial countries.

Another area in which support for a coherent family policy in the United States has been emerging is day care. In fact, our nation's employers have been developing day-care programs over the past decade (Kate, 1992). About 3 percent of the nation's employers sponsor day-care centers for their employees' children, and another 9 percent offer at least some employee financial assistance for day care or information and referral services to guide parents in finding day care for their children. Furthermore, 61 percent of employers provide indirect day-care assistance in the form of flexible work schedules, flexible leaves, and part-time work for parents of young children. Not surprisingly, employers with large numbers of women of childbearing age in their work force are most likely to have some day-care policy, and it is the better-paid and more powerful employees who are most likely to be offered these services by employers. The motivation for employers to sponsor these programs is in good part pragmatic: Research has shown that the problems employees face in arranging care for their children tend to result in absenteeism, tardiness, low morale, and productivity problems. Also, recruiting new employees is easier when an employer can offer child-care services to prospective employees, especially in heavily female segments of the labor market such as nursing. As one authority on workplace issues put it:

> The organizations that provide a child-care benefit recognize that family and work life are no longer separable, that tensions between them affect the work performance of employees, and that it may be in the organization's best interest to do what it can to alleviate those tensions. (Auerbach, 1990: 391)

This may be increasingly true in the future because young women will likely make up a large proportion of new entrants into the labor pool. Laissez-faire advocates would argue that this largely private-sector initiative is the most appropriate way to handle day care policy: Let employers respond to the needs of their employees. Child care should become another fringe benefit—like health-care insurance and vacation time—that is negotiated between employer and employee.

Both the state and the federal governments provide funding for child care, but often as a part of programs with goals separate from child care itself. For example, the Head Start program, which is basically a poverty program, serves a child-care function for some poor families (see Chapter 5). Community Development

Changes in the family, especially increases in divorce and single parenthood, have made more women the sole breadwinners for their families, which makes them more vulnerable to discrimination and inequality based on gender (Chapter 7). Family problems are exacerbated by drug and alcohol addiction (Chapter 10) because poor parents are more likely to become addicted, and domestic violence is associated with drug and alcohol addiction.

Block Grants, which focus on the economic development of communities (see Chapter 12), can be used in part to construct nonprofit child-care facilities. The Family Support Act of 1989, which reformed the welfare system with work requirements, provides child-care services for welfare parents who are in job training programs. Half of the states also provide some support for day care through their tax codes. In addition, all state governments provide some funds for the training of child-care workers or the provision of child-care services, although state funding sometimes goes to only a limited number of people, such as the very poor.

There are other state and federal supports for child care, but the point is that there is not one coherent policy on the issue as is found commonly in other advanced industrial nations. Instead, the United States has scattered and piecemeal day-care programs that are parts of other programs. There is as yet no consensus in the United States that day-care services should be available to all families, irrespective of their economic circumstances.

Another controversy in current child-care policy is over *privatization:* Should policies encourage the private sector to develop and provide the services people want, or should the government directly provide the services? Privatization policies provide parents with vouchers to purchase child care or tax credits for money spent on child care, and then parents seek the services where they wish, often from private, profit, or nonprofit centers. Needless to say, laissez-faire advocates support this approach. Interventionists argue that programs such as Head Start, for which the government runs the child-care centers, are preferred because their mission is focused exclusively on providing the best services available without interference from the desire to make a profit. As we saw earlier, there is some evidence that nonprofit and government-run centers do provide better services than for-profit centers. Nevertheless, this controversy has still not been resolved in the United States.

Summary

1. The family is a social institution based on kinship that functions to replace members of society and to nurture them.

2. In the United States today, people practice monogamy, and egalitarianism is encouraged. Families vary in configuration but usually fall into one of three categories: extended, nuclear, or modified extended.

3. The functionalist perspective posits that some form of the family exists in all societies because the family performs certain basic functions that are essential to human survival and the maintenance of society.

4. The conflict perspective views the family as serving the interests of the dominant groups in society, and the version of family most prominent in society is usually the one that is consistent with the values and benefits of the dominant groups. The dominant form of family also benefits particular economic interests.

5. The interactionist perspective points to the fact that what is considered the family is a matter of social definition, becoming a part of the social reality that people create and live by.

6. Marriage and family relationships are popular in the United States today, but these kinds of intimate associations are more likely to be participant-controlled rather than parent-run, the latter being more common prior to the Industrial Revolution.

7. The divorce rate in the United States has risen considerably during this century but has stabilized in the last two decades. Sociologists identify certain changes in society brought about by industrialization as the cause of this rise in the divorce rate. Some couples are at considerably greater risk of experiencing divorce than others. Widespread divorce has some negative consequences, both for the parents and the children.

8. There are many different family lifestyles that have emerged over the past few decades. These lifestyles are considered by many to be another dimension of the problems surrounding the family today. Among them are dual-career families, singlehood, cohabitation, single parenthood, and gay families.

9. Violence among family members is common in the United States, usually occurring between married couples or directed at dependent children or the elderly.

10. Most sociologists are confident that the family will survive as a social institution, but that family relationships will be pluralistic in the future, with different forms of family existing side by side, each having an attraction for some segment of the populace. Steps are being taken in the United States to lower the rate of family violence. A continuing concern regarding the configuration of families in the future relates to children: locating suitable environments for children to grow up in.

STUDY AND Review

Key Terms

blended family

cohabitation

dual-career family

egalitarian family

extended family

family

modified extended family

monogamy

nuclear family

patriarchy

pluralistic family

polygamy

refined divorce rate

serial monogamy

Multiple-Choice Questions

1. Which of the following perspectives would argue that family institutions exist in society because families make important contributions to human survival and the maintenance of society?
   a. The functionalist perspective.
   b. The conflict perspective.
   c. The interactionist perspective.
   d. The extended family perspective.

2. Which of the following is *not* a conclusion of the research regarding the impact of day care cited in the text? In comparison to children raised at home:
   a. Day-care children are as attached to their parents.
   b. Day-care children do as well in intelligence and psychosocial development.
   c. Day-care children are as sociable.
   d. Children enrolled in day care at a young age may become more aggressive.
   e. All of the above were conclusions cited in the text.
3. By the early 1990s, the most common household had which of the following compositions?
   a. Male head of household, no spouse present.
   b. Female head of household, no spouse present.
   c. A one-person household.
   d. A married couple household.
   e. Two or more unrelated people in a household.
4. Which of the following statements is true regarding the marital status of people in the United States today as compared to 50 years ago?
   a. A substantially smaller percentage of people are married today.
   b. A substantially larger percentage of people are divorced today.
   c. A substantially larger percentage of people are single today.
   d. A substantially larger percentage of people are widowed today.
5. The likelihood in the United States today that a marriage will end in divorce is closest to which of the following figures?
   a. 15 percent.
   b. 30 percent.
   c. 50 percent.
   d. 65 percent.
   e. 85 percent.
6. All of the following were identified as placing a couple at a higher risk of divorce *except:*
   a. Social differences between the couple.
   b. High socioeconomic standing.
   c. Young age at marriage.
   d. Whirlwind romances.

7. Over the past 50 years, the percentage of married women who work outside the home has:
   a. Declined steadily.
   b. Increased steadily.
   c. Increased until 1970 and then declined.
   d. Increased until 1970 and then leveled off.
   e. Remained level until 1960 and then increased.
8. Which of the following family lifestyles appears to be on the decline?
   a. Cohabitation.
   b. Single parenthood.
   c. Dual-career families.
   d. None of the above appears to be declining.
9. Given the research findings on spouse abuse, which of the following women would most likely be at risk of being abused by a spouse?
   a. A woman whose spouse has traditional, nonegalitarian views toward sex-role relationships.
   b. A woman with high levels of education and other economic resources.
   c. A woman with an elaborate social network of friends and relatives.
   d. A woman with little education whose husband was well educated.
10. Based on the research on family violence, which of the following does the text conclude to be a key element of the abuse of spouses, children, and the elderly?
    a. The high divorce rate.
    b. The growth in nuclear families.
    c. The inequitable distribution of power and resources in the family.
    d. A resurgence in patriarchy.

True/False Questions

1. Extended families are more functional in industrial societies than are nuclear families.
2. Of the three sociological perspectives, the functionalist perspective would most clearly take the stance that a particular form of the family exists in society because that family form benefits the powerful groups in society.
3. Young people today, when compared to their parents, have fewer negative attitudes toward staying single.

4. "Parent-run" courtship is more prominent today than it was in preindustrial United States.
5. Even though it is difficult for parents to remain together in a conflict-ridden marriage, research shows that children are almost always better off when such parents stay together rather than divorce.
6. Children's negative reactions to divorce can be reduced if the amount of conflict between divorcing parents is kept low.
7. More adults are single (never married) today than was the case fifty years ago.
8. Looking at the trends in divorce and single motherhood, the text predicts that the proportion of single-parent families will decline in the future.
9. Levels of child abuse are higher among the poor than they are among the affluent.
10. In comparison to the United States, most other industrial nations take a more extreme laissez-faire position in regard to government support for families and children.

Fill-In Questions

1. The _____ family is one in which elaborate networks of visitation and support are found among extended relatives but each nuclear unit lives separately.
2. Since the 1930s, the average size of households in the United States has _____ .
3. When marital partners are chosen primarily on the basis of the individual desires of the prospective mates, this is called a _____ courtship process.
4. A marriage system that allows people to have more than one spouse, but not at the same time, is called _____ .
5. In terms of age, it is those who are _____ at the time of marriage who are at the highest risk of experiencing divorce.
6. A _____ family is one that results when people experience a series of divorces and remarriages.

7. The most common living arrangement for children and teenagers in the United States today is to be living with _____ .
8. The elderly person who is least likely to experience abuse is the elderly person who lives _____ .
9. According to the text, the family organization that seems to be developing in modern industrial societies is the _____ family.
10. In terms of who provides day-care services, laissez-faire advocates would probably support the _____ of day care.

Matching Questions

_____ 1. patriarchy

_____ 2. interactionist perspective

_____ 3. courtship in preindustrial United States

_____ 4. a family system in which people can have more than one spouse at a time

_____ 5. status conferral

_____ 6. palimony

_____ 7. Murray Straus and Michael Gelles

_____ 8. nuclear family

_____ 9. serial monogamy

_____ 10. family inheritance

A. family as socially defined
B. polygamy
C. cohabitant support payments
D. male domination
E. married couple and children
F. U.S. marriage system
G. parent-run
H. perpetuation of social inequality
I. studies of marital violence
J. a function of the family

Essay Questions

1. Select one of the sociological perspectives and describe its view of the family as an institution in society. When would that perspective define the family as a social problem?
2. Assess the issue of whether children sent to day care are reared as effectively as children raised in the home. Summarize the research on both sides of the issue.
3. How have attitudes toward marriage and having children changed over the past fifty years in the United States?
4. Describe the four social conditions discussed in the text that account for the rising divorce rate over the past century.
5. What are the social characteristics of couples who are at the greatest risk of experiencing a divorce?
6. Describe the trends in single parenthood in the United States today. Why, and under what conditions, does single parenthood become a social problem?
7. What are the social conditions that increase the likelihood of child abuse in a family?
8. What is likely to happen to divorce rates in the future in the United States? What could be done to bring those rates down?
9. What is being done, and what could be done, to reduce family violence in the United States?
10. What are the differences between the social policies of the United States regarding families and children and the equivalent policies in other industrial nations?

Answers

Multiple-Choice
1. A; 2. E; 3. D; 4. B; 5. C; 6. B; 7. B; 8. D; 9. A; 10. C

True/False
1. F; 2. F; 3. T; 4. F; 5. F; 6. T; 7. F; 8. F; 9. T; 10. F

Fill-In
1. modified extended
2. declined
3. participant-run
4. serial monogamy
5. very young
6. blended
7. both parents
8. alone
9. pluralistic
10. privatization

Matching
1. D; 2. A; 3. G; 4. B 5. J; 6. C; 7. I; 8. E; 9. F; 10. H

For Further Reading

Brigitte Berger and Peter L. Berger. *The War Over the Family: Capturing the Middle Ground.* New York: Anchor Press/Doubleday, 1983. A controversial book in which two well-known sociologists argue that the traditional nuclear family should be embraced as a repository of important personal values and social virtues. It is a spirited defense of the embattled nuclear family.

Stephanie Coontz. *The Way We Never Were: American Families and the Nostalgia Trap.* New York: Basic Books, 1992. This enlightening book by a historian debunks the many myths that people hold regarding how much better shape the institution of the family was in the United States in earlier times.

John Crewdson. *By Silence Betrayed: Sexual Abuse of Children in America.* Boston: Little, Brown, 1987. This book is based on interviews with abused children, the people who abuse them, and those who prosecute and defend the abusers. Crewdson is a Pulitzer-Prize-winning journalist who has written a disturbing account of the problem.

Leon Dash. *When Children Want Children: The Urban Crisis of Teenage Childbearing.* New York: William Morrow, 1989. This is an interesting book on the extent of teenage parenting and the difficulties that teen mothers face, as well as the problems created for society.

Andrew M. Greeley. *Faithful Attraction.* New York: Tor Books, 1991. This sociologist marshals survey data to present a positive image of the family: most people getting married, being satisfied with their spouses, and not having extramarital affairs. This is a good antidote to the "family in crisis" view that is often presented.

Robert B. Hill et al. *Research on the African-American Family: A Holistic Approach.* Westport, Conn.: Auburn House, 1993. This is a comprehensive review of the current research on the strengths and weaknesses of the black family in the United States today. It gives a thorough review of the social conditions in the black community and society at large that have shaped the black family.

Phyllis Moen. *Working Parents: Transformations in Gender Roles and Public Policies in Sweden.* Madison: University of Wisconsin Press, 1989. This book explores some innovative social policies in Sweden that are focused on encouraging women to have children and continue working. Some of the policies might be useful to consider for the United States.

Leslie A. Morgan. *After Marriage Ends: Economic Consequences for Midlife Women.* Newbury Park. Calif.: Sage, 1991. This book analyzes the social and demographic differences between women who divorce and those who stay married and looks at the economic consequences for the women who divorce.

Daniel Patrick Moynihan. *Family and Nation: The Godkin Lectures, Harvard University.* San Diego: Harcourt Brace Jovanovich, 1985. A very important statement by a sociologist-politician wherein the author claims that poverty among children is exacerbated by the disintegration of the traditional family structure and the growth of single-parent families. Moynihan's social policy recommendations are certain to be controversial.

Arlene Skolnick. *Embattled Paradise: The American Family in an Age of Uncertainty.* New York: Basic Books, 1991. This thought-provoking book includes some history of the American family in the twentieth century. It takes a generally positive view of the changes that have occurred and criticizes the "decline of the family" moralizers for not seeing the benefits of the new changes.

FOUR *CHAPTER* *Health and Illness*

What problems does the United States confront in the area of health and illness? While the health-care system in the United States can do some marvelous things, Joseph Califano, Jr., who has worked on health-care policy for many decades, summarizes the problems as colossal costs, inefficiency, waste, and abuse (Califano, 1994). The costs of health care have truly skyrocketed. In 1960, health-care expenditures amounted to $142 for each person in the United States; now that amount has exploded to $3,607—a sixteenfold increase! Many billions of dollars are spent each year on coronary bypass surgery, but Califano claims that many of these surgeries could have been avoided by using less invasive—and less expensive—medical procedures to manage patients' condition. A recent estimate is that as much as 30 percent of coronary bypass surgeries may be totally unnecessary (Anstett, 1992).

As all this money is spent on health care, it is not exactly clear what benefit people in the United States receive: They pay twice as much for their per capita health bill as do people in France, yet French males live longer than males in the United States. In addition to costs, another dimension of the problem of health and illness has to do with an unhealthy lifestyle. Too many people in the United States smoke and drink to excess and gorge themselves on foods that contribute to problems of obesity and high blood pressure. Thirty-eight percent of the United States populace has high blood pressure, and 26 percent is overweight (National Center for Health Statistics, 1992).

Yet another dimension of the problem is whether people have access to the health-care services and resources that they need to remain healthy or overcome illness and injury. Although people in the United States spend billions on coronary bypass surgery, infant mortality rates are distressingly high, especially among minority groups. The infant mortality rate in Washington, D.C., the capital of the United States, is as high as the infant mortality rate in Russia and some of its former territories such as the Ukraine and Belarus—countries suffering from severe political dislocation and economic downturn (U.S. Bureau of the Census, 1994: 854–55). These high rates persist in the United States even though there are relatively inexpensive ways to reduce them, such as providing all pregnant women with prenatal care and making nutrition programs available to all newborn infants.

This chapter addresses these and other problems related to health and illness in the United States. Califano (1994) believes that the health-care system in the United States needs radical surgery to overcome the problems. This chapter will assess both the problems and the solutions. It begins by developing an understanding of the role of health-care institutions in society.

Perspectives on Health Care

People tend to view health and illness as biological phenomena. However, health and illness also have a very important social dimension, and this is what we need to focus on as we approach problems surrounding health and health-care delivery. Social factors, for example, influence what diseases people contract, who receives health care, and who benefits from the type of health-care organization that is dominant in society. The sociological perspectives can help us analyze how social factors shape social problems in this area.

The Functionalist Perspective

Disease is a threat to the social order because those who are ill may be unable to make useful contributions to society. People who are ill may not be able to raise food, build houses, drive trucks, or rear children as they are expected to. This makes them burdensome and nonproductive. In extreme cases, ill health can threaten the very survival of society. Many Native American groups, for example, were decimated by infectious diseases, such as venereal disease, during their early contact with European explorers to the New World. Some people today feel that a nuclear war would cause so much injury and disease that the survival of some societies would be threatened. So disease can be viewed as a social problem when it threatens the ability of a group to survive and prosper.

Given these consequences of disease, sociologist Talcott Parsons (1951) argued that being healthy is the preferred or most functional human condition. When people are ill, they can no longer fulfill their expected role obligations. Society responds to this, Parsons argued, by casting them into a "deviant," or socially disvalued, role. Society must help these deviants to become "normal" again. Ostracizing or imprisoning sick people, which is a common

Myths & FACTS

ABOUT HEALTH AND HEALTH CARE

Myth: The poor in the United States receive shoddy health care, finding it difficult to see a doctor or gain admission to a hospital.

FACT: Some poor people are quite a bit more likely than the affluent to see a doctor or be hospitalized. Government health insurance for the poor has given some of them far more access to health care than ever before, although it may be of lower quality than the care available to more affluent Americans.

Myth: Women are healthier than men (or vice versa).

FACT: Reality is complicated on this issue. Men have higher mortality rates, but women are more likely to have acute, non-life-threatening illnesses. Men, on the other hand, tend to have higher rates of serious, chronic illnesses. So the facts on gender and health depend on how one measures "health."

Myth: Controlling physicians' fees would stop the rise in medical costs.

FACT: Although it would help, physicians' services account for less than one of every five dollars spent on health care. And the proportion of the health-care dollar spent on physicians' fees has declined considerably over the past forty years.

Myth: Thanks to modern science, people today have a healthy diet and can look forward to a long life.

FACT: People in most hunting-and-gathering societies probably had healthier diets than most people in the United States have today. They ate a wide range of fruits, nuts, grains, and other plant foods and relied on meat relatively little. Hunters and gatherers could, if they survived infancy and childhood, look forward to a relatively long life. However, the hunters and gatherers still died at a younger age than most people today, and the quality of their lives in terms of their health status was not nearly as good.

---

response to many deviant behaviors, is ineffective. Instead, sick people are given a special social role, the sick role, which is intended to facilitate their return to health. The **sick role** refers to *a set of expectations intended to guide the behavior of people who are ill.* People who occupy the sick role are excused from their normal role obligations to the extent that the illness calls for, and they can claim assistance and sympathy from others. However, they are also expected to seek competent care and to cooperate with those who are trying to cure them.

The function of the health-care system, then, is to return people to normal social functioning. The system becomes a social problem when it fails to perform this function effectively. Ideally, people who need health-care services would receive exactly what they need, no more and no less. To the extent that this ideal is not reached, social disorganization exists. This chapter will review the extent to which the health-care system in the United States deviates from this ideal. We will also look for the sources of the disorganization. One source is the lack of integration between different parts of the social system. For example, health care in the United States is operated largely as a profitmaking institution, as is the rest of our economy (see Chapter 2). Because large sums of money can be made from medical services and products, there is considerable abuse in these areas, such as unnecessary surgeries and the overutilization of pharmaceuticals. In addition, people who are unable to pay for services often do not receive adequate medical care. The point is that, in some situations, the profit-making dimension of the health-care system is not well integrated with, and may work against, the goal of achieving the highest possible level of health.

The Conflict Perspective

Health and health care are highly valued in all societies, and they are also scarce resources. Interest groups compete with one another to gain what they feel is their fair share of those resources, as they do with other scarce resources. Staying healthy depends on having access to adequate food, satisfactory employment conditions, clean water, and good health care. Generally, as we shall see, people with higher social and economic standing in society have greater access to these resources, and they are generally healthier than the less affluent. For example, high infant mortality among the poor is not surprising, from the conflict perspective, because the poor are less able to afford nutritious food, sanitary living conditions, access to prenatal care, and the other things that reduce infant mortality.

In addition to the issue of whether groups receive services is the problem of how much those services will cost—in both monetary and non-monetary terms—and who benefits most from health-care treatment. In this context, the health-care system is an arena for competition among a variety of groups: health-care consumers, doctors, nurses, hospital administrators, medical technicians, pharmaceutical companies, and a host of others. People must pay, in some fashion, for health-care goods and services, and many people make a living through providing those goods and services. Naturally, what benefits one group, such as low health-care costs for the consumer, may work to the disadvantage of other groups, such as doctors and nurses. Beyond money, prestige and power are also involved in the health-care delivery process.

The inequitable distribution of money, prestige, and power in the health-care system, then, is viewed as a social problem by those groups who feel they are receiving less than their fair share of resources. From the conflict perspective, however, there is no state of the system that is "preferred" or necessarily beneficial to all. If some group gains additional benefits, other groups must lose something. What determines who gains and who loses is the exercise of power. Groups have various power strategies available to them. Nurses and doctors, for example, can go on strike or in other ways withhold their services in order to force concessions from competing groups. Recently, many doctors began refusing to provide obstetrical services because of the substantial increase in malpractice insurance for that specialty. Another power strategy is to influence Congress and state legislatures to approve legislation that benefits particular groups. In fact, many interest groups in the health field have formed political action committees to collect contributions and press their interests. The American Medical Association and other physicians' groups have been very effective at lobbying over the years, partly because of the substantial economic resources of their constituents. For example, the AMA has to date successfully fought all efforts to establish a national health insurance program.

The Interactionist Perspective

The interactionist perspective emphasizes that sick people are cast into a social role, part of which has been described as the sick role. This role may include socially devalued and stigmatized elements. A person with venereal disease, for example, may be viewed as immoral, whereas the mentally ill are seen as dangerous. In other words, we attach social meanings—sometimes very negative ones—to various illnesses, and we expect people to behave in conformity to those meanings. For example, some health-care institutions treat people in a dehumanizing and impersonal fashion, which can lead to low self-esteem and a negative self-concept and may drive people away from seeking the health care they really need. Likewise, the staff in a mental hospital expects its patients to be dependent and confused, and the patients often conform to those expectations.

So from the interactionist perspective, the health-care system is considered a social problem when it produces stigmatized and devalued behavior or self-concepts among either the providers or consumers of health care. This perspective is particularly useful in understanding the societal reaction to some diseases, such as Acquired Immune Deficiency Syndrome (AIDS), and to mental illness, discussed later in this chapter. The Policy Issues insert on pages 124 and 125 focuses on the societal reaction to the AIDS epidemic.

According to the interactionist perspective, people attach social meanings to illnesses and disabilities. When these meanings are negative, people may be stigmatized and discriminated against by others. These attitudes have limited the opportunities of many disabled people and deprived society of the contributions they have to offer.

Health, Illness, and Society

One of the central problems related to health and health care is that there are a variety of social factors—things that we have some control over—that can lead to illness. In this section, we will look at how the diseases that are a threat to us have changed over time and how social and lifestyle factors can put us at greater risk of illness.

Health and Societal Development

Most diseases can be classified as acute diseases or as chronic ones. **Acute diseases** are *those with fairly quick, and sometimes dramatic and incapaci-tating, onset and from which a person either dies or recovers.* They are often caused by an organism or parasite that infects or invades the body and disrupts its functioning, such as with influenza, tuberculosis, and gastroenteritis. **Chronic diseases,** such as heart disease and cancer, *progress over a long period of time and often exist long before they are detected.* Early symptoms of these diseases are often absent or easily ignored. They are usually caused by a mixture of biological, social, and environmental factors.

In preindustrial societies, infectious and parasitic diseases posed some of the more serious health threats (Dunn, 1978; Black, 1978). Diseases such as influenza, diphtheria, and

AIDS is now the leading cause of death among young adults. Over 200,000 people in the United States have AIDS and close to 2 million are infected with the HIV virus; forty thousand new infections occur each year (Kolata, 1995). This will translate into massive health-care costs as these people develop full-blown AIDS. Sadly and outrageously, this devastating epidemic gained a foothold in the United States in part because society failed to show a serious interest in attacking it when it first appeared. The reasons for this are enlightening in terms of understanding how human beings respond to illness and sick people.

Diseases such as the Bubonic Plague and AIDS involve a complex intertwining of biology with political, social, and cultural considerations. As the interactionist perspective suggests, health, illness, and disease are given meaning by people in a particular social and cultural environment, and how we treat those who are ill is a function of these meanings. The impact of social and cultural forces on the treatment of the ill is especially evident in seriously threatening diseases (Sigerist, 1977). Among the Kubu people of Sumatra, for example, serious diseases that produced high fevers were viewed as highly threatening. In fact, they so frightened the Kubu that the sick person was shunned—isolated completely—as if he or she were dead. The ancient Babylonians had a different view of disease: It was punishment for sin and wickedness—it was believed that people who suffered pain and discomfort were paying for their sins. Because of the spiritually unclean nature of sick people, they were marked by the Babylonians with a stigma. They were not physically shunned, but they were socially isolated until they had made some atonement for their sins. More recently, and continuing into the twentieth century, a disease like leprosy has provoked reactions of both stigmatization and shunning or isolation.

We might be tempted to think that, by the end of the twentieth century, our reactions to disease

have become more "rational" and "scientific" than those of the Kubu or the ancient Babylonians. Yet social life is complex, and people's reactions to disease are no exception. In the case of AIDS, many social and cultural factors came together to produce a significant delay in the attack on the disease. When AIDS cases first began to appear in the United States around 1980, the first thing that sociologists, epidemiologists, and other medical researchers from the Centers for Disease Control (CDC) noticed was that healthy gay men and intravenous drug users were dying of unusual infectious diseases rarely seen in humans before (Shilts, 1987). What became clear very quickly from looking at these early victims and their lifestyles was that AIDS might be transmitted through sexual contact. As one sociologist at the CDC put it, after looking at the lifestyles of the early victims and the spread of the disease: "It looks more like a sexually transmitted disease than syphilis" (Shilts, 1987: 87).

Despite the growing scientific evidence in the early 1980s about the mode of transmission of AIDS and the ominous realization about the potentially monstrous dimensions of this epidemic, tragedy was heaped upon tragedy when research and policy development were delayed as the disease spread. The reasons for this delay were complicated, but some of them are strikingly similar to the reactions to disease among the Kubu and ancient Babylonians. First of all, stigmatization of the supposedly unclean or morally suspect clearly played a role: The disease was linked with homosexuality and illegal drug use. Many people in positions of political and economic power either felt that these were powerless groups whose problems need not be seriously attended to or that they were disreputable groups whose lifestyles ought to be discouraged if not eradicated. In fact, some fundamentalist religious leaders declared that AIDS was punishment for the sins of homosexuals—not a far cry from the ancient Babylonian belief about disease. One conservative columnist wrote: "The poor homosexuals—they have declared war upon nature, and now nature is exacting an awful retribution" (quoted in Shilts, 1987: 311). Some people believed that these groups were sufficiently unrespectable that they were getting what they deserved, and the government need not respond too quickly to the growing epidemic.

A second reason for the delayed response to AIDS was the Reagan administration policy of smaller government and greater austerity in social and health programs. The first AIDS victim in the United States appeared in 1980, and the Reagan administration entered office in 1981. The competition for government funds in the early 1980s was fierce, and AIDS researchers typically lost out in the battle. A third reason for the delay had to do with urban politics. New York City had the largest number of AIDS cases in the country, yet New York Mayor Edward Koch refused to do anything about it for a number of years, apparently because of the belief that support for gay causes would link him with the gay rights movement and hurt his chances for reelection. Fourth, the politics of gay communities figured into the delay. There were intense conflicts among gays over how, or whether, to respond to the AIDS epidemic. Some gays proposed closing gay bathhouses on the grounds that these places, where unprotected sex and multiple sexual partners were common, helped spread the disease. The owners of the baths objected strenuously, as did many gays who felt that such a move would be an attack on their sexual freedom and an attempt to restrict the open expression of their sexual orientation. As a consequence, the gay community found itself divided and unable to launch a united campaign for more research and programs on AIDS.

The overall consequence of these political and social factors was that AIDS research and programs were delayed significantly and the disease gained a substantial foothold. Had the government acted as quickly and aggressively as it has with other diseases (such as Legionnaire's Disease in the 1970s), the spread of AIDS would have been much less substantial. Once the cause of the disease and the mode of transmission were established, steps were taken to control it. The gay community, in particular, has emphasized health education, the practice of safe sex, and a change in sexual lifestyles as ways of preventing the spread of the disease. And this effort has resulted in dramatic declines in risky sexual behavior among some gay men, although there is evidence of a "relapse" to unsafe practices when public concern over AIDS is less prominent (Lifson, 1992). Among intravenous drug users, their sexual partners, and their babies, however, incidence of the disease continues to grow (Kolata, 1995). Currently in the United States, three-quarters of the people newly infected with the AIDS virus are drug addicts, either heroin addicts who share infected needles or crack addicts who have unprotected sex with multiple partners. Heterosexual transmission of AIDS is growing, with a quarter of the new infections resulting from heterosexual contact; another quarter of new infections are among gay men. Worldwide, 60 percent of HIV infection results from heterosexual intercourse.

So, AIDS is a huge epidemic by any standards, and its magnitude has been exacerbated by the complex social and political forces that influenced society's response to the disease. The reaction to AIDS brings home to us how much people in the United States are like the Kubu, the Babylonians, and all other human groups. Human response to disease is shaped not only by the biomedical nature of disease but also by the social meanings we impart to disease and its victims. By understanding this, we are better able to shape a more rational health policy that can effectively attack disease and protect health.

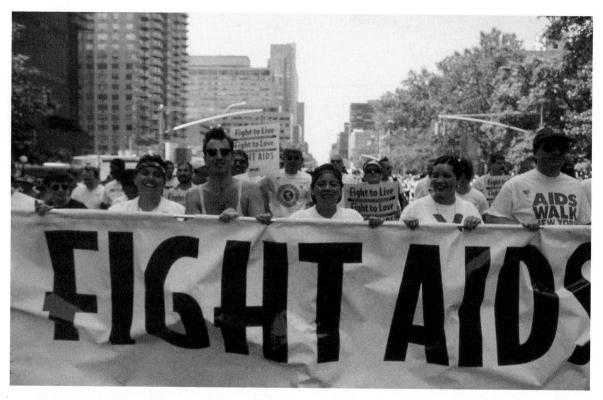

Political attention to the AIDS epidemic developed slowly. Without question, demonstrations and protests by AIDS activists have been critical in focusing societal resources on attacking this serious health problem.

typhoid could strike quickly and were highly contagious and often fatal, especially among infants, the weak, and the elderly. Accidents such as drowning or burns also took their toll, as did cannibalism, infanticide, and human sacrifice. All of these threats added up to a life expectancy in preindustrial societies that was rather short by today's standards, probably around twenty-five to thirty-five years. However, this short life expectancy was due in good part to high rates of infant and childhood mortality; if one survived the illnesses of infancy and childhood, one had a reasonable chance to live much longer (Antonovsky, 1972).

With the emergence of industrial societies, there has been a dramatic increase in life expectancy, to around seventy-five in the United States today (U.S. Bureau of the Census, 1994). The death rate has also changed appreciably, dropping from 17 deaths per 1,000 people in the United States in 1900 to 8.5 deaths today (see Figure 4.1). The declining death rate and increasing life expectancy can be attributed in good part to two related factors: declines in infant and childhood mortality and changes in lifestyle.

Infant mortality today is less than one-sixth of what it was a century ago. So a newborn infant today has a far better chance of surviving than did infants in earlier times, and this means that someone born today has a better chance of living into old age. For those who survive through childhood, however, industrialization has led to considerably smaller increases in longevity over that of their preindustrial counterparts. A study in Massachusetts, for example, revealed that the life expectancy of fifteen-year-olds in 1869 was only five years less than that of fifteen-year-olds a century later (Vinovskis, 1978). Furthermore, there was virtually no increase in the life expectancy of thirty-year-olds between 1869 and 1969. Another study showed that people born in the United States in 1980 can expect to live twenty-four years longer than those born in 1900. Someone who was twenty years old in 1980, however, could expect to live only about twelve years longer than a twenty-year-old

could in 1900 (National Center for Health Statistics, 1984). This illustrates that a major benefit of industrialization in terms of health and longevity is that we have a much greater chance of living through infancy and childhood. Industrialization provides less benefit in terms of longevity once we reach adulthood.

The second key factor in increasing longevity has been changes in people's lifestyles. In fact, this has probably been at least as important as medical treatments offered by modern medicine (McKeown, Brown, and Record, 1972; McKeown, Brown, and Turner, 1975). Industrialization has made available better diets, improved sanitation, better sewage disposal, and cleaner water. Consequently, people are exposed to fewer infectious and parasitic diseases and are better able to resist those to which they are exposed. The death rate for scarlet fever, for example, had dropped

FIGURE 4.1 Birth and Death Rates in the United States, 1910–1994. *Sources:* U.S. Bureau of the Census, *Statistical Abstract of the United States, 1982–83* (Washington, D.C.: U.S. Government Printing Office, 1982), p. 60; U.S. Bureau of the Census, *Statistical Abstract of the United States, 1992* (Washington, D.C.: U.S. Government Printing Office, 1992), p. 64; National Center for Health Statistics: Births, Marriages, Divorces, and Deaths for January 1995. *Monthly Vital Statistics Report,* Vol. 44, No. 1, DHHS Pub. No. (PHS) 95–1120 (Hyattsville, Md.: Public Health Service, July 20, 1995).

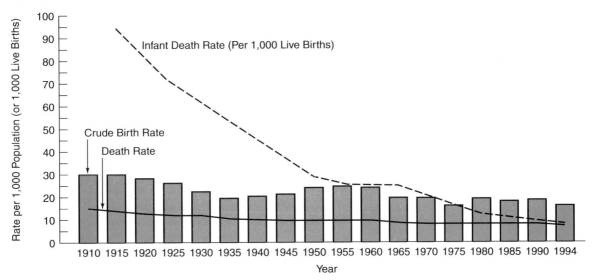

to practically zero by the 1940s, when effective medical treatment for this disease first became available (McKinlay and McKinlay, 1977).

Despite declining mortality rates and increasing longevity, we must all die someday, and the diseases we die of today are different from those of the past. In 1900 in the United States, the top three killers were acute infectious diseases, which accounted for well over twice the number of deaths caused by heart disease and cerebrovascular disease (see Figure 4.2.) Today, four of the five leading causes of death are chronic diseases, the fifth being accidents. So acute infectious diseases have become relatively unimportant in terms of mortality, and chronic diseases confront society with a different set of problems than did the acute ones in an earlier era (Mumford, 1983). Chronic diseases develop over a long period of time, may go unnoticed until extensive dam-

age has occurred, and are often associated with people's lifestyles. Effective treatment of such diseases calls for continual rather than intermittent health care and may require that people change their lifestyles. Furthermore, the most effective and least expensive way of dealing with most chronic diseases is probably **preventive medicine,** *changes in lifestyle or other steps that help avoid the occurrence of disease* (McKinlay, 1986). Yet modern medicine is not organized around prevention but rather toward **curative** or **crisis medicine:** *treating people's illness after they become ill.* Modern medicine arose early in the twentieth century when acute infectious diseases were the major health problems, and medical education trained doctors with a "crisis" orientation. This is an effective approach with such infectious diseases as influenza, pneumonia, or diphtheria, in which medical measures introduced after a person

FIGURE 4.2 Leading Causes of Death in the United States, 1900 and 1994. *Sources:* U.S. Bureau of the Census, *Vital Statistics Rates in the United States, 1900–1940* (Washington, D.C.: U.S. Government Printing Office, 1943), pp. 210–215; National Center for Health Statistics: Births, Marriages, Divorces, and Deaths for January 1995. *Monthly Vital Statistics Report,* Vol. 44, No. 1, DHHS Pub. No. (PHS) 95–1120 (Hyattsville, Md.: Public Health Service, July 20, 1995).

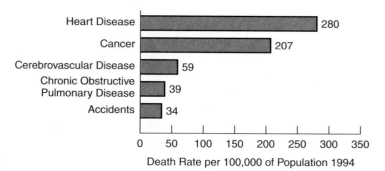

becomes ill can often return the person to complete health. With chronic diseases, however, much damage has already been done—and often cannot be reversed—by the time symptoms manifest themselves and medical intervention occurs. A person who suffers a heart attack, for example, may already have severe blockage of coronary arteries, and the damage typically cannot be completely undone with such modern medical measures as angioplasty or coronary artery bypass surgery. To date in the United States, preventive medicine has had a considerably lower priority—in terms of research and program funding, the construction of medical facilities, and the allocation of health-care personnel—than has crisis-oriented medicine. In fact, Joseph Califano argues that our crisis orientation in the United States has led to a "sick"-care system rather than a "health"-care system:

> the obsession of health care reformers with the delivery of medical care for the sick. This love affair has relegated the commonsense alternatives of disease prevention and health promotion to the role of dowdy wallflowers. (Califano, 1994: 130)

He argues that we should move from sick care to health care by promoting disease prevention and health promotion through changes in people's lifestyles.

So we have come to depend on medical practitioners intervening after we have become sick and returning us to health. Some have argued that this dependence has become pathological because it blinds people to the part that they can play in maintaining and protecting their own health (Illich, 1976). Believing that "miracle" medicine can save them under virtually any circumstances, people may continue to smoke, overeat, and eat foods high in cholesterol. Too late they find out that medicine may be able to help them but it often cannot "save" them. People suffering with emphysema from smoking all their lives can gain some extra years of life from oxygen tanks and respirators, but there is no way that the damage to their lungs can be undone. People want to believe in the myth of miracle medicine, and medicine itself often helps to perpetuate it.

So one of the major problem areas in the health-care system in the United States today is that the health-care organization has not adapted to the changing nature of the diseases we face. Another problem is that, although death rates are down and life expectancy is up, people in the United States are not so well off when compared with some other countries. For example, the life expectancy of women in fifteen other nations exceeds that of women in the United States, whereas men in the United States have shorter life spans than their counterparts in twenty other nations (see Figure 4.3 on p. 130). Men in Cuba and Costa Rica and women in Hong Kong and Greece live longer than men and women in the United States. Likewise, the United States has a higher infant mortality rate than seventeen other nations (see Figure 4.4 on p. 131). In fact, infant mortality rates in the United States are almost *twice* as high as in Japan. Part of the reason the health status of the United States is this low is that certain social and cultural factors have a detrimental impact on the health of many of its people.

Social Factors in Health and Illness

Who suffers from higher rates of illness and death? We will look at the four major sociocultural factors that have the greatest impact on health and illness.

Socioeconomic Status *Socioeconomic status* (SES) refers to people's position in society as measured by their income, educational attainment, and occupational status. The effect of SES on health is very clear: Those who are lower on such things as income, educational achievement, and occupational status generally have substantially higher disease rates and death

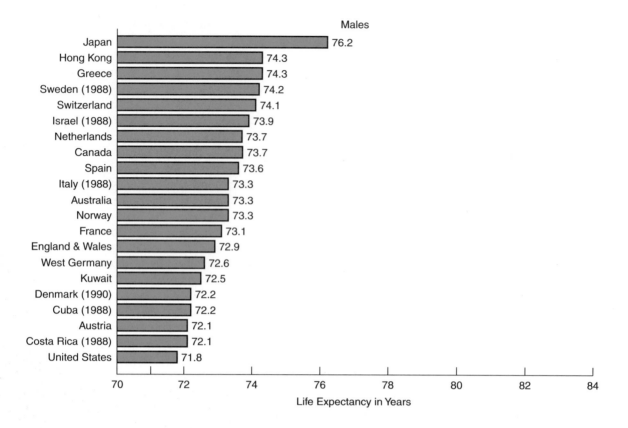

Males

Country	Life Expectancy
Japan	76.2
Hong Kong	74.3
Greece	74.3
Sweden (1988)	74.2
Switzerland	74.1
Israel (1988)	73.9
Netherlands	73.7
Canada	73.7
Spain	73.6
Italy (1988)	73.3
Australia	73.3
Norway	73.3
France	73.1
England & Wales	72.9
West Germany	72.6
Kuwait	72.5
Denmark (1990)	72.2
Cuba (1988)	72.2
Austria	72.1
Costa Rica (1988)	72.1
United States	71.8

Life Expectancy in Years

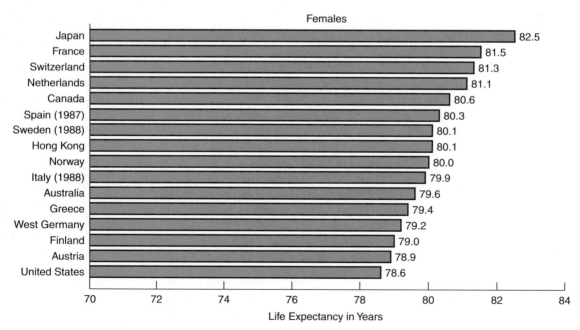

Females

Country	Life Expectancy
Japan	82.5
France	81.5
Switzerland	81.3
Netherlands	81.1
Canada	80.6
Spain (1987)	80.3
Sweden (1988)	80.1
Hong Kong	80.1
Norway	80.0
Italy (1988)	79.9
Australia	79.6
Greece	79.4
West Germany	79.2
Finland	79.0
Austria	78.9
United States	78.6

Life Expectancy in Years

FIGURE 4.3 Life Expectancy at Birth in the Countries with the Highest Life Expectancies, by Sex (for 1989 unless other year mentioned). *Source:* National Center for Health Statistics, *Health, United States, 1992,* DHHS Pub. No. (PHS) 93–1232 (Hyattsville, Md.: Public Health Service, 1993), pp. 42–43.

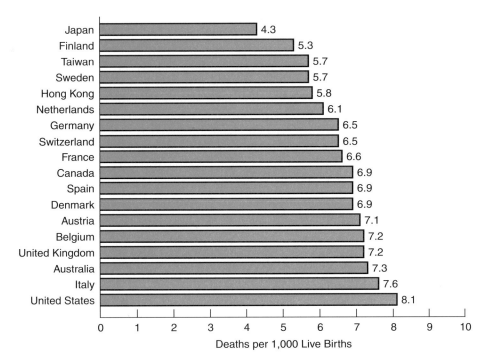

FIGURE 4.4 Infant Mortality Rates: Selected Countries, 1994. *Source:* U.S. Bureau of the Census, *Statistical Abstract of the United States, 1994* (Washington, D.C.: U.S. Government Printing Office, 1994), pp. 854–855.

rates than do their more affluent counterparts (Freund and McGuire, 1991; Aday, 1993). With very few exceptions, the incidence of diseases such as cancer, heart disease, diabetes, high blood pressure, arthritis, and many others is higher among those in the lower SES ranges. Infant mortality is also substantially greater among children born into low SES families. One of the major reasons for the substandard health status of the poor is that they live under conditions that substantially increase their general susceptibility to disease (Syme and Berkman, 1979). They live under less sanitary conditions, have less nutritious diets, and are less likely to take preventive health actions such as obtaining routine physical examinations. Re-

garding infant mortality, poor women are less likely to have prenatal checkups and more likely to have poor diets that result in infants with low birth weights. These things contribute to infant mortality. Furthermore, despite the considerable advances brought about by Medicare and Medicaid, many poor people are not covered by these programs, and some health care still depends on out-of-pocket costs, which the poor usually cannot afford. Finally, the medical care that the poor do receive is likely to be of lower quality. They are more likely to be treated in a hospital outpatient clinic or emergency room where continuity of care, follow-up treatment, and patient education are less common than in a physician's office.

Gender   Women appear to be healthier than men, especially if we consider longevity as the key measure of health. The life expectancy of women today is seven years greater than that of men, compared with only three years more at the turn of the century (Figure 4.3; National Center for Health Statistics, 1984). Women also have lower rates of most serious chronic illnesses. What accounts for these differences? First, it may well be that women are biologically more capable of survival than are men (Waldron, 1986). Males have higher death rates than females at every age, including deaths of fetuses. This suggests that women may have some sort of biological advantage in comparison with men, but the explanation is more complex than this. Higher mortality among males is also due to traditional sex-role definitions that encourage males to be aggressive and to seek more stressful and dangerous occupations where they might, for example, come in contact with industrial carcinogens. In addition, the lifestyles of men have traditionally been less healthy than those of women. For example, men drink more alcohol and smoke more tobacco. One health researcher concluded that "Cigarette smoking is the primary cause of men's excess lung cancer and emphysema mortality. . . . The total pathological effect of smoking . . . makes a major contribution to the sex differential in total death rates" (Waldron, 1986). Although the gap between men and women in smoking and drinking has narrowed, it is still there. Finally, cultural definitions of women as the "weaker sex" may lead women to respond more quickly to symptoms and to seek medical care earlier in an illness episode. If so, this treatment may enhance the likelihood of effective medical intervention for women.

In the realm of mental illness, women also have higher rates of psychological disorders, especially for neuroses, anxiety disturbances, and depression. Part of the reason for this is that sex-role socialization seems to lead men to turn to drugs or alcohol in stressful situations. Women, on the other hand, are more stigmatized for doing this and are more likely to cope with stress through symptoms of depression or other mental disorders. Many of the symptoms of these mental disorders—dependence, withdrawal, self-devaluation, indecisiveness—are characteristics that have traditionally been a part of the stereotype of women. So women have been socialized to behave in ways that, when used as means of coping with situations, are seen as symptomatic of mental illness (Franks and Rothblum, 1983).

Race   Most studies of the relationship between health status and race have involved comparisons between African Americans and Anglo Americans. All these studies reach distressingly similar conclusions: African Americans are at a serious disadvantage when it comes to health, having considerably higher death rates, shorter life expectancies, and more serious life-threatening health conditions such as hypertension and diabetes than do whites (Manton, Patrick, and Johnson, 1987). One major reason for this difference, of course, is that race is associated with socioeconomic status, with blacks being considerably lower in SES on the average than whites (Keil et al., 1992). Yet even when researchers control for SES, some racial differences persist. This is probably accounted for by the unique social position of African Americans: The combination of years of racial oppression, poverty, and physically demanding occupations probably works to generate more stress in the lives of blacks than in other racial groups at the same SES level. This stress, in turn, produces greater susceptibility to disease. Minorities other than blacks also suffer substantial health problems. Native Americans, especially those on reservations, have disproportionately high mortality rates from such things as accidents, alcoholism, and suicide, and this occurs because of longstanding problems of poverty and unemployment (Young, 1994).

Lifestyle Factors Industrialization has unquestionably improved people's lives, but it has also created health hazards, largely unknown in preindustrial societies, that contribute to death and misery. For example, a substantial proportion of all human cancers are caused in part by environmental conditions, such as air pollution or chemicals in the water and soil (Proctor, 1995). (Solutions to problems of environmental pollution are discussed in Chapter 13.) Occupational stress is linked to heart disease and hypertension (House, 1974; Schnall and Kern, 1986). Unemployment, or even the threat of it, is associated with many physical and mental disorders (Kessler, House, and Turner, 1987). The use of alcohol, tobacco, and other drugs can also cause serious health problems. There even appears to be an association between health and the quality of a person's family life: People who are married and have children are healthier than people who are single or have no children (Verbrugge, 1983). Finally, as Figure 4.2 illustrates, accidents have become one of the leading causes of mortality in modern society.

We could go on at length on this topic, but the point should be clear: There are many elements of our lifestyle that adversely affect our health. Any overall solution to health problems must take into account the ways in which people's lives and social circumstances can be changed to improve their health.

Mental Illness

In the past forty years, the number of people seeking help for psychological distress, either mild or severe, has increased more than four times. This increase, however, does not necessarily mean that more mental illness exists today. Instead, people are more willing to seek help for psychological distress today because attitudes toward mental illness have changed,

and there is less stigma attached to seeking mental health services. Some special issues arise when looking at the problem of mental illness and what to do about it.

The Nature of Mental Illness

There is substantial agreement about the basic nature of most physical disorders: Some malfunction or pathology has occurred to a person's body. For example, organic malfunction includes such things as a broken leg or an injury to the eye that impairs sight. The cure of such ailments involves, at least in part, some repair work on the person's body, such as setting the leg in a cast or performing surgery on the eye. With mental illness, however, there is more controversy about its basic nature. In fact, there are three positions on this issue (Cockerham, 1996).

The Medical Model One position—very popular among psychiatrists, psychologists, nurses, and other providers of mental health services—is to view mental disorders as having the same basic nature as physical disorders: A person's normal personality and psychological processes have malfunctioned and produced pathological behavior. This behavior is a symptom of the underlying disturbance in the person's psyche, and the mental "disease" can be cured by doing some repair work on the person's psyche, using drugs or possibly surgery. If left untreated, the condition will become progressively worse. Those persons who hold this position may disagree among themselves on the causes of mental disorders. Some would argue they are caused by biochemical imbalances or genetic traits; others would assert that mental illness grows out of disturbed interpersonal relationships. In fact, different disorders might have different causes, some biological in nature and others social. Proponents of the medical model would agree, however, that the disorder is located inside the person and that effective treatment would involve "repairing" the affected individual, possibly through drugs or surgery.

Some mental disorders do appear to have genetic or biochemical causes, at least in part, and the medical model has produced some remarkable advances in treating these disorders. It has also resulted in some effective drugs to treat the symptoms of mental disorders that are caused by environmental factors such as disturbed interpersonal relationships. However, the medical model has its limitations, and if one relies on it too heavily, it can lead to a misunderstanding of some aspects of mental disorders. In particular, its emphasis on the idea that the focus of mental illness is "inside" the person can restrict focus and lead to a disregard for the many factors in the social environment that contribute to mental problems themselves and how we define them. The other two positions on this issue round out the medical model by using the sociological perspectives to place more stress on the processes occurring outside the individual—in social interaction and the social environment.

Mental Illness as Deviance The second position on the nature of mental illness focuses on the fact that the symptoms of mental illness show up in a person's behavior, and human behavior, according to the interactionist perspective, is based on shared social expectations. This insight has led some sociologists to suggest that some of the disordered behavior of the mentally ill reflects not the inner workings of a twisted psyche but a person's efforts to conform to social expectations. Sociologist Thomas Scheff (1984), for example, based his view of mental illness on the interactionist perspective. He argued that the behavior of the mentally disturbed violates normal social conventions, so his view is that of mental illness as "deviance." For example, the person who shouts obscenities on a crowded street violates

norms about appropriate behavior in that setting. When we notice these transgressions, we try to understand the behavior, especially if it is threatening, by labeling the person. In this case, we might label the person as drunk. If this individual is not under the influence of alcohol and we cannot come up with another reasonable explanation for his behavior, we might then conclude that the person is mentally disturbed. Why else would he shout obscenities in public? The label of "mental illness" offers us some comfort that we understand the person's behavior and that the world is a predictable and comprehensible place.

Scheff argues that at times everybody engages in behavior that could be labeled as mental illness. In many cases, these behaviors are not noticed by others and are called **primary deviance:** *the violation of social norms in which the violator is not labeled as a deviant.* In other cases, such behavior might be attributed to something other than mental illness, such as overwork, drunkenness, or some physiological ailment. However, in a few cases, people are given the label of "mentally ill," and to be so labeled is to be cast into a social role with certain expectations associated with it. Depending on the circumstances, we may expect those labeled as mentally ill to be dependent, helpless, or even dangerous; we may even make it difficult for them to behave otherwise. For example, we might deprive them of some household or occupational duties. Then, a *self-fulfilling prophecy* may occur as the person begins to live up to our expectations. Scheff calls this **secondary deviance:** *behavior that a person adopts in reaction to being labeled as mentally ill.* This self-fulfilling prophecy is most likely to result when people are experiencing some personal crisis and they are especially sensitive to the reactions of others and vulnerable to any signs of disapproval.

Scheff readily admits that some behavioral disturbances have organic, biological, or psychological causes. His point is that sporadic violations of norms are organized into a stable pattern of behavior when people conform to the expectations of the social role of the mentally ill. Furthermore, he argues that mental disorders with such internal causes can be perpetuated and extended through the emergence of secondary deviance. When mental health professionals label someone as mentally ill, they may be contributing to the emergence of secondary deviance. So Scheff shifts our focus away from the individual in understanding mental disorders and toward social relationships. The Applied Research insert provides a case study of the impact of some of these processes.

Mental Illness as Problems of Living   Psychiatrist Thomas Szasz (1970; 1987) provides the third position on the nature of mental illness, and it is very different from those previously discussed. He believes that mental disorders should not be viewed as "illnesses" at all but rather as problems of living: expressions of the fact that human life is a continual struggle to decide how to live and relate to others. Human existence means making choices about what makes life meaningful and valuable. Life is not, says Szasz, without considerable stress, anxiety, and conflict—nor should it be.

Szasz feels that the medical model of mental disorders is not only incorrect but also a potentially dangerous myth that can lead us to seek medical solutions to personal and ethical problems. If a psychiatrist classifies your behavior as a mental disorder, this is a value judgment regarding how you should lead your life. It limits your own exercise of judgment and freedom of choice. Furthermore, defining behaviors as symptoms of a mental disorder can lead to the dangerous step of absolving people of responsibility for their behavior. If one is not responsible for the nausea and fever that accompany influenza, then should a father be held responsible for the rage and child beating that accompany the "illnesses" of personality disorders? Szasz believes that people should be

held accountable for the social and ethical choices they make in their lives.

These three positions taken together provide a more complete view of mental disorders than does only one or two of them. Each makes us aware of different things about the problem of mental illness. The medical model suggests that we can clearly define what mental illness is and unambiguously state that certain behaviors are pathological. Scheff and Szasz claim that social reality is more complex than this. What is considered pathological in one context is viewed as normal in another. Furthermore, there is a danger, they argue, that we will abdicate in making moral choices in our own lives by turning the decision over to mental health "professionals" who are more than ready to tell us the "healthiest" way to live our lives. So it is important to approach the problem of mental illness by using all three perspectives.

The Treatment of Mental Disorders

Problems with Diagnosis   Mental health professionals use many concepts to describe the mental disorders that they believe exist: schizophrenia, depression, paranoia, and the like. They assess the existence of these disorders by observing people's behavior. Psychiatric diagnosis basically involves linking the behavioral display of a particular person with one or more diagnostic categories. If this diagnostic process is to be useful, it must be reliable, which means that the same diagnosis is made of the same patient by different professionals.

Unfortunately, psychiatric diagnoses are not nearly as reliable as we would hope. Recent reviews of studies spanning many decades found only a few studies in which reliability of the diagnoses was above the minimum level acceptable for good scientific research (Kirk and Kutchins, 1992). In some cases, psychiatrists reached the same diagnosis in only one of every three cases. In the American Psychiatric Association's most recent version of its

APPLIED RESEARCH
Labeling and Depersonalization in Mental Hospitals

To understand a social problem, it is sometimes helpful to view it from the perspective of its victims, whether they be AIDS sufferers, crime victims, or mental patients. D. L. Rosenhan and his associates (1973) did this with a careful observational study of mental institutions. They used a type of research called "participant observation," in which the researchers take part in the daily activities and routines of the people being studied. To do this, Rosenhan's researchers sought entrance into mental hospitals as patients. Their goal was to see first if they would be admitted and then how they were treated after admission. The people who sought admission were, as far as could be determined, sane. In fact, three were psychiatrists and one was a psychologist. The results were quite disturbing and sent howls of protest through the psychiatric community.

Each researcher, called a "pseudopatient" by Rosenhan, approached a hospital seeking voluntary admission. During their intake interviews, they described having vague symptoms, such as hearing unclear voices that said words sounding like "empty" and "hollow." All except one of the pseudopatients were admitted with a diagnosis of schizophrenia and remained hospitalized for an average of nineteen days. Once admitted, the pseudopatients acted normally, making no special effort to convince the staff that they were mentally ill. A review of the records gave no indication that any staff members developed any suspicions that

the pseudopatients might be sane. The pseudopatients were eventually discharged with a diagnosis of schizophrenia "in remission."

Rosenhan's research makes us painfully aware of some disturbing dimensions of the mental health system. First of all, the ability to detect mental illness and to diagnose it reliably is distressingly weak. In other words, it is sometimes difficult for mental health professionals to detect the sane from the insane. To be sure, they can diagnose extreme cases, such as a suicidal person or someone in a catatonic stupor. With less extreme symptoms, however, it is more difficult to separate the actions of mentally healthy people from those of the "insane." Mental health professionals also find it difficult to say reliably which mental disorder is involved in a particular case. (Although all of Rosenhan's pseudopatients presented the same symptoms, eleven were diagnosed as schizophrenic and one as manic-depressive psychotic.) Does this mean that perfectly sane people might be thought to be insane, be institutionalized, and have rights taken away from them? It undoubtedly has happened and could happen again. In addition, Rosenhan's findings raise the concern that people with serious mental disorders might not be receiving treatment or, more likely, be treated for the wrong disorder.

The second dimension of Rosenhan's research is that it documents the power of labeling in mental health settings. Once the pseudopatients were

---

Diagnostic and Statistical Manual of Mental Disorders (called the DSM-IV), studies of reliability with more positive results are reported, but even here there were few findings with more than 80 percent agreement; a few had as low as 30 percent agreement. In addition, these studies were limited in scope and not well controlled (American Psychiatric Association, 1994).

The unreliability of psychiatric diagnoses is a serious problem because it throws into question whether mental health professionals can accurately detect mental disorders. If they cannot accurately detect them, can they possibly treat them effectively? Furthermore, with such unreliability, it may well be that some people are being treated for the wrong disorder while others are being treated who have no disorder given the label of "insane," no one questioned that label. Because the institution had officially labeled the people, apparently no one believed the diagnoses incorrect. Furthermore, all of the pseudopatients' behavior was interpreted in the context of assuming that they were, in fact, insane. "Normal" behavior was either overlooked or interpreted as further symptoms of the mental disorder. For example, the pseudopatients openly took notes to record their observations for the research project. Rather than questioning this unusual behavior, the staff accepted it as the bizarre actions of the insane. Because the people were already judged to be "crazy," the staff did not think it possible that there was a sane reason for their note taking. As the interactionist perspective suggests, the label, once successfully applied, becomes the social reality to which people respond. What shapes behavior is what people believe to be true.

Rosenhan's pseudopatients made another disturbing observation during their research: These mental institutions contained powerful sources of depersonalization for their patients. The interactionist perspective points out that people gain a sense of positive self-regard when others treat them in a loving, respectful way. We get feedback about ourselves from the way others interact with us. **Depersonalization** refers to *feelings of detachment from people and social groups that give life meaning and provide a sense of importance and self-worth.* The pseudopatients found themselves

and other patients being dealt with in a condescending, insulting, and thoroughly negative manner. They saw patients being ignored or treated like children. They saw patients being undressed in semipublic rooms in total disregard of their privacy or their desire to control what happened to them. The impact of all this was a virtual assault on the patients' self-concept: The patients showed few signs of independence and autonomy and few feelings of self-worth. For most patients, some degree of depersonalization had set in. In fact, a self-fulfilling prophecy had occurred: The patients became the kind of people that the staff treated them as. Such characteristics as autonomy, confidence, and self-control—things we associate with mentally healthy people—declined among those in the institutions. This depersonalization does not always occur, and it does not have to occur (Weinstein, 1990b). However, the features of many institutional settings increase the likelihood that it will occur. For example, lack of staff and resources can make it difficult to provide a less depersonalizing environment.

Participant observation research such as Rosenhan's is extremely valuable in understanding social problems because it offers a perspective that is often neglected—the perspective of the victim. There is real truth to the saying that you cannot truly understand a person until you have walked in his or her shoes.

at all. In addition, this unreliability may reflect the fact that the medical model of mental illness, on which these diagnostic categories rest, is not a very useful vehicle for understanding some mental disorders.

Community Treatment In the past forty years, something called the "community mental health movement" has arisen and has come to play a

key role in the delivery of mental health services (Mechanic, 1989; Carling, 1995). Growing in part from the kinds of concerns expressed by people such as Szasz and Scheff, its basic thrust can be summarized in a few statements:

1. Mental health services should be delivered to a total community rather than just to individuals.

2. Services should be delivered in the community where people live rather than in state hospitals or other institutional settings removed from the community.

3. Sources of stress or other problems in the community that have implications for mental health should be detected and attacked.

4. Preventive services should be delivered as well as crisis-oriented ones.

In other words, the community treatment approach assumes that the whole community is its clientele. In addition to traditional therapies such as psychotherapy, community mental health centers should offer vocational placement, compensatory education, or other programs that would alleviate stress and help people lead more fulfilling lives. This should result in improved mental status for individuals. So the community approach tends to promote social change as well as individual adjustment.

Some of the goals of the community mental health movement appear to have been at least partially achieved. There are about as many mental hospitals today as forty years ago, but they are much smaller. Furthermore, although the rate of admission to psychiatric hospitals has not declined, the length of stay has dropped dramatically. Most striking of all, a substantial shift has occurred in where mental health services are delivered. Today, only about 11 percent of psychiatric services are delivered in mental hospitals, compared with 56 percent forty years ago. Today, people are usually treated in the psychiatric wards of general hospitals or as outpatients in hospitals or community mental health centers. In fact, this shift has been so dramatic that it has been called the "deinstitutionalization" of the mentally ill. In addition, the community mental health movement has provided psychiatric services to the aged, the poor, the underprivileged, and other groups that had in the past been underserved in this realm.

Not everyone has been enamored with the community approach (Brown, 1985). Some critics have charged that the process of deinstitutionalization did not commence when community mental health centers were established in the 1960s; rather, it began a decade earlier when drugs that control violence and depression became available. These drugs controlled the most disruptive symptoms of mental disorders, and they made it possible for some people to live in the community. The community mental health approach has also been criticized on the grounds that it does not accomplish many of its innovative goals, such as reducing community stressors or promoting social change, but rather ends up providing the traditional types of therapies to individuals. Yet another criticism of the community mental health approach is that it releases mental patients into the community without regard to the therapeutic value of the setting in which they will live. Living in the community may not always be the most desirable alternative for those who are mentally ill. As one study of newly released mental patients living in the community found: "For those without supportive homes to which to return or without sufficient competencies with which to sustain themselves independently in the community, community life is often difficult and dissatisfying" (Sommers, 1988: 225). All too often, critics charge, there are few coordinated follow-up services available in the community. Finally, the basic philosophy of keeping the mentally ill in the community has been questioned on the grounds that, if the community environment contributes to the mental disorder, then we may be simply compounding the problem by leaving people in the community.

Problems in Health Care

We have seen how a variety of social and cultural factors can contribute to the health problems of the United States. We have also discussed some special problems associated with mental illness in the United States. There are some other major problems associated with health and illness: rising costs, a lack of access to health care, poor quality services, and sexual inequality in the health field.

Rising Health-Care Costs

For most of the twentieth century, the rise in the cost of health care has been remarkably rapid and consistent. In 1970, it cost about $74 to stay in a major hospital for one day. By 1992, the average cost of a one-day hospital stay had risen to an astounding $820 (U.S. Bureau of the Census, 1994: 127). Per capita expenditures for health care have increased over thirtyfold since 1950 (see Table 4.1). We now pay $3,607 each year for health-care goods and services for each man, woman, and child in the United States—over $14,000 a year for a family of four. Inflation accounts for some of this increase, but inflation during the same period increased overall prices only about four times. What accounts for the skyrocketing growth in health-care costs? There are a number of factors involved (McCue, 1989).

First and probably most important is the fact that there has been a growing demand for health-care services, and a basic economic

TABLE 4.1 National Health Expenditures in the United States, 1940–1994, Expressed in Percentages

Variable	1940	1950	1960	1970	1980	1994
Percentage of GNP	4.0%	4.6%	5.2%	7.2%	9.1%	13.8%
Per capita expenditures	$29	$78	$142	$334	$1,054	$3,607
Percentage spent for						
Hospital care	25.0	30.7	32.9	37.4	41	36.4
Physicians' services	24.4	22.4	21.6	19.4	18.9	19.4
Dentists' services	10.4	7.8	7.5	6.5	6.2	4.3
Other professional services	4.5	3.2	3.3	2.0	2.3	6.0
Drugs and sundries	16.0	13.7	13.9	10.3	7.6	8.4
Eyeglasses and appliances	4.6	3.9	2.9	2.6	2.0	1.4
Nursing home care	.7	1.5	1.9	5.5	8.2	7.9
Other health services	2.4	3.3	4.0	3.2	2.4	2.1
Expense for prepayment and administration	4.1	3.6	3.9	3.6	3.7	5.3
Government public health activities	4.0	2.9	1.6	2.1	2.9	2.8
Research and medical facilities construction	3.5	7.0	6.6	7.4	4.8	3.1

Sources: Robert M. Gibson and Charles R. Fisher, "National Health Expenditures, Fiscal Year 1977," *Social Security Bulletin,* 41 (July 1978), p. 15; Sally T. Burner and Daniel R. Waldo, "National Health Expenditure Projections, 1994–2005." *Health Care Financing Review,* 16 (Summer 1995), pp. 221–236.

principle is that increasing demand for something tends to push up prices. Our population is larger, more affluent, and older, and these factors tend to increase the demand for a finite amount of health-care goods and services. Affluent people can afford more and better health care, and they are more knowledgeable about what services are available. Older people have more health problems and require more health-care services. These services are also more widely available today because there are more physicians and more hospital services available in suburbs and small towns.

Second, and probably equally important, is the availability of diagnostic and treatment procedures that were unheard of five, ten, or twenty years ago, and these procedures can be very costly. Premature babies who would have died two decades ago are now saved in expensive neonatal intensive care units (but at a high cost: from $200,000 to $1 million for an infant who weighs only one pound at birth). Laser surgery, CAT scanners, cobalt treatment, ultrasound, coronary bypass operations, angioplasty procedures, magnetic resonance imaging—these and many other procedures did not exist a few years ago. Some feel that heart transplants will be routine in the not too distant future, and they now can cost upwards of $300,000 apiece.

Third, health care is a labor-intensive industry—it requires many people to provide health care—and the cost of health care rises quickly when health-care providers lobby for higher salaries. Nurses, nurses' aides, medical technologists, and many others feel they have been underpaid in the past and are demanding salaries they believe to be commensurate with their training and responsibilities. In addition, physicians' incomes have been rising at a much faster rate than the incomes of most workers: Surgeons' and radiologists' incomes nearly doubled during the 1980s, whereas full-time male workers' incomes went up by 40 percent and full-time female workers' by only 12

percent (Anstett, 1992). Also, savings through automation are not as easy to achieve in the health field as in other industries. Advances in health technology often involve completely new procedures, which call for new technicians, rather than replacing something that had been done less efficiently by older technology. So, improvements in health technology often result in the need for more, not fewer, workers.

Fourth, economic competition and the check on costs that this can afford are weaker in the health field than in other economic areas. This means that physicians and hospitals can raise costs with less concern about market considerations. The ways in which the health field diverges from the ideal of free competition are discussed in the Policy Issues insert.

Fifth, there is a tendency to overutilize health-care services and even to perform completely unnecessary diagnostic and treatment procedures. One reason for this involves the way we pay for health care, which leaves both the physician and the patient with little reason to show constraint in the use of services. The most common mode of payment is through **third-party medicine,** in which *the patient pays premiums into a fund and the doctor or hospital is paid from this fund for each treatment provided the patient.* The first two parties in the transaction, of course, are the patient and the doctor or hospital. The third party might be a private health insurance company or a government program such as Medicare or Medicaid. The basic flaw in such payment schemes is that the party paying the bill—the third-party source of funds—does not participate in the decision about how much or what kinds of services to provide. Patients have already paid their premiums and do not have to pay more as additional services are rendered, and physicians and hospitals benefit financially when more services are provided. The result is the performance of too many and sometimes completely unnecessary medical procedures. In 1992, for example, *Consumer Reports* published a study concluding that as much as 20 percent of all surgeries and medical services provided in the United States are unnecessary, costing health-care consumers $130 billion each year (Anstett, 1992). This problem is especially serious with very profitable procedures, such as coronary artery bypass surgery, of which 30 percent may be unnecessary, and cesarean births, of which 50 percent may be unnecessary (Barron, 1989).

Finally, there are a number of other factors contributing to increasing costs. The number of malpractice suits and the size of the financial judgments against physicians in these litigations have increased. Consequently, malpractice premiums for physicians rose by 18 percent per year in the 1980s, with some specialties seeing much greater increases (Brostoff, 1992). This rise in costs is then passed on to the health-care consumer. In addition, as we mentioned above, crisis medicine tends to be more expensive in the long run than preventive medicine, but our health-care system still tends to emphasize the former. Finally, there are many powerful interest groups benefiting from rising costs: physicians, hospital administrators, the pharmaceutical industry, and so on. Health-care consumers benefit most from controlling costs, but they have yet to organize into a powerful lobby group.

For some critics of our health-care system, the problem of rising costs is only a symptom of deeper, structural problems that must be attended to. The Policy Issues insert analyzes the role that the corporatization of health care and the profitmaking nature of the system may play in exacerbating the problem.

Access to Medical Services

Many people in the United States do not have easy access to medical care when they need it (Wolfe, 1994). Because health care is a commodity sold in the marketplace, those who can afford to pay get medical services, whereas those who cannot afford it are left to fend for themselves. The high cost of health care means that only the wealthiest can afford to pay out of their own pockets for medical services. Most rely on health insurance, either purchased by themselves or provided by an employer. The poor and less well-to-do, who cannot find jobs that provide health insurance, are out in the cold. This situation has been eased somewhat with the introduction of programs of publicly financed health insurance such as Medicaid. Since these programs became available in the 1960s, the health-care utilization rates among the poor have increased considerably. When looking at people with equivalent health status, however, the poor still have considerably less access to health care than do the nonpoor. In addition, less than one-half of the poor are eligible for Medicaid. As a consequence, fully one-third of the poorest in the United States younger than age sixty-five have no health insurance coverage at all; for them, access to medical care is quite limited. In addition to the poor, there are others who find themselves without health insurance: laid-off employees; people who retire before they are eligible for Medicare; young people who are too old for coverage under their parents' health insurance plan; and widows, widowers, and divorced people who had depended on their spouses' health insurance. Altogether thirty-seven million Americans, or 15 percent of our populace, are without health insurance (Lindorff, 1992).

One critic of the health-care delivery system argues that the United States has a four-tier health-care system (Steinberg, 1985). The top tier consists of people with full health insurance coverage or some other means to pay for necessary care. They have complete access to excellent health care. Below them reside those with limited health insurance coverage, who do not have complete access but do have their essential health needs taken care of. The

Much of the health-care system in the United States is profit oriented, and health-care providers sometimes closely watch the profit margin when they make medical decisions. Consider these examples:

1. A young woman is admitted to a for-profit hospital in Tennessee with a life-threatening irregular heartbeat. When the hospital learns that her health insurance only covers 80 percent of her hospitalization and that, being of modest means, she would be hard pressed to pay the remaining 20 percent, they recommend she be transferred to a nearby university hospital. When that hospital has no room for her, the for-profit hospital discharges her with medications to take at home—a move that independent medical experts called "totally inappropriate" for "a patient who is a candidate for sudden death" (Lindorff, 1992: 16).

2. One hospital sent some of its physicians a memo informing them that their position at the hospital would be terminated if they did not admit more patients. It also kept a physician profile showing how many patients each one admits, how long the patients stay, and whether they pay their bills. Physicians who admit the "wrong" kind of patient—the really sick, the elderly, the expensive, and the ones whose bill is not paid fully by someone—find they lose their privileges at the hospital.

3. Some hospitals refuse to treat ailments that are expensive and unprofitable. Many have closed their emergency rooms because these attract people of modest means who do not have health insurance and cannot pay their bills.

The hospitals involved in these practices are privately owned and intended to make a profit for their investors, just like a bakery or a tavern. In other words, health-care institutions are a part of the capitalist economic system of the United States described in Chapter 2. Now this is not new. After all, physicians have been business entrepreneurs in this country since its founding, pharmaceutical companies have always tried to make a profit selling people drugs, and there have always been privately owned hospitals. What is different today is the size and scope of the privatization and corporatization of health care in the United States. In the past, nonprofit hospitals were run by communities or by religious or service organizations. Their primary goal was to provide for all of the health needs of a community. Although such hospitals can still be found today, the hospital industry is slowly being taken over by national corporations that own chains of hospitals and manage local hospitals from a centralized business office (one in four acute care hospitals is now investor owned). In these corporate settings, control and authority over medical decisions and issues is gradually shifting from the hands of patients, physicians, and community leaders to corporate headquarters and medical industry entrepreneurs, and the primary motivation of these corporations is to increase corporate profits. The public sector of community and nonprofit hospitals is being forced to adopt some of the same strategies or be run out of business.

The corporate takeover of hospitals began with the emergence of Medicare and Medicaid, which meant that there were huge profits to be made treating the recipients of these programs. By the 1980s, in the Wall Street world of medicine, patients were known as "revenue bodies," hospitals were "profit centers," and the goal was to "maximize the return on each admission." What has emerged is a rather chilling trend: "Charging every penny that can be charged for patient care, and avoiding as much as possible the treatment of patients unable to pay. It also means marketing, or offering paying patients what they *think* they need, while eliminating services a community might *really* need but which aren't profitable" (Lindorff, 1992: 18). So young professionals with good health insurance get valet parking and luxurious birthing rooms, but poor pregnant women, even when they have Medicaid, find that they are not welcome. And the professionals have to travel further to find a community hospital that offers emergency services when they have an accident.

There are, of course, benefits to this privatization. Especially for those with good health insurance or the wealthy who can afford to pay on their own, medicine in the United States provides some excellent services. As we saw in Chapter 2, capitalism is based on the assumption that competition and profit seeking will work in the interests of the consumer by providing the widest range of goods and services at the lowest price. These incentives should, in theory, encourage private health-care businesses to provide high-quality, inexpensive health care.

However, it does not seem to work out that way (Lindorff, 1992). In areas where many hospitals compete with one another for patients, both for-profit and nonprofit hospitals charge about the same for various procedures; when there is no competition, for-profits actually charge more for services than do the nonprofits. It seems that, in a noncompetitive environment, the temptation to raise

One of the key trends of the past few decades has been the concentration of health-care resources and decision making in the hands of large corporations in the United States. Many critics blame this privatization and corporatization for the problems of rising costs and reduced accessibility of health care.

charges, and thus increase profits, is too great to resist. The overall lower costs of nonprofit hospitals is especially surprising because they do not dump expensive services such as obstetrics in the way that the for-profits have.

The privatization and corporatization of health care also means that those who cannot afford health care—the poor who do not qualify for Medicaid and those who do not have health insurance on the job—do not have access to the health services they need. Even those with Medicaid find that they have limited access to the system because corporate hospitals and doctors prefer to serve those whose insurance will pay higher fees for services than will Medicaid. In addition, expensive medicine, such as obstetrics and emergency medicine, gets dumped onto publicly owned hospitals, which further taxes their ability to provide quality care to their patients. And some question whether profit seeking by doctors and hospitals always works in the best interests of the patient. As one health economist put it: "The real threat to health care is when the doctors' and the hospitals' interests become aligned against the interests of the patient. It's possible that the corporations could usurp the physicians' power" to act as an advocate for the patients (quoted in Lindorff, 1992: 86).

Dr. Arnold S. Relman (1980), editor of the presti New England Journal of Medicine, calls this a **medica industrial complex:** *a coincidence of interests betwee physicians and other health-care providers and the in tries producing health-care goods and services, with b parties profiting from the increased use of these com modities while the health-care consumer pays enorm costs for inadequate care.* This is analogous to the mi tary-industrial complex discussed in Chapter 2. It can lead to a conflict of interest because many of the bus nesses are owned by doctors or employ doctors. Like other enterprises, these businesses stand to increase their profits by "selling" as much of their commodity they can, just as a person who sells cars profits by increasing sales. This raises the question of whether he care decisions are motivated by the health needs of th consumer or by the profit needs of the medical–indus complex.

Looking at these problems with a privatized health care system, some critics have argued that they arise, part, because health care is different from other segm of the economy: It has elements that make it less sub to the laws of competition and the marketplace.

third tier consists of those on Medicaid, who have access to the health-care system if they can find someone to offer treatment or nursing homes that will admit them. Some Medicaid recipients find it difficult to locate physicians who will treat them. At the bottom of the system are the uninsured for whom access to health care is practically nonexistent.

Another dimension of access to health care is the availability of services. In this regard, it has been residents of the inner city and rural areas who are underserved. Physicians prefer to practice in locales where they would like to live and can find a profitable clientele, and neither the inner city nor rural areas can satisfy this prefer-

ence. Native American youth in rural areas have been heavily affected by this; they are isolated from services and the services available tend to focus more on the health needs of children and adults (Davis, Hunt, and Kitzes, 1989).

Quality of Medical Services

Rising costs and the intense competition among hospitals may be affecting the quality of health care in the United States. To keep costs down and profits up, hospitals have responded by cutting back on services to patients (Gordon, 1995). For example, the number of regis-

1. Ninety percent of the U.S. populace is covered by some form of third-party insurance, which means that they do not have to pay for many health-care goods and services out of their pockets. Because they do not pay directly, they have less incentive to shop around for the best buy.
2. In most economic situations, consumers decide how many goods or what kinds of services they will purchase. Health-care consumers, however, are heavily dependent on their doctors—the very ones who benefit economically from the provision of services—for expert advice on what they need.
3. Many practices common in other realms are not available in medicine. Consumers cannot, for example, test a health-care service before purchasing nor can they obtain a money-back guarantee to protect against faulty procedures.

Despite these differences between health care and other economic spheres, health care is still largely a private-enterprise, profit-making activity in the United States. Many critics consider this profit-making nature of the health-care system as a major factor leading people to pay more for lower quality health care than they should.

There is contentious debate about what, if anything, to do about all these problems. Relman has urged the American Medical Association to discourage physicians from commercially exploiting health care by being financially involved in health-care businesses. Other critics, such as Ivan Illich (1976) and Robert Sherrill (1995), believe that the capitalist nature of our health-care system is the fundamental problem. For these radical critics, only a complete restructuring of the system can prevent widespread abuses and exploitation. Some of these critics call for much more government involvement in protecting health-care consumers, controls over excess profit-making in health care, and possibly even a socialized health-care system. Current social policy tends to support the profit-oriented nature of the system, but changes could occur in the future.

tered nurses has been cut significantly, and their work has been taken over by lower-paid but less highly trained nursing assistants and technicians. Registered nurses are also given responsibility for supervising these less-trained workers, further taking away from their direct contact with patients. The Health Care Financing Administration has cited these and other cutbacks as among the reasons for a decline in services to the point of increased injury and suffering to patients in some hospitals.

Cutbacks such as these, along with the highly bureaucratic organization of the health-care system, can result in highly impersonal and even dehumanizing health-care services.

The standardization and routinization of health care can benefit the health-care system because it is less expensive. Yet it can lead patients to feel dissatisfied, lonely, and frightened. However, if people receive expert medical treatment, does it matter if they are emotionally dissatisfied by the experience? Much evidence indicates that it does (Mumford, Schlesinger, and Glass, 1982; DiMatteo and DiNicola, 1982). Studies of the "placebo effect" document that what people think and feel about their treatment—their faith that they will be cured—increases the likelihood of a cure. Other research shows that patients who receive group or emotional support from friends or health-care providers recover more quickly from illness, injury, or surgery. In addition, research shows that people who are emotionally satisfied with their treatment by a hospital or doctor are more likely to follow their doctor's medical advice. So, how the health-care system treats people does matter: People who are dehumanized are less likely to respond to treatment and less likely to do what their doctors recommend medically.

Gender Inequality in Health Care

Gender inequality pervades the health-care system in the United States, with widespread ramifications. First, the health-care industry is male-dominated, with men holding most of the prestigious, high-paying, and powerful positions (see Figure 4.5). Men make up 78 percent of today's physicians, for example, whereas 94 percent of the registered nurses are women. Almost all dentists are men, whereas practically all dental assistants and dental hygienists are women. Clearly, the health-care system involves men in positions of authority telling women what to do. This was not always the case. In the nineteenth century, women working as midwives or other types of healers provided much of the medical care for families. As more medical schools opened in the late 1800s, women were excluded

FIGURE 4.5 Men and Women in Health Occupations, 1994. *Source:* U.S. Department of Labor, Bureau of Labor Statistics, *Employment and Earnings,* Vol. 42, No. 1, January 1995, pp. 175–180.

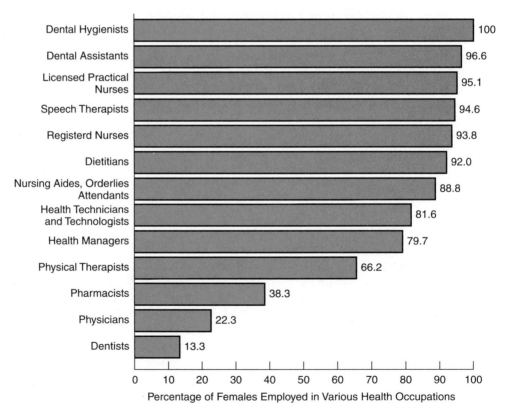

Percentage of Females Employed in Various Health Occupations

from most of them. By the turn of the century, legislation banned the "practice of medicine" by anyone not trained in a state-approved medical school. The result: Women were effectively banned from the practice of medicine. During the first half of the twentieth century, medical schools admitted few, if any, women. Even through the 1960s, medical and dental education were male preserves: Although a few women were admitted, they were often met with hostility or demeaning jokes, making the difficult road through school even tougher. It has not really been until the last fifteen years that medical and dental education have opened up to women. Today about one-third of both medical and dental students nationwide are women (see Figure 4.6). There has been little change, however, in the sparse numbers of men in nursing schools.

One reason for concern about male dominance in the health field is that it has severely restricted women's access to lucrative and prestigious occupations. These issues of economic discrimination are discussed in more detail in Chapter 7. Another reason for concern is that male dominance may have had a detrimental effect on the health and health care of women in the United States (Scully, 1994). Male physicians over the years held the same stereotypes about women that other men did, and this influenced what physicians defined as illness and what treatments they made available. For example, one stereotype viewed menstruation as "unclean" or "abnormal," and physicians contributed to this view by "medicalizing" menstruation or defining it as a medical condition or weakness calling for some intervention. In the nineteenth century and well into the twentieth century, menstruation has been viewed as a pathological condition sometimes having serious consequences and influencing women's ability to think and make decisions. In fact, the reputed ill effects of women's reproductive biology have been an important staple in a sexist ideology justifying the inequitable treatment of

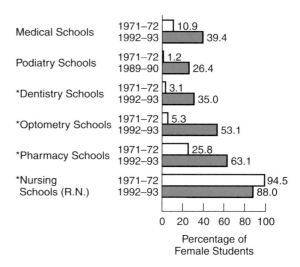

FIGURE 4.6 Enrollment of Women in Schools for Health Occupations, United States, Academic Years 1971–1993. * First-year enrollment only *Sources:* National Center for Health Statistics, *Health, United States, 1990,* DHHS Pub. No. (PHS) 91–1232 (Hyattsville, Md.: Public Health Service, 1993), p. 172; National Center for Health Statistics, *Health, United States, 1994,* DHHS Pub. No. (PHS) 95–1232 (Hyattsville, Md.: Public Health Service, 1995), p. 210.

women. From the late 1800s until recently, the very process of childbirth itself has been viewed as a medical procedure rather than the profoundly natural and personal event that it really is. Women were routinely given powerful anesthetics that prevented them from experiencing the birth of their children. Then they might not even be permitted to see their infants for a few days after birth, interfering with the bonding that occurs between mother and child soon after birth. More recently, the number of cesarean births has grown from 5 percent to almost 25 percent of all births, giving the United States the highest rate of such births (Taffel et al., 1991). Some cesareans, of course, are medically justified, but there is much suspicion that some are performed for the convenience of medical personnel, to protect against malpractice suits, or because doctors and hospitals are reimbursed more for surgical births. In any event, the mother loses control of the birth process when it becomes overly medicalized. Over the years, then, male dominance in medicine has meant that men have been the "authorities" telling women about their own bodies, and what the men told the women sometimes did more to bolster inaccurate stereotypes or line the pockets of physicians than to benefit the health of women.

The medical procedure that is among those most likely to be performed unnecessarily—the hysterectomy—affects only women. Conservatively, one-third of all hysterectomies over the years were probably medically unjustified (Stroman, 1979). Some observers have questioned whether a medical profession dominated by women would have so routinely performed such surgeries. In addition, feminists argue that medical research has been dominated by the sexist assumption that it is the woman's responsibility to orchestrate birth-control efforts. Consequently, most birth-control research has been on female contraceptive devices rather than finding effective procedures for male contraception.

Bioethics: Technology and Health

Modern technology has opened up some wonderful opportunities, but it also confronts us with some difficult and potentially frightening issues. The final chapter of this book deals with the impact of science and technology on our lives, but here we want to address a few special concerns that relate to health issues. **Bioethics** refers to *the study of ethical questions that relate to the life and biological well-being of people* (Brody and Engelhardt, 1987). It involves an intertwining of ethical, medical, and biological considerations. We will discuss three major issues in this realm: the prolongation of life, the distribution of limited medical resources, and ge-

netic screening. Keep in mind that these ethical issues have come to the fore, in part, because of the very success of science and medicine in attacking illness and injury.

The Prolongation of Life

When people die, their respiratory, circulatory, and nervous systems—the major life-sustaining body systems—normally fail at about the same time. With modern technology, however, respiration and circulation can be machine assisted far beyond the point at which the body itself could sustain them. These machines do not provide medical treatment but merely assist the body to stay "alive." Thus, severely injured, critically ill, or very old people can be kept alive for long periods of time. A particularly disturbing case gained prominence in California in 1984 (Malcolm, 1984). A seventy-year-old man was hospitalized with five normally fatal diseases, including inoperable lung cancer. He could not breathe on his own, so a machine breathed for him through a passage in his neck. Other tubes fed him and drained his wastes. Electronic monitors warned nurses of any change in his condition. Everyone involved agreed that the man would never leave his hospital bed alive. Both the man himself and his wife requested that the breathing machine be turned off so that he could die naturally. His physicians refused the request on the grounds that the man would die if removed from the machine. They even tied his arms down so that he would not be able to remove the tubes himself. The man's wife sued the hospital to have the machines turned off, but the man died before the case was resolved. His medical and legal bills were estimated to be over $500,000. A similar dilemma is faced by relatives and medical personnel who must decide whether to withhold life-prolonging medical treatment from loved ones.

The expense of such life-support systems can devastate a family's finances. There is also a tremendous psychological burden for the family who has to watch a loved one go through a prolonged period of debilitation before death. Finally, from the individual's perspective, there is the loss of dignity that comes from helplessness. Even if comatose, many would prefer not to end their lives with tubes inserted in their bodies and machines powering their hearts—almost as if the body must fight against modern technology in order to die.

Technology has made the line between life and death more vague. It has become a difficult practical matter to say exactly when death occurs in many cases. The same technology can maintain the lives of terminally ill or comatose people, even when there is little or no hope of recovery. This situation creates a dilemma regarding who should decide whether to discontinue life support. Parents or relatives would seem to be the natural ones to make such decisions, but they could be swayed by such considerations as the psychological or economic costs of maintaining a critically ill relative over time. Medical personnel also play a role in such decisions. But their mission is to save lives, and they may be rightly concerned about civil or even criminal suits resulting from their decisions in such cases. As a consequence, their choices may not be in the patients' best interests.

A number of developments have had an impact on this problem of the artificial prolongation of life. One has been the emergence of social movements whose major theme is "death with dignity." Those involved have lobbied for the acceptance of "living wills," in which people state, while they are still healthy, the conditions under which medical efforts to save their lives should be stopped. A few states have accepted these living wills as legal documents, but their ultimate legality is likely to be debated in the courts. Another development has been the acceptance of a revised definition of death, which used to be defined as the cessation of breathing and heartbeat. The newer approach defines death as the prolonged absence of brain waves, or "brain death." This gives physicians some legal standing in withholding life-sustaining efforts from those who show virtually no possibility of recovery. A final development has been the establishment of panels in hospitals to make recommendations about decisions of whether to withhold treatment or turn off life-support equipment. The panels are made up of doctors, nurses, social workers, psychologists, and even laypeople. These panels relieve physicians of the difficult burden of making such decisions alone, and, by including many different opinions, they reduce the likelihood that personal bias will result in judgments at variance with the patient's interests.

Whom Shall We Treat?

As we have seen, health care is expensive and is becoming more costly all the time. A part of the problem is the growing number of technologically complex and costly procedures that are available. This raises the question of whether we can afford to provide these treatments to everyone with a medical need for them (Merrill and Cohen, 1989). After all, the money we spend on health care is money we cannot spend on defense, social services, automobiles, and recreation. In 1989, for example, $700 of the cost of each automobile Chrysler produced went to pay health-care premiums for Chrysler workers, retirees, and their families (Iacocca, 1989). This plan provides excellent health-care coverage for Chrysler workers, but it means more expensive cars and less money for auto consumers to spend on other items. One option, of course, is to limit the availability of some medical procedures, possibly the more expensive ones. But how do we decide to whom these procedures will be made available? Such decisions rest on some "principle of social justice." There are a number of these principles that can serve as the basis of medical allocation decisions (Veatch and Branson, 1976; Hingson et al., 1981).

1. *Ability to pay:* offer services to those who can afford to pay part or all of the costs.

2. *Merit:* offer services on the basis of people's merits, such as their achievements or societal contributions.

3. *Utilitarian:* offer services to those who would provide the greatest benefit—in economic, personal, or social terms—to the greatest number of people should they live.

4. *Compensatory justice:* offer services to those who have already suffered some social wrongs or have been deprived of resources.

5. *Egalitarian:* offer everyone who needs services an equal opportunity to receive them.

Which of these principles, or combinations of principles, would you use to allocate health-care resources? The egalitarian concept is probably the most popular one in the United States. In fact, some physicians in the 1960s chose kidney dialysis patients on the basis of a random lottery. The point, of course, is that, as medical technology becomes more expensive, we may have to decide how to limit its use by adopting some principles of social justice on which to rest the allocation process.

Genetic Screening

Medical technology has advanced to the point where we can determine many things about the health status of a fetus through intrauterine testing (Kimbrell, 1993). Amniocentesis, for example, is a procedure in which amniotic fluid is withdrawn from around the fetus and analyzed for abnormal cells and genetic content. Such procedures can determine the sex of the child and whether the child suffers from a number of serious defects or disorders such as Down's syndrome or cystic fibrosis. When the fetus is found to have some serious problem, especially one for which there is no known treatment, the parents are confronted with a potential dilemma: Should they continue the

pregnancy? For people strongly opposed to abortion, of course, the answer is yes. For others, however, the prospect of raising a retarded or severely ill child may be sufficiently difficult or disturbing that abortion is considered a viable option. So genetic screening, made possible by advances in medical technology, confronts people with ethical dilemmas that were much less common in the past.

Amniocentesis also raises a future problem that could be disturbing. Because we can learn the sex of a fetus, might this information be used in deciding whether to continue a pregnancy? Would a couple desperately wanting a boy abort a female fetus? In a society placing more value on males than females, would people continue having abortions until the woman was pregnant with a male fetus? Would cultural values or fashions determine whether people continue pregnancies with a fetus of a given sex? These are not, of course, problems at the moment in the United States, but the technology is very new. And it does raise some disturbing possibilities. As we will see in Chapter 15, genetic engineering on a substantial scale may be possible in the near future, with disturbing social implications.

Future Prospects

In attacking the problems of the cost of, access to, and quality of health care, there is an overriding issue to be resolved: Is health care in the United States a right or a privilege? One view is that access to high-quality health care should be a fundamental right of all members of society. We have reviewed the functionalist argument that the health status of citizens is central to the maintenance of society. Society needs to ensure that people are healthy so that they can make contributions to the maintenance of society. The opposing view is that access to health care should be a privilege of those with resources to obtain it. Like the conflict perspective, this position holds that health care is a valued commodity to be distributed to those who can afford it. This reflects the capitalist and market foundations of our economy: Health care is merely another economic service, and it can be most efficiently produced and distributed through competition in the marketplace.

Although most industrial nations today view health care as a citizen's right, there is still some controversy regarding this in the United States. The lack of resolution of this issue is reflected in the programs proposed to solve problems in the health area.

Publicly Funded Health Insurance

One approach to increasing people's access to health care is through publicly funded health insurance.

Medicare and Medicaid Two government programs that have probably had the most profound effects on health-care delivery in the United States are Medicare and Medicaid, both established in 1965. These programs are based on the assumption that all people have a right to medical treatment irrespective of their financial circumstances. **Medicare** is *government health insurance for those over sixty-five years of age.* This program pays some of the costs for hospitalization, nursing-home care, and some home-health care. For a monthly fee, the elderly can also purchase medical insurance from Medicare that will cover other services such as doctors' fees and outpatient services. **Medicaid** is *a joint federal–state program to provide medical care for low-income people of any age.*

These two programs have gone a long way toward reducing the differences in the use of health-care services between the affluent and the poor. Unlike in the past, the poor today visit doctors and enter hospitals more frequently than the well-to-do. To that extent, these two programs have achieved one of their major

goals, which was to make health care available to all citizens regardless of financial circumstances. But these plans are not without their problems. First they are very expensive and growing more expensive. Medicare expenses rose from $7 billion in 1971 to over $130 billion today—a fourteenfold increase in a little over two decades. Medicaid payments are about $100 billion (U.S. Bureau of the Census, 1994: 115). Both payment schemes were originally designed as third-party arrangements, and this accounts for some of their high costs. A second problem, especially with Medicaid, has been fraud, committed by both recipients and providers of health care. Some physicians have provided unneeded treatments, and some medical laboratories have routinely charged for tests never performed. Some abuse is inevitable in such large programs, but it has been extensive and expensive (Jesilow, Pontell, and Geis, 1993). A third problem is that some providers have refused to treat Medicaid and Medicare patients because of delays in receiving payments or because the payments were inadequate. Medicaid has been criticized over the years for paying physicians too little for services. Medicare began a new fee schedule in 1992 that sometimes reimburses physicians less than half what they charge their private paying patients. Physicians claim they cannot even cover their overhead with what the programs pay (Freudenheim, 1992). This problem may be creating a two-tiered health-care system in which Medicare and Medicaid patients receive lower-quality care by lower-paid physicians in crowded settings, whereas people with private health insurance have good quality services available to them. Finally, as we have seen, the eligibility level for Medicaid in most states is so low that people who truly need it do not have access to it. Raising the eligibility ceilings would provide health insurance to many who currently have no insurance whatsoever.

A number of efforts have been made to control the skyrocketing costs of Medicaid and

Medicare. Some states have developed "preferred provider" programs for Medicaid in which a hospital or a group of doctors agrees to provide all health-care services to Medicaid recipients in a particular geographic area, receiving, in return, one annual, lump-sum payment. This arrangement encourages the providers to prevent costs from exceeding the annual amount that they are paid because they will not receive any additional payments and are contractually required to provide services. For Medicare, the federal government instituted a new payment mechanism in the early 1980s called diagnostically related groupings, or DRGs. This strategy involves placing each hospitalization episode into one of about 450 diagnostic groupings. Then all treatments in a single diagnostic grouping receive the same reimbursement, whether any particular case actually costs more or less. If a case costs more to treat, the hospital must make up the difference; if it costs less, the hospital keeps the surplus. The purpose is to offer doctors and hospitals a financial incentive for keeping an eye on lowering costs. Opponents of the DRG approach argue that people's illness episodes are too individualized to be treated in this assembly-line fashion: Some people bleed more, others take longer to recuperate, and others are fast healers. Furthermore, doctors would have to consider DRGs when they make diagnoses rather than being guided solely by the condition of their patients. The program seems to have produced a few changes in what doctors and hospitals do: Hospital stays for the elderly are shorter than they used to be, hospitals are trying to draw in more patients to take up the slack, and hospitals have aggressively developed outpatient services (Freund and McGuire, 1995).

National Health Insurance Medicare and Medicaid amount to government health insurance for the poor and the elderly. Some have proposed that these benefits be extended as a right to all citizens through **national health insur-**ance: *government health insurance covering all citizens* (Intriligator, 1993). Great Britain had such a program as early as 1911. In fact, the United States is alone among the industrial nations in not providing some form of national health insurance or health service. National health insurance would alleviate a number of problems. It would ensure health insurance coverage to the many people who do not currently have any, such as low-income people ineligible for Medicaid and people who are between jobs. It would also give the government a more direct means of controlling health-care costs. Finally, it would reduce the likelihood of a two-tiered health-care system. However, national health insurance, if designed as a third-party payment system, could be costly if it did not include some cost containment mechanisms, such as DRGs.

While some support for a program of national health insurance persists in the United States, such a program has never come close to adoption. The relatively low level of enthusiasm for extending publicly financed health care to all people suggests that some ambivalence remains regarding whether health care is a right or should be a privilege. As the International Perspectives insert points out, this contrasts sharply with the approach taken in many other societies. However, as health-care costs continue to rise in the United States and both employers and employees are squeezed to pay health insurance premiums, people may take another look at national health insurance as a mechanism for spreading the costs out over all people.

Compulsory, Employer-Financed Health Insurance

Some would prefer that the government not get involved in the actual provision of health insurance but rather just ensure that all citizens have access to some health insurance. Because many of the currently uninsured have jobs with no health insurance benefits, one proposal is to have the government require that all employers provide comprehensive health insurance for their employees. The Clinton administration proposed a version of this in 1994.

The government could pay the insurance premiums of those who don't work or work for employers who are too small to afford health insurance. Such a program would be expensive, of course, and it would put a burden on small businesses. In addition, the consumer would pay for it through higher prices for goods and services. Yet it would provide all people with access to health care. It is also more acceptable than programs such as national health insurance to many laissez-faire advocates because it accomplishes the goal with minimal government involvement. In fact, something similar could be done with Medicare and Medicaid: Instead of the government providing the insurance, the government could pay the private health insurance premiums for those who are eligible for the programs.

Access to Health Services for Special Groups

Providing more extensive health insurance coverage is a major way to increase access to services. However, there are other barriers that reduce access, such as the isolation of Native Americans on reservations. These problems need to be approached by developing very focused programs for delivering services to particular groups. One program, for example, focused on the health needs of Native American teenagers, by providing substance abuse counseling, suicide prevention services, and pregnancy testing—thereby addressing problems that many young Native Americans in rural areas are likely to confront (Davis, Hunt, and Kitzes, 1989). Services were provided in the local school to make them readily available in an isolated community with few health resources. Access to health services can also be limited if health providers and institutions behave in an arrogant or insensitive manner to people of particular groups. Native American utilization of health services has been limited by the feeling that Anglo providers are insensitive or judgmental. Community involvement in the development and operation of health services can go a long way toward reducing this problem.

HMOs and Managed Care

In discussing Medicaid, "preferred provider" programs were mentioned. When these kinds of arrangements emerged many decades ago, they were called health maintenance organizations, or HMOs, and they represented an alternative to traditional health insurance for financing health care. A **health maintenance organization** is *an organization that agrees to provide for all of a person's health-care needs for a fixed premium.* Whereas health insurance is third-party medicine involving a separate payment for each service rendered, HMOs receive a set fee and agree to take care of all of a person's health needs for that fee. In so doing, the HMO assumes a financial risk that the services they give patients might cost more than the premiums the HMO takes in. If this happens, the HMO loses money, so the HMO has an incentive to control costs that the physician or patient in third-party medicine does not have.

In the last decade, a number of trends discussed in this chapter—the corporatization of health care, increased competition in the health-care field, and rising costs—has led to the emergence of what is now called **managed care:** *these are organized like HMOs, with networks of hospitals and doctors who provide all of the health-care needs for large groups of people for a flat fee* (Eckholm, 1994; Miller and Luft, 1994). Some HMOs and managed-care systems own their own hospitals and the health-care providers, including physicians, are employed by the system. People with managed care typically have a

INTERNATIONAL PERSPECTIVES
Paying for Health Care in Other Societies

Earlier in this chapter, two rather disturbing facts emerged. One is that the United States doesn't come off very well in international comparisons of health status. For example, in comparison to most other industrial nations, people in the United States live shorter lives and lose more infants to death. The second disturbing fact is that we pay more for our health care than do these other nations. Why do these other nations pay less and get more? Some critics attribute this to the largely unregulated, laissez-faire nature of the U.S. health-care system which leaves many people with limited or no access to the health-care system.

In Sweden, France, Australia, Germany, Canada, and many other nations, health services are paid for with money collected by the government (Cockerham, 1994). This is similar to Medicare and Medicaid in the United States. Employers and employees pay taxes that are placed in a fund from which medical bills are paid. Canada, for example, provided hospital insurance for its citizens beginning in 1961 and physician's care insurance in 1971 (Bennett and Adams, 1993). The entire population is covered and 95 percent of hospital and physician costs are paid by federal or provincial taxes. There are some amenities, such as private hospital rooms and cosmetic surgery, that the system does not pay for. Everything else is covered, and Canadians hardly ever even see a hospital bill. Patients can choose their own physicians, and physicians are private, self-employed practitioners, not government employees. Hospitals operate on a budget that is set largely by provincial governments. So, Canada has an essentially private health-care system that is paid for almost entirely by public money.

One way in which this universal coverage can be paid for is by keeping costs down. For example, in Canada, the government sets all doctor and hospital fees, and physicians can't charge more for services than the insurance will pay. Canadian physicians do not earn the lucrative incomes that American physicians do, although physicians are still among the highest paid professional groups in Canada. However, Canadian doctors do not have to worry about billing patients, preparing insurance forms, or writing off bad debts. Another way Canada pays for its system is through progressive taxes, or tax rates that increase with income, to pay health insurance premiums. This makes for a larger kitty from which to pay for health care. In the United States,

limited choice of doctors to select from, and the managed care system exercises tight control over medical treatments and, therefore, costs. Two-thirds of the people who work at medium and large companies in the United States today are enrolled in managed care health systems rather than traditional health insurance. Health Maintenance Organizations are a form of managed care. While most HMOs were originally not-for-profit organizations, today most are for-profit. Insurance companies, traditional HMOs, and hospitals have taken the lead in developing managed care plans and offering them to employers, usually at a lower price than the employer would pay for traditional health insurance.

One of the motivations for developing HMOs and managed-care systems has been cost containment, and studies of HMOs indicate that they are less expensive than traditional health insurance (Brown et al., 1993). Those enrolled have lower hospitalization rates and undergo fewer unnecessary surgeries. These benefits may derive from the HMO's mode of health insurance premiums tend to be the same, irrespective of people's income.

Of course, you can't spend less on health care and cover more people, as the Canadians do, without some costs. One cost is that there are sometimes waits for hospital beds and some types of surgical procedures, especially nonemergency surgeries. In addition, some state-of-the-art technology, such as magnetic resonance imaging (MRI) machines, is not as widely available as in the United States. Yet another cost is the higher taxes to pay for the universal government-provided coverage.

These costs, however, don't seem too painful because Canadians still live longer and have less infant mortality than do citizens in the United States. In addition, health-care financing programs should be looked at in terms of *who* bears the costs since the costs of any program will have to be borne by someone. Currently, in the United States, those who benefit the most are the affluent, those fortunate enough to have good, employer-provided health insurance, and the elderly with Medicare. A shift to a Canadian-style system would mean redirecting some of the benefits from those groups to the poor, the unemployed, the underemployed, and other marginal groups. So, it comes down to *how*

health care will be rationed, not whether it will be rationed. Will some poor and unemployed be denied basic health care, such as prenatal care or frequent doctor visits for sick people? Or will some of the affluent be denied rapid access to elective surgeries or exotic technologies, such as coronary bypass surgery for elderly patients?

Sweden has a truly socialized health-care system, with the government nationalizing most health-care facilities and employing health-care workers. Health services are free to anyone who needs them, and little money changes hands between patient and health care providers. Taxes support the health-care system, and Sweden does have high taxes. However, the Swedes are also among the healthiest people in the world. They live three years longer than people in the United States and have half the infant mortality. Sweden is an interesting contrast with both Canada and the United States in that it runs a generally effective, socialized system of health care in a capitalist country.

Canada and Sweden suggest some of the ways in which health care can be made more available to all citizens, recognizing that there are advantages and disadvantages to each approach.

financing, which gives the HMO an incentive to economize, or from their greater utilization of preventive health care. However, it may also be that, when these studies were done, healthier people joined HMOs, which accounted for their lower costs. The managed care systems of today have not yet been extensively studied in terms of these outcomes.

However, managed care has been criticized on a number of grounds. It does nothing to help those without health insurance, and its oversight of medical decisions threatens the in-

dependence and autonomy of medical practitioners. That independence is also threatened because, in some communities, managed care enrolls so many people that insufficient business is left for physicians who are not part of the managed care system. To make a living, doctors have little choice other than to sign with the managed care system and accept whatever pay and working conditions are dictated. This means that control over medical decisions has shifted dramatically from the hands of many dispersed doctors and local hospitals to the hands of the directors of these huge corporate empires. And these health empires have been merging at a rapid rate, with the result that the system is moving toward an oligopoly (see Chapter 2). Some managed care systems have also been criticized for aggressively competing for contracts, offering employers low premiums, and pressuring doctors to limit medical procedures and hospitals to cut staff and costs in order to come in under cost and make a profit.

So, the kind of health care that more and more people receive today is determined by a contract negotiated between their employer and a national (or global) corporate health care system (Woolhandler and Himmelstein, 1994). HMOs and managed care systems are also competing for Medicare business and may try to encroach on Medicaid in the future. At this point, it is unclear what all the benefits and disadvantages of managed care are or whether the former outweigh the latter. For the moment, policy action seems focused more on managed care than on other alternatives such as national health insurance.

Social Control of Health Care

The health-care system in the United States is capable of delivering very high quality health care. However, as the increase in malpractice suits and other evidence suggests, incompetence and poor quality services do exist. Efforts to deal with this problem have focused on detecting such poor quality when it does occur and preventing incompetent practitioners from continuing to practice medicine. One major approach toward this has been peer review, in which physicians are watched by their peers and incompetence or poor clinical judgment brought to people's attention. This approach can work, especially in group medical practices where there are a number of partners in practice together who have an interest in seeing that good quality medical care is provided.

However, research shows that, although physicians are willing to criticize one another in informal discussion groups, they are much more reluctant to do so as part of formal proceedings where a physician might be sanctioned for poor procedure (Millman, 1977).

Another approach to the social control of health care is to create an oversight structure that is independent of physicians themselves. This was done in 1970 when the government established Professional Standards Review Organizations that were to evaluate the care given to patients of Medicare and Medicaid. Today, many insurance companies have their own quality review organizations to assess the care given to patients they insure, and managed care systems engage in aggressive oversight of physicians' medical decisions. A major motivation for some of this review is cost control, but it also focuses on the quality issue. Another step toward creating more independent oversight structures was taken in 1990 when the National Practitioner Data Bank began full operation (Harty, 1991). This data bank lists all medical malpractice awards or settlements against health-care professionals and any disciplinary proceedings, including denial of hospital privileges to physicians. Health-care facilities are required by law to consult the data bank when making decisions about medical privileges. The goal is to make it more difficult for health-care professionals to get privileges in another hospital or other health facility after getting into trouble somewhere else. However, access to the list is limited to doctors and hospitals; the general public cannot consult it when making decisions about choosing health-care providers.

New Health-Care Practitioners

Another approach to lowering costs and increasing accessibility to health care is to expand the types of providers giving primary care and reduce dependence on highly trained and expensive specialists. For example, a new specialty called "family practice" began in the 1960s and was intended to increase the ranks of primary-care physicians. After medical school and a year of internship, family practice physicians go through a residency program in which they receive advanced training in a broad range of medical specialties. This enables them to treat many health problems themselves and to refer more complex cases to the appropriate specialist.

Until recently, there has been a shortage of physicians in the United States, especially in rural and inner-city areas. To alleviate this problem, the government has supported the development of physician extenders, practitioners trained to perform some of the simple and routine health-care tasks traditionally accomplished by physicians. Nurse practitioners (NPs), for example, are registered nurses with advanced training that in some cases includes the master's degree in nursing. Physicians' assistants (PAs) have some medical training and can work only under the supervision of a physician. NPs and PAs do such things as conduct routine physical examinations, provide simple emergency and prenatal care, and the like. They normally work under the guidance of a physician and may serve as the patient's initial contact with the health-care system. In these ways, nurse practitioners and physicians' assistants provide medical doctors with more time to make complex diagnostic and treatment decisions. Studies show that NPs and PAs can do the things they are trained for as well as physicians can, and they can do them at substantially less cost (Robyn and Hadley, 1980).

Other alternatives exist to highly trained, specialized, and expensive physicians in the delivery of health-care services. Midwives, for example, deliver babies in many rural areas as safely as do physicians in hospitals, especially when life-saving technology is not immediately needed during the delivery (Durand, 1992). In fact, physicians tend to make more life-saving interventions that are not necessary, and this actually increases the risk to the mother and infant. Health policymakers had hoped that alternative healers, such as NPs, PAs, and midwives, would produce less reliance on traditionally trained physicians and thus make health care more accessible and less expensive. This may not be happening, however, to the extent that it could. One reason is that some doctors are reluctant to accept these personnel, believing that only physicians are competent to provide key medical services. In addition, a surplus of physicians is now emerging, at least in some specialties. As this occurs, physicians may come to see these other providers as competition for a shrinking health-care dollar. So the situation remains unsettled.

Self-Care and Changing Lifestyles

Social commentators such as Ivan Illich (1976) and Joseph Califano (1994) have severely criticized the health-care system in the United States for creating as much illness as it cures. It creates illness, for example, when a hospital patient gets an infection or suffers complications in surgery. This is called *iatrogenic illness:* illness or injury that arises while receiving treatment. However, a more subtle form of iatrogenesis can occur when the health-care system and cultural values convince people that they must rely on medical professionals to remain healthy or to overcome illness. People see themselves as virtually helpless without medical support. When these beliefs predominate, people tend not to do things that might enhance their health status. To overcome this problem, Illich and Califano argue, people should rely more on self-care and lifestyle change as a way to improved health.

We have seen that one of the major causes of many chronic illnesses is the lifestyle of many people today: they eat, drink, and smoke too much; they suffer periodic stresses of divorce or unemployment; and they pollute the environment. People can improve their

Society's health problems are exacerbated by increases in drug abuse (Chapter 10), because intravenous drug users are at a high risk of contracting the AIDS virus and spreading the epidemic by sharing dirty needles. The amount of illness and injury people have to cope with is also increased considerably by environmental pollution (Chapter 13), violent crime (Chapter 9), and violence, war, and terrorism (Chapter 14).

health status if they attack these problems. In fact, this whole text relates to health problems to the extent that improvements in the physical and social environment have beneficial health consequences.

Summary

1. From the functionalist perspective, illness threatens the survival of society because sick people cannot accomplish essential tasks. The health-care system becomes a problem when it fails to return sick people to normal social functioning.

2. From the conflict perspective, health and health care are scarce resources that interest groups compete over. The inequitable distribution of these resources will reflect the overall inequitable distribution of resources in society. This becomes a problem when some group feels that it is not receiving its fair share of these resources.

3. The interactionist perspective recognizes that illnesses involve a network of social meanings and social expectations. Health care can be considered a social problem when it produces stigmatized or devalued self-concepts among consumers of health care.

4. Diseases can be classified as acute or chronic, with the former contributing more to the death rate in preindustrial societies. In in-

dustrial societies, the death rate drops substantially and life expectancy increases. This is due largely to declines in infant and childhood mortality and changes in lifestyle.

5. The four major sociocultural factors that affect health and illness are socioeconomic status, gender, race, and lifestyle.

6. There are three positions regarding the nature of mental illness: The medical model views mental disorders as having the same basic nature as physical disorders; interactionists view mental illness as people's response to the expectations associated with being in the role of mentally ill; Szasz views mental illness as a problem people face when making choices about their lives.

7. Given the unreliability of psychiatric diagnoses, there is some debate over whether mental health professionals can accurately detect mental disorders. There has been a trend over the past thirty years toward a treatment approach known as community mental health, which involves delivering services to a whole community and providing treatment in the community.

8. There are a number of problems associated with health and illness in the United States: Health-care costs have been rising rapidly; some people do not have access to the health services that they need; the quality of some health services is low; there is substantial gender inequality in the health-care field.

9. Bioethics refers to the study of ethical questions that relate to the life and biological well-being of people. Three major issues in this realm are whether to prolong the life of someone who is terminally ill; how to distribute limited medical resources; and how extensively to engage in genetic screening.

10. A central issue in deciding how to attack problems in the health-care field is whether access to health care should be every citizen's right or whether it is a privilege of those who can afford to pay for it. Problems in this field have been attacked through publicly funded health insurance, the emergence of health maintenance organizations and managed care systems, the elaboration of societal control over health-care providers, the development of new health-care practitioner roles, and changes in people's lifestyles.

STUDY *Review*

Key Terms

acute disease
bioethics
chronic disease
crisis medicine
curative medicine
depersonalization
health maintenance
  organization
managed care
Medicaid

medical-industrial
  complex
Medicare
national health
  insurance
preventive medicine
primary deviance
secondary deviance
sick role
third-party medicine

Multiple-Choice Questions

1. The concept of the sick role is associated most clearly with which of the following perspectives?
   a. The functionalist perspective.
   b. The conflict perspective.
   c. The managed care perspective.
   d. The deinstitutionalization perspective.

2. Which of the following statements would be most consistent with the interactionist perspective on health care institutions?
   a. Health and health care are scarce resources, and interest groups compete with one another to gain a share of them.
   b. Disease is a threat to the social order because those who are ill are less able to make useful contributions to society.
   c. People attach social meanings to various illnesses and expect people to behave in conformity with those meanings.
   d. The health-care system involves an inequitable distribution of money, prestige, power, and other resources.

3. The most common cause of death in the United States today is:
   a. Acute disease.
   b. Cancer.
   c. Influenza and pneumonia.
   d. Heart disease.
   e. Cerebrovascular disease.

4. Which of the following statements is true regarding the impact of social factors on health?

a. Men live longer than women.
b. The poor have higher death rates than do the affluent.
c. When looking at African Americans and Anglo Americans in the same social class, no differences in disease or death rates are found.
d. All of the above are true.
e. Only b and c are true.

5. Which of the following is *not* a criticism offered in the text for the community mental health approach to treating mental illness?
   a. It relies too heavily on the medical model.
   b. It does not accomplish many of its innovative goals.
   c. It sometimes releases mental patients to community settings that are not therapeutic for the patients.
   d. Few coordinated follow-up services exist for ex-patients in the community.

6. Which of the following are factors that have contributed to rising health-care costs?
   a. A growing demand for health-care services.
   b. The growth of new diagnostic and treatment procedures.
   c. Weak economic competition in the health-care field.
   d. All of the above are such factors.
   e. Only b and c are such factors.

7. Concern over male dominance in the health field has been raised for all of the following reasons *except:*
   a. It restricts women's access to lucrative occupations.
   b. It may have had a detrimental effect on the health care received by women.
   c. It contributes to the problem of the medical-industrial complex.
   d. It may lead to unnecessary treatments for women's health problems.

8. Which principle of social justice is most commonly used in the United States to decide how to allocate medical treatments?
   a. Merit.
   b. Egalitarian.
   c. Utilitarian.

d. Compensatory justice.
e. Secondary deviance.

9. Which type of health-care financing arrangement pays for all of a person's health-care needs for a fixed premium each month or year?
   a. Medical-industrial complex.
   b. National health insurance.
   c. Third-party medicine.
   d. Socialized medicine.
   e. Health maintenance organizations.

10. Which of the following was *not* cited as a disadvantage in the Canadian health-care system in comparison with the United States?
    a. Higher taxes.
    b. Patients sometimes wait for hospital beds.
    c. Some advanced technology is not as widely available.
    d. Health-care costs are higher.

True/False Questions

1. Most of the women who contract AIDS do so because of sexual contact with another woman.
2. The transition from preindustrial to industrial societies has been associated with a shift from chronic diseases to acute diseases as the most serious health threat.
3. As far as offering people a longer life, changes in lifestyles associated with industrialization have been more important than modern medical treatments.
4. Modern medical practice in the United States is organized more around preventive medicine than around crisis medicine.
5. Thomas Scheff's view of mental illness as "deviance" is based on the interactionist perspective more than the other two sociological perspectives.
6. The medical model of mental illness assumes that the basic nature of mental disorders is directly analogous to physical ailments.
7. National health expenditures today constitute a smaller percentage of the gross national product than was the case fifty years ago.
8. According to the text, the two groups in the United States that have been the most severely

underserved by the health-care system are inner city residents and those residing in rural areas.

9. One of the problems with the Medicaid program is that eligibility levels are so high that many nonpoor families are eligible for it.

10. According to the text, the health-care system in Canada is an example of a truly socialized health-care system.

Fill-In Questions

1. According to the _____ perspective, the role of the health-care system in society is to return people to their normal social functioning.

2. The kinds of diseases that pose the most serious health threats to preindustrial societies

   are _____ .

3. If a person labeled mentally ill becomes dependent on others for assistance because those others will not let the person do things for him- or herself, this dependence would be an

   example of _____ deviance.

4. The _____ approach to treating mental disorders assumes that the whole community is the client of the mental health provider.

5. When a patient pays premiums to a fund and the hospital or doctor is paid from this fund for each treatment provided the patient,

   this is a system of _____ medicine.

6. The _____ is the phenomenon in the health-care field that is analogous to the military-industrial complex.

7. The health occupation that has the largest percentage of females employed in it is

   _____ .

8. Two of the bioethical issues discussed in the

   text are _____ and

   _____ .

9. Medicare and Medicaid amount to

   _____ for the elderly and the poor.

10. _____ is illness or injury that occurs while a person is receiving medical treatment.

Matching Questions

_____ 1. secondary deviance

_____ 2. heart disease

_____ 3. crisis medicine

_____ 4. deinstitutionalization

_____ 5. third party in health financing

_____ 6. compensatory justice

_____ 7. Medicare

_____ 8. Thomas Szasz

_____ 9. preferred provider programs

_____ 10. physicians' assistants

A. mental ilness as problems of living
B. curative medicine
C. health insurance company
D. government health insurance for the elderly
E. chronic disease
F. HMOs
G. shift in mental health treatment settings
H. self-fulfilling prophecy
I. physician extender
J. principle to allocate health resources

Essay Questions

1. What concepts and assumptions does the interactionist perspective use to analyze and understand social problems in the health-care field?

Use the example of AIDS to illustrate your answer.

2. Describe the impact of industrialization on human health and health-care institutions.
3. What is the impact of a person's socioeconomic status on that person's likelihood of getting sick or dying? Why does SES have this impact?
4. How do gender and race influence a person's chances of getting sick or dying? Why do these characteristics have this impact?
5. What is the community mental health approach to the treatment of mental illness? What are the advantages and disadvantages of it?
6. Explain why health-care costs have been rising in the United States over the past fifty years.
7. How much gender inequality exists in the health-care system in the United States? Why is it considered a problem?
8. Explain what problems are created by the privatization and corporatization of health care in the United States.
9. Raise some of the benefits and some of the disadvantages of organizing health care around national health insurance or around health maintenance organizations.
10. What new health-care practitioners have emerged in the past few decades? Why have they emerged and what benefits do they offer?

Answers

Multiple-Choice
1. A; **2.** C; **3.** D; **4.** B; **5.** A; **6.** D; **7.** C; **8.** B; **9.** E; **10.** D

True/False
1. F; **2.** F; **3.** T; **4.** F; **5.** T; **6.** T; **7.** F; **8.** T; **9.** F; **10.** F

Fill-In
1. functionalist
2. acute; or parasitic and infectious
3. secondary
4. community treatment; or community mental health
5. third-party

6. medical-industrial complex
7. dental hygienists
8. prolongation of life, whom to treat, and genetic screening
9. government health insurance
10. iatrogenic illness

Matching
1. H; **2.** E; **3.** B; **4.** G; **5.** C; **6.** J; **7.** D; **8.** A; **9.** F; **10.** I

For Further Reading

Ronald L. Braithewaite and Sandra E. Taylor, eds. *Health Issues in the Black Community.* San Francisco: Jossey-Bass, 1992. This comprehensive book of readings covers many of the health issues that confront the African American community in the United States and makes recommendations for how things could be improved.

Gena Corea. *The Invisible Epidemic: The Story of Women and AIDS.* New York: HarperCollins, 1992. This disturbing book documents how gender influences the provision of health care and the medical paternalism that pervades our health care system. It reports how medicine underreports and misdiagnoses AIDS in women, with tragic results.

Rael Jean Isaac and Virginia C. Armat. *Madness in the Streets: How Psychiatry and the Law Abandoned the Mentally Ill.* New York: The Free Press, 1990. In this book, a sociologist and a journalist combine forces to provide a history of the deinstitutionalization of the mentally ill and a strong criticism of the policy on the grounds that it really means doing little for the mentally ill.

John Mirowsky and Catherine E. Ross. *Social Causes of Psychological Distress.* New York: Aldine de Gruyter, 1989. These authors present convincing evidence to show that mental illness, especially depression and anxiety, are profoundly influenced by some very important social conditions.

Vicente Navarro. *Crisis, Health, and Medicine: A Social Critique.* New York: Tavistock, 1986. This is a sophisticated and fundamental criticism of our health-care system that sees the profit orientation as one of its key problems.

William A. Rushing. *The AIDS Epidemic: Social Problems of an Infectious Disease.* Boulder, Colo.: Westview Press, 1995. This is a recent and comprehensive assessment of AIDS in society, including social factors in the spread of the disease as well as how society has reacted to it.

Victor W. Sidel and Ruth Sidel. *A Healthy State: An International Perspective on the Crisis in United States Medical Care.* Rev. and Updated ed. New York: Pantheon Books, 1983. A very readable comparative perspective on our own health-care system. By looking at other countries and our own health-care system through history, the Sidels offer a unique view on problems we face today.

Paul Starr and Walter Zelman. *The Logic of Health-Care Reform.* Grand Rounds Press/Whittle Direct Books, 1992. Starr is a sociologist, and both authors were members of President Clinton's health-care team. They propose using global budgeting and managed competition to reform the health-care system.

Elliot S. Valenstein. *Great and Desperate Cures: The Rise and Decline of Psychosurgery and Other Radical Treatments for Mental Illness.* New York: Basic Books, 1986. This book provides a history of various somatic treatments for mental illness that have become popular at some time, especially psychosurgery. It is a cautionary tale, suggesting that the forces that make "desperate" cures popular tend to recur in new forms.

Howard Wolinsky and Tom Brune. *The Serpent on the Staff: The Unhealthy Politics of the American Medical Association.* New York: Putnam, 1994. While the authors do show a clear bias against the AMA, they also make many important points and provide useful information about the role of that organization in shaping health-care policy in the United States.

FIVE *CHAPTER Poverty*

When it comes to economic resources, the United States is truly a nation of contrasts. We are, few would dispute, among the wealthiest nations in the world. We produce more goods and services for each man, woman, and child than do most other nations. The signs of this opulence are not difficult to find. There are palatial mansions and fine automobiles. Expensive restaurants and clothing stores cater to the whims of those with large sums of money to spend. There are those who ski in the Alps, the Andes, and the Rockies—all in one season, if not one month. Most people in the United States, of course, do not share in such unbelievable wealth, but most are nevertheless quite comfortable materially, with spacious homes, more than adequate diets, and audiovisual entertainment centers in their homes.

Amidst this wealth, however, one in seven people lives below the officially defined poverty level. This includes one of every three African Americans and Hispanic Americans, and one of every four Mississippians (U.S. Bureau of the Census, 1994: 476–77). Despite the material opulence in the United States, the Annie E. Casey Foundation released a disturbing report in 1995 exposing the fact that one of every three children in Mississippi, Louisiana, and Washington, D.C. was growing up in poverty (Kids Count . . . , 1995). Despite the promises of virtually all politicians to ease the problem of poverty, the poverty rate has increased over the past twenty-five years. In fact, some people in the United States are so impoverished that they do not even have homes, living instead on sidewalks, in train stations, in steam tunnels, or in parks.

Why should we be concerned with the problem of poverty? Why not relegate the poor to the dustbin of underachievers who are reaping the just rewards of people who are unwilling to work or have little to offer society? There are a number of reasons why all people should pay attention to this problem. Some people are poor, as we will see, not through any fault of their own but because societal barriers make it difficult if not impossible for them to improve their circumstances. In short, there is a discrepancy between our ideal culture, which calls for equal opportunity for all, and our real culture, in which social forces prohibit some people from improving their lot. Beyond this, there are a number of practical concerns about the widespread existence of poverty: Unemployment, welfare, and other social costs of the poor are a substantial burden on all people; crime, illness, and other costly social conditions are linked with poverty; and poverty is a potential seedbed for social unrest and even outright rebellion that could threaten the political and social order.

This chapter first discusses what constitutes poverty in the United States and how extensive it is. Then it examines the social characteristics and circumstances of those who are poor. This examination is followed by an analysis of the causes of poverty using the sociological perspectives. The chapter concludes with a look at current and future policies that might alleviate the problem of poverty.

The Extent of Poverty

Defining Poverty

People often think of poverty in terms of deprivation—being short of food, for example, or not having enough money to buy adequate clothing. This is somewhat misleading, however. There have been many societies in which people, by our standards today, were severely deprived, yet poverty did not really exist. The reason is that virtually everyone was so deprived. In societies in which there was little accumulation of food or material resources, everyone had pretty much the same access to the resources available. When a surplus of resources exists, however, it is possible for some people to accumulate more than others. There then emerges a system of **social stratification,** *the ranking of people into a hierarchy in which the resources considered valuable by society are unequally distributed.* With this development, people could be differentiated from one another based on how much of those valuable resources they possessed. Those with the least could be defined as "poor": so deficient in resources that they could not maintain a lifestyle considered minimally acceptable in that society. Thus, **poverty** *does not refer to a deprivation of resources alone but to an uneven distribution of the resources available.*

Defining poverty becomes even more complex, however, when we try to specify what a "minimally acceptable lifestyle" is. In fact, there is probably no completely satisfactory definition of poverty. Three such definitions are widely used today (Ruggles, 1990).

Absolute Deprivation Some definitions of poverty attempt to establish an economic level below which people are unable to achieve the basic necessities of life. But what are the "necessities" of life? A reliable automobile? A juicy

Myth: The poor are a drain on the public treasury that affluent citizens have to support out of their hard-earned dollars.

FACT: Both the poor and the affluent in the United States are a drain on the treasury, and both pay to support it. While some poor people receive welfare and other government assistance, the affluent receive government handouts such as loans for college students, price-support payments to farmers, and tax deductions for meals and entertainment expenses connected with business. If tax deductions for home mortgage interest are considered to be a government housing subsidy, then families earning more than $50,000 per year receive more than half of all such federal subsidies. In addition, when all taxes—on income, sales, investments, and so on—are looked at, there is considerable debate over whether the affluent or the working poor pay a larger percentage of their income in taxes. So, the similarity is that both the affluent and the poor receive public assistance in the United States; the difference is that the poor are labeled disreputable and stigmatized for doing so.

Myth: Receiving welfare payments encourages women to have more children, to leave their husbands, and to avoid work.

FACT: While these beliefs about the negative effects of welfare are strongly entrenched in the public mind, the best social research on the topic suggests that most are wrong. Women on welfare actually have a lower birthrate than non-welfare women of equivalent age and social standing. Welfare also has little effect on whether women marry or divorce. Life on welfare is a difficult struggle, both physically and psychologically, and few people seek it out voluntarily. The one part of the myth that does hold some truth is the work disincentive: Welfare does encourage people to avoid work but for reasons different from what is often thought. Welfare recipients avoid work because much of what they earn is lost due to reduced welfare benefits and lost government health insurance. So, they simply do not get ahead by working in many cases. Given these disincentives to work, it is surprising that as many welfare recipients do leave welfare for work.

steak? A summer vacation at the beach? While recognizing that "necessities" is a somewhat relative term, we can nonetheless define it in terms of a diet, clothing, housing, medical care, and the like that will enable people to remain healthy and productive. Nutritionists, for example, can tell us what constitutes a minimally adequate diet. You do not need a steak to maintain health, but the human body does need a certain amount of protein, vitamins, and minerals from some food sources. Likewise, a house without indoor plumbing might be viewed as unacceptable in modern times because of the health hazard it creates. The point of this **absolute definition of poverty** is that *it establishes a fixed economic level below which people are considered poor, and this level does not necessarily change as society on the whole becomes more or less affluent.*

Government programs for the poor in the United States are based on this absolute definition of poverty. For such programs, a fixed annual income cutoff point is established below which people will be unable to purchase what are considered the necessities of life. In the 1960s, Mollie Orshansky, then a social research analyst with the Social Security Administration, developed an ingenious and somewhat objective technique for establishing the poverty level, a technique still in use today (Ruggles, 1990). It is based on how much it costs to buy a nutritionally adequate diet. Once the amount of money necessary for this has been established, it is multiplied by three to arrive at the poverty income, based on the fact that the average family in the United States spends one-third of its income on food. Thus, three times the cost of food is assumed to provide adequate income for food, housing, medical care, and the other necessities of life. Actually, the poverty level is a series of income cutoffs based on factors that can increase a family's cost of living, such as the size of the family, the number of children present, and the cost of living in the community where the family resides.

Relative Deprivation   We pointed out earlier that poverty is not just the absence of resources; it also involves the inequitable distribution of resources. According to the **relative definition of poverty,** *people are poor relative to some standard, and that standard is partially shaped by the lifestyles of other citizens.* A lack of indoor plumbing is considered a sign of poverty today, whereas a century ago that was the norm for many people. But people usually compare themselves with their contemporaries, not their predecessors. People look around and see what most others have and assess their own lives based on that comparison. To take this relative nature of poverty into account, one suggestion might be to define the poor as those families who are on the lowest end of the income scale, say the 15 percent of the people with the lowest income. Or, the poor may be defined as people in those families with incomes less than one-third of the median family income in the United States. In 1992, this was

$10,000 and included about 15 percent of the populace. Such a definition means that poverty would always exist, irrespective of how affluent society became. The poor would be those who share least in such affluence. In fact, using the relative definition, poverty could be eliminated only if the inequitable distribution of resources was eliminated.

Cultural Definitions   Absolute and relative approaches to poverty define it as the economic resources necessary to achieve a certain lifestyle. However, some have argued that poverty is a cultural as well as an economic condition (Hayes, 1970). The **cultural definition of poverty** *views poverty not only in terms of how many resources people have, but also in terms of why they have failed to achieve a higher economic level.* For example, some people are poor because they have no skills that would enable them to get a job. Others are poor because they have young children at home and cannot afford day care while they work. Still others are poor because they have chosen to go to college and endure temporary low income in order to enhance their earning power in the future.

Using this cultural definition of poverty, the poor are identified as those who are permanently and unwillingly poor. These are people who are likely to remain poor for a long time, possibly generations, and it is toward them that poverty programs should be directed. This would probably include most of the people who are defined as poor when using purely economic criteria, but it would exclude people such as college students who temporarily and willingly choose poverty. The rationale for this is that the real problem of poverty lies with the chronic long-term poor. College students who are poor, although suffering some personal troubles, are not really a societal problem because they will likely improve their circumstances in a relatively brief period. This cultural definition of poverty avoids the rigidities of strict economic definitions and enables us to direct resources toward the entrenched problem of poverty.

Which one of the above definitions of poverty is used, of course, depends on people's values. The absolute definition is used in many social policy decisions today, and it reflects widely held values in the United States regarding the role of the government in poverty problems. It especially reflects the belief of many that the government should provide equal opportunities for people to achieve resources rather than ensure an equitable distribution of those resources. In this view, the government's role is to provide people with the minimum necessary resources that will enable them to achieve on their own. Whether people then realize such achievement is regarded by many as a personal matter.

The Extent of Poverty in the United States

The official poverty level in the United States, then, is based on the absolute definition of poverty. In 1993, a nonfarm family of four people with an annual income of less than $14,763 was considered by the government to be poor (see Table 5.1). This meant that more than thirty-nine million people in the United States —approximately one out of every seven citizens—were living in poverty. Throughout the

TABLE 5.1 Persons Below Poverty Level: 1960–1993.

| Year | Persons Below Poverty Level | | Average Poverty Income Cutoffs for Nonfarm Family of Four | Median Family Income of all Families |
	Number (millions)	Percentage of Total Population		
1960	39.9	22.2	$3,022	$5,620
1966	28.2	17.3	3,223	6,957
1970	25.4	12.6	3,968	9,867
1975	25.9	12.3	5,500	13,719
1980	29.3	13.0	8,414	21,023
1981	31.8	14.0	9,287	22,388
1982	34.4	15.0	9,862	23,433
1983	35.5	15.3	10,178	24,549
1984	33.7	14.4	10,609	26,433
1985	33.1	14.0	10,989	27,735
1986	32.4	13.6	11,203	29,458
1987	32.5	13.5	11,611	30,853
1988	31.7	13.0	12,092	32,191
1989	31.5	12.8	12,675	34,213
1990	33.6	13.5	13,359	35,353
1991	35.7	14.2	13,924	35,939
1993	39.3	15.1	14,763	36,959

Source: U.S. Bureau of the Census, *Statistical Abstract of the United States, 1994* (Washington, D.C.: U.S. Government Printing Office, 1995), pp. 474, 480.

1980s, the poverty rate remained considerably higher than it had been in the 1970s. In 1993, the poverty rate was 15.1 percent—one of the highest rates since the mid-1960s, and more people were poor in 1993 than in any year since the 1960s. Furthermore, the gap between the nonpoor and the poor has been growing as the median family income has increased at a faster rate than the poverty cutoff. The poverty cutoff income was 54 percent of median family income in 1960, whereas it was 39 percent in 1993 (see Figure 5.1). So, using the relative definition of poverty, the poor are worse off today than thirty years ago.

Another way to assess the status of the poor relative to an earlier time is to look at what per-

FIGURE 5.1 Comparison of Median Family Income and Official Poverty Cutoff for a Family of Four, 1960–1993. *Source:* U.S. Bureau of the Census, *Statistical Abstract of the United States, 1995* (Washington, D.C.: U.S. Government Printing Office, 1995), pp. 472, 480.

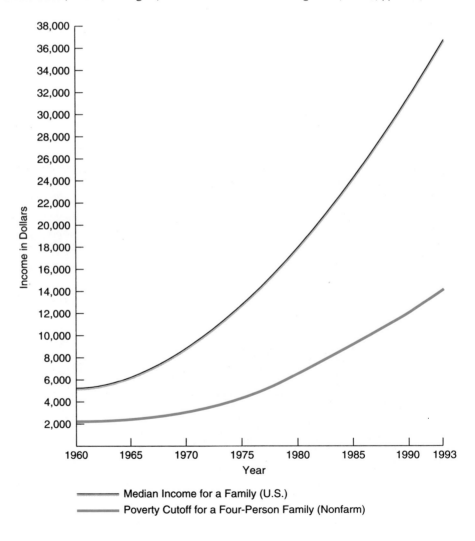

Median Income for a Family (U.S.)
Poverty Cutoff for a Four-Person Family (Nonfarm)

centage of the total income in the United States goes to poor families. Once again, the poor seem worse off today. As Figure 5.2 shows, the percentage of income going to the poorest families has declined since the 1960s. Today, the poorest 20 percent of families receives less than 5 percent of the total income while the wealthiest 20 percent receives over 46 percent. Furthermore, these disparities have increased over the past three decades. In fact, the only group who saw their share of the total income increase significantly is the wealthiest 20 percent of families. The maldistribution of resources is even more striking when one looks at wealth (earned income plus stocks, savings, equity in a home, and other economic resources) rather than just income. The top 20 percent of U.S. households possess 80 percent of the total

wealth (Wolff, 1995). This topic has been hotly debated, but most analysts agree with what Figure 5.2 suggests: in the last 30 years in the United States, the rich have gotten richer and the poor have gotten poorer (Danziger and Gottschalk, 1993). Also, poverty seems to have become more chronic, with people who fall into poverty today remaining poor for longer periods than was true in the 1960s and 1970s (Devine, Plunkett, and Wright, 1992). As if all this were not enough, poverty also seems to have become more dysfunctional for the individual and society, with the drug epidemic and the growth in homelessness hindering individual efforts to overcome poverty and confronting society with serious challenges.

The absolute approach to defining poverty provided by the Orshansky poverty cutoffs is

FIGURE 5.2   Percent Distribution of Aggregate Income to Families from the Poorest 20 Percent to the Richest 5 Percent, 1965–1993. *Source:* U.S. Bureau of the Census, *Statistical Abstract of the United States, 1978* (Washington, D.C.: U.S. Government Printing Office, 1978), p. 455; U.S. Bureau of the Census, *Statistical Abstract of the United States, 1995* (Washington, D.C.: U.S. Government Printing Office, 1995), p. 475.

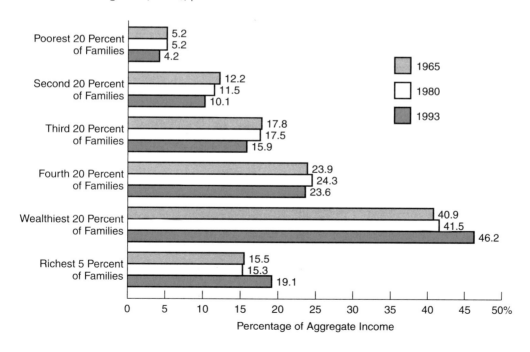

used by the government for making social policy decisions, such as who is eligible for various government programs. These cutoffs, however, do have flaws as an accurate measure of people's economic circumstances. One such flaw is that the assumptions for establishing the poverty thresholds were defined in the 1950s and 1960s based on family consumption patterns and basic needs of that era, and things have changed since then. For example, the poverty index relies on the purchase of food in determining the poverty level. However, for some poor people, especially in urban areas, other expenses such as housing can consume a larger share of the family income than they do for the average family in the United States. In earlier decades, families spent 34 percent of their income on housing, whereas today it is more like 42 percent. Despite changes such as these, the poverty cutoffs are still based on the old assumptions. One expert estimates that today's poverty line would have to be 50 percent higher to be comparable, in terms of the ability to buy food and other basic needs, to the standard established in 1963 (Ruggles, 1990). This means that a family of four in 1993 would really need $21,500 to maintain the same standard of living as a poverty-level family in the 1960s. If this were the poverty cutoff in 1993, the poverty rate would be between 20 percent and 25 percent instead of 14 percent.

A Global View of Poverty

By the standards of many nations around the world, many poor in the United States would be considered reasonably well off. Some people in other nations live in absolute poverty that is so stark and dehumanizing that it is difficult for people in the United States to imagine. For these people, survival itself is a struggle. Few, if any, of the poor in the United States would fall into this category. In nations such as Bangladesh and Somalia, as many as 75 percent of the people may live in absolute poverty; in El Salvador, it is nineteen percent, and in Brazil

and Venezuela, over five percent (Kurian, 1984). Compared to these nations, the United States is well off. However, as Figure 5.3 demonstrates, it is not so well off when compared to other industrial nations. In that comparison, U.S. poverty rates tend to be significantly higher, especially among children.

Figure 5.2 shows a very lopsided distribution of wealth in the United States. Are we out of line in this regard in comparison to other nations? It depends on who we compare ourselves to (World Bank, 1989; Wolff, 1995). In many less developed countries around the world—such as Kenya, Peru, Brazil, and Panama—the wealthiest 20 percent of the families nab 60 percent or more of the family income. In Brazil and Panama, the poorest 20 percent of the families receive only 2 percent of annual income—a very small share indeed! So, the United States has a more equitable distribution of wealth than do these nations. In comparison to other wealthy nations in the world, however, the U.S. income distribution is somewhat lopsided. In only three of the twenty wealthiest nations do the top 20 percent of the families receive as large a share of income as in the United States; in none of these twenty nations does the bottom fifth receive as small a share as in the United States. For example, the wealthiest 1 percent of households in the United States possess nearly 40 percent of the nation's wealth. By contrast, the wealthiest one percent of households in Britain possess only 18 percent of that nation's wealth. In addition, trends of the past century have produced higher levels of inequality in the United States while the trend in Britain has been toward reducing levels of inequality.

Who Are the Poor?

A few years ago, a popular bumper sticker read: "I fight poverty . . . I work!" Implied in this is a characterization of the poor as lazy and somewhat disreputable people who are poor be-

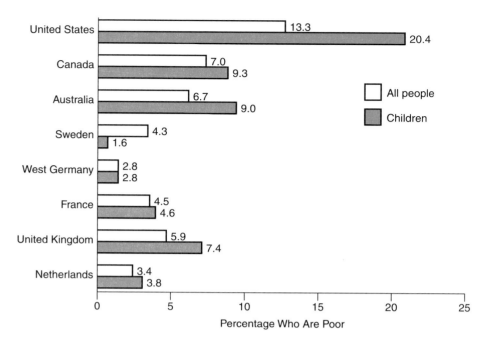

FIGURE 5.3 Poverty Rates in Selected Industrial Countries, mid-1980s. *Source:* Reprinted with permission of M.E. Sharpe, Inc., Publisher, 80 Business Park Drive, Armonk, New York, 10504, from *Challenge*, Vol. 35, January/February 1992, p. 31.

cause of their own unwillingness to work for a living. This highly stigmatizing view of the poor is quite popular in the United States, where a majority believes that a willingness to work is the primary ingredient necessary to achieve at least a modest degree of success (Smith and Stone, 1989). Assessing the veracity of these beliefs is central to developing a social policy for the United States regarding poverty. A first step in this direction is understanding who the poor people are in this country.

Social Characteristics

Racial and Ethnic Minorities   Contrary to what many people believe, most of the poor in the United States—66.5 percent—are white (see Figure 5.4 on p. 174). Looking at each racial group separately, however, nonwhites are more likely to be poor than are whites. Although 33.3 percent

of African Americans and 29.3 percent of Hispanic Americans are below the poverty cutoff, only 11.6 percent of whites are at that income level (see Figure 5.5 on p. 174). About 23 percent of American Indians have incomes below the official poverty level. Asian Americans as a group also have higher levels of poverty than whites—17.9 percent of Asian-American families (Lee, 1994). Some groups have quite high poverty levels, with 61.5 percent of all first-generation Laotian and Cambodian families living in poverty, as well as 25 percent of all first-generation Vietnamese families. For Asian Americans, poverty is closely linked with the recency of their immigration experience. So although nonwhite families constitute a relatively small proportion of our populace, they contribute disproportionately to the ranks of the poor.

The reasons for these racial and ethnic differences are complex and will be dealt with in

RACE

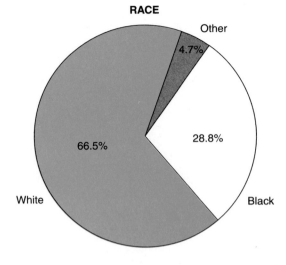

Other 4.7%

28.8%

66.5%

White

Black

AGE

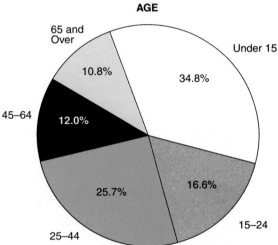

65 and Over 10.8%

Under 15 34.8%

45–64 12.0%

25.7%

16.6%

25–44

15–24

FIGURE 5.4 People Living Below the Poverty Level by Race and Age, as a Percentage of All Poor People, 1992. *Source:* U.S. Bureau of the Census, Current Population Reports, Series P-60, No. 185, *Poverty in the United States, 1992* (Washington, D.C.: U.S. Government Printing Office, 1993), p. xi, i.

families to advance from poverty. Hispanics, especially those of Mexican and Puerto Rican ancestry, have also experienced a great deal of discrimination in their efforts to establish a niche in the United States. American Indians have confronted some unique problems in the form of the reservation system and the Bureau of Indian Affairs (BIA), which were intended to work for the benefit of Indians but seem instead to have worked to their disadvantage.

Children Over one-third of the poor are children under the age of fifteen, and more than half of these children live in single-parent families headed by women. Almost one-half of all black children and more than one-third of all Hispanic children live in poverty, which will

FIGURE 5.5 Percentage of People in Various Groups Below the Poverty Level, 1992. *Source:* U.S. Bureau of the Census, Current Population Reports, Series P-60, No. 185, *Poverty in the United States, 1992* (Washington, D.C.: U.S. Government Printing Office, 1993), pp. 1–14.

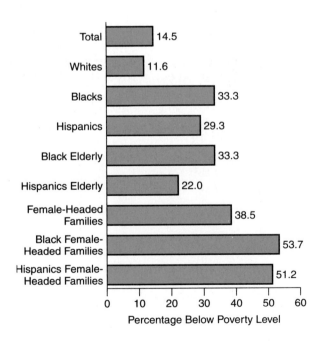

Group	Percentage Below Poverty Level
Total	14.5
Whites	11.6
Blacks	33.3
Hispanics	29.3
Black Elderly	33.3
Hispanics Elderly	22.0
Female-Headed Families	38.5
Black Female-Headed Families	53.7
Hispanics Female-Headed Families	51.2

more detail later in this chapter and in Chapter 6. However, a key factor in all cases has been oppression and discrimination. African Americans have felt the brunt of slavery and, after the abolition of slavery, decades of severe oppression during which it was difficult for black make it more difficult for the next generation of racial and ethnic minorities to lift themselves out of poverty (see Figures 5.4, 5.5, and 5.6). Children living in large families are especially likely to live in poverty. This is so because economic resources must be spread more thinly in a large family and because the mother is less able to work outside the home when she has many children. The large number of children among the poor serves to deflate the belief that poverty derives from a lack of initiative because we presume that children are not responsible for supporting themselves. This tendency toward poverty shows no sign of ceasing for the youngest of the U.S. citizenry. Poverty rates among children have remained unchanged or increased slightly since the late 1960s (Duncan and Rodgers, 1991). A major reason for the persistently high poverty among children is changes in the family structure in the United States—higher divorce rates, more children born to unmarried women, and more female-headed families (Eggebeen and Lichter, 1991). All this means that children today are more likely to live in a single-parent household headed by a woman. In 1992, 54 percent of children living in such families were poor—more than five times the rate for children in two-parent households (see Figure 5.6). In addition, the parents of poor children today are younger—the teenage pregnancy rate is far higher than that in most other industrial nations (see Chapter 3). Finally, young workers today earn relatively less than did young workers in the past. The consequence of all this is that poor children today have fewer resources available to them and live in worse circumstances than did poor children thirty years ago.

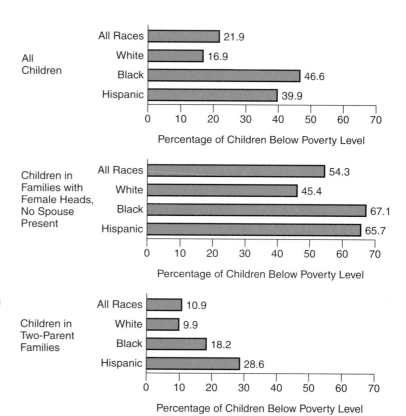

FIGURE 5.6 Percentage of Children Younger Than 18 Living Below the Poverty Level, 1992. *Source:* U.S. Bureau of the Census, Current Population Reports, Series P-60, No. 185, *Poverty in the United States, 1992* (Washington, D.C.: U.S. Government Printing Office, 1993), pp. 1–14.

The Elderly Although poverty among the elderly is relatively low, it is higher than among non-elderly adult Americans, and the figure is much higher for African-American, Hispanic-American, and female elderly. The special problems of the elderly are dealt with in more detail in Chapter 8.

Women A development that has been viewed with some alarm in recent years is what has been labeled the "feminization of poverty," referring to the growing number of women among the poor. Despite the increasing emphasis on equality between the sexes in recent years, women, especially those who head their own households, have made little progress. In 1992, for example, 14.5 percent of all people lived below the poverty level, whereas in single-parent families headed by a woman it was 38.5 percent. Things may actually be getting worse in some respects: In 1959, 23 percent of all families in poverty were headed by women; by 1992, this figure had grown to 53 percent. However, the poverty rate in single-parent female-headed families is now lower than it was in 1959

but a little higher than it was in the late 1970s (see Figure 5.7). As is discussed in Chapter 3, the growth in single-parent female-headed families is due to changes in the structure of the family in the United States which can be traced back to at least the 1930s (Barrington and Conrad, 1994). Basically the family has gotten smaller, due to divorce, the decline in extended families, and increasing childbearing by single women. Because of global economic competition and other factors discussed in Chapter 2, young men today are over twice as likely to earn poverty-level wages compared to 30 years ago and thus be less able to support a wife or children. For this and other reasons, husbands, grandmothers, unmarried aunts, and other unattached females have departed from the family, leaving women alone to raise their children. These women alone offer their families substantially less economic support than do women who also have an economically productive husband, grandmother, or aunt living in the family and helping out. In addition, the incomes of women still lag far behind those of men (a topic discussed in more detail in Chap-

FIGURE 5.7 Poverty Rate of Single-Parent Families Headed by a Woman, 1959–1992. *Source:* U.S. Bureau of the Census, Current Population Reports, Series P-60, No. 185, *Poverty in the United States, 1992* (Washington, D.C.: U.S. Government Printing Office, 1993), p. xvi.

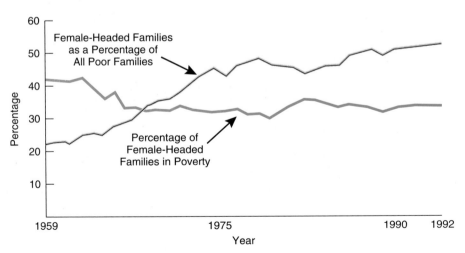

ter 7). Evidence indicates that growing up in a female-headed family increases the risk that children will still be poor as adults (McLanahan and Sandefur, 1994). However, this is probably caused primarily by the decreased availability of economic and other resources in such families rather than to the absence of a father figure.

Central-City and Rural Dwellers   Poverty tends to be concentrated in certain places in our country, particularly in the centers of our cities and in rural areas. Almost 40 percent of the poor live in central-city areas, places with high unemployment and few places to find work (U.S. Bureau of the Census, 1991a: 54). As we will see in Chapter 12, businesses and industries have left the cities for the suburbs in large numbers, leaving fewer jobs behind. The jobs that remain tend to be white-collar occupations requiring some college education, which the poor are unlikely to have. This is particularly true of the older cities of the Northeast and Midwest.

One-quarter of the poor live outside metropolitan areas (Duncan, 1992). Pockets of poverty can be found in rural parts of the South, Southwest, the Ozarks, Appalachia, and the Upper Great Lakes region. Blacks living in farming communities are especially hard hit by poverty. Small plots of land and poor soil make for a meager existence for these farmers. In nonfarming rural areas, people do a variety of things to survive, such as mining and lumbering. The

This homeless mother and her children, camping under a freeway bridge in Oregon, had a home until the mother lost her job. They illustrate the fact that many of the poor are children living in single-parent families headed by women who can't find work to support their families.

Many of the poor are disabled, making it difficult, and in some cases impossible, for them to support themselves entirely through work.

rural poor face problems similar to but more intense than their central-city counterparts. Employment opportunities are scarce and transportation is often a costly hindrance. Unemployment is high and the jobs that can be found are likely to be low paying.

The Disabled   Poverty is often associated with physical disability. Twenty percent of the poor are too physically disabled to work and another 8 percent have partial disabilities that prohibit them from doing the work that they did before becoming disabled. Blacks, Hispanics, and people over the age of forty-five are most likely to

have such disabilities. Four and a half million people receive medical assistance from Medicaid because they are blind or totally disabled. At least 80 percent of Medicaid expenditures go to the elderly, the disabled, or children (U.S. Bureau of the Census, 1994: 116). These figures lead us once again to recognize that poverty is often not a problem of failed ambition or motivation but rather one of people being victimized by social or personal tragedy.

Social Circumstances

There is considerable mythology surrounding the circumstances under which poor people live. Because most poor are "invisible" or conveniently out of sight to most people in the United States, it is easy to believe that the poor lead a leisurely, if spartan, lifestyle while feeding at the public trough (Harrington, 1984). Reality is actually quite different from this.

The Working Poor   Despite common misconceptions, many adults below the official poverty level actually work for a living. Approximately 60 percent of poor families earn wages from work, with about 20 percent having at least one member working year-round full-time (U.S. Bureau of the Census, 1991a: 127). Only one-third of poor families receive cash public assistance income, although others receive such government assistance as unemployment benefits, Social Security payments, disability assistance, government pensions, and the like. Fully one-quarter of all poor families receive no noncash benefits, such as food stamps or Medicaid, from the government (U.S. Bureau of the Census, 1994: 374). So, income earned from work is essential for many poor families to support themselves.

Once again, the picture of the poor presented by this research does not support the image that many people have. The poor are not, in general, people who are able but unwilling to support themselves, although some such people might be found. Rather, they are people who are mostly unable to work because of age or disability or who work at low-paying or part-time jobs with wages insufficient to lift them out of poverty (Rank, 1994). The number of poor males who are able to work but do not is low. There are more able-bodied poor women who do not work, but this is most often because they have young children at home to care for, lack the job skills to find a decent job, and would lose government health insurance for their children if they worked.

The Illiterate In 1985, education critic Jonathan Kozol published a book titled *Illiterate America,* wherein he reports that sixty million Americans—more than one-third of the entire adult population of the United States—are illiterate. Kozol calculates that

> Twenty-five million American adults cannot read the poison warnings on a can of pesticide, a letter from their child's teacher, or the front page of a daily paper. An additional 35 million read only at a level which is less than equal to the full survival needs of our society. (Kozol, 1985: 12)

According to Kozol, 16 percent of white adults, 44 percent of blacks, and 56 percent of Hispanic citizens are functional or marginal illiterates. One-half of the heads of households classified below the poverty level cannot read an eighth-grade book, and more than one-third of mothers who receive support from welfare are functionally illiterate. There can be no question that the problems of illiteracy and poverty are inextricably linked. In the 1970s, Kozol estimates, $6 billion yearly went to child welfare costs and unemployment compensation, because illiterate adults were unable to perform at standards necessary for available employment.

The Unemployed About 48 percent of the householders in poverty-level families do not work; 57 percent of householders in female-headed households do not work (U.S. Bureau of the Census, 1991a: 103, 127). Fifty percent of the poor who do not work are either ill, disabled, or retired or have looked for but could not find work; another 32 percent were prevented from working by child-rearing or other family obligations. Others have given up on trying to find work after years with no success. The official unemployment rate in 1993 was 6.7 percent, which translates into 8.7 million people who are looking for work but cannot find it. Many of these people are among the poor.

An unemployment rate of 7 percent or more means that people who are poor will find it exceedingly difficult to improve their lot by finding well-paying jobs. The unemployed receive unemployment benefits for a time, but these are exhausted eventually. When they do end, the unemployed person may still have payments to make on a home mortgage or an automobile loan. Some of the unemployed become eligible for welfare assistance when unemployment benefits end, but not all unemployed are eligible for welfare. To be eligible, people may have to sell their homes and use up most of their savings. Temporary unemployment, then, could devastate a family that had worked and accumulated resources over the years.

As we move further into a postindustrial social organization, there will be larger numbers of industrial workers who are "displaced" by the movement from an industrial to an information-based society (see Chapter 2). In addition, technological innovations such as computerization and robotization are responsible for the displacement of previously employed workers, and many U.S. jobs have been exported overseas where labor and other costs are lower. As a consequence, employment in some industries declined substantially in the 1980s and 1990s: Employment in the steel industry dropped from almost six hundred thousand in the late 1970s to three hundred thousand by the end of the 1980s; during the same period, the textile industry experienced a decline from nine hundred thousand workers to seven hundred thousand (Aronowitz and DiFazio, 1994). Although there has been job growth in other segments of the

This is a shelter in New York City for homeless families. On any given night in the United States, forty percent of the homeless are families, and as many as fifty thousand are children.

economy, it has tended to be in service occupations, which pay considerably less and have fewer employee benefits, such as retirement plans.

The Homeless   Some of the poor are homeless, with no permanent residence. The most careful estimates by sociologists are that as many as four hundred thousand Americans may be homeless on any given night, with as many as fifty thousand of them being children (Jencks, 1994). Other estimates are higher, but it is a difficult thing to measure with any precision. A more disturbing fact is that 40 percent of the homeless are families—parents and children out on the street—double the percentage of a decade ago. It is a disturbing problem whose

causes can be found in recent social trends, especially the decline in the number of industrial jobs that pay a living wage (see Chapter 2), the flight of jobs from the cities where poor people live, the contraction of social welfare, increases in poverty, and the decline in the amount of low-income housing available (Shinn and Gillespie, 1994; Schutt, 1990). These factors coming together mean that more people are wandering the countryside, searching for a job and living out of their car or truck. Some sleep on park benches, in subway stations, or in steam tunnels. Some eventually land a job and find housing, but others live on the streets for years. Homelessness is also linked with the trends in our health-care institutions discussed in Chapter 4: At least one-quarter of the homeless are mentally ill people who were released from mental hospitals because of the process known as "deinstitutionalization," the emphasis on treatment in the community rather than in institutions. As we saw, many of these former mental patients receive little in the way of psychological or financial assistance.

The Causes of Poverty

Programs intended to alleviate poverty must rest on a clear understanding of its causes, and those causes are complex. People often focus on the weaknesses or failures of individuals as the causes of poverty. He is poor, people say, because he is unwilling to work, or she is poor because she had too many children and did not pursue her education. Although there may be some truth to these statements in particular cases, they ignore the part that societal factors play in generating widespread poverty. The three sociological perspectives remedy this by focusing on various elements of the structure of our society that contribute to producing poverty. It is these structures that social policy makes an effort to change in order to alleviate poverty.

The Functionalist Perspective

The Stratification System
Functionalists argue that stratification exists because it makes some useful contribution to the ongoing maintenance of society. According to sociologists Kingsley Davis and Wilbert Moore (1945), for instance, all societies must ensure that people will fill essential positions and perform important tasks. Somebody must produce food, build shelter, heal the sick, and raise the young. If these tasks are not accomplished, society cannot survive. However, some positions and tasks are more important or more difficult than others. For example, physicians are more crucial than janitors, and it takes more skill to be a judge than an assembly line worker. Some positions call for scarce natural talents or qualities, whereas others require extensive and difficult training. The stratification system serves to motivate people to occupy and work hard at all of these essential positions. People who fill the more difficult or more essential tasks are given greater rewards—both economic and social—as a consequence.

Thus, the stratification system in society is an essential mechanism for differentially allocating rewards in order to motivate people to perform socially useful tasks. Furthermore, according to the functionalist view, people who do not perform useful tasks should receive fewer rewards. Poverty, then, is society's mechanism to discourage people from neglecting their social duties. If those who do not work were to receive the same rewards as those who do, then many people would choose not to work and society might be threatened.

There has been an ongoing debate over Davis and Moore's functionalist approach to poverty: Are rewards really related to the importance of a position or to the scarcity of qualified personnel to fill it? There does appear to be a relationship between the contributions that people make to society and the rewards they receive (Cullen and Novick, 1979). However, some studies have found that the importance of positions is unrelated to the rewards people receive (Wanner and Lewis, 1978). In addition, a study of public school teachers over a forty-year span showed little support for the functionalist prediction that incomes of teachers would be higher when the supply of teachers was scarce (Betz, Davis, and Miller, 1978). Thus, although these functionalist factors may play a part in causing poverty, there are clearly many exceptions in which people receive low rewards for some other reason. Even when the functionalist argument is true, it cannot account for the vast disparities between the well-to-do and the poor. Clearly, some people earn far more than would seem warranted by their contribution to society and others make far less. When the link between what a person does and what he or she receives becomes vague or broken entirely, then social disorganization can result. People no longer believe that work will be rewarded, and the stratification system no longer serves as the motivation that it is intended to be. In addition, if people are prevented from making a contribution—because of discrimination in the job market, for example—then a similar sense of disorganization can occur.

The Economy According to the functionalist perspective, society is made up of many interrelated and interdependent parts, and a change in one part can have implications for the other parts. In the realm of poverty, normal and sometimes desirable changes in the economy can affect the level of poverty. One of these changes has to do with inflation. Many economists believe that unemployment is related to inflation. As unemployment drops, more people are working and have money to buy things. This demand for goods causes prices to rise, producing inflation. To reduce inflation, then, it may be necessary at times to let unemployment increase. This was the policy followed by the Reagan administration in the 1980s. Inflation dropped, but unemployment and poverty increased (see Table 5.1). In this view, then, a certain amount of poverty is an unfortunate side effect of maintaining other elements of the economy.

Another important source of economic change has been technological innovation, which has brought such improvements as automation. But automation can throw people out of work and reduce the number of jobs in the economy, contributing to the problem of poverty. The automobile industry, for example, has automated in response to foreign competition. As a consequence, many of the auto workers laid off during the recessions of the 1980s and 1990s will never be called back to work in the auto plants. Many of these workers will find work elsewhere, but in the interim their lives have been dramatically dislocated. Because

such automation is constantly replacing workers somewhere in the economy, it always contributes to the level of unemployment and poverty.

In addition to automation, another type of economic change is the rise and decline of various economic sectors. The ghost towns in California attest to the once-booming and now largely dead gold mining in that state. For a good part of this century, heavy industries such as steel and automobile manufacturing were booming. In the past few decades, these industries have been on the decline. Other industries, especially service industries and computers, have surged to prominence. These changes also result in dislocations as some communities experience high levels of unemployment as their industries decline. People in these communities, too, will likely find work elsewhere, but before they do, they will also contribute to unemployment and poverty.

These kinds of changes, some economists argue, are necessary for a healthy economy, but their cumulative impact is to increase rates of unemployment and poverty. This is sometimes called **structural unemployment** because *it is a part of the very structure of the economy*. Some of the growth in economic inequality described previously in this chapter is undoubtedly due to these kinds of structural changes (Murphy and Welch, 1993). The decline in high-paying industrial jobs, the increase in lower-paying service jobs, and the importance of skills such as computer literacy have all imperiled workers at the lower end of the income scale. People without skills find fewer jobs today that pay a reasonable wage, meaning that they are worse off than their counterparts of thirty or forty years ago.

The Functions of Poverty According to some functionalists, one of the reasons that poverty persists is that it performs some positive functions for society or at least for some groups in society. Although it is difficult to think of poverty in this light, this view illustrates a point that has been made elsewhere: Social conditions or practices that some find undesirable or

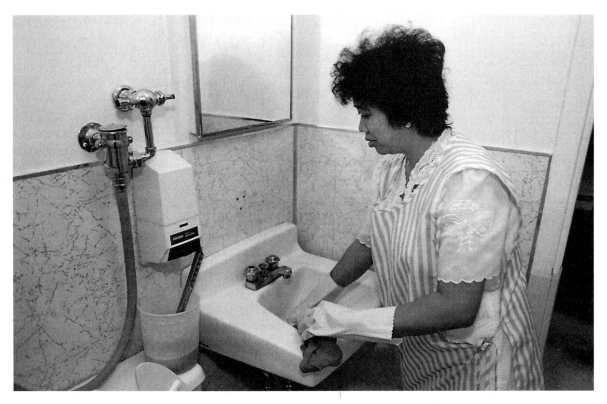

Cleaning bathrooms in a convalescent home, as this woman does, doesn't pay much. People without educational credentials or some job skills find that there are few jobs for them in the U.S. economy that pay a reasonable wage.

even repugnant, such as poverty or crime, may nonetheless make a positive contribution to society. How can poverty be functional? Herbert J. Gans (1971) suggests that among the benefits to society from poverty are

1. The existence of poverty ensures that society's "dirty work" will be done. There are many boring, underpaid, or undignified occupations that most people would prefer not to do, even though they need to be done. Jobs such as washing dishes, scrubbing floors, or picking farm produce would probably go undone unless people either received high wages to do them or had no other choice. The poor have little choice and are essentially coerced into taking these "dirty" jobs.

2. Poverty subsidizes many of the activities of the more affluent because the poor are willing to work for low wages. For example, the poor do domestic work and housecleaning for the affluent, which frees the affluent to engage in professional, cultural, or leisure activities.

3. Poverty creates jobs for all those people who serve the poor, such as social workers, or who protect society from them, such as police and corrections officers.

4. Poverty creates a market for inferior goods and services that others will not buy. The poor buy day-old bread, run-down automobiles, and secondhand clothes. They also rent deteriorating apartments in run-down neighborhoods that would otherwise go vacant. Needless to say, the people who sell these goods and services benefit from the poor.

5. The poor help to support and symbolize the status of the nonpoor by serving as the official "losers" or "underdogs" in the societal race for success. In a hierarchical society such as ours, someone has to be on the bottom, and this lets everyone else know where they stand. Relative to the poor, the nonpoor can feel that they have "made it."

Other functions of poverty could be listed, but the point should be clear: Poverty exists in part because it performs positive functions for many groups in society. Not that these groups consciously wish poverty to continue or actively campaign for its persistence. They may not even be aware of the extent to which they benefit from poverty. But it does mean that these groups feel little pressure to alleviate poverty. In fact, although we have discussed this issue under the functionalist perspective, it has elements of the conflict view of poverty, to which we now turn our attention.

The Conflict Perspective

Most conflict views of poverty derive at least in part from the view of Karl Marx, and his position contrasts sharply with that of the functionalists. Marx viewed society as involving a constant struggle between social classes over scarce resources, with some groups managing to capture more of these resources than others. This results in the inequitable distribution of resources that makes up the stratification systems of modern societies. Yet this unequal distribution, said Marx, has little to do with rewarding talent or filling important positions. Instead, people gain desirable positions in the stratification system through coercion, exploitation, and possibly inheritance. Once their position is acquired, they work to protect it against inroads by less fortunate groups. This can be done in many ways. For example, employers seek the cheapest labor possible because this increases

their profits. The tax system is used to benefit the more affluent who can use tax loopholes, unavailable to the less affluent, to avoid paying their share of income tax. Even the legal system tends to benefit the affluent. The crimes they commit, such as business fraud, are less likely to be detected and punished than are the crimes of the poor, such as assault and armed robbery.

It should not be surprising that the affluent benefit in these ways, because it is the affluent who write the tax laws, design the legal system, and pay the police to enforce the law. For Marx, the affluent are merely using the resources available to them to protect their own position. There is an even more subtle way in which dominant groups can protect their position: They can convince subordinate groups that the existing distribution of resources is "natural" or preferable to any other. This is done in part by persuading the poor that they, too, can become affluent. Through schools and the media, for example, people can be taught to believe that everyone will be successful if they apply themselves. The implication of this belief, of course, is that poverty is caused by one's not having worked hard enough. Being poor, then, is one's own fault. This belief deflects people's attention from the societal structures and barriers that contribute to maintaining some groups in power. Poverty is viewed as a personal problem rather than a societal one, and the poor are less inclined to demand changes in the system.

Once people have become successful, they tend to pass on their success to their children, and this makes it more difficult for people on the bottom to move up. **Social mobility** refers to *the movement of people from one social position to another in the stratification hierarchy.* Although upward social mobility is fairly widespread in the United States, our stratification system is also characterized by considerable stability with a high degree of occupational inheritance. Most of the mobility that occurs is short range, such as the child of a blue-collar worker who advances to a somewhat better-paying blue-collar job. For the most part, children tend to take jobs that are not too different in socioeconomic status from those of their parents (Featherman and Hauser, 1978; Hout, 1988). Furthermore, children of the affluent have much greater access to a good education, which has become a key requirement for success. In fact, a national tragedy is the fact that our society spends considerably less on the education of poor children, who are more desperately in need of these resources, than it does on the education of affluent children. And relatively little is being done to rectify this (Kozol, 1991). All of this means that the poor do not have the same chances for mobility as the more affluent. By virtue of being born poor, they are already at a serious disadvantage. Even the intelligent and capable among the poor suffer such disadvantages, for the stratification system tends to perpetuate itself.

From the conflict perspective, issues of poverty and inequality need to be assessed from a global vantage point, as was done in Chapter 2. The emerging global economy pits large corporations in a competition out of which some people benefit while others suffer from an inability to find a job that will enable them to support themselves and their families in a dignified fashion. The search around the world for higher profits and lower labor costs means persistent, and in some cases grinding, poverty for those who do not have the skills, the social background, or the good fortune that would enable them to benefit from the global economy. For the United States, this loss of good-paying jobs has been one of the reasons for the growth of an "underclass" of poor who do not have the education or skills that are essential to landing a good job today. For some in this group, poverty has become a permanent, intergenerational problem (see Applied Research insert).

The Interactionist Perspective and Cultural Analysis

The functionalist and conflict perspectives focus on the role of social and economic structures in creating poverty. By contrast, the interactionist perspective focuses on the importance of the subjective element of social reality—how people define themselves and their opportunities through day-to-day social interaction with others around them. This has led to a **cultural analysis of poverty** that focuses on *the values, attitudes, and psychological orientations that may emerge among groups of people who live under conditions of poverty* (Marks, 1991). The basic idea is that people who live in poverty develop a cultural orientation that helps them adapt to their life circumstances in a way that enables them to still feel good about themselves. However, elements of this cultural orientation can make it more difficult for poor people to improve their circumstances. Anthropologist Oscar Lewis (1966) was one of the first to speak of a "culture of poverty"—the beliefs, values, and norms that emerge among the long-term poor and help them adapt to their circumstances. The poor tend to be isolated from centers of power and decision making in society and from influential groups and organizations. As a result, their cultural orientation tends to emphasize fatalism and powerlessness, feeling that they have little control over what happens to them. In addition, the experiences of the poor have shown them that, despite their own efforts, the future is unlikely to get a lot better for them. So, their cultural orientation tends to be present-oriented—seeking enjoyment now—because they see little point in sacrificing for a future that looks bleak.

More recently, William Julius Wilson (1991) has suggested that prolonged joblessness contributes to this cultural orientation by leaving people with a general sense that they are unable to achieve goals that they might set for themselves, that there is little point in making efforts or taking on challenges. Another element of this cultural context applies to African Americans, whose ancestors were brought to this country against their will, suffered slavery, poverty, and racial oppression over the centuries, and were forcibly kept out of the mainstream in the

APPLIED RESEARCH
The Underclass in the United States

For some people, poverty is a temporary status out of which they will ultimately move. For other people, poverty is more permanent, sometimes persisting from one generation to the next. This latter group has presented researchers and policymakers with the greatest challenge in terms of relieving poverty. In fact, some researchers have labeled this group an "underclass," implying that they inhabit a quasi-permanent, underprivileged nether region from which escape is, at best, difficult.

Most sociologists consider the underclass to be not only people who are poor, or those who have been poor for a long time; in addition, the underclass is a group whose members are severely disadvantaged, isolated from mainstream society, and living in communities with limited access to the resources that might enable them to improve their lot. For this underclass, chronic unemployment is the norm, crime is taken for granted, and welfare is a fact of life (Marks, 1991; Devine and Wright, 1993). Only about 3 percent of the poor would be considered members of the underclass, and they account for a disproportionate share of problems such as teen pregnancies, crime, and drug abuse (Mincy, 1994).

What accounts for the emergence of the underclass in the United States? Sociologist William Julius Wilson (1978; 1987) attributes it to some fundamental structural changes in the economy over the past several decades. One such change is the transition from a product-based manufacturing economy to an information-based service economy. People in the underclass are without the skills or work experience useful in the latter type of economy, which places more emphasis on verbal talent and educational qualifications than on physical brawn and manual labor. Another basic change in the U.S. economy has been the relocation of industries away from the communities where poor people live. This has occurred for a number of reasons, such as government policies providing funds to build new housing in the suburbs and freeways

to get there (see Chapter 12). The outcome has been that factories, businesses, and jobs have fled poor neighborhoods and relocated in nonpoor areas. This has been especially disastrous for African Americans who, because of discrimination in housing, have been forced to live in segregated neighborhoods where there are few good jobs (Massey, 1990).

The labor market in modern industrial economies has also changed in such a way that people with no work skills or little education are hard pressed to compete successfully for most jobs. At one time, there were ample jobs for people with strong backs and a willingness to work. By contrast, in today's economy, in which a high school degree (and, increasingly, post-high school training) is the entry-level requirement for most jobs, people who lack these credentials are relegated to the lowest-paying jobs or, increasingly, to no jobs at all. So, given these structural changes in our economy, the underclass consists of those marginally skilled people who have little opportunity to gain the education or skills necessary to succeed in modern industrial economies.

Furthermore, changes in the communities in which poor people live have contributed to the perpetuation and expansion of the underclass. In particular, as employers have abandoned the inner city, so too have the working- and middle-class people who held those jobs, leaving behind the poorer residents. When the working people and nonpoor leave, so do many of the small businesses and merchants, who prefer to locate elsewhere. The consequence is that poor neighborhoods eventually contain mostly the poor and the unemployed. In addition, without working people living in the community, there are fewer respectable role models for the young to look up to. The role models remaining are more commonly those who do not work, who commit crimes, or who take drugs. When the youth in poor communities look around, they see little reason to have high aspirations because none of the people they see in their community seems to have achieved any success (Wilson, 1991; Mead, 1994).

Sociologist Christopher Jencks (1992) points to some additional things that help perpetuate the underclass: Because of stereotyping and racism, employers are reluctant to hire blacks. After all, even though jobs have left a community, ghetto residents can seek jobs outside their neighborhood, even in the suburbs. But Jencks points to research showing that employers direct hiring efforts toward white neighborhoods and prefer not to recruit inner-city blacks, especially males (Neckerman and Kirschenman, 1991). Employers may perceive young black males as less skilled, educated, or trustworthy than white workers. In addition, cultural conflict and racism may also be involved. In the 1980s and 1990s, ghetto culture has emerged as a distinct cultural phenomenon in the United States, in part because blacks have not been permitted to assimilate into the mainstream Anglo culture as many ethnic minorities have. This ghetto culture involves a distinctive manner of speaking (such as black English), new modes of cultural expression (such as rap music), a different type of interpersonal demeanor (which Anglos often interpret as hostile and aggressive, especially when exhibited by young males), and an acute awareness that blacks in the United States today still suffer serious discrimination if not outright oppression. According to Jencks, this has an impact on employers:

> Employers' distaste for ghetto culture does not seem to me to have declined. Indeed, it may have increased. A generation ago, most employers expected young ghetto blacks to "know their place." Today employers anticipate that ghetto blacks will be far more assertive. Few employers want unskilled workers who are assertive, regardless of their race. Even fewer want assertive workers from an alien culture they don't understand. (Jencks, 1992: 128–129)

Jencks sees this as symptomatic of a basic cultural conflict. One consequence of all this is the profound difficulty blacks, especially young males, have in finding and keeping jobs that will enable them to support a family.

Using their research as a foundation, Wilson, Jencks, and other sociologists have made recommendations to Congress and other government agencies about what to do about the underclass. Their recommendations basically suggest ways in which the negative impact of the economic structural changes on people's lives can be alleviated. In particular, they have focused on programs to provide people with the education and skills necessary to find good jobs in a postindustrial society. They point out that programs that expand job opportunities for those with good job qualifications, such as college graduates, will not have an impact on the underclass. Wilson even criticizes affirmative-action programs on the grounds that they benefit affluent minorities rather than the underclass. What is needed are programs to provide people with the basic literacy skills, a high school diploma, or other qualifications needed to gain entry into our modern service-based economy. For, despite all the crime, single parenthood, and other behaviors among the poor that mainstream culture frowns on, research clearly shows that poor people cling to conventional behaviors when they see a chance of succeeding. As sociologist Herbert Gans puts it: "only when the poor lose the struggle to escape poverty do they give up mainstream behavior" (Gans, 1992: A56). Research shows that people in the underclass, especially the youth, want to work and are willing to work (Freeman and Holzer, 1986). It is not desire or ambition that they lack, but rather the opportunity to find jobs that pay enough to enable them to support their families in a respectable fashion.

United States. Among some of these poor people there has developed a conflictual subculture that defines their circumstances as due to the racial oppression and dominance exercised by more powerful groups. As they see it, it is racism and discrimination that control and limit their lives (Peterson, 1991b).

With such a cultural orientation, poor people may despair of ever improving their lot. They may see little point in making efforts to change their circumstances because their fate, they believe, is out of their control. They may not sacrifice for the future because they see no link between present effort and future gain. If racial discrimination, over which they have no control, severely limits any opportunities they might have, then they may see little point in continuing with school or applying for a job that they probably will not get. In fact, if things are that hopeless, they may find that it may make more sense to rip the system off through crime or other means and enjoy what they can. When such a cultural orientation develops, argue proponents of cultural analysis, poverty may become, to a degree, self-perpetuating. The values and norms that make up this orientation may get passed on unwittingly from one generation to the next. When this happens, poverty can become a vicious, difficult-to-break cycle.

Cultural analysis has been controversial because it seems to "blame the victim": Poor people are blamed for their own difficulties by arguing that poverty is due to the character flaws of, or lack of effort by, those affected (Ryan, 1976). However, that is not the point of cultural analysis. Rather, it argues that certain social conditions—discrimination, lack of opportunity, social isolation—can produce a culture of poverty, and this culture in turn perpetuates the victimization of the poor. It is flaws in the social system that are at the root of the problem and that must be changed to combat poverty.

A second reason the culture of poverty thesis has been controversial is that research suggests that it applies only to a limited number of poor people. In fact, the traits that characterize the culture of poverty are probably found among less than half of all poor people and are more common among some poor, such as Hispanics, than among other poor people (Irelan, Moles, and O'Shea, 1969; Kutner and Kutner, 1987; Mead, 1994). Research also shows that some poor people do improve their lives, despite the culture of poverty. So, although the culture of poverty may inhibit some poor people from making things better for themselves, its impact on perpetuating poverty in general is probably limited, although not unimportant. Many things other than this cultural orientation make life difficult for the poor and account for their limited capacity to improve their lot.

Future Prospects

Support for the fight against poverty remains high in the United States. In a 1994 survey, 80 percent of the people surveyed agreed that the government has a responsibility to try to do away with poverty (Kull, 1994). Remarkably, considering the mood toward welfare in the 1990s, this support is higher than it was in the mid-1960s when only 70 percent agreed with that statement. Along with this, however, there has been a dramatic decline over the same period in people's confidence that the government can do the job properly. So, people continue to embrace the values that underlie poverty programs, but they are frustrated with the government's record of achievements in those programs. With these public sentiments in mind, the remainder of the chapter reviews what has been done and what could be done to alleviate the problem of poverty.

Full Employment

Because poverty is related in part to unemployment, it seems sensible to promote policies that encourage **full employment:** *a situation in which everyone or nearly everyone who wants to work can find a job.* Although most politicians would probably support such a concept, the controversy is over how to do it. The Reagan and Bush administrations promoted an essentially laissez-faire approach to full employment. At the foundation of this approach is the idea that the government should play only a limited part in matters of unemployment and poverty. According to this view, the poor benefit from a free and growing economy because the wealth such an economy produces "trickles down" to the poor in the form of more jobs created by economic expansion. Government spending and regulations increase the cost of doing business, make products and services more costly, and thus reduce the level of economic activity. Another element of this laissez-faire approach is to support lower taxes as a way of encouraging economic activity. Lower taxes mean that people earn more for their work and will thus work harder. It also means that people have more money to spend for goods and services or to invest. President Clinton has taken a more interventionist stance on the issue of full employment by using government spending as a way to stimulate economic growth and the development of new jobs. The interventionist approach also stresses the provision of education and training to people so that they have the skills and credentials that will assist them in getting jobs. So, interventionists envision government programs as a key element, although not the only one, in helping achieve full employment.

Certainly, any program that proves effective at creating more jobs would probably receive widespread support, but some cautions about such programs are in order. First, most of the poor, as has been seen, are not able-bodied nonworkers. Rather, they are people who would be largely unaffected by the creation of more jobs: children, the elderly, the disabled, and women raising their children alone. Second, many of the jobs created are likely to be low-paying, unskilled, or part-time jobs that will not pull people out of poverty (Rank, 1994). Third, having tried both laissez-faire and interventionist strategies to promote full employment over the decades, it

appears that neither is a panacea for the problem of poverty. If anything, unemployment in the United States seems to have increased somewhat over the years despite these policies.

Education, Training, and Jobs

Some social policies aimed at reducing poverty focus on preparing the poor to compete effectively in the job market. The idea is that, for some poor people, the major factor holding them in poverty is that they lack the education, skills, or motivation to find and keep good-paying jobs. A number of programs have been created over the years to focus on these issues.

Head Start The Head Start program was established by the Economic Opportunity Act of 1964. This program is based on the belief that people fail in life because their access to conventional channels to success—especially education—is blocked. The presumption is that poor children live in an environment, especially at home, that discourages educational achievement, initiative, and a positive self-concept. By intervening on behalf of these poor children, it is argued, the intergenerational cycle of poverty might be broken. Head Start provides preschool children with enrichment and early learning experiences that middle-class children presumably receive at home.

Although early reports on the impact of Head Start were not favorable, research over the past two decades has shown that the program does achieve many of its goals. Children enrolled in Head Start, when compared with other poor children who do not have such preschool experience, show clear benefits (Parker, Piotrkowski, and Peay, 1987; Lee et al., 1990; Besharov, 1992). Head Start children are less likely to be assigned to special education classes or to be kept back a grade in school. They also do better on mathematics achievement tests and show more improvement in IQ scores, and they are less likely to repeat a grade, get in trouble with the law, or become teenage mothers. Head Start children also have a better family life and a more positive self-concept. Finally, as young adults, the Head Start children may be more likely to go to college or to hold a steady, skilled job. With benefits such as these, it seems that children who are exposed to such preschool educational experiences will be better equipped to avoid poverty as adults. The extensive evaluation of Head Start is important in assessing solutions to social problems such as poverty.

Jobs Programs   Whereas Head Start is an indirect, long-term approach to the problem of poverty, other programs have involved more direct and immediate efforts to train people and to find them jobs. In the 1970s and 1980s, programs such as WIN (Work Incentive Program) and CETA (Comprehensive Employment and Training Act) provided job training and work experience for people on welfare and assisted them in finding jobs. They provided on-the-job training and temporary public-service jobs. They also provided the young and criminal offenders with special services. The programs actually helped relatively few people find permanent jobs and get off welfare, and the jobs they did get often paid less than welfare. Because of their lackluster results, both programs were eliminated.

In 1982, the Reagan administration established its own program, the Job Training Partnership Act or JTPA (Kellam, 1992). One key feature of this approach was that some of the training was provided by programs run by private industry with federal funds. The belief was that this private-sector involvement would result in better training and the creation of more jobs. The JTPA also included a Dislocated Worker Program to provide retraining for the displaced workers (discussed in Chapter 2) who were laid off from industries that face substantial foreign competition, such as the steel and automobile industries. However, the JTPA also seems to have fallen far short of its goals. Many of the trainees have been people with high school degrees who probably would have gotten jobs on their own, and most would have been hired and

trained by their employers even if JTPA funds had not been available. In addition, the JTPA has not created many new high-paying jobs, and most trainees end up in minimum-wage jobs.

In 1988, a major piece of welfare legislation with significant provisions for training and jobs programs became law. The Family Support Act represented a considerable shift from past policy on welfare and poverty ("Congress Clears . . . ," 1988). Basically, it involved a transformation of the welfare system from an emphasis on income maintenance to an emphasis on education and training in order to help people find jobs. The new law requires states to operate a Job Opportunities and Basic Skills (JOBS) program. These programs require single parents on welfare whose children are older than three either to find a regular job or to enroll in educational and job-training courses that are provided by federal and state governments. Earlier job training and welfare programs did not have this coercive element. In some cases, welfare recipients will be required to participate in community work activities or other unpaid work to continue receiving welfare payments. States must provide child care for parents who work or attend courses, provide continuing eligibility for Medicaid health-care coverage for families, and offer transportation and other support to the participants. The overall design of this "workfare" law is to discourage long-term dependency on welfare and to foster a transition to job-holding independence. Many states have established similar compulsory training programs and work requirements as a part of their welfare systems.

Social scientists have been evaluating these new workfare approaches to job training and welfare since the early 1980s, and a body of evaluation research results now exists that enable us to draw some conclusions about their effectiveness (Friedlander and Burtless, 1995; Nightingale and Haveman, 1995). Generally, the programs achieve modest positive outcomes. If the programs are designed well, people in them are more likely to find employment and to earn more than are people who do not have access to such programs. Program participants are also more likely to stay off welfare. However, on the negative side, program participants do not find better jobs because of the program than they would have without it and they are not better off financially: Any earnings gains from work tend to be offset by lost welfare benefits. Furthermore, much of the increase in earnings goes to a fairly small group of program participants, and the many others show little earnings benefit. Finally, the workfare programs show little success with the very disadvantaged who are likely to be dependent on welfare for a long time. So, the effects of switching to a workfare program are modestly positive, complicated, and clearly no panacea. A major reason for only modest improvement is simple: Many people are on welfare because there are insufficient jobs for those with few work skills, and fewer jobs still that pay better than welfare. Providing people with job training is not a great help if the jobs do not exist. In addition, the research shows that effectiveness depends on resources expended: the better programs spent more on education, training, and job search activities. The overall conclusion is that welfare programs designed like workfare will probably not dramatically reduce poverty because of the persistence of the basic structural problems that make it difficult for some people to get a job that will support their families at a decent level.

However, irrespective of whether the new workfare policy gets people off welfare or gets them jobs, it clearly represents a shift in sentiment in the United States regarding welfare: Rather than viewing welfare as a right of people who have fallen on hard times, it is now organized as a privilege for those who can demonstrate that they are making an effort to help themselves.

Income-Maintenance Programs

Modern governments have taken on the responsibility of assisting those in need through a variety of programs that provide them with some minimal level of resources. In the United States, these programs can be divided into two general categories: social insurance and public assistance. **Social insurance** refers to *programs offering benefits to broad categories of people, such as the elderly or injured workers, who presumably were working and paying for the insurance before becoming eligible for it.* There is no "means" test to receive social insurance; that is, there is no income minimum necessary to be eligible. Also, one can receive outside income while insured, and there is little stigma associated with it. In fact, 80 percent of the social welfare dollar is spent on the nonpoor. **Public assistance,** which is what most people mean when they use the term *welfare,* refers to *programs in which a person must pass a "means" test to be eligible.* Those whose assets are above a certain level are not eligible.

There are various social insurance programs in the United States. At both the federal and state levels, over $600 billion were spent on such programs in 1991 (U.S. Bureau of the Census, 1994: 370–75). Among the best known and most expensive are

1. *Social Security.* Old Age, Survivors, and Disability Insurance (OASDI), commonly referred to as "Social Security," is intended to provide income for retired or disabled workers and their survivors. It also provides unemployment compensation and benefits to workers for on-the-job injuries. Benefits also go to dependent spouses over age sixty-two and dependent children under age eighteen. Social Security benefits lift as many as fifteen million people a year out of poverty, making it one of the government's most effective weapons against poverty. Because Social Security is primarily focused on the elderly, it is discussed in more detail in Chapter 8.

2. *Medicare.* Medicare is a health insurance program for the elderly and for some others who are receiving Social Security. It also provides supplementary medical insurance in return for a monthly premium. Medicare is discussed further in Chapters 4 and 8.

There are also a variety of public-assistance programs, costing at least $200 billion in 1991.

1. *Supplementary Security Income.* Supplementary Security Income (SSI) is given to certain categories of poor people with little income and few assets. To be eligible, one must be over sixty-five, blind, or disabled.

2. *Aid to Families with Dependent Children.* Aid to Families with Dependent Children (AFDC) is a combined federal-state program to provide assistance to parents or guardians who do not have the financial resources to support their children. It also covers families in which the father is disabled and thus unable to support his children.

3. *General Assistance.* General Assistance (GA) is for people ineligible for SSI or AFDC. GA is funded by state or local governments, but only about half the states have GA, and the amount of assistance and the eligibility requirements are highly variable from one locale to another.

4. *Medicaid.* Medicaid is a program providing medical and hospital services to people who cannot pay for them themselves. Generally, Medicaid goes to people who meet the means test for other public-assistance programs, but it can also go to people who can provide for their own economic support except for necessary medical care.

5. *Noncash Benefits.* A number of public-assistance programs provide poor people with resources that are not direct cash payments. For example, food stamps are given to people on public assistance. There is also housing assistance for the poor, either in the form of public housing with low rents or government assistance in paying rent for housing in the private sector. There is also a school lunch program to assist poor children in receiving a good diet.

The history of income-maintenance programs in the United States shows some significant changes in both policies and attitudes toward welfare over the years (Skocpol, 1995). Many modern government support programs, such as Social Security, were established during the New Deal of the 1930s. These programs were clearly designed to assist what some people considered the "deserving" poor, those who had worked to support themselves but who, because of age, disability, or loss of a spouse, were in difficult times. The goal of the programs was to keep these people from falling into poverty or help them out of poverty. Even Aid to Dependent Children, which is what AFDC was called then, was originally intended for widowed mothers, not for single or divorced mothers. Single and divorced mothers along with marginally employable men were considered by many to be the "undeserving" poor, who were perceived as being partially responsible for their plight or at least capable of improving their circumstances on their own. Most people at the time believed that single motherhood and divorce were wrong and that women could and should avoid these plights. If they did not avoid them, they did not deserve government assistance.

The Great Society programs of the 1960s tended to get away from distinctions between "deserving" and "undeserving" people. Instead they focused on helping all poor people rise out of poverty by providing opportunities to all. Single or divorced mothers and any other poor people could get government assistance. Since the 1960s, disillusionment has grown among many people in the United States regarding income-maintenance programs, especially considering that poverty has not been eliminated. What has emerged from this disillusionment seems to reflect the earlier distinction between deserving and undeserving people. While social insurance programs such as Social Security and Medicare have been fairly successful in resisting pressures to cut their budgets, states and the federal government have felt much freer to slash AFDC and GA rolls and to find ways to deny or restrict benefits to people. Many people believe that at least some recipients of these programs could make it on their own and that waste and fraud are rampant. As a result, many people have been dropped from public-assistance rolls in the 1980s and 1990s. Some states have tightened restrictions on recipients: reducing benefits if a teenage parent drops out of school, denying additional benefits to women who have additional children, or dropping teenage mothers from welfare unless they live with a parent or guardian. Although some of the policies may have some beneficial outcomes, they clearly arise from a frustration over the continuing growth in welfare costs and the inability of such programs to reduce levels of poverty significantly.

Yet, the picture of poverty and welfare in the United States is complex because, despite all of this hesitancy, expressed support for poverty programs remains strong in the United States. In a 1994 survey, 78 percent of those interviewed believed that we should spend the same as we currently do or more for a host of poverty programs (Kull, 1994). Surprisingly, 76 percent of those questioned expressed similar support for AFDC, probably the most controversial and maligned poverty program. The support for poverty programs is virtually unanimous when these programs are seen as moving people toward productive employment. Thus, almost no one believes that we should cut funds for job training programs, such as the Jobs Corps, or educational programs, such as Head Start.

One policy outgrowth of all these sentiments of support and resistance was the Family Support Act of 1988, mentioned in the preceding section. This Act attempts to transform welfare from an income-maintenance system to one that stresses education, training, and assistance in job searching. As mentioned, this "workfare" approach represents a shift in public sentiment from viewing welfare as a "right" of those who have fallen on bad times to a "privilege" that can be revoked. The legislation also attacks welfare dependency through the work-incentive elements previously described and by requiring states to spend 55 percent of their welfare budget on those showing long-term de-

pendency on welfare. This is an effort to tackle the most intractable cases of welfare dependence; it assumes that those who are dependent for only short periods will have a good chance of getting off welfare despite what the government does. The law provides for extending welfare benefits to families in which both parents are unemployed, so that fathers will not leave their families in order to make them eligible for benefits. The law also contains stiff measures to enforce child-support payments in the hope that some families could be kept from going on welfare to begin with.

Welfare has always been a controversial topic in the United States, and some sharply contrasting views of welfare are presented in the Policy Issues insert. The International Perspectives insert explores how such issues are dealt with in other societies.

Collective Action

Many of the programs intended to alleviate poverty have been designed by politicians, economists, sociologists, and other experts who are not themselves poor. This raises the question of whether these experts have different interests from the poor or whether they have an accurate and sincere understanding of poverty and its related problems. Leslie Dunbar (1988), who has interviewed many poverty-stricken people at length, believes that policymakers and the general public hold inaccurate stereotypes of the poor as unthinking, unambitious, irresponsible, and possibly even dangerous social misfits. In reality, after listening to poor people speak, Dunbar found that the poor value many of the same things that the non-poor do, such as ambition, self-reliance, and family life. Most want to work and support themselves, but because of bad luck or circumstances, they find themselves destitute. If policymakers and the public misunderstand the poor and have different interests than they do, then the programs these officials develop may

POLICY ISSUES
Does Welfare Work?

There are probably very few people who are satisfied with our current system of public welfare. Some are inclined to view those on welfare as cheats, chiselers, and lazy loafers who have found a free meal at the public trough. Others see welfare recipients as victims: people who, by virtue of disability, discrimination, or some other reason, cannot find and keep a job that will provide them with a minimally decent lifestyle. Which of these views is most accurate is a topic of considerable debate. In fact, reality is probably more complex than either of these stereotypes. Two opposing views of our welfare system are presented by policy analysts Charles Murray (1984) and Christopher Jencks (1992).

Although there may be some lazy people collecting welfare, Charles Murray does not believe that laziness need really be considered in understanding why people choose welfare over work. Rather, he argues, the welfare regulations are such that, for some people, going on welfare may be the most rational economic choice to make. First, AFDC payments, along with such in-kind income as food stamps and Medicaid, often amount to more each month than a person can make at the low-paying jobs that are available to people with little education and few skills. Because those low-paying jobs are often boring and unpleasant, why should a young man or woman work if he or she can stay home and collect more income from public assistance? In addition, people can supplement their welfare income by working, and for each dollar they earn, they lose considerably less than a dollar in AFDC. And if a woman on AFDC lives with a man without being married, what he earns is not deducted from her public assistance. As a final critique of the welfare system, Murray argues that when people go on welfare, they become dependent on it and lose the values of hard work and self-sufficiency that would enable them to support themselves. In fact, the more welfare we provide, the more dependent people become and the more poverty we create.

Murray's solution to this problem is extreme, but he believes it is defensible. It is very consistent with the laissez-faire approach to social problems: Dismantle the entire federal welfare system and income-support structure for working-age people! These people would have to find a job, locate family or friends who can assist them, or get assistance from local public or private social service agencies. He proposes this not out of callous disregard or anger at "welfare loafers" but from the recognition that the current welfare regulations make it preferable, in the short term, for some people to choose welfare over work. If federal welfare payments were removed, some recipients would face only inconvenience because their payments were only for a short period or constituted only a small portion of the income available to them. Other recipients will have to scramble around to find a job or a relative to support them. This will definitely involve great disruption for some of them, but it will also have the long-term benefit of changing their behavior in positive ways. Parents, not wanting to support their adult children or grandchildren, will apply greater pressure to avoid pregnancies or to get a job. A single adult woman will probably want to avoid such dependence on her parents. To be sure, some will have to work for lower wages at dissatisfying jobs for a time. However, many of these people—not all, Murray recognizes, but many—will find that they have acquired some skills after a time and can move on to better jobs. They will also have acquired a sense of independence and pride in supporting themselves.

Christopher Jencks defends the record of achievements by the federal welfare system. First, he argues, it has substantially improved the circumstances of many of the truly needy among the elderly, the disabled, and children. Furthermore, Jencks and other researchers present evidence that disputes many of Murray's points. For example, there is little evidence that the availability of AFDC leads women to go out and have children out of wedlock. Over the past thirty years, rates of single parenthood have increased steadily, whereas welfare benefits have gone up and down. If Murray is right that welfare produces more births and out-of-wedlock children, then higher welfare benefits should lead to higher birth rates. They do not. Many states with high welfare benefits have lower fertility among welfare recipients than states with low welfare benefits (Rank, 1994). In addition, women on welfare actually have a lower birthrate than nonwelfare women of equivalent age and social standing. The reality, says Jencks, is that the increase in single-parent families has been a broad cultural trend that shows up in both welfare and nonwelfare women. It reflects a more tolerant attitude toward sex and reproduction, a growing cultural individualism, and a greater commitment to personal freedom. And these trends have affected the decisions of all women in the United States.

This same research shows that welfare also has little effect on whether women marry or divorce. Welfare payments do enable poor women to get out of undesirable marriages and avoid rushing into a second marriage to support themselves and their children. However, Jencks sees these outcomes as benefits because getting out of, or staying out of, a bad marriage probably reduces the levels of child abuse and child abandonment by poor parents. As for the argument that welfare breeds dependency and increases poverty, political scientist Sanford Schram (1991) presents data showing the opposite: when welfare spending *declines,* the poverty rate tends to go up.

Jencks also does not believe that economic growth will do much to reduce welfare loads because most of the poor—the elderly, the disabled, and women heading their own households—are precisely the groups that benefit least when economic conditions improve. In addition, welfare mothers cannot support their families on their AFDC payments. The truth is that many welfare mothers work! Despite Murray's and others' image of welfare mothers choosing leisure and indolence over hard work, reality is more complex. Many welfare mothers supplement AFDC payments with wages from low-paying jobs; many get support from parents or boyfriends; a few turn to selling drugs or prostitution to narrow the gap between what AFDC

pays and what they need to support their children. In short, they work—and show considerable initiative in coming up with supplemental income in a difficult situation.

Given these realities, Jencks says, dumping welfare altogether would be destructive and mean spirited. However, "any successful social policy must strike a balance between collective compassion and individual responsibility" (Jencks, 1992: 87). Based on the assumption that it is better to work and help yourself, Jencks' basic premise is that people who work should always be better off than those who do not work and receive welfare. This might mean providing such assistance to low-income workers as health insurance, child-care assistance, housing subsidies, and the like. One reason women choose welfare over work is that they lose Medicaid and some of their AFDC payments when they work (Rank, 1994). This means that, for these women, working typically means being less well off, or at least not much better off, than when they are receiving only welfare benefits. This is a strong disincentive to work. So, says Jencks, take this out of the equation by offering health insurance and other assistance to working mothers. Once again, the reality is that many welfare mothers do work; Jencks policy would provide even more encouragement for these habits of work and self-sufficiency.

Another sociologist, Nathan Glazer (1995), goes further than Jencks and argues that welfare recipients should be encouraged to work even if they are not better off than when receiving only welfare. The reason for this is that such behavior reinforces an important social value, namely, that work and self-support are desirable goals to strive toward in and of themselves, even when they do not result in improvements in a person's circumstances. Some policy analysts argue that even nonpaying work, such as learning parenting skills or doing voluntary community service, can have positive benefits for welfare recipients. It can improve self-esteem, encourage a greater responsibility toward family, and engender a sense of community involvement and support (Maynard, 1995).

INTERNATIONAL PERSPECTIVES
Poverty and Welfare in Other Societies

Poverty rates tend to be higher in the United States than in many other industrial countries, especially Germany, Switzerland, the Netherlands, and the Scandinavian countries (Rodgers, 1990). Practically all of these societies also provide more comprehensive assistance to low income individuals, the poor, and single parents. And they take a very different approach to issues of welfare and public assistance than does the United States. For one thing, these industrial nations focus on preventing social problems, including poverty and crime, by assisting people to avoid poverty. For example, they have housing programs and child or family allowances that go to the nonpoor as well as the poor. In this way, people can avoid tumbling into self-perpetuating poverty if they come on hard times. A second difference is that many of the assistance programs in these nations are universal rather than "means tested" as in the United States. In many countries, for example, all families receive some child or family allowance, although the amount varies by income level. Such universal programs are more effective at preventing social problems, they receive more widespread public support because everyone gains from them, and those who receive "welfare" are less likely to be stigmatized.

A third difference in the approach of these countries, especially Japan and the Scandinavian countries, is to use public resources and government intervention to keep unemployment as low as possible. In 1991, Sweden's unemployment rate was 2.1 percent while Switzerland's was an unbelievable 1.4 percent! (Compare those figures with figures in the United States in Chapter 2.) Low unemployment can be a significant factor in keeping poverty down. A final difference with the U.S. approach is that all of these other industrial countries make health care services available to both the poor and the nonpoor. In the United States, many people stay on welfare rather than work because

they lose Medicaid eligibility if they work. The jobs available to the poor are not likely to have health insurance as a benefit and pay too little to enable them to purchase health insurance, which is quite expensive. So, the choice for the poor in the United States is often either to work but forego health insurance or to get health insurance by not working and remaining eligible for welfare.

Countries that spend more on public assistance don't necessarily have lower rates of poverty (Lawson and George, 1980). This is probably because there are powerful structural and economic determinants of poverty that are unaffected by increasing levels of welfare expenditure. One such structural factor is the number of single-parent families, which is linked with higher poverty levels. In the United States, 9 percent of all households are single parent as compared to 3 percent in Sweden, 5 percent in the Netherlands, and 2 percent in Japan (U.S. Bureau of the Census, 1994: 857). Another reason why welfare expenditures don't clearly reduce poverty is that, in many of these industrial countries, a good portion of social welfare dollars is not directed at the poor but at assisting people who work to keep working and achieve a satisfactory lifestyle. For example, we saw in the International Perspectives insert in Chapter 3 that many European societies provide family benefits, such as day care and maternity leave, to everyone, even those who could afford to get them on their own. So, some nations have high public assistance expenditures and low poverty rates because some of the public assistance is directed at the nonpoor.

So the experiences of these other industrial nations suggest that it is not necessarily the amount of public assistance that reduces poverty but rather the approach taken: universal programs that focus on reducing social problems and unemployment and that make health care available to all.

Poor people become more deeply entrenched in poverty when segregation into urban ghettos (Chapter 12) makes it more difficult for them to find jobs and when corporate concentration of power (Chapter 2) makes it easy to close factories and move them away from where the poor live.

not necessarily further the interests of the poor. So the poor may need to take matters into their own hands through some collective action that would further their interests. In fact, the poor have done this periodically. The original war on poverty of the 1960s was in part a reaction to the focus of the civil rights movement aimed at the problems of poor African Americans. Since then, groups such as the United Farm Workers Union and the National Welfare Rights Organization have lobbied and protested in support of policies that are in the interests of the poor. Richard Cloward and Frances Fox Piven (1974) suggest that a coalition of poor groups and civil rights organizations could be an effective weapon to bring about change. A strategy such as this has its dangers, of course. It could create a backlash against the poor and result in - substantial reductions in public assistance. However, it does illustrate the point that disadvantaged groups in the United States have traditionally used collective action as one avenue to pursue their interests. The poor have not utilized this strategy as much as they might.

Summary

1. Poverty arises not from a deprivation of resources alone but from an uneven distribution of the resources available in a society. The system of social stratification in society refers to the ranking of people into a hierarchy in which the resources considered valuable by society are unequally distributed.

2. There are three widely used definitions of poverty: One is based on absolute deprivation, the second on relative deprivation, and the third on cultural elements. Most social policy on poverty in the United States uses the absolute definition.

3. Poverty is more common among some racial and ethnic minorities than among whites; among children than among adults; among female-headed households than among male-headed households; and among central-city and rural dwellers. Among the poor can also be found the working poor, the illiterate, the unemployed, and the homeless.

4. From the functionalist perspective, poverty exists to discourage people from neglecting their social duties. If people do not contribute to society, they are "punished" by receiving little in terms of wealth, status, or other rewards. In addition, poverty exists because it performs some positive functions for society.

5. From the conflict perspective, poverty exists because some groups are deprived of the opportunity to accumulate the resources that would make possible a minimally acceptable lifestyle. The affluent gain their positions through coercion, exploitation, or possibly inheritance, and then they use their position to protect what they have from inroads by the less fortunate. The poor are those with little power and few resources.

6. According to the interactionist perspective, living in poverty can lead the poor to define situations or interpret reality in ways that

make it more difficult for them to improve their circumstances. A part of this is called the culture of poverty, or values and norms that help the poor adapt to their life circumstances. This should not be interpreted, however, as a "blame the victim" argument.

7. One approach to reducing poverty is to strive for full employment, a situation in which nearly everyone who wants to work can find a job. How to achieve this, or whether it can be achieved, remains controversial.

8. Another approach is to provide the education and training that will prepare the poor to find and keep jobs. Head Start seems to have been fairly successful at this. Other jobs programs, however, have had mixed success.

9. To assist the poor, a variety of income-maintenance programs has been made available. The two general types are social insurance and public assistance. There is considerable debate over whether welfare is beneficial or detrimental to people and society.

10. Some have argued that the only effective way for the poor to get programs that truly benefit them is through collective action.

STUDY *and Review*

Key Terms

absolute definition of poverty

cultural analysis of poverty

cultural definition of poverty

full employment

poverty

public assistance

relative definition of poverty

social insurance

social mobility

social stratification

structural unemployment

Multiple-Choice Questions

1. Cultural definitions of poverty are distinct from the other definitions used because the cultural definitions consider:
   a. Relative deprivation.
   b. Why people have failed to achieve a higher economic level.
   c. An absolute level of deprivation.
   d. A fixed level below which people are considered to be poor.
   e. Social stratification to be central.

2. Which of the following statements is true regarding the poverty rate in the United States today?
   a. It is at its lowest point since 1960.
   b. It is at its highest point since 1960.
   c. It is higher than in all but a few years since 1970.
   d. Fewer people are poor today than in the 1970s.

3. Which of the following groups has experienced the largest increase in its percentage of the aggregate income in the United States since 1965?
   a. The poorest 20 percent of families.
   b. The second 20 percent of families.
   c. The third 20 percent of families.
   d. The fourth 20 percent of families.
   e. The wealthiest 20 percent of families.

4. People in which of the following groups have the highest rate of poverty?
   a. African-American female-headed families.
   b. Hispanic elderly.
   c. White elderly.
   d. Children.
   e. Hispanic children in two-parent families.

5. Which of these statements is most consistent with the functionalist perspective regarding the reason that poverty exists?
   a. Dominant groups protect their position and resources against inroads by less fortunate groups.
   b. Welfare systems produce dependency in people.
   c. The cultural orientation emerges when people live in conditions of poverty that discourage them from work.
   d. Poverty makes a useful contribution to the ongoing maintenance of society.

6. The cultural analysis of poverty has been controversial for all of the following reasons *except:*
   a. It gives support to the functionalist perspective on stratification.
   b. It seems to blame the poor for their own difficulties.
   c. It seems to apply only to a limited number of poor people.
   d. Some poor people do improve their lives despite the culture of poverty.

7. Sociologists attribute the emergence of an underclass of poor people in the United States to all of the following *except:*
   a. Inadequate funding for Aid to Families with Dependent Children.
   b. Fundamental structural changes in the economy of the United States.
   c. Changes in the communities in which poor people live.
   d. The relocation of industries away from the communities where poor people live.

8. Which of the following programs to assist the poor is still in operation?
   a. CETA.
   b. WIN.
   c. Head Start.
   d. All of the above are still operating.
   e. Only a and c are still operating.

9. Which of the following is classified as a "social insurance" program?
   a. Aid to Families with Dependent Children.
   b. Social Security.
   c. Medicaid.
   d. Supplemental Security Income.
   e. General Assistance.

10. Which of the following best characterizes the attitudes of people in the United States today regarding poverty programs?
    a. All such programs should be reduced drastically.
    b. Most such programs should be eliminated.
    c. Support is strong for programs that move people toward productive employment.
    d. Programs that help children should be kept but the rest should be eliminated.

True/False Questions

1. Using the absolute definition of poverty, poverty could be eliminated only if the inequitable distribution of resources were to be eliminated.
2. Since 1965, most analysts agree that the distribution of resources among the wealthy and the poor has become more equitable.
3. In making policy decisions, such as who is eligible for various government social programs, the absolute approach to defining poverty is typically used.
4. According to the text, the majority of homeless people are homeless because they suffer from a severe mental disorder which makes it difficult for them to hold a job or maintain a home.
5. Regarding social mobility, sociologists have found that, for the most part, people in the United States tend to take jobs that are not too different in socioeconomic status from those of their parents.
6. Research shows that most people in the underclass, especially the young, are unwilling to work and this accounts for their poverty status.
7. The text concludes that programs to promote full employment will probably not eliminate the problem of poverty.
8. Evaluations of workfare programs have shown that poor people in such programs are more likely to find employment and get off welfare than people without access to such programs.
9. People in the United States tend to be less supportive of public assistance programs than they are of social insurance programs.
10. Research shows that nations that spend more on public assistance usually have lower rates of poverty.

Fill-In Questions

1. The _____ definition of poverty compares people to some standard based partially on the lifestyles of other people.
2. The ranking of people into a hierarchy in which the resources considered valuable by society are unequally distributed is called a system of _____ .
3. In terms of racial designations, the majority of all poor people in the United States are _____ .
4. Davis and Moore's approach to understanding poverty would be classified as deriving from the _____ perspective.
5. Unemployment that occurs because of normal changes in the structure of the United States economy is called _____ .
6. The set of beliefs, values, and norms that emerges among the long-term poor and helps them adapt to their circumstances is called the _____ .
7. The _____ program was established in 1964 and provides poor preschool children with enrichment and early learning experiences that middle-class children presumably receive at home.
8. Three education and/or job training programs that are still in operation are _____ , _____ , and _____ .
9. Social Security and Medicare are classified as _____ programs.
10. _____ advocates the extreme laissez-faire position of dismantling the entire federal welfare system and income-support structure for working-age people.

Matching Questions

____ 1. social stratification
____ 2. cultural analysis of poverty
____ 3. Head Start
____ 4. Supplemental Security Income
____ 5. absolute definition of poverty
____ 6. homeless mentally ill
____ 7. functionalist perspective
____ 8. Medicare
____ 9. underclass
____ 10. functions of poverty

A. interactionist perspective
B. public-assistance program
C. fixed-income cutoffs
D. Kingsley Davis and Wilbert Moore
E. hierarchy of inequality
F. long-term, severely disadvantaged poor
G. social-insurance program
H. Herbert J. Gans
I. deinstitutionalization
J. educational program for poor children

Essay Questions

1. Discuss the different ways of defining poverty, pointing to the drawbacks of each one. Which definition is currently used for social policy decisions in the United States?
2. Summarize the research on the social characteristics of the poor in the United States.
3. What accounts for the increase in homelessness in the United States in recent decades?
4. What answers does the functionalist perspective offer on the issue of why poverty exists in society?
5. What are the positive functions that poverty can perform for society?
6. What criticisms have been made of the cultural analysis of poverty?
7. What recommendations have sociologists made to assist the underclass in their rise out of poverty?
8. What are the principles that underlie the workfare approach to public assistance? How well does it work?

9. Make both the laissez-faire and interventionist arguments on the issue of whether welfare works or not.
10. Describe how policies on poverty and welfare are dealt with differently in industrial societies other than the United States.

Answers

Multiple-Choice

1. B; 2. C; 3. E; 4. A; 5. D; 6. A; 7. A; 8. C; 9. B; 10. C

True/False

1. F; 2. F; 3. T; 4. F; 5. T; 6. F; 7. T; 8. T; 9. T; 10. F

Fill-In

1. relative
2. social stratification
3. white
4. functionalist
5. structural unemployment
6. culture of poverty
7. Head Start
8. Head Start, JTPA, JOBS
9. social insurance
10. Charles Murray

Matching

1. E; 2. A; 3. J; 4. B; 5. C; 6. I; 7. D; 8. G; 9. F; 10. H

For Further Reading

Mary Jo Bane and David T. Ellwood. *Welfare Realities: From Rhetoric to Reform.* Cambridge, Mass.: Harvard University Press, 1994. This book summarizes recent research on issues of welfare dependency and welfare reform and suggests some interesting new policies. These policy analysts went to work for the Clinton administration in 1993.

Alex Kotlowitz. *There Are No Children Here: The Story of Two Boys Growing Up in the Other America.* New York: Doubleday, 1991. This is a very sensitive and wrenching description of what it is like to grow up poor and African American in Chicago. It helps the reader to see, through the eyes of the poor, what it is like to be poor.

Elliot Liebow. *Tell Them Who I Am: The Lives of Homeless Women.* New York: The Free Press, 1993. This is an enlightening and compassionate look at the lives of women who are homeless—how they got that way and how they cope with it. Liebow is an anthropologist who did participant observation research to uncover this aspect of life in the United States.

Kevin Phillips. *The Politics of Rich and Poor: Wealth and the American Electorate in the Reagan Aftermath.* New York: Random House, 1990. This commentator argues very strongly and convincingly that the 1970s and 1980s were a period of income redistribution in the United States, with wealth flowing away from the lower and middle classes and into the hands of the very well-to-do.

Valerie Polakow. *Lives On the Edge: Single Mothers and Their Children in the Other America.* Chicago: University of Chicago Press, 1993. This book provides an excellent description of life for poor single mothers in a very affluent nation. It dispels many of the myths surrounding childbirth and welfare among the poor.

Richard H. Ropers. *Persistent Poverty: The American Dream Turned Nightmare.* New York: Plenum, 1992. This is a good analysis of how poverty results from long-term economic, social, and political policies and trends rather than from the inadequacies or shortcomings of the poor themselves.

Rob Rosenthal. *Homeless in Paradise: A Map of the Terrain.* Philadelphia: Temple University Press, 1994. This applied sociologist offers an intriguing glimpse of the homeless in an otherwise wealthy community in California. He looks at why they become homeless, what it's like to live on the street, and some of the problems social scientists confront in studying homelessness.

Susan Sheehan. *Life For Me Ain't Been No Crystal Stair.* New York: Pantheon, 1993. This insightful book gives us a window into the world of poverty by describing life for a teenage girl growing up poor in the streets of New York City.

SIX CHAPTER *Race and Ethnic Relations*

A central value in the United States is equality—the belief that people should be treated with dignity and respect and have access to social opportunities regardless of their particular racial, ethnic, religious, or sexual group membership. In addition, Americans take pride in boasting of how a "little person on the bottom can make it" in their country. For example, both Ronald Reagan and Bill Clinton were born into quite humble circumstances, and both have accumulated considerable wealth and power during their lives, ultimately being elected to the highest public office in the land. Their lives, along with the lives of such people as Abraham Lincoln, John D. Rockefeller, Andrew Carnegie, and H. L. Hunt, support the contention that opportunity awaits those who want to work hard. Yet how true is this?

One of the most fascinating and enriching aspects of life in the United States is the great physical and cultural diversity of the peoples who have settled here. This diversity has provided the United States with a large range of lifestyles. At the same time, however, it has been a major source of divisiveness and conflict for our society. Despite our cultural emphasis on equality, groups with different traditions, values, and languages have struggled with one another over power, privileges, and prestige. In fact, U.S. history has been a chronicle of unequal treatment of racial minorities, stretching from the enslavement of black Africans for the benefit of white Europeans settling the New World to the persisting barriers to advancement that confront some black, Hispanic, and Asian Americans today. More often than not, one group has tried to impose its own way of life on other groups. Events, from the civil rights movement during the 1950s and 1960s to the highly destructive riot in south central Los Angeles in 1992, all document why race and ethnic relations persist in being regarded as a social problem in the United States.

Characteristics such as race and ethnicity are called *ascribed statuses* because they are assigned to people and represent social positions over which people have little or no say about occupying. Whether the people occupying these statuses like it or not, such positions can and do serve as the basis for unequal treatment of groups, functioning as criteria for allocating resources and determining life chances and lifestyles. Such groups are referred to by sociologists as minority groups, and a discussion of what constitutes a minority group is our first topic in this chapter.

Minority Groups

A **minority group** is *a group whose members share distinct physical or cultural characteristics; are denied access to power and resources available to other groups, and are accorded fewer rights, privileges, and opportunities* (Marden, Meyer, and Engel, 1992). In the United States, black, Hispanic, Vietnamese, and some white ethnic groups such as rural Appalachians are considered minority groups because each has lower levels of educational and occupational attainment than other groups, and each has fewer opportunities. Chapter 7 will show that, despite their numerical majority in our population, women are also considered a minority group because they have been denied equal access to education, jobs, and important positions that men have controlled for some time. Then, Chapter 8 will consider the plight of the young and the old who can also be considered minorities because they are sometimes exploited and deprived of rights and privileges because of their age. This chapter, however, focuses only on minorities whose disadvantaged status arises from their racial or ethnic group membership.

The term *minority group,* then, refers not to numerical size but to one's position in the stratification system of society. A rather extreme case from recent history of a numerically large group of people being dominated by a much smaller group can be found in South Africa's traditional system of *apartheid* (Adam and Moodley, 1986). About 85 percent of South Africa's population is made up of black Africans. Under *apartheid,* these people had virtually no power, and a system of legal segregation maintained a rigid separation between the social worlds of blacks and whites. Blacks could not vote, they received limited educations, they were restricted to certain occupations, their travel in their own country was rigidly controlled, and they could live only in certain designated areas. The dominant group in South Africa has been the white Afrikaners, a small group of descendants of early Dutch or Huguenot immigrants, who possessed virtually complete control over the political, economic, and social life of South Africa. Although change has been occurring in South Africa in the 1990s, as recently as the late 1980s black South Africans could not vote for central government candidates, residential and school segregation still existed, and legislation placed 87 percent of South African land in white

Myths & FACTS

ABOUT RACE AND ETHNICITY

Myth: The Civil Rights Act, affirmative action, and other social policies have eliminated racism in the United States.

FACT: While the amount of overt prejudice and discrimination against racial minorities has declined in the past few decades, research still finds considerable racism and discriminatory practices. Recent studies, for example, document discrimination against African Americans still occurring in housing and employment (Neckerman and Kirschenman, 1991; "Study Finds . . . ," 1991).

Myth: If people insist on retaining a strong racial or ethical identity, then ethnocentric tendencies make conflict, and sometimes violence, an inevitable development in such multiracial or multiethnic societies.

FACT: While such conflict and violence are all too common, political and social structures can be created that minimize the likelihood of it. Switzerland, for example, is made up of three distinct ethnic groups. Yet, they have overcome conflicts and work together peacefully and cooperatively because of a political system that ensures the participation and influence of minorities.

Myth: Native Americans live comfortably with the benefits they receive from the government for

being Indian and with the proceeds from the gambling casinos that are now permitted on some reservation lands.

FACT: Of all American minorities, native Americans remain among the poorest. As a group, they suffer very high unemployment rates and have a median income that is less than half the national average. More than one-third of all native American families live below the official poverty level. Native Americans living on reservations tend to be worse off than their non-reservation counterparts, with large families often living in small, dilapidated homes.

Myth: Nonwhites in the United States continue to lag behind whites in education, income, and occupational status in the 1990s.

FACT: Contemporary reality is more complicated than this. African Americans, for example, have made considerable improvement, and their educational levels are coming very close to those of whites. Cuban Americans, Chinese Americans, and Japanese Americans are among the best educated groups in the United States. However, inequities persist. For example, African Americans and Hispanic Americans still lag considerably behind whites in average family income.

---

hands. These arrangements made South Africa one of the most rigidly stratified societies in the world. As we saw in Chapter 5, social stratification refers to the ranking of people into a hierarchy in which the resources considered valuable by society are unequally distributed. Ascribed characteristics such as race and ethnicity often determine a person's position in

the stratification system, as they did, and still do, in South Africa. But the terms *race* and *ethnicity* can be easily misunderstood.

Race and Ethnicity

People use the term *race* quite freely and often with only a vague understanding of its precise meaning. Scientists use the term *race* as a biological concept to identify a population that differs from others in terms of certain key genetic, hereditary traits. There is much controversy among anthropologists and biologists, however, over whether there are any traits unique to particular races in the world today. Certainly some traits ar more common in some races than others. But with extensive interbreeding among the racial groups throughout human history, genetic traits and characteristics have tended to spread around the world. However, although the biological reality of race may be hazy, its social reality is not. In fact, sociologists' definition of race is based on people's *belief* in racial differences: A **race** is *a group of people who are believed to be a biological group sharing genetically transmitted traits that are defined as important.* Thus, race is a social category because people make important distinctions between people on the basis of such presumed biological differences, even when these differences are actually vague or nonexistent.

An **ethnic group** is *a people who share a common historical and cultural heritage and sense of group identity and belongingness.* Groups that share distinctive cultural traits such as a common language, national origin, religion, or a sense of historical heritage have been a major source of diversity that has enriched all of our

As this march of Ku Klux Klan members in Washington, DC illustrates, white supremacist groups have continued to find support among some people in the United States, suggesting that some degree of racism persists.

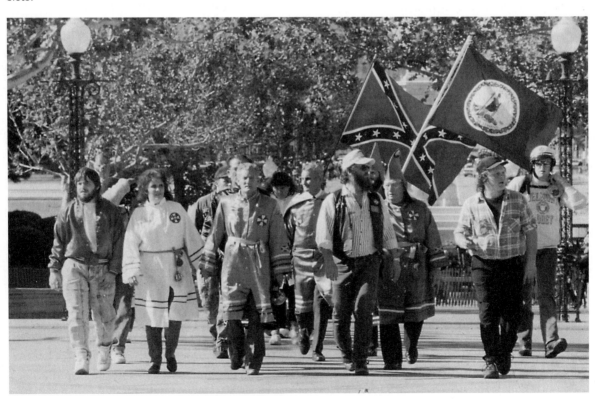

lives. Hispanic Americans, Polish Americans, Gypsies, the Amish, and the Jews are but a few of the many ethnic groups in the United States that have made significant contributions to our way of life. On the other hand, much of the tension, conflict, and violence that have been part and parcel of U.S. history and still characterize social life today have focused on ethnic differences.

Racism

The subordination and oppression of minority groups is commonly supported by an ideology that assumes that members of the minority are innately inferior and thus deserving of their subordinate status. **Racism** is *the view that certain racial or ethnic groups are biologically inferior and that practices involving their domination and exploitation are therefore justified.* Racist ideologies in Nazi Germany justified genocidal attacks on the Jews, just as racism in the United States has been at the core of discrimination against African Americans, Asians, and other racial groups. For example, in 1979, five social activists, mostly black, were killed in Greensboro, North Carolina, by a group of Nazis and Ku Klux Klan members, motivated in part by racist beliefs, who were later acquitted of murder charges in the slayings (Wheaton, 1987).

Despite the highest hopes of many people about equality, racism persists in some parts of the United States. At this point in the discussion, it is helpful to understand how this kind of ideology arises and, in particular, how prejudice and discrimination develop and affect minority groups.

Sources of Prejudice and Discrimination

Prejudice and discrimination are closely intertwined, so much so that people are likely to view them as the same thing. In reality, they are quite distinct. A **prejudice** is *an irrational attitude toward certain people based solely on their membership in a particular group* (Levin and Levin, 1982). Individuals are "prejudged" on the basis of whatever undesirable characteristics the whole group is presumed to possess. Prejudices can be positive, but they are also often negative. **Discrimination,** on the other hand, refers to *behavior, particularly unequal treatment of people because they are members of a particular group.* The type of discrimination we are most concerned with is the denial of equal access to resources, privileges, or opportunities, practices that are often based on illogical and irrational grounds.

The relationship between prejudice and discrimination is complex. Although they are likely to go together, Robert K. Merton (1949) has demonstrated that sometimes they do not. In fact, people may combine prejudice and discrimination in four different ways. The most desirable combination, from the point of view of political and social values in the United States, is the *unprejudiced nondiscriminator* who accepts other racial or ethnic groups in both belief and practice. The *prejudiced discriminator,* on the other hand, has negative feelings toward a particular group and translates these sentiments into unequal treatment of people in that group. Members of the Ku Klux Klan, for example, have a strong prejudice against blacks and members of other racial groups; they advocate segregated schools and neighborhoods. These first two possibilities involve a consistency between belief and practice, but there are other possibilities. The *prejudiced nondiscriminator* is a kind of "closet bigot" who is prejudiced against members of some groups but does not translate these attitudes into discriminatory practices. A landlord, for example, may be prejudiced against Asian Americans, yet still rent apartments to them because of laws forbidding housing discrimination. Because there are now many laws against discrimination that are strictly enforced, the incidence of this kind of relationship between prejudice and discrimination is likely to increase. The *unprejudiced discriminator* treats the members of some groups unequally because it is convenient or advantageous to do so rather than out of personal antipathy toward them. Salespeople in a real estate agency, for example, may have no personal prejudices but still decline to show houses in certain neighborhoods to African Americans because of the prejudices of people who already live in those neighborhoods.

Next, the major sources of prejudice and discrimination and some of their consequences—the factors that lead them to be viewed as social problems—are reviewed.

Social Sources

Problems of poverty and discrimination are closely linked because the result of discrimination is often that minorities are poor, with little access to valued resources. Because of this, prejudice and discrimination can be understood in part through the theoretical explanations of wealth and poverty presented in Chapter 5: the functionalist, conflict, and interactionist perspectives. That discussion will not be repeated here. Instead, some additional elements of the perspectives that apply especially well to problems of prejudice and discrimination will be presented.

Ethnocentrism   **Ethnocentrism** is *the tendency to view one's own group or culture as an in-group that follows the best and the only proper way to live.* An **in-group** is *a group that we feel positively toward and identify with, and that produces a "we feeling."* Feeling positively about one's own group, of course, is good because it gives one a sense of belonging and self-worth. For functionalists, ethnocentrism is functional because it produces loyalty, cohesiveness, and strong group ties. All this helps groups stick together and achieve their goals. It can, however, lead one to believe that other groups—especially those that are very different—have unfavorable characteristics. If one's own way of life is the only proper way to live, it seems that other lifestyles are improper. This can be used to justify unfair,

hostile, and even genocidal attacks on other groups. Under Adolf Hitler, for example, the Nazis were so thoroughly convinced of the superiority of the alleged Aryan "race" that the Jews became a despised out-group. Likewise, many Europeans who came to the Americas as colonists believed that their European heritage contained all that was wise and desirable, and these racist beliefs fueled their treatment of the people who inhabited the New World. So if ethnocentrism gets out of hand, it can become dysfunctional and create social disorganization in the form of hostility, conflict, and discrimination, which can threaten the social order. Although ethnocentrism can have these negative consequences, according to functionalists, such outcomes are not inevitable if people are aware of and guard against them.

Competition   According to the conflict perspective, prejudice and discrimination arise when groups find themselves in competition with each other. This competition is often economic, for jobs or land, but it can also be based on noneconomic valued resources, such as access to attractive marriage partners or the right to practice a preferred religion. The more intensely groups compete, the more threatening each group becomes to the other and the more likely negative and hostile views are to emerge. When there are obvious differences between the groups, such as in skin color or religious practices, these can become the focus of prejudice. Discriminatory practices may emerge, sanctioned by law or custom, as a way to limit the access of the less powerful group to the scarce resources. Prejudice and discrimination can arise from competitive situations in a number of specific ways (Olzak, 1992).

One type of competitive situation has been called a split labor market by sociologist Edna Bonacich (Bonacich, 1972). A **split labor market** is *one in which there are two groups of workers willing to do the same work, but for different wages.* In a split labor market, lower-priced laborers have a competitive advantage because employers prefer to hire them. Higher-priced workers find their position threatened by those willing to work more cheaply. In such a situation, the higher-priced workers will be inclined to discriminate against the inexpensive laborers in an effort to exclude them from certain occupations. Bonacich argues that this is a key factor in much racial, ethnic, and sexual antagonism because the presumed biological differences between the two groups can serve as the focus of discrimination and can be justified on racist grounds. If people believe that members of a particular racial group are lazy or untrustworthy, then this is a rationale for excluding them from jobs that demand hard work and trustworthiness. Likewise, if people believe that women are best suited for clerical and secretarial positions, then this belief can be used to discriminate against them when they try to get more lucrative jobs in construction or the professions (Cheng and Bonacich, 1984; Boswell, 1986).

Another type of economic competition is one in which a powerful group exploits a weaker one for its own gain. A clear case of this would be the relationship between the slaveholder and the slave in which the former gains substantially from the relationship, to the detriment of the latter. Slavery in the United States was clearly a form of economic exploitation supported by racist beliefs about the inferiority of blacks. Many of the poor today suffer a similar kind of exploitation because their work at low-paying and demeaning jobs benefits the more affluent in society (see Chapter 5). A variant of this type of exploitation is **internal colonialism,** in which *a subordinate group provides cheap labor that benefits the dominant group and is then further exploited by having to purchase expensive goods and services from the dominant group* (Doob, 1993). For example, the poor in the United States not only provide cheap labor but also purchase expensive health care, televisions, food, and other products that provide substantial profit to dominant groups.

Socialization Once patterns of prejudice and discrimination arise, they become incorporated into the values and norms of the group. Prejudice and discrimination toward particular groups then become legitimated, transmitted to new members through the socialization process, and frequently internalized. A study of regional differences in prejudice toward African Americans during the 1960s, for example, found, not surprisingly, that there was greater prejudice in the South, especially within the states of the old Confederacy (Middleton, 1976). It also found, however, that people who lived in the South as children and then moved to other regions were less prejudiced than those who remained in the South. In the same way, people who grew up outside the South and then moved there were more prejudiced than those who remained outside the South. In other words, people tend to adopt the prejudiced beliefs, values, and norms that are considered appropriate in the groups they belong to.

Institutionalized Discrimination Prejudice and discrimination sometimes become incorporated into social policies and practices, and this can result in the perpetuation of prejudice and discrimination through **institutionalized discrimination:** *the inequitable treatment of a group resulting from practices or policies that are incorporated into social, political, or economic institutions and that operate independently from the prejudices of individuals.* One form of institutionalized discrimination is the use of physical size requirements as qualifications for certain jobs. Many police departments, for example, set minimum height requirements for police officers. Asian Americans have protested against this because Asians are, on the average, shorter than whites and many therefore cannot qualify for police work. Discrimination in this form may not be direct; people may not be excluded from jobs because of their race. Rather, it is the minimum entrance requirements that effectively bar most members of a particular minority group from the jobs while serving as a barrier to only a few people in the dominant group. Through institutionalized discrimination, social inequality can persist long after prejudicial attitudes may have changed. In fact, much of the civil rights effort in the United States over the past thirty years has been concentrated on eliminating this kind of discrimination.

Psychological Sources

A number of psychological factors can play a part in the emergence of prejudice and discrimination.

Stereotyping One psychological factor involves the human tendency to categorize. The physical and social world is sufficiently complex that we need to simplify it by thinking in terms of general categories or by lumping together the elements that have something in common. Categories, however, can become *stereotypes*— rigid and oversimplified images in which each element or person in a category is assumed to possess all the characteristics associated with that category. Because some Jews work in banking, for example, some people might assume that all Jews are proficient in financial matters. Thus, stereotyping can contribute to prejudice and discrimination.

Frustration and Aggression Prejudice and discrimination can arise when people become frustrated by their inability to achieve sought-after goals. Psychologists have shown that frustration can lead to aggression in both overt and covert forms (Baron and Richardson, 1994). Aggression can be expressed by direct physical assaults or through prejudice or discrimination. One form this aggression can take is *scapegoating*, or placing the blame for one's troubles on an individual or group incapable of offering effective resistance. This happened, for example, in the southern United States between 1880 and 1930 when thousands of blacks were lynched by angry mobs of whites, many of whom were suffering from unemployment or other economic difficulties. Such racial hatred and discrimination can serve as a form of release for frustrated people, offering the hope, however false, that they are attacking the true source of their difficulties.

The Authoritarian Personality Another psychological approach has been to search for personality types that are more prone toward prejudice and discrimination. For example, motivated by the dread that the events of Hitler's Germany in the 1930s might occur again, a group of social scientists initiated a research project that ultimately found a series of personality characteristics, now called the authoritarian personality, that tend to be associated with prejudice (Adorno et al., 1950). The **authoritarian personality** is characterized by *a rigid adherence to conventional lifestyles and values, admiration of power and toughness in interpersonal relationships, submission to authority, cynicism, an emphasis on obedience, and a fear of things that are different.* Authoritarians tend to be suspicious, anti-intellectual, and insecure about their own self-worth. They are also likely to be conformists and upset by ambiguities, preferring a world characterized by absolutes with few gray areas. Numerous studies over the years have documented the link between authoritarianism and prejudice. Furthermore, this relationship has been discovered in many cultural contexts, such as white prejudice against blacks, Arab prejudice against Jews, and Israeli prejudice against Arabs (Hanson, 1975; Dekker and Ester, 1991; Kluegel and Bobo, 1991).

The sources of prejudice and discrimination are complex, resulting from the intertwining of numerous sociological and psychological factors. Most sociologists hold that social factors such as ethnocentrism, competition, socialization, and institutionalized discrimination play the most important roles in that these "set the stage" for the operation of psychological mechanisms. Without this social underpinning, prejudice and discrimination resulting from the psychological mechanisms alone would likely be sporadic and unorganized. This is exemplified by the example of lynchings of African Americans by whites mentioned earlier. Research makes clear that the frustration that helped create such horrid aggression was produced in part by the economic competition that existed in some communities in the South between whites and African Americans. In locales where there was less of such competition, lynchings were substantially less common, although they did occur (Soule, 1992). Unfortunately, the social sources of prejudice and discrimination are all too often present, and the consequences can be devastating both to society and individuals.

Consequences of Discrimination

Prejudice by itself can be relatively harmless, but it can become destructive when it fuels discrimination. Discrimination marks the spot where the social problems surrounding race and ethnic relations begin. In modern societies, discrimination against minorities has had a detrimental impact, although some groups benefit in the short run. First and most important, discrimination forces some groups into a disadvantageous position in the stratification system and adversely affects their life chances. Chapter 4 showed that discrimination results in higher rates of illness, injury, and death for minorities. This chapter will show that most minorities in the United States enjoy fewer socioeconomic resources and opportunities than do members of dominant white groups. Being deprived of these opportunities can produce simmering resentments that periodically erupt in destructive violence.

A second consequence of discrimination is its effect on people's views of themselves. Those who feel the brunt of discrimination may come to accept the devalued and stigmatized view of themselves that is implied by their being powerless and on the bottom of society. Minority

youth, for example, often have more negative self-concepts and a poorer sense of self-worth than do nonminority youth. This does not always occur, and the negative consequences can be overcome by supportive families, high-quality schools, and a minority culture that insulates people from the negativism implied by low social standing. Yet the research is clear that racism can and does result in lower self-esteem among minorities in some contexts (Pallas et al., 1990; Martinez and Dukes, 1991). And people with negative views of themselves and their worth may contribute less to society, and may exacerbate existing social problems through criminal behavior, long-term poverty, domestic violence, child neglect, and the like.

A third consequence of discrimination is that it creates tense, hostile, and sometimes violent encounters between dominant and minority group members, thus destroying trust, communication, and cooperation. In settings such as school or the workplace where members of different groups interact, discrimination makes it difficult for people to work together. In a relevant investigation, sociologist Albert Szymanski (1976) reported that white workers in the United States actually lose economically rather than gain from discrimination against nonwhite workers. The reason for this is that discrimination increases hostility and reduces the possibility of cooperation between lower-paid whites and non-whites, making it more difficult for either group to work toward better economic conditions for themselves. Collective action on the part of whites and non-whites, such as unionization, becomes less feasible when the two groups are split from one another by hostility.

A final consequence of discrimination is that it can undermine our social and political values and institutions. Because the United States professes to value equality and human dignity, the violation of these values because of racism and discrimination can generate cynicism regarding political and economic institutions. It can also threaten the legitimacy of those institutions if people see them merely as tools to benefit those fortunate enough to have acquired some power in society. From the functionalist perspective, this may represent the most serious of trends to combat—when people begin to lose faith in the system's core values and foundation, that system's survival may be in jeopardy.

With this understanding of prejudice and discrimination and their consequences, it is time to look at how these factors affect different minority groups in the United States. The situation is not a pretty one nor one to be proud of. Keep in mind that there are racial and ethnic groups that do not receive treatment here, as this discussion focuses on those that are the largest numerically or have encountered some of the most severe problems.

Racial and Ethnic Minorities in the United States

The United States is, of course, a land of foreigners. The only difference between groups in this regard is the time of their arrival. Even the group with the deepest roots in American soil, who claim the title "native" Americans, are descendants of immigrants who traversed the Bering Straits land bridge from Asia to the Americas tens of thousands of years ago. Beyond immigrant status, however, there is considerable variation in the positions of racial and ethnic groups in the United States today.

African Americans

African Americans comprise the largest nonwhite minority group in the United States, numbering approximately thirty-two million, or about 12.4 percent of our total population in 1992 (U.S. Bureau of the Census, 1994). They are also one of the oldest minority groups, with the first blacks arriving from Africa in 1619, not long after the first permanent European settlers in the New World. They are also the only minority group to have been enslaved in the United States. When the British colonized the New World, they followed the practices of the Spanish and Portuguese before them in bringing black African slaves to the New World (Westermann, 1955; Phillips, 1963).

Technically, all African Americans gained their freedom with the end of the Civil War. However, after a short period during which African Americans exercised a degree of freedom and political control, white Southerners began to reassert their dominance when federal troops left the South in 1877. In 1896, the Supreme Court ruled in *Plessy v. Ferguson* that it was constitutional to provide "separate but equal" public facilities for members of different races, and the era of widespread legal segregation began. For six decades, the *Plessy* case served as the foundation for discrimination against African Americans in schools, housing, and other areas. During this sixty-year period of time, a split labor market in black–white relations prevailed in the United States (Marks, 1981). Because of deteriorating race relations after the *Plessy* decision and economic distress in the South, a massive migration of young southern blacks to eastern and midwestern cities began. This was the beginning of large black ghettos in cities such as New York, Detroit, Boston, and Chicago. These concentrations of blacks in cities would later serve as an important mobilizing element in the efforts of African Americans to gain equality.

The 1950s and 1960s were a period of considerable change in the lives of African Americans (Bloom, 1987). In the *Brown v. The Board of Education* decision of 1954, the U.S. Supreme Court ruled that the "separate but equal" doctrine was unconstitutional. The southern states were ordered to integrate their schools "with all deliberate speed," but this process turned out to be rather slow. However, the civil rights movement emerged and, along with more militant black groups, initiated a drive for more economic and social opportunities for African Americans. Out of the demonstrations, protests, and rioting came the Civil Rights Act of 1964 and the Voting Rights Act of 1965. Later, affirmative-action programs and school busing would be used to provide greater opportunities for African Americans.

The position of African Americans has improved substantially over the past three decades. For example, the number of blacks enrolled in college has increased six times since 1960, whereas enrollment of whites has only tripled; African Americans now constitute 10 percent of all college students, compared to 6 percent in 1960 (U.S. Bureau of the Census, 1994). The number of African Americans in professional occupations also increased at a much faster rate than among whites. The percentage of blacks registered to vote has doubled, and the number of blacks holding elected political office has increased by five times.

The current picture, however, is by no means one of unblemished progress because African Americans still lag behind many other groups in terms of access to education, power,

and economically rewarding jobs (see Table 6.1 and Figure 6.1), For example, although the average income of African Americans has climbed in the past thirty years, the income of white people has also increased, and the position of African Americans relative to that of whites has changed very little. The ratio of black-to-white income is virtually the same as it was thirty years ago. Although channels of mobility are open to some blacks, others are trapped in poverty or in occupations that offer little prestige or hope for advancement (see Chapter 5). By the 1990s, for example, the number of African Americans in poverty is actually higher than it had been in 1965, with the poverty rate being three times as high as for whites (U.S. Bureau of the Census, 1994).

This lagging achievement is not due to a lack of aspirations, since research shows that African-American youth actually have higher educational and occupational aspirations than do white youth (Solorzano, 1991). Somewhere along the way, these high aspirations get side-

TABLE 6.1 Income of White, Black, and Hispanic Families, 1960–1993

Year	Median Income			Ratio of Black to White Income	Ratio of Hispanic to White Income
	White	Black	Hispanic		
1960	$ 5,835	$ 3,230	NA*	.55	
1965	7,251	3,993	NA*	.55	
1970	10,236	6,279	NA*	.61	
1975	14,268	8,779	$ 9,551	.61	.67
1980	21,904	12,674	14,716	.58	.67
1985	29,152	16,786	19,027	.58	.65
1993	39,300	21,542	23,654	.55	.60

*Data not available

Source: U.S. Bureau of the Census, *Statistical Abstract of the United States, 1985* (Washington, D.C.: U.S. Government Printing Office, 1984), p. 446; U.S. Bureau of the Census, *Statistical Abstract of the United States, 1995* (Washington, D.C.: U.S. Government Printing Office, 1995), p. 474.

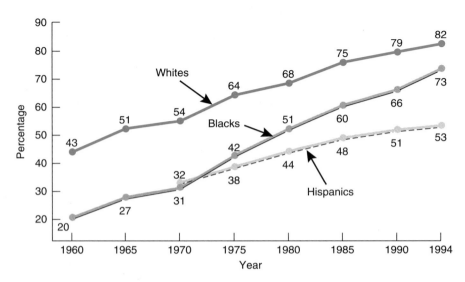

FIGURE 6.1   People Completing Four Years of High School or More, by Race or Ethnicity, Among People Aged Twenty-Five Years and Older, 1960–1994. *Source:* U.S. Bureau of the Census, *Statistical Abstract of the United States, 1995* (Washington, D.C.: U.S. Government Printing Office, 1995), p. 157.

tracked before becoming reality. The Policy Issues section in this chapter will explore some reasons for the slow improvement in the circumstances of African Americans. However, a clearly overriding factor is that prejudice and discrimination against African Americans have been deeply embedded in U.S. history since the period of slavery and, although improvements have occurred, racism is still a powerful force in the United States (Neckerman and Kirschenman, 1991; Hacker, 1992). As just one illustration of this, a report published in 1991 documented persisting discrimination against black Americans attempting to rent or purchase a home ("Study Finds . . .", 1991). Researchers sent a black person and a white person, with the same income and educational levels, to inquire about the same housing. In over half of the cases, the black person experienced discrimination by being told the housing was no longer available when it actually was available, being charged more

rent, being shown fewer housing units, or being steered to housing in predominantly minority neighborhoods. Clearly, as this and other research shows, African Americans are still not treated equally, nor are their opportunities the same as those for whites.

Hispanic Americans

Hispanic Americans, or Latinos, are Americans whose ancestral home is Mexico, Central America, South America, or the Caribbean. They include Mexican Americans (Chicanos), Cubans, and Puerto Ricans. (Some members of this ethnic group prefer to be called Hispanic and others Latino; there is no consensus about a proper designation. This text will use Hispanic as the primary designation because it is the term used by the Census Bureau from which many of the data in this chapter were obtained.) In 1993 there were twenty-three million Hispanic Americans in the United States, or about 9 percent of our population. There are also an estimated three to six million Hispanics in the United States illegally.

The largest Hispanic group in the United States, almost two-thirds of the total, is the Mexican Americans (see Figure 6.2). This group has a long history of settlement in the United States (Moore, 1976; Acuna, 1987). In fact, there have been Spanish communities located throughout what is now the American Southwest since before Mexican independence from Spain in 1821. However, as the white population in the Southwest grew during the 1800s, the economic prospects for these early settlers declined. Light-skinned, pure Spanish settlers who had adopted the white lifestyle were accepted into the white world, but the darker-skinned settlers who maintained their heritage, especially those with some Indian heritage, were viewed as inferiors and bore the brunt of prejudice and discrimination (Vigil, 1980). Following the Mexican Revolution in 1909, hundreds of thousands of Mexican peasants migrated to the Southwest, where there was much demand for inexpensive labor because of expanding agriculture and railroads. The status of these more recent migrants to the United States, however, was low, although perhaps slightly higher than it had been in Mexico. The Depression of the

Louis Farrakhan addresses the Million Man March on Washington, DC, in 1995. This march was in part a reaction to persisting prejudice and discrimination against African Americans in the United States.

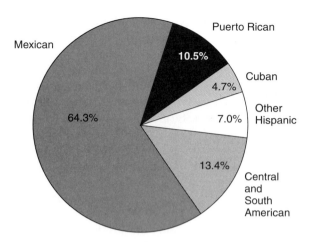

FIGURE 6.2 Percentage Distribution of Hispanic Americans by Type of Spanish Origin, 1993. *Source:* U.S. Bureau of the Census, *Statistical Abstract of the United States, 1994* (Washington, D.C.: U.S. Government Printing Office, 1994), p. 51.

1930s resulted in a decline in farm work, driving many Mexican Americans into the cities to seek employment or public relief. The first urban barrios, or Spanish-speaking neighborhoods, began to spring up in such cities as Denver, Phoenix, and Los Angeles.

Since World War II, the position of Mexican Americans has changed substantially. First, their numbers have grown steadily because of a continuing stream of migrants from Mexico and a high birthrate among Mexican Americans. By 1980, this group made up almost 20 percent of the California population and had larger concentrations in many urban areas in the Southwest: 62 percent of El Paso residents, for example, were of Spanish heritage. Second, in part as an outgrowth of the civil rights movement, the Chicano movement gained support in the 1960s in championing the rights of all Hispanics. Cesar Chavez organized the United Farm Workers to fight for better pay and working conditions for Chicano farm workers, and Reyes Lopez Tijerina started *La Alianza Federal de Mercedes* to demand the return to Chicanos

of land in the Southwest deeded to their ancestors in the Treaty of Guadalupe Hidalgo in 1848.

In the past two decades, Mexican American efforts have focused more on conventional politics and consciousness raising than on confrontation (Hero, 1992). A number of Chicano organizations, such as the Mexican American Political Alliance (MAPA) in California, were founded in the 1960s and continue to be powerful forces on the political scene, pursuing the interests of Mexican Americans as a group. Consciousness raising and ethnic awareness have been encouraged by Chicano student organizations in high schools and colleges and by pressures for bilingual education in communities with large concentrations of Mexican Americans.

Puerto Rican Americans are the second largest Hispanic group in the United States, comprising 10.5 percent of all Hispanics. Puerto Ricans were granted U.S. citizenship, as a group, in 1917. A small number of Puerto Ricans immigrated to the mainland United States before World War II, mostly attracted by farm-labor jobs but a few by factory work in the East. Following World War II, this immigration increased dramatically, in large part because of the chronically depressed economy of Puerto Rico. Puerto Ricans have tended to settle in New York City and Chicago (Fitzpatrick, 1987).

Mexican Americans and Puerto Rican Americans today face much the same problems as African Americans: poverty, low educational levels, and poor health in comparison to Anglos (see Table 6.1 and Figures 6.1 and 6.3). For example, two out of five Puerto Rican families in the United States live in poverty, and just 53 percent of Americans of Spanish origin have completed four years of high school or more, whereas 82 percent of whites have done so. As with African Americans, the incomes of Hispanic families have persistently lagged behind those of white families, remaining at less than 70 percent of white incomes for the past twenty years and actually declining over the years.

Hispanics in the United States today are a diverse group. In addition to the variation among groups already mentioned, for example, Cuban Americans have generally been different from other Hispanics in that they come from more middle-class and affluent origins. Despite their diversity, some Hispanic groups may be moving toward a more common Latino ethnic identity and consciousness (Totti, 1987). Being of a different color, having a common origin in the "south," speaking a common tongue, many sharing the experience of discrimination and outsider status—all this may be forging an ethnic awareness that spans the diversity found in such groups as Mexican Americans and Puerto Ricans. In fact, the term *Latinismo* has been coined to describe a sentimental and ideological identification and loyalty that transcend individual Latin ethnic groups in the United States (Padilla, 1985). This emerging Latin consciousness may be in part political, that is, may reflect a realization that advantage can be gained in the struggle for equality and fair treatment by combining forces behind a common symbol. However, Latinismo also represents an identification with and devotion to the collective concerns of Spanish-speaking peoples in the United States. Groups such as the League of United Latin American Citizens and the Latino Urban Political Association have emerged to represent all Latin ethnic groups, while groups such as MAPA and the Puerto Rican Organization for Political Action devote some attention to the concerns of particular nationalities. All of these groups recognize that Hispanics—who soon may be the largest ethnic minority in the United States—can become an effective force for political and social change if they can get beyond their differences and combine their forces.

Native Americans

During the fifteenth and sixteenth centuries, there were probably between one million and ten million native Americans living in North America (Snipp, 1989). By the late 1800s, there were only about 250,000. After the founding of the United States, the federal government was required by the U.S. Constitution to negotiate treaties with native American groups, but this did not prevent whites from robbing Indians of their land. In 1824, the Bureau of Indian Affairs (BIA) was created by Congress as a division of the War Department to seek a military solution to what many Congressmen referred to as the "Indian problem." By 1830, Congress suc-

FIGURE 6.3 Percentage of Families in the United States with Incomes Below the Poverty Level, by Race, 1959–1993. *Source:* U.S. Bureau of the Census, *Statistical Abstract of the United States, 1995* (Washington, D.C.: U.S. Government Printing Office, 1995), p. 484.

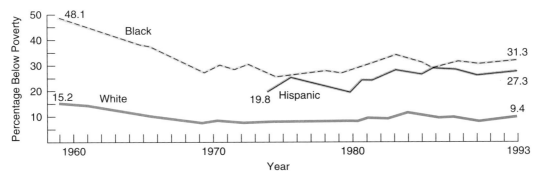

cumbed to pressures for opening up more Indian lands to white settlement and ordered the BIA to relocate all Indians west of the Mississippi River. It was not until 1924 that Congress passed the Indian Citizenship Act, granting U.S. citizenship to all native Americans. In 1968, Congress enacted the Indian Civil Rights Act, which extended the basic human rights guaranteed by the Bill of Rights to persons living on tribal lands. Although this undoubtedly had many positive benefits, it may have had the negative effect of undermining tribal control and unity among native American groups who possessed their own judicial systems based on tribal customs (Schaefer, 1993).

By the 1990s, there were 2.1 million native Americans in the United States (U.S. Bureau of the Census, 1994: 17). In 1983, 2.3 percent of American land, fifty-three million acres, was still being managed by the Bureau of Indian Affairs "on behalf of" native Americans. In 1980, there were 350,000 American Indians, Eskimos, and Aleuts living on reservations in the United States (Thornton, 1987). The BIA, now part of the Department of the Interior, has conservation as its prime directive rather than economic development. This deemphasis on economic matters has contributed to the problems of native Americans by making it more difficult for them to improve their economic position (Guillemin, 1980).

Native Americans suffer significant social, economic, and health disadvantages in comparison to other ethnic and racial groups (Snipp, 1989; Young, 1994). Nonreservation Indians are somewhat better off than their reservation counterparts, but half of all Indians live on reservations that are in rural areas. They suffer high levels of unemployment, low levels of income, and poverty rates disproportionate to their numbers in the population. They are also less likely to graduate from high school than people in most other groups. A comprehensive survey in the 1990s of adolescents attending school in reservation communities serviced by the Indian Health Service docu-

mented the extensiveness of these problems (Blum et al., 1992). When compared with rural white adolescents, the native American youth were much more likely to be in poor health, suffer sexual abuse, attempt suicide, commit suicide, eat a poor diet, and suffer severe emotional distress.

The 1960s were years when many minority groups began to resist oppression, and native Americans were among them. In 1969, a group of Indians seized Alcatraz Island to call attention to their exploitation. In 1973, members of the American Indian Movement (AIM) staged an armed takeover of Wounded Knee, South Dakota, where hundreds of native Americans had been killed by whites in the late nineteenth century. These protests may be in part responsible for some recent court decisions ruling that Indian tribes should receive payment for land taken from their ancestors during the nineteenth century. Still, there is a lingering feeling among many native Americans that exploitation continues, albeit in more subtle ways than before (Prucha, 1985).

By the 1990s, the native American community in the United States was growing in number and showing renewed pride in their history and culture (Fost, 1991). While many serious problems persist, a college-educated middle class of native Americans has emerged, and the number of businesses owned by Indians is increasing significantly. Tribes on reservations have been able to exploit gambling and tourism to create jobs, and some have built successful manufacturing businesses. These foundations suggest that a cohesive native American culture will grow in the future and may make it possible for more native Americans to succeed on tribal lands.

Asian Americans

Between 1820 and 1970, more than one million legal immigrants from China, Japan, the Philippines, Hong Kong, Korea, and India came to the United States—a mere 3.7 percent of all immigration taking place during that period (see Figure 6.4). The heaviest migration of Chinese to the United States occurred between 1849 and 1882 (Daniels, 1988). Although racial prejudices existed toward the Chinese prior to 1849, once their immigration began in large numbers, these sentiments intensified. There was a feeling among many people that the Chinese would deprive whites of jobs in mining and railroading, another illustration of the split labor market discussed earlier. These feelings culminated in the Chinese Exclusion Act of 1882, which prohibited the entrance of Chinese laborers into the United States for ten years.

Between 1882 and World War II, racist attitudes in the United States characterized the Chinese as a "yellow peril." Many Chinese returned to their own country because of this hostility. Those who remained were forced to move to ghettos called Chinatowns. Chinese people were often referred to with the pejorative term *coolies,* and the racism toward Chinese often implied biological differences between Chinese and Anglos. An anthropological study in 1877, for example, concluded, "It is true that ethnologists declare that a brain capacity of less than 85 cubic inches is unfit for free government, which is considerably above that of the coolie as it is below that of the Caucasian" (quoted in Miller, 1969: 145).

These anti-Chinese attitudes persisted in the United States until the 1940s. Following Japan's attack on Pearl Harbor, hostilities shifted toward the Japanese, and the Chinese came to be regarded in a more positive way. In 1943, the Chinese remaining in the United States were granted citizenship. Between 1950 and 1970, Chinese Americans became upwardly mobile, with children of the original immigrants attending colleges and universities

FIGURE 6.4 Immigrants to the United States, by Country of Last Permanent Residence, 1820–1990. *Sources:* U.S. Department of Justice, *1984 Statistical Yearbook of the Immigration and Naturalization Service* (Washington, D.C.: U.S. Government Printing Office, 1984), pp. 4–5; U.S. Bureau of the Census, *Statistical Abstract of the United States, 1994* (Washington, D.C.: U.S. Government Printing Office, 1994), p. 11.

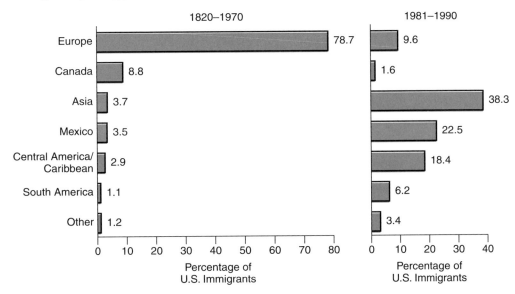

and moving into professional and technical positions. Today, the socioeconomic status of Chinese Americans, especially those who have been in the United States for some years, is considerably above the average for Americans as a whole (Hirschman and Wong, 1986; Barringer, Takeuchi, and Xenos, 1990).

The peak period of Japanese immigration to the United States began after the Chinese Exclusion Act, between 1880 and 1924. Unlike the Chinese, Japanese immigrants were permitted to bring their wives with them, which aided in the formation of stable Japanese families, and early relations between Americans and the Japanese were positive. After Pearl Harbor, Japanese Americans were the object of considerable discrimination, being forced to sell their property and being interned in concentration camps (Kitano, 1976; O'Brien and Fugita, 1991). Along with the enslavement of blacks and the genocidal attacks on native Americans, the imprisonment of Japanese Americans—none of whom had been proven disloyal to America—stands as one of the darkest examples of racism in U.S. history.

After release from the concentration camps after the war, Japanese Americans led successful lives, exceeding many whites in occupational achievements, and most Americans appear to have a high regard for Japanese Americans today (Ima, 1992; Barringer, Takeuchi, and Xenos, 1990). Still, there are occasional flare-ups of the racism that was so prevalent during World War II.

Significant immigration from Asia to the United States has continued in recent decades (Min, 1994). For example, in the 1970s and 1980s, tens of thousands of refugees entered the United States from Vietnam, Laos, and Cambodia as well as other parts of Asia. These recent immigrants have largely followed the route of their predecessors as far as integrating themselves into the United States, taking undesirable jobs that most workers tend to reject or opening small businesses to make a living. Although there is little widespread discrimination

against Asian immigrants, violence does occur. In the 1992 riot in south central Los Angeles, for example, Korean American businesses were apparently targeted for looting and burning by African American and Hispanic American rioters who were angry over what they perceived as mistreatment of blacks and Hispanics by Korean store owners. This reflects the economic sources of racial discrimination and conflict discussed earlier. Blacks and Hispanics find themselves in a position of economic subordination to Korean store owners. This has led to stereotyping on both sides, with Koreans accusing African Americans and Hispanics of stealing and African Americans and Hispanics accusing Koreans of selling poor products at high prices and refusing to hire African American or Hispanic employees. Exacerbating this situation is the fact that Koreans have little contact with African Americans and Hispanics outside of this economic (merchant–customer) context. The importance of this situation is explored in more detail in the Applied Research insert (see pp. 226-227).

So the experiences of the various racial and ethnic groups in the United States have been quite variable. Some of the implications of this variation are discussed in the Policy Issues insert in this chapter.

Today's Immigrants

In 1965, a totally revamped immigration act removed all racial and ethnic quotas for immigrants to the United States. As a consequence of this act and other trends, today's immigrants are quite unlike those of the past (see Figure 6.4). For most of U.S. history, over three-quarters of the immigrants have been from Europe, with very small proportions coming from Asia or Central and South America. Today, less than 10 percent come from Europe, 38 percent come from Asia, and another 47 percent from Mexico and Central and South America.

Figure 6.4 does not include people who have entered the United states illegally. Esti-

This Cambodian Buddhist Temple in Massachusetts shows the extent to which immigrants to the United States have changed: Today they come mostly from Asia, and Central and South America, rather than from Europe as in the past.

mates place the number of people in the United States illegally at between two and four million, most from Mexico and Central and South America (Morganthau, 1993). The impact of illegal immigrants on the United States is complex. On the positive side, they take low-paying and difficult jobs that many U.S. citizens seem disinclined to do. In other words, these immigrants perform many of the functions that poor people have traditionally served, as discussed in Chapter 5. On the negative side, some illegal immigrants take jobs that citizens might be willing to hold, and it is very costly to society to try to contain illegal immigration with a border patrol and other activities. While

it is very difficult to control illegal immigration, laws now prohibit the hiring of illegal aliens, and employers who do so can be fined and imprisoned (Schaefer, 1993). Some states have also stopped providing educational, health, and social services to illegal immigrants and their children.

In recent years, smaller and less publicized episodes of immigration have created problems of prejudice and discrimination. For example, tens of thousands of immigrants from middle eastern, mostly Arab, countries have settled in Detroit and southeast Michigan. Most Arab immigrants have headed for the Detroit area because earlier Arab immigrants settled there,

The experiences of the various racial and ethnic groups in the United States have been quite different. Some, such as Japanese and Chinese Americans, have become quite successful, whereas others, such as African Americans and Puerto Rican Americans, still lag behind on most indicators of socioeconomic status. Why the different outcomes? The answer to this lies, in part, in the cultural experiences of different groups.

The oppression of Japanese Americans has certainly been severe: incarceration in relocation camps during World War II without benefit of formal charges or a trial. They were considered a security threat, even though none of them was actually proven to be such a threat. They were sent thousands of miles to bleak camps; many lost all their possessions, including home and property; some families were separated. This was clearly a racist operation because no Italians or Germans—including those who were aliens—were treated similarly. Yet despite such ill treatment, five decades later Japanese Americans are one of the best-educated groups in the United States and have one of the highest median incomes of all groups. As a group they are solidly middle class.

What accounts for the rise of Japanese Americans since World War II? A good part of it has to do with the cultural context and heritage of Japanese Americans (Kitano, 1976, Shibutani, 1978). First, there is a work ethic in Japanese culture that is quite congruent with the values regarding work found in dominant groups in the United States. Thus, Japanese culture imbued Japanese Americans with cultural orientations that increased their chances of gaining an education or making money in the United States. Second, the Japanese family is highly valued, and family reputation and goals are regarded as more important than individual ones. Individuals gain a sense of self-worth from family membership, and they work hard to avoid bringing shame or disrepute to their family by their own failings. Individual success reflects positively on the family. Third, the Japanese who came to the United States never identified with the lower classes, even when living in poverty. They perceived themselves as successful and respectable, and they passed on middle-class expectations and aspirations to their children. They never developed the cultural orientation described in Chapter 5 that makes achievement more difficult. With a cultural heritage like this, young Japanese Americans are fairly well equipped to compete in various economic arenas if given the opportunity to do so.

So, the Japanese experience suggests that "cultural legacy" is the key factor: The values, skills, and traditions that people bring with them play a big part in their success. This has certainly also played a part in the experiences of some recent immigrant groups, such as Koreans, Vietnamese, Arabs, and Cubans. These immigrants often were part of the business and professional classes in their native lands, and this background endowed them with an entrepreneurial spirit, an educational background, or some business experience that made it easier for them to do well in the United States. Yet cultural legacy does not always carry the day. For example, in Ireland and other European countries in earlier centuries, Protestants were generally more prosperous than Catholics. Yet Irish Catholic immigrants to the United States have done better than Irish Protestant immigrants (Jencks, 1992).

So, although cultural legacy can play an important part, we need to look at other factors, some of which may be unique to particular groups. One is the mutual aid organizations that spring up to provide support for some immigrants. Koreans and some other recent immigrants, for instance, have been able to raise venture capital among friends and family within the ethnic community and sometimes from relatives in their native lands. In other cases, immigrants have ties to the business community in their native lands, which provide them with information and support in starting a new business (Katz and Ryan, 1992). In the case of Cuban immigrants to south Florida in the 1960s and 1970s, some early immigrants were well educated and experienced in business and were able to find important positions in banking and commerce. In the name of ethnic solidarity, they then assisted later Cuban immigrants who had less education and fewer resources with which to get a start in business in the United States (Portes and Stepick, 1993).

Some differences between the experience of African Americans and that of other immigrant groups help explain why the black struggle for success has been so difficult (Jencks, 1992). One is that, unlike most other immigrants, blacks came involuntarily. European and Asian immigrants saw migration as a new opportunity to be seized and planned to adapt and make the United States their home. Those who did not like it or did not do well could return from whence they came. Not so for African Americans. Many Africans were forcibly torn from their native lands, with little regard for their culture or their heritage, and were given no freedom to achieve or develop in the land to which they were brought. Slaves from many different cultural backgrounds were forced together. Slaves were strongly disciplined for showing initiative or independence, and there was often little regard for the integrity of the black family. Whatever entrepreneurial spirit existed in their native cultures was largely destroyed during the slave experience.

A second difference is that African immigrants had, at best, an ambivalence toward the legitimacy of the social and legal institutions that enslaved them. For many it was outright hostility and resentment. As a consequence, the African American culture that emerged incorporated this resentment and tolerated if not admired resistance to what some perceived as illegitimate social institutions. A third difference is that European immigrant groups, if they shed their ethnic heritage, could become "just plain Americans" and participate in the American success story. Because of visible differences, blacks were never allowed to do this and so there was less incentive to adopt mainstream culture. Fourth, the mutual supports that some ethnic groups could offer their members have been almost nonexistent among African Americans. Living in poverty in the United States with no link to their native lands meant that there was nowhere to turn for investment loans or other supports.

A final reason for the relatively slow improvement in the circumstances of African Americans is that they still suffer under persistent discrimination in the realms of occupation, education, and housing. This was described earlier in the discussion of African Americans in the United States. African Americans, and to a lesser degree Hispanics, are still not treated equally, nor are their opportunities the same as those available to white Americans (Hacker, 1992). It has only been in the past few decades that the structures of racial discrimination and oppression have begun to be dismantled. If this dismantling continues and a cultural environment emerges that is supportive of African-American achievement, the circumstances of African Americans will likely improve. The African-American experience teaches that the factors shaping outcomes for various immigrant groups are complicated, and not all immigrant groups have the same opportunities.

and thus a supportive network exists for the new immigrant. There have been sporadic but serious conflicts between Arab American store owners and African American patrons in the Detroit area that mirrors the black–Korean conflict mentioned earlier in Los Angeles. Once again, there is economic competition in a superior–subordinate relationship. The result has been isolation, stereotyping, and occasional violence. Because the role of social contact and social isolation is so important in intergroup relations, we will explore it in more detail in the Applied Research insert in this chapter.

Future Prospects

Assimilation or Pluralism?

A review of the history of racial and ethnic minorities in the United States shows that relations between minority and dominant groups have taken a number of different forms (Simpson and Yinger, 1985). For blacks, for example, *segregation* from whites in schools, housing, and transportation has been common and still lingers in some realms today. For many minorities, *subjugation,* in the form of subordination and exploitation, has been a major problem. The grisly experiences of native Americans came close to *genocide,* or the annihilation of an entire group. Estimates are that at least two-thirds of the native American population was annihilated by the direct and indirect actions of white Europeans, with some tribes being completely eliminated. Today, however, the most common relationships between racial and ethnic groups in the United States involve assimilation and pluralism. **Assimilation** is *the process by which a racial or ethnic minority loses its distinctive identity and way of life and becomes absorbed into the dominant group.* Despite the considerable amount of assimilation that has occurred in the United States, there are still many racial and ethnic minorities that preserve their heritage. This pattern of intergroup rela-

tions is called **pluralism,** *which exists when a number of racial and ethnic groups live side by side, each retaining a distinct identity and lifestyle while still participating in some aspects of the larger culture.*

What pattern of minority–majority relations is most desirable in the United States—assimilation, pluralism, or some other? People's response to this question is often colored by a misconception about what has happened historically. The United States is often referred to as a melting pot in which the beliefs, values, and lifestyles of many different racial and ethnic groups have been blended together into a unique mix that is called "American." If this had occurred, it would be a form of assimilation in which all groups change to some degree in creating an American identity. Actually, the experience of most immigrants to the United States has come closer to what Milton Gordon has called *Anglo conformity:* To share fully in the American dream, immigrants have been required to renounce their ancestral culture in favor of the beliefs, values, and lifestyle of the dominant WASPs, the white Anglo-Saxon Protestants (Gordon, 1964). These WASPs were among the earliest European immigrants to North America. They came from the British Isles and Germany, and they dominated political, economic, and social life in the United States from the sixteenth through the nineteenth centuries. The WASPs were sufficiently fearful of people who immigrated after them—from places such as Ireland, Italy, and Eastern Europe—that they attempted to "Americanize" them rather than let them build their own social institutions and way of life. Many people today still insist on a version of Anglo conformity by arguing that groups such as Hispanics and Asians should learn English and not be given a bilingual education.

Although Anglo conformity worked for quite a while, it has not persisted. Over time, the original WASP group became such a small minority that it became more difficult for it to force its lifestyle on others. The outcome, at least to this point, is that the United States remains a

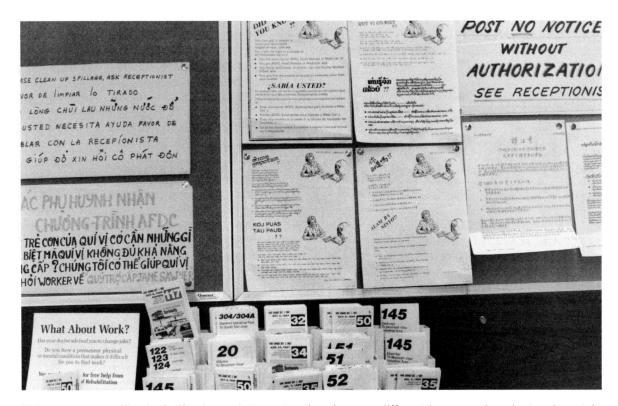

This government office in California needs to post notices in many different languages in order to adequately serve its clientele. This attests to the extent of racial, ethnic, and cultural pluralism that exists in the United States today.

highly pluralistic society with many distinct racial and ethnic subcultures. Furthermore, some minorities, especially among African Americans and Hispanics, who were never allowed to assimilate by the dominant white groups, prefer it that way. Whether pluralism is desirable, however, is a matter of considerable controversy (Pettigrew, 1988; Triandis, 1988). Many people argue that extensive pluralism will promote tensions that could flare into conflict in the future. They point to the efforts of French Canadians in Quebec to secede from Canada as the kind of problem that pluralism can generate. In fact, concern over this has become so strong in some groups that, by the mid-1990s, twenty-two states had passed laws making English the official lan-

guage of state business. Proponents of pluralism, on the other hand, contend that racial and ethnic diversity contributes to the richness of U.S. culture and symbolizes the nation's roots as open to the oppressed of all lands. Furthermore, ethnic identity can be a source of pride and positive self-regard for individuals, and speaking in one's native tongue can play an important part in this. Among Latinos, for example, speaking Spanish and having a large and powerful Spanish-language media in the United States are sources of cultural pride and ethnic identity (Totti, 1987).

The past few decades have generally been a time of improvement in the relationship between minorities and dominant groups in the

Combating Prejudice and Discrimination

The horror of the genocidal attack on Jews and other ethnic groups during World War II dramatically portrayed the extremes to which prejudice and racism might go. One positive spinoff from these atrocities was that they pushed many European and American social scientists to conduct research on the sources of prejudice and discrimination, and many of the results of that research have been summarized in this chapter. The findings of this body of research can also be applied to seeking ways of combating racism.

How do we reduce racist attitudes and encourage people to view members of another racial or ethnic group more positively? A program at a summer camp for children showed one way to achieve this (Clore et al., 1978). The camp included equal numbers of black and white children, and they came from all levels of the socioeconomic hierarchy. In the camp, all children had the same rights and same work duties. There was also an equal mix of blacks and whites among the administrators and counselors in the camp, so the authority structure of the camp was not racially biased. In other words, blacks were as likely to exercise power over the children as were whites. During their one-week stay at the camp, children were required to work on cooperative tasks involving group, rather than individual, goals.

What did the camp accomplish? Basically, children who entered the camp with negative attitudes toward members of the other race showed positive improvements in their views by the end of their stay. Why did this change occur? The answer to this question is complex. The results of past research and the outcomes of current programs, such as the one described above, are very clear in showing that intergroup contact can reduce prejudice if the conditions of the contact are right (Brewer and Miller, 1988; Sigelman and Welch, 1993). Contact should have these characteristics if it is to reduce prejudice:

1. The contact should have high "acquaintance potential," which means that people have the time and opportunity to get to know one another and have some personal and intimate associations.
2. The contact should be between people of equal status, rather than a low-status minority interacting with a higher-status member of the dominant group.
3. The behavior of the minority-group person in the contact should contradict the stereotype held of members of that group.
4. As a part of the contact, the people should work toward cooperative and interdependent

United States. Many of the more explicit forms of discrimination have been reduced, and these changes have lessened the inequalities that exist in the stratification system. In addition, racial and ethnic minorities in the United States today are more organized, confident, and optimistic than they were in the past.

The New Racism

Have we entered a new era of race relations in the United States where we can say that racism is mostly a thing of the past? To answer this question, we must clarify the meaning of the term *racism*. Many whites interpret this to mean support for white superiority or white supremacy, or a devaluing of or hostility toward people because of their race. This idea of racism focuses on individual attitudes and beliefs, and whites believe that this kind of racism has declined or largely disappeared. One thing that does seem clear is that blatant expressions of racism—blanket, negative castigations of all members of a particular racial or goals rather than competitive ones; that is, no one in the group can achieve his or her individual goals unless everyone works together and achieves their goals.

5. The contact situation should have the support of legitimate authorities, such as a school or church, and should involve social norms dictating friendliness and respect between people.

One can readily see that many of these features were built into the children's summer camp described above. One can also recognize that many everyday interpersonal contacts between members of different races violate these principles. Black and white prison inmates, for example, live together in intimate contact, but it is a very tension-filled contact with little inducement for cooperation or interdependence. Many races intermingle in schools, but school is often highly competitive. And how often is the equal status element violated when a black or Hispanic person deals with a white teacher, a white social worker, or a white prison guard?

We cannot, of course, change all these settings. On a smaller scale, however, we can structure social situations over which we do have control with the above principles of intergroup contact in mind. This was done very well in the children's

summer camp. A similar approach has been used successfully many times with adults in the form of small-group interaction and sensitivity training. The goal of these efforts is to bring members of different races together for lectures, discussions, and group activities over a period of days or weeks. Through the use of role playing and other group techniques, participants are encouraged to explore stereotypes, diagnose interracial problems, and cooperatively develop strategies for alleviating those problems. This was done, for example, in Houston in the late 1960s when police–community relations became very tense and hostile following a violent clash between black college students and police in which one police officer was killed. Hundreds of police and community residents participated in the program, and it had a positive effect on people's attitudes and reduced the number of citizen complaints against the police (Bell et al., 1969).

What has been learned about the impact of intergroup contact on prejudice and discrimination can be used to bring about other structural changes in society. School integration, for example, brings students of different races together. The research offers a pretty good idea how to do this so that the positive impact is maximized.

ethnic group—are limited mostly to a few, relatively marginal groups, such as skinheads or the remaining remnants of the Ku Klux Klan.

Many African Americans, on the other hand, define racism as institutional racism or discrimination that is built into the systems of power and social institutions of a society. In one interview, for example, African American college students clearly saw the white-dominated power structure on their campus as racism, even though particular white college administrators or faculty might not have expressed

racist attitudes themselves (Bunzel, 1991). With this view of racism, many African Americans believe that racism is still pervasive in the United States because whites still retain thorough control over political and economic institutional structures.

Some social scientists argue that blatant racism has merely been replaced by a new form of racism, sometimes called *symbolic racism,* in which hostility toward particular groups is expressed not directly but through opposition to policies or practices that benefit those groups

(Sears, 1988). One could express prejudice toward African Americans, for example, by opposing affirmative-action or school-busing policies that are intended to provide major benefits to African Americans. Furthermore, this symbolic racism is rationalized on the basis of support for mainstream American values, such as self-reliance, hard work, obedience, and discipline. The idea is that if African Americans worked hard, were obedient, and engaged in disciplined behavior, they would not need affirmative action to get ahead. However, the symbolic racism thesis argues that the real source of people's feelings toward African Americans and affirmative action is still racism against blacks.

The symbolic racism thesis is difficult to assess, in part because the weaknesses of surveys on racism make it hard to tell whether opposition to a policy is genuine or a symptom of deeply felt prejudice. Recent surveys attempting to do so have produced equivocal results—some evidence supports the idea, other evidence does not (Sniderman et al., 1991; Sidanius, Devereux, and Pratto, 1992). So, we cannot say with certainty how much levels of racism have declined in the past few decades. It may be that some (or much) of that decline has merely represented a shift from overt racism to a more covert form.

Race Relations Today: Race or Class?

As discussed earlier, some minority groups, such as African Americans, still lag significantly behind other groups on various indicators of socioeconomic status. There is considerable debate over whether this is because of racial discrimination or because of the class position held by many African Americans, which places them in a weak situation from which to compete for jobs and income.

Sociologist William J. Wilson argues that class, rather than race, is the more important factor in determining the social positions of African Americans today (Wilson, 1978; 1987).

Wilson certainly does not deny that racial antagonism is still with us, or that substantial discrimination against and oppression of African Americans not only has clouded U.S. history but also lingers today. But he points out that the real problem today lies in the continuing existence of an "underclass" of poor, marginally skilled African Americans who have little opportunity to obtain the education and skills necessary to succeed in a modern industrial society (see the Applied Research insert in Chapter 5). Such an underclass can also be found among Puerto Ricans and some other Hispanic groups (Tienda, 1989). Wilson attributes the persistence of this underclass to basic changes in the structure of the U.S. economy, including the relocation of industries away from the communities where many minorities live and a labor market in which people with few job skills or little education are limited to low-paying work with little opportunity for advancement. The primary barrier that this underclass faces, argues Wilson, is the lack of appropriate job-related skills, not racial discrimination. Blacks or Hispanics with job skills or a college education, he argues, will enjoy opportunities and privileges similar to those of their white counterparts in the class hierarchy and will probably not face significant discrimination even if economic conditions deteriorate.

On the other side of this argument are sociologists Joe Feagin and Melvin Sykes (1994) who argue that racial oppression is still a key factor influencing race relations in the United States. They argue that African Americans are still oppressed and discriminated against because of their race, although the forms and mechanisms of racial oppression may have changed since the 1950s and 1960s. One difference today is that the overt individual racism of the past has declined considerably, but there is still widespread, institutionalized racism in which such things as residential and school segregation place barriers before the advancement of many African Americans but few whites. Another difference today is that more

African Americans have made it into the middle class, and this can justify the belief that we have eliminated discrimination and achieved equality. If this is true, then the many African Americans who do not make it can be blamed for their own failures: Their poor work attitudes, lack of job skills, or dependency on government help, it is argued, renders them unable to help themselves. This is the cultural analysis explanation of poverty that was discussed in Chapter 5. So, although a few superior African Americans have the wherewithal to make it, the reasoning goes, most are doomed to failure.

Contributing to this view that most African Americans do not have the qualities that enable whites and a few African Americans to succeed, according to Christopher Jencks (1992), is a cultural conflict that also involves elements of individual racism: Many whites find the black urban culture of the 1990s alien and threatening (see Chapter 5). Because of this they are less likely to hire African Americans, particularly young males. In addition, says Jencks, employers have other motivations for discriminating against African Americans in hiring. For example, an employer might believe that an African-American employee will drive away white customers. This was done in professional sports for many years when owners and managers believed that white fans would not pay to see black players. This still occurs today when companies refuse to hire African Americans for highly visible positions, such as receptionist or salesperson, when customers are white.

After Feagin and Sykes interviewed hundreds of middle-class African Americans—who are presumably the ones least affected by race, according to Wilson—they concluded "few middle-class African Americans interviewed . . . see the significance of racism in their lives declining" (1994: 12). For all these reasons, Feagin and Sykes argue that "race" still very much determines the position of African Americans as a group.

So, controversy continues over whether the continuing chasm between the achievements of African Americans and whites is predominately due to "class" or to "race." Although it may be difficult to resolve the proportionate role of each, it is certain that each plays some part. The issues involved are important because the contrasting positions on this controversy point to very different policy recommendations for its solution. The discussion now turns to the policies put forth in the past few decades, and still under debate, to improve race relations in the United States.

Collective Protest and Civil Rights Legislation

The civil rights movement of the 1950s and 1960s marked the beginning of some significant developments in racial and ethnic discrimination in the United States (Morris, 1984). By the end of the 1960s, as a result of protests and demonstrations, laws had been established that made it illegal to discriminate against people in jobs, housing, schools, or public facilities on the basis of race or ethnicity. Voting rights legislation was also passed to ensure that adults in the United States did not confront barriers to the voting booth. These laws have become the tools for bringing about impressive improvements in the problem of discrimination. Educational, employment, and housing opportunities are now available to minorities who, three decades ago, would have had those doors to opportunity completely closed. Despite advances, however, discrimination persists. Although it is illegal, some employers and landlords still turn away African Americans, Asians, or others because of their race. This discrimination is difficult to eliminate because it is often hard to prove that denial of a job, for example, was motivated by an applicant's minority-group membership rather than by the superior qualifications of another applicant. So civil rights legislation has been a good foundation, but additional efforts have been made to eliminate the lingering effects of discrimination in the form of affirmative action.

Affirmative Action

Affirmative-action legislation requires schools and employers to take active efforts to seek qualified minority applicants for openings and even to establish hiring and admissions practices that give a preference to minorities. In some cases, this may call for establishing quotas whereby a certain proportion of openings will go to minority applicants, even if that necessitates hiring a less qualified minority applicant over a more qualified white applicant. The rationale underlying affirmative action is the belief that a school or business with few minority students or employees is itself evidence that discrimination has occurred. The burden is then on the school or the employer to prove that they have not discriminated by actively seeking out minorities.

Some argue, however, that affirmative action has produced *reverse discrimination,* according to which whites are passed over for jobs or positions in school in favor of nonwhites who are sometimes less qualified than the white applicants. The best-known reverse discrimination case to date is that of Allan Bakke, a white male who was initially denied admission to the medical school at the University of California at Davis. He alleged he was a victim of reverse discrimination because several minority students with lower grades and lower scores on the Medical College Admissions Test were accepted ahead of him under the university's minorities quota policy. In the *Bakke* decision in 1978 and later rulings, the Supreme Court ruled that strict racial quotas are unconstitutional but that race can be used as one among many criteria in admissions decisions. During the 1980s and 1990s, however, programs to encourage hiring preferences based on race have been scaled back, and the courts have weakened the legal foundations that minorities successfully used to bring affirmative-action lawsuits against employers or schools. The overall trend during the Reagan and Bush years was toward a weakened affirmative-action policy. By the mid-1990s, some affirmative-action programs were being completely dismantled.

Despite the controversy, affirmative-action legislation probably has made it possible for some minorities to overcome persisting discrimination and obtain jobs or entrance into schools that they probably would not have obtained otherwise. At the same time, affirmative action has produced considerable resentment among whites, especially males, over what they see as unfairness to them and opportunities lost because minorities have been treated preferentially. Whites generally favor affirmative-action programs that provide training and education for minorities to help them compete for jobs; what they do not like is preferential hiring where less qualified minorities are hired before more qualified whites. Many whites also feel that they have personally suffered because of this reverse discrimination (Lynch and Beer, 1990; Bunzel, 1991). This has produced feelings of frustration, resentment, anger, and cynicism among many whites toward social and political institutions and policies. At the same time, the perception arises that minorities can only succeed if they have help—that they are not capable of succeeding on their own. Christopher Jencks (1992) argues that the way affirmative action has evolved—particularly toward reverse discrimination and quotas—has produced a situation where both whites and minorities feel that they are being hurt by the system. In addition, the resentment felt by whites probably increases feelings of hostility toward minorities, which is not surprising because this is precisely the kind of competitive situation that produces feelings of prejudice.

Some economists, such as Thomas Sowell (1981), argue that minorities would be best served by a laissez-faire economic system in which people compete for jobs on the basis of their own abilities and wits. This has certainly been true for some immigrant groups, such as

Irish and Jewish Americans, both of whom ended up at least as well off as those who discriminated against them when they were still new immigrants to the United States. But these groups suffered only sporadic discrimination, not the nearly universal and persistent discrimination that African Americans have faced. Under these conditions, says Christopher Jencks, laissez-faire policies will not achieve equal opportunity, and some form of affirmative action through government intervention is called for. However, he also agrees that reverse discrimination or separate standards for particular groups are counterproductive in the long run. He argues for affirmative-action "targets": soft quotas that employers make a good-faith effort to meet. As long as the effort is made, failure to meet the precise numerical goal is not seen as failure. This policy keeps government pressure on employers to seek out minority employees without forcing employers to make unfair or irrational decisions.

Affirmative action is a policy that does not ignore race but rather takes it into account when making decisions about hiring, promotion, or entrance into schools. The International Perspectives section explores a policy in another society that takes ethnicity into account in an effort to accommodate minorities in a political system.

School Programs and Busing

In 1966, sociologist James Coleman and his colleagues published a report on school segregation that quickly became known as the "Coleman Report." In it, they presented data that showed extensive segregation in schools in the United States and that documented that African Americans performed more poorly than other racial or ethnic groups. These African-American students, Coleman and his coauthors argued, suffer from poor facilities and teachers and from school and home environments that provide little motivation to the students to excel. They also showed that

African-American students who attend desegregated schools with a better "motivational atmosphere" showed improved academic performance. The motivational atmosphere in the school basically had to do with the proportion of lower-class to middle-class pupils in the school. African Americans attending schools with a "middle-class" atmosphere did better than African Americans attending schools with a "lower-class" atmosphere. In part because of the Coleman Report, a number of programs were developed to assist minority and white students in improving their academic performance and possibly their career opportunities. Some programs focused on compensatory education to make up for the deficiencies students might experience because of a poor school or home environment. Other programs focused on school integration, sometimes by busing students from one school to another. The employment of busing to achieve school integration has since become a highly controversial issue in U.S. education. Such integration, it was believed, would not only improve the performance of minority students, but also reduce prejudice and discrimination in the long run.

In the late 1960s, court-ordered school busing was instituted. After thirty years of experience with school busing to achieve integration, it remains a highly controversial policy. One reason for the controversy is that schools in the United States remain highly segregated because of the residential segregation that persists between whites and African Americans (Rivkin, 1994). And this residential segregation may have been enhanced over the years by "white flight" in reaction to compulsory school busing. White flight refers to white students leaving certain school districts for suburban or private schools to avoid either busing or integration. Research clearly shows that whites do tend to avoid schools in which the majority of students is African American or Hispanic (Rossell, 1990; Smock and Wilson, 1991). The controversy enters when trying to determine how much of this

INTERNATIONAL PERSPECTIVES
Switzerland: Cooperation in a Multiethnic Society

In 1993, President Clinton proposed Lani Guinier for the post of Assistant Attorney General for Civil Rights and ran into a hailstorm of opposition. Some of the opposition was because Ms. Guinier had explored in her writings some radical proposals for giving minorities some influence on the political system. One alternative she explored, for example, was "cumulative voting," in which voters might cast more than one vote for a single candidate for office. It could work like this: If five city council seats are vacant, each voter could cast five votes. They could cast one vote for each of the five or all five votes for one candidate. By cumulating their votes on one candidate, a racial or ethnic minority that constituted only a small percentage of the population in the city might be able to elect a candidate. Without cumulating, their numbers are so small that they are unlikely to elect any candidate. Cumulative voting and other proposals explored by Guinier were focused on identifying political structures that give minorities a share of political power and that avoid completely disenfranchising groups that happen to be small in size. Such proposals are highly controversial in the United States, but a look at how such issues are handled in other societies can be instructive.

Switzerland is often pointed to as a model of effective pluralism because it is made up of three distinct ethnic groups—German, French, and Italian—that work together peacefully and cooperatively. Prior to the nineteenth century, ethnic conflict in Switzerland was constant and often violent (Steiner, 1990; Schmid, 1981): Interethnic relations, dominated by German-speaking Swiss, at times verged on civil war. Intense and bitter religious conflict between Catholics and Protestants also contributed to the strife. Ethnic and linguistic equality was imposed on Switzerland by the French, who conquered Switzerland in 1798. Finally, a brief civil war in the 1840s ended with the adoption of a Constitution in 1848 that continued the protection of linguistic minorities and created a system of power sharing among ethnic groups that has enabled the Swiss to live in peace and harmony for the last 150 years.

The basic assumption of this power-sharing system is that all three language groups are assured of representation in the government. The Swiss Federal Council, the executive body of Switzerland, includes members from all three ethnic groups, in rough proportions to their numbers in the population. The chairmanship of the Council (equivalent to the U.S. presidency) is rotated to a different ethnic group each year, assuring each ethnic group a turn in that important position. The parliament is elected by proportional representation, with each ethnic group being represented in the legislature in proportions approximate to its

white flight is due to busing. From reviewing the research it seems reasonable to conclude that, although busing is not the sole culprit, it has made a significant contribution to the flight of whites from many public school districts (Carr and Zeigler, 1990; Armor, 1991). In any event, some courts have interpreted the research to mean that busing produces white flight and thus helps to resegregate the schools. Based on this, by the 1990s, some courts have allowed school districts to dismantle busing programs in order to stop white flight and avoid further resegregation of their schools.

Has school integration achieved its goals? In terms of school achievement, some studies have found improvements with integration and others have not (Rist, 1979; Longshore and Prager, 1985; Armor, 1989; Entwisle and Alexander, 1994). Overall, integration has probably made modest improvements in school achievement by African Americans, especially when students are integrated in the early grades. The size in the population. Civil service positions and military appointments are also made with proportional representation in mind. All three languages are considered the national languages of Switzerland. The Swiss political system is one of decentralized federalism, with the governments of each canton, or district, having autonomy in the conduct of many of their affairs. Thus, each canton, dominated by a particular ethnic group, controls its own schools and police.

The pluralist Swiss system amounts to what would be called a quota system in the United States. In contrast to Swiss power sharing, the United States and many other nations tend more toward a system of power competition, according to which each group strives to concentrate as much power in its own hands as it can. Such competition can lead to instability and chaos and often leaves minorities largely disenfranchised and dissatisfied.

Swiss pluralism works for a number of reasons. First, since the three ethnic groups are of European heritage, they share a lot of common history and culture, despite their differences. Second, the three ethnic groups have been settled in the region for centuries, and compromises and accommodations have been worked out over the years. Third, the Swiss state has been stable for a number of years, without the political instability that can serve as fertile ground for ethnic conflict. Fi-nally, the Swiss ethnic minorities did not have to go through a protracted or bitter struggle for their rights that could have left simmering antagonisms.

Because of these factors, some have argued for Swiss "exceptionalism": The Swiss experience is unique and cannot serve as a model for other societies where conditions make solutions to racial and ethnic conflicts much more difficult to find. But Jurg Steiner (1990), who has studied the Swiss, says they are not a different or "naturally peaceful" people. Rather, from experience over a long period, they have created a system that reduces conflict between groups and produces greater cooperation, stability, and prosperity. As one expert who studied the Swiss experience put it, the lesson to learn from Switzerland is that "successful democratic pluralism depends on minorities being continually accommodated within the political system" (Schmid, 1981: 155). The United States is certainly different from Switzerland, and Swiss structures would not necessarily achieve the same outcomes in the United States. However, the Swiss experience does suggest that it could be of value to explore whether new political or social structures could help our pluralist society function with more harmony and less feelings of disenfranchisement among some minorities.

reason that the impact has not been more uniformly positive is because so many other factors—socioeconomic status, family background, racial tensions in the schools, and the manner in which integration is accomplished—also influence achievement. However, there are signs that school integration may produce benefits beyond its impact on school achievement. Research suggests that school integration has helped to reduce racial isolation in the United States, and that this will reduce racial tensions and stereotyping in the future (Hawley et al., 1983). Research also suggests that the experience in desegregated schools has an impact on African Americans later in life: They are more likely to attend predominantly white colleges, socialize with whites outside of school, and live in integrated neighborhoods as adults (Braddock, Crain, and McPartland, 1984; Braddock, 1985).

However, the consequences of social policies are often complex. As just mentioned, while school integration has some benefits, court-ordered busing to achieve integration has also contributed to greater racial isolation by increasing residential segregation. This has led to a search for ways to encourage voluntary school integration. To achieve this, some school districts have established "magnet" schools that offer special programs, such as computer training or performing arts, to attract students. Students from anywhere in a school district can choose to attend these schools. With the proper choice of attractive programs, a school could attract students with a mix of racial and ethnic heritages. Some policy analysts believe that such voluntary programs can achieve a modest degree of racial integration while avoiding the white flight and hostility often associated with court-ordered busing (Armor, 1995).

Improving the Economy

Those who view contemporary racial problems as a "class" problem and those who take the laissez-faire approach to solving social problems argue that improvements in the U.S. economy will narrow many of the disparities between dominant groups and minorities. Differences in family income, for example, or education or life expectancy can be narrowed if people have access to better jobs and can improve their lifestyles. This does not deny the occurrence of discrimination or exploitation in the past, but it does say that the future calls for different emphases. The government's role in the future, they argue, should be focused on improvements in the economy. Some of the specific proposals have been reviewed in Chapter 5 and need not be repeated here.

There have been many improvements in race relations in the United States in the past two decades. Although there is much in U.S. history to be lamented, people can be proud of the recent advances. Yet there are reasons for uncertainty about the future. Whereas racial violence has been limited of late, periodic outbursts document that such violence is just below the surface. The riot in south central Los Angeles in 1992 was the most recent manifestation of the anger and resentment that can trigger such violence. (The reasons for this outburst are analyzed in detail in the Applied Research insert in Chapter 14.) The same thing happened in Miami in 1989 when a police officer shot and killed a black man on a motorcycle. These violent riots express the anger that many minority youths feel about their position and opportunities in the 1990s. They illustrate the potential for racial conflict that simmers below the surface despite the improvements that have been made. This suggests that the po-

LINKAGES

The current pattern of racial segregation in housing between cities and suburbs in the United States was underwritten by the urban policies of the federal government going back into the 1930s (Chapter 12). By building freeways to the suburbs and providing mortgage loans to whites (but not African Americans) to buy houses in the suburbs, the government helped create the racial isolation that persists today. This racial segregation in turn has made poverty more extensive and entrenched for African Americans (Chapter 5) because it magnifies the difficulties they confront in finding jobs.

tential for prejudice, discrimination, and racial violence is still very strong and can be rekindled if the proper social conditions arise.

Summary

1. A minority group is a group whose members are viewed by dominant groups as inferior because of certain characteristics. They have less access to power and resources than do other groups, and they are accorded fewer rights, privileges, and opportunities.

2. A race is a group of people who is believed to be a biological group sharing genetically transmitted traits that are defined as important. An ethnic group comprises people who share a common historical and cultural heritage and sense of group identity and belongingness. Racism is the view that certain racial or ethnic groups are biologically inferior and that practices involving their domination and exploitation are therefore justified.

3. Prejudice and discrimination result from different social and psychological sources. Among the social sources are ethnocentrism, competition, socialization, and institutionalized discrimination. Psychological sources include stereotyping, frustration and aggression, and the authoritarian personality.

4. Discrimination has a number of consequences, including an adverse effect on people's life chances and an increase in tension and hostility in society.

5. Among racial and ethnic groups in the United States, African Americans and Hispanics are the largest nonwhite minorities, and they lag considerably behind other groups in access to education, power, and economically rewarding jobs. One of the most important reasons for this is the long history of discrimination and oppression suffered by both groups, making it difficult for them to improve their position in society.

6. Native Americans experience some of the worst conditions of all minority groups in the United States. Some Asian Americans, on the other hand, have been able to attain a degree of affluence despite the substantial prejudice and discrimination they have experienced.

7. Today, the most common types of relationships between dominant and minority groups in the United States are assimilation and pluralism. Although most minority groups have experienced some degree of assimilation, there is considerable emphasis today on the pluralistic nature of society. There is considerable debate over whether racism in the United States has declined, or just changed to a more subtle and symbolic form. There is also controversy over whether ongoing socioeconomic differences between the members of dominant and minority groups is a result of racial discrimination or class position.

8. Civil rights legislation, affirmative-action programs, school programs and busing, and efforts to improve the economy are techniques that have been used in trying to improve race and ethnic relations in the United States.

STUDY AND Review

Key Terms

assimilation

authoritarian
  personality

discrimination

ethnic group

ethnocentrism

in-group

institutionalized
  discrimination

internal colonialism

minority group

pluralism

prejudice

race

racism

split labor market

Multiple-Choice Questions

1. Polish Americans would most clearly be:
   a. A racial group.
   b. An ethnic group.
   c. An authoritarian group.
   d. An example of internal colonialism.
   e. A split-labor group.

2. A negative attitude toward certain people based solely on their membership in a particular group is called:
   a. Prejudice.
   b. Discrimination.
   c. A minority group.
   d. Pluralism.
   e. Segregation.

3. Joseph has a negative stereotype toward and dislikes all people from the Middle East, but he does not discriminate against them in hiring for his store because of the laws against it. In Robert Merton's classification, he would be called:
   a. An unprejudiced nondiscriminator.
   b. A prejudiced discriminator.
   c. A prejudiced nondiscriminator.
   d. An unprejudiced discriminator.

4. Which of the following is a type of economic exploitation between a dominant group and a minority group?

   a. Ethnocentrism.
   b. Assimilation.
   c. Institutionalized discrimination.
   d. Internal colonialism.
   e. Genocide.

5. The split-labor market could be best characterized as:
   a. Two groups of workers willing to do the same work but for different wages.
   b. Exploitation of a subordinate group by a dominant group for the benefit of the dominant group.
   c. An unprejudiced person who is a discriminator.
   d. Institutionalized discrimination by a dominant group against a minority group.

6. All of the following are true about Hispanic Americans *except:*
   a. They are the second largest minority group discussed in the text.
   b. The largest group among Hispanics is Mexican Americans.
   c. They suffer from low educational levels in comparison to whites.
   d. The gap between Hispanic and white income has narrowed substantially in the past thirty years.

7. Which of the following groups was once placed in concentration camps in the United States?
   a. Japanese Americans.
   b. Chinese Americans.
   c. African Americans.
   d. Hispanic Americans.
   e. Arab Americans.

8. According to the text, which of the following elements of Japanese-American culture contributed to their success in the United States?
   a. Their Samurai tradition.
   b. Their worship of nobility.
   c. Their work ethic.
   d. Their value of the family.
   e. Both c and d.

9. Over the history of the United States, the experience of most immigrants to this country comes closest to:
   a. A melting pot.
   b. Ethnocentrism.
   c. Anglo conformity.
   d. Genocide.
   e. Both a and c.
10. The text concludes which of the following regarding the impact of school integration programs on the performance of minority students?
   a. The amount of white flight from cities is reduced.
   b. Minorities show modest improvement in school performance.
   c. Minorities show dramatic improvement in school performance.
   d. Hostility between minorities and whites increases.

True/False Questions

1. Race and ethnicity are ascribed statuses.
2. Groups such as the gypsies and Jews would be classified by sociologists as races.
3. From the functionalist perspective, ethnocentrism is always considered to have negative consequences for members of an in-group.
4. The text concludes that racism does lower the self-esteem of minorities in some contexts.
5. African Americans were the only minority group to be enslaved in the United States.
6. Because of casino gambling and other economic enterprises on Indian reservations, income and educational levels on reservations now approach those for society as a whole.
7. According to the text, the most common relationship between racial and ethnic groups in the United States today is segregation and subjugation.
8. Contact between different racial and ethnic groups can reduce prejudice if the contact has high "acquaintance potential."
9. The text concludes that "race" is more important than "class" in determining the social position of African Americans in the United States today.

10. The civil rights legislation established in the 1960s has virtually eliminated discrimination on the basis of race and ethnicity.

Fill-In Questions

1. Sociologists' definition of "race" is based on people's _____ that there are biological differences between the races.
2. _____ is the view that certain racial or ethnic groups are biologically inferior and can be discriminated against because of this.
3. Fred and Mary believe that their high school is superior to all the other high schools in their district. This is an example of the tendency toward _____ .
4. In a split-labor market, the group that receives the brunt of the discrimination is the _____ .
5. The ruling in which the U.S. Supreme Court declared the "separate but equal" doctrine to be unconstitutional was _____ .
6. U.S. citizenship was granted to all Native Americans in the decade of the _____ .
7. In recent decades, the largest percentage of immigrants to the United States has come from the geographical region of _____ .
8. _____ racism is racism expressed not directly but through opposition to policies or practices that benefit a particular race.
9. _____ discrimination occurs when affirmative-action quotas result in qualified majority-group members being excluded from a job because of their race.
10. _____ occurs when white students leave a school district for suburban or private schools in order to avoid school busing or school integration.

Matching Questions

_____ 1. MAPA

_____ 2. *apartheid*

_____ 3. competition causes discrimination

_____ 4. psychological source of prejudice and discrimination

_____ 5. Ashanti

_____ 6. Cesar Chavez

_____ 7. assimilation

_____ 8. WASPs

_____ 9. the *Bakke* court decision

_____ 10. James Coleman

A. legal segregation in South Africa
B. large African tribe
C. a blending of racial and ethnic identities
D. the authoritarian personality
E. Hispanic political group
F. study of segregation in schools
G. Hispanic labor organizer
H. reverse discrimination
I. earliest European immigrants to North America
J. conflict perspective

Essay Questions

1. What is ethnocentrism? What role does it play in prejudice and discrimination?
2. How does socialization influence prejudice and discrimination?
3. According to the text, what detrimental consequences does discrimination have for society?
4. Describe the prejudice and discrimination experienced by Japanese Americans and Chinese Americans since first immigrating to this country.

5. Why has the experience of African Americans been different from that of other immigrant groups to the United States?
6. Characterize the patterns of minority–majority relations in the United States today and in the past.
7. What characteristics of the contact between racial groups are most likely to reduce prejudice between the groups?
8. What are the arguments for and against affirmative action programs?
9. Is the situation of African Americans in the United States today mostly a function of "race" or "class"? Make arguments for both sides of this issue.
10. What does the text conclude regarding whether racial integration of the schools has achieved its goals?

Answers

Multiple-Choice

1. B; 2. A; 3. C; 4. D; 5. A; 6. D; 7. A; 8. E; 9. C; 10. B

True/False

1. T; 2. F; 3. F; 4. T; 5. T; 6. F; 7. F; 8. T; 9. F; 10. F

Fill-In

1. belief
2. racism
3. ethnocentrism
4. lower-priced workers
5. *Brown v. the Board of Education*
6. 1920s
7. Asia
8. symbolic
9. reverse
10. white flight

Matching

1. E; 2. A; 3. J; 4. D; 5. B; 6. G; 7. C; 8. I; 9. H; 10. F

For Further Reading

Martin Carnoy. *Faded Dreams: The Politics and Economics of Race in America.* New York: Cambridge University Press, 1994. This book reports grim findings but a somewhat optimistic assessment of race relations in the United States. Much depends, according to the author, on whether the government takes the initiative in pushing for more social and economic equality.

Stephen S. Fugita and David J. O'Brien. *Japanese American Ethnicity: The Persistence of Community.* Seattle and London: University of Washington Press, 1991. Focusing on the experiences of Japanese Americans, these sociologists investigate the factors that influence whether an immigrant group maintains a viable community or becomes completely assimilated by the dominant group.

Jonathan Kozol. *Savage Inequalities: Children in America's Schools.* New York: Crown, 1991. This book explains why, if you are born poor and minority in the United States, the schools will not be of great assistance in climbing out of poverty. The schools Kozol describes, whose students are mostly poor and mostly African American, are in horrendous shape. The students who need societal help the most get the least in terms of good quality education.

Douglas S. Massey and Nancy A. Denton. *American Apartheid: Segregation and the Making of an Underclass.* Cambridge, Mass.: Harvard University Press, 1993. As the use of "apartheid" in the title implies, these authors see the United States as a rigidly segregated society. They discuss the reasons for this, disputing much of Wilson's argument that racial discrimination is not the major factor determining the position of African Americans in the U.S. today.

David Milner. *Children and Race.* Beverly Hills, Calif: Sage Publications, 1983. A very readable book summarizing the research on how children develop racial attitudes as they grow up. The author also discusses the impact of racism on the psychological development of black children and some educational programs to promote positive race relations.

Earl Shorris. *Latinos: A Biography of the People.* New York: W. W. Norton, 1992. This excellent book explores the lives and history of the fastest growing minority group in the United States, the descendants of the Spanish conquest of the native American peoples. Through wonderfully insightful biographical sketches, the author communicates the complex diversity today in the group that is given the single designation of "Latino."

David E. Stannard. *American Holocaust: Columbus and the Conquest of the New World.* New York: Oxford University Press, 1992. This book catalogues an "unbroken string of genocidal campaigns" by the Europeans against the native peoples of the Americas after Columbus's voyages. The author attempts to explain the brutality and devastation that occurred in terms of European attitudes toward race, religion, war, and conversion.

Ronald Takaki. *Strangers from a Different Shore: A History of Asian Americans.* Boston: Little, Brown, 1989. This is an acclaimed history of Asian immigrants to the United States. The author argues compellingly that all Asian immigrants have had to confront the reality that the dominant groups in the United States have always viewed this country as a fundamentally white society.

Ronald Takaki. *A Different Mirror: A History of Multicultural America.* Boston: Little, Brown, 1993. This is a very readable history of the United States from the perspectives of the various immigrant groups that came to our shores. It begins with the Wampanoag Indians of Massachusetts watching the first Europeans arrive and closes with the Los Angeles riot of 1992.

CHAPTER SEVEN

Gender and Social Inequality

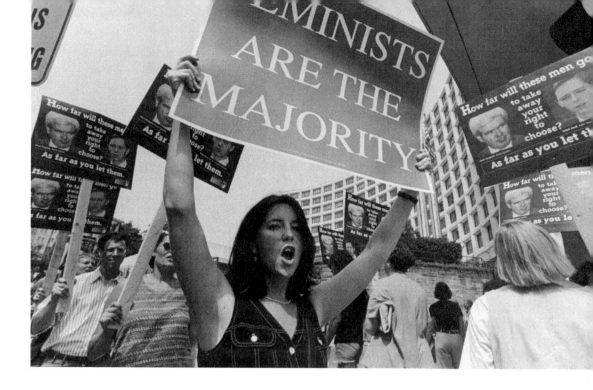

It is difficult, maybe impossible, for those who have not experienced discrimination and oppression to truly comprehend what they are like. This may account for why many men tend to take sexual harassment and assault less seriously than do women: Most men have not experienced these things. Recent highly publicized cases have brought these issues into the forefront: the Mike Tyson rape case, the Senator Packwood sexual harassment charges, the raucous Clarence Thomas—Anita Hill sexual harassment hearings, and the accusations in the 1991 Tailhook scandal that naval officers sexually assaulted twenty-six women—including some of their fellow naval officers—at a wild party. Men's and women's reactions to such episodes are sometimes divided by chasms of misunderstanding. Many men tend not to see such episodes as earthshaking; women are outraged that men do not understand how important the issues are (Johnson, Stockdale, and Saal, 1991).

In some ways, sexual harassment and assault may be an appropriate microcosm in which to view inequalities between the genders. This is partly because men and women tend to perceive them very differently, but also because they can function as weapons of oppression, tools that discourage women from taking jobs or entering other arenas that had been the exclusive domains of men.

The evidence is clear that sexual harassment on the job is pervasive. Ninety percent of the companies on the Fortune 500 have received complaints of sexual harassment from employees, and more than one-third of these companies have been sued over harassment (Sandroff, 1988). A report on sexual harassment in the military, released in 1991, stated that "the majority of women (64%) and 17 percent of men reported experiencing some form of sexual harassment ranging from jokes to actual assault while on duty" (Martindale, 1991: 201). In 1991, a California commission held hearings on the issue of why so few women take jobs in the construction trades. What they heard from the women who testified was of a systematic, unrelenting campaign of sexual harassment, sometimes bordering on terror, perpetrated by their male coworkers to drive women out of these jobs (French, 1992). The men were verbally hostile and pinched and fondled the women as they tried to do their jobs. Male workers urinated next to the women and hung lewd pictures in the women's toilet. The women were constantly confronted in the workplace with pinup calendars and close-up pictures of female genitals. The nasty comments and teasing were constant. One electrician was doused with water as she worked on live electrical wires, putting her life in danger. All this treatment seemed to reflect a campaign by the male workers to drive women out in order to preserve a bastion of "maleness" into which women did not intrude. And this testimony, remember, was being given in 1991, not 1961! Practically all women who have worked for any length of time can recall their own experiences with sexual harassment.

Sexual harassment and job discrimination are two elements of the problem of social inequality based on sexual status. Although many strides have been made in the past few decades to provide women with the same opportunities as men, the examples just discussed illustrate that the problem lingers. This chapter will review the reasons why such inequality occurs, its dimensions in the United States, and what can be done to alleviate it.

Men and Women in Society

Sex is an *ascribed status:* It is a position in society that is assigned to a person; people have virtually no control over their ascribed statuses. Unlike achieved statuses, such as one's educational level or occupation, there is little, if anything, that people can do to alter their sexual status. Sex is also a *master status* because it has considerable social significance in all societies. It is a central determinant of how people view themselves and how others respond to them, and it frequently serves as a basis for social differentiation. In fact, gender inequality is an important element of the stratification system in society. In some societies discrimination based on sexual status is so irrevocable that women have virtually no chance to improve their status. Gender inequalities are typically justified by **sexism,** *an ideology based on the belief that one sex is superior to and should dominate the other sex.* To understand how sexual status shapes the structure of society, it is helpful to understand why sex is an element of social differentiation in societies at all. This chapter will examine four different views on this issue.

The Biological Perspective

One perspective on the role of sexual status in determining one's position in society is that innate biological differences between men and women shape the contributions each can make to society. One question this raises, of

Myths & FACTS

ABOUT GENDER INEQUALITY

Efforts have been under way around the world during the past few decades to reduce the disadvantages suffered by women, and one can receive the overall impression that significant progress has been made. And, in fact, many gains have been made. As with many social problems, however, the reality is more complex than first impressions might suggest, and the overall record of efforts to reduce gender inequality is spotty. Many statements of fact, if not qualified, are so misleading as to almost constitute myths.

Myth: Women have taken their place in the work force with men, holding more varied jobs and earning higher pay relative to men than ever before.

FACT: More women work, but their pay still lags significantly behind that of men doing the same work. This is true in virtually all industrial nations, with women in Japan earning only 46 percent of what men do. Also, many low-paying, low-prestige jobs are still female ghettos, with 99 percent of secretaries, 96 percent of receptionists, and virtually 100 percent of dental hygienists in the United States in the 1990s being women.

Myth: More women are seeking political office than ever before.

FACT: Women, who make up 51 percent of the U.S. population, held 7 percent of the seats in the U.S. Senate in 1993 and a paltry 10 percent of the seats in the House of Representatives. Women do well in Cuba and Finland, where they hold one-third of the parliamentary seats, but in some African and Arab nations, there are no women in parliament.

Myth: By the 1990s, the United States had become solidly supportive of equal rights for women.

FACT: The Equal Rights Amendment to the Constitution, which would prohibit discrimination on the basis of gender, has yet to be approved.

Myth: The courts have ruled that barring women from service and community organizations such as Rotary and the Kiwanis violates antidiscrimination laws. Thus, women now have the same access as men to community and business arenas.

FACT: This is true in communities that have antidiscrimination laws. In the thousands of communities where there are no such laws, however, women can be and are excluded from such organizations. In fact, former presidents Reagan and Bush belong to a very influential social club, the Bohemian Club, at which many very powerful businessmen and politicians gather and to which women are completely excluded as members.

---

course, is: What precisely are the biological differences between the sexes? Modern research has documented some differences and shown that allegations of other differences are not supported by the available evidence. These findings are summarized in Table 7.1. Are these differences caused by biology? In only a few realms is there any evidence that they are (McCoy, 1985; Fausto-Sterling, 1992). Higher levels of aggressiveness in males, for example, are very common in other species, such as rhesus monkeys, and it is almost universal in human cultures. Levels of aggressiveness can also be affected by changes in sex hormones.

TABLE 7.1 Gender Differences and Similarities

Physical Attributes

Strength	Males taller, heavier, more muscular.
Health	Females less vulnerable to illness and disease, live longer.
Activity level	Some evidence that preschool boys more active during play in same-sex groups; sex differences for school-age children are qualitative, not quantitative.
Manual dexterity	Women excel when speed is important; findings hard to interpret.

Abilities

General intelligence	No difference on most tests.
Verbal ability	Some evidence that females acquire language slightly earlier; males more often diagnosed as having reading problems; females excel on various verbal tests after age ten or eleven.[a]
Quantitative ability	Males excel on tests of mathematical reasoning from the start of adolescence.[a]
Spatial-visual ability	Males excel starting in tenth grade, but not on all tests or in all studies.[a]
Creativity	Females excel on verbal creativity tests, but otherwise no difference.
Cognitive style	Males excel on spatial-visual disembedding tests starting at adolescence, but no general differences in cognitive style.

Personality Characteristics

Sociability	No consistent findings on infants' responsiveness to social cues; school-age boys play in larger groups; women fantasize more about affiliation themes, but there is no evidence that one sex wants or needs friends more.
Empathy	Conflicting evidence; probably depends on situation and sex of participants in an interaction.
Emotionality	Self-reports and observations conflict; no convincing evidence that females feel more emotional, but they may express certain emotions more freely.
Dependence	Conflicting findings; dependence appears not to be a unitary concept or stable trait.
Susceptibility to influence	Preschool girls more obedient to parents; boys may be more susceptible to peer pressure; no overall difference in adult susceptibility to persuasion across different settings in laboratory studies.
Self-esteem and confidence	No self-report differences in self-esteem, but males more confident about task performance; males more likely to take credit for success, less likely to blame selves for failure.
Nurturance	No overall differences in altruism; girls more helpful and responsive to infants, small children; some evidence that fathers are as responsive to newborns as mothers are, but issue of maternal versus paternal behavior remains open.
Aggressiveness	Males more aggressive from preschool age on; men more violent, more likely to be aggressive in public, more likely to be physically aggressive in situations not involving anger.

Values and Moral Perceptions

	Some controversial evidence that males and females approach choice and conflict somewhat differently. Males seem more likely to emphasize abstract standards of justice, fairness, balancing of individual rights. Females seem more likely to emphasize the ethics of care, human attachments, balancing of conflicting responsibilities.

[a]Differences statistically reliable but quite small.

Source: From *The Longest War: Sex Differences in Perspective,* Second Edition, by Carol Tavris and Carole Wade, copyright © 1984 by Harcourt Brace Jovanovich, Inc., pp. 42–43. Reprinted by permission of the publisher.

Thus, there is the suggestion, but by no means conclusive proof, that higher levels of aggressiveness in males are in part biological. In terms of the differences in verbal and spatial-visual ability, some evidence suggests that the brains of males and females are organized differently in this regard. In men, verbal skills are focused on one side of the brain and the spatial-visual skills on the other. In women, each skill can be found on both sides of the brain. This difference in the organization of the brain may account for why women tend to have more verbal skills and men are more adept at spatial-visual tasks. With regard to greater upper-body strength, this is probably attributable to the higher levels of the hormone testosterone among males.

So there undoubtedly are some biological differences between men and women that have implications for social behavior. However, the differences are far fewer and much smaller than were once thought to be the case. Furthermore, the differences appear to relate to general tendencies, such as aggressiveness, rather than to specific social behaviors, such as fighting or playing football. In addition, despite any biological differences, men and women are highly flexible and extremely malleable in terms of what they are capable of doing. Most of our behavior is learned rather than biologically programmed, which means that men can learn to behave in a stereotypically female fashion, and women can learn to behave in ways that we would expect men to behave (Tavris, 1992). A final point is that the differences between men and women refer to average levels of performance, which ignores the significant overlap between the sexes. Many women, for example, are more aggressive than some men, and some men are less aggressive than many women. Because of this, sexual status alone is a rather poor basis for establishing social policy or allocating social tasks and rewards.

The Functionalist Perspective

Functionalists argue that some tasks were allocated to men and others to women in preindustrial societies because such arrangements were more convenient and practical (Ford, 1970; Giele, 1978). On the whole, males are physically stronger than women and free of the responsibility of bearing and nursing children. Women, on the other hand, were expected to have many children during their lives and to spend much of their adult lives either pregnant or rearing their children. In addition, women were a more valuable reproductive resource in that the loss of a woman, as in war, would reduce the reproductive potential of society. The loss of a man, on the other hand, could easily be made up for through increased sexual activity on the part of other men. There would be no loss in the overall reproductive potential of society. Given these considerations, functionalists argue, it was more practical in preindustrial societies to assign to men tasks, such as hunting or felling trees, that are physically demanding and might draw one away from home for long periods. Men were also assigned the dangerous tasks, such as protecting the group against attack from enemies. Women, on the other hand, who were limited by pregnancy and the need to nurse their young, were considered better suited to such tasks as gathering roots or berries, cooking food, and making pottery. Once these sex-role distinctions had become firmly established as a part of a group's tradition, they were then supported by strong group norms that made these differences independent of their origins. They came to be seen as the "natural" ways for men and women to behave rather than as practical means of accomplishing societal tasks (Brown, 1970; O'Kelly and Carney, 1986).

Industrialization ushered in a number of significant social changes: the separation of work from family life, smaller families, and a longer life expectancy. As a consequence, women tended to be isolated in the family and given prime responsibility for homemaking and child-rearing duties, whereas men went out and worked. Sex roles became divided along the lines of instrumental and expressive tasks (Parsons and Bales, 1950). **Instrumental tasks** refer to *the goal-oriented activities of the group, such as hunting, building something, or managing a work team.* Males were seen as having responsibility for most of these tasks. **Expressive tasks** refer to *activities focused on the relationships between people—maintaining happiness, harmony, and emotional stability.* These tasks were seen as primarily a woman's responsibility. In fact, for men, it became a status symbol to have a wife who did not work. A nonworking wife was taken as an indication of how capable the man was at producing economically and supporting his family. To justify this division of tasks, sexist beliefs emerged that a woman's place was in the home and that women were not biologically equipped for most forms of male work. However, in most preindustrial societies, women were not removed from economically productive roles. Much of what they did, such as gathering roots, tending crops, or herding flocks, contributed significantly to the economic support of the group. They were by no means limited to child rearing or expressive tasks. Likewise, men were by no means limited to instrumental tasks in preindustrial societies (Murdock, 1934).

From the functionalist perspective, then, a social problem exists when the sex-role division of labor is no longer consistent with the needs of a particular society. To confine women to child rearing or expressive activities would waste a valuable resource. In industrial societies, families have few children today, and they have many supports, such as day care, to help in raising them. So it is no longer necessary for adults—either male or female—to devote their lives to such tasks. It would be better if they used their intellectual, creative, and productive abilities to make additional contributions to so-

ciety. Because the birthrate is low and most jobs in industrial societies are not dangerous, there is no need to protect women as a reproductive resource, as was the case in the past. In addition, great physical strength is no longer necessary for most jobs in a highly automated, technological society. For all of these reasons, functionalists argue, it is not particularly useful to use sex as a criterion for allocating jobs today. It would be more functional to assign tasks based on individual abilities.

The Conflict Perspective

Many sociologists have questioned whether the fact of a woman having children is the central element in shaping sex roles in society and especially whether it explains the continued existence of sex stratification. For example, sociologist Randall Collins (1971) has argued that there is an inherent conflict of interest between men and women and that sex roles can serve as a mechanism by which one group dominates the other. In part, this domination results because males in general are physically stronger than women, which better equips them to use power to their own advantage and gain dominance. But the situation is more complex than this. Through the socialization process, a subtler form of power is exerted and control achieved: People learn to want those things that are in the interests of the dominant group in society. In most societies, women have learned to accept the dominance of males and their own subordinate positions because they believe such dominance is appropriate and even desirable or because they feel they have no other choice.

The economic competition discussed in Chapter 6 also contributes to sexual inequality. In simple hunting and gathering societies, there is a division of labor based on sex, as we have seen, but there is also considerable equality between men and women. The reason for this is that women produce as much as and sometimes more than men. Gathering nuts, roots, and berries produces a steady and dependable food supply, whereas the results of hunting can be very sporadic. It might be days or weeks before men can fell some game. In the interim, women provide food for the group. In agricultural societies, men tend to dominate economic productivity, in good part because their physical strength and freedom from child-bearing duties enable them to engage in extensive, heavy labor that might take them away from home for hours or days at a time. This leaves women economically subordinate and unequal. As functionalists point out, this inequality continues into early industrial societies as men work and women stay home. This arrangement benefits men, of course, because they have a corner on the prestigious and powerful positions in society, and most men wish to continue those social practices.

The dominance of men has continued well into the twentieth century in the United States. During World War II, for example, large numbers of women joined the work force, replacing men serving in the military and showing they were capable of performing many traditionally male jobs (Van Horn, 1988). Most people assumed that these women were housewives who had no financial need to work, but who were doing their part for the war effort, and who wanted to return to their traditional roles after the war. In fact, government and industry, through such groups as the Office of War Information and the War Advertising Council, mounted a propaganda effort to encourage the public to believe this. Reality for many of these working women, dubbed "Rosie the Riveters," was quite different: Many of them were married and needed these well-paying, previously all-male jobs to support their families; some were single parents or single women for whom these jobs were their sole source of economic support; and many of these women wanted to continue in these jobs after the war. Despite the fact that these women had shown themselves to be capable of performing well in traditionally

male jobs, there was a backlash against them when the war ended and returning servicemen competed with the women for jobs. Many people felt that the women had done their duty and now should return to their homes and families ("where they belonged") and make jobs available for returning servicemen. Public pressure and job discrimination resulted in most of these women leaving the traditionally male jobs (Honey, 1984). From the conflict perspective, then, sexual differentiation becomes the "battleground" for a struggle over scarce resources—in this case, for jobs and prestige. However, this economic competition for jobs—a form of the split labor market discussed in Chapter 6 because women are typically paid less than men—was translated into the sexist ideology that women were incapable of performing the jobs as well as the men.

From the conflict view, sexual inequality becomes a social problem when some group—in this case, women—realizes it is being exploited and that something can be done about it. In the past thirty years, women have come to realize that their inferior status has been caused by male domination, not biological inheritance. Once this realization emerged, sexual inequality came to be viewed as a social problem and entered the arena of public debate.

The Interactionist Perspective

According to the interactionist perspective, human beings relate to one another on the basis of symbols that have social meaning within a given culture or society. Those social meanings are created, communicated, and reinforced as people interact with one another on a daily basis. So we can understand a lot about the creation and maintenance of gender inequality if we watch how men and women interact in various settings. Probably the most important symbol system for human beings is language. Interactionists point out that many values, beliefs, and social meanings find ex-

Women were allowed to hold many traditionally male jobs during World War II when men were unavailable, but the women were forced out of the jobs when the men returned—a clear reflection of gender dominance and inequality, according to the conflict perspective.

pression in different language forms, and an analysis of some of these forms suggests a continuing sex bias in many languages, including English. For example, the sex-specific pronouns *he* and *his* can be used when referring to both men and women, and this convention in English may be a veiled way of maintaining male dominance. Recent investigations suggest that such sexist language is still very much with us and show conclusively that use of the generic *he* does create predominantly male images in people's minds, especially for men (Gastil, 1990; Switzer, 1990). When people read or hear

he, instead of *she* or *they*, they think of men, and this can be a symbolic reinforcement of the exclusion of women from many aspects of society. This linguistic usage, then, may reinforce and help perpetuate sexist thought and action, especially among men, by encouraging a predominantly male imagery when thinking about activities or realms of which both men and women might be a part.

The conversational styles of men and women can also reflect and reinforce gender patterns of dominance and subordination (Spenser and Drass, 1989; Tannen, 1994). Such styles, for example, can have direct implications for gaining and keeping positions of leadership in groups. One investigation focused on the order in which people speak in mixed sex groups (Aries, 1985). In general, men initiate more conversation and receive more interaction than women. People who initiate the most interaction in groups take up the most time and are considered by others in the group to be leaders. So if women are taught to be submissive or timid around men, they may be less likely or less able to assume leadership in groups. As another example of the effect of conversational styles, it is widely believed in the United States that women talk more than men (the stereotype has it that women "chatter on" about frivolous subjects), yet many investigations of conversational behavior in mixed groups show that men talk more than women and interrupt while others are talking more than women do. Men also answer questions not addressed to them and continue talking when there is an overlap in conversation. The impact of these different patterns of conversation on gender inequality is quite direct:

> The beliefs that women talk too much and talk about insignificant subjects function to keep women quieter than they might be and to allow men to monopolize social conversations and work groups. The expectation that whatever a woman says is trivial and unimportant creates insecurity, timidity in presenting ideas, and lower feelings of self esteem. . . . The lack of authority attached to female speech patterns lowers a woman's chances for success in many fields. (Kirsh, 1983: 74–75)

So it is through interaction patterns such as these that beliefs and practices regarding gender inequality are maintained and reinforced. In preindustrial societies, the roles of men and women were relatively clear-cut and accepted by most people, even though those roles reflected substantial inequality. In modern industrial society, however, the social structure is changing at a rapid pace, and forms of sexual differentiation formerly accepted are now challenged by many people. So gender inequality becomes a social problem when there is a lack of consensus and a lack of shared expectations about the roles of men and women in society. As expectations change, so too do people's self-concepts in relationship to their sexual status—these are more likely to be uncertain and ambiguous.

The Socialization of Men and Women

The belief is strong that being born male or female automatically implies specific behavioral differences between people. Yet scientific research has demonstrated that most of our behavior as males and females is not a function of biology but rather of learning. This leads to the distinction that sociologists make between *sex* and *gender. Male* and *female* are used as sex-related terms—the innate, biological feature of sexual identity. **Sex** refers to *the biological role that each of us plays, such as in reproduction. Masculine* and *feminine,* on the other hand, are used as gender-specific terms. **Gender** refers to *learned behavior involving how we are expected to act as males and females in society.* One of the key issues in analyzing gender inequality is how we learn to be masculine and feminine and how this learning contributes to sexual differentiation and inequality. This learning occurs in good part through the socialization process, with three major agencies of socialization being primarily responsible: the family, the schools, and the media.

The Family

Infancy represents the most crucial period for human development because patterns of personality and behavior are established during these years. These early years are also extremely important in the establishment of beliefs about appropriate masculine and feminine behavior. There is a growing body of literature that clearly demonstrates how parents are likely to treat male and female infants and young children in ways consistent with how they view masculinity and femininity. For example, fathers are typically "rougher" with boys and more gentle with girls, and both mothers and fathers tend to speak more softly to girls than to boys (Rossi, 1984; MacDonald and Parke, 1986).

By the age of three, children have acquired a gender identity, which means that they can correctly label themselves as male or female. But at this point, their identity is oversimplified and highly stereotyped. It is also based more on such things as hairstyle or dress than on an accurate awareness of genital differences between the sexes. Once the child's gender identity has been established, he or she then attempts to master the behaviors that are associated with that gender. Behaving "like a boy" or "like a girl" becomes rewarding because it brings approval from adults and peers. Parents today still tend to encourage boys to engage in instrumental play, such as building something, whereas girls are encouraged toward expressive play, such as making themselves look attractive.

Even in childhood, it appears that male activities are valued more than female ones (Martin, 1990). For example, girls often display a fondness for the higher prestige of the masculine role by becoming "tomboys." "Tomboyism" is acceptable to a much greater extent than a little boy's being a "sissy." In fact, girls are more prominent in boys' games than boys are in girls' games—testimony to the less negative reactions to "tomboys" than to "sissys." Other investigators have discovered that boys play more competitive games than girls and that girls typically do not learn how to deal with direct competition (Best, 1983; Berliner, 1988). Children learn from their family experiences what it

means to be male and female, and these are extremely strong influences.

The Schools

A very significant part of the socialization process occurs in the schools. School systems are characteristically staffed in such a way that children's perceptions of masculinity and femininity are reinforced. Although most elementary schoolteachers are female, most elementary school principals are male. Thus, from the beginning of school, children see men in positions of authority and dominance over women (Richmond-Abbott, 1992). In addition, schools and teachers treat children very differently based on their gender, with significant consequences for what children learn about gender (Best, 1983; Thorne, 1993; Benokraitis and Feagin, 1995). Investigations have shown that female teachers are more likely to encourage independence and assertion in boys than in girls. Teachers also tend to view girls as less creative than boys, to provide less attention to girls, and to reward female students for conforming and male students for being aggressive. The way teachers do this is quite subtle. Dependence in girls, for example, is encouraged by not sending them off to work on their own, although boys often work alone. As for aggressiveness, boys often have to misbehave to gain their teacher's attention, whereas girls who are quiet and demure are more likely to receive attention from the teacher. So teachers, often without realizing it, reward their students for behaving in a fashion consistent with their own sex-role stereotypes.

Two or more decades ago, the images of males and females presented in school textbooks typically reinforced traditional stereotypes: Males were pictured far more often than females, males were pictured in many occupations and women in few of them, and female pronouns such as *her* were uncommon. But have there not been changes in all this in the

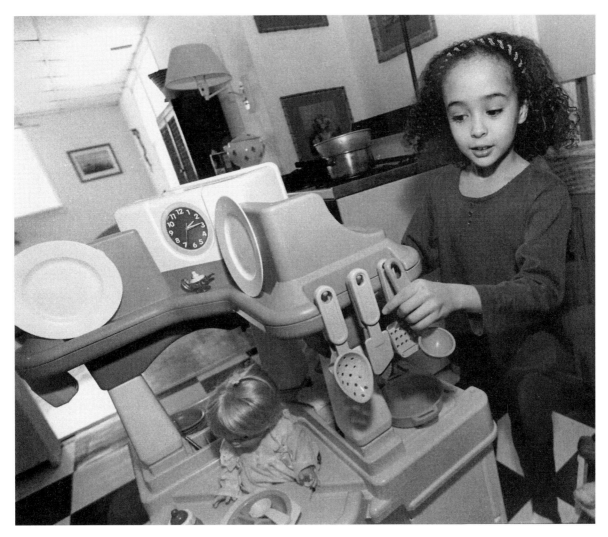

One of the ways that society socializes the young is by encouraging boys and girls to play at different kinds of activities both at school and home. This can produce lifelong preferences that appear inborn but are actually a product of social experience.

past twenty years? Not as many as one might think. Things have improved, especially when efforts are made to produce materials that are nonsexist in their presentation. However, stereotyping still persists. Recent studies of children's picture books, for example, find that more women are portrayed than in the past but still less often than men (only one-third of the illustrations are of women), almost no women are portrayed as working outside the home, women are still shown in fewer occupations than men, and women are portrayed as less brave and adventurous and more helpless (Williams, Jr. et al., 1987; Peterson and Lach, 1990; Purcell and Stewart, 1990). Furthermore, although men are sometimes portrayed as expressing their emotions, denying one's feelings is still characterized in these books as a normal aspect of maleness. Even college textbooks are not immune to these influences. Recent studies of the pictorial content of texts for college-level psychology and sociology courses found that women are shown less often than men and are portrayed more passively and negatively than men (Ferree and Hall, 1990; Peterson and Kroner, 1992). For example, the psychology texts portray women as the victims of mental disorders and the clients in therapy, whereas men are pictured as the therapists. All these portrayals help to perpetuate the cultural stereotype that men tend to be stronger, more active, and working in the world to solve problems, whereas women are more likely to be weaker, more passive, and focusing their interests around home and family.

Because young schoolchildren are at a very formative and impressionable stage in life, the impact that these school experiences have on them is substantial and long-lasting. Evidence shows that sexist treatment in the schools does result in lower self-esteem for female grade school and high school students (Martinez and Dukes, 1991; Sadker and Sadker, 1994). Even at the college level, as the Applied Research insert in this chapter suggests, the interaction between faculty and female students can involve strong doses of sexism, with potentially detrimental influences on female students' performance. At the same time, it has been shown that college experiences have a liberalizing effect on men's and women's gender-role attitudes, especially for those who go on to graduate (Funk and Willits, 1987).

The Media

The media is an extremely important influence on gender role socialization through its portrayals of men and women. Despite the fact that *Cosmopolitan* magazine is allegedly a publication for "modern women," for example, the cover photographs generally focus on very seductive women wearing clothing that is sexually suggestive. In popular romance novels, women are typically portrayed as the victims of male aggression, and this victimization is usually attributed to the nature of their relationship to the aggressors (which is an excellent example of "blaming the victim," as discussed in Chapter 6). The impact of these books is significant, because millions of people read them every year. In a recent investigation of men and women in newspaper photographs, it was determined that men appear in the photos far more often than women, and that men are typically portrayed in professional roles, whereas women are cast in domestic roles (Luebke, 1989).

Perhaps the most significant media influence on young people is television. It has been estimated that between kindergarten and sixth grade, children watch from ten to twenty-five hours of television every week. In fact, "children spend more time watching television than they do reading books, listening to the radio, or going to the movies" (Richmond-Abbott, 1992: 98). Despite the fact that television has "cleaned up its act" to some extent, this powerful medium still overwhelmingly portrays stereotyped gender roles. Investigations of television programs reveal that many of them present a grossly distorted view of family life, with 75 percent of male roles portrayed in prime time reflecting the images of unmarried men who are "tough" and "cool." Even on public television, there have been strong indicators of sexual differentiation—the female puppets on *Sesame Street* have been observed to portray predominantly strident, loudmouthed types. Over the last three decades, only 20 percent of the characters on prime time television shows were female, and most of the women shown were young, unemployed, family-bound, and in comic roles (Richmond-Abbott, 1992).

There have, of course, been improvements in the portrayal of women in the movies and on television over the past decade. Two of the most popular network shows in recent years, *Roseanne* and *Murphy Brown,* have featured strong and positive female characters in their starring roles. Yet, a study commissioned by the Screen Actors Guild and released in 1993 found that only one out of three roles in prime time is played by women, and that anchors, newsmakers, and authorities on television news shows are overwhelmingly white men. The portrayal of women in children's shows was even more lopsided, according to the report (Gunther, 1993). So, some of the old stereotypes linger, and evidence shows that they affect youngsters' attitudes about these matters. A longitudinal study of sex-role attitudes of teenagers found that watching a lot of television did not make boys more sexist. However, the teenagers who had the least sexist attitudes to begin with—fairly intelligent girls—were most affected by television: Those who watched it a lot developed more sexist attitudes (Morgan, 1972). This again illustrates the subtle ways in which people can develop views of the world that help maintain patterns of dominance and subordination.

The Extent of Gender Inequality in the United States

Although women are a numerical majority in the United States, they comprise a minority group, and there are a number of important similarities between women and other minorities (see Chapter 6). Like African Americans, women still have unequal access to valued resources and suffer discrimination on many fronts. Although this chapter will focus primarily on the way in which women suffer from gender inequality, it will also look at some ways in which men have been discriminated against by unreasonable differentiation based on sex.

Economic Discrimination

Women occupy a subordinate position in comparison to men on virtually every dimension of socioeconomic status (SES). The three main dimensions of SES are education, occupation, and income.

Education Education has long been a key channel of social mobility in the United States, particularly for members of minority groups or others who were disadvantaged. Today, a college education is especially important in gaining prestigious and powerful positions in society, but higher education has never been equally available to all. Until about 1850, women were almost completely excluded from colleges. It was assumed that women needed less education because their careers would be as homemakers and mothers. In fact, in 1873, the U.S. Supreme Court ruled that an Illinois woman could be denied a license to practice law on the grounds that she was female. One Supreme Court justice of the era defended this stance by saying, "the paramount mission and destiny of women are to fill the noble and benign offices of wife and mother. This is the law of the Creator" ("The Brethren's First Sister," 1981: 17).

Since 1950, the number of people twenty-five years of age and older with some college training has quadrupled, and there have been dramatic increases in the proportion of women who pursue some form of advanced education in the United States. The percentage of doctoral degrees going to women has grown from 14 percent in 1971 to 37 percent today, and 43 percent of law degrees go to women today, compared with only 5 percent in 1970 (U.S. Bureau of the Census, 1994: 189–91). Still, many more men attain these degrees than do women, and as Figure 7.1 (on p. 256) illustrates, the percentage of men who complete college still considerably exceeds that of women. Although women have gained on men in college graduation rates in the past thirty years, a significant gap still exists. The

Blatant forms of discrimination are probably the easiest to eradicate. Although women could be rejected for admission to medical school seventy years ago, legislation now prohibits such overt gender discrimination. However, the manner in which men and women are treated in college classrooms can also amount to gender discrimination if women are treated in such a way that the classroom takes on a powerful negative educational atmosphere for them. Some behaviors that are offensive to women are fairly obvious: professors using sexist humor to "spice up" dull lectures or diverting a discussion about female students' school work to one about their physical attributes or appearance. While most college professors probably avoid such blatantly offensive behaviors, there may still be subtle ways in which male students are favored in the classroom over female students, even though many professors and students may not be consciously aware of them. In fact, a report by the Association of American Colleges' Project on the Status and Education of Women (1982) suggested that there was a "chilly climate" in the college classroom for women. It cited the following behaviors by professors as instances of sexism that help create that chilling effect:

- calling directly on male students but not on female students.
- "coaching" male but not female students to work toward a fuller answer by probing for additional elaboration or explanation.
- waiting longer for men than for women to answer a question before going on to another student.

- interrupting women students or allowing them to be disproportionately interrupted by peers.
- responding more extensively to men's comments than to women's.
- using classroom examples that reflect stereotyped ideas about men's and women's social and professional roles, as when the scientist, doctor, or accountant is always "he" and the lab assistant, patient, or secretary is always "she."
- using the generic "he" or "man" to represent both men and women, as in "When a writer is truly innovative, what criteria can we use to measure his achievement?"

The report provoked considerable debate and numerous research efforts to assess the extent and exact forms that such "chilly" behaviors might take (Constantinople, Cornelius, and Gray, 1988; Crawford and MacLeod, 1990). The research consistently shows that male students do dominate college classroom discussions. However, there is less evidence that it is the "chilly" behavior of male college professors that elicits greater participation from the male students. Some colleges may have a classroom atmosphere that is generally friendlier to male students, but in most colleges the sex of the professor does not seem to be a big factor in producing the dominance of males—it occurs in the classrooms of both male and female professors. It may be that males come to college more prepared to actively and aggressively project themselves into classroom discussions, and the professors in turn may respond more positively to those students, irrespective of sex, who show such

problems that women face in getting an education, especially in a professional school, can often be subtle and difficult to detect. For example, one study of admission to medical school found that the personal interview part of the admissions process counted more heavily for fe-

male than for male applicants (Clayton, Baird, and Levinson, 1984). Furthermore, the women were rated lower on the average on these interviews than were men. This suggests that these interviews, which are very subjective assessments by those doing the interviewing, serve as a mechinitiative and speak up in the classroom. Male college students may behave differently from their female counterparts in this regard because of the general socialization experiences discussed elsewhere in this chapter, or because they were encouraged to do so in grade-school and high-school classrooms.

Whatever the reasons for gender differences in the classroom, colleges and professors need to look at things they can do to encourage more classroom participation from female students. A helpful finding in some of this research is that female professors create an atmosphere in the classroom in which students feel more comfortable interacting, and they elicit more student participation than do male professors. Female professors seem to be more aware of the interpersonal dynamics in the classroom that might discourage participation. Their male counterparts might be able to learn something from them.

The college climate is chilly for female faculty as well as for female students. Even women who receive their doctoral degree and land a position teaching at a university discover their experiences finding and securing a job tend to be different from those of their male counterparts (Gallagher et al., 1992). The women are more likely to choose a college teaching job on the basis of where their husband can find work, whereas men are freer to choose jobs that will provide the most benefit to their careers. This means that the first job these women get after completing their training is at a lower status university than the men get, and it means that women who

change jobs experience more downward mobility in their subsequent jobs than do men. This illustrates how the interlinkage of the institutions of education, the economy, and the family have different effects on men and women. Even after receiving high educational degrees that make them eligible for good jobs at prestigious universities, women are more constrained in their choices by demands of childbearing and rearing than men are. Women are expected to accommodate their career aspirations to family needs, and if a conflict arises, wives are more often expected to adapt their careers to their husbands' advancement than vice versa.

Despite laws that prohibit any preferences concerning hiring, promotions, and salary, women are still underrepresented in jobs in higher education (Benokraitis and Feagin, 1995). Twelve percent of the presidents of colleges and universities, including those that are all female, are women. Figures regarding academic rank are particularly revealing: Eighty-five percent of academics holding the rank of full professor are male; it is only in the least well-paid and least secure jobs—instructors and lecturers, who are often forced to accept part-time appointments—that the proportions of female faculty begin to equal those of the male faculty.

So, although advances have been made, research documents that sexism persists in higher education, although in much more subtle forms than in the past.

anism to limit women's opportunities to enter medical school. An interesting related issue is that among African Americans, men are slightly worse off in terms of educational achievement than women, suggesting that decades of oppression and racial discrimination have made it especially difficult for black males to be upwardly mobile (see Chapter 6).

Work and the Workplace While women constitute about 45 percent of the labor force in the United States, they are concentrated at the

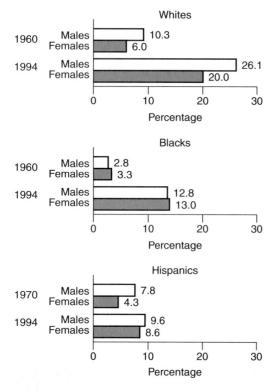

Whites

1960 Males 10.3
Females 6.0

1994 Males 26.1
Females 20.0

Percentage

Blacks

1960 Males 2.8
Females 3.3

1994 Males 12.8
Females 13.0

Percentage

Hispanics

1970 Males 7.8
Females 4.3

1994 Males 9.6
Females 8.6

Percentage

FIGURE 7.1 Percentage of People, Aged 25 Years or Older, Completing Four Years or More of College, by Sex and Race, 1960 and 1994. *Source:* U.S. Bureau of the Census, *Statistical Abstract of the United States, 1995* (Washington, D.C.: U.S. Government Printing Office, 1995), p. 157.

lower end of the status hierarchy. Table 7.2 illustrates that women tend to hold jobs such as secretary or receptionist, which provide relatively low income and prestige. The better occupations, such as physician or lawyer, are held primarily by men. Evidence suggests that some of this difference, even in the 1990s, is the result of discrimination in hiring practices. Some employers still prefer to hire men for jobs requiring technical or managerial skills based on the gender-role stereotype that men are more competent at such tasks. This is especially true when there is no evidence to suggest superior job performance on the part of either the male or female applicant for a job (Gerdes and Garber, 1983; Zebrowitz, Tenenbaum, and Goldstein, 1991). Table 7.2 illustrates that the job opportunities for women have improved since the 1970s, with considerably more women moving into such lucrative jobs as lawyer, physician, or engineer. But the dark side of the issue is that the low-paying and low-prestige jobs are still almost exclusively filled by women. In addition, research shows women who take traditionally male, blue-collar jobs encounter a very hostile climate in terms of how they are treated by their male coworkers and supervisors. These women, as a result, are less satisfied with their jobs and experience more stress at work than do women in traditionally female jobs (Mansfield et al., 1991).

Even when educational opportunities are available to women, their chances for success in an occupation are often blocked by obstacles that men usually do not face, such as subtle forms of discrimination in hiring and promotion practices. In the legal profession, for instance, access to jobs in large law firms is one of the major routes to success, but for many years such law firms closed their doors to women. In 1968, one woman lawyer (now a federal district judge) was told by a law firm that "we don't hire women; the secretaries might resent it" ("The Brethren's First Sister," 1981: 17). There has been an upsurge in the number of women lawyers in recent years—from 2.8 percent of the profession in 1970 to about 25 percent today. Yet women still make up only about 2 percent of the partners in the largest law firms, and research documents that, into the 1990s, women lawyers still are discriminated against in promotions in major U.S. law firms (Spurr, 1990; Bernstein, 1996). A 1995 report by a government commission found further evidence that women were discriminated against in promotions to senior management positions in industry (Glass Ceiling Commission, 1995). While women make up 40 percent of the work force, they constitute less than 5 percent of senior managers. In addition, the commission's investigation found evidence that the disparity was due to discrimination: Male senior managers refused to promote women and other minorities because they viewed such promotions as a direct threat to their own advancement.

Another obstacle that women face in the occupational realm is that they tend to be saddled, more so than men, with familial obligations (Ferree, 1991; Spade and Reese, 1991). Even when both spouses work, and even though men have taken on more responsibilities for these tasks in recent decades, women are still expected to take on more responsibility for raising the children, keeping up the home, and taking care of sick relatives. In fact, research shows that the cost of child care is an important reason why women sometimes quit the jobs they do get (Maume, 1991). Even among college-educated people, it is the rare couple who has a truly symmetrical relationship in which both partners share equally in household and work responsibilities.

Even women who start their own business are at a disadvantage in comparison to men (Loscocco et al., 1991). They have more difficulty securing capital from banks and contracts

TABLE 7.2 Employment Positions Held by Women, 1976–1994

Some Jobs Show Changes			Some Jobs Show Little Change		
	Percentage of Jobs Held by Women			Percentage of Jobs Held by Women	
Employment Positions	1976	1994	Employment Positions	1976	1994
Cashiers	87.7%	79.8%	Secretaries	99.0%	98.9%
Food counter clerks	85.5	70.2	Receptionist	96.2	96.4
Food service workers	68.7	57.9	Child-care workers	98.2	97.3
Real estate sales	41.2	48.4	Typists	96.7	94.1
Accountants and auditors	26.9	51.8	Bank tellers	91.9	90.4
Cleaning service workers	33.5	45.2	Bookkeepers	90.0	91.9
Financial managers	24.7	49.1	Health-service workers	86.2	87.9
College and university teachers	31.3	42.5	Hairdressers, cosmetologists	88.0	90.6
Lawyers and judges	9.2	24.8	Librarians	82.4	84.1
Physicians	12.8	22.3	File clerks	85.5	78.9
Police and detectives	3.7	12.2	Schoolteachers (except college and university)	70.9	74.9
Engineers	1.8	8.3	Social workers	61.0	69.3
Firefighters	0.0	2.1	Construction trades	1.6	2.2

Source: U.S. Department of Labor, Bureau of Labor Statistics, *Employment and Earnings,* Vol. 24, No. 1, January 1977, pp. 8–9; Vol. 42, No. 1, January 1995, pp. 175–180.

from the government, in part because of the belief that female-owned businesses are more likely to fail. Women are more often excluded from social networks where contacts are made and business deals can be discussed. Women also tend to start small businesses, which are more likely to fail than large businesses, and they go into business sectors where profits tend to be lower and failure rates higher, such as services or retail trade. Finally, women have less experience in the business world than do men. All these factors combined result in women's businesses being less profitable and more subject to failure.

Income   Classical economic theory claims that wages are determined by the competitive forces of supply and demand. Employers are rational and pay workers what they are worth in terms of the employer's ability to produce goods and services for a price that consumers are willing to pay. In this view, discrimination in pay based on gender or other characteristics is irrational and thus will not persist in the long run. Many economists and much sociological research suggest that this is a very simplistic view of the factors that influence the setting of wages (Jacobs and Steinberg, 1990; Peterson, 1990). In addition to market forces, income levels are also influenced by how much power different groups of workers possess and by cultural stereotypes of what different workers are worth as well as by the traditional levels of pay for different jobs. The effect of these "irrational" factors on women has been that they are paid considerably less than men.

In 1992, the median income for males working year round and full time in the United States was $30,358; for females, it was only $22,173 (U.S. Bureau of the Census, 1994). Women's income is 71 percent of men's income, and this has changed only slightly since 1970 (see Table 7.3). Such gender inequality is found in virtually all industrial nations, with women in Australia doing best by earning 79 percent of what men make and in Japan doing

worst with 46 percent of men's incomes (Rosenfeld and Kalleberg, 1991). This is a substantial difference. Even if we look at income levels of male and female workers in the same occupational categories who work year round and full time, women earn substantially less than men in every job category (see Table 7.4). Some of these differences in income result from the fact that most men have been working longer than women and thus have gained seniority and salary increases that have boosted their income. However, studies that have taken this into account still conclude that women have tended to earn less than men for doing the same job. A recent study by the U.S. Department of Education, for example, looked at the experiences of men and women who graduated from high school in 1972 and thus would be in the middle of their careers at the time of

TABLE 7.3 Ratio of Female/Male Median Income by Age, 1970 and 1992, Among Year-round, Full-time Civilian Workers

Age	1970	1992
All ages	0.59	0.71
15 to 19 years	0.96	0.93
20 to 24 years	0.74	0.93
25 to 34 years	0.65	0.83
35 to 44 years	0.54	0.69
45 to 54 years	0.56	0.64
55 to 64 years	0.60	0.64
65 years and over	0.72	0.61

Sources: U.S. Bureau of the Census, *Statistical Abstract of the United States, 1989* (Washington, D.C.: U.S. Government Printing Office, 1989), p. 448; U.S. Bureau of the Census, *Statistical Abstract of the United States, 1994* (Washington, D.C.: U.S. Government Printing Office, 1994), p. 472.

the study (Adelman, 1991). What they found was that women on the whole did better in high school and college than men did, they finished college faster, and they had more positive attitudes toward their educational experience. However, by the midpoint in their careers, the women earned less than the men and were more likely to be unemployed. The study looked at comparable men and women, such as those who had no children and had been working equal lengths of time, but still found pay inequities: In only seven of the thirty-three occupations studied did pay equity between men and women occur. The other twenty-six occupations showed men making significantly more than women. No occupation showed women making more than men. Even among men and women in the same age brackets, income differences persist (see Table 7.3). Al-

though there is little sex-based difference in income between teenagers, differences emerge among young adults and grow larger among older adults. It is safe to say, then, that not a lot of improvement has occurred, and the prospects for income equality in the near future are not great.

Chapter 6 discussed social inequality based on race and ethnicity. People in whom a subordinate racial or ethnic status is combined with a subordinate sexual status are even worse off than women in general. Sixty percent of elderly black women who live alone are living in poverty, and minority women who work earn less than do their male counterparts or white women (see Figure 7.2). Clearly, minority women in the United States are in a weak and vulnerable position when it comes to competing for economic resources. Even when they have

TABLE 7.4 Median Annual Income for Year-round Full-time Workers, by Sex and Occupational Category, 1992

Occupational Group	Female Income	Male Income	Ratio Women/Men
Professional specialty	31,261	44,015	0.71
Executive, administrators, and managerial	27,695	42,509	0.65
Sales	17,924	31,346	0.57
Precision production, craft and repair	19,045	28,923	0.66
Service workers	12,931	20,606	0.63
Technical and related support	24,797	32,720	0.76
Administrative support	20,321	27,186	0.75
Machine operators, assemblers, and inspectors	15,714	23,884	0.66
Transportation and material moving	20,131	25,787	0.78

Source: U.S. Bureau of the Census, *Statistical Abstract of the United States, 1994* (Washington, D.C.: U.S. Government Printing Office, 1994), p. 431.

FIGURE 7.2 Median Weekly Earnings of Full-time Workers, by Sex and Race, 1994.
Source: U.S. Department of Labor, Bureau of Labor Statistics, *Employment and Earnings,*
Vol. 42, No. 1, January 1995, p. 215.

full-time jobs, they tend to be concentrated in those jobs with the lowest income or prestige (Higginbotham, 1987; Blea, 1991).

Discrimination in the Military

Even women who choose the military as a career do not have the same opportunities as men. Although they constitute 11 percent of the armed services, they are currently barred from serving in many combat positions (Spitzer, 1992). In 1993, the Clinton administration opened some, but not all, combat positions to women. This is important because serving in combat positions is one of the best ways to advance one's career in the military. The partial ban on women in combat units continues to exist despite the fact that, during the Gulf War of 1991, female soldiers found themselves in combat, performed well by all standards, and were killed in action and taken prisoner by enemy troops. In fact, a poll taken

during the Gulf War indicated that half the U.S. public feels that women should have combat assignments if they want them (Fuentes, 1991). The major arguments against women in combat positions, especially ground infantry units, is that they do not have the physical strength or aggressive nature needed for the job, that they would disrupt the cohesiveness and "bonding" that occurs among men in combat and is important to combat success, and that it violates deep-seated cultural values regarding manhood and womanhood in Western civilization. Supporters of equal opportunities for women argue that women can be trained for the strength and aggressiveness and that they proved themselves in the Gulf War. Furthermore, there is no reason to believe that women could not "bond" in a military unit as well as men. The major stumbling block, according to this view, is that fighting and military combat are one of the last bastions where men can maintain a separate

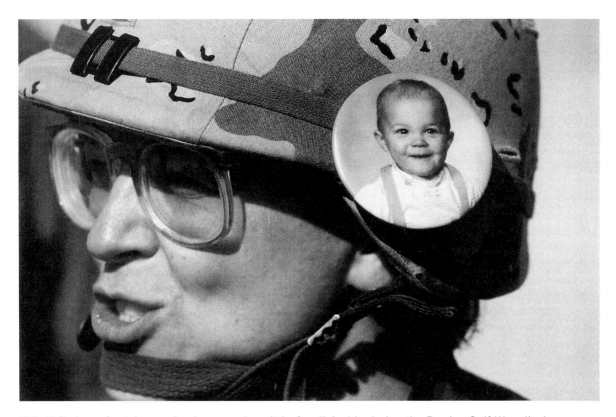

This U.S. Army Captain, serving in a supply unit in Saudi Arabia during the Persian Gulf War, displays a photo of her daughter. Clearly, occupational opportunities for women in the U.S. military are greater than ever.

"male" world into which women are not allowed. Of course, a major factor fueling the movement of women into the military over the past thirty years has been the needs of the military itself, which is ultimately concerned with finding a sufficient number of educated and motivated recruits. Along these lines, three factors are propelling the greater utilization of women: the all-volunteer military; the increasingly high-tech workplace, which calls for brains and dexterity more than brawn; and the increasing feminization of the work force. Given these trends, the military may see that it is in its own interests to expand opportunities for women, maybe by opening up more combat positions to them in the future.

Other Types of Discrimination

Discrimination on the basis of gender is not confined to education, occupation, and income. There are various other ways in which women are placed at a disadvantage in the United States. For example, the U.S. legal system has built into it a great deal of discrimination against women. In 1990, most states provided husbands with some loopholes to avoid prosecution for raping their wives (Russell, 1990). In eight states, men cannot be charged with raping their wives as long as they are living together and the wife has not filed for divorce or protection. Twenty-six other states allow charges of marital rape but with exemptions. Depending on the state, for example, a man cannot be charged with raping his wife unless he has kidnapped her or threatened her with a weapon; some of these states do not permit rape charges if the wife is unable to consent to having sex because she is drugged or unconscious. Only sixteen states accord wives the same protection as other women by treating marital rape like any other rape.

Women have also experienced discrimination in the realm of retirement income. Retirement plans have traditionally paid women a smaller monthly income than they pay to men with the same accumulated retirement assets. This inequity has been based on the fact that women live longer, on the average, than men. The rationale has been that women will draw the same total assets from their retirement plan as men, but they will draw it out in smaller amounts over a longer period. Women, of course, have complained that this penalizes them for being healthy. They have also argued that there are many other criteria than gender that could be used to determine retirement income, such as genetic susceptibility to disease such as heart disease or behavioral factors such as smoking.

Gender Inequality Involving Males

Most discussions of gender inequality focus on women, but men also suffer from unreasonable gender differentiation. Some have even spoken of a "masculine mystique" and the "myth of masculinity": a set of stereotypes about men, such as their being strong, dominant, tough, unemotional, and so forth (Kimmel and Messner, 1992). Socially imposed expectations concerning male behavior can be as limiting for men as the stereotypes involving females have been for women. In terms of professional ca-

reers, for example, male secretaries were often regarded as social oddities not that long ago. Men who entered such unconventional male roles had to be prepared for incredulous and sometimes even abusive reactions from others. At that time, most men probably did not even consider a profession such as nurse or secretary, even at times when jobs for college graduates in nursing were plentiful and other jobs were scarce. Still, today, very few men go into nursing (see Chapter 4).

The stereotypical male role also limits the opportunities open to men in terms of domestic activities, emotional expression, and relationships with children. Not that many years ago, if a male executive were to ask his employer for paternity leave, his boss would probably have laughed. Today, leaves of absence for new fathers are becoming more common. At the same time, there is still a form of institutionalized discrimination involved, because the man who takes such a leave often loses ground in the competition for advancement and seniority. Although there are very few males who identify themselves occupationally as "house husbands," it is more common than it once was for men to accept equal responsibility with their partners for domestic tasks (Lewis, 1984; McCall, 1988). In fact, despite the cultural assumption that work is the chief activity for men, one investigation found that 90 percent of the male respondents to a survey expressed strong attachments to their roles as husbands and fathers and defined their marital and parental roles as the most important (Cohen, 1987).

Other forms of discrimination against men can be found. For example, some states have laws that make it a punishable offense for men (and presumably other women) to use obscene language in the presence of females. Many insurance companies charge higher automobile insurance premiums to young males because of the higher rate of automobile accidents among that group. Thus, a young man who is a careful driver is penalized by virtue of his gender.

Finally, men but not women are required to register for the military draft, and only men could be inducted into the military should the draft itself be reinstated. Women are not required to make any equivalent contribution to national public service. This is true despite the fact that a public opinion poll during the Gulf War in 1991 showed that half of those surveyed believe that any future draft should include women (Fuentes, 1991).

A Global Perspective on Gender Inequality

The general patterns of gender inequality found in the United States are reproduced in other societies around the globe. The overall conclusion, as stated by the Secretary General of the United Nations, is that "the majority [of women] still lag far behind men in power, wealth and opportunity" (United Nations, 1991: v). Over the past few decades, a growing number of women have entered the work force, but in some areas their share of the labor force is still quite small: 17 percent in North Africa and Western Asia and 29 percent in Latin America (in the United States, it is 45 percent). In Algeria, women make up only 9 percent of the work force and in Egypt only 10 percent. In some areas, like the former Soviet Union and sub-Saharan Africa, women actually have lost a little ground since 1970, seeing their share of the labor force decline. However, women are also the most affected by economic recession: They are hired later when jobs are expanding and are let go quicker when jobs contract. For the women who do work, they generally have the less prestigious and lowest-paying jobs, a situation found in nations at all levels of development. In industrialized nations, such as Japan and South Korea, women earn about one-half of what men do, but this is also true in less developed nations, for example, Cyprus. In Iceland, women earn 90 percent of what men do, compared to 71 percent in the United States.

In all parts of the world, the rate of illiteracy is higher among women than men, with the rate almost twice as high for women in Asia. Also, in most places women lag behind men in enrollment in high school and college, although in 33 countries more women enroll in higher education than men (including the United States and many nations in Asia, Latin America, and the Caribbean). In addition, around the world, women in educational occupations tend to be employed at the lower levels, teaching in primary schools rather than in the more prestigious and higher-paying post-secondary school postions.

Worldwide, women are poorly represented in political positions where important decisions are made (United Nations, 1995). Women make up fewer than 10 percent of all members of parliaments or congresses in the world. Women do fairly well in some countries: Finland, Norway, Romania, and Cuba have one-third of their parliamentary seats filled by women. Some African and Arab nations have no women in parliament, and Japan's Diet is made up of less than 2 percent women. The United States does a little better than this, with 10 percent representation following the upsurge of women elected to Congress in the 1990s, but it still lags significantly behind the more advanced nations.

Finally, poor women in many Third-World nations have been among the major victims of the capitalist world economy that is described in Chapter 2. As noted there, the spread of capitalism to many nations has uprooted people from their traditional lands, with many migrating to towns or cities looking for work. The women among these migrants have been a significant source of cheap and docile labor for agribusiness and export industries. Traditional cultures do not encourage women to seek high levels of education or pursue careers. Yet their families permit, and sometimes encourage, them to seek the low-paying factory or agricultural jobs they can get because the families desperately need the income. Traditional gender roles encourage the women to be subservient to their fathers and husbands and to provide whatever economic support they can. Women who cannot find such jobs sometimes resort to joining the burgeoning sex industry in nations such as Thailand. Thus, patriarchy and traditional gender relations conspire to push these women into exploitative jobs in the global economy, and global corporations take advantage of this in order to maximize profits and exercise control over labor.

The International Perspectives section explores the issue of gender equality in various societies and suggests some reasons for variations in the levels of such inequality.

The Future of Gender Inequality

Gender inequality is more widely recognized as unacceptable today than in the past. One reason for this is that more women around the world are working outside the home or finding themselves the sole support of their families. For these women, the kinds of discrimination discussed in this chapter represent a serious problem that could threaten their ability to provide for their family. A second reason for the growth in opposition to gender inequality has been the efforts made by women and men around the world to draw attention to the inequities and change the social practices that support them. An assessment of the future of gender inequality can begin with a look at the worldwide feminist movement.

Collective Action and the Feminist Movement: A Global Struggle

The **feminist movement,** or **women's movement,** refers to *the collective activities of individuals, groups, and organizations whose goal is the fair and equal treatment of women and men around the world.* This movement has not been limited to

the United States, or even western democracies. Certainly, the democratic, egalitarian, and individualist ideologies that emerged in Europe and the United States in the seventeenth and eighteenth centuries have been influential in many parts of the world. However, many nations have used their own religious beliefs and traditions, combined with ideas from elsewhere, to justify gender equality. The Arab world, for example, was certainly influenced by European belief and example in the 1800s and early 1900s (Hourani, 1991; Barakat, 1993). Yet, there are many in the Arab world who argue that Islamic traditions themselves support the emancipation of women and that the substantial subordination of women in the Arab world is the result of a misinterpretation of the Koran, the Islamic holy book. For instance, one of the pioneers of Arab feminism, Qassem Amin, published a book in 1899 titled *The Liberation of Women* that called for extending to women most of the same rights that men enjoyed. Anticolonialist movements in places such as Palestine, Egypt, and Iraq mobilized women in support of nationalist causes, and this effort produced a variety of women's organizations that have continued the struggle for gender equality (Najjar, 1992). In 1923, Arab feminists convened at a women's conference in Rome, and in 1944 an Arab women's conference held in Cairo called for women to have the same marital rights as men, including the right to initiate divorce. Even such tradition-bound societies as China and Cuba have an active feminist movement which has at times gained significant support from the Communist government (O'Kelly and Carney, 1986).

Stirrings of feminist activity could also be found in the United States in the 1800s when women such as Susan B. Anthony and Elizabeth Cady Stanton campaigned for women's right to vote. Finally, in 1920, the Nineteenth Amendment to the Constitution—the Women's Suffrage Amendment—was passed. In the first half of the twentieth century, the nation became involved in two world wars, and these events took most of the attention away from women's rights for decades. In the late 1940s, fueled by women's work experience during World War II, women renewed the campaign for equal rights, but were beaten back by the conservative champions of another movement: the "return to normalcy" (Deckhard, 1979). Women were pressured to quit jobs that they held while American men had been at war and to return to the home so that the country could resume "normal" operations again.

In 1963, a well-known advocate of women's rights, Betty Friedan, wrote a book titled *The Feminine Mystique.* She took issue with the assumption that women "belong in the home," and her argument became the classic indictment of the presumption that women function best as mothers and homemakers. In 1966, Friedan and other feminists organized the National Organization for Women (NOW). At the time, this body of activist women was regarded as radical in mission, but many observers feel that "its style was actually somewhat conservative, and it stressed working through established legislative channels to achieve rights for women" (Richmond-Abbott, 1992: 354).

NOW concentrated much of its efforts toward passage of the Equal Rights Amendment, a constitutional amendment that would have banned discrimination based on sex. The ERA stated very simply: "Equality of rights under the law shall not be denied or abridged by the United States or any state on account of sex." In 1982, the deadline for ratification passed on the ERA because an insufficient number of states were willing to endorse it. The ERA was viewed by many as the Emancipation Proclamation for women. Proponents of the ERA viewed its defeat as a significant setback for the women's rights movement, and it certainly suggests that sentiment still lingers in the United States against complete equality for women. But again, reality is probably more complex than this. Some people opposed the ERA because they believed that existing legislation protected women adequately and that the amendment was re-

dundant, whereas others thought it would produce unisex bathrooms and sanction homosexual marriages. Some women opposed it because they did not want to give up special privileges that they do receive, such as preference in child custody and divorce award cases. So, people opposed the ERA for many reasons, some of them having little to do with resistance to equality for women (Richmond-Abbott, 1992).

Seen from another perspective, the ERA issue is one of *status politics:* Opposition to or support for the amendment is in part a controversy over who has the power to enforce their definition of appropriate sex-role behavior on society. Beyond any practical effect it might have, passage of the ERA would symbolically demonstrate the power of NOW and other feminist groups. Likewise, the defeat of the ERA shows that people supporting more traditional definitions of the sexes have the power to draw the line somewhere. According to the status politics point of view, the passage of legislation is as important as a symbolic demonstration of the exercise of power as it is for its practical outcome (Scott, 1985).

The experience with the ERA in the 1980s suggests the possibility of a "backlash" against feminism—a resistance to further steps toward gender equality and possibly even a rollback of some of the gains. Along these lines, journalist Susan Faludi (1991) points out that those opposed to further advances even try to blame the feminist movement for whatever difficulties modern women experience. Feminism has raised unrealistic expectations among women, these opponents argue, and thus created more dissatisfaction and unhappiness. Despite these developments, feminists in the United States and around the world have created a global network to work toward gender equality, often working through international organizations like the United Nations or independent nongovernmental organizations (NGOs) discussed in Chapter 2. The United Nations formed its Commission on the Status of Women in 1946 to monitor the treatment of women and promote

When we look at cultures other than our own, it is not hard to find women being treated, even today, in ways that people in the United States would find abhorrent. In Bangladesh, for example, mothers with limited resources give their sons the first pick of the food available whereas daughters have to be satisfied with what is left over. Since Bangladeshi culture discourages women from doing paid work outside the home, males are seen as the more important breadwinners in the family and are thus fed and cared for with more zeal. As a consequence, Bangladeshi girls are often underfed and suffer stunted growth. In Saudi Arabia, religious police, or Mutawin, patrol in jeeps looking for women who are not properly attired, according to the Islamic code. Unacceptable attire, which might mean having an ankle visible beneath the mandatory long black robes, is met with harassment and in some cases arrest (Hijab, 1988; Sadik, 1989). Such cultural beliefs and practices are reflected in women's and men's opportunities in the workplace. In Bangladesh, less than 10 percent of adult women work, compared to well over half of women in the United States. In Saudi Arabia, women and men are segregated in many workplaces and schools.

A close look at these and other examples of gender inequalities in many cultures makes one thing clear: While gender inequality is pervasive, and often more extensive than in the United States, it is also complicated and influenced by many factors. One such factor is religion. Both Bangladesh and Saudi Arabia are Islamic countries, and Islamic societies have tended to keep women subordinate and out of the labor force. At the same time, there are many modern and well-educated women in such Islamic countries and many Muslim men who support greater education of and opportunities for women (Hourani, 1991). In fact, many Muslims interpret parts of the Koran (the Islamic holy book) as giving religious affirmation to gender equality. So, the picture is one of a tension between an admittedly very strong and pervasive social custom of male dominance on the

one hand, and the desire of some women and men to open up a broader range of opportunities for both genders on the other hand. Which of these tendencies predominates shifts over time. But this fluctuation in attitude is also true in the United States. We have documented in this chapter a move toward greater gender equality in the United States. But some people have detected a backlash against equality that seems to have brought considerable resistance to further advances for women—a tension like that in Islamic countries, although at a different level (Faludi, 1991).

Another factor that influences gender equality is wealth and modernization, with the wealthier and more industrialized nations according more equal opportunities to women. Yet, Saudi Arabia, one of the wealthiest nations in the world, is also one of the more patriarchal. Even among the industrialized nations, levels of gender equality vary. In countries like the United States, Canada, and Sweden, for example, over half of all women work. However, in Belgium and the Netherlands—both modern, industrial nations—the figures are 28 percent and 37 percent, respectively (U.S. Bureau of the Census, 1991: 847). In these two societies, special cultural traditions have produced less support for women working outside the home, especially after they have children. Religion also influences practices in industrial nations, with heavily Catholic countries like Italy, Ireland, and Spain having only about one-third of all women in the work force.

Although opportunities for women seem to increase with industrialization, in some traditional societies women end up worse off, at least in the short run, as the economy shifts from agricultural to industrial production. "As agriculture becomes more mechanized and less labor intensive, men tend to take over the mechanized farming jobs. Women may be displaced or relegated to routine tasks associated with agriculture, such as the sorting of coffee beans. As women lose jobs in the agricultural sector, there are generally few employment opportunities for them in the indus-

Some Islamic societies have tended to keep women in a subordinate status, symbolized by the required wearing of long black gowns that fully cover the body and veils that cover the face.

trial sector, as men are preferred" (Stockard and Johnson, 1992: 78). This trend may reverse, as it did in the United States as the expansion of industrial and service sectors of the economy provided a new source of jobs for women. However, this same pattern may not prevail in all societies. In addition, as we have seen in this chapter, the jobs that become available to women as industrialization proceeds tend to be at the low end of the pay and prestige scale. The fact that more women work does not mean that gender equality has been achieved.

So, patterns of gender inequality are complex and influenced by many elements of a culture, such as religious beliefs, wealth, level of industrialization, and other factors. How much gender inequality exists in a particular society depends on that society's unique blend of all those elements at a given time. This cross-cultural and international viewpoint serves as a warning not to oversimplify the reasons for gender inequality or the patterns that it can take.

women's rights in all nations (United Nations, 1991). There followed a series of steps to expand the arenas in which nations were to be encouraged to accord equal treatment to women. In 1952, for example, the Convention on the Political Rights of Women established the mandate that all women should have the right to vote, hold office, and exercise public functions. Later conventions extended equal rights to women in marriage and in choosing divorce. The period from 1975 to 1985 was called the United Nations Decade for Women. A Nairobi World Conference on Women in 1985 approved even more stringent and detailed plans for governments to ensure that women have equal rights in education, training, and employment; to attack negative stereotypes and perceptions of women; to encourage men and women to share domestic responsibilities; and to collect statistics to monitor the situation of women. Further steps were made at the UN Conference on Women in Beijing in 1995. Of course, all member nations of the United Nations are not strongly enthusiastic about the advancement of gender equality, but a host of women's NGOs has maintained pressure on the United Nations to encourage nations on these issues. The outcome of these pressures has been the achievement of important victories in the quest for gender equality in many nations, although much gender inequality still persists on a global scale.

This global movement for greater gender equality has produced some very significant developments that affect the status of women in the United States.

Changes in the Law

Over the past twenty years in the United States, a significant amount of legislation has been approved that contributes to the reduction of gender inequality. Legislation prohibits discrimination in loan eligibility based on sex or marital status. Title VII of the 1964 Civil Rights Act makes illegal any sex discrimination in em-

ployment practices. Title IX of the Educational Amendments Act specifies that any educational institution discriminating on the basis of sex will be denied federal aid. Other examples of legislation that helps women are the Displaced Homemaker Act (which assists women who have divorced but have few skills with which to support themselves) and legal provisions for wives who have been abused by their husbands.

A new idea for reducing the economic inequities suffered by women has emerged, called "comparable worth." The basic idea is that people whose jobs make equivalent demands on them and that call for similar skills, education, or responsibility should receive roughly similar pay; in other words, "equal pay for comparable worth" (England, 1992). For example, a judge in Seattle ruled in 1983 that the state government was in violation of Title VII of the 1964 Civil Rights Act because it routinely paid jobs performed mostly by women less than those performed mostly by men. His ruling was based in part on a comparison of state jobs in terms of "worth points," with points given for such things as knowledge and skills required, mental demands, accountability, and working conditions. Since then, twenty-two states have begun to reassess their pay schedules with these ideas in mind. In fact, in Ontario, which is one of Canada's largest provinces, the Ontario Pay Equity Act, covering 1.7 million workers in public and private settings, now demands adherence to the principle of comparable worth (Freudenheim, 1989).

It has been a highly controversial development with opponents arguing that it is impossible to really compare the "worth" of different jobs and that the free market should determine what people are paid. These opponents argue that, if women are dissatisfied with the low pay in some jobs, they should compete for the higher-paying jobs. Some even suggest that such interference with market mechanisms would disrupt the whole economic system. Supporters argue that women face more barriers in the competition for jobs and that comparable worth would help overcome generations of discrimination in the way salaries are set. So far, comparable worth has not substantially altered the position of women in society, but it is likely to become a central issue over the next decade (Aldrich and Buchele, 1986; Peterson, 1990).

Changes in the Workplace

As the number of women in the work force has increased and as they have moved into more traditionally male occupations, some new issues have risen to prominence, especially some more subtle and unexpected barriers to advancement that affect women in the 1990s. One study of male and female managers in large business concerns, for example, found that the women promoted to middle-management positions by male supervisors were the less aggressive, less threatening women who did not rock the boat or "make waves" (Harlan and Weiss, 1981). However, these middle-management positions were dead ends for these women because supervisors wanted more aggressive and dynamic people for top positions. This same research also disputed the belief that sexism in the workplace would decline as more women were employed. They found that resistance to women declines at first, but as the proportion of women passes 15 percent, renewed resistance emerges because men feel their opportunities are being reduced due to competition with women. Research has also found that when many women are employed in the same job, that job comes to be defined as a woman's job. Once this happens, the job tends to be devalued, with less pay and a smaller budget than when more men held that position (Baron and Newman, 1990; Reskin and Roos, 1990).

Another emerging reality concerning women in executive management positions is that many who occupy these positions are "bailing out" of the managerial work force because trying to combine full-time, demanding careers with being wives and mothers has proved too difficult. A recent study showed that the rate of turnover in management positions is nearly three times higher among women than among men, and many women who take maternity leave do not return to work (Schwartz, 1989). In addition, young women appear to be less drawn to high-powered business careers in the 1990s than they were in the 1970s. For example, women today make up a smaller proportion of applications to graduate programs in business than six years ago (Cowan, 1992). It seems that women today are less willing to make as many compromises in the family area as some young women did twenty years ago.

To alleviate this tension between work and child rearing, it has been suggested that corporations offer women two career tracks. One, called career-primary, would involve the conventional expectations placed on male employees: career comes first, no time out for personal reasons, and work on nights and weekends if corporate needs demand it. The second track, called career-and-family or the "mommy track," would allow women to pursue careers while also devoting themselves to their families. For example, maternity leave would not be frowned on and excessive demands would not be placed on the women's free time. Critics of such proposals argue that those in the career-and-family track would be discriminated against in any event through smaller pay increases or reduced opportunity for promotion. In fact, research shows that women who interrupt their careers for family reasons, such as raising children, never catch up, in terms of income or promotions, to their female counterparts who stay on the job (Jacobsen and Levin, 1992). Apparently, their employers think they are not as serious about or as committed to their jobs. So, the career-and-family track would likely produce the same old outcome: Women who choose to have children would be discriminated against because they did not follow the male model of career development.

Despite this, we can predict that women will continue to join the work force in even larger numbers. Substantial improvement is al-

POLICY ISSUES
Fighting Sexual Harassment in the Workplace

Since the Anita Hill–Clarence Thomas hearings, the climate in the workplace certainly seems to have changed in relation to how people of different sexes treat one another. Both men and women seem more willing to report episodes of sexual harassment and assault. In fact, in 1992, it came out that a number of women serving in the military in Saudi Arabia and Iraq during the Gulf War were subjected to sexual assault—not by the enemy but rather by their fellow soldiers! Such behavior is now more likely to come under the harsh glare of publicity, and lawsuits have made sexual harassment expensive for employers to ignore. In 1980, the Equal Employment Opportunity Commission placed sexual harassment under the Civil Rights Act of 1964 as a form of civil rights violation. The Civil Rights Act of 1991 provided beefed-up protection and additional legal weapons in the fight against sexual harassment in the workplace. Some states also have strong antidiscrimination statutes that include sexual harassment. However, because of stringent standards set by the courts, winning a sexual harassment case is not easy. In particular, many courts require that harassment be so severe

that a "reasonable employee" would find her or his psychological well-being and work performance seriously affected because of it, but some of the behaviors that women find demeaning and disturbing are not perceived by judges and juries to be that serious ("Sexual Harassment . . . ", 1991).

Part of the problem with sexual harassment is that men and women tend to perceive behaviors quite differently. Most men and women agree that demanding sexual favors as a condition of employment or promotion is wrong. However, the Equal Employment Opportunity Commission also defines as harassment behaviors that create a "hostile" environment that makes it more difficult for people to do their job. So, repeated sexual advances by a coworker, even if not linked to employment or promotion, could constitute harassment because they are disturbing to the woman and create an environment in which it is difficult for her to work. And this is where men's and women's perceptions tend to differ. Many men see such behaviors as relatively harmless and claim they would even be flattered if they were the recipients of such actions by coworkers. Most women, on the other

ready observable. Nearly one-third of the small businesses in the United States today belong to women, up from 23 percent in the early 1980s. Some labor experts project that this may hit 40 percent by the year 2000 (O'Hare and Larson, 1991). This growth has been impressive, and credit and capital are now more available to women who wish to start or expand a business. In addition, research shows that college-educated women are becoming much more like their male counterparts in terms of the emphasis they place on work as being essential to a person's life and happiness (Fiorentine, 1988). As these changes occur, mechanisms are developing to overcome some of the barriers

that women have faced in the past. For example, women are excluded from fewer of the social and business networks that can assist one in a career or business. Because of court challenges based on antidiscrimination legislation, women have gained access to some chapters of such organizations as Rotary, the Lions Club, and the Kiwanis where businesspeople often gather. And it makes a big difference to success in business. As one businesswoman put it after she joined Rotary, "Suddenly I was having lunch every week with all the movers and shakers in town. Now they think of me when business opportunities come up" (quoted in Zane, 1991: 35). In addition, new networks have hand, find such behaviors disturbing, insulting, and offensive, and such behaviors do create a "hostile" atmosphere in many women's minds. This is why, during the Anita Hill–Clarence Thomas confrontation, we repeatedly heard women exclaim about men: They just don't get it. In other words, men just fail to understand why women find such behaviors offensive, demeaning, and maybe even frightening.

To give both men and women a better perspective on women's views of these issues, attorneys William Petrocelli and Barbara Kate Repa (1992), experts on the legal issues of sexual harassment, suggest the following simple test to help decide whether a remark or a behavior is appropriate:

1. Would you say or do the same thing in front of your spouse?
2. How would you feel if the same remarks or behavior were directed at your mother, sister, wife, or daughter?
3. How would you feel if a man made the same remarks or took the same actions toward you?

If your reaction to any one of these questions is negative, then the remark or behavior might well be seen as inappropriate harassment by a female coworker.

Many employers have been taking steps that experts recognize will reduce the likelihood of sexual harassment or assault occurring in the workplace: have a written and publicized policy against such actions, vigorously enforce the policy, educate employees about what constitutes harassment and how to file a complaint about it, and provide sincere and significant top-management support for the policy (Webb, 1991; Powell, 1993). Such steps should make the workplace of the 1990s a much more hospitable one for women. However, as we saw in Chapter 6, discrimination, as well as harassment, tends to rear its ugly head when competition between groups grows fierce. As more women enter the work force and take jobs traditionally held by men, harassment may emerge as a response to threatened losses. So additional vigilance may be necessary to alleviate this problem.

emerged to help women. For example, WomenVenture is a nationwide organization that offers seminars and workshops to women on how to start or expand a business, as well as financial backing to twenty-five hundred businesswomen each year. Such organizations and contacts can make the difference between advancement and stagnation in one's business or career. The opportunities for advancement for women in the 1990s will undoubtedly improve with the further availability of such supports for women. However, thousands of clubs and organizations still do not admit women because there are no state or local antidiscrimination laws to force them to do so. In fact, former Presidents Ronald Reagan and George Bush belong to an elite businessmen's social club, the Bohemian Club, which refuses to admit women.

Sexual harassment and assault are serious problems that women face in the workplace, making work for them more difficult and demeaning and in extreme cases impossible. As the Policy Issues insert in this chapter shows, some important strides have been made in overcoming this problem.

The Changing Face of Politics

One image from the Anita Hill–Clarence Thomas confrontation in 1991 was unforgettable: a black woman confronting a panel of the all-white, all-male faces of the members of the Senate Judiciary Committee. It brought into stark reality the truth that, although women make up 51 percent of our populace, very few of them are among our elected representatives at the national level. Of the one hundred senators, the number of women among them fluctuated from a low of none to a high of two between 1970 and 1992, rising to seven in the 1994 election (U.S. Bureau of the Census, 1994). However, this hides some very dramatic gains that women have made in politics over the past few decades. In 1970, only twenty-five women ran for seats in the U.S. House of Representatives; by 1992 this had increased six times, to 150 women. Although only 10 percent of the representatives in 1994 were women, that is almost four times greater than the 2.7 percent of twenty years earlier. Gains have been especially impressive at the state and local levels. Twenty years ago, women made up less than 5 percent of all state legislators, compared with 18 percent today. Twenty years ago, a paltry 1 percent of the mayors of cities of more than thirty thousand people in the United States were women; today the figure is 17 percent. Although women are still far underrepresented in politics, they are beginning to move into more powerful and nationwide political positions. It takes time to get significant numbers of women entrenched in the political system to the point where they can make a run for a Senate seat. We will likely see more of this in the future.

Masculine, Feminine, or Human?

Some of the problems surrounding gender inequality may arise in part because of the oversimplified view that people tend to have of gender, seeing things as either male or female, but not both. In reality, each individual can be seen as a combination of both feminine and masculine characteristics. In fact, masculinity and femininity may not be polar opposites but rather two independent sets of characteristics. So, for example, some very feminine women may have few masculine characteristics, whereas other very feminine women might have many masculine traits. In fact, the word **androgyny** (from the Greek *andro*, "male," and *gyn*, "female") has been coined to describe *a condition where male and female characteristics are not rigidly assigned and there is a blending of the traits, attitudes, and roles of both sexes*. From this perspective, people explore a broad range of gender-role possibilities and choose emotions and behaviors without regard to gender stereotypes. This does not mean that gender distinctions disappear but that one's biological sex becomes a less rigid determinant of which masculine and feminine traits a particular individual will exhibit. This means that people can be more flexible in their role playing and express themselves in a variety of ways other than the traditionally masculine or feminine ways. The trends toward gender equality discussed in this chapter may make more of this flexibility possible in the future. People may be more free to choose roles or tasks at which they are most competent and express emotions or attitudes with which they feel most comfortable—all without regard to whether they will be ridiculed for choosing the "wrong" roles or emotions for their sex.

In fact, some evidence suggests that sex-role traditionalism, where males exhibit a largely masculine/instrumental orientation and women a mostly feminine/expressive orientation, is less common today. Some research shows that women are more inclined than in the past to take on traditionally male orientations, and other research suggests that men today are more likely to express androgynous or feminine orientations (McBroom, 1984; Hyde, Krajnik, and Skuldt-Niederberger, 1991). However, it is probably too soon to say how extensive or enduring these trends will be.

Using the interactionist perspective, the social problem of sexual inequality will be alleviated only when there is shared consensus about expectations for men and women in society.

Gender inequality and fewer opportunities for women can lead
some poor women (Chapter 5) toward prostitution and pornography (Chapter 11) as ways to support themselves and their
families. This is especially tempting for poor single mothers
whose opportunities are severely limited. Prostitution and
pornography are in great demand by men, but the women who
satisfy that demand are considered morally tainted by those
same men.

L I N K A G E S

This could be achieved by reestablishing traditional sex roles or by changing to something
closer to androgyny—as long as there was consensus about these expectations. On the other
hand, there must be consistency between gender roles and the other roles that people perform. We could not, for example, expect
women to exhibit a certain kind of self-concept
as women—passive, dependent, less intelligent—and then be required to have a contradictory self-concept in some other role that
they play, such as business executive or soldier.
As women and men move into nontraditional
roles in society, their self-concepts and identities will be changed by their experiences in
these new roles. As this occurs, our values about
existing sources of sexual inequality will also be
likely to change. But only the future will reveal
the extent to which these changes will alter the
present fabric of sexual differentiation.

Summary

1. Sex is an ascribed and a master status. The
text examines four different views of sex as an
element of social differentiation: the biological
perspective, which assumes that innate biological differences between men and women shape
the contributions that each can make to society; the functionalist perspective, which argues
that a problem exists when the sex-role division
of labor is no longer consistent with the needs

of a particular society; the conflict perspective,
which views sexual inequality as a problem
when some group (women) realizes it is being
exploited and strives to do something to
change the situation; and the interactionist
perspective, which emphasizes social definitions and symbolic representations of appropriate behavior for males and females in trying
to understand sexual inequality.

2. Male and female are sex-related terms; gender refers to learned behavior involving how we
are expected to act as males and females in society. One of the key issues in analyzing gender
inequality is how we learn to be masculine and
feminine and how this contributes to sexual
differentiation and inequality. This learning occurs through the socialization process, with
three major agencies of socialization being primarily responsible: the family, the schools, and
the media.

3. Sexual inequality is widespread in the
United States and around the world. Women
occupy a subordinate position in comparison
to men on virtually every dimension of socioeconomic status (SES). Discrimination on the
basis of sex is not confined to education, occupation, and income. Women also experience
unequal treatment in the military and before
the courts. Sexual inequality also affects men
when they are discouraged from pursuing certain kinds of jobs and can be drafted into the
military when no equivalent service is asked of
women.

4. The future of gender inequality will depend on the progression of the feminist movement and how much collective action is mobilized around the world to deal with the various forms of discrimination. Changes in the law and new legislation affecting women, such as comparable worth, will also be important. The workplace is changing, with increasing numbers of women joining the labor force. Any meaningful changes in the situation surrounding sexual inequality will involve a redefinition of both masculinity and femininity.

STUDY A N D *Review*

Key Terms

androgyny

expressive tasks

feminist movement

gender

instrumental tasks

sex

sexism

women's movement

Multiple-Choice Questions

1. Regarding biological differences between men and women, the text draws which of the following conclusions?
   a. The differences are actually larger than was once thought.
   b. The differences refer to averages which ignore the significant overlap between the sexes.
   c. Relatively little human behavior is learned through socialization.
   d. There has not been much research on the differences between the sexes.
2. Which of these statements would be most consistent with the conflict perspective?
   a. The sex-role division of labor is a social problem when it is no longer consistent with the needs of society.
   b. Sexual differentiation is a "battleground" for the struggle over scarce resources.
   c. Beliefs about sexual inequality are maintained and reinforced through patterns of social interaction.
   d. Innate biological differences between men and women shape the contributions each can make to society.
3. Research on conversational styles supports the conclusion that:
   a. Men talk more than women in mixed-sex conversations.
   b. Women talk more than men in mixed-sex conversations.
   c. Women interrupt more than men do in mixed-sex conversations.
   d. Both a and c are supported.
   e. Both b and c are supported.
4. Which of the following is *not* an agency of socialization that the text considers primarily responsible for learning during the socialization process?
   a. The family.
   b. The media.
   c. The schools.
   d. The churches.
5. Regarding the socialization of children, the text concludes that:
   a. Boys are more prominent in girls' games than girls are in boys' games.
   b. Most elementary school teachers treat boy students and girl students the same.

c. In childhood, male activities tend to be more valued than female activities.

d. Children's books have eliminated most stereotyped images of the sexes.

6. Among which of the following groups does a higher percentage of women graduate from college in the United States than the percentage among men?
   a. The elderly.
   b. Whites.
   c. Hispanic Americans.
   d. The poor.
   e. African Americans.

7. Classical economic theory claims that wages are determined by which of the following?
   a. The competitive forces of supply and demand.
   b. How much power different groups of workers possess.
   c. Cultural stereotypes of what different groups of workers are worth.
   d. Both a and b are consistent with classical economic theory.
   e. a, b, and c are consistent with classical economic theory.

8. Which of the following is *not* true regarding the gender inequalities suffered by males in the United States today?
   a. Men but not women must register for the military draft.
   b. More women attend law school than do men.
   c. Men are sometimes charged more for automobile insurance than are women.
   d. Socially imposed expectations limit the freedom of men to choose stereotypically female occupations.

9. Which of the following is currently *not* being implemented as a social policy in the United States?
   a. Comparable worth.
   b. The 1964 Civil Rights Act.
   c. The Equal Rights Amendment.
   d. The 1991 Civil Rights Act.

10. A situation in which male and female characteristics are not rigidly assigned but instead there is a blending of the traits of both sexes is called:
    a. A master status.
    b. Comparable worth.

c. Sexism.
d. Androgyny.
e. Instrumental tasks.

True/False Questions

1. Gender is an ascribed status, but it is not a master status.
2. The text concludes that there are no biological differences between men and women that have any social significance.
3. The functionalist perspective argues that it is more functional in industrial societies to assign tasks to people on the basis of individual abilities rather than ascribed characteristics.
4. Stereotyped views of gender roles have been largely eliminated in children's textbooks but can still be found in college-level textbooks.
5. Male predominance in social interaction in college classrooms does not seem to occur in the classrooms of male professors only but is also found in classrooms with female professors.
6. There is a higher proportion of college graduates among women today than among men.
7. The percentage of secretaries who are men has remained virtually unchanged over the past twenty years.
8. One argument that is made for not allowing women into combat units in the military is that their presence would interfere with the male bonding that is important to combat success.
9. The quest for gender equality is a global movement rather than one limited to western or industrial nations.
10. According to the text, androgyny is a thing of the past.

Fill-In Questions

1. A person's educational level is an

   _____ status.

2. _____ is an ideology that justifies the domination of one sex over the other because of the presumed biological inferiority of the subordinate.

3. Building a house or managing the activities of a work team are tasks that sociologists call _____ tasks.

4. The study of the conversational styles of men and women provides evidence for the _____ perspective.

5. The learned behavior involving how we are expected to act as males and females is referred to by sociologists as _____ .

6. The three main dimensions of socioeconomic status are education, _____ , and _____ .

7. The employment position that has the highest percentage of jobs held by women is _____ .

8. Currently, women earn approximately _____ percent of the income of men in the United States.

9. The idea that people whose jobs make equivalent demands on them should receive roughly similar pay is called _____ .

10. Women currently constitute _____ percent of the United States Senate.

Matching Questions

_____ 1. Equal Rights Amendment

_____ 2. NGOs

_____ 3. a person's occupation

_____ 4. maintaining harmony in a family

_____ 5. Rosie the Riveter

_____ 6. Anita Hill

_____ 7. blending of traits of both sexes

_____ 8. WomenVenture

_____ 9. prohibits gender discrimination in education

_____ 10. myth of masculinity

A. international pressure groups
B. expressive task
C. sexual harassment
D. androgyny
E. achieved status
F. Title IX of the Educational Amendments Act
G. stereotypes about men
H. status politics
I. World War II workers
J. helps women in business

Essay Questions

1. What conclusions does the text draw regarding the impact of biological differences between men and women on social behavior?

2. According to the conflict perspective, what are the reasons for sex stratification in society?

3. What does research show about the impact of gender on conversational styles? What is the importance of these gender differences?

4. Describe the ways in which schools contribute to the problem of gender inequality.

5. What is the "chilling effect" on the classroom described in the text? Why does it happen and what are its consequences?

6. Describe the impact of gender and race on people's educational opportunities and accomplishments in the United States.

7. What are the arguments for and against women serving in combat positions in the military?

8. Describe the kinds of gender inequality that confront women in Third-World nations around the globe.

9. What are ways to reduce levels of sexual harassment in the work place?

10. What changes have occurred in the work place in the United States as far as gender inequality is concerned?

Answers

Multiple Choice
1. B; 2. B; 3. A; 4. D; 5. C; 6. E; 7. A; 8. B; 9. C; 10. D

True/False
1. F; **2.** F; **3.** T; **4.** F; **5.** T; **6.** F; **7.** T; **8.** T;
   9. T; **10.** F

Fill-In
1. achieved
2. sexism
3. instrumental
4. interactionist
5. gender
6. occupation, income
7. secretaries or dental hygienists (Ch. 4)
8. seventy-one
9. comparable worth
10. seven

Matching
1. H; **2.** A; **3.** E; **4.** B; **5.** I; **6.** C; **7.** D; **8.** J;
   9. F; **10.** G

For Further Reading

Nancy Bonvillain. *Women and Men: Cultural Constructs of Gender.* Englewood Cliffs, N.J.: Prentice Hall, 1995. This is a very enlightening book that explores issues of gender and gender inequality in many cultures around the globe and in societies at many different levels of development, from hunter-gatherers to industrialists. It provides a very complete and sophisticated view of gender in society.

Anne Campbell. *Men, Women, and Aggression.* New York: Basic Books, 1993. This provocative book takes the position that high levels of aggression in males are not a function of biology but of learning. Men learn while growing up to use aggression as a tool to get their way whereas women do not learn this.

Arlie Hochschild with Anne Machung. *The Second Shift: Working Parents and the Revolution at Home.* New York: Viking, 1989. This book is about who cares for children, who does the housework, and whose career suffers as it becomes increasingly normal for both men and women to work outside the home. Hochschild has been in this domestic bind herself, so she can speak forcefully on the basis of her research and her personal experience.

Ethel Klein. *Gender Politics: From Consciousness to Mass Politics.* Cambridge, Mass.: Harvard University Press, 1984. An excellent overview of the use of the political process to achieve more equality for women. This is a good historical overview of the women's rights movement.

John Nicholson. *Men and Women: How Different Are They?* New York: Oxford University Press, 1984. In this book, a British psychologist explores the origins of male dominance in different societies, focusing on the question of whether this phenomenon is an inevitable consequence or the result of aspirational differences between men and women.

Peggy Orenstein. *Schoolgirls: Young Women, Self-Esteem, and the Confidence Gap.* New York: Doubleday, 1994. This book documents the decline in self-esteem and self-confidence that many girls experience as they go through adolescence by looking in-depth at the lives of girls at two schools.

Peggy Reeve Sanday. *Fraternity Gang Rape: Sex, Brotherhood, and Privilege on Campus.* New York: New York University Press, 1990. Rape may be the ultimate form of control that men exercise over women. This book documents how college women are controlled by it and some of the social and cultural dynamics that encourage gang rapes on campus.

Deborah Tannen. *Talking from 9 to 5: How Women's and Men's Conversational Styles Affect Who Gets Heard, Who Gets Credit, and What Gets Done at Work.* New York: William Morrow, 1994. Building on the interactionist perspective's focus on conversational styles shaping and reinforcing gender patterns in society, this excellent book describes some of the complexity of these processes in the work place and the consequences they can have.

Naomi Wolf. *The Beauty Myth: How Images of Beauty Are Used Against Women.* New York: Morrow, 1991. This is an intriguing book about how our culture encourages a conception of beauty that tends to coerce women into doing things that are not in their best interests. It is a thoughtful illustration of how cultures can exercise social control in very subtle and often unrecognized ways.

Julia T. Wood. *Gendered Lives: Communication, Gender, and Culture.* Belmont, Calif.: Wadsworth, 1994. This book provides a comprehensive overview of the multitude of ways that gender pervades people's lives and profoundly shapes their thoughts, feelings, and behaviors—often in ways of which they are totally unaware.

CHAPTER EIGHT

Age and Social Inequality

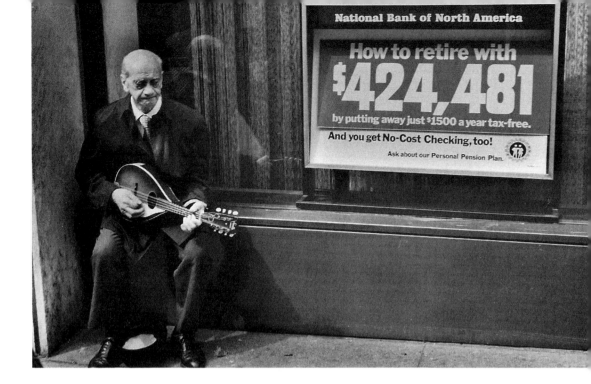

Most cultures contain positive images of both the young and the old. In the United States, for example, we call youth the "tender years" or the "springtime of life," implying that the young are more innocent and less troubled than older people and possess as yet unrealized potential and promise. The later years in life are referred to as the "golden years," and old people are presumed to have gained more wisdom and patience than the young. But beyond these positive images, the young and the old share something considerably less valued: They bear the brunt of inequitable treatment in society. They are more likely than other age groups to be unemployed; they experience discrimination in the job market and other realms; they can experience victimization and exploitation by others in degrading ways; and they are more likely than others to be excluded from the adult world of work, contribution, and responsibility.

All these things afflict the young and old by virtue of their age. In this chapter, we will document the extent of these problems and what can be and is being done about them. First, however, we need to understand the way in which age—an ascribed status like race and sex—influences a person's position in society.

Age, Life Course, and Social Structure

Gerontology is the *scientific study of aging.* It began as the study of why some people are especially long lived, but it now focuses on all the biological, psychological, and social aspects of growing old (Atchley, 1994). It studies people of all ages because the process of aging begins the day we are born. As people age, societies tend to carve out their lives into a series of stages, with different things being expected of them at each stage. The content of these stages depends on a person's biological age and the social needs of a particular society. All these stages taken together constitute the **life course** or **life stages,** which is *a succession of statuses and roles that people in a particular society experience in a fairly predictable pattern as they grow older.* Biology plays an important role in the life course, especially at the beginning and the end. As infants and young children, each of us is highly dependent on others for our survival, and thus the statuses that are open to us are limited. In very old age, physical deterioration may limit our capabilities and again make us dependent on others. Society cannot rely on us during these periods to the extent that it can during other stages of the life span. Between infancy and very old age, however, the social structure is more important than biology in shaping the life span. Thus, although biology does play a role, we should be cautious about viewing life-span stages as biologically created. Rather, they make up a socially approved sequence of stages, adjusted for certain biological limitations, that guides people's behavior as they live their lives. The sociological perspectives provide insight into how society shapes the life course.

The Functionalist Perspective

Functionalists argue that the stages of the life course are intimately related to the social needs of particular societies. For this reason, the stages that occur may differ substantially from society to society (Aries, 1962; Flacks, 1971). In preindustrial societies, for example, people usually learn how to fill adult positions fairly early in life. The technology is relatively simple, so little training or education is required. People do not need to know how to read or write in order to make contributions to society. So the transition from childhood to adulthood generally occurs early, somewhere between age eight and the mid-teens. People continue to work as they grow old, being limited only by physical infirmity. Only among small groups within society, such as a ruling group or a priesthood, is inactivity or nonproductivity common among older adults.

Industrial societies, on the other hand, with a complex technology and an elaborate division of labor, need a highly educated and well-trained work force. Thus, training and education must be more extensive than in preindustrial societies. Furthermore, the sophisticated technology of industrial societies makes it possible for a small number of people to provide all of the goods and services that are needed. As a consequence, it is not necessary for all adults to participate in the work force. These factors contribute to two major differences in the life course of industrial societies in contrast to preindustrial ones. First, the age at which people are allowed to enter the adult world is postponed in industrial societies (Kett, 1977). Childhood continues into the early teens and is followed by a new stage in life, adolescence, which runs roughly from thirteen to eighteen years of age. Adolescence is viewed as a time of preparation for adulthood, in terms of both education and psychological maturation. Adolescents are not considered adults and are not expected to assume adult responsibilities, such as supporting a family. They are also not ac-

Myth: Teenagers are too young to have achieved maturity, and this is why they are required to stay in school rather than work for a living or begin raising a family.

FACT: In preindustrial societies, most people have joined the adult world of work by their teenage years and may have even begun raising a family. Industrial societies have created a new social category called adolescence, consisting of people who are biologically mature but still considered dependent and emotionally immature. The purpose of this category is to allow for an extended period of education and to reduce competition with adults for existing jobs.

Myth: In the past, people respected their elders because this was the right thing to do.

FACT: Respect for elders flowed in part from the fact that older people in the past controlled many political, social, and economic resources and thus could demand respect from younger people.

Myth: The exploitation of child labor in the United States is largely a thing of the past.

FACT: Although child-labor problems have been reduced, there are currently few restrictions on youngsters working in some jobs, such as farm laborer. It is estimated that one quarter of the farm laborers in the United States may be under age sixteen.

Myth: The elderly consider their low financial status to be their most serious problem.

FACT: In one survey, only 17 percent of people over sixty-five thought money was a serious problem for them. However, a majority of younger people think money is a problem for the elderly.

Myth: Because most people in the United States today have retirement plans where they work, retirement income for the elderly in the future will not be a problem.

FACT: Less than half of working people today have retirement plans. In addition, some people do not work for a company long enough to have retirement funds vested (or become their own personal property), so they end up with meager pension resources.

corded many adult privileges, such as being able to vote or join the adult work force on a full-time basis. The second difference between the life stages of industrial and preindustrial societies involves old age (Plakans, 1994). In industrial societies, most men and women are encouraged to leave the work force, or forced from it, long before they die, often when they are still healthy and capable of working. Presumably, younger workers are more healthy and vigorous and make a better contribution to the work world. But irrespective of the capabilities of older workers, retirement serves as a way of reducing the number of workers who are competing for a limited number of jobs.

From the functionalist perspective, the treatment of the young and the old becomes a social problem when it is inconsistent with their capabilities and development, both biological and social. When age is used as an arbitrary criterion for inequitable treatment, it is dysfunctional and can lead to social disorganization. If young people, for example, are prevented from gaining prestige by joining the work world, they may turn to drugs or crime as a way of gaining a sense of self-importance. Likewise, forced retirement among the elderly can lead to depression and alcoholism. So societies need to provide socially acceptable statuses for their members at every stage of life and make available opportunities to achieve socially desired goals (Riley, Kahn, and Foner, 1994). People need to feel that they are making an important contribution to society. With the transition from a preindustrial to an industrial social order, however, something has been lost. A degree of social disorganization has arisen as there are more and more young and old people with fewer and fewer contributions that they are allowed to make to society. They do not work, head families, or rear children. As we mentioned when discussing both race and sex, it is probably most functional in modern societies to allocate tasks and roles on the basis of abilities rather than ascribed statuses.

In addition, each stage in a person's life should be integrated with other stages. One stage might be a preparation for later stages, whereas another stage is viewed as a reward for earlier contributions. This continuity in life motivates people to perform well by making their tasks at one stage in life understandable and meaningful in terms of their place in the whole life course. Thus, a comfortable old age might be seen as a reward for earlier contributions. For some, however, old age is not viewed as an outgrowth of earlier life stages, and this lack of continuity can be a social problem.

The Conflict Perspective

The position of the young and the old in modern societies is not unlike that of other minority groups (see Chapters 6 and 7). They have less access to social, political, and economic power, and they are dominated by groups with more resources. This has not always been the case. In most preindustrial societies, the elderly held considerably more power because they owned and controlled many economic resources, especially property. In addition, kinship ties were much more important then than today, and people often needed the support of their parents to get a start in life. It was from their parents that young adults learned a trade or acquired some land to farm. This meant that sons and daughters were economically dependent on their parents. In such a situation, social customs and laws tended to support and reinforce the dominant position of the elderly in society. In other words, respect for the elderly in preindustrial societies flowed from their control over political, social, and economic resources. Such respect may have been functional for the times, but it was enforced through custom and law.

In industrial societies, people are not as heavily dependent on their parents to make a living. Trades can be learned in school, and most people will be salaried employees of a corporation or government agency. So entry-level positions in the economy can be gained with little if any parental support. In addition, family ties in general have become less important. As a consequence, kinship ties are not a source of power and prestige for many elderly. The outcome of all this is that the status of the elderly has declined because they no longer hold positions of economic power, and their children are no longer dependent on them for their economic livelihood.

From the conflict perspective, then, the position of any age group in society is determined by the social, political, and economic resources that group has access to. The access of the young and old to jobs and other sources of social and economic reward has been restricted because this exclusion benefits the large group of people in early to middle adulthood. In an economic system with a scarcity of jobs, this helps to reduce competition. Fewer young workers enter the labor market, and older workers are forced out by retirement in order to open positions for younger adults.

Society, of course, does not couch these social practices in such contentious terms. Rather, cultural norms hold that the restrictions placed on the young and old are for their own benefit. The young, it is said, need time to grow and mature because people in their teens do not have sufficient biological development to take on adult responsibilities. Likewise, the old suffer some physical deterioration, such as failing eyesight or loss of hearing, that makes them less able or willing to work. An ideology emerges to legitimize these social practices, just as sexism justifies discrimination against women and racism justifies the domination of particular racial groups. **Ageism** refers to *an ideology, or set of beliefs, holding that people in a particular age group are inferior, have negative attributes, and can be dominated and exploited because of their age* (Laws, 1995). The term was originally coined to describe reactions to the elderly, but it applies to any age group that experiences such prejudice and discrimination. In addition, like sexism and racism, ageism is often defended on biological grounds. In fact, one of the travesties of our treatment of the elderly is the all-too-quick assumption that any failing or memory loss is due to irreversible biological senility. With such beliefs, age becomes an important factor in differentiating among people in society.

Furthermore, the young and old are taught to expect these restrictions for themselves. The young, it is alleged, deserve a carefree adolescence. For the old, retirement is claimed to be a reward for a long life of productive work. In short, the victims are taught to desire precisely those things that work to the benefit of other groups.

The Age Structure of Society

Demography is *the study of the size, composition, and distribution of human populations and how these factors change over time.* Demographers have found that societies vary in the proportions of their populations that are at different stages in the life cycle. They refer to this as the **age structure** of society, *the distribution of people into various age categories.* In preindustrial societies, such as the United States of more than a century ago, the age structure is "bottom heavy" with young people representing a large proportion of the population (see Figure 8.1 on p. 284). In such societies, as much as 40 to 50 percent of the populace might be fifteen years of age or under with less than 6 percent being older than age sixty-five. The reason for this, which will be discussed in more detail in Chapter 12, is that preindustrial societies have high birthrates and high death rates. Many people are born, but a smaller proportion of them live into old age than in industrial societies. Industrial societies, with lower birthrates and a longer life expectancy, tend to "age," making their populations "top heavy." Older people make up a growing proportion of the populace. Today, 26 percent of the United States population is under age eighteen, compared with almost 13 percent sixty-five or older (see Figure 8.2 on p. 285). This is quite a dramatic shift from a preindustrial United States, and this trend will intensify. By the year 2050, when the younger students reading this book will be among our senior citizens, the young and the old will come very close to constituting equal proportions of our populace: 23 percent and 20 percent, respectively. In that year, there will be eighty million people over age sixty-five in the United States, compared with only three million in 1900 and thirty-two million today.

From their analysis of the age structure of society, demographers can develop a very important statistic called the **dependency ratio,** which *shows the relative size of the group in our society that is economically dependent for support on others who are working.* The dependency ratio is often calculated by comparing the number of people over sixty-five with the number between eighteen and sixty-four. Of course, not all people over sixty-five are unemployed and dependent and not all between eighteen and sixty-four are working. But this comparison gives us an approximation of the trends occurring (see Figure 8.3 on p. 285). In 1900, the dependency ratio

FIGURE 8.1 Age–Sex Population Pyramids for the United States: 1900, 1940, 1994. *Sources:* U.S. Bureau of the Census, *Census of Population: Characteristics of the Population* (Washington, D.C.: U.S. Government Printing Office, 1940, 1970); U.S. Bureau of the Census, *Statistical Abstract of the United States, 1995* (Washington, D.C.: U.S. Government Printing Office, 1995), p. 15.

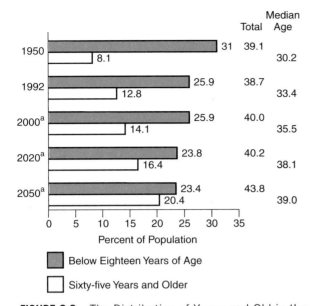

	Total	Median Age
1950	31	39.1
	8.1	30.2
1992	25.9	38.7
	12.8	33.4
2000ᵃ	25.9	40.0
	14.1	35.5
2020ᵃ	23.8	40.2
	16.4	38.1
2050ᵃ	23.4	43.8
	20.4	39.0

Percent of Population

■ Below Eighteen Years of Age

□ Sixty-five Years and Older

FIGURE 8.2 The Distribution of Young and Old in the United States, 1950–2050. ᵃEstimates based on the assumption that the population reaches zero growth around the middle of the twenty-first century.
Sources: U.S. Bureau of the Census, *Statistical Abstract of the United States, 1978* (Washington, D.C.: U.S. Government Printing Office, 1978), pp. 8–9; U.S. Bureau of the Census, *Statistical Abstract of the United States, 1994* (Washington, D.C.: U.S. Government Printing Office, 1994), pp. 13–16.

in the United States was 7, meaning that there were seven older people for each one hundred people between eighteen and sixty-five. Today the ratio is about 20. By the year 2050, projections suggest that it will be 40, or four older persons for every ten adults of working age. However, the traditional dependency ratio may underestimate the proportions of dependents to workers because there is a tendency today for a growing number of people to enter the labor force at an older age than eighteen and retire younger than sixty-five. If we assume that people begin work at age twenty and retire at sixty, then the dependency ratio gets even larger. So, as society ages, those who are dependent become a significantly larger proportion of the populace.

The major concern about this issue, of course, is whether or at what level society can or will support such a large dependent population. It also raises the question of whether working people will be willing to continue supporting a growing number of elderly at a high standard of living. Potentially, it sets one interest group against another. Later in this chapter, we will address some possible solutions to the

FIGURE 8.3 Dependency Ratio in the United States, 1900–2050. *Source:* U.S. Department of Health and Human Services, *Aging America: Trends and Projections,* DHHS Pub. No. (FCoA) 91–28001 (Washington, D.C.: Department of Health and Human Services, 1991), pp. 18–19.

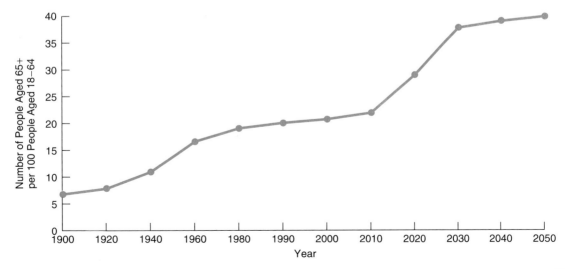

problems created by shifts in the age structure of the United States.

Problems of the Young

Human beings remain dependent on others after birth for much longer than is the case with most species. Infants are completely defenseless and must rely totally on others for their survival. Through most of childhood, human beings are immature and their development would be seriously threatened were they not supported by others. In modern industrial societies, as has been seen, this dependence is extended into adolescence, during which physically mature human beings are denied complete access to the adult world. This extended period of dependence is beneficial in many ways, but it also makes the young easy targets for inequitable treatment. And throughout history, ageist ideologies have been around to justify the unequal treatment of the young on the grounds that they are too immature and irresponsible to fend for themselves and need protection from adults (Gillis, 1974; Purdy, 1992). Parents or other guardians are given authority over children, sometimes to the point of seeing children as the property of their guardians. In their position of authority, parents can expect the complete obedience of their children. Overall, this physical, economic, and social dependence places the young at considerable risk of being discriminated against, exploited, and even assaulted. This section will review the major kinds of discrimination and exploitation experienced by children and youth in the United States and around the world.

Economic Exploitation

Children in most societies participate in some form of economic productivity, but it is usually by joining with family members in hunting or farming. In some cases, however, children work in nonfamily settings as wage laborers (Bequele and Boyden, 1988). They work in mines, in factories, and as self-employed workers engaging in street trades. Many of these children confront terrible economic exploitation: working long hours in potentially harmful environments for relatively little pay. In nineteenth-century England and the United States, for example, children worked in factories for eleven or more hours per day. Toddlers barely three years old worked in cotton mills, crawling on the floor and retrieving cotton waste. Young boys were hired as chimney sweeps because their small bodies enabled them to climb up chimneys, sweeping away soot with their clothes. In the early part of this century, children as young as four years of age were hired to shuck oysters and peel shrimp in Gulf Coast canneries (Paradise, 1922).

Such severe economic exploitation of children is not often found in the United States today, but it is, unfortunately, all too common in many nations around the globe, especially in developing countries (U.S. Department of Labor, 1994a). In Africa, one-third of all children work; in Latin America 15 to 20 percent of children work. While it is impossible to say exactly what proportion of these children are exploited, the great majority work long hours for substandard wages in conditions that are often unhealthy. Child workers are often beaten or otherwise abused, and they typically do not receive an adequate education that would better prepare them to support themselves as adults. In some cases, children are in debt bondage, which occurs when, to secure a loan, a person offers his or her own labor or the labor of others in payment of a loan. If interest on the loan is sufficiently high, the labor will never be able to pay it off, and the person is, in effect, a slave. Parents in places such as India and Pakistan sometimes offer their children's labor to secure such loans, placing their child in virtual slavery. An international human rights organization reported on such a case in Pakistan in the 1990s. A seven-year-old boy named Anwar was found weaving carpets in his village for twelve to sixteen hours each day, six or seven days a week. He was given some food, little free time, and no medical assistance. He was never asked if he wanted to work but was told that he had to work until he earned enough to pay off a family debt. If he made a mistake in his weaving, he was fined and the debt was increased. If he worked too slowly, he was beaten with a stick. When he ran away because of the beatings, the police apprehended him and returned him to the carpet looms. Export industries in which child labor is often

When this young boy was four years old in Pakistan, he was chained to a loom and forced to work for six years making carpets. Such exploitation occurs because, among other reasons, poverty forces families to send their children to such work.

used are garment making, carpet making, shoemaking, and furniture building.

There are a number of reasons why such child exploitation exists. For one thing, poverty forces families to exploit their children to survive. For another, factory owners find children an easy and profitable group to exploit. Children are much more vulnerable than adults and far less likely to protest their conditions successfully. With the intense competition in the world economy described in Chapter 2, some employers find it impossible to resist the temptation to exploit children. A third reason why child workers are exploited is that the public is often indifferent to the issue or, in some nations, believes that child labor among the poor is just "the way things are."

Legislation has been adopted in most countries in the past fifty years to control the labor exploitation of the young (Bequele and Boyden, 1988; U.S. Department of Labor, 1994b). In the United States, the Fair Labor Standards Act of 1938 outlawed the employment of people younger than sixteen years in some industrial settings, and it has since been amended numerous times to prohibit child labor in many other circumstances, especially occupations with hazardous conditions. However, child labor is by no means a thing of the past. In fact, families sometimes have to put everyone to work—including the children—to keep out of poverty. In 1990, a congressional committee investigating child labor heard of a fifteen-year-old boy working in a bakery who died when pulled into a dough-mixing machine, a thirteen-year-old boy whose leg was torn off by a blowing machine while working in a car wash, a fifteen-year-old girl whose finger was cut off in a slicing machine at a fast-food restaurant, and a fourteen-year-old boy who worked thirteen hours a day picking strawberries, inhaling pesticides, and earning "at best" $2.80 per hour (Lantos, 1992). The number of violations of federal child-labor laws more than doubled during the 1980s, mostly for working youngsters too many hours per day, too late at night, or in hazardous jobs with dangerous equipment. However, current legislation places few restrictions on youngsters working in some jobs, including that of farm laborer. It is estimated that one-quarter of the farm laborers in the United States may be under age sixteen. These children work in hot, unpleasant conditions for low wages and receive few, if any, benefits such as retirement or health insurance. Many agricultural states have no minimum age for farm laborers, and state laws often do not apply to the children of migratory farm laborers.

Child laborers around the world work in jobs that pay the minimum wage or less and offer few benefits. In the United States, fast-food restaurants, self-serve gas stations, and grocery stores employ youngsters of high school age or younger as a means of reducing costs and maintaining flexibility in their work force. Adolescents are much less likely than adults to demand pay increases or to view such fringe benefits as retirement pensions to be important. They are also less concerned about unionization and long-term job security. The young are more likely to go quietly if released from a job.

Child-labor laws are intended to protect young people from exploitation, and compulsory school attendance laws are meant to offer them important opportunities in life. Some young people, however, feel that these legal statutes are themselves discriminatory because they prohibit them from working. The notion that people should not begin full-time, adult work until after they are eighteen years of age is a product of the last half century. There are many people under eighteen today who would prefer to work than attend school. Through legislation or social pressure, most youths feel compelled to remain in school and work at part-time, low-paying jobs.

Family Instability

Many young people in the United States and other nations grow up in family settings that are less stable and supportive than would be desir-able for effective childrearing. Chapter 3 reviews the extent of divorce and single parenthood and the problems associated with them. Children often suffer when a divorce occurs, even if the divorce is necessary. Many children of divorce have strong emotional problems, do less well in school, and are more prone to delinquency and other kinds of behavior problems. This is not to say that a single parent cannot provide the necessary environment for good childrearing; they can and some do. However, the research does suggest that children are often worse off when raised by one parent than two (McLanahan and Sandefur, 1994; Bruce, Lloyd, and Leonard, 1995). The difficulties of children in single-parent families are due to three factors: low income, inadequate parental guidance, and less access to community resources. If single parents can overcome these difficulties, then their children can do quite well. Nevertheless, as rates of divorce and single parenthood increase, more children are living in family environments that are less than stable or that do not provide them with all the economic and social resources that would enable them to develop to their full potential.

Poverty

Partly because of the higher rates of divorce and single parenthood, many young people today are at risk of growing up in poverty. The statistics on poverty among children are reviewed in Chapter 5. The poverty rate among children is higher today than it was twenty-five years ago: 22 percent today as compared to 14 percent in 1969. And it is twice as high as the poverty rate among the elderly. Almost one-half of all African-American children live in poverty, and two-thirds of all African-American and Hispanic-American children in single-parent families live below the poverty level.

More than one-third of the nation's poor people are under the age of sixteen, and the children of the United States are worse off than children in most other industrial nations (see

Figure 5.3). What accounts for these appalling circumstances among our nation's young? Although some teens earn income, the economic circumstances of children are determined almost entirely by that of their parents—another manifestation of their dependency. And some critical trends of the past few decades, already reviewed in Chapters 3 and 5, have contributed to the growing poverty among children. Unemployment has increased and family incomes have not grown and in many cases have declined. More children today live in single-parent families, which have much higher poverty rates than two-parent families. These economic circumstances that children confront are especially troubling because children, for the most part, cannot walk away from them or work to improve their lives as some adults can. They are heavily dependent on adults. Poverty is simply something they must live with until they become adults, and often they face further poverty in adulthood because their poverty-stricken childhood failed to provide them with the resources and the motivation to achieve as adults.

Sexual Exploitation

Children and adolescents are highly susceptible to sexual exploitation in a variety of forms. This has at times come to light in an especially grisly fashion when people working in day-care centers are arrested for criminal sexual assault on

These poor children in Kentucky remind us that one of the major problems confronting the young is poverty. The poverty rate among children is higher today than it was 25 years ago.

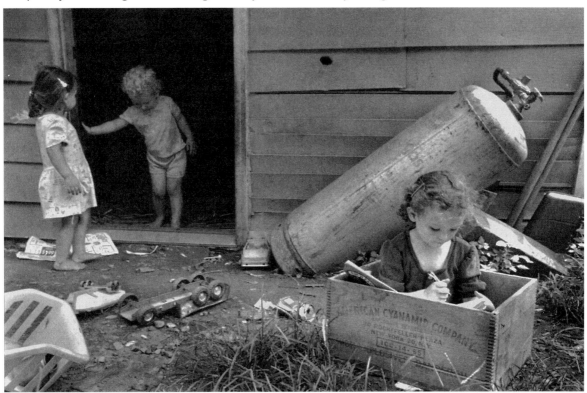

How Well Off Are Children and Youth in the United States?

Are children and youth in the United States better off in the 1990s than they were in earlier decades? Many have computers, VCRs, and compact discs, along with many other luxuries and technological wonders of the age, but overall, has life for the young gotten better or worse? Economists Victor R. Fuchs and Diane M. Reklis (1992: 41) give a gloomy answer: "American children are in trouble. . . . Many observers consider today's children to be worse off than their parents' generation in several important dimensions of physical, mental, and emotional well-being." They reach this conclusion by looking at statistics that can give a glimpse of prevailing social trends. These are among the trends that contributed to their depressing assessment:

- Since 1960, the performance of children and youth on standardized aptitude tests in the United States has declined steadily.
- Since 1960, the teen suicide rate has tripled.
- Since 1960, the teen homicide rate has almost tripled.
- Since 1960, obesity is up sharply, especially among children.
- The percentage of children living in poverty dropped until 1970 and has increased steadily since then.
- Since the mid-1970s, reports of child abuse have tripled.

- Since 1960, the proportion of children who live in a household without an adult male present has tripled.

The Fordham Institute for Innovation in Social Policy has combined data on these kinds of trends with data on drug abuse and high school dropout rates among teens and developed an Index of Social Health for Children and Youth, a composite score on how well children in the United States are doing (Miringoff, 1992). The Index documents that the social health of youth has declined dramatically in the last twenty years. In fact, 1990, the last year for which data are available, was the worst year since 1970. In 1970, the Index stood at 77, with a higher score indicating greater social health; by 1990, it had plummeted to 44 (see Figure 8.4). On the whole, and despite the substantial affluence in the United States, life for its children and teenagers appears to have gotten demonstrably worse over the years. Some positive trends have occurred over the past thirty years, such as declines in infant and child mortality, but the number of negative trends is disturbing, especially in what is one of the wealthiest and most powerful nations in the world. Also, some of these indicators, such as teen suicide and homicide, clearly point to the significant failure of our society to provide for its young.

children under their care. Children are especially susceptible to such abuse for two reasons. First, parents often find it very difficult to admit that their children might be exposed to such treatment at schools to which they themselves have sent them. Second, assailants can easily manipulate children with threats of reprisal if the children reveal what has happened.

The more common form of sexual exploitation of the young is sexual assault by a parent, adult relative, or guardian. Sexual assault can involve sexual intercourse, fondling, or indecent exposure. Once again, the young are at a disadvantage, especially when assaulted by a family member or relative, because the attack is often couched as an expression of love or affec-

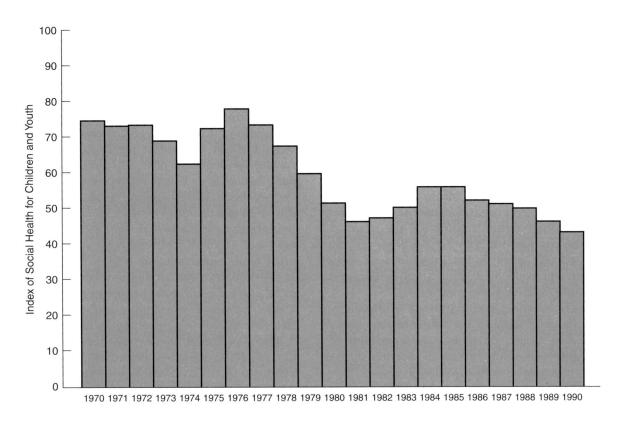

FIGURE 8.4 Index of Social Health for Children and Youth in the United States, 1970–1990. *Source:* Marc L. Miringoff, *The Index of Social Health, 1992: Monitoring the Social Well-Being of the Nation* (Tarrytown, N.Y.: Fordham Institute for Innovation in Social Policy, 1992), p. 8.

tion. This often inhibits the child from reporting the assault. Such attacks can continue for years because children are often afraid of hurting the adult by reporting the incidents.

Adolescents are susceptible to yet another version of sexual exploitation: prostitution and pornography. Teenage runaways, for example, find it difficult to support themselves through legitimate jobs, which are likely to be either unavailable or low paying. Such teenagers are sought after by pimps and pornographers because they are defenseless and exploitable. The teenagers are afraid to go to the police and have no other adults to protect them. In large cities such as New York, Chicago, and Los Angeles, prostitutes as young as twelve years old—both male and female—can be found. There are even organized rings nationwide to provide the services of young prostitutes to those who desire them (Campagna and Poffenberger, 1988). Such youngsters typically lack the economic and social resources necessary to extricate themselves from these situations and are likely to continue being exploited until arrested.

Child Abuse

Because of their dependent status, it is often children who experience the brunt of their parents' frustrations or failures. Too often, this reaction takes the form of child abuse. As with sexual exploitation, children are usually too weak and defenseless to protect themselves against such abuse. In addition, their fear of their parents is often mixed with love, making it especially difficult for them to seek assistance. The problem of child abuse is discussed in more detail in Chapter 3.

The Applied Research insert in this chapter discusses some of the evidence that social scientists use to document the condition of children and youth and assess whether things are getting better or worse.

Problems of the Elderly

The problems confronting the elderly in the United States and around the world have received increasing attention in the past thirty to forty years. This section will review the nature and extent of these problems.

Work and Retirement

In all societies, what people do to make a living is important to them. Work provides an economic livelihood, and it is a major source of self-esteem and sense of personal self-worth. For many, the work world is a source of intrinsic satisfaction, whereas for others it is a place to meet and be with friends. Yet, many people have been, and some still are, forced out of work because of their age. Actually, mandatory retirement was largely eliminated in the United States when the Age Discrimination in Employment Act of 1967 was amended in 1986. In only a few occupations, such as airline pilot, does mandatory retirement still exist. Yet, some people still find themselves forced out of a job because of their age. Companies may do this as a way of reducing costs or saving on retirement benefits. After all, younger workers are cheaper than older workers because younger workers have smaller incomes and place less strain on company resources such as health costs. Companies may deliberately "restructure" as an excuse for the wholesale dismissal of older workers. Thousands of complaints of such age discrimination are made to the Equal Employment Opportunity Commission each year.

Although there is no mandatory retirement age today for most people in the United States, few people continue working after age sixty-five: only about 16 percent of all men and 8 percent of all women (U.S. Bureau of the Census, 1994: 395). In contrast, 60 percent of the men older than sixty-five in 1900 continued working. Indeed, a majority of people in the United States believe that a person ought to be able to continue working at any age if he or she wishes to and is able to do so. In addition, studies show that as many as one-quarter of retired people wished they were working in some capacity (Burkhauser and Quinn, 1994). Since most older people are retired, a major concern is whether retirement has a beneficial or detrimental impact on people's lives. One view is that occupational roles and identities are so important and pervasive that their loss has very negative consequences. In their place, the retiree is left with an ambiguous status that gives life little direction and whose social prestige is difficult to determine. In fact, gerontologist Ethel Shanas (1972) has called retirement a "roleless" role to emphasize the point that what society expects of a retiree is much less well defined than are most social roles. Despite this, however, retirement for many is a positive experience (Atchley, 1994). According to a summary of research on the topic, people are likely to enjoy retirement if

> (1) retirement is voluntary rather than forced; (2) one's income and health are good enough to live comfortably in retirement; (3) work is not the most important thing in one's life; and (4) some preparation and planning for retirement have occurred. (McConnell, 1983: 340)

There have been a number of suggestions for changing retirement practices to make the transition to retired status easier and more gradual. One such proposal has been to shift to a system of gradual retirement in which people continue to work as long as they are able but for a decreasing period of time each year (Burkhauser and Quinn, 1994). This would allow for a steady adjustment to the status of retiree but would still open up jobs for younger workers. Although some employees can arrange such gradual retirements, there are no serious proposals to make them a widespread part of the economy.

Poverty and Financial Problems

The poverty rate among people over sixty-five years of age in the United States was 12.9 percent in 1992, only slightly above that of people between the ages of eighteen and sixty-four, which was 11.7 percent. As Figure 8.5 shows, this represents astonishing progress over thirty years ago when 28 percent of the elderly were poor—almost three times higher than nonelderly adults. So the elderly have come a long way. However, as Figure 8.6 illustrates, the annual income of a family headed by a person sixty-five years of age or older is considerably

FIGURE 8.5 Poverty Rates of Elderly and Non-Elderly Adults, 1966–1992. *Source:* U.S. Bureau of the Census, Current Population Reports, Series P-60, No. 185, *Poverty in the United States, 1992* (Washington, D.C.: U.S. Government Printing Office, 1993), p. ix.

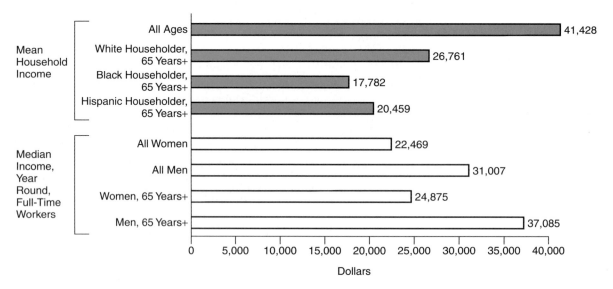

FIGURE 8.6 Income and Age, 1992. *Source:* U.S. Bureau of the Census, *Statistical Abstract of the United States, 1994* (Washington, D.C.: U.S. Government Printing Office, 1994), pp. 466, 472.

less than that of other families. In addition, Figure 8.7 demonstrates that some groups among the elderly are not doing so well. Poverty rates are still unacceptably high among older women living alone, older African Americans, and older Hispanics. Three-quarters of the poor among the elderly are women (Meyer, 1990). This reiterates the point made in Chapters 6 and 7 about the impact of sexism and racism on the position of minority-group members and shows that a considerable number of older people in the United States are at a financial disadvantage.

There are a number of reasons to be cautious, however, in comparing the economic circumstances of older and younger people. One reason is that, when we look at total wealth or total net worth, the elderly are in some ways better off than younger adults (Peterson, 1991a). During the 1980s, for example, the net worth of families headed by someone over sixty-five increased, whereas the net worth of

families headed by someone fifty-five or younger decreased. In addition, the share of the total wealth going to the elderly went from 26 percent in the 1960s to 33 percent today, whereas adults aged thirty-five or younger got only 6 percent of that wealth then and today. So the elderly seem to have cornered a substantial, and growing, portion of society's wealth over the last three decades. A big reason for this is that the elderly have accumulated resources over their years of living, especially equity in a home. A second reason for caution in comparing the economic circumstances of the old and the young is that the elderly tend to have fewer expenses than do younger adults. Older people are more likely to have paid off their home mortgages and to have fewer, if any, childrearing expenses.

When the elderly do experience economic difficulties, it is usually for one of two reasons. First, the elderly are more likely than other adults to be outside the work force and thus prevented

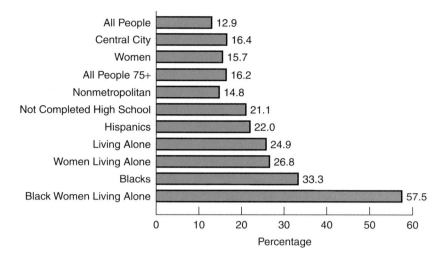

All People	12.9
Central City	16.4
Women	15.7
All People 75+	16.2
Nonmetropolitan	14.8
Not Completed High School	21.1
Hispanics	22.0
Living Alone	24.9
Women Living Alone	26.8
Blacks	33.3
Black Women Living Alone	57.5

Percentage

FIGURE 8.7 Percentage of Elderly Below the Poverty Level, by Selected Characteristics, 1992.*
*Unless otherwise noted, data are for age 65+.
Source: U.S. Bureau of the Census, Current Population Reports, Series P-60, No. 185, *Poverty in the United States, 1992* (Washington, D.C.: U.S. Government Printing Office, 1993).

from earning a high income. Only 17 percent of the income of people aged sixty-five years or older comes from earnings (see Figure 8.8). The rest of their income is from Social Security, retirement benefits, assets, or public assistance. The elderly who do work full-time earn as much as, if not more than, younger workers (see Figure 8.6). However, the elderly are discouraged from working because they lose some of their Social Security benefits if they earn more than a certain amount of income each year (Gustman and Steinmeier, 1991).

A second reason for the economic difficulties of some elderly is that they have worked for years at jobs with no retirement pension plan or with few benefits. In 1960, for example, only 37 percent of all nongovernmental employees had retirement programs where they worked; by the 1990s, this had increased to only 40 percent (U.S. Bureau of the Census, 1978: 344; U.S. Bureau of the Census, 1994: 379). This could continue as a problem in the future since, in the 1980s and 1990s, companies have cut costs by reducing the amounts that they put into employee retirement plans and requiring employees to match contributions (Uchitelle, 1995). Also, many companies have dropped pension

plans that make the company responsible for paying a set annual income to a retiree and replaced them with plans that provide less security and fewer guarantees regarding what a

FIGURE 8.8 Income Sources of People Aged 65 and Older, 1988. *Source:* Susan Grad, *Income of the Population 65 or Over, 1988,* Pub. No. 13-11871 (Washington, D.C.: U.S. Social Security Administration, June 1990).

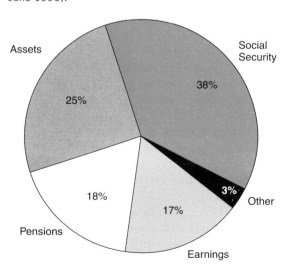

retiree's income will be. Only one-sixth of all income available to the elderly comes from pensions (see Figure 8.8). As a consequence, some elderly find themselves heavily dependent on Social Security or other transfer income from the government. What is ironic about this situation is that, from its inception in 1935, Social Security has not been intended to serve as a person's sole retirement income, but rather as a supplement to other sources of financial support. Social Security payments are low, therefore, and those solely dependent on them are in difficult financial straits. Women, especially, are likely to have inadequate retirement incomes because most retirement plans, including Social Security, are tied to the extent of paid labor a person has done during his or her life. Women, when compared with men, tend to work less, get paid less when they work, and change jobs before gaining ownership of their pension resources. As a result, women have smaller pension resources available to them than do men (Meyer, 1990).

Social Isolation

In preindustrial societies, older people normally remained with their families because few other alternatives existed. Today, however, an aging person is much more likely to live apart from family: Thirty percent of the elderly lived alone in 1994 compared with 18 percent in 1960 (see Figure 8.9). Living alone is especially common among women and the very old. Yet, living alone does not automatically mean loneliness or social isolation. In fact, research indicates that loneliness and isolation are not a problem for most elderly, at least not most of the time (Atchley, 1994). Only 13 percent of the older people surveyed by the National Council on Aging viewed loneliness as a serious problem. Older people maintain relatively extensive contacts and involvements with friends and acquaintances, albeit fewer than do younger people. People in advanced old age (older than

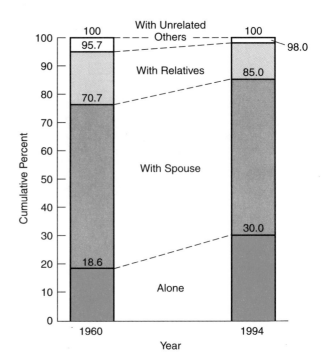

FIGURE 8.9 Distribution of the Elderly by Living Arrangements, 1960 and 1994. *Sources:* Congressional Budget Office, *Changes in the Living Arrangements of the Elderly: 1960–2030* (Washington, D.C.: U.S. Government Printing Office, March 1988), p. 3; U.S. Bureau of the Census, *Statistical Abstract of the United States, 1995* (Washington, D.C.: U.S. Government Printing Office, 1995), p. 56.

seventy-five years) and those with serious physical ailments are most likely to suffer from severe social isolation. It is these elderly who are least likely to visit friends, go to the library, or attend social events. In addition, socioeconomic status plays an important part in this. Middle-class elderly have more friends, are more likely to develop new friendships, and visit their friends more often than do their working- and lower-class counterparts (National Council on Aging, 1975; Atchley, 1994). The differences are not a result of financial status but rather are attributable to the social skills acquired by middle-class people that enable them to develop and maintain friendships more easily.

Domestic Violence

Chapter 3 discusses the problem of the physical and psychological abuse of older people by their caretakers. Just as the dependence of the young makes them vulnerable to abuse, the elderly who are dependent on others for care face the same problem. Some abuse of the elderly results from the stress or frustration of taking care of an older parent or grandparent who is physically or mentally impaired. The burden at times becomes too much, and the nuclear family does not provide the extensive support network that would help spread these stresses over many people. Abuse of the elderly also occurs when it is the caretakers who are dependent on those they care for, possibly for financial support. The dependence of a younger adult on an older adult can lead to pent-up frustration that may find release in violence, especially when the caretaker has personal or financial problems or abuses drugs or alcohol.

Health Problems

Health is one of the major problems faced by the elderly. Paying for the health care of the elderly poses considerable difficulty for society as a whole, as the discussion of Medicare in Chapter 4 demonstrates. Medicare currently costs over $125 billion each year, which translates into almost $500 for every man, woman, and child in the United States. Forty percent of all hospital beds occupied each day are filled by people older than sixty-five years. Almost half of people older than sixty-five years in the United States experience some limitation in their activities because of chronic illnesses, with many of these limitations being major ones. Overall, the health-care expenditures of the elderly are three and one-half times greater than those of people under sixty-five. Medicare

and other government health insurance pays for 63 percent of these costs, but 28 percent of the health expenditures of the elderly are paid out of their own pockets (U.S. Department of Health and Human Services, 1991). These costs are likely to increase in the future as the number of very old people, those over eighty years of age, increases.

Because the elderly face such severe health problems and also because our culture places such value on youthfulness and physical fitness, the elderly are especially susceptible to quackery that promises to alleviate their pain and improve their functioning. The elderly are the victims of 60 percent of all health-care fraud and are cheated out of billions of dollars each year (Atchley, 1994). Some of these practitioners promise magical remedies for serious conditions, such as arthritis, that medical science cannot currently cure. Other unethical practices focus on diseases that medicine can treat, and they tempt people to use fraudulent cures in place of those known by medicine to be effective.

The reason that the elderly are especially susceptible to such fraud is that they suffer from many more painful and chronic diseases than do younger people. Loneliness and social isolation can also make them easy marks for a friendly and glib salesperson who is willing to show them some sympathy and understanding. Mental deterioration and social isolation may also cloud the judgment of some older people, leading them to make decisions that they might not otherwise make.

Fear of Crime

Older people commit relatively few crimes. Their arrest rate is less than one-tenth that of people in their twenties, and the median age of people in jail is twenty-five years. As we will see in Chapter 9, crime tends to be a problem of the young. Instead, the elderly tend to be the victims of crime, or at least many elderly fear that they will be (Ward, LaGory, and Sherman, 1986; Webb and Marshall, 1989). Actually, the rate of crime perpetration against the elderly has dropped about 25 percent over the past two decades (U.S. Bureau of the Census, 1991: 181). Despite this, one poll found that crime was considered by older people to be one of the most serious problems that they face, more severe than health, poverty, or loneliness (Schack and Frank, 1978). Street assault, such as purse snatching, is one of the more common crimes perpetrated against older people, and it is one that they particularly fear. The problem of crime victimization among the elderly arises in part because some older people find themselves living in neighborhoods that, although once middle class and respectable, have deteriorated over the years. However, the elderly also are the victims of crime committed by their families and caregivers, which was discussed in the section on domestic violence. The elderly also are the victims of health-care fraud, just discussed, as well as other types of fraud, such as fraudulent business practices.

Institutions and Nursing Homes

There are more than 33,000 nursing homes in the United States with 1.7 million residents (U.S. Bureau of the Census, 1994: 132). Yet most older people do not live in nursing homes or other extended-care facilities. In fact, only about 5 percent do. However, between 40 percent and 60 percent of the elderly will live in a nursing home for at least some time before they die (Kane, 1994). So the reality for most elderly in the United States is that they will likely spend their final days, if not their last years, in such institutions. This is especially true for women, those with fewer financial resources, and people with fewer social ties in the community.

The overriding concern with nursing homes is whether they offer the elderly a pleasant and healthy environment. Many residents are sick and vulnerable, making them easy targets for exploitation by the unscrupulous. In some homes, the elderly suffer from unappetizing and poorly prepared food, dark corridors and stairwells, and severe boredom and apathy. Sometimes basic physical care, such as prompt assistance to the bathroom, is slow or lacking. Residents are sometimes tied to their beds or wheelchairs or given powerful tranquilizing drugs in circumstances that are more for the benefit of the staff than the safety of the residents (Kolata, 1991). Elderly nursing-home residents also sometimes suffer from physical and psychological abuse at the hands of nursing home personnel (Pillemer and Moore, 1990). Medical care can be poor and dental care scarce.

Such conditions exist for a number of reasons. First, in profit-making, or proprietary, institutions, there is a tension between the necessity of making a profit and the desire to provide services to the residents. Medicaid and private insurance carriers pay for people's nursing-home care on a flat-fee basis, meaning a set per diem charge for each resident. If the facility actually spends less to care for a resident, it keeps the difference. This means that the less care provided, the greater the institution's profits. And three-quarters of the nursing homes in the United States are proprietary institutions (U.S. Bureau of the Census, 1994: 124). So there is a built-in incentive to watch carefully the extent of services provided. There are also, of course, incentives to provide good care because many groups, including the government and relatives of the residents, are watching over the institution. Whenever those oversights are lacking, however, the potential for exploitation is there.

A second reason for poor conditions in nursing homes is that they have difficulty hiring and keeping qualified staff (Kane, 1994). People with little or no training in health care or gerontology are often hired because they will accept low salaries and cannot find other work. Such people are not likely to have the empathy that can lead to good care or the professionalism that will result in innovative programs in the home. Because of low pay and poor working conditions in nursing homes, there is often a high turnover rate among the skilled nursing staff. This makes it extremely difficult to maintain the continuity of care and the leadership that would help sustain adequate and innovative services.

A particularly pernicious problem that can occur in nursing homes is *depersonalization,* which is discussed in the context of mental institutions in Chapter 4. It refers to the feeling of detachment from the people or social groups that give life meaning and provide people with a sense of importance and self-worth (Coe, 1978). Institutions can take control over people's lives, regulating what and when they eat and when various activities will occur. The residents can be treated as dependent and helpless individuals. When this happens, a self-fulfilling prophecy can occur: The residents become products of the institutional treatment and view themselves as dependent and powerless. This is especially true in all-encompassing institutions such as nursing homes, particularly those with a highly authoritarian and impersonal organization. The residents respond by withdrawal or extreme depersonalization. For example, they may stop thinking of themselves in terms of social statuses such as mother or husband. In extreme cases of depersonalization, a person can drift into a psychotic world

Approximately one-half of the elderly will live in a nursing home for some time before they die, and nursing homes are often unpleasant, and sometimes unhealthy, places for the elderly to be.

of delusions that represents a complete break with reality.

The behavior that is symptomatic of depersonalization is often attributed to senility in an ageist attempt to claim that physiological deterioration accounts for such behavior in nursing homes. In many cases, however, this is incorrect. Instead, the people affected are responding to their social surroundings, with depersonalization being their reaction to their treatment by the institution. Such depersonalization can be avoided, but it is costly. To do so calls for skilled nursing care and other changes in the institutional environment. One such change, for example, is to develop programs that involve residents in interesting or important group activities, such as discussion groups on how to run the nursing home, groups to plan musical shows, or trips for bowling and other activities. In fact, such activities are so important that the government now mandates that all nursing homes provide such activities (Voelkl et al., 1995). The goal is to enhance social involvement and people's sense of self-worth and social connection.

Future Prospects

Reducing Risks for Children and Youth

Many social policies over the past few decades have focused on reducing the risk that children and youth will be exposed to poverty, family violence, sexual exploitation, and other forms of discrimination and exploitation. Many of these programs are discussed elsewhere (e.g. Chapters 3, 4, and 5), and those discussions need not be repeated here. One of the major emphases in the United States has been to provide the supports to children and their families that will make child development and socialization a more positive and fruitful experience. However, one important development has made this effort less effective than it might be: In the struggle for a share of society's resources, chil-

dren and youth in the United States have not done nearly as well as some other interest groups. Although the United States spends more on government programs for children now than thirty years ago, government programs that benefit adults have grown at a much faster pace. In addition, people over age sixty-five have gained the largest increase in government support. The government spends more on the health-care needs of the elderly during the last year of life than it spends on *all* the health care of *all* children. Overall, the government spends eleven times as much on each person over sixty-five as on each under eighteen (Hewlett, 1991). The Policy Issues section in this chapter explores the issue of whether the current allocation of resources to different age groups is the most effective.

Economic Resources of the Elderly

Social policy regarding retirement in the United States rests on the assumption that the elderly's economic support will consist of three elements: personal pensions, Social Security, and accumulated savings and assets.

Retirement Pensions As has been seen, some elderly have little or no income from personal retirement pensions. In the 1970s, the government tried to alleviate this problem by passing legislation that requires employers with more than ten employees to offer their workers a pension plan. This legislation also regulated the "vesting" of pensions. A "vested" pension is one that is the property of the employee rather than the company, so that the employee keeps the accumulated funds in the plan even if he or she no longer works for that company. In the past, some pension plans were never vested so that people had to keep working for a particular company until they retired in order to receive retirement benefits. All too often, people would work for a company for many years, only to be laid off in their fifties and lose all their retirement income. In fact, some companies have been accused of purposely laying off older workers to save the pension money. Federal legislation now requires that pensions be vested in the employee after five years of employment.

Legislation has also been enacted to protect some older women, especially those who were homemakers throughout their lives and never established a pension plan of their own (Rankin, 1985). Such women are dependent on their husbands' retirement, but some husbands chose—without consulting their wives—to have retirement benefits end at their death. These women, who often outlive their husbands, find themselves with no pension after their husbands die. The Retirement Equity Act of 1984 requires employees to take their retirement in a form that provides the spouse with a pension after the worker's death, unless the spouse agrees in writing to another arrangement.

Current legislation involving retirement plans is a vast improvement over the far less regulated environment of the past. Still, however, many people find themselves with few accumulated pension funds when they retire. Some people jump from one job to another every few years and never achieve a vested pension plan. This problem could be considerably alleviated by shortening the vesting period to two to four years of employment. This would provide many more workers with retirement income, but it would also cost employers more and possibly increase prices.

Social Security   The Old-Age, Survivors, Disability, and Health Insurance Program (OASDI) is discussed briefly in Chapter 5. OASDI, popularly known as Social Security, was first established by Congress in 1935. It is a compulsory retirement insurance program, meaning that all qualified employees and their employers must contribute. Currently, income up to $55,500 is taxed for Social Security at a rate of 15 percent. (If you pay Social Security taxes, the amount is shown in the box labeled "FICA" on your pay stub.) The employer and the employee each pay half of the tax, with self-employed persons paying the full tax at a lower rate. When people retire, they receive monthly benefits based mainly on total contributions they made to Social Security over the years.

Social Security income constitutes 38 percent of all the income available to the elderly. Although Social Security was never intended to be a person's sole retirement income, it is for some people, and Social Security payments are barely sufficient to live on. For example, in 1993, the average monthly benefit for a retired worker and spouse was $1,145, for an annual income of $13,740—poverty-level income (U.S. Bureau of the Census, 1995: 380). Many elderly receive much less than this average. So retirees who must rely exclusively on Social Security are in desperate straits.

Social Security has at times run into trouble as the number of people receiving benefits from the program grew (Axinn and Stern, 1990). In some years, the system paid out more than it collected. Changes were made in the 1980s to alleviate this problem. Among the changes were trimmed benefits, higher Social Security taxes, taxes on some Social Security benefits, lower benefits to early retirees, and a gradual rise in the age at which full benefits could be received. The goal was to encourage older people to keep working and be less reliant on Social Security, and it worked. Social Security now runs surpluses, and it should do so for some years. The basic problem remains, however: The population is aging, with the elderly growing in proportion to those still working. Unless we reduce the benefits to the recipients or raise the taxes on working people, the system will eventually be jeopardized once more.

Savings and Assets   Savings and accumulated assets, such as stocks and bonds, are a third source of economic support in retirement, but many elderly do not have any significant amount of such assets (U.S. Department of Health and Human Services, 1991). This is especially true for minority elderly, among whom

Age or Need? Policies for the Elderly and Youth

In the past fifteen years, many social programs have been cut or eliminated in an effort to reduce budgets and institute laissez-faire policies regarding government support for those in need. During the period, Social Security and Medicare have probably been affected less than other government programs. In fact, over the past few decades, Social Security and Medicare have become increasingly generous to the elderly. As Figure 8.10 shows, these two programs have been consuming a larger and larger proportion of the federal budget—32 percent by the 1990s. By the end of the twentieth century, more than one of every three federal budget dollars will probably go to these two programs that support primarily the elderly. The sacrosanct status of programs for the elderly can probably be attributed to two things. First, there was a time, not too many decades ago, when the elderly were much worse off than today and undoubtedly deserved a large share of societal largess. Second, as we have seen, the elderly have become a powerful interest group nationally, and politicians are hesitant to oppose them.

However, the circumstances of the elderly have changed over the past thirty years, and this is leading some policymakers and gerontologists to rethink our approach to programs for the elderly (Crystal, 1986; Longman, 1987). Many elderly today are quite comfortable, with retirement plans that offer them a lifestyle that they enjoy. In fact, as we have seen, most elderly people do not view financial problems as being among their more serious concerns. This has led gerontologist Bernice Neugarten to comment that "age itself is becoming a poor indicator of an older person's circumstances and needs" (Neugarten, 1982: 25). Yet the vast array of social programs that has been established since the Great Depression to help the elderly—in income maintenance, housing, health services, social services, and the like—has utilized chronological age as an easy criterion for eligibility. This may

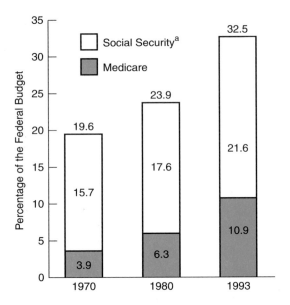

FIGURE 8.10 Medicare and Social Security as a Percentage of the Total Federal Budget, 1970–1993. [a]Includes only old age and survivors' insurance. *Source:* U.S. Bureau of the Census, *Statistical Abstract of the United States, 1995* (Washington, D.C.: U.S. Government Printing Office, 1995), pp. 109, 333, 335.

be a convenient way for legislators or administrators to develop and run programs, but we need to assess whether it is the most equitable and efficient utilization of societal resources.

There are, as we have seen, groups of elderly who are still very much in need; but age-based services may actually draw resources away from those elderly who are in most desperate need of help. It also draws resources away from other groups whose needs may be greater than the needs of some elderly. Earlier, this chapter demonstrated that the social health of youth in the United States seems to have deteriorated over the past few decades, whereas the circumstances of the elderly have gotten better. If Neugarten's policy of focusing on need rather than age is adopted, then resources now flowing to the elderly might be rechanneled toward needy youth. Resources must be spread more thinly if they have to cover a whole age category, such as all elderly, rather than being directed toward those with identifiable needs irrespective of age.

Neugarten makes the point that advocates of age-based legislation may be perpetuating ageism and age discrimination at the same time that they claim to be advocates for the elderly. This can occur because age-based policies can help to perpetuate the misperception of "the old" as a homogeneous group with numerous problems not experienced by other age groups in society. This can reinforce the notion that "being old" is a highly stigmatized status. People identify "old age" itself as a social problem rather than focusing on those conditions, such as poverty or physical infirmity, that can be found among all age groups, although possibly more often among the old. Thus, Neugarten argues, we should focus on poverty, not old age, as the key social problem in devising social policy.

Neugarten's position could translate into social policy in a number of possible ways:

1. Medicare could be made available to all people over sixty-five, but the financially independent elderly might pay a higher deductible, a larger percentage of their charges, or possibly monthly premiums for the coverage.
2. Social Security could be based on need, with the poor elderly receiving larger payments and the well-to-do-elderly receiving little or no Social Security.

These are merely some suggestions for social policy to stimulate thought about Neugarten's ideas. Certainly, some policies would be difficult to establish, especially because current workers have already contributed to Social Security in anticipation of receiving support from it in their old age. They might be understandably reluctant to drop Social Security and forego that source of retirement income. However, these are technical problems that can be solved. The more difficult hurdle is to decide whether policies should be based on age or need.

Neugarten's position is a controversial one because there are many groups whose interests would be threatened if policies and programs were to become based on need rather than age. Her position is also a complex one because it causes us to assess the many other ways in which age is used as a legal and administrative criterion. Is it equitable, for example, to allow sixteen-year-olds to drive a car but prohibit fifteen-year-olds from doing so, or to require teens to attend school until a certain age. There are, of course, good reasons for teenagers to stay in school, but the point here is that society does place these people in a dependent position, which encourages them to view themselves as dependent and less mature than adults. Until now, age sixteen was the point after which society would no longer force youngsters into a dependent status. Now, however, some states are beginning to stretch that point: A few states have passed laws that withdraw the driver's licenses of teens who drop out of high school before graduating. These practices raise critical questions of equity: Is it fair to treat members of a group in this fashion merely because of their age? It also makes one wonder what the future holds: Will the line be stretched even further? Might society eventually revoke the driver's licenses of students who drop out of college? Once one begins to view age as an ascribed status that may be an inappropriate criterion for allocating most resources and privileges, many social practices may need scrutiny.

probably less than 20 percent have such assets. If people who are able could be encouraged to save and accumulate assets while working—beyond money put into a pension or Social Security—this would help alleviate the financial problems of some older people. In the past two decades, the government has moved to encourage this by allowing various types of tax-deferred savings and investment plans that have tax benefits that make them attractive. Individual Retirement Accounts (IRAs) are available to anyone. Some employees are also allowed tax-deferred supplemental retirement accounts (SRAs), while self-employed people can set up self-employment pensions (SEPs). There are limits on how much money can be placed into these plans and severe penalties if any of the money is withdrawn before a person is fifty-nine and one-half years old. By the early 1990s, IRA accounts alone had a total value of over $800 billion (U.S. Bureau of the Census, 1994: 513, 532).

These tax-deferred savings and investment plans have become very popular and will be an important element in the economic picture of many retired people in the future. In fact, the government could further encourage such personal saving for retirement by allowing people to put a larger proportion of their income into such plans than they currently do. However, such encouragements to save only help those with money to save, that is, the more affluent. Only 23 percent of households in the United States have an IRA—only 5 percent of African-American households and 7 percent of Hispanic-American households.

Health Care of the Elderly

The availability of health care to the elderly has been vastly improved through the Medicare and Medicaid programs. Recall from Chapter 4 that Medicare is a program of health insurance for people over sixty-five, whereas Medicaid is health insurance for the indigent. These programs have gone a long way toward relieving the financial burden of health care for the elderly and they have made the decision of whether to seek health services an easier one for older people to make.

These programs, however, are not without their problems. First, they do not cover all services. The elderly still pay substantial out-of-pocket health-care costs. Supplemental health insurance can be purchased through Medicare, but the recipient must pay a monthly premium for this coverage. A second problem is that Medicare is very costly for society. It currently costs $122 billion, as compared with $7 billion in 1970 (U.S. Bureau of the Census, 1994). That represents a seventeenfold increase in twenty years. However, despite the budget cutting that hit social programs in recent decades, Medicare emerged relatively unscathed. This suggests that the benefits provided are not likely to be significantly reduced in the future, although expenditures for additional benefits will probably be scrutinized very closely. In any event, Medicare makes it possible for people to worry less about whether they will have access to needed health care in their old age.

Living Arrangements of the Elderly

Because old people are increasingly unlikely to live with and be cared for by their children, where do they live? A number of alternative living arrangements have arisen.

Retirement Communities   The elderly who are healthy and financially secure most commonly live in their own home or apartment. Over the past few decades, planned retirement communities have evolved for those who can afford them. These communities are often owned by private development corporations and include many easily accessible amenities such as golf, tennis, and community centers. There is also sometimes restricted access in order to ease the residents' fears of victimization. Also, children and adolescents are not allowed to live in some of these communities. These communities appeal to elderly people because they can associate with others in their age group in a safe and relaxed atmosphere.

Despite their appeal, these planned communities have been criticized on the grounds that they isolate the elderly into a segregated subculture. We know from considerable research that stereotypes, often quite negative ones, develop between groups that have little communication and social contact. Chapter 6 demonstrates that this is an element in creating and maintaining patterns of prejudice and discrimination against racial and ethnic minorities. If such stereotyping occurs, taking the form of ageism discussed earlier, it can lead to prejudice and discrimination against the elderly. So planned retirement communities, which create geographical and social isolation, may contribute to misunderstanding and possibly even hostility between the elderly and younger people.

Age-Integrated Housing

For the last two decades, Maggie Kuhn, founder of the Gray Panthers, an advocacy group for the elderly, has promoted what she called "shared housing" arrangements for herself and other old people (Danigelis and Fengler, 1990). Shared housing involves a number of people, both young and old, sharing a home and the various chores and responsibilities of home ownership. Proponents of such arrangements believe they offer many advantages to the elderly, including social ties to replace the family. In a shared housing setting, there are young people to make difficult repairs and do hard labor; there are people present to alleviate feelings of isolation; and there is help for the elderly if they develop some activity limitations. These arrangements also reduce the segregation and stereotyping that may result from age-segregated housing.

Age-integrated housing arrangements can take forms other than shared housing. They might involve a community with separate houses or apartments that are available to people of all ages. Proponents of such living arrangements have argued that they offer the elderly stimulation, novelty, and the delight of relating to people of all age groups. However, the evidence is not clear on whether age-integrated settings or age-segregated settings are more beneficial to the elderly (Burby and Rohe, 1990). Elderly in age-segregated housing seem more satisfied with how their living arrangements are managed and are more active and involved with people around them. But the impact is not great, and there are some negatives, such as a greater fear of crime in age-segregated settings.

Government-Subsidized Housing

The housing priority of the many elderly with low or moderate incomes is very basic: to find a place to live that is safe, clean, and affordable. The government has offered assistance in this area for many years, including such things as building low-income housing, offering rent supplements for private apartments, and providing mortgage insurance for elderly with low or moderate incomes (Kerschner and Hirschfield, 1983).

While these government programs have gone a long way toward helping the elderly acquire decent housing, problems remain that need to be addressed. For example, the problem of crime is still sizable in the deteriorating neighborhoods and public housing projects in which many elderly people live. In addition, much of the public housing already constructed is beginning to deteriorate and is badly in need of repairs. Finally, elderly homeowners on fixed incomes are especially hard hit by rising property values. When property values increase at rapid rates, some elderly can no longer afford houses that they have lived in for many years because the taxes are so high.

Supported-Living Environments

One of the difficult problems elderly people face is coping with the physical infirmities that can accompany aging. These infirmities have a particular impact on the ability of people to live independently. Family members, especially adult daughters, provide most of the care for aging parents in

INTERNATIONAL PERSPECTIVES
Public and Familial Assistance for the Elderly in Other Societies

Around the world and throughout history, families have provided much of the support people need in their old age, and we often hear calls in the United States for a return to family values. However, today's families may not be able to play such a central role because family structures have weakened in virtually all societies in the modern world (Kosberg, 1992). Even in more traditional and highly religious societies such as China or Mexico the family is changing as these societies industrialize and modernize: Families have become smaller, the elderly are less revered and more likely to live alone, and marital disruption is more common. All these factors suggest that modernization has caused pervasive changes in the family that make it a less than complete or perfect support for the elderly. In addition, in all societies, some elderly do not have families, while some families are too poor to offer much assistance. In other cases, the elderly do not get along with younger members of the family and may even suffer abuse at their hands. Finally, in societies as different as Argentina, Sweden, and the United States, surveys show that many elderly do not *want* to be dependent on their adult children or other family members. For all these reasons, a shift of responsibility for caring for the elderly has been occurring in all societies, with the government becoming increasingly active in providing this assistance.

One form of government assistance to the elderly is public pensions. The United States has one of the lowest mandatory contribution rates to a public pension plan (Social Security) of all the industrialized countries. Furthermore, our public pension policy leaves some elderly with little or no pension income because the amount of income a person receives from Social Security depends on their lifetime work and earnings. Such a policy discriminates against those, often women, who never worked or who worked part-time or intermittently. In practically all societies, women are given primary responsibility for taking care of home and family. In the majority of cases, this can be done only by cutting back on paid employment. Societies such as Israel, the United Kingdom, and the Scandinavian countries try to alleviate this problem by also providing a universal pension that is payable to all citizens who reach a certain age, irrespective of whether or how much they have worked (Nusberg, 1984; Cnaan, Olsson, and Wetle, 1990). In Israel, for example, this universal pension provides all individuals with 16 percent of the median income of employed persons, while couples receive 24 percent. Swedish policy provides for three sources of income: a flat-rate pension for all citizens, an earnings-related pension for those who have worked, and mandatory worker pensions provided by employers and trade union organizations. With this system, destitution among Swedish elderly is practically nonexistent.

Since public pensions are rarely large enough to provide for all the needs of the elderly, many industrial nations, like France and Sweden, require almost universal private pension coverage for employees through nationally negotiated agreements. While less than one-half of U.S. workers have

the United States (Abel, 1991). This places a considerable burden on those family members, and some supports for them have developed, such as in-home physical therapy or other assistance. But often the infirmities become too much for family members to handle, and they must turn to some kind of institutional setting for the elderly person.

In the past few decades, a variety of such institutional settings has emerged to help the elderly cope with infirmity (Struyk et al., 1989). Taken together, they are called *supported-living* private pension coverage, 90 percent of workers in Sweden and 80 percent in the Netherlands have that coverage. Switzerland actually has an amendment in its constitution that mandates that all workers will have pension coverage.

To provide protection for women and men with meager work histories, Germany, New Zealand, and Canada split pension credits accumulated during a marriage at the time of a divorce. This is sometimes done for both public and private pensions, and it means that a nonworking spouse shares in the pension accumulation of the working spouse. For earnings-related public pensions, Switzerland and the United Kingdom permit people to use a deceased or former spouse's earnings record at the time the marriage ended to calculate retirement benefits. In some cases, if a wife's earnings record does not qualify her for a pension, she can combine it with her husband's earnings record. Programs of this sort have been considered in the United States but not yet implemented.

In order to assist retirees in maintaining something close to their preretirement lifestyle, some societies set goals for how much of a worker's preretirement income should be replaced by the combination of public and private benefits. In the Netherlands, for example, the goal is that retirement pay be 70 percent of a retiring worker's final pay, while in Switzerland it is 60 percent. In addition, to ensure that all work contributes to a worker's retirement pay, many societies have much more liberal vesting policies. In Sweden and Switzerland, for example, for workers who have

reached their late twenties, full vesting occurs as soon as one begins to work or within a few years of employment. This means that people who switch jobs after a few years still accumulate some retirement funds that are permanently their own. This especially benefits women, who are more likely to work for short periods and to switch jobs.

All industrialized countries recognize the value of maintaining the elderly in their own homes because it is more humane and less expensive than caring for them in a nursing home or other institutional setting. Denmark, Norway, and Sweden, for example, provide such things as chore and escort services, meals-on-wheels, laundry services, counseling, transportation, friendly visiting services, and other practical but essential supports that allow older people to continue living in their homes as they become more frail and limited. In some cases, these services are universal rather than age-based or income-based—anyone with functional impairments is eligible for them. This increases political support for them and encourages people to view them as a right of citizenship rather than a welfare handout. While these services are free to those with low incomes, others pay according to their abilities which helps defray the costs of the programs and reduces demand. Some of these services are available to the elderly in the United States, but these other societies have a much more elaborate infrastructure of such services. This infrastructure ensures that these services are more universally available and that the goal of maintaining the elderly in their own homes is more achievable.

environments because all provide some level of support for people who cannot or do not want to live independently. Some of these homes are nonprofit institutions run by religious groups, business organizations, or labor unions for the benefit of their members. Others are

commercial or proprietary institutions that are run to make a profit for their owners. The range of support they provide is quite varied. At one extreme are homes for the aged that care for reasonably healthy people who no longer want responsibility for running a home and caring for themselves. At the other extreme are nursing homes that take people who have severe physical limitations and require extensive support. In some homes, people purchase or rent an apartment with cooking facilities and can either cook for themselves or eat in a dining area with the other residents. There are homes that will accept people with greater physical limitations, such as those confined to a wheelchair or who use a walker. These homes are designed to be barrier free and may still offer separate, fully equipped apartments for their residents. Some homes provide the whole range of support. People can enter when they are reasonably healthy and be assured of support by the community if their physical status deteriorates.

The care and programs available in these living environments are quite variable. Generally, the nonprofit homes run by religious groups or labor unions have the financial resources and the motivation to provide excellent care and a wide range of services. Other homes charge high fees and still find it difficult to provide high-quality care. This is especially true of proprietary institutions that cater to low- and moderate-income groups. To alleviate these problems, the government has developed an elaborate set of regulations to be followed in order for a home to be licensed. It has also developed programs to train nursing-home personnel and nursing-home inspectors.

The previous International Perspectives insert (see pp. 306–307) provides a comparison of financial and other services available to elderly in the United States with those in some other societies.

Collective Action

There is little doubt that it has been older people themselves who have been the most vocal about the treatment of the elderly in the United States. The elderly have shown, and continue to show, signs of increasing political activism, and even radical militancy, focused on changing traditional conceptions of old age

and advocating social policies that might alleviate the problems of the elderly (Wallace et al., 1991). Two popular organizations promoting the interests of the elderly are the American Association of Retired Persons (AARP) and the National Retired Teachers Association (NRTA). These groups offer many programs and services for the elderly, such as courses in income tax preparation and public speaking. They have also been very active at the local, state, and national levels in lobbying for programs that are beneficial to the elderly.

The Gray Panthers is a group that is considerably more extreme than AARP or NRTA. The group, whose official name is Consultation of Older and Younger Adults, believes that the problems of the aged stem from some basic defects in the social structure. The most fundamental defect, they argue, is our emphasis on materialism and the consumption of goods and services, rather than on the quality of life and personal relationships. In a materialist society, the elderly are viewed as useless because they are less economically productive. Because of this, they are abandoned, like worn-out automobiles. The Gray Panthers hope to liberate people from what they perceive as outmoded ways of thinking about the elderly and to encourage independence and self-determination among the elderly.

These various groups and social movements have been quite successful in protecting and advancing the interests of the elderly. For example, when many social programs were being severely trimmed by the government, Medicare, Social Security, and other programs providing benefits for the elderly suffered the least. A primary reason for this was that politicians were concerned about the strong reaction they could expect from the very well organized groups backing the elderly. Such successes are likely to enhance support for groups such as AARP, NRTA, the Gray Panthers, and other groups working for the elderly. In addition, the elderly have more financial and economic resources available today than they did decades ago, and this will be even more true in the future. They

Providing support and assistance to the elderly has contributed to skyrocketing health-care costs because Medicare has become so expensive and increased demand considerably for health-care services (Chapter 4). At the same time, the elderly are more likely to be battered and injured by a caretaker who abuses drugs or alcohol (Chapter 10).

also have more time to pursue their interests than do younger people who must work. Finally, older people take their duty to vote much more seriously than do younger people. In the 1992 presidential election, only 45 percent of the people in their early twenties bothered to vote, whereas 70 percent of the people over sixty-five did so (U.S. Bureau of the Census, 1994: 287). This affords the elderly considerably more political clout. People between fifty and sixty-five also vote in large numbers, and these people are also concerned about issues related to the elderly because they will soon be in that group.

This group of people aged 50 and older comprises a substantial voting bloc.

So collective action on the part of the elderly is likely to continue as one of the most powerful forces working against ageist attitudes and social policies in the United States.

Summary

1. Gerontology is the scientific study of aging. All societies carve out people's lives into a series of social stages, and this is called the life

For the elderly who are healthy and can live independently, life is often fulfilling and rewarding. In fact, the elderly have become very effective advocates in pursuing their own interests through collective action.

course. The life course is determined in part by biology and in part by the needs of a particular society.

2. Functionalists argue that the stages of the life cycle are intimately related to the social needs of a particular society. The life cycle in preindustrial societies differs significantly from that in industrial societies.

3. From the conflict perspective, the position of the young and old in society is related to their access to social, political, and economic power. The elderly have less power today than in the past because they control fewer resources and the young are less dependent on them.

4. Ageism refers to the ideology holding that people in a particular age group are inferior, have negative attributes, and can be dominated and exploited because of their age. The age structure of industrial societies is becoming more "top heavy" as these societies age and their dependency ratios grow larger.

5. Throughout history, there have been ideologies that justified the inequitable treatment of the young. The major problems facing the young are economic exploitation, family instability, poverty, sexual exploitation, and child abuse.

6. The elderly in the United States face a number of serious problems: they are less likely to work and have to adapt to retirement; they are poorer than other adults; they suffer from social isolation, especially when they are very old; they are sometimes victims of domestic violence; they have more health problems than others and are more susceptible to fraud and quackery; they fear being the victims of crime; and they are in danger of being exploited in poorly run nursing homes when they need some type of supportive living environment.

7. An important issue in social policy regarding age is to find an equitable distribution of resources between the young and the old.

8. Efforts to improve the economic status of the elderly have focused on ensuring that more people have personal pension plans and that the plans provide more adequate support. It has also been suggested that Social Security could be improved and put on a more sound financial basis. Policies have also been established to encourage people to increase their assets for retirement through tax-deferred savings and investments.

9. The health care available to the elderly has been increased substantially with the establishment of Medicare and Medicaid. Also, numerous new approaches to the living arrangements of the elderly have alleviated the problems of isolation and infirmity in old age.

10. Much of the attention focused on problems of the elderly has arisen because the elderly have been very vocal about things that work against their interests. Through moderate and radical political activity the elderly have gained much and protected what they have fairly effectively.

STUDY AND *Review*

Key Terms

ageism

age structure

demography

dependency ratio

gerontology

life course

life stages

Multiple-Choice Questions

1. The scientific study of aging is called:
   a. Demography.
   b. Androgyny.
   c. Life course.
   d. Ageism.
   e. Gerontology.

2. According to the functionalist perspective, the treatment of the young and the old is considered a social problem when:
   a. It leads to social disorganization.
   b. The young and the old have little power.
   c. There is an absence of ageism.
   d. The young and the old believe they do not have a fair share of society's resources.
3. Ageism is like racism in that both:
   a. Use race as a criterion for discrimination.
   b. Use both race and age as criteria for discrimination.
   c. Derive from the functionalist perspective.
   d. Use biological grounds to defend inequitable treatment of groups.
4. The dependency ratio in the United States today is approximately _____ people older than age 65 for each one hundred people between ages eighteen and sixty-four.
   a. Three.
   b. Twenty.
   c. Sixty.
   d. Eighty.
   e. Cannot be determined.
5. In the United States today, which of the following is true regarding retirement policies?
   a. Retirement is mandatory at age sixty-five.
   b. Retirement is mandatory at age seventy.
   c. Retirement is not mandatory at any age for people in most occupations.
   d. All companies are required to provide pensions for their employees.
6. Which of the following is true of poverty rates among those older than sixty-five years of age in the United States today?
   a. The rates are only slightly higher than those for adults aged eighteen to sixty-four.
   b. The rates are much higher than those for adults aged eighteen to sixty-four.
   c. The rates are higher than they were thirty years ago.
   d. The rates are slightly lower than those for adults aged eighteen to sixty-four.
7. The largest source of income for people older than age sixty-five in the United States is:
   a. Pensions.
   b. Social Security.
   c. Assets.
   d. Earnings from work.
   e. Medicare.
8. Regarding the elderly and crime, which of the following statements is true?
   a. The elderly fear they will be the victims of crime.
   b. The crime rate among the elderly has gone up.
   c. The crime rate among the elderly is about the same as that among the young.
   d. The rate of crimes committed against the elderly has been increasing.
9. What proportion of the total federal government budget is consumed by Medicare and Social Security together?
   a. Five percent.
   b. Fifteen percent.
   c. Thirty percent.
   d. Fifty percent.
10. Age-segregated housing for the elderly produces which of the following outcomes in comparison with age-integrated housing?
    a. Less fear of crime among the residents.
    b. Less activity and involvement for the residents.
    c. More satisfaction with living arrangements.
    d. Higher rates of crime among the residents.

True/False Questions

1. According to sociologists, biology plays a relatively small role in shaping the life course in human societies.
2. The transition from childhood to adulthood occurs earlier in life in industrial societies than it does in preindustrial societies.
3. As societies industrialize, their age structures tend to become more "top heavy" rather than "bottom heavy."
4. One of the reasons that children in single-parent families face difficulties is that such families are more likely to have low incomes.
5. Research shows that retirement for most elderly is a negative experience.
6. When one looks at total wealth and not just annual income, the elderly are better off than younger adults.

7. The largest share of the income of people older than sixty-five years comes from earned income from work.
8. Approximately one-half of all older people will live in a nursing home at some point before they die.
9. One criticism of retirement communities for the elderly is that they isolate the elderly into a segregated subculture in society.
10. The elderly are much more likely to vote in elections than are people in their early twenties.

Fill-In Questions

1. The _____ is a succession of statuses and roles that people in a particular society experience in a fairly predictable pattern as they grow older.
2. The new stage in the life course that is found in industrial societies but not preindustrial ones is called _____ .
3. The dependency ratio in preindustrial societies tends to be _____ than the same ratio in industrial societies.
4. Since what society expects of people who retire is much less well defined than are most social roles, retirement has been called _____ role.
5. Feelings of detachment that can arise in nursing homes and mental institutions are called _____ .
6. A _____ is a pension that is the property of an employee rather than the company the employee works for.
7. _____ are tax-deferred savings or investment plans that have some tax advantages.
8. _____ is a government health-insurance program for people older than age sixty-five.
9. _____ is a popular organization promoting the interests of the elderly.
10. Political activism and radical militancy on the part of the elderly themselves are examples of _____ among the elderly.

Matching Questions

_____ 1. Age Discrimination in Employment Act

_____ 2. adolescence

_____ 3. nursing homes

_____ 4. an aging population

_____ 5. shared housing

_____ 6. ageism

_____ 7. demography

_____ 8. child exploitation

_____ 9. IRAs

_____ 10. Gray Panthers

A. stage in the life course
B. a higher dependency ratio
C. depersonalization
D. prejudice
E. debt bondage
F. retirement savings
G. study of human populations
H. radical activism for the elderly
I. age-integrated housing
J. eliminates mandatory retirement

Essay Questions

1. How do the life stages in industrial societies differ from the life stages in preindustrial societies? Why do these differences occur?
2. Describe the age structure and the dependency ratio in preindustrial and industrial societies. How do they differ from one another?
3. Explain why the economic exploitation of child laborers occurs in the United States and other nations.
4. Explain why children in the United States are at such risk of living in poverty.
5. Is retirement a good or a bad thing? Make the argument for both sides of this issue.
6. What is the poverty status of the elderly? What other kinds of financial difficulties do they confront?
7. Describe what problems are found in nursing homes, and explain why these problems exist.

8. Describe the three elements that make up the economic resources of the elderly. What current policies are in place or proposed to make these elements an even stronger source of support for the elderly?

9. What is the policy debate over whether programs for the elderly should be based on age or need? What arguments are there in favor of need-based policies?

10. In what kinds of collective action have the elderly engaged? How effective have they been and why?

Answers

Multiple-Choice
1. E; **2.** A; **3.** D; **4.** B; **5.** C; **6.** A; **7.** B; **8.** A; **9.** C; **10.** C

True/False
1. F; **2.** F; **3.** T; **4.** T; **5.** F; **6.** T; **7.** F; **8.** T; **9.** T; **10.** T

Fill-In
1. life course or life stages
2. adolescence
3. lower
4. roleless
5. depersonalization
6. vested pension
7. IRAs or SRAs or SEPs
8. Medicare
9. AARP or NRTA
10. collective action

Matching
1. J; **2.** A; **3.** C; **4.** B; **5.** I; **6.** D; **7.** G; **8.** E; **9.** F; **10.** H

For Further Reading

Advisory Council on Social Security. *Social Security and the Future Financial Security of Women.* Washington, D.C.: Advisory Council on Social Security, 1991. This is an excellent report that documents the financial difficulties that older women will confront well into the next century and what can be done about it.

Phillippe Aries. *Centuries of Childhood: A Social History of Childhood.* New York: Random House, 1962. An excellent history of how childhood has been viewed in many different cultures.

Joel Best. *Threatened Children: Rhetoric and Concern About Child-Victims.* Chicago: University of Chicago Press, 1990. This is a very good book on the "constructionist" approach to social problems, emphasizing the point made in Chapter 1 that conditions do not become social problems until an influential group defines them as such. The author focuses particularly on the various threats and dangers, such as abuse and kidnapping, that confront children in our society.

Karen A. Conner. *Aging America: Issues Facing an Aging America.* Englewood Cliffs, N.J.: Prentice-Hall, 1992. This book offers a good overview of the many problems that confront the elderly and what can be done about them.

Donna Dickenson and Malcolm Johnson. *Death, Dying and Bereavement.* Newbury Park, Calif.: Sage, 1992. This book deals with topics surrounding death: what happens socially when people die, the process of bereavement, euthanasia, and so on. These topics may be closer to the experience of the elderly, but they can also be issues for the young.

Peter B. Doeringer, ed. *Bridges to Retirement: Older Workers in a Changing Labor Market.* New York: ILR Press, 1990. This book explores a topic mentioned in this chapter: innovative policies toward retirement.

Carroll L. Estes. *The Long Term Care Crisis: Elders Trapped in the No-Care Zone.* Newbury Park, Calif.: Sage, 1993. This sociologist explores the problems with institutional care of the elderly in hospitals or nursing homes and suggests improvements in current policies.

Carl Husemoller Nightingale. *On the Edge: A History of Poor Black Children and Their American Dreams.* New York: Basic Books, 1993. This is a thought-provoking book about the circumstances of African-American children today—showing how they are very much products of their culture, but the culture conspires against their advancement.

Susan Sheehan. *Kate Quinton's Days.* Boston: Houghton Mifflin, 1984. This is an absorbing look at what it is like for one person to be very old. It is often not pleasant reading, but it forcefully makes us confront the realities of how we treat some old people.

CHAPTER NINE
Crime and Delinquency

When novelist Chip Elliott and his wife, a psychiatrist, moved to Los Angeles in the late 1970s, they were hoping to lead pleasant, quiet lives. They were young and embarking on promising careers. Both would certainly have regarded themselves as peaceful people. The world of assaults, street crime, juvenile gangs, and handguns all seemed far away. In a short time, however, the Elliotts found out otherwise. Their neighborhood turned out to be a battleground for two juvenile gangs: "When they shot at each other—as they did less than one week after we had moved in—they shouted to us . . . to get out of the way. We did" (Elliott, 1981: 33).

The Elliotts' home was broken into and some of their friends were robbed. Going against their previous values, they purchased handguns and even obtained permits to carry them. Walking home one night, Elliott was confronted by five young men. Elliott was carrying a 9mm automatic pistol.

> We were directly under a streetlight and less than fifty feet from an intersection thick with traffic. Their leader pulled a kitchen knife, smiled at me, and said: "Just the wallet, man. Won't be no trouble." That was a very long moment for me—it was supposed to be one of those moments that are charged with electricity. It wasn't. It was hollow, silent, and chilly. I pulled the automatic, leveled it at them, and said very clearly, "You must be dreaming." The leader smiled again, muttered an obscenity, and began to move toward me with the knife. His buddies laughed. I aimed the automatic at the outer edge of his left thigh and shot him. I backed off and walked away with the gun still in my hand. I remember thinking, shouldn't I call a doctor? And then I thought, would he have called a doctor for me? And I kept on walking. I am not proud of this. I did not swallow it easily either. More than a year passed before I talked about it with anybody, even my wife. But I did it. And I could do it again if I had to. (Elliott, 1981: 33–36)

Elliott's experience graphically illustrates the problems of crime and delinquency and their impact on people. When Elliott moved to Los Angeles he did not own a gun. A growing fear of crime, however, drastically changed both his attitudes and his behavior. He adapted by buying a pistol, and having to use that pistol was the price he paid for living in a dangerous society.

Elliott's experience also highlights an element of the sociological view of deviant behavior that was discussed in Chapter 1. Elliott shot a person and then walked away. Does that make him a deviant? Some people would argue that under the circumstances it does not, just as most would say that the young men who attempted to rob him at knifepoint were deviant. In other words, it is not the act itself that is deviant; rather, it is our interpretation of it or judgment about it that makes it deviant. Deviance exists in the social context of an event rather than in the act itself.

This chapter will try to understand and find solutions to various types of crime. Not all crime is as graphic, violent, or public as the ones Elliott experienced. We need to remember that crimes are committed by people wearing business suits and in corporate board rooms, and they can be just as harmful to society as violent street crime. This discussion of crime and delinquency begins by examining different explanations of these behaviors.

Explanations of Crime

Like all behavior, crime and delinquency are complex, and many people find them hard to understand. In fact, because crime and delinquency are often so frightening, it is tempting to settle for overly simple explanations of them. Over the years, many people have sought *biological explanations* of crime, which view criminal behavior as arising, at least in part, from a person's physical or biological makeup. Some people, it is argued, are simply biologically less capable of conforming their behavior to conventional norms (Wilson and Herrnstein, 1985). Decades of research results, however, have shown that biology makes, if anything, only a small contribution to the crime problem. Criminologists today agree that criminal behavior is for the most part due to psychological and social forces (Gottfredson and Hirschi, 1990; Chambliss, 1991).

Unlike their biological counterparts, *psychological approaches* to crime still receive considerable support. From this perspective, criminality is linked to personality disorder or maladjustment, often developing during childhood. Evidence in support of such connections comes from research on personality defects and disorders among delinquents, mental disease in prisoners, and studies of psychopathic and sociopathic personalities (Med-

Myth: There is a clear line between the "criminal element" in society and the law-abiding and respectable people. If we could put that criminal element behind bars, the crime problem would be solved.

FACT: Once again, social reality is far more complex than many commonsense beliefs would have it. It turns out that many crimes are committed by people who are otherwise considered quite respectable by themselves and many others. For example, who commits vandalism? Teenage punks? Hostile and alienated losers? Social psychologist Philip Zimbardo conducted an intriguing study of people who vandalized automobiles in New York City (Zimbardo, 1973). After seeing many stripped and battered automobiles on his way to work, he decided to observe who the vandals were. He bought an old car, left it on a street near New York University, and watched from a hidden location. Within ten minutes, the first vandals appeared: a father, mother, and their eight-year-old son! The mother served as lookout while the father and son removed the battery and radiator. Later, another vandal was pushing an infant in a baby carriage. There followed a virtual parade of people who removed everything of value from the car and then began battering what was left. These vandals were often well dressed and chattered amiably with passersby as they toiled. Zimbardo's research leads to the conclusion that many criminals not only appear quite respectable but also probably consider themselves quite law abiding.

Myth: Crimes are committed by the less educated members of society, whereas those fortunate enough to attend college understand the importance of obeying the law.

FACT: College students in the state of Michigan were asked to indicate which criminal activities they had engaged in (see Table 9.1 on p. 318). Their responses showed that every student who responded could have been jailed for at least one year for offenses they had committed. Michigan is probably no different in this regard than any other state.

Some groups may commit more crimes than others, or more of certain types of crime, but the crime problem is by no means limited to one or a few groups. The social factors that lead people to commit crimes are very complex and affect all of us to a degree. If all the criminals were behind bars, would anyone be left on the outside? Probably not many.

nick, Moffitt, and Stack, 1987; Eysenck and Gudjonsson, 1989). Although sociologists recognize the importance of personality and psychological processes in people's lives, such explanations offer only a partial understanding of crime and delinquency. In many cases, people who commit crimes are free from the psychological disorders that are presumed to cause crime, and people with those disorders often do not commit crimes. In other cases, it can be the criminal lifestyle, along with the stigma and fear of imprisonment, that leads

TABLE 9.1 Criminal Activities Under the State of Michigan Penal Code

1. You attempt to physically strike another person but do not succeed.
   (Sec. 750-81/750.92: Attempted Assault and Battery)

2. During a fight, you break your opponent's nose.
   (Sec. 750.81a: Assault and Battery with Bodily Harm)

3. You set fire in a wastebasket located in a public restroom.
   (Sec. 750.73-.81: Arson)

4. You intentionally damage somebody else's property
   (Sec. 750.377a: Malicious Destruction of Property)

5. You knowingly trespass on another person's property.
   (Sec. 750.552: Trespass)

6. You write a check, knowing that it exceeds the amount you have in your account.
   (Sec. 750.218: False Pretenses)

7. You shoplift minor articles (candy bar, cigarettes, magazines).
   (Sec. 750.356: Larceny)

8. You purchase a compact disc player that you know or believe is stolen.
   (Sec. 750.535: Receiving Stolen Property)

9. You hide in the trunk of a friend's car in order to gain entrance to a drive-in movie without paying the admission fee.
   (Sec. 750.292–93 Failure to Pay)

10. You participate in sexual activity with an animal.
    (Sec. 750.158: Crime Against Nature)

11. You are married, and you have voluntary sexual intercourse with a person other than your spouse.
    (Sec. 750.29: Felonious Adultery)

12. You engage in an act of sexual intercourse for money.
    (Sec. 750.44: Soliciting and Accosting)

13. You participate in procuring a prostitute for another person or direct that person to a place of prostitution.
    (Sec. 750.450: Aiders and Abettors)

14. You engage in sexual intercourse with any female under the age of 16 years.
    (Sec. 750.13: Enticing Away Female Under the age of 16)

15. You are involved in a fight involving two or more persons in a public establishment.
    (Sec. 750.167: Disorderly Conduct)

16. You use obscene, profane language in the presence of women and children.
    (Sec. 750.337: Improper Language)

17. You throw an empty can of soda out the window of your car.
    (Sec. 752.901: Littering)

18. You play poker for money at a friend's home.
    (Sec. 750.301: Accepting Money or Valuable Thing Contingent on an Uncertain Event)

19. You hide a firearm or knife with a blade exceeding three inches on your person while outside of your home.
    (Sec. 750.227: Concealed Weapons, Carrying)

Source: Michigan Compiled Laws, Vols. 38–39 (St. Paul, Minn: West Publishing Company, 1987).

people to develop unique personality characteristics rather than the other way around (Jeffrey, 1967). In addition, many of the psychological maladjustments that lead to crime are the products of social circumstances, and social conditions also contribute to the cause of crime in many cases where psychological factors do not come into play. So, social conditions contribute substantially to the level of crime in society. Therefore, policy designed to reduce crime needs to focus on the social conditions that produce it, and the sociological approaches to crime provide the basis for doing this. These perspectives emphasize the role of culture, social structure, and social interaction in bringing about criminal and delinquent behavior.

The Functionalist Perspective

An early functionalist, Emile Durkheim, provided one of the explanations for high levels of crime in industrial societies. One of the key features of industrial societies, he argued, is the weakening of many of the social bonds important in preindustrial societies. Ties to family, community, and church become less important in industrial societies as families become smaller and workers more mobile and independent of their families (see Chapter 3). People are more free to pursue their own needs and fulfill their own desires; they are less constrained by the need to please relatives or account to a priest or minister. But this freedom has its costs. The reduction in social constraints also results in a degree of social disorganization as people pursue needs and goals that may be detrimental to the overall good of society. After all, bonds to family and church were one of the key mechanisms constraining people from committing crimes or engaging in other socially disapproved activities. When those bonds are weakened or removed, a certain amount of crime and social disorder will result. For Durkheim, then, crime is one of the costs that we pay to live in the type of society that we do, and recent research comparing many different societies supports his theory (Leavitt, 1992). More recently, Durkheim's views have been applied to juvenile delinquency in the form of a "social control" theory of delinquency. The basic idea is that the chances of delinquency occurring can be reduced if youngsters maintain attachments and commitments to the conventional world of their parents, schools, and peers (Hirschi, 1969; Agnew, 1991).

Another influential functionalist approach to crime and delinquency is sociologist Robert K. Merton's **anomie theory** (1968), which posits that *inconsistencies and contradictions in the social system contribute to many forms of crime.* Merton observed that *people in the United States are taught to strive for certain goals but are not always provided with the culturally approved means necessary to attain these goals.* Merton referred to *such inconsistencies and the confusion they can cause in people* as **anomie.** In the United States, for example, an important cultural goal is success, which is defined largely in material terms. One culturally approved way to become successful is to get an education and work in some legitimate occupation. Some people, however, are prevented from succeeding in this fashion because of poverty, discrimination, or some other social condition. When people are thus hindered from achieving desired goals, deviance in one of its many forms may result. Deviance is the person's "mode of adaptation" to the anomie, although the person may not think of it this way.

Merton called the most common mode of adaptation to anomie *innovation,* according to which people pursue the cultural goals through illegal or other socially disapproved means. This is likely to occur when people feel that legitimate routes to success are closed and that their only option is to turn to illegitimate ones. People who are unemployed or underemployed, for example, can provide for their families and themselves through robbery or burglary. Likewise, a person running a marginal business concern can survive by cheating on taxes or using deceptive advertising practices. Recent research on crime supports anomie theory. For example, crime rates, especially for property crimes, are higher in communities with greater economic inequality or with a larger disparity between incomes among groups. In such cities, the less fortunate can readily see the affluence around them, and some turn to crime to improve their own circumstances (Simons and Gray, 1989). Crime also goes up when there is an economic recession (Devine, Sheley, and Smith, 1988). Crime rates are high among the unemployed and low among the employed (Allan and Steffensmeier, 1989; Lafree, Drass, and O'Day, 1992).

The importance of anomie theory for understanding crime should be clear: Much criminal activity derives from the social and economic conditions of U.S. society. With high unemployment and reduced government spending on social services, economic disparities are exacerbated. In fact, criminologist Elliott Currie has argued that the low crime rate in industrial societies such as Japan results in part from their programs promoting high employment and the fact that income disparities are much smaller than in the United States (Currie, 1985).

The functionalist perspective also emphasizes the interrelatedness of the various parts of the social system. Changes in one part bring about changes in other seemingly unrelated parts. Certain social trends and changes that are found in affluent industrial societies have increased the opportunities for committing certain kinds of crime, particularly burglary, larceny, and theft (Cohen and Felson, 1979; Cohen, Felson, and Land, 1980; Miller and Ohlin, 1985). For example, the number of women working has increased dramatically in the past three decades; there has been an increase in the number of households with only one adult member; and people take more vacations now than in the past. The result of these three trends is that homes are much more likely to be left unattended for a part of the day and therefore become tempting targets for burglars. There has also been tremendous growth in consumer spending for items such as televisions and automobiles that are likely objects for theft. In short, the rise in crime results in part from increasing opportunities made available by trends that many people view as desirable. Unless alternative means of controlling such crimes are found, people may have to settle for the realiza-

tion that some crimes represent an unfortunate by-product of an affluent and leisured lifestyle.

The Conflict Perspective

In reviewing the functionalist argument, conflict theorists observe that the analysis of the "crime and delinquency problem" tends to focus heavily on criminal behavior that is more likely to occur among the less powerful groups in society: the young, the poor, and the nonwhite. In fact, the Federal Bureau of Investigation's Crime Index, the most widely publicized statistic on the amount of crime, emphasizes crimes such as assault, which the less well-to-do are more likely to commit, rather than embezzlement, gambling, or tax evasion, which are committed more by middle-class and "respectable" people. The so-called crime and delinquency problem, then, as it is defined by the police, the courts, and the public, results from the activities of the less fortunate in society.

From the conflict perspective, the legal and criminal justice systems are geared to benefit the dominant groups in society (Quinney, 1974; Kennedy, 1990). Laws, after all, are mechanisms whereby some groups exercise control over the activities of other groups. Generally, it is the powerful who establish legislation defining what activities will be considered criminal and who decide what the penalties will be for those crimes. Thus, removing a television from a store is regarded as criminal, whereas polluting a stream may not be. Armed robbery can bring a fifteen-year prison sentence, whereas price fixing that costs the public millions of dollars in excess expenditures may be punished with a light prison sentence or a fine.

It is also the powerful who can get the police to enforce the laws against some crimes while ignoring other infractions of the law. The powerful also determine the extent of resources that will be devoted to controlling particular types of crime. There are, for example, periodic and highly publicized drives against robbery, prostitution, and drug offenses. In 1989, the Bush administration declared "war" on illegal drugs, proclaiming that this problem was the United States' number one crime issue. One does not, however, often see a politician launch such a campaign against corporate crime. From the conflict perspective, then, the social problem of crime is not simply a matter of social disorganization; it is also influenced by the preferences, predilections, and interests of various groups in society (Caringella-Macdonald, 1990).

Conflict theorists who have been influenced by the writings of Karl Marx view the causes of crime very differently from the functionalists. These conflict theorists blame certain characteristics of capitalism as an economic system (Headley, 1991). Capitalism is characterized by a constant search for greater profits, or at least a struggle against falling profits. This process can be especially fierce in a worldwide economy such as we have today where countries at many different levels of development compete with one another. In the process, capitalists search for ways to enhance profits by reducing costs through mechanization or automation of work or through relocation to areas where resources and labor are cheaper. Both mechanization and relocation put people out of work or force people into competition for lower-wage jobs. Because this process is a continual one, capitalism inevitably contains recurring cycles in which people are thrown out of work and communities are decimated by the loss of jobs. These inherent features of capitalism, then, mean that certain levels of poverty and the crime associated with it will always be with us, although which groups or communities are affected may shift over time.

In addition, capitalists need to sell their goods to make a profit, so capitalists must instill in people a desire for the many products that capitalism can produce. At the same time, capitalists attempt to keep wages low to reduce the costs of production. A mass of unemployed people also benefits a capitalist economy by serving as a cheap labor force when new workers are needed. The unemployed also serve as a lesson to employed workers: Do not demand too high a salary or you, too, may be among the unemployed. The result, according to sociologist William Chambliss (1975: 151), is a contradiction: "capitalism creates both the desire to consume and—for a large mass of people—an inability to earn the money necessary to purchase the items they have been taught to want." For these people, crime is one way of resolving this dilemma. Unlike anomie theory, however, Marxian conflict theory does not assume that the problem can be alleviated through full employment; rather, it sees these contradictions as inherent in a capitalist economy.

The Interactionist Perspective

Interactionist approaches do not dispute the sources of crime pointed to by the functionalist and conflict views. But interactionists see these views as incomplete because they do not explain how a person becomes criminal or why one poor person responds to anomie through crime and another does not. To understand this, we need to look at the socialization and interaction processes that influence people's daily lives.

Cultural transmission theories posit that *crime and delinquency are learned and culturally transmitted through socialization.* The most influential of these theories is the **differential association theory,** developed by criminologist Edwin Sutherland in the 1920s and 1930s. According to Sutherland, *crime and delinquency are learned in interaction with other people, for the most part within intimate primary groups such as families and peer groups* (Sutherland and Cressey, 1978). There are two elements of this learning process. First, people learn the specific techniques for engaging in criminal behavior. For example, by becoming a member of a delinquent gang, a person might learn how to buy drugs or where to obtain weapons. Learning these things makes it more possible and likely that a person will engage in some criminal or delinquent acts. Second, people learn to value criminality more highly than conventional behavior. By associating with other people who engage in criminal behavior, people are more likely to learn to view these activities as desirable and learn a rationale for why they are preferable to a more conventional way of life. Delinquent gangs or prison inmates, for example, may value a lifestyle in which a person makes money the "easy way"—through crime—and to denigrate the "chumps" who work every day for a small wage. Someone who falls in with groups such as these may well be influenced by their values. Whether people become criminals or delinquents depends on the extent and intensity of contacts with groups that value a particular form of criminality and on the age at which the contacts occur. It also depends on whether a person identifies with these criminals. Association with such people without identification is not likely to result in valuing criminal behavior.

According to cultural transmission theories, then, learning to be criminal or delinquent involves mechanisms of socialization similar to those associated with learning any social status. If people have close group ties with others who conform to established group values, they are likely to learn to conform to that lifestyle. Those who associate with criminal or delinquent groups are more likely to adopt criminal or delinquent values.

Another interactionist approach to understanding crime and delinquency is labeling theory, which shifts attention away from the individual transgressor and toward the ways that others react to the deviant (Cavender, 1991). **Labeling theory** suggests that *whether other people define or label a person as deviant is a critical determinant in the development of a pattern of deviant behavior.* According to this theory, many people engage in activities that are defined as criminal, at least occasionally. In all likelihood, you

have engaged in actions that have been so defined (recall the criminal activities listed in Table 9.1). Few of us, however, are caught and labeled—either by our friends or by official agencies—as criminals or delinquents. Labeling theorists refer to this *violation of social norms in which a person is not caught or is excused rather than labeled as a deviant* as **primary deviance** (Lemert, 1951). But the theory does not attempt to explain this type of behavior. Labeling theory concentrates on **secondary** or **career deviance**—*the deviant behavior that a person adopts in response to the reaction of others to his or her primary deviance.* Consider how this could happen.

We know that shoplifting among teenagers, at least of small items, is not uncommon. Imagine that a teenager, possibly out of curiosity or on a dare from peers, engages in a single act of shoplifting. This would constitute primary deviance, because there has been no labeling and no change in the teenager's or the community's image of him or her. If, however, the young person's shoplifting is brought to the attention of the police, they may begin the labeling process by notifying the young person's parents. If this label becomes "public," it is quite likely that some stigma will attach to this teenager's reputation—perhaps a criminal record.

One key consequence of this labeling process is its effect on a person's self-concept: Because the teenage years are formative ones in terms of personal identity, the person may respond to others' reactions, at least in part, by accepting their judgment. After all, the stigma associated with deviant labels such as "criminal" and "delinquent" implies something very negative about people who behave in that fashion. The terms *murderer, thug, robber,* and *thief* suggest the strong emotions that underlie these deviant labels, and such labels can affect the way people view themselves. A second key consequence of labeling involves the effect that labeling has on people's social relationships. If the criminal activity becomes publicly known, some of the person's conventional friends may shun him or her out of fear for their own reputations. The person may also find it difficult to develop new friends, at least among conventional peers, finding acceptance, instead, among youngsters who are already engaging in delinquent or criminal actions on a widespread scale.

As a result of these changes in self-concept and social contacts, labeling theorists argue, the likelihood of a deviant career developing is increased. Thus, labeling can perpetuate crime and delinquency because, once people have been labeled, they have fewer alternatives, and the deviance becomes a part of their social identity. This represents secondary deviance because it results from a person's efforts to cope with the responses of others to their primary deviation. It also represents, in a sense, a *self-fulfilling prophecy* in that the deviant label helps to bring about the pattern of career deviance that people thought they were merely identifying when they first attached the label (Heimer and Matsueda, 1994).

These major sociological theories of crime and delinquency should help us to better understand why sociologists take the position that criminal behavior is *relative*. According to anomie theory, what is defined as criminal or delinquent depends on what are considered socially approved means and goals in a particular society. Conflict theorists see crime and delinquency within a framework of definitions and judgments that are formulated and enforced by those people in powerful positions in society. For cultural transmission theory, criminality is a result of socialization, and people are capable of learning a wide variety of things. Finally, labeling theory makes us aware that being identified as deviant depends, among other things, on the resources a person possesses and his or her ability to avoid the negative aspects of being labeled. As we review the different types of crime, keep in mind that the line between criminality and acceptable behavior, between delinquency and nondelin-quency, is shifting and vague rather than clear and obvious.

Types of Crime

A **crime** is *an act that violates a criminal code enacted by an officially constituted political authority.* The Federal Bureau of Investigation (FBI) publishes an annual document called the Uniform Crime Reports (UCR) that summarizes crime statistics collected by the FBI each month from law enforcement authorities in more than sixteen thousand cities and towns. In the UCR, the FBI distinguishes between what are called Part I, or more serious criminal offenses, and Part II, or less serious offenses (see Table 9.2 on p. 324). Part I offenses are considered more serious because many believe they pose the greatest and most direct threat to personal safety and property. The FBI also publishes the Crime Index, which is the official crime rate typically reported in the media. The Crime Index comprises the number of Part I offenses known to the police for every one hundred thousand people in the United States.

Violent and Property Crime

Violent crimes such as murder, assault, robbery, and rape are clear violations of group norms and the law. There were over twenty-three thousand murders committed in 1994, along with over one million aggravated assaults (Federal Bureau of Investigation, 1995). Murders tend to be situational, in that they often occur as a result of some dispute, frequently trivial, over money or some element of personal demeanor; they are only rarely planned in advance. The victim is usually a relative, friend, or acquaintance of the assailant. In 1994, one-third of all homicides arose from an argument, whereas only 20 percent occurred during the commission of a felony. Assaults are much more likely to involve strangers than are murders. In addi-

TABLE 9.2 Classification of Criminal Offenses by the Federal Bureau of Investigation

Part I Offenses		Part II Offenses
Murder and nonnegligent manslaughter	} violent crimes	Other assaults
Forcible rape		Forgery and counterfeiting
Robbery		Fraud
Aggravated assault		Embezzlement
		Stolen property; buying, receiving, possessing
		Vandalism
Burglary	} property crimes	Weapons; carrying, possessing, and so on
Larceny-theft		Prostitution and commercialized vice
Motor vehicle theft		Sex offenses (except forcible rape and prostitution)
Arson		Drug abuse violations
		Gambling
		Offenses against family and children
		Driving under the influence
		Liquor laws
		Drunkenness
		Disorderly conduct
		Vagrancy
		All other offenses (except traffic)
		Suspicion
		Curfew and loitering law violations
		Runaways

tion to these offenses, there are more than a half million robberies every year, some of which involve personal injury to the victims.

Forcible rape, another violent criminal offense, occurs when an assailant sexually assaults another person. In 1994, there were more than one hundred thousand rapes known to the police in the United States, but many estimates place the actual number much higher because victims may be reluctant to report the crime. According to survey results, rape is the crime that women, especially those under thirty-five years of age, fear the most. Especially in urban areas, this fear affects their daily lives as they avoid going out alone, refuse to enter certain neighborhoods, and install deadbolt locks in their homes (Gordon and Riger, 1989). In addition to the physical danger and degradation experienced by rape victims, the act also has a political element in that it symbolizes and reinforces the power and domination of the assailant over the victim. As one social scientist put it regarding female rape victims: "Rape is to women as lynching was to blacks: the ultimate physical threat" (Brownmiller, 1975: 254). Only in recent decades, because of pressure from women's groups, have states begun to make raping one's wife a crime (Russell, 1990). Yet, not all states have done so. In eight states in 1990, men could not be charged with raping their wives as long as they were living together and the wife had not filed for divorce or protection. Twenty-six other states allowed charges of marital rape but with exemptions. Depending on the state, for example, a man could not be charged with raping his wife unless he had kidnapped her or threatened her with a weapon; some of these states did not permit rape charges if the wife was unable to consent to sex because she was drugged or unconscious. Only sixteen states accorded wives the same protection as other women by treating marital rape like any other rape. So some states still seem to believe that a wife is, to a degree, the "property" of her husband, at least for sexual access, a view that outrages many women and men.

Although people are most alarmed about violent crime, they are much more likely to be victims of property crimes in which the costs are usually economic rather than physical. Three million burglaries, eight million thefts, and one and one-half million auto thefts are reported to the police each year. There are hidden costs of property crime that are frequently underestimated, such as the enormous amount of money that citizens pay in insurance premiums to protect property from burglary, theft, and arson.

Organized Crime

Much of the crime so far described is sporadic and individualized in nature, such as the lone mugger or the small group of juveniles who rob homes. There are, however, forms of criminal activity that benefit from large-scale organization. For example, gambling and prostitution can be highly profitable to those who organize them. Other crimes, such as drug smuggling, involve large overhead costs (front money to purchase the drugs, for instance) that are difficult to fund without some organization. This leads to organized crime or *syndicates:* criminal operations in which several criminal groups coordinate their illegal activities. Although a great deal of criminal activity in the United States is organized to some degree, there is considerable debate about the structure and extent of this kind of crime. One view is illustrated by the image of the Mafia, consisting of a nationwide alliance of families, based on kinship and ethnic solidarity, that coordinate their criminal actions and control large areas of criminal activity. Whether the Mafia or La Cosa Nostra was ever as powerful and consolidated as its portrayal in the media suggests is subject to debate, but it is probably not nearly that large, cohesive, or controlling today (Abadinsky, 1994). Organized crime today also includes many other racially or ethnically based criminal gangs, including Asian organized crime, Colombian drug trafficking organizations, and Hispanic street gangs. Many of these gangs operate in local or regional criminal markets, although some do gain a national reach (Delattre, 1990). In addition to illegal activities, organized crime also develops interests in legitimate business, such as real estate, trucking, and food processing, at least in part as mechanisms to launder the vast sums earned through their illegal activities (Santino, 1988). The amount of money that flows into the coffers of organized crime is difficult to determine because of its hidden nature, but one government estimate placed it at between $26 billion and $67 billion annually (Zawitz et al., 1988). This is probably a conservative estimate.

The social context of organized crime must be kept in perspective. Organized crime does perform functions for society. After all, if there were no demand for the services it provides, it would perish. In addition, organized criminals may well have alliances with government and law enforcement groups in order to operate as freely as they do. What is perhaps even more unsettling is that the benefits of organized crime stretch far beyond the core criminal elements. Some legitimate business interests, political figures, labor leaders, and other respectable citizens undoubtedly share in the profits of organized crime, sometimes unknowingly, thus contributing to its ongoing activities (Fijnaut, 1990).

White-Collar Crime

White-collar crimes are offenses committed by people in positions of respect and responsibility during the ordinary course of their business (Sutherland, 1949; Coleman, 1989). One such offense is antitrust violations, or attempts by businesses to monopolize a segment of the economy. White-collar crime can also take the form of price fixing, in which competitors agree to sell their products for a price higher than they would be able to in a truly competitive market. In the mid-1970s, for example, a price-fixing scheme involving the four major breakfast cereal makers in the United States is estimated to have cost the public some $128 million. Another type of white-collar crime is the fraudulent use of funds. In 1985, E. F. Hutton, one of the nation's largest investment firms, was convicted of an elaborate fraud in which it shuffled millions of dollars among numerous banks and bank accounts, making the funds appear to be in more than one bank account at a time. Hutton collected $8 million in interest on the same money from more than one bank. Finally, white-collar crime can take the form of fraudulent insurance claims, which amount to an $11 billion loss each year.

While people express most concern about violent crimes, crimes such as fraud that do not involve any violence are also very burdensome to society. This man was arrested for defrauding people of $8.5 million by selling them nonexistent precious metals.

As these illustrations should make clear, white-collar crime can be very costly to society. Despite this, the FBI classifies most white-collar crimes as less serious offenses. The public in both the United States and Canada also seems to view most white-collar crimes as less serious than other crimes (Cullen, Link, and Polanzi, 1982; Goff and Nason-Clark, 1989). Occasionally, corporate criminals go to jail: During the past decade, a chairman of LTV Corporation was sentenced to four years for insider stock trading and a Tennessee financier was given twenty years for financial irregularities. Between 1987 and 1990, Michael Milken, Ivan Boesky, and a number of other influential and wealthy stock traders were sent to prison for securities fraud, illegal insider trading in stocks, and various other violations of the securities laws (Stewart, 1991). But critics argue that these tend to be the exception rather than the rule and that the law is very lenient on white-collar criminals, especially the influential ones.

Victimless Crime

Victimless crimes are offenses such as gambling, drug violations, and prostitution, in which the "victims" are willing participants in the crime (Schur, 1965; Stitt, 1988). In 1994, more than one million arrests were made for these crimes (Federal Bureau of Investigation, 1995). There are obviously far more victimless crimes than these statistics suggest because many offenses are never reported to the police. Although no accurate estimates of the total number of victimless crimes are available, it is safe to say that most Americans have participated in such offenses, if only by betting in a football pool or purchasing small quantities of marijuana. When highly desired goods and services are made illegal, a black market is likely to develop to provide them. One of the controversies about having victimless crimes on the books is whether the government ought to be controlling what some people feel are personal or moral issues, such as gambling, drug use, or prostitution. A second controversy is that, because victimless crimes are illegal, people sometimes commit additional crimes, called "secondary crimes," while doing the victimless crime. Thus, an addict may rob to buy drugs, which are very expensive in part because they are illegal. If the victimless crimes were legal, less secondary crime might occur. Finally, victimless crimes are related to public corruption in that bribes are sometimes given to police or other public officials to ignore the illegal flow of drugs, sex, or gambling.

Juvenile Delinquency

A juvenile delinquent is a young person who has committed a crime or has violated a juvenile code. *Youthful offenders* are young people, in most states between the ages of seven and seventeen, who commit offenses for which, if they were adults, they could be tried in a criminal court. *Status offenders* are young people who commit specific acts that are prohibited by the juvenile code, such as running away from home, incorrigibility, truancy, or sexual promiscuity. Status offenses are not considered criminal when committed by an adult.

According to official statistics, juveniles under the age of eighteen are responsible for committing 30 percent of all Part 1, or serious, crimes, although youth between ten and seventeen years of age make up only about 12 percent of our population (Federal Bureau of Investigation, 1995). They are arrested for over 40 percent of the vandalism and auto thefts and 32 percent of the robberies in our society. People in this age category are responsible for 16 percent of all murders, 36 percent of all burglaries, and around 16 percent of rapes and aggravated assaults. And the rate of delinquency may be on the rise. In 1960, there were twenty cases of delinquency before the courts for every one thousand young people. By the 1990s, that number had increased to fifty-one cases for each one thousand juveniles each year (U.S. Bureau of the Census, 1984: 182; U.S. Bureau of the Census, 1994: 213). Most delinquent acts, however, are status offenses.

The Crime Rate in the United States

Between 1970 and 1980, according to the FBI, the rate of Crime Index offenses rose by a startling 49 percent. However, the 1980s were another story: Crime Index offenses actually dropped by 2 percent between 1980 and 1990. Most of this drop was accounted for by the drop in property crimes. During the 1980s, violent crimes rose by 22 percent, but this was less of an increase than the 64 percent rise in the 1970s (see Figure 9.1). So far in the 1990s, the crime rate has stayed level or declined slightly. Yet, the crime rate is still far higher than it was in previous decades. If crimes were evenly

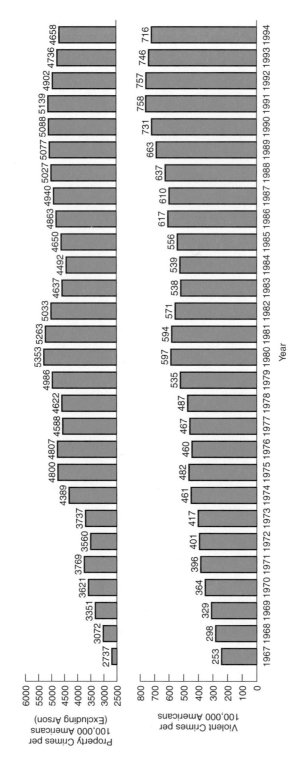

FIGURE 9.1 Rates of Violent and Property Crimes per 100,000 People in the United States, 1967–1994. *Sources:* U.S. Bureau of the Census, *Statistical Abstract of the United States, 1980* (Washington, D.C.: U.S. Government Printing Office, 1980), p. 182; Federal Bureau of Investigation, *Uniform Crime Reports: Crime in the United States, 1994* (Washington, D.C.: U.S. Government Printing Office, 1995), p. 58.

spaced throughout the day, in 1994, there would have been one serious crime about every two seconds of each day and one violent crime approximately every seventeen seconds (Federal Bureau of Investigation, 1995).

Some of these increases, however, need to be placed in perspective. They may in part reflect changes in the likelihood of reporting crimes rather than actual increases in crime. Rape, for example, has traditionally been a vastly underreported crime. With more public discussion of rape in the 1970s and 1980s and strong pressure from feminist groups, both the police and the public have become more sensitive to the problems of rape victims. Many hospitals provide counseling for rape victims, and many states have rules that limit the use of information about a victim's previous sexual activities as evidence in court. These changes have encouraged more women to report rapes, and this undoubtedly accounts for some, although not all, of the increase in reported rapes.

Another reason for caution about UCR crime statistics is that they are based on crimes known to the police, and considerable crime is not brought to the attention of the police. Such unreported crime is not reflected in these statistics, which are conservative indicators of the crime problem in the United States. It is estimated, for example, that only 45 percent of the violent crimes are reported to the police and as few as 28 percent of the thefts (Maguire and Flanagan, 1991: 254). When the reported and unreported crimes are put together, it is clear that the United States has a considerable crime problem and people are concerned about it.

Who Are the Criminals?

Studying crime can be difficult, especially when trying to determine the social characteristics of those who commit crimes. One approach is to look at the official statistics on who has been arrested, but we know that many people who commit crimes are never arrested. Another approach is to use self-reports of people about the crimes they have committed, but many people will be reluctant to admit they have committed crimes. However, combining these and other methods of measuring crime, sociologists have gained a fairly good picture of the characteristics of those who commit crimes.

At the outset, however, it is important to recognize that patterns of criminality are not to be confused with the causes of crime. For example, the fact that nonwhites are disproportionately represented in the commission of violent crimes does not imply that there is something about race itself that causes this kind of criminality (Duster, 1987). What is critical in explaining high levels of crime are the social factors linked to race in our society: economic deprivation, lifestyle differences, educational level, and so forth. In addition, the members of some social groups may be more likely to be arrested and processed by criminal justice agencies, thus injecting an element of bias into crime statistics. For example, some crimes such as embezzlement are "hidden crimes" in the sense that they are less likely than homicide or assault to come to the attention of the police. When an embezzler is discovered, the victim-employer may not call in the police for fear that it will hurt the business's reputation. Homicide, on the other hand, is virtually always brought to the attention of the police by someone. So people committing hidden crimes are less likely to be arrested than people committing more noticeable crimes. If members of one group are more likely to commit hidden crimes and members of another group commit more open crimes, then the latter group will get arrested more often. So especially when using arrest records, one group will appear to be more criminal than another because of its differential treatment by the police and the courts. With these thoughts in mind, we will look at four social characteristics that are closely associated with crime.

Gender

Gender is the single social factor that is most predictive of patterns of criminal behavior. Males have higher rates of involvement than females in practically all forms of criminality. In 1994, 80 percent of all people arrested for a crime were males—five times as many males as females. There are approximately four boys referred to the juvenile court for every girl so referred. Even crimes that do not involve aggressiveness or violence—larceny, fraud, embezzlement—are still more likely to be committed by males (see Table 9.3). The only offenses that females are more likely to be involved in are prostitution and being runaways. Although it is possible that women receive preferential treatment in the criminal justice system or that women are more likely to engage in "hidden" crimes, there is evidence against this (Bishop and Frazier, 1984; Steffensmeier and Allan, 1988). Males are disproportionately represented in most forms of criminal activity even if such sex preferentials occur. The male propensity toward crime is probably in part a function of the male's

These 3 young men are accused of killing an elderly man. Age and gender are closely associated with involvement in crime.

TABLE 9.3 Total Arrests, Distribution by Sex and Race, 1994

Offense Charged	Percent male	Percent female	Percent White	Percent Black
TOTAL	**80.0**	**20.0**	**66.6**	**31.3**
Murder and nonnegligent manslaughter	90.1	9.9	41.7	56.4
Forcible rape	98.9	1.1	56.1	41.7
Robbery	90.8	9.2	37.5	60.8
Aggravated assault	83.4	16.6	58.9	39.2
Burglary	89.6	10.4	67.4	30.6
Larceny-theft	66.7	33.3	64.5	33.0
Motor vehicle theft	87.6	12.4	57.3	40.1
Arson	85.3	14.7	75.1	23.0
Violent crime[a]	86.0	14.0	53.4	44.7
Property crime[b]	73.1	26.9	64.4	33.1
Crime Index total[c]	76.6	23.4	61.4	36.3
Other assaults	81.3	18.7	63.2	34.6
Forgery and counterfeiting	64.3	35.7	63.6	34.4
Fraud	60.6	39.4	62.2	36.5
Embezzlement	58.8	41.2	65.5	32.9
Stolen property; buying, receiving, possessing	86.6	13.4	57.7	40.5
Vandalism	87.2	12.8	74.7	22.8
Weapons; carrying, possessing, etc.	91.9	8.1	57.2	41.1
Prostitution and commercialized vice	38.6	61.4	62.1	35.6
Sex offenses (except forcible rape and prostitution)	91.6	8.4	76.2	21.6
Drug abuse violations	83.5	16.5	60.6	38.4
Gambling	85.2	14.8	49.5	45.7
Offenses against family and children	79.2	20.8	63.8	33.0
Driving under the influence	85.8	14.2	87.7	10.1
Liquor laws	80.4	19.6	83.3	13.6
Drunkenness	88.4	11.6	80.6	16.8
Disorderly conduct	79.1	20.9	65.0	33.2
Vagrancy	79.2	20.8	57.4	40.3
All other offenses (except traffic)	82.1	17.9	62.2	35.9
Suspicion	84.3	15.7	49.6	49.6
Curfew and loitering law violation	71.2	28.8	75.9	21.0
Runaways	43.1	56.9	77.3	19.1

[a]Violent crimes are offenses of murder, forcible rape, robbery, and aggravated assault.
[b]Property crimes are offenses of burglary, larceny-theft, motor-vehicle theft, and arson.
[c]Includes arson.
Source: Federal Bureau of Investigation, *Uniform Crime Reports: Crime in the United States, 1994* (Washington, D.C.: U.S. Government Printing Office, 1995), pp. 234–235.

role in which daring, action, and aggressiveness are viewed positively and sometimes take a criminal form. However, with some crimes, such as fraud, forgery, and auto theft, crime rates are growing much faster among women than men.

Age

Table 9.4 shows the percentage of all people arrested in 1994 who were younger than age twenty-five. To put the numbers in this table in perspective, people younger than twenty-five constitute only 36 percent of the U.S. population but 55 percent of the arrests for Crime Index offenses. Clearly, crime is a "young person's game." There are a number of possible explanations for this. It may be that young people are more likely to be arrested for committing a crime than are older people. Or it may be that older people are actually less likely to engage in criminal activity (Rowe and Tittle, 1977). Young people's higher rates of criminal conduct may be due to opportunity and physical capability: Young people are more likely to commit visible offenses such as property crimes and robbery than "hidden" crimes such as embezzlement, price fixing, or corporate malfeasance. In addition, young people have the strength, agility, and stamina to commit crimes such as burglary and robbery.

Important social policy considerations flow from the link between age and crime. Crime rates go up when teens and young adults, who commit lots of crimes, grow as a proportion of the population. This is what happened in the 1960s and 1970s: People fourteen to twenty-four years grew from 15 percent of the U.S. populace to 20 percent in 1980, and the crime rate doubled during that period (see Figure 9.1). Since 1980, the proportion of people in that same age group has dropped to 14 percent. So, as young people constitute a smaller proportion of the populace, the crime rate should go down, or at least go up less rapidly.

And, as we have seen, it appears to have done that during the 1980s and 1990s.

Socioeconomic Status

The relationship between socioeconomic status (SES) and criminality has been one of the more controversial issues in modern-day criminology. Some research has shown that lower-class people have higher rates of crime commission than do middle-class and more affluent people; other research concludes that little evidence exists for a consistent or strong association between SES and rates of crime commission (Tittle, Villemez, and Smith, 1978; Elliott and Huizinga, 1983; Tittle and Meier, 1990). So, the relationship between social class and crime is probably more complicated than a straightforward association. Official crime statistics show that lower-class people are more likely to commit crimes, but research shows clearly that lower-class people are also more likely to be arrested. Therefore, it may be that arrest is more common among the lower class rather than that actual rates of crime commission are higher. In addition, lower-class people are more likely to commit highly visible and violent crimes, such as homicide or assault, that are more frequently reported to the police (Huff-Corzine, Corzine, and Moore, 1991), whereas some hidden crimes, such as embezzlement and fraud, may be more common among the middle class. Other hidden crimes, such as vice offenses, may be as common in the lower class as in the middle class. Therefore, there may be some social class variation in the types of crimes committed but not in the overall numbers of criminal acts committed. At this point, a reasonable conclusion is that the the relationship between SES and crime is weak and complicated.

Race

As we indicated at the outset of this discussion, official statistics show that African Americans are disproportionately involved in crime (Tonry,

TABLE 9.4 Percentage of All Arrests Accounted for by Persons Under 18, 21, and 25 Years of Age, 1994

Offense Charged	Percentage of total		
	Under 18	Under 21	Under 25
TOTAL	18.6	31.1	45.3
Murder and nonnegligent manslaughter	16.8	38.7	57.8
Forcible rape	16.3	28.2	42.1
Robbery	32.0	49.8	64.3
Aggravated assault	15.6	26.9	41.5
Burglary	36.2	51.1	62.8
Larceny-theft	33.4	45.6	56.1
Motor vehicle theft	44.1	60.3	71.9
Arson	55.3	63.4	69.7
Violent crime[a]	19.4	32.5	47.2
Property crime[b]	35.1	48.2	59.0
Crime Index total[c]	30.9	44.0	55.8
Other assaults	17.3	26.8	41.1
Forgery and counterfeiting	7.5	21.5	39.2
Fraud	5.6	15.9	33.2
Embezzlement	6.9	22.4	40.8
Stolen property; buying, receiving, possessing	26.8	44.8	59.8
Vandalism	47.0	59.9	70.5
Weapons; carrying, possessing, etc.	24.5	41.8	58.9
Prostitution and commercialized vice	1.2	7.5	22.5
Sex offenses (except forcible rape and prostitution)	17.6	25.5	36.2
Drug abuse violations	11.7	26.9	43.2
Gambling	9.4	19.5	30.1
Offenses against family and children	4.6	11.8	25.2
Driving under the influence	1.0	7.0	22.6
Liquor laws	22.2	61.7	71.9
Drunkenness	2.6	9.9	23.2
Disorderly conduct	22.8	36.6	52.2
Vagrancy	17.1	29.3	40.6
All other offenses (except traffic)	11.3	23.9	40.1
Suspicion	15.0	25.1	38.7
Curfew and loitering law violations	100.0	100.0	100.0
Runaways	100.0	100.0	100.0

[a]Violent crimes are offenses of murder, forcible rape, robbery, and aggravated assault.
[b]Property crimes are offenses of burglary, larceny-theft, motor vehicle theft, and arson.
[c]Includes arson.
Source: Federal Bureau of Investigation, *Uniform Crime Reports: Crime in the United States, 1994* (Washington, D.C.: U.S. Government Printing Office, 1995), p. 233.

1995). They make up about 12 percent of our population but account for 31 percent of all arrests for all crimes. Table 9.3 indicates that African Americans are particularly likely to be arrested for robbery, murder, and gambling. Only in the cases of liquor law violations and driving under the influence of alcohol are their arrest rates proportionate to or lower than what would be expected given their numbers in the populace.

Detailed analysis through victimization surveys indicates that black–white differences in criminal behavior are real, rather than merely reflecting criminal justice system biases such as the likelihood of arrest (Hindelang, 1981). Still, as was pointed out earlier, this does not imply that race is a causal variable. The social environment of African Americans is primarily responsible for crime rate differences (Duster, 1987). In addition, African Americans are lower in socioeconomic standing, so they are less likely to be involved with "hidden" and "respectable" crimes, which we have seen result in greater economic losses than all other types of criminality combined. Because we are aware of black–white differences in criminal behavior, African Americans may be more closely watched than whites by law enforcement agencies, which would lead to higher arrest rates.

Who Are the Victims?

We sometimes focus so closely on people who commit crimes that we forget the victims of their actions. In 1992, ninety-one out of every one thousand Americans were crime victims (U.S. Bureau of the Census, 1994: 203). But race and sex play a part in this, with males and blacks considerably more likely to be victims. One hundred ten of every one thousand black males, for example, were crime victims. Homicide rates, especially, show the gruesome consequences of race. Black males are eight times more likely to be the victims of homicide than are white males,

and black females are five times more likely to be victims than white females. For some crimes, such as robbery and larceny, poorer households were more likely to be victimized, whereas the affluent were more likely to experience auto theft.

One very important correlate of victimization is its relationship to participation in criminal and delinquent activities: Offenders are often the victims of other criminals (Fagan, Piper, and Cheng, 1987).

The Criminal Justice System

The criminal justice system includes the police, the courts, the prisons, and other institutions whose task is to control crime in society. There is much debate over how effectively it achieves its goals in the United States. Critics argue that the system operates in a fashion that substantially departs from the fairness and impartiality that is demanded by the Constitution and our cultural heritage. A few detractors even claim that the criminal justice system actually contributes to the crime problem in the United States. This discussion will focus on certain elements of the system that relate to these problems.

The Police

When a crime is committed, the first and perhaps most crucial link that most citizens have with the criminal justice system is the police. In the United States, police have a great deal of discretion in dealing with offenses that come to their attention. Sometimes, the police may even help to negotiate some type of informal agreement between the complainant and the accused, a procedure that is well short of actually arresting and booking a suspect. This may appear surprising to some, because it is often assumed that police take pride in "busting" all crimes. In fact, there are so many minor violations of the law occurring on a daily basis that police agencies would be helplessly swamped if they tried to pursue every one of them. One investigation found that in New York City there was only one arrest for every five felonies known to the police. In some of these cases, the police undoubtedly chose not to pursue the case, possibly realizing that they had little chance of solving it (Shipp, 1981). However, the exercise of discretion by the police is not influenced solely by judgments of the seriousness or solvability of the crime, as one might expect, but also by subtle social factors. For example, a study of police response to domestic disputes found that police were far more likely to arrest someone when the dispute occurred in a poor neighborhood (Smith and Klein, 1984). In middle-class neighborhoods, police put in more effort to find solutions to the dispute short of arrest. Thus, social factors influence the discretionary behavior of police in ways that affect the crime statistics discussed earlier.

The police in our society are confronted with a confusing dilemma (Kupelian, 1992). On the one hand, they are under constant pressure to combat crime, but they are also expected to protect the constitutional and personal rights of suspects and other citizens. The public demands that order be maintained but also creates procedural laws, such as due process, that may make it more difficult for the police to achieve that order. Police often attempt to keep the peace by ignoring or circumventing the procedural rules that are designed to govern their activities. As a result of this dilemma, the police tend to feel isolated and frustrated. This can generate feelings of alienation and separation from other groups in society. The danger is that a "we" versus "they" mentality might emerge—the "they" including all citizens, not just the criminals. To the extent that this happens, it may interfere with the ability of police to do their jobs and make them less sensitive to the needs and rights of suspects, victims, and the citizenry.

The Courts

As illustrated in Figure 9.2, there is substantial case attrition following arrest. Of one hundred

FIGURE 9.2 Typical Disposition of 100 Urban Felony Arrests. *Source:* Adapted from Barbara Boland and Ronald Stones, *The Prosecution of Felony Arrests* (Washington, D.C.: Department of Justice, Bureau of Justice Statistics, 1986).

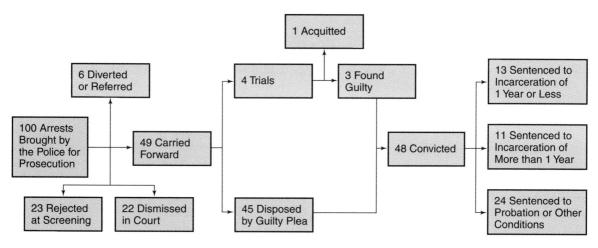

typical felony arrests brought by the police to the prosecutor, fewer than half result in conviction. After arrests are made by the police, the court system utilizes an adversary model in evaluating guilt or innocence. The prosecution is pitted against the defense, and a judge or jury is utilized to settle the "dispute" (Sykes and Cullen, 1992). The office of prosecuting attorney is perhaps the most powerful position in the criminal justice system. Prosecuting attorneys have the power to determine which cases will be pursued and with how much vigor. Most importantly, prosecuting attorneys are political figures—they are either elected or appointed to office—and have a keen awareness of how they achieved their positions in the first place. To keep influential groups or their elective constituencies happy, prosecutors exert enormous pressure on the police. One criterion used to evaluate police departments is the number of arrests that eventually result in convictions. Should a prosecuting attorney see fit not to seek convictions for a particular type of offense, then the police will spend little time dealing with cases of this type. By like token, if a prosecutor shows favoritism for a given offense, then police will regard these as "good busts" and alter their law enforcement patterns accordingly. Once again, discretionary elements enter into the battle against crime. As we have seen, it is usually more politically profitable to attack "street" crime committed by the less fortunate because this is the crime that frightens the middle class and affluent groups who put prosecuting attorneys in office.

Defense attorneys represent the other part of the court system. Ideally, counsel for the defense is responsible for representing their client's interests before the criminal justice system. In reality, there are considerable pressures on defense attorneys to place as much emphasis on "negotiating justice" as on ensuring due process for their clients. Defense attorneys often have close ties with judges, prosecuting attorneys, police, and others working in the criminal justice system. They work daily with these people on many cases and need their cooperation and good will to do their work. In fact, defense attorneys are as much a part of the legal system as they are the adversarial representatives of their client. Because of this, they come under considerable pressure to help the system run smoothly, which may mean encouraging their clients to accept a guilty plea or a plea bargain. If they do not appear cooperative, the prosecutor's office has many resources that can be used or assistance that can be withheld that could make the defense attorney's job more difficult. So, negotiation between the prosecutor and the defense counsel becomes the most sensible alternative open to many of those charged with a crime. Court-appointed defense attorneys make sure that even poor defendants have representation in court, but the defendant's best interests may not be served when the overriding pressure on both prosecution and defense is to dispose of cases on a crowded court docket quickly and smoothly.

A third important ingredient in the court system is *bail:* money or credit deposited with the court to ensure that people released while awaiting trial will ultimately appear for trial. Bail is based on a core tenet of the U.S. legal system: A person is considered innocent until proven guilty in a court of law. Given the presumption of innocence, a person should not be punished by a jail term prior to trial. One major problem with bail is that it is obviously prejudicial to the disadvantaged who often cannot afford to post bail. Failure to "make bail" represents a form of punishment prior to conviction, which appears to violate the "presumption of innocence." Another major problem with bail is that it can be used as a means of "preventive detention" rather than merely to ensure appearance for trial. In fact, the Comprehensive Crime Control Act of 1984 allows judges in federal courts to consider issues other than likelihood of court appearance in setting bail. Federal judges can now consider the likelihood that a person will commit another offense while out on bail in deciding whether to set bail and how high to set it. Although this applies only in federal courts, it may serve as a model for state criminal justice codes. It is a revolutionary change in our court system in that it allows the court to incarcerate someone for a crime he or she has not yet committed but a judge feels reasonably sure will be committed if the person is set free.

Another element of the court system is plea bargaining: an informal agreement among the defense, the prosecution, and the court that is not legally binding. Plea bargaining is involved in over 90 percent of all convictions for criminal offenses. In exchange for a plea of guilty, suspects may receive special considerations from the court, such as the dropping of some charges, a more lenient sentence, or the reduction of a charge to a lesser offense. This accounts for further attrition in the criminal justice system. As Figure 9.2 shows, of the forty-nine felony arrests carried forward, forty-five (over 90 percent) were disposed of through a guilty plea, and a large percentage of these cases involved the reduction of the original charge to a misdemeanor. Approximately 4 percent of all felony arrests result in a trial verdict of guilty or innocent. In another type of plea bargain, a suspect who pleads guilty to multiple charges may be sentenced to serve them concurrently. Plea bargaining has been criticized because it involves an "informal dispensing of justice," as issues such as local politics, community norms, and the perceived needs of criminal justice bureaucracies take precedence over established judicial principles such as due process of law.

A final element of the court system is the sentencing of convicted criminals, and there appears to be considerable inequity here also. With homicides, for example, one would expect the same crime to receive the same punishment. But there is much disparity. A person is far more likely to receive the death penalty for homicide—in some states, more than eight times as likely—when the victim is white rather than black (Joyce, 1984; Heilbrun, Foster, and Golden, 1989). Studies of sentencing in a number of states document that African Americans and Hispanics are given heavier sentences by judges than are whites and serve more time in prison than do whites. This is true even when comparing those who have committed comparable felonies and have similar criminal records (Petersilia, 1985). All this discriminatory treatment may reflect unconscious racism on the part of prosecutors, judges, and juries, or it may be that mostly white jurors tend to identify with white victims and deal more harshly with those who victimize whites. In either case, it leads many people to question whether justice is fairly and impartially dealt by the courts.

The Prisons

The United States currently imprisons a far larger proportion of its population than ever before, with the rate of incarceration having more than tripled since 1975 (see Figure 9.3). For much of this century, the rate of incarceration was fairly steady, fluctuating around one-third of what it is now, even in the difficult economic times of the Great Depression of the 1930s. Since 1975, the rate has increased steadily and disturbingly. Even more distressing is that the United States now incarcerates more of its citizens than almost any other nation in the world, and far more than any of the other modern industrial nations (Selke, 1993). What is happening here? It is partly due to a rising crime rate, of course. However, another contributing factor was the emergence of crack cocaine in the 1980s and the explosion in drug arrests. More people were taking drugs, and the drug use led to more secondary crimes to support people's drug habits. In addition, the federal government put millions of dollars into the war on drugs, which encouraged the police and other officials to aggressively pursue drug users. Yet another factor contributing to the

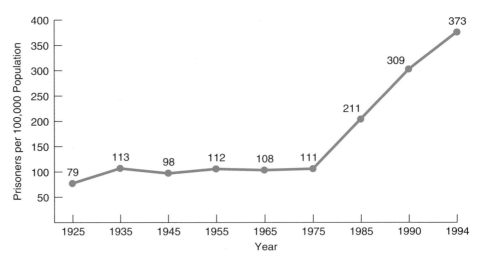

FIGURE 9.3 Sentenced Prisoners in State and Federal Institutions, 1925–1994.
Sources: Prisons 1925–1981 (Washington, D.C.: Department of Justice, Bureau of Justice Statistics, 1982); "Prisoners in 1993," *Bureau of Justice Statistics Bulletin* (Washington, D.C.: U.S. Government Printing Office, 1994).

explosion in incarceration is a growing frustration with and anger against crime felt by many people, which in turn has made "getting tough on crime" very popular. A recent survey, for example, found that three-quarters of all Americans feel that the courts do not deal harshly enough with criminals (Cohn, Barkan, and Halteman, 1991). People in the United States have become very receptive to sending more people to prison for longer periods of time as a way of controlling crime. This has produced a crisis of overcrowding in many of our prisons unheard of in our history.

This overcrowding is dangerous because it increases unrest among inmates and produces a climate in which violence is more likely. Riots, escapes, and hostage taking become more of a problem. Prison overcrowding also makes it more difficult for correctional officers and prison administrators to manage the prisons. All this makes prisons more costly to run. In addition, many question whether it is moral to imprison people in circumstances that are cruel

and unusual; that may promote mental disorders; where degrading sexual assaults are common; where stabbings, beatings, extortion, and murder are routine and rampant.

Prison crowding also makes it far more difficult for prisons to achieve one of their major goals: the rehabilitation of the inmates. So far, prisons have failed miserably at rehabilitation. **Recidivism** refers to *the repeat of an offense after having been convicted of a crime,* and the rate of recidivism is very high. In 1991, eighty percent of all inmates in state prisons were recidivists—they had been convicted and sentenced to either prison or probation for a crime before the one currently sending them to prison (U.S. Bureau of the Census, 1994: 216). Two-thirds of people released from prison are rearrested for a felony within three years. Critics of the criminal justice system point to these figures as evidence that prisons have failed in their efforts to rehabilitate. One controversial development that might affect these problems is discussed in the Policy Issues insert in this chapter.

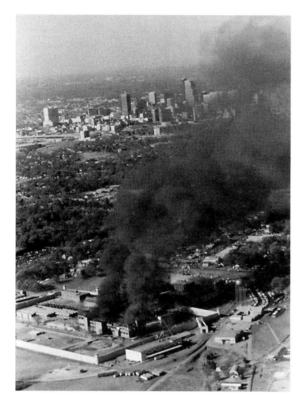

A federal prison in Atlanta burns out of control after the inmates siezed control of much of the prison. Overcrowding in prisons contributes to inmate unrest, which can take the form of violence, riots, and escape attempts.

Critique of the U.S. Criminal Justice System

The criminal justice system itself is viewed by some as a culprit in creating crime. Some critics have gone so far as to label the criminal justice system a "nonsystem." Quoting from the National Commission on the Causes and Prevention of Violence:

> A system implies some unity of purpose, an organized interrelationship among component parts. In the typical American city, and state, and under federal jurisdiction as well, no such relationship exists. There is, instead, a reasonably well-defined criminal process. . . . The inefficiency, fallout, and failure of purpose during this process is notorious. (As quoted in Cole, 1989: 144)

According to Jeffrey Reiman, a professor of criminal justice:

> The goal of our criminal justice system is not to reduce crime or to achieve justice but to project to the American public a visible image of the threat of crime. To do this, it must maintain the existence of a sizable population of criminals. To do this, it must fail in the struggle to reduce crime. (Reiman, 1996: 1)

Reiman employed a novel approach in constructing this view of the criminal justice system. He asked a group of graduate students to design a correctional system "that would maintain and encourage the existence of a stable and visible 'class' of criminals" rather than reduce and prevent crime (Reiman, 1979: 2–4). This is the system the students sketched:

1. It would contain many irrational laws, such as those governing gambling and other victimless crimes, that make many people "criminals" for behaviors that they regard as normal and that increase their need to engage in secondary crime, such as stealing, in order to pay gambling debts.

2. It would give police, prosecutors, and judges broad discretion to decide who gets arrested, charged, and sentenced to prison. In this way, almost everyone who ended up in prison would be aware of others who committed the same kind of offense and did not become incarcerated, creating a sense of bitterness and hostility toward the unjust nature of the system.

3. It would make the prison experience painful and demeaning, so that whatever deterrent effect imprisonment may have is counteracted by the lack of privacy and control over one's actions that could enhance self-control.

4. Prisoners would not be trained in marketable skills nor provided with jobs upon release. Further, their prison records would follow them wherever they go, making a return to noncriminal behavior more difficult.

Privately Operated Correctional Facilities: Who Is Accountable for the Welfare of the Incarcerated?

Prisons and jails in the United States have historically been under the jurisdiction of federal, state, or local governments. Recently, however, there has been a trend toward contracting with privately owned, profit-oriented companies to provide these services. This move began during the 1980s, when government-run facilities were fast becoming overcrowded and some jurisdictions turned to the private sector to help them out. By the early 1990s, forty-four private corrections facilities were being operated by fourteen different companies with a total of thirteen thousand four hundred inmates (Shichor, 1995). Some were regular jails and prisons, whereas others were detention centers for the Immigration and Naturalization Service. There are also more than two thousand private juvenile detention facilities.

The Corrections Corporation of America (CCA) owns sixteen of these facilities, located in Texas, Tennessee, and North Carolina (Ramirez, 1994). The CCA is responsible for supervising more prisoners than any other single private concern and has become both a target of criticism and a model for other corporate operators. CCA and others who run jails claim that they can do the job more cheaply than the government does. The federal government, for example, spends $26 per day to keep each resident in an immigration detention center. CCA charges the government only $23 per day to house the same residents. In a juvenile detention center it runs, CCA charges the state only one-half of what it costs to keep each juvenile in a state training school. Proponents of privately owned prisons also claim that they are free of political interference and patronage that make public prisons costly and inefficient. They also point to the high recidivism rate to show that public prisons have not done such a hot job at corrections work.

Many experts in the field, however, are skeptical of whether privately owned detention facilities should be used at all (Shichor, 1995). One general concern is whether it is ethical to allow a private company to oversee the removal of the rights and freedoms of a human being. Because it is only the legally constituted government that can take away a person's freedom, some question the constitutionality of giving private individuals the state's authority to deprive people of their freedom. Supporters of the privatization of prisons recognize that these issues are important but also argue that the state does not abdicate any authority when it contracts with private corporations to run prisons. It is still the state that *imposes* punishment by determining who will go to prison and for how long. The state then delegates to a private corporation the power to *administer* the punishment. Yet, opponents of privatization argue that the correctional staff, even a private one, performs a quasi-judicial function when it disciplines inmates, metes out punishment, and advises parole

Reiman concludes that, in short, the system that the students described is a portrait of the criminal justice system in the United States today. The system creates an image that crime is a threat from the poor so that discontent and hostility are directed away from those in positions of power and toward the poor. A large convict population gives the appearance that crime is being controlled while at the same time the prison system increases recidivism.

Future Prospects

The question of how to deal with the crime and delinquency problem in the United States is highly controversial. However, our analysis of boards. Some of this disciplining and punishing is a part of the day-to-day operation of the prison and is neither mandated by nor reviewed by the courts or other state authorities. The director of the National Association of Criminal Justice Planners commented: "We're talking about taking away people's liberties, and I have real questions about the propriety of anyone but the state doing that" (Tolchin, 1985).

A more practical issue in regard to the privatization of prisons is whether a profit-oriented institution might not be motivated to enhance its profit margin to the detriment of the inmates. The fear is that it will be the residents and their rehabilitation that will suffer to achieve lower costs and greater profits. Recall the discussion of capitalism, competition, and free enterprise in Chapter 2. Unlike other realms in which private enterprise operates, however, the recipients of services in this realm—the inmates—do not have the freedom to "shop around" for the best proprietors of correctional services. What does the research show about private prisons? Research on juvenile facilities concludes that the private outfits pay their correctional officers less than public ones, provide more meager training and fringe benefits, and have fewer services, such as psychological counseling, for residents. Some also tend to reduce the quality and number of staff and programs as a way to maintain profits (Shichor and Bartollas, 1990). On the other

hand, a recent review of the research comparing private correctional facilities with public ones concludes that, overall, the former exhibit "somewhat lower costs and higher quality of services" (Shichor, 1995: 231). However, these conclusions are highly qualified because relatively few research evaluations have been done and because the research is often done on juvenile facilities and community programs which probably cannot be generalized to adult mainline prisons. The final conclusion is that we do not yet have enough research from which to make clear-cut recommendations about when private prisons are beneficial in comparison to public ones.

Another practical issue regarding private prisons is accountability: Who will take responsibility for the welfare of the incarcerated? When inmates in private prisons have filed formal grievances about conditions they believed were dangerous or unhealthy, the private contractors have tended to refer the complaints to the government agency under whose authority it incarcerates people. The government agency, in turn, tends to refer the problem back to the private contractor who has day-to-day responsibility for taking care of the inmates. Despite these and other problems, the pressure to privatize prisons is strong as states strive to save money in times of financial difficulties.

the sociological perspectives along with our assessment of various problems related to crime point to a number of promising reforms that deserve consideration.

Social Reform

Given the role of poverty and economic inequities in fostering crime, it is plausible that reducing poverty and the economic disparity between the affluent and the poor would help reduce some forms of crime and delinquency. Especially important along these lines would be to provide equal educational and occupational opportunities for all Americans. Given Elliott Currie's analysis of crime in Japan discussed earlier, it may be possible to reduce poverty and economic disparity through programs that

INTERNATIONAL PERSPECTIVES
Crime in Other Societies

It is sad to admit, but the United States is a disturbingly crime-ridden society when compared to most societies around the world. This chapter showed that the United States puts more of its citizens in prison for committing crimes than does any other nation. This high rate of incarceration reflects the fact that crime rates in the United States are very high. If we compare the United States with Japan, another affluent, industrial nation, the United States comes off poorly (Currie, 1985; Thornton and Endo, 1992). Overall, there are twelve hundred crimes committed for each one hundred thousand persons in Japan; this compares to almost five thousand crimes per one hundred thousand population in the United States! The United States has eighteen times more rapes, ten times more homicides, six times more burglaries, and nine times more drug-related offenses.

What accounts for this dramatic contrast? To answer this question, we need to look at how Japanese culture and society differ from our own. One widely recognized difference is that Japanese society places much more emphasis on the importance of group and family while the United States emphasizes individualism and personal autonomy. Individual Japanese feel a strong obligation to their family and society, and families feel a strong

sense of responsibility for the behavior of their members. Each family member bears a share of the responsibility for preserving the reputation of the family and avoiding bringing disgrace to it by doing something that might be socially disapproved, like committing a crime. This means that informal mechanisms of social control, such as threatened exclusion from the group, can more effectively control crime in Japan than in the United States.

Another difference is that Japanese culture instills a strong sense of respect for laws, rules, and customs. Respect for and obedience to the law is seen as part of a citizen's social obligation, probably deriving from Confucian teachings about uprightness, duty, and obligation. In Japan, people obey the law because of this obligation, not just out of fear of authority or punishment; in the United States, people are more inclined toward cynical violation of the law if they feel they can get away with it.

A third difference between Japan and the United States is that Japan is a much more racially and culturally homogeneous society where there is considerable consensus regarding desirable values and appropriate behaviors. This removes one important source of misunderstanding, tension, and

encourage fuller employment—government and private-sector programs to create new jobs and to provide job training to those without adequate job skills (Currie, 1985). In addition, the jobs people get must pay a living wage so that people can support their families. Furthermore, sociologist Mark Colvin (1991) recommends that we fight crime by investing in the institutions that prepare people for productive roles in society: families and schools.

Many of these proposals have been discussed in other chapters in this book, such as job-training programs, Head Start, and so on. It is failures in educational institutions and families that have contributed to the inability of many young people to find and make use of legitimate avenues to opportunity. These calls for social reform are an attempt to attack the social and structural conditions that have created much, although not all, of our crime problem. The conflict that exists in the United States. Without these social fault lines, Japan offers its citizens a much more cohesive and supportive neighborhood and community environment.

A final difference is that Japanese society is much more *supportive* of individuals and their families than is the United States. Through economic and social policies, Japan strives toward full employment of its workers and tries to create a stable connection of workers to the workplace. Consequently, the income distribution in Japan is much more equitable than in the United States, and no severely deprived and permanently disadvantaged underclass exists. These supportive policies create the foundation for the emergence of strong and stable family and neighborhood ties, which in turn exert strong social controls over misbehavior. In addition, Japan, along with many western European industrial nations, has social policies that cushion the disruptions and hardships that can accompany the loss of work. These nations, for example, give more generous unemployment benefits and distribute them to more unemployed workers than does the United States. Because of this, less disruption of family and communal roles accompanies unemployment. This is important because it is not just economic circumstances that motivate crime; the

destruction of family and communal supports that can accompany unemployment also reduces controls over misbehavior. As Elliott Currie (1985: 130) puts it: "Social policies that strip away those cushions—or that disrupt the stability and effectiveness of communal networks of support and care—are likely to aggravate the impact of economic insecurity on crime."

When considered separately, each of these elements of Japanese culture may make only a small contribution to the low Japanese crime rate; however, in combination they advance us a good way toward understanding the yawning gulf between crime in the United States and crime in Japan. They also emphasize the sociological perspective on crime—namely, that crime emerges from particular social and cultural conditions and that crime can be reduced by changing those conditions. Some of the elements of Japanese social structure that have insulated them from high crime in the past seem to be changing, and Japan may confront rising crime in the future. However, the contrast between the two cultures provides us with significant insight into the link between social structure and crime.

International Perspectives insert explores in more depth the differences between Japan and the United States in this regard.

Legalization of Some Crimes

Some have proposed that we should legalize many of the victimless crimes, such as gambling, prostitution, and some drug violations. This would reduce the secondary crime associated

with these offenses and free the police and courts to attack more serious and dangerous crimes. This measure would also remove these activities from the black market and the hands of organized crime and place them in the public realm, where they can be regulated and taxed. Legalizing these "crimes without victims" does not imply societal support of such activities; they might still be considered by many as serious social problems. Rather, legalization involves the recognition that the criminal justice system should deal with controlling behavior that threatens public order, not with regulating people's morality. Legalization is also an admission that the criminal justice system has been unable to control these crimes effectively.

Better Law Enforcement

Arresting people who commit crimes reduces the likelihood that those individuals will commit crimes in the future (Smith and Gartin, 1989). Society should provide the resources that enable the police to do their job. In fact, we have made considerable strides in the past few decades toward a better-equipped, better-trained, and more highly educated police force in the United States. An increasing number of police departments, for example, require their officers to have a college education. Whether this makes them more effective at controlling crime we will only know through future research (U.S. Department of Justice, 1992).

A fairly recent program to make the police more effective has been introduced into a number of police departments. It is based on research showing that a large number of crimes such as robberies and burglaries are committed by a rather small number of people. The police should have a much greater impact on crime by focusing their resources on catching, convicting, and imprisoning these "career" criminals than by imprisoning someone who only occasionally commits a crime (Swickard, 1986). This effort has been enhanced through the use of computer technology to coordinate the investigations of various precincts and departments. All too often in the past, police in different precincts were looking for the same suspect without realizing it and sharing information. With respect to juvenile delinquency, recent investigations have emphasized that our society should focus on the termination of delinquent careers at their

commencement rather than "going easy" on delinquency (Conrad, 1985).

Judicial Reform

There are a number of reforms that might be considered for our judicial system to enhance its effectiveness in controlling crime (U.S. Department of Justice, 1992).

1. Provide swift, certain, and fair punishment. Swift and certain punishment is more effective in controlling crime than are overly long and counterproductive prison sentences. There is little evidence that severity of punishment reduces crime or the rate of recidivism.

2. Provide equitable punishment, whether the crime occurs on a slum street or in a corporate boardroom. Disparities in punishment resulting from the racial, sexual, or socioeconomic characteristics of the offender should be carefully monitored and controlled. This means that society needs to make a serious effort to control white-collar crime, which we have been rather lax about until now. Disparities in punishment lead those who are punished to view the criminal justice system with a jaundiced eye. As more than one inmate has been heard to say: "I'm not in prison because I committed a crime; I'm here because I'm poor (or black)."

3. Narrow the discretionary options of police officers, prosecutors, and judges and develop procedures to hold them accountable to the public for the fairness and reasonableness of their decisions and actions.

4. Provide all criminal defendants with truly equal legal counsel to reduce the inequities in convictions and sentences.

5. Establish fixed, or determinate, sentences and eliminate parole. The Comprehensive Crime Control Act of 1984 did this for federal crimes beginning in 1986. The rationale for this is that parolees often commit crimes. A study by the Bureau of Justice Statistics found that 28 percent of those who entered state prisons in 1979 would still be serving time in the mid-1980s for their previous offense if they had served the maximum number of years to which they were sentenced (Werner, 1985). Opponents of determinate sentencing argue that it removes the flexibility that the criminal justice system now has to reward inmates who have demonstrated good behavior and who appear to be rehabilitated.

Although all these reforms are valuable to consider, one must not become entranced by the simple notion that throwing more people in prison for a longer period of time will significantly reduce the crime problem. Many criminologists feel that such a prison-based criminal justice policy is a costly delusion (Selke, 1993; Irwin and Austin, 1994). There is little evidence that fear of prison alone will substantially reduce the crime rate. Professor of law and criminology Norval Morris says that people "have an exaggerated belief in the efficacy of imprisonment" to control crime (quoted in Butterfield, 1992: 4). He points out that, although the prison population has more than doubled since 1980, the crime rate has not gone down (see Figure 9.1). Furthermore, throwing more people in prison or giving them longer sentences is enormously expensive. Ten years ago, criminologist Elliott Currie (1985) estimated that tripling the current prison population would cost $70 billion immediately and $14 billion in annual operating costs. Such costs could be justified if it resulted in substantial reductions in crime, but this is unlikely. And prison expansions bleed funds away from social and economic programs that might improve conditions for the urban poor and other high-crime groups and thus decrease crime by attacking its roots. Finally, imprisoning people causes untold human suffering and dislocation to both the prisoners and their families and should be used only when necessary for public safety or when it has proven deterrent value.

This is not to say that prison is always ineffective but that it should be balanced by efforts to change the conditions that produce crime. Ironically, however, many people in the United States seem angry about spending on social reform but eager to spend on prison construction. The Applied Research insert discusses the efficacy of capital punishment.

Prison Reform

Prisons and prison programs should be designed so that they have the greatest chance of rehabilitating prisoners and reducing recidivism. Research has shown that some things seem to work (Gendreau and Ross, 1987; Andrews et al., 1990). For example, effective rehabilitation programs are those that focus on changing behaviors and beliefs conducive to crime, that provide carefully planned and structured programs that do not reinforce criminal responses, and that concentrate resources on offenders who are most likely to return to crime. Correctional programs should promote rather than undermine personal responsibility and provide offenders with real opportunities to succeed in legitimate occupations. These might include increased occupational training and counseling while imprisoned, work release, and other alternatives to incarceration. The crowding in prisons should be reduced to eliminate the degrading conditions under which many prison inmates live.

Environmental Opportunities

Efforts should be made to reduce the environmental opportunities for committing crime (Crowe, 1991). This can take the form of better physical security, such as burglar-proof locks; better detection of crime through such mechanisms as burglar alarms and antishoplifting tags in stores; and improved surveillance, such as better street lighting.

APPLIED RESEARCH
Does the Death Penalty Deter Crime?

One of the more controversial elements of the criminal justice system in the United States is the use of the death penalty for certain crimes. In the 1930s and 1940s, more than one hundred prisoners a year were executed in the United States. Quite a few more blacks were executed than whites, even though blacks constituted a relatively small proportion of our populace. The number of executions has since gone down substantially— there were only thirty-one in 1992 (U.S. Bureau of the Census, 1994: 218). However, there were two thousand five hundred prisoners on "death row" that year. Almost half of them are nonwhite, and this points to one of the arguments against the death penalty: The poor and nonwhite are more likely to be executed than are affluent whites. It seems that the well-to-do can afford the legal battle to avoid the death sentence, and judges and juries—which are mostly white—may be more inclined to sentence nonwhites to death. Another argument that is made against the death penalty is that it does not achieve one of the goals of punishment: to deter others from committing crimes. Over the past fifty years, quite a lot of social research has focused on this latter issue.

If capital punishment deters crime, then we should be able to assess its impact by comparing homicide rates in states that have capital punishment with those in states that do not. If it deters, then states with capital punishment should have lower homicide rates. Another approach would be to look at states that once had the death penalty but abolished it and states that were once without it and instituted it. Once again, this before–after comparison should show lower homicide rates when a state has capital punishment, if such punishment deters crime. The overall conclusion from many studies of these types is that the death penalty seems to have no deterrent effect, or at least we cannot find much evidence of it

(Schuessler, 1952; Sellin, 1959; Bedau, 1967; Bailey, 1974; Cochran, Chamlin, and Seth, 1994).

Although many states have the death penalty on the books, some states are much more likely to actually execute people for certain crimes. Maybe it is the death penalty in action that deters crime rather than its mere existence in law. To evaluate this possibility, we can compare the number of murderers who have actually been executed in each state. Studies that have done this find no relationship between the use of capital punishment and homicide rates or at best a very weak and confusing relationship (Lempert, 1983; Peterson and Bailey, 1991). Where a relationship is found, it is small and sometimes in the opposite direction from what we would expect: In some years, states with many executions actually have higher homicide rates than states with fewer executions. Finally, maybe the use of the death penalty has to be widely publicized for it to deter crime. Once again, research findings have been inconsistent on this (Bailey, 1990; Stack, 1990).

So, we cannot clearly say at this point whether or under what conditions the death penalty does deter homicide. However, the research does clearly show that homicide rates are linked to a variety of social factors. For example, states with low income and educational levels, high unemployment, and a highly urbanized population tend to have higher homicide rates. Research to date suggests that directing our resources toward these problems is likely to make a more significant impact on homicide rates than would executing more murderers. As Elliott Currie suggests, overreliance on a punishment-based criminal justice policy may not be the most efficient utilization of resources for all crimes (Currie, 1985).

Through applied research efforts such as these, we can assemble a body of observations about the outcome of various strategies and poli-

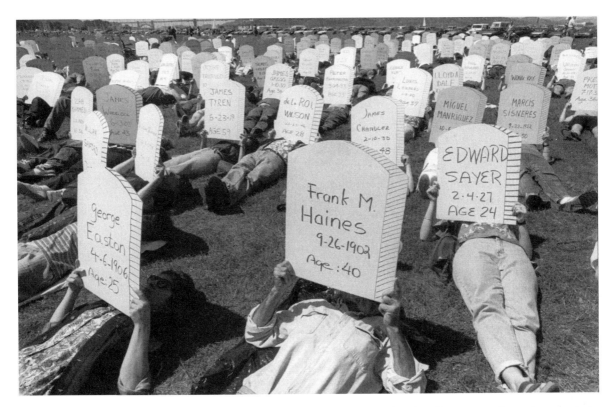

Anti–death penalty protestors form a mock cemetery with headstones bearing the names of people executed by the state of California. There is much controversy over whether capital punishment is an effective deterrent against crime.

cies related to social problems. This assessment of outcomes can then be used in evaluating criminal justice policy. This is not the whole story, however, because there may well be reasons other than deterrence for having capital punishment. The death penalty can satisfy people's needs for retribution against someone who has committed the most

heinous of crimes, and it may serve to affirm symbolically society's moral outrage over such offenses and support for those who are victims of such crimes (Finckenauer, 1988). At this point, however, observational evidence suggests that capital punishment does not serve as a deterrent to homicide.

LINKAGES

The level of crime in the United States is significantly increased by the persistence of entrenched poverty (Chapter 5) and the spread of illegal drugs (Chapter 10). At the same time, high rates of crime make parts of our cities into dangerous places to live (Chapter 12), and throwing criminals in prison can disrupt family lives (Chapter 3).

Victim Restitution

States should be encouraged to establish victim restitution programs in which the victims of crime are provided with some compensation for their loss. Oftentimes the victims of crime feel more assaulted by the criminal justice system than by the perpetrator. Once the many social sources of crime are recognized, it should be clear that society has some responsibility to the victims who unwittingly suffer as a consequence of society's failings.

Citizen Action

In many communities, citizens have decided to take matters into their own hands. Some are motivated by the belief that the police are too weak, corrupt, or politically hampered to deal with crime effectively; others feel that the police are overwhelmed by a tenacious problem that cannot be solved without the help of the citizenry. Whatever their beliefs, these groups have endeavored in a number of ways to assist in protecting people from crime. Some programs involve citizen patrols of neighborhoods or buildings, reporting any suspicious activities to the police. Most are unarmed and avoid confronting suspects themselves, except in an emergency. One of the most well known of these groups is the Guardian Angels, originally formed in New York City but now found in many other cities as well (Perry and Pugh, 1989).

Which of the reforms discussed in this chapter will have the most beneficial effect on the crime problem and on inadequacies in the criminal justice system can be determined only after programs have been initiated and evaluated. What should be clear is that only a broad-based and coordinated attack is likely to have a significant impact. If all these suggestions were incorporated into our attack on the crime problem, we would undoubtedly make a significant dent in it. Still, given our understanding of crime based on the sociological perspectives discussed in this chapter, some crime will probably persist, and we will need to make continuing efforts to cope with it.

Summary

1. Biological explanations of crime, which view crime as arising from people's physical constitution or genetic makeup, have been largely discounted by criminologists today. Psychological approaches receive more support, but they are seen as offering only a partial understanding of crime and delinquency. Social policy designed to reduce crime needs to focus on the social conditions that produce it.

2. The functionalist perspective views crime as arising in part from the weakened impact of bonds to family, church, and community. Another functionalist approach is anomie theory, which views crime as a consequence of the inconsistency or confusion between the goals people are taught to strive for and the culturally approved means they have available to achieve these goals.

3. Conflict theorists point out that it is powerful groups in society who decide which crimes will be considered serious problems and who will be arrested and sent to jail for committing crimes. Conflict theorists also blame certain contradictions in capitalism as a source of crime.

4. The interactionist perspective emphasizes the differential association theory, which points to how people learn whether to value criminal or conventional behavior through interaction with others in intimate groups. Labeling theory shows how a pattern of criminal behavior (career deviance) can arise because a person has been labeled by the police or others as a criminal or deviant.

5. The Federal Bureau of Investigation classifies crimes into Part I and Part II offenses. Juvenile delinquency involves the committing of a crime by a juvenile or the violation of the juvenile code. The crime rate in the United States has been rising for a number of decades, but the rise appears to have leveled off some in the 1980s and may even be declining a little in the 1990s.

6. Four social characteristics are closely associated with crime: Men commit more crimes than women; people between fifteen and thirty years of age account for most criminals; people of low social standing may commit more crimes than people of higher social standing and they certainly commit different types of crimes; African Americans are more likely to be involved in criminal activity than are whites.

7. There are a number of problems associated with the criminal justice system in the United States. The police have a great deal of discretion—maybe too much—in how they do their job, and police feel they do not receive the support of the public or the courts. The courts exercise discretion regarding which cases will be pursued and with how much vigor, and there is much "negotiated justice." The use of either bail or plea bargaining has been criticized.

8. Prisons are overcrowded and do not seem to be very successful at rehabilitation. The criminal justice system overall has been criticized for making it appear that we are attacking crime when little is actually being done to control it.

9. To control crime, we need most of all to carry out social reforms that will have an impact on the social conditions that cause crime in the first place. Some crimes could be legalized, thus freeing the police to deal with more serious crimes. The police could institute new law enforcement procedures that would enable them to catch serious criminals. Many judicial reforms could be carried out that would make the courts more effective. We could also reform our prisons, reduce the opportunities to commit crimes, and provide for victim restitution. In some communities, citizens have begun to work with the police to control crime.

STAND Review

Key Terms

anomie

anomie theory

career deviance

crime

cultural transmission
  theories

differential
  association theory

labeling theory

primary deviance

recidivism

secondary deviance

Multiple-Choice Questions

1. With regard to a biological explanation of crime, sociologists have concluded that:
   a. Biology explains a substantial amount of crime.
   b. Biology plays no role in causing crime.
   c. Biology makes, at best, only a small contribution to the crime problem.
   d. Biological explanations are more important than psychological ones in understanding crime.

2. The concept of "anomie" is linked with which theoretical perspective in sociology?
   a. The functionalist perspective.
   b. The conflict perspective.
   c. The interactionist perspective.
   d. The biological perspective.
   e. The psychological perspective.

3. Conflict theorists argue that the causes of crime can be found in:
   a. The labeling process.
   b. Certain characteristics of capitalism.
   c. Biological inadequacies of individuals.
   d. Weakened social bonds in industrial societies.

4. A violation of social norms for which a person is not caught, or is excused rather than labeled, is referred to as:
   a. Relative deviance.
   b. Secondary deviance.
   c. Tertiary deviance.
   d. Career deviance.
   e. Primary deviance.

5. Which of the following is true of homicides?
   a. They are rarely planned in advance.
   b. The majority occur during the commission of a felony.
   c. The majority of homicide victims are strangers to their assailants.
   d. The majority are committed as a part of organized crime activities.

6. Which of the following are considered "victimless" crimes?
   a. Gambling.
   b. Prostitution.
   c. White-collar crimes.
   d. All of the above are considered "victimless."
   e. Only a and b are considered "victimless."

7. Regarding the relationship between socioeconomic status and crime, the text concludes that:
   a. Lower-class people commit more of almost all types of hidden crimes.
   b. The relationship between SES and crime is a strong one.
   c. There is social class variation in the numbers of criminal acts committed but not the types of criminal acts committed.
   d. Lower-class people are more likely to commit highly visible and violent crimes.

8. A person is sent to prison for committing a felony, is released, and then commits another felony after release. This would make this person:
   a. A primary deviant.
   b. An anomie deviant.
   c. A recidivist.
   d. A secondary deviant.

9. The text recommends all of the following to help in the fight against crime and delinquency *except:*
   a. Reduce poverty.
   b. Give longer prison sentences for most crimes.
   c. Legalize some crimes.
   d. Promote personal responsibility among prison inmates.

10. According to the text, prisons and prison programs should be designed so that they:
   a. Rehabilitate prisoners.
   b. Increase recidivism.
   c. Reinforce criminal responses.
   d. Increase secondary deviance.

True/False Questions

1. For sociologists, a behavior can be inherently deviant, without regard to people's interpretation or judgment of the behavior.
2. Anomie theory can lead to the conclusion that large disparities between income groups can cause crime.
3. Cultural transmission theories posit that crime can be blamed on certain characteristics of capitalism as an economic system.
4. People in the United States view most white-collar crimes as less serious than other crimes.
5. Crime rates are rising faster among men than among women for all types of crime.
6. When responding to a domestic dispute, police are more likely to arrest a suspected abuser in a poor neighborhood than in a middle-class neighborhood.
7. People are more likely to receive the death penalty for homicide when the victim is white rather than when the victim is black.
8. Prison populations in the United States have grown in part because people are receptive to giving criminals longer prison sentences.
9. Effective rehabilitation programs in prisons are those that concentrate resources on offenders who are most likely to return to crime.
10. Research has shown that states that institute the death penalty experience a significant drop in their homicide rates.

Fill-In Questions

1. According to _____ approaches to crime, criminality is linked to personality disorders or maladjustments.

2. _____ refers to the inconsistencies and contradictions in the social system and the resulting confusion experienced by people.
3. The most important mode of adaptation, according to Robert Merton, and the one that might take the form of crime, is called

   _____ .
4. The differential association theory of crime is

   one example of a _____ theory.
5. If a drug user is discovered and responds to the discovery by becoming more closely involved with other drug users, this would be an

   example of _____ deviance.
6. Antitrust violations are one type of

   _____ crime.
7. Young people who commit acts that are prohibited by the juvenile code but are not considered criminal when committed by an adult

   are called _____ offenders.
8. The single social factor that is most predictive of patterns of criminal behavior is

   _____ .

9. _____ is money or credit deposited with the court to ensure that people released while awaiting trial will appear for their trials.
10. According to the text, the criminal justice system should provide punishment that is

   _____ and _____ .

Matching Questions

_____ 1. organized crime

_____ 2. recidivist

_____ 3. sociopathic personalities

_____ 4. Emile Durkheim

_____ 5. plea bargaining

_____ 6. forcible rape

_____ 7. fraudulent insurance claims

_____ 8. Corrections Corporation of America

_____ 9. social reform

_____ 10. labeling theory

  A. syndicates
  B. psychological approaches to crime
  C. Part I offense
  D. white-collar crime
  E. repeat offender
  F. functionalist perspective
  G. private prisons
  H. reducing poverty
  I. informal dispensing of justice
  J. interactionist perspective

Essay Questions

1. Describe the psychological approaches to crime. How do sociologists assess them as explanations of crime?
2. Explain crime from the conflict perspective.
3. According to the differential association theory, what is the explanation for why some people commit crimes and others do not?
4. Describe the effect of gender and age on people's likelihood of committing crimes.
5. Describe the relationship between socioeconomic status and crime.
6. What are the causes of the burgeoning prison population in the United States since 1980?
7. Make arguments both for and against the use of private prisons in the United States. What does research show about how well these prisons work?
8. Why is the crime rate in Japan so much lower than it is in the United States?
9. What social reforms are suggested in the text to help reduce the crime rate in the United States?
10. Make arguments both for and against the use of the death penalty for some crimes in the United States. What does research show about the impact of the death penalty?

Answers

Multiple-Choice
1. C; **2.** A; **3.** B; **4.** E; **5.** A; **6.** E; **7.** D; **8.** C; **9.** B; **10.** A

True/False
1. F; **2.** T; **3.** F; **4.** T; **5.** F; **6.** T; **7.** T; **8.** T; **9.** T; **10.** F

Fill-In
1. psychological
2. anomie
3. innovation
4. cultural transmission
5. secondary
6. white-collar
7. status
8. gender
9. bail
10. swift, certain, equitable, or fair

Matching
1. A; **2.** E; **3.** B; **4.** F; **5.** I; **6.** C; **7.** D; **8.** G; **9.** H; **10.** J

For Further Reading

Edmund G. (Pat) Brown with Dick Adler. *Public Justice, Private Mercy: A Governor's Education on Death Row.* New York: Weidenfeld and Nicolson, 1989. As governor of California, Brown commuted the sentences of twenty-three men on death row and sent thirty-six to the gas chamber. This experience had a profound impact on him personally and he conveyed this in this compelling book.

Robert J. Bursik, Jr. and Harold G. Grasmick. *Neighborhoods and Crime: The Dimensions of Effective Community Control.* New York: Lexington Books, 1993. This book looks at the causes of crime and suggests some programs for changing communities to help reduce the amount of crime.

Geoffrey Canada. *Fist Stick Knife Gun: A Personal History of Violence in America.* Boston: Beacon, 1995. This is an excellent and personal account of the subculture of violence that some young people in the United States today confront as they grow up.

Gilbert Geis, Robert Meier, and Lawrence Salinger. *White Collar Crime: Classic and Contemporary Views,* 3rd ed. New York: The Free Press, 1995. These authors provide an extensive overview of the problem of white-collar crime.

Liz Kelly. *Surviving Sexual Violence.* Minneapolis: University of Minnesota Press, 1989. This book views violence against women as running along a continuum from subtle threats to physical attacks. The author uses both feminist theory and sociological research to understand the violence women experience and to show the powerful strategies they use to cope with and survive the violence they face.

Coramae Richey Mann. *Unequal Justice: A Question of Color.* Bloomington: Indiana University Press, 1993. This book provides a thorough exploration of the link between minorities and crime in the United States. It explores reasons for the relationship and the response of society to minority crime.

Russell Mokhiber. *Corporate Crime and Violence: Big Business Power and the Abuse of the Public Trust.* San Francisco: Sierra Club Books, 1988. A muckraker's view of white-collar and corporate crime: Thirty-six cases are described in which corporate misconduct killed people or significantly harmed the environment.

Felix M. Padilla. *The Gang as an American Enterprise.* New Brunswick, N.J.: Rutgers University Press, 1992. This is an ethnography of second-generation Puerto Rican youth in Chicago who belong to a gang called the Diamonds. It chronicles all facets of gang life, from how youth get drawn into gangs to their illegal drug selling.

Wilbert Rideau and Ron Wikberg. *Life Sentences: Rage and Survival Behind Bars.* New York: Times Books/Random House, 1992. This is a moving book by two men who spent many years in prison, each convicted of murder. It is an excellent insider's view of prison life, making a convincing argument against our desire to lock criminals in prison and throw away the key.

CHAPTER TEN
Alcohol and Other Drugs

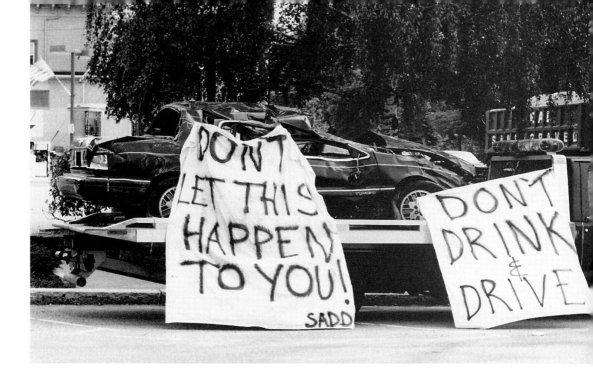

In 1982, well-known actor and former *Saturday Night Live* star John Belushi died from an injection of heroin and cocaine, a combination known as a "speedball" in drug circles. In 1984, David Kennedy, the twenty-eight-year-old son of Senator Robert F. Kennedy and nephew of President John F. Kennedy, died in a hotel room from a combined dose of cocaine, a narcotic painkiller called Demerol, and an antipsychotic tranquilizer known as Mellaril, which had been prescribed for Mr. Kennedy by a physician. In 1993, the movie star River Phoenix died of an overdose of cocaine and heroin or morphine. In 1995, Jerry Garcia, leader of the rock group The Grateful Dead, died while a resident in a drug treatment program, and baseball great Mickey Mantle died of cancer, partly the result of years of alcohol abuse. The only thing that distinguishes these deaths from others attributable to drug abuse is that these men were wealthy and famous. Deaths related to drug abuse or overdose occur routinely in the United States, although rarely with the attention surrounding these cases. The notoriety of the people mentioned publicized the horrible consequences that can result—to people of both high and low social standing—when drug use gets out of control.

Use of drugs in one form or another is widespread in human societies. Most societies condone the use of certain drugs, at least by some groups. Such drug use is generally regulated, either through law or social convention, because the unregulated use of mind-altering substances can have damaging effects on society. For example, drug users may not work, or they may fail to support their families. They may even become dangerous to themselves or others. This common societal ambivalence toward drug use—condoning it on the one hand, but controlling it on the other—points to one of the controversial elements of the problem of alcohol and drug use: drawing the line between what is acceptable use and what is not. In Chapters 1 and 9, we describe the relative nature of deviant behavior. In this chapter, we focus on this issue specifically in the context of drug use. In the United States, opinions about drug use vary widely. At one extreme, some groups call for a complete ban on all drugs, including alcohol. Other groups believe that some drugs—alcohol and marijuana are most commonly mentioned—can be used safely by mature people. At the other extreme, a few groups argue that adults should be free to use any drug they please as long as they do not become a danger to others.

These issues of social definition are central to understanding the problem of drug abuse in the United States and to developing sensible social policies to deal with it. These issues will be addressed first, before considering the extent and nature of the drug problem in the United States.

Drugs and Their Consequences

What is a drug? Strictly speaking, a **drug** is *any substance that, when consumed, alters one or more of the functions of the human body* (Milby, 1981). This definition covers a wide range of substances, from cocaine to medicines for the control of cancer to high blood pressure medications. It also includes many everyday foods along with beverages such as tea, coffee, and cola that contain the mild stimulant caffeine. Does this make your aunt, who drinks two six-packs of caffeine-laced cola each day, a drug addict? Not by most definitions. The effects of most of these everyday substances are rather mild, and their use or withdrawal does not normally create major disruptions in people's lives. The drugs that constitute a social problem are typically limited to the **psychoactive drugs:** *those that can produce major alterations in the mood, emotions, perceptions, or brain functioning of the person who takes them* (Edwards, 1983; Schuckit, 1989).

Drug Use and Abuse

The use of psychoactive drugs is not, by itself, a social problem. After all, as we have noted, most societies approve the use of some such drugs. In our society, for example, the moderate use of alcohol is accepted by many groups. Alcohol consumption is even incorporated into the Roman Catholic ritual of the Mass. Few would argue that these uses of psychoactive drugs constitute a social problem. Where, then, is the line between acceptable drug use and drug abuse? This is a very controversial question. The World Health Organization defines drug abuse as the excessive use of a drug in a way that is inconsistent with medical practice (Milby, 1981). However, this definition, with its emphasis on the medical consequences of behavior, seems overly broad. Heavy smoking, for example, would by this definition be drug abuse because physicians warn against it, but

Myth: The drug abuse problem in the United States today is of epidemic proportions, with more people using and abusing drugs than ever.

FACT: Although today's drug abuse problem is serious, it is probably not a lot more serious than it was a century ago. Then, marijuana, cocaine, and various narcotics were legal and widely available, and many people were addicted to drugs.

Myth: Heavy use of heroin clouds judgment and reduces inhibitions, and this is the prime reason heroin addicts commit crimes.

FACT: Heroin addicts are as likely to be high on alcohol as heroin when they commit crimes, and in fact many heroin addicts drink alcohol before committing crimes in order to bolster their courage.

Myth: The most serious drug problem that the United States faces is the flow of heroin, cocaine, and marijuana into the United States from overseas.

FACT: In terms of the number of people affected and the economic costs to society, most specialists on drug problems consider alcohol abuse to be the most severe drug problem we have. In addition, a drug such as heroin is probably less harmful to its user's health than is alcohol, and many have argued that heroin should be treated by society like alcohol: as a legal but highly controlled substance.

Myth: Addiction to heroin and other narcotics produces the most severe and dangerous physical withdrawal symptoms.

FACT: Withdrawal from addiction to barbiturates (sedatives and painkillers), which can be purchased legally in the United States, is much more dangerous than withdrawal from heroin, a substance that is illegal.

few are likely to call heavy smokers "drug addicts." Rather, we need to consider drug use in the context of particular cultural or subcultural norms and values. From this viewpoint, **drug abuse** is *the continued use of a psychoactive substance at a level that violates approved social practices.* Typically, use of a substance meets social disapproval when it has negative consequences for people's health, endangers their relationships with other people, or is threatening to others in society. Even people's belief that the substance has these consequences can produce social disapproval. As we will see, cultural norms regarding drug abuse are by no means completely rational. These norms are influenced as much by history, religion, and cultural values as they are by the actual damage drugs do to a person's health or social relationships.

Much of the concern about drugs of abuse relates to their effects on people, such as drug dependence, drug addiction, and a tolerance to drugs. Some drugs produce **dependence,** or *a mental or physical craving for the drug and withdrawal symptoms when use of the drug is stopped.* Dependence and its withdrawal symptoms can be physical, psychological, or both. Alcohol withdrawal, for example, can lead to convulsions, hallucinations, and insomnia on the physical level and nervousness and a reduced sense of self-worth on the psychological level. The withdrawal symptoms of a drug are often the opposite of the effects of taking the drug. For example, alcohol, which helps a person relax, can lead to insomnia and anxiety when use is discontinued. Drug dependence and drug abuse are not the same thing, although they are often related. A severely depressed person, for example, may become highly dependent on antidepressant medications prescribed by a physician, but this would not be considered drug abuse because the physician's diagnosis and treatment prescription make this a socially approved use of a drug. Neither are drug abuse and drug addiction synonymous. **Drug addiction,** as used by professionals in the field, refers to *physical dependence on a drug.* Although most drugs of abuse are physically addicting, some, such as the hallucinogens, are not.

Often associated with dependence on a drug is **tolerance:** *physical changes that result in the need for bigger and higher doses of the drug to achieve the same effect.* This occurs because, with continual use of some drugs, the liver destroys the drug more quickly and the nervous system's response to the drug is diminished. So more of the drug is needed for the same "boost." It is also possible to develop cross-dependence and cross-tolerance. **Cross-dependence** occurs when *the withdrawal symptoms of one drug are alleviated by another drug in the same pharmacological class.* **Cross-tolerance** is found when *a tolerance built up to one drug leads to a reduced response to another drug in the same pharmacological class.*

The Societal Costs of Drug Abuse

The consumption of alcohol and other drugs takes a costly toll from our society.

1. *Accidents.* Each year, from one-third to one-half of the drivers in fatal traffic accidents have been drinking, and between sixteen thousand and thirty thousand people die in traffic accidents involving alcohol (U.S. Bureau of the Census, 1994: 633). Alcohol consumption is also associated with airplane and occupational accidents. Marijuana impairs motor skills, reduces judgment, and affects time and distance estimation, and thus increases the danger of accidents (Sutton, 1983).

2. *Crime.* In well over half of the homicides in the United States, either the victim, the perpetrator, or both were drinking at the time of the crime. People who commit rape are also disproportionately likely to have been drinking before the crime or to be alcoholics. Studies of heroin addicts in treatment programs have found that most addicts commit crimes to support their habit (Inciardi, Horowitz, and Pottieger, 1993). Thirty-six percent of all convictions for federal offenses in the United States today are for drug offenses, up from 18 percent in 1980 (U.S. Bureau of the Census, 1994: 212). In most large cities, over half of the people arrested for all crimes test positive for some illegal drugs.

3. *Family Problems.* Alcoholics are seven times more likely to become separated or divorced from their spouses than are other people, and 40 percent of the family court problems involve alcohol in some fashion. Studies find that between 29 and 71 percent of spouse abusers were drinking at the time of the attack (Martin, 1993).

4. *Work Problems.* Alcohol abusers have twice the rate of work absenteeism as other workers and cause many other problems at work. In 1989, for example, the captain of the oil tanker *Exxon Valdez* was under the influence of alcohol at the time the ship went aground and released millions of gallons of oil into the Alaskan coastline, causing a terrible environmental disaster.

5. *Health Problems.* Most psychoactive drugs, especially if taken continually or in large quantities, produce severe health problems and even death. Alcoholics and heroin addicts, for example, have far higher death rates from many illnesses than do people who abuse neither drug.

Placing a dollar figure on these and other costs of drug abuse is necessarily approximate and tentative, but it helps to highlight the dimensions of the problem. One estimate of the core costs for alcohol abuse alone in the United States was $86 billion! This is what it cost society to diagnose, treat, and care for alcoholism and alcohol-related illnesses and deaths and to cover the costs of lowered work productivity (Rice, Kelman, and Miller, 1991). Add in another $58 billion for the abuse of other drugs, and the cost to society becomes an astounding $144 billion. Estimates of losses in work and productivity alone because of drug abuse were over $99 billion per year (Scanlon, 1991).

The Extent of Drug Abuse in the United States

People in the United States consume many different kinds of drugs; some are legal and others are illegal. These various drugs differ from one another in their chemical composition and their social, psychological, and medical consequences. The major classes of drugs that are problems in the United States will be discussed.

Alcohol

Alcohol is a psychoactive drug that any adult in the United States can purchase legally without a prescription. There is little debate that it constitutes our most severe drug problem. According to a survey conducted by the National Institute on Drug Abuse, 5 percent of all adult Americans are heavy drinkers, consuming five or more drinks at one sitting at five or more times each month (National Institute on Drug Abuse, 1991). Overall, people fourteen years of age and older in the United States consume an

The social characteristics of age and gender are associated with alcohol and drug abuse: Young people and males are more likely to be involved than are older people and females.

average of 2.7 gallons of alcohol per person per year. This is a particularly impressive amount considering that about one-third of the adult population drinks no alcoholic beverages whatsoever. Furthermore, the young also drink a lot. In 1992, almost 4 percent of all high school students drank every day, and almost one-third of all high school seniors reported episodes of heavy drinking in the preceding two weeks (see Figure 10.1; Johnston, O'Malley, and Bachman, 1993).

The consumption of alcohol by itself is not a social problem. Many people use it throughout their lives without running into any difficulties, or at least the particular effects are not defined as problems. However, the continuous or excessive consumption of alcohol, commonly termed "alcoholism," is likely to create

problems. Actually, attempts to define alcoholism have created much controversy. One approach is to define it by the amount of alcohol consumed or the alcohol blood levels of a person. However, many alcoholism treatment specialists feel that these definitions have weaknesses because they ignore the social definitions of what is considered too much alcohol or the social consequences of consuming a certain amount of alcohol. The most popular definition of **alcoholism** is *the consumption of alcohol at a level that produces serious personal, social, or health consequences, such as marital problems, occupational difficulties, accidents, or arrests* (Ray, 1983; Schuckit, 1989). In this definition, there is no set level of alcohol consumption that distinguishes the alcoholic from the nonalcoholic. Alcoholics are people who cannot stop drink-

FIGURE 10.1 Trends in Thirty-Day Prevalence of Daily Use of Marijuana and Alcohol, by Sex, Among High School Seniors, 1975–1992. *Source:* Lloyd D. Johnston, Patrick M. O'Malley, and Jerald G. Bachman, *National Survey Results on Drug Use from the Monitoring the Future Study, 1975–1992: Volume I, Secondary School Students,* National Institute on Drug Abuse, NIH Pub. No. (ADM) 93–3597 (Washington, D.C.: U.S. Government Printing Office, 1993), p. 106.

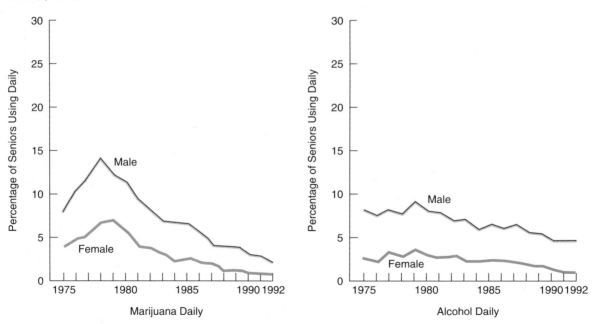

ing before the detrimental consequences, such as losing their jobs or being arrested, occur.

The popular image of the alcoholic is the stumbling-down drunk and the skid-row bum, but such people probably make up less than 5 percent of all alcoholics (Scanlon, 1991). An estimated 15 percent of male drinkers and 6 percent of female drinkers in the United States become alcohol abusers. This means that about eighteen million people in the United States are either addicted to alcohol or drink enough to cause problems for themselves and other people. Who are these alcoholics? Alcoholism counselors are quick to point out that alcoholism knows no age, sex, race, or social class bounds, and this is certainly true to the extent that alcoholics can be found in virtually all social groups. Yet this statement also hides the reality that people with certain social characteristics are much more likely to become alcoholics (Haglund and Schuckit, 1981; Flewelling, Rachal, and Marsden, 1992):

1. *Sex.* Men are far more likely to become alcoholics than are women. This is due in part to the fact that alcohol consumption and drunkenness have been more socially acceptable for men than for women.

2. *Socioeconomic Status.* Rates of alcoholism are higher among people with lower levels of income and education. This may be due in part to the abilities of people with higher socioeconomic standing to avoid being publicly labeled as alcoholics.

3. *Religion.* There are strong associations between religion and alcohol consumption. Most Jews, for example, consume alcohol, but heavy drinking among this group is relatively infrequent. Catholics, on the other hand, have many drinkers and much higher rates of heavy drinking, especially among French and Irish Catholics.

4. *Age.* Alcohol abuse is a more serious problem among younger than older people. Among people between the ages of eighteen and thirty-four,

one-quarter to one-half admit to having some alcohol-related problems, such as automobile accidents while drunk or missing work because of drinking (Schuckit, 1989). After age thirty-four, heavy drinking declines, and by age sixty-five the proportion of heavy drinkers is about one-third what it is in the younger groups. Surveys of high school seniors reveal that almost 5 percent report daily or near daily use of alcohol, whereas a significantly higher proportion report occasional heavy drinking. Fifty-one percent of high school seniors have used alcohol in the last month, and over 40 percent of college students have consumed five or more drinks in one sitting during the previous two weeks. However, surveys over the past two decades suggest that alcohol consumption among adolescents as well as adults has declined, in some cases significantly, since the early 1980s (see Figure 10.1, Figure 10.2 on p. 362, and Tables 10.1 and 10.2 on pp. 364–366).

Marijuana and Hashish

Marijuana is a preparation made from the Cannabis plant, usually consumed by smoking it like tobacco (Milby, 1981; Milhorn, 1994). The primary psychoactive ingredient of Cannabis is tetrahydrocannabinol, or THC, which is concentrated in the resin of the plant. The potency of marijuana depends on how much of the resin is present. Hashish is a concentrated form of the resin taken from the flowers of the plant. It is either eaten or smoked and is very potent. It is difficult to classify marijuana in relationship to other psychoactive drugs. It has sedative properties at the doses usually consumed in cigarette form, but it also has definite hallucinogenic properties when taken in stronger doses.

The level of marijuana use in the United States is far lower than that of alcohol. By 1992, less than 5 percent of college students used marijuana on a daily basis, and somewhere between one-third and one-half of all adults have ever used marijuana (see Figure 10.3 on p. 363

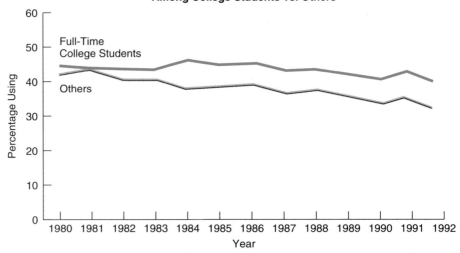

Trends in Two-Week Prevalence of 5 or More Drinks in a Row Among College Students vs. Others

Full-Time College Students

Others

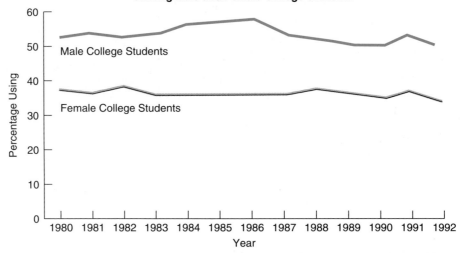

Trends in Two-Week Prevalence of 5 or More Drinks in a Row Among Male and Female College Students

Male College Students

Female College Students

FIGURE 10.2 Use of Alcohol Among College Students, 1980–1992. *Source:* Lloyd D. Johnston, Patrick M. O'Malley, and Jerald G. Bachman, *National Survey Results on Drug Use from the Monitoring the Future Study, 1975–1992: Volume II, College Students and Young Adults,* National Institute on Drug Abuse, NIH Pub. No. (ADM) 93–3598 (Washington, D.C.: U.S. Government Printing Office, 1993), p. 187.

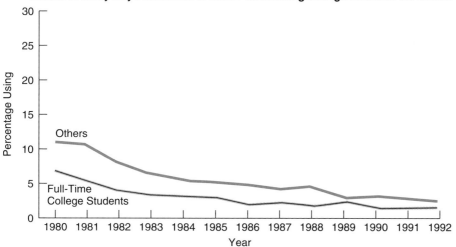

Trends in Thirty-Day Prevalence of DAILY Use Among College Students vs. Others

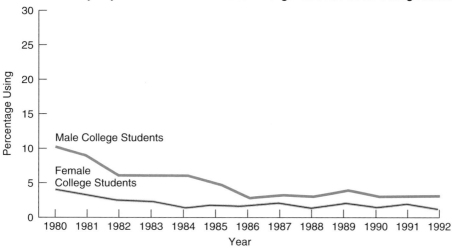

Trends in Thirty-Day Prevalence of DAILY Use Among Male and Female College Students

FIGURE 10.3 Marijuana Use Among College Students, 1980–1992. *Source:* Lloyd D. Johnston, Patrick M. O'Malley, and Jerald G. Bachman, *National Survey Results on Drug Use from the Monitoring the Future Study, 1975–1992: Volume II, College Students and Young Adults,* National Institute on Drug Abuse, NIH Pub. No. (ADM) 93–3598 (Washington, D.C.: U.S. Government Printing Office, 1993), p. 175.

TABLE 10.1 Drug Use Among High School Seniors, 1975–1992

A. Percent Who Used at Least Once in Last Thirty Days

	Class of 1975	Class of 1977	Class of 1979	Class of 1981	Class of 1983	Class of 1985	Class of 1987	Class of 1989	Class of 1992
Approx. N =	(9400)	(17100)	(15500)	(17500)	(16300)	(16000)	(16300)	(16700)	(15800)
Marijuana/Hashish	27.1	35.4	36.5	31.6	27.0	25.7	21.0	16.7	11.9
Inhalants	NA	1.3	1.7	1.5	1.7	2.2	2.8	2.3	2.3
Amyl & Butyl Nitrites	NA	NA	2.4	1.4	1.4	1.6	1.3	0.6	0.3
Hallucinogens	4.7	4.1	4.0	3.7	2.8	2.5	2.5	2.2	2.1
LSD	2.3	2.1	2.4	2.5	1.9	1.6	1.8	1.8	2.0
PCP	NA	NA	2.4	1.4	1.3	1.6	0.6	1.4	0.6
Cocaine	1.9	2.9	5.7	5.8	4.9	6.7	4.3	2.8	1.3
Heroin	0.4	0.3	0.2	0.2	0.2	0.3	0.2	0.3	0.3
Other opiates[a]	2.1	2.8	2.4	2.1	1.8	2.3	1.8	1.6	1.2
Stimulants[a]	8.5	8.8	9.9	15.8	8.9	6.8	5.2	4.2	2.8
Sedatives[a]	5.4	5.1	4.4	4.6	3.0	2.4	1.7	1.6	1.2
Barbiturates[a]	4.7	4.3	3.2	2.6	2.1	2.0	1.4	1.4	1.1
Methaqualone[a]	2.1	2.3	2.3	3.1	1.8	1.0	0.6	0.6	0.4
Tranquilizers[a]	4.1	4.6	3.7	2.7	2.5	2.1	2.0	1.3	1.0
Alcohol	68.2	71.2	71.8	70.7	69.4	65.9	66.4	60.0	51.3

(continued)

and Table 10.2 on p. 366). Rates of marijuana use are far higher among younger than older people. Among those between eighteen and twenty-five years of age, 11 percent are current users, compared with only 3 percent of those over twenty-six. Although these levels of use are much higher than those prior to the 1970s, usage peaked in the late 1970s and declined steadily and substantially since then (see Tables 10.1 and 10.2 and Figure 10.3). Usage rates are now lower than at any point since 1975. Males are also more likely to use marijuana than are females, and it is less common among college students than others.

In the low potencies found in some marijuana, the drug produces feelings of pleasant euphoria and well-being, along with sleepiness, heightened sexual arousal, increased sense awareness, difficulty in keeping track of time, and a decrease in short-term memory. Marijuana intoxication can also impair a person's ability to carry out complex tasks. However, some marijuana today is far more potent than the marijuana of earlier decades, and large amounts of this highly potent marijuana can lead to intense emotional reactions, substantial distortions in perception, a "panic" that one has lost control of oneself, and vivid hallucinations. It can even lead to a psychotic reaction, usually in people with a history of mental instability. Long-term marijuana use may also damage the lungs and immune system and affect long-term memory. However, marijuana is a fairly mild drug when used in moderation

B. Percent Who Used Daily in Last Thirty Days (or Used 20 or More Times in Last 30 Days)

	Class of 1975	Class of 1977	Class of 1979	Class of 1981	Class of 1983	Class of 1985	Class of 1987	Class of 1989	Class of 1992
Marijuana/Hashish	6.0	9.1	10.3	7.0	5.5	4.9	3.3	2.9	1.9
Inhalants	NA	0.0	0.0	0.1	0.1	0.2	0.1	0.2	0.1
Amyl & Butyl Nitrites	NA	NA	0.0	0.1	0.2	0.3	0.3	0.3	0.1
Hallucinogens	0.1	0.1	0.1	0.1	0.1	0.1	0.1	0.1	0.1
LSD	0.0	0.0	0.0	0.1	0.1	0.1	0.1	0.0	0.1
PCP[a]	NA	NA	0.1	0.1	0.1	0.3	0.3	0.2	0.1
Cocaine	0.1	0.1	0.2	0.3	0.2	0.4	0.3	0.3	0.1
Heroin	0.1	0.0	0.0	0.0	0.1	0.0	0.0	0.1	0.0
Other opiates[a]	0.1	0.2	0.0	0.1	0.1	0.1	0.1	0.2	0.0
Stimulants[a]	0.5	0.5	0.6	1.2	0.8	0.4	0.3	0.3	0.2
Sedatives[a]	0.3	0.2	0.1	0.2	0.2	0.1	0.1	0.1	0.1
Barbiturates[a]	0.1	0.2	0.0	0.1	0.1	0.1	0.1	0.1	0.0
Methaqualone[a]	0.0	0.0	0.0	0.1	0.0	0.0	0.0	0.0	0.1
Tranquilizers[a]	0.1	0.3	0.1	0.1	0.1	0.0	0.1	0.1	0.0
Alcohol	5.7	6.1	6.9	6.0	5.5	5.0	4.8	4.2	3.4

[a]Only drug use that was not under a doctor's orders is included here.

Source: Lloyd D. Johnston, Patrick M. O'Malley, and Jerald G. Bachman, *National Survey Results on Drug Use from The Monitoring the Future Study, 1975–1992: Volume I, Secondary School Students,* National Institute on Drug Abuse, NIH Pub. No. 93–3597, 1993, pp. 77–78.

and in low potency. Its use leads to only mild levels of tolerance. Some argue that there is no physical dependence at all with marijuana (Milby, 1981). Withdrawal symptoms, if they occur at all, appear to be quite mild.

Some studies have concluded that chronic marijuana users, especially among adolescents, may develop what has been called an amotivational syndrome, characterized by a lack of goals, apathy, sluggish mental responses, and mental confusion (Cohen, 1982). Such investigations have been criticized, however, on the grounds that many of the behaviors associated with this syndrome are socially acceptable and even valued in the subculture of some chronic drug users. So these behaviors may not be responses to the drug but to the social expec-

tations present in a subcultural milieu. In addition, this syndrome probably affects a small number of chronic users—one study estimates 3 percent—and it disappears without any treatment being given for it, even when marijuana use is continued (Halikas et al., 1982).

There has been some debate over the years about whether marijuana use can lead to the use of other drugs such as cocaine or heroin (Botvin, 1990). Clearly, people who use these other drugs often use marijuana first. However, there is no convincing evidence that marijuana itself causes a person to turn to these other drugs. Rather, the social circumstances or personal problems that incline certain people toward drug abuse probably lead to marijuana first, possibly because of its accessibility. Even if

TABLE 10.2 Drug Use by Type of Drug and Age Group, 1974–1992

A. Those Who Have Ever Used a Drug

Drug	Percentage of Persons 12–17 Years of Age			Percentage of Persons 18–25 Years of Age			Percentage of Persons 26 Years of Age and Older		
	1974	1979	1992	1974	1979	1992	1974	1979	1992
Marijuana/Hashish	23.0	30.9	10.6	52.7	68.2	48.1	9.9	19.6	33.0
Cocaine	3.6	5.4	1.7	12.7	27.5	15.8	0.9	4.3	11.4
Inhalants	8.5	9.8	5.7	9.2	16.5	9.8	1.2	3.9	3.7
Hallucinogens	6.0	7.1	2.6	16.6	25.1	13.4	1.3	4.5	7.7
Heroin	1.0	0.5	0.2	4.5	3.5	1.3	0.5	1.0	0.9
Nonmedical use of any psychotherapeutics	—	7.3	10.2	—	29.5	15.6	—	9.2	11.5
Stimulants	5.0	3.4	2.1	17.0	18.2	6.8	3.0	5.8	6.7
Sedatives	5.0	3.2	1.5	15.0	17.0	3.2	2.0	3.5	3.8
Tranquilizers	3.0	4.1	1.6	10.0	15.8	6.8	2.0	3.1	5.3
Analgesics	—	3.2	3.9	—	11.8	8.7	—	2.7	5.1
Alcohol	54.0	70.3	39.3	81.6	95.3	86.3	73.2	91.5	88.1

B. Those Who Have Used a Drug at Least Once in the Past Month

Drug	Percentage of Persons 12–17 Years of Age			Percentage of Persons 18–25 Years of Age			Percentage of Persons 26 Years of Age and Older		
	1974	1979	1992	1974	1979	1992	1974	1979	1992
Marijuana/Hashish	12.0	16.7	4.0	25.2	35.4	11.0	2.0	6.0	3.2
Cocaine	1.0	1.4	0.3	3.1	9.3	1.8	a	0.9	0.5
Inhalants	0.7	2.0	1.6	a	1.2	0.8	a	0.5	0.2
Hallucinogens	1.3	2.2	0.6	2.5	4.4	1.3	a	a	a
Heroin	a	a	0.1	a	a	0.2	a	a	a
Nonmedical use of any psychotherapeutics	—	2.3	2.7	—	6.2	2.6	—	1.1	1.0
Stimulants	1.0	1.2	0.2	3.7	3.5	0.7	a	0.5	0.2
Sedatives	1.0	1.1	0.4	1.6	2.8	0.6	a	a	0.3
Tranquilizers	1.0	0.6	0.2	1.2	2.1	0.6	a	a	0.4
Analgesics	—	0.6	0.8	—	1.0	1.2	—	a	0.7
Alcohol	34.0	37.2	15.7	69.3	75.9	59.2	54.5	61.3	50.1

[a]No estimate.

Source: U.S. Bureau of the Census, *Statistical Abstract of the United States, 1994* (Washington, D.C.: U.S. Government Printing Office, 1994), p. 141.

marijuana were not available, such people would probably abuse other drugs eventually, such as alcohol, heroin, or cocaine. In addition, obtaining marijuana often brings the user into contact with people who also know how to obtain and use other drugs. It is probably these associations, not the marijuana itself, that produce the link between use of one drug and use of another.

Stimulants

There are enough stimulants produced legally in the United States each year to provide fifty doses to every person. About one-half of these legal stimulants find their way into the illegal drug trade (Schuckit, 1989). The term **stimulant** refers to the many *drugs whose major effect is to stimulate the central nervous system.* They can increase one's alertness, reduce fatigue, enhance a person's mood, and create a sense of excitement. They can also produce euphoria, confidence, a heightened sense of sexuality, increased energy, and restlessness. Low doses of some stimulants, such as cocaine, can lead to enhanced motor performance, but higher doses result in a deterioration in performance and, at an extreme, convulsions. The stimulants produce tolerance, cross-tolerance, and physical and psychological dependence. Stimulants have many legitimate medical uses in the treatment of narcolepsy (falling asleep without warning), hyperactivity in children, and obesity. However, they are also widely abused.

Cocaine is a stimulant derived from coca leaves and has become the third most popular psychoactive drug in the United States after alcohol and marijuana (Erickson et al., 1987). By the 1990s, more than 10 percent of all adult Americans aged twenty-six and over had tried cocaine, compared with around 1 percent in the mid-1970s. Among young people aged eighteen to twenty-five years old, almost 16 percent had used it in 1992 compared with 12 percent in 1974. However, there seem to be fewer current users now: 1.8 percent of the eighteen to

twenty-five year olds used cocaine in the last month in 1992 compared with 3.1 percent in 1974. In fact, cocaine use seemed to have peaked between 1980 and 1985 and has shown a substantial decline since then (see Tables 10.1 and 10.2, and Figure 10.4 on p. 368). However, there is evidence that the decline in cocaine use is among casual users rather than heavy users or addicts. This is suggested in Table 10.1, for example, which shows that the rate of daily use of cocaine has not dropped much, whereas the rate among those who used cocaine in the last thirty days—presumably the casual users—has dropped significantly. In addition, although equal proportions of whites, African Americans, and Hispanic Americans have tried cocaine, whites are less likely to be current users than are the other two groups. So, cocaine use among whites tends to be more short-lived and probably more experimental (U.S. Department of Health and Human Services, 1994: 30–31).

Cocaine used to be an expensive drug, and this limited its use. However, drug entrepreneurs discovered ways to produce cheap and potent drugs from cocaine (Lerner and Raczynski, 1988; Witkin, 1991). In the 1970s, they discovered a recipe for cocaine "freebase," in which a chemical process was used to "free" base cocaine from cocaine hydrochloride powder (called "powder" or "blow"), turning the cocaine powder into smokable "crack" cocaine. (The term *crack* comes from the cracking sound cocaine makes when heated.) Crack (called "rock cocaine" or "hubbas") gives an intense high—almost instantaneously because it is smoked—and is extremely addictive. Crack addicts sometimes engage in "binging," taking high doses in rapid succession, as often as every ten minutes. Crack is sometimes used with other drugs, such as when combined with heroin to make a "speedball" that gives a quick and potent high (McDonnell, Irwin, and Rosenbaum, 1990). It is also cheap enough to be available even to poor people with a few extra dollars in their pocket. Cocaine powder costs $75 a gram, whereas one hit of crack is as little

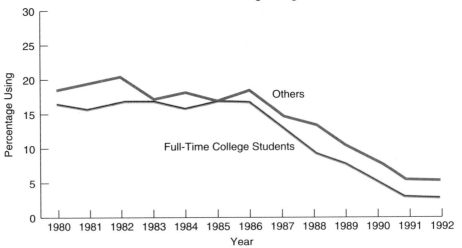

Trends in Annual Prevalence Among College Students vs. Others

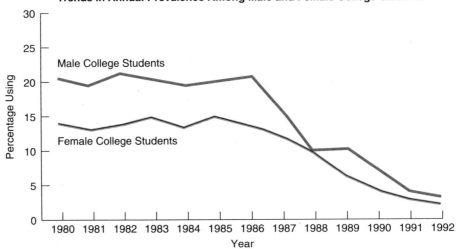

Trends in Annual Prevalence Among Male and Female College Students

FIGURE 10.4 Cocaine Use Among College Students, 1980–1992. *Source:* Lloyd D. Johnston, Patrick M. O'Malley, and Jerald G. Bachman, *National Survey Results on Drug Use from the Monitoring the Future Study, 1975–1992: Volume II, College Students and Young Adults,* National Institute on Drug Abuse, NIH Pub. No. (ADM) 93–3598 (Washington, D.C.: U.S. Government Printing Office 1993), p. 180.

as $5. Because of this, crack has been an especially cruel plague for many poor communities. Even mothers receiving welfare can afford crack if they neglect their personal needs and those of their families. Consequently, some poor women have become addicted to crack, given birth to children who are addicted, and then neglected and even abandoned their children as their crack habits spun out of control. Under these circumstances, the problems of poverty and drug abuse become intertwined and mutually reinforcing. Another characteristic of crack is especially important in terms of criminal behavior: Heroin is a depressant, which means that addicts are lethargic and mostly immobile during their "highs." Cocaine, on the other hand, is a stimulant, and crack addicts are far more likely to be paranoid and highly active.

Cocaine can be absorbed into the body in many different ways, but the most common ways are to to sniff or "snort" it into the nostrils, to smoke it (as in the use of crack), or to inject it intravenously. Prolonged snorting of cocaine can destroy the mucous membranes of the nose and eventually the septum. High doses or chronic use can produce a schizophrenia-like or paranoid psychotic reaction, manic-like states, severe depression, and panic states. Crack especially can be extremely dangerous. For

Among the people in this crack house in Brooklyn are a prostitute and a person infected with the AIDS virus, pointing to some of the health dangers that can surround the use of cocaine in the United States.

example, the heart rates of users can increase abnormally, which in some cases can lead to cardiac arrest and death. Cocaine can produce as much dependence, tolerance, and withdrawal in those who use it as does heroin (Hasin et al., 1988). Finally, for those who take cocaine intravenously, there is the danger of AIDS infection when dirty needles are shared with other users.

Amphetamines are synthetic central nervous system stimulants. The effects of amphetamines are longer lasting than cocaine, but the two types of stimulants are quite similar in other respects. Some amphetamine abuse arises when people use these stimulants to help them accomplish socially acceptable tasks, such as studying long hours for an examination, putting in extra hours at work, or trying to lose weight. For these people, the drug may have been obtained through medical prescriptions or it might have been bought on the black market. These socially acceptable uses of amphetamines, however, can readily become abuse. Because tolerance develops, legitimate users may increase the dosage to the point at which withdrawal symptoms occur if use is discontinued. In addition, amphetamines are highly addicting, and this can make quitting very difficult. A far more destructive type of amphetamine abuse is by "speed freaks" who take massive doses, often through intravenous injections, several times a day. This "run" might result in the person staying awake for many days (Milhorn, 1994). Sleeping and eating very little, people's judgment becomes impaired, and they feel overconfident, paranoid, and nervous. The feelings of overconfidence can lead to accidents. At the end of a "run," users will "crash," sleeping for long periods.

Heavy users of stimulants, especially cocaine and amphetamines, are much more likely to commit crimes and be involved in violence than are users of most other psychoactive drugs (Eckerman et al., 1971; Goldstein et al., 1991). Part of this is the stimulant effect of the drugs themselves, which can lead people to feel delu-

sional, overly courageous, impulsive, or panicky. But violence also occurs because "speed freaks" and crack cocaine users must participate in a criminal subculture where hustles, coercion, fraud, and violence are routine practices in the illegal drug business (U.S. Department of Justice, 1992). In addition, prostitution, robbery, and violent crimes are ways of getting money to buy drugs and support oneself. Interestingly, heavy drug users among males were most likely to be the perpetrators of violence, whereas among women drug users were the victims of violence. To oversimplify somewhat, the male users robbed stores and the female users got beat up by their spouses or lovers.

Depressants

The main effect of **depressants** is the opposite of stimulants: *They depress the central nervous system (CNS), along with having some analgesic, or painkilling, properties.* Alcohol is a depressant that we have discussed in a separate section. In addition, depressants include almost all sleeping medications (hypnotics or barbiturates) and antianxiety drugs (or the minor tranquilizers).

Barbiturates are a class of CNS depressants that are used as sedatives or painkillers. They can have effects similar to alcohol, particularly in reducing people's inhibitions. This can lead some to relax and others to become highly active, even aggressive. Their effects range from slight lethargy or sleepiness, to various levels of anesthesia, and finally to death from respiratory and heart depression. Among the many barbiturates are pentobarbital (Nembutal), secobarbital (Seconal), and amobarbital (Amytal). They can produce physical addiction, tolerance, cross-tolerance, and psychological dependence. Addiction to barbiturates is so severe that withdrawal is more dangerous than withdrawing from narcotics. Withdrawal can be accompanied by anxiety, nausea, cramps, hallucinations, and even fatal convulsions. Another serious problem with barbiturates is overdose. Especially with someone who uses a lot of depressants, including alcohol, it is easy to forget how much one has taken and inadvertently take too much. With their depressant effect, an overdose of barbiturates can slow a person's breathing and heart rate to the point where coma or death occurs. An overdose of barbiturates is also a common means of committing suicide (Lettieri, 1978).

An especially serious problem with barbiturates and other depressants is what drug abuse specialists call *potentiation*. This refers to what occurs when two depressants are taken at the same time: The effect of the combination is greater than would be expected from the action of either drug separately. The outcome can be an unexpected lethal dose. For example, people who consume a lot of alcohol—a depressant drug—and then decide to take a few sedative pills to sleep may inadvertently kill themselves due to respiratory failure or go into an irreversible coma. This lethal combination of barbiturates and alcohol is not uncommon.

In earlier decades, barbiturates were often obtained legally through a physician's prescription and then used in ways for which they were not medically prescribed. Today, however, barbiturates are not prescribed as commonly as in the past, having been replaced by other drugs, including tranquilizers (Milhorn, 1994). As a consequence, use of barbitiates has declined, especially among the young (see Tables 10.1 and 10.2).

The minor tranquilizers have many of the same effects as barbiturates, but in addition they can reduce anxiety and tension and produce a sense of well-being. They include such drugs as diazepam (Valium), chlordiazepoxide (Librium), and meprobamate (Equanil or Miltown). The minor tranquilizers are also characterized by addiction, tolerance, and severe withdrawal symptoms. In one year, more than two billion tablets of Valium were prescribed by physicians in the United States (Schuckit, 1989). Medical use of tranquilizers is more common than sedatives. For many, this means taking tranquilizers to relieve the stresses and anxieties and to get over the "rough spots" of modern life. The danger, of course, is that a pattern of abuse can set in, often before the person realizes what has happened. Also, the combination of tranquilizers with other depressants can be deadly: It was a combination of alcohol and tranquilizers taken at a party that is suspected of sending Karen Ann Quinlin into a decade-long coma that ultimately resulted in her death in 1985.

The nonmedical use of sedatives and tranquilizers is more likely to occur among young adults (see Table 10.2). Such use is also more common among whites than among nonwhites (U.S. Department of Health and Human Services, 1994).

Some barbiturate-like drugs were developed as nonaddicting and safe substitutes for barbiturates. Most have turned out to be very different indeed, sharing many dangers with barbiturates. This is especially true for methaqualone (Quaalude, Sopors), which has been widely abused. First introduced in 1965, it was not a controlled substance and was prescribed widely by many physicians who thought it was safe and nonaddicting. The effects of methaqualone are much the same as those of other sedatives and hypnotics, although with a possible greater loss of motor coordination. This can lead to a substantial loss of control, which led to the slang name "wallbanger" for the drug because of the tendency for users to bump into walls. By 1973, methaqualone's dangers were apparent and it was declared a controlled substance. But much damage had already been done. Methaqualone found its way into the black market. Soon after its introduction in both the United States and Great Britain, "ludes" or "sopors" became appealing to teenagers, heroin abusers, and just about anyone who wanted an inexpensive, but quite potent, "downer." The large market for methaqualone is partly due to its reputation as an aphrodisiac that can enhance people's sexual abilities and pleasure. In fact, some called it "heroin for lovers." However, the most it probably does along these lines is to reduce inhibitions.

Narcotics

Narcotics or **opiates** are *drugs whose main use is as analgesics or painkillers.* These include natural substances (opium, morphine, and codeine), minor chemical alterations of those natural substances (heroin, Dilaudid, and Percodan), and synthetic drugs (Darvon and Demerol). In addition to reducing pain, they produce drowsiness, mood changes, euphoria, and reduced mental functioning with high doses. They also depress the central nervous system and heart activity. The opiates produce tolerance and cross-tolerance. They are also highly addictive, with physical dependence developing very quickly. For example, therapeutic doses of morphine given four times a day to relieve pain will produce mild withdrawal symptoms after only three days (Schuckit, 1989). Opiates can be ingested in a variety of ways: orally (especially the synthetic opiates), intranasally ("snorting," as with morphine and heroin), by smoking (opium), or intravenously ("mainlining," as with heroin).

Some opiate abusers misuse painkillers that they began taking for medical reasons. Health-care providers, especially physicians and nurses, have a high rate of such analgesic abuse, possibly because of its easy availability to them. Other opiate abusers purchase their narcotics in the street market. Most illegal opiates enter the United States from the Orient, the Middle East, or South America. Many street abusers begin with the occasional use of opiates and then progress to daily use, with tolerance and dependence growing rapidly. Daily heroin users who are physically addicted may spend $50 to $100 per day to support their habits. However, the image of the addicted narcotic addict should not be overdrawn. Some heroin users never progress beyond occasional use, called "chipping," and they continue this for many years, without physical addiction, and while

maintaining a family, a circle of friends, and a job. They may spend as little as $15 to $20 for heroin on the days that they use it. This suggests that opiates, like alcohol, can be used semiregularly by some people while maintaining respectability and social stability and without contributing to a social problem (Johnson, 1984). As for the link between crime and heroin abuse, it is clear that heroin addicts commit many crimes (Lerner and Raczynski, 1988; Deschenes, Anglin, and Speckart, 1991). However, as the Applied Research insert indicates, alcohol—a legal psychoactive drug—plays an important role in this criminal behavior.

There are probably seven hundred thousand heroin addicts in the United States (Peirce, 1992). Yet relatively few people have ever tried heroin. Among young adults—the heaviest users—only 1 percent claim to have ever used it, and that figure may be declining (see Table 10.2). There are other indications that heroin use has declined. For example, the number of arrests involving opiates has dropped, as has the number of cases of hepatitis and opiate-related mortalities. Still, the morbidity and mortality rate for street abusers of opiates is high, usually due to dirty needles and impure drugs. In addition, addicts who are accustomed to heavily diluted heroin may suffer an overdose if they happen to purchase some high-quality heroin. Finally, because of sharing dirty needles with HIV-infected drug users, heroin addicts run a considerable risk of HIV infection and thus contracting AIDS. One estimate is that half of the heroin addicts in New York City are infected with the HIV virus (Dole, 1991).

Heroin and many other opiates are far less damaging to the human body than are alcohol and tobacco (Trebach, 1982). Withdrawal from the opiates is also less dangerous than withdrawal from barbiturates or alcohol. In fact, opiate addicts can lead reasonably normal lives if they have a steady supply of the drug, use clean equipment, and know how to administer it properly. Many of the street abusers' problems arise from the illegality of the drugs: the high prices of black market drugs, the violence associated with the street drug trade, the varying quality and purity of drugs bought on the street, and the difficulty of keeping injection equipment sterile.

Hallucinogens

Hallucinogens, also called **psychedelics,** are *drugs that produce hallucinations, often of a visual nature.* Unlike marijuana, whose effect at normal doses is to change a person's mood or feelings, the hallucinogens produce illusions and hallucinations even at low doses. Awareness of sensory input and mental activity is intensified, thoughts are turned inward, and users are less able to differentiate between themselves and their surroundings. Hallucinogens have no accepted medical use in which their benefits outweigh their disadvantages. Examples of hallucinogens are: lysergic acid diethylamide (LSD), psilocybin, peyote, mescaline, diethyltryptamine (DET), and a phenylisopropylamine known as DOM or STP. Some, such as LSD and STP, are synthetic, whereas others are plant products (peyote and mescaline come from cacti, and psilocybin comes from mushrooms—although not the ones sold by your friendly grocer). All are taken orally. Tolerance to hallucinogens builds up rapidly, and there is cross-tolerance between most hallucinogens (although not, as some believe, between hallucinogens and marijuana). There is no physical dependence or withdrawal.

The popularity of hallucinogens peaked in the 1960s, and their use has since been somewhat supplanted by stimulants and depressants. As Table 10.2 shows, about 13 percent of young adults have tried hallucinogens, but relatively few use them regularly. This may be because their hallucinatory effect makes it difficult to relate to others, especially people who are not also hallucinating. The hallucinations make normal activities—such as shopping, going to class, and the like—almost impossible to accomplish.

One problem with hallucinogens bought on the street is that you may not know what drug has actually been purchased. What a seller hawks as mescaline may actually be PCP or LSD. In addition, hallucinogens are sometimes adulterated with other drugs, such as amphetamines. This makes it difficult for users to know exactly what drug they are taking, and thus their reaction to it may be unpredictable, unpleasant, or dangerous (Jackson and Jackson, 1983). Another problem with hallucinogens is that usage can precipitate psychoses, with wild hallucinations, paranoid delusions, and mania. These psychoses are not common and usually clear within hours or days. If the psychoses persist, it is usually because of a preexisting psychiatric condition.

One of the most widely abused drugs, after alcohol, cocaine, and marijuana, is phencyclidine (PCP). It is inexpensive and relatively easy to synthesize by amateurs. As a consequence, it is often sold by street dealers as some other, more expensive, drug such as THC or LSD. PCP, often called "angel dust" on the street, was first introduced as a CNS depressant that was an anesthetic with some desirable properties. However, the drug was soon discovered to cause postoperative agitation and hallucinations in many patients, so medical use of PCP was discontinued. On the street, PCP was first used to adulterate other drugs, but then came to be abused as a hallucinogen in its own right, which is why it is discussed here rather than with the depressants. The usual way of taking PCP is orally or through smoking, but it can also be injected or sprayed on other drugs. The evidence is still unclear as to whether PCP causes physical or psychological dependence, and there do not seem to be any withdrawal symptoms.

PCP in low doses creates a sense of euphoria, a lack of coordination, and an agitated emotional state. Moderate doses create a drunken-like condition with perceptual illusions. At still higher doses, PCP can produce psychosis. Especially with people who go on "runs" of two or three days of continual PCP ingestion, highly agitated and even violent be-

The Role of Alcohol in the Crimes of Heroin and Cocaine Addicts

In much popular imagery, the stereotype of the "drug addict" is of a person crazed by heroin or cocaine who commits crimes to support his or her habit with little regard for the victims of his or her actions. In fact, as we have seen, heroin and cocaine addicts do commit many crimes. Yet this stereotype is oversimplified in at least one dimension: It ignores the fact that heavy users of heroin and cocaine tend to be polydrug users, including heavy alcohol use. Many substance abuse programs have ignored the role of drugs other than heroin or cocaine in the criminal activities of addicts. As a consequence, they have been less effective in attacking the problem.

Social researchers at the Interdisciplinary Research Center for the Study of the Relations of Drugs and Alcohol to Crime have undertaken a series of investigations designed to gather more information about the relationship between the use of alcohol among active heroin users and their criminal activity (Strug et al., 1984). The researchers interviewed fifty-nine active heroin users recruited from the streets of Manhattan regarding the nondrug-related crimes that they had committed during the thirty-six hours prior to being interviewed. The investigators also asked about the users' drug and alcohol consumption patterns before and after committing crimes. These fifty-nine heroin users reported committing 103 nondrug crimes during the thirty-six hours before the interviews. Furthermore, intensive interviews were conducted with eleven heavy-drinking heroin users who had criminal records concerning the role that alcohol played in their criminal behavior patterns.

The researchers learned that alcohol, not heroin, was the drug that these addicts had used most frequently during the thirty days before being interviewed, and they were more likely to report being under the influence of alcohol than any other drug. Nearly 70 percent of these people had consumed alcohol on twenty-six or more of the prior thirty days. Although they used alcohol more frequently than heroin, they felt that they had been dependent on heroin for a longer period of time than any other drug, including alcohol. According to the investigators, this may be explained by the fact that alcohol use is so common and socially acceptable in society that dependence on the substance is less likely to be recognized. In fact, one of the men characterized himself as a "light drinker" even though he consumed three pints of wine per day. Among the eleven "heavy drinkers" in the group, the range of alcohol con-

havior can occur. These people are often seen in hospital emergency rooms. One study found that 80 percent of the acute psychiatric admissions to one hospital in Los Angeles had detectable levels of PCP in their blood (Aniline et al., 1980). Law enforcement officials experience serious problems in subduing suspects who are using PCP because the suspects are often very difficult and dangerous to stop.

Another drug abused for its hallucinogenic properties is amyl nitrite or butyl nitrite, used medically to increase the blood flow for people suffering from acute angina pain. It causes slight euphoria and slows down time perception. Abuse of these substances, often called "poppers" on the street, first appeared among homosexuals who believed that it postponed sexual orgasm and increased sexual pleasure. Use then spread to other groups as young people learned of its hallucinogenic value. However, poppers do have negative side effects, including nausea, dizziness, faintness, and a drop in blood pressure.

A new drug, MDMA, reportedly offers the euphoric rush of cocaine and certain mind-expanding qualities of hallucinogens. MDMA, sumption was from three to twelve pints of wine each day.

Regarding crime, the respondents reported being high on some drug during 37 percent of the crimes they committed. Of these crimes committed while on drugs, the perpetrator was high on alcohol alone or alcohol in combination with other drugs 63 percent of the time. The men reported that consuming alcohol near the time of their crimes "provided them with calmness and courage, and allowed them to take bigger risks which, in their opinion, also allowed them to perform better" (Strug et al., 1984: 561). As one man put it: "Liquor puts 'a gorilla' on my back. I get more 'hard' as they say." Another said: "I would not have broken into that van if I was sober, because it might have belonged to somebody on the street." With respect to the use of money gained through criminal activities, in 93 percent of these occasions, the income was used to purchase alcohol and/or other drugs. The respondents were as likely to spend their criminal income on alcohol as on heroin.

The researchers also discovered that the need for money to buy alcohol was one of the motives for these men to commit their crimes. Although the general public tends to think that the high cost of heroin makes heroin addicts particularly prone to committing income-producing crimes, the economic resources of these addicts are so meager that the regular use of alcohol alone can generate the need to commit crimes. In a study of drugs and violence among cocaine users, the researchers concluded that alcohol, not cocaine or heroin, was "the major contributor" to violence resulting from the effect of the drug on people's thinking and behavior (Goldstein et al., 1991: 365). The drug users did engage in criminal violence to support their drug habit, but the majority of the violence they engaged in was produced by the effect of alcohol on the body rather than done to get money to buy drugs.

So based on this research, we begin to see that the addict-criminal may be as "crazed" on alcohol as on heroin or cocaine. Alcohol use served both as a very important motivation to commit crimes and as a key facilitator of criminal and violent behavior. When looking at the problem of drug use and crime, then, we are led to wonder whether alcohol—a legal drug—is more of a problem than heroin and cocaine. However, as these researchers note, most drug treatment programs do not provide for rehabilitation from alcohol.

known as "ecstasy" on the street, can be easily manufactured from readily available chemicals. Substances like MDMA have been called the "designer drugs" because they can be manufactured so easily from available chemicals, and they are rarely detected in ordinary drug tests.

Explanations of Drug Abuse

The search for explanations of drug abuse has spanned many decades, and we have learned a great deal. One thing that has become quite clear is that drug abuse is a very complicated process. Many factors—biological, psychological, social, and cultural—contribute to the problem. There is no one source of the problem and no one quick fix that will solve it.

Biological Explanations

There is now impressive evidence to suggest that heredity influences the likelihood of some people becoming alcoholic (Blum and Payne, 1991; Milhorn, 1994). People with an alcoholic parent are as much as six times more likely to become alcoholic themselves, even when raised apart from their biological parents in a nonalcoholic family. Although this heritability is found among men, it is not yet clear whether it applies to women.

The reasons for this susceptibility are still under debate (Schuckit, 1989). Alcoholics may develop a tolerance to alcohol more quickly, they may metabolize alcohol more quickly, or they may possess an inherited nutritional deficiency that is made up by alcohol. However, one very important point—especially when considering social policy relating to alcoholism—is that 60 to 65 percent of alcoholics do not exhibit this genetic link, and some alcoholics with the genetic link only became heavy drinkers under certain environmental conditions. As for biological mechanisms involved in addiction to drugs other than alcohol, there are a number of theories relating to tolerance, drug metabolism, and the like, but there is little evidence that such factors make some people more biologically susceptible to drug addiction (Milby, 1981).

Psychological Explanations

Psychological approaches to drug abuse posit that abuse arises from some psychological process or is the result of some emotional or personality disorder. Social learning or reinforcement theories, for example, argue that people will repeat those actions that provide them with some reward or pleasure (Ray, 1988). Drugs provide experiences that some people find pleasurable: euphoria, relaxation, ease of tension, even hallucinations might be enjoyable to some. So people who feel uncomfortable at parties, for example, may find that alcohol, marijuana, or a depressant relaxes them so that they can talk, dance, and enjoy themselves. Drug use may then become a habitual way they relax or enjoy themselves. Given the number of stressful and tense situations that some people face in their daily lives, it is not surprising that the reinforcing properties of alcohol and other drugs can have these effects.

Psychodynamic theories claim that drug abuse is a consequence of flaws or weaknesses in people's personalities (Collins and Marlatt, 1983; Light, 1986). It may be, for example, that alcoholics are exceedingly dependent personalities who experienced rejection by their parents during childhood and have a compulsive need for love. The excessive use of alcohol can serve as a means of relieving anxiety when those unrealistic needs are not met. Another psychodynamic approach claims that it is a need for power, not dependency, that underlies excessive alcohol use. While drinking, men can fantasize about how strong and powerful they are and thus ignore feelings of weakness and inadequacy. Many studies have found that opiate addicts have very high rates of mental disorders, especially depression (Rounsaville et al., 1984).

Although personality and psychological processes are undoubtedly important in the lives of individuals, they are probably not sufficient, by themselves, to explain a deviant behavior such as drug abuse. For one thing, psychological factors by themselves would produce an abuse problem that is sporadic and intermittent. Yet the societal drug problem is continuous and persistent because there are many social and cultural factors contributing to it. In addition, psychological problems have social sources, often in family experiences, and these social factors should be the focus of social policy. Finally, research results on the psychology of addiction have been contradictory. Some addicts exhibit psychological maladjustment, whereas others do not.

Sociological Explanations

Sociological explanations of drug abuse focus on the role of culture, social structure, and social interaction in precipitating drug abuse. We will review the insights that the three sociological perspectives shed on this problem.

The Functionalist Perspective The functionalist approach focuses on the strains, inconsistencies, and contradictions in the social system that can contribute to the drug problem. In Chapter 9, Robert Merton's anomie theory of deviance and crime was discussed. It posits, in brief, that an inconsistency occurs when people are taught through the socialization process to pursue certain socially approved goals, such as success, but then are denied access to socially approved means of achieving those goals. Examples of people in anomic situations would be those who want to go to college but cannot afford it, a person whose business has failed, or a parent whose child has died. People can adapt to this anomie in many ways, such as crime, resignation, or outrage. Merton labeled one mode of adaptation *retreatism:* the rejection of the culturally approved goals and the importance of achieving them through the culturally approved means. Retreatists "drop out" or try to escape, and for some, this means using drugs or alcohol in the search for solace and forgetfulness.

Another mode of adaptation to anomie, discussed in Chapter 9, is *innovation:* an acceptance of the cultural goal of success but the use of socially disapproved, possibly illegal, means to achieve it. People in poor communities might be drawn into the illegal drug trade as a way to attain material success that would be more difficult or impossible to attain in conventional ways. Their benefiting from the drug trade helps to perpetuate the illegal drug business.

Functionalists also point to another inconsistency in the United States: There is no clear normative consensus regarding which drugs are socially acceptable and which are not. Some subcultures in the United States approve of the use of alcohol, others cocaine, and still others the hallucinogens. This lack of consensus regarding drugs opens the door for new drugs to find acceptance. When a new drug such as PCP or crack becomes available, it exists in a normative vacuum, with no norms prescribing or proscribing its use. Because other drugs are widely used, it is likely that some susceptible individuals will adopt the new drug as acceptable.

The Conflict Perspective   The drug abuse problem is shaped in part by the exercise of social, political, and economic power. As we saw in Chapter 9, it is powerful groups in society that are in a position to define which crimes or which drugs will be sanctioned and made illegal. Over the years, powerful and respectable people have used alcohol, and it was not, until recently, even considered a "drug" to be linked with substances such as heroin and cocaine. In the 1980s and 1990s, the War on Drugs has not attacked alcohol but rather cocaine and heroin. In fact, drug enforcement authorities have been criticized for what appears to be a war against mostly young male African Americans and Hispanics. The vast majority of those arrested in the War on Drugs are African American and Hispanic even though there are as many white drug users as African American and Hispanic. This could be interpreted to mean that the authorities may be more interested in creating the appearance of fighting drugs by attacking drug use among poor and minorities while largely ignoring the much more considerable drug use, both legal and illegal, among more affluent and influential groups. In the past twenty years, marijuana has gained a more respectable status—and legal penalties for its use have been reduced in many jurisdictions—primarily because middle-class, college-educated people have taken up its use. So what is considered a dangerous drug whose use is to be sanctioned by society depends on which groups have most control over the political and legal apparatus. The assessments of the danger of drugs and stigma attached to them are often unrelated to the actual danger they represent. We have seen that some illegal and highly stigmatized drugs are actually fairly safe, whereas some clearly damaging drugs such as alcohol and barbiturates are legal and less stigmatized.

The conflict perspective points to another element of the drug abuse problem: Some groups benefit in economic and other ways from the consumption of drugs by others, and it is in their interests to make drugs available

Two young lawyers in San Francisco lay out some lines of cocaine for their friends at a party while thousands of miles away a Bolivian peasant family, children and all, trudges along a dusty path into an isolated field. The two scenes seem worlds apart, but they are intimately linked through the political economy of the worldwide drug trade. The term *political economy* refers to the way in which politics and the exercise of power influence the production and distribution of economic resources. Bolivia exports $4 billion of cocaine each year—its biggest single export (Bagley and Walker, 1994; U.S. Department of Justice, 1992). For a poor country like Bolivia, that is big business. For many Bolivian peasants, their very survival depends on cultivating the drugs that feed the acquired illicit tastes of those lawyers along with the many other people in the United States who use cocaine or smoke marijuana. Marijuana and cocaine produce more foreign exchange for Bolivia than do coffee and cut flowers, the country's two chief legal exports. At least five hundred thousand Bolivians depend on the coca trade for their livelihood. Illicit drugs worldwide may generate annual revenues of $500 billion. As one Bolivian peasant farmer put it: "I don't care how much pressure [the United States] puts on us to stop growing coca, we will never give this up because we have no other means to survive" (Sims, 1995). Farmers in many other countries that export illegal drugs to the United States would echo those sentiments.

All coca leaf and much marijuana are grown in Central and South American countries, primarily Belize, Bolivia, Colombia, Jamaica, Mexico, and Peru (U.S. Department of State, 1991). In Asia, the major drug producers are Myanmar (Burma), Laos, Thailand, Pakistan, Iran, and Afghanistan. This is where most opium poppies are grown (see Figure 10.5). One goal of American drug enforcement policy is to reduce the overseas production of drugs and their importation into the United States. In fact, by law, the president of the United States is required to cut off foreign aid to countries that do not make progress in reducing their drug crops. This leaves the United States with the dilemma of

whether to reduce economic assistance and other types of foreign aid to countries that do not cooperate. This is a controversial policy issue because a cut in foreign aid is considered a hostile move by countries with whom the United States is friendly and may disrupt other elements of our foreign policy. In addition, such cuts may exacerbate a major factor underlying the international drug trade: Poverty and economic underdevelopment make the growing and selling of drugs a way for some people to survive. A cut in aid may hinder efforts at improving the economies of these countries and thereby create more fertile ground for drug production.

Why do these countries refuse to cooperate? Part of the reason is the difficulty of controlling the illicit growing of marijuana, coca, and opium poppies. Much of the cultivation takes place in isolated, hard-to-reach parts of these countries, and the law enforcement authorities are often not equal to the task. In addition, the criminals running the illegal drug traffic are powerful, sometimes more powerful than the government. In Bolivia and Burma, for example, wealthy and well-organized drug traffickers have actually taken control of the areas where drugs are produced, killing government officials or soldiers who enter without permission. In Colombia, many judges, politicians, police officers, and other government officials have died in drug-related assassinations. Often, the governments have been corrupted by bribes from drug traffickers or by direct participation of government officials in the traffic. Finally, the drug crops, although illegal, are often a significant source of economic support and foreign dollars. To successfully control the drug trade would be a severe economic blow to these countries. Only once, in Turkey in the early 1970s, was the United States effectively able to pressure a nation to reduce its drug production. But the Turkish farmers who grew opium poppies also grew other cash crops, and their livelihoods were therefore not threatened. They could shift their productive efforts to other crops with little disruption.

When we understand the extent to which the drug problem in the United States is linked with

Major Cocaine-Smuggling Routes into the United States

DEA Quarterly Intelligence Trends

FIGURE 10.5 Drug Smuggling Routes into the United States.

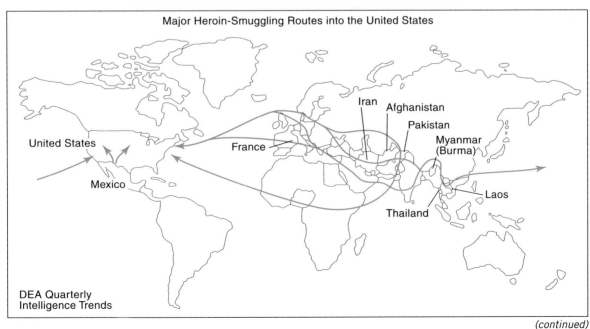

Major Heroin-Smuggling Routes into the United States

DEA Quarterly Intelligence Trends

(continued)

worldwide political and economic issues, the complexity of the problem becomes more clear. Lest we think that the political economy of drugs is primarily a foreign problem, estimates place marijuana as the largest cash crop in California, and 25 percent of the demand for marijuana in the United States is satisfied by marijuana grown in the United States (Kupfer, 1989). For some remote counties of northern California and rural Appalachia, growing marijuana is very lucrative for those willing to take the risk, and their profits help support other local businesses, such as small-town banks. If we look at legal drugs, the political economy of the drug problem becomes even more clear. Bars and liquor stores in the United States have an annual retail trade of over $34 billion dollars, whereas the sale of alcoholic beverages in the United States totals about $18 billion a year (U.S. Bureau of the Census, 1994: 786). In addition, the pharmaceutical industry benefits from the sale of stimulants, depressants, and other legal drugs. Although none of these industries encourages drug abuse, they

nonetheless thrive from swamping the United States in drugs and from reducing any controls that might limit the extent of drug abuse. The tobacco industry, for example, fought against a ban on the advertising of cigarettes on television, but it lost. Currently, the liquor industry is opposing proposals for a similar ban against alcohol advertising. It is in its interest to encourage people, through extensive advertising, to use alcohol. People who sell beer, wine, and liquor spend $239 million a year on newspaper and magazine advertising and $428 million on television advertising.

So a key element of the drug problem in the United States is the many sources—domestic and international, legal and illegal—that give people a host of opportunities to purchase and use drugs. Controlling the drug problem depends on our ability to reduce these sources of supply. Yet so many powerful interest groups benefit from policies that make it difficult to reduce the supply that there is some pessimism about how successful these efforts can be.

and to encourage their use. This issue is discussed in the Policy Issues insert in this chapter.

The Interactionist Perspective The interactionist approach is based on the premise that drug use and abuse arises from the social influences and pressures that can be found in particular contexts. Recall from Chapter 9 that cultural transmission theories view crime and drug abuse as learned behaviors that are transmitted through the socialization process of a particular culture or subculture. This learning occurs mainly in intimate groups, such as with family or friends, where people learn what drugs to use, where to buy them, how to use them, and even what the "high" from a particular drug is supposed to feel like. They also learn to value

the use of particular drugs. A person being introduced to cocaine, for instance, might be told by experienced users that cocaine is good because it makes one more perceptive, creative, and energetic, whereas alcohol is a downer. In other words, drug subcultures are important in promoting and maintaining patterns of abuse. People must have the opportunity and encouragement to use drugs and the willingness to take the consequences. Sociologists Richard Cloward and Lloyd Ohlin (1960), for example, have argued that youngsters with close ties to conventional groups and little access to drugs will not respond to teenage adjustment problems by turning to drugs. Instead, they will find other outlets for their energies or anxieties. It is the youths without access to legitimate opportunities and with some entrance into a drug subculture who are in danger of developing a pattern of drug abuse. Even an "alcoholic personality" may be somewhat immune from becoming an alcoholic if he or she is involved in a subculture in which drinking is severely sanctioned (Miller, 1984).

This cultural transmission of values regarding drug use can be illustrated by comparing patterns of alcohol use among some ethnic groups in the United States. Some groups, such as Jews and Italians, incorporate alcohol into family activities in a closely regulated fashion. Alcohol is consumed in moderation as a part of family rituals such as meals or picnics. This teaches youngsters to value the moderate use of alcohol and to view alcohol consumption as appropriate only in particular social contexts. Among such groups, many people use alcohol, but rates of alcoholism are fairly low. Among the Irish, on the other hand, it is acceptable for males to drink outside of the family context, and drinking is viewed as an approved way of reducing frustrations or tensions.

Future Prospects

Drug abuse is a serious and complex problem for which there is no quick and easy solution. In fact, there probably are no solutions that will completely eradicate the problem from the United States. Yet some things can be done to keep it under reasonable control and to mitigate some of its more serious consequences. These programs focus on either prevention or treatment. We will review the major efforts in both of these directions.

Prohibition: The War on Drugs and Alcohol

One of the major preventive efforts of current social policy toward drugs of abuse is the legal prohibition of their use. Most such drugs, with the exception of alcohol, are illegal (when not used for medical reasons) and carry criminal penalties for their use. Does prohibition work? Not by most assessments (Duke and Gross, 1993). The effort to prohibit the use of alcohol through the Eighteenth Amendment to the U.S. Constitution (ratified in 1920) was an abysmal failure. People continued to drink, and organized crime flourished by supplying the "bootleg" liquor. The amendment also produced a certain cynicism toward law and government, as violations of the law were open and flagrant. The hypocrisy of the law was finally recognized by 1933 when the Eighteenth Amendment was repealed.

A similar experience has occurred over the past few decades as marijuana has become more popular. Although still illegal just about everywhere in the United States and carrying stiff prison terms in some jurisdictions, the use of marijuana flourishes. It is cheap, easy to obtain, and few people are punished for using it. There are lessons to be learned from our experience with alcohol and marijuana. When a practice is widespread, viewed as socially acceptable and even desirable by powerful groups, and brings economic gain to some interests, it is extremely difficult to eradicate through legislation. Laws will probably stop some people from using and abusing these drugs, and proponents of prohibition support it for this reason: They believe that it reduces the drug problem to below what it would be without such prohibition (Crowley, 1988).

In fact, the War on Drugs of the past decade was carved into law in the Anti-Drug Abuse Act of 1988. More police and narcotics agents have been sent out to track down drug users, stiffer and mandatory prison sentences have been given to those convicted, and boats and planes have swarmed over the Caribbean and Central America to catch drug importers. Despite spending billions of dollars each year, not much has changed. Casual use is down, but the crack cocaine and heroin epidemics are still blighting parts of our cities, and our prisons are bursting at the seams with people doing time for drug offenses. There are probably as many hardcore

Hundreds of cases of beer are destroyed in Pennsylvania during the period when alcohol was prohibited in the United States. Prohibition has proven to be a controversial and not very effective means of dealing with alcohol and drug abuse.

addicts as before, and there are as many drugs being produced in, or shipped into, this country as before. Illegal drugs are as easy to get today as before the War on Drugs. In addition, experts who have studied the changing trends in drug use do not attribute the decline in drug use in the past decade to vigorous law enforcement (Jacobsen and Hanneman, 1992). Instead, the drop in use has probably been due to the decline in the social acceptance of drugs, which had an impact on the casual users but not the serious drug addicts. Yet, despite the doubts of experts regarding the effectiveness of prohibi-

tion to control drug use, this policy still attracts considerable public support.

Legalization

Opponents of prohibition point not only to its ineffectiveness but also to the fact that it infringes on the rights of people who use drugs without abusing them (Duke and Gross, 1993). As we have seen, many people use alcohol, marijuana, cocaine, LSD, and even narcotics in a limited and periodic fashion for recreational purposes. The effects of some currently illegal drugs, such as marijuana, are mild and cause little damage when used in moderation. So proponents of legalization argue that marijuana and possibly other drugs should be treated much like alcohol: as legal but highly controlled substances. In fact, although no state has fully legalized marijuana, at least eleven states have *decriminalized* its use, or made simple possession of it for one's own use either a misdemeanor or a noncriminal offense punishable by a fine.

Proponents of legalization also point to the problems created because of the illegality of some drugs—their high cost and the crime and violence associated with obtaining them. Legalization, they argue, is one way of alleviating these problems. Both with the prohibition of al-

cohol in the 1920s and with the illegal drugs today, powerful and violent crime syndicates emerged to supply these substances. Because of the enormous amount of money involved, such organized crime can also have a corrupting influence on law enforcement agencies and elected officials. This has happened in South America and in the United States, where some drug enforcement agents have been found guilty of drug trafficking. If drugs were legal, they could be supplied by legitimate corporations; crime syndicates would not move in and other problems created by the illegality of drugs would be reduced. It has also been suggested that legalizing marijuana, the mildest of the illicit drugs, would have another advantage: It would help sever the connection of mari-

Dogs are used to search out drugs being smuggled into the United States. The results of such drug interdiction programs have been meager, with most drugs eluding such interdiction efforts.

juana use with drug dealers. The first drug that young people use is typically either alcohol or marijuana. With marijuana illegal, the only place youngsters can obtain the substance is from drug dealers, who naturally would like to encourage young people to experiment with other more expensive, and more dangerous, drugs such as cocaine. If marijuana could be purchased legally, one less incentive for involvement with drug pushers would exist. The International Perspectives insert describes the experiences of some other societies that have legalized or decriminalized some drugs.

The closest the United States comes to legalizing drugs (other than alcohol) is the methadone maintenance program. Methadone is a synthetic opiate that is prescribed for addicts who enroll in government-sponsored treatment programs. Methadone is itself highly addicting and leads to withdrawal, but its benefits over heroin are that the effects of methadone last longer (twenty-four hours as opposed to six hours for heroin) and people do not develop tolerance to methadone. What is called a "blocking dose" of methadone will block the euphoric effects of heroin, thus negating the motivation for continuing heroin use. The goal of the methadone maintenance program is to lower the dosage of methadone to a "maintenance" level at which withdrawal symptoms are prevented and there are few undesirable side effects. Methadone also does not induce much of a "high," so the person is sufficiently clear-headed and coherent to hold a job and lead a normal life. In addition, enrollees in maintenance programs are provided with various social services, including family counseling and job training, in an effort to attack the many elements of the drug abuse problem.

Methadone maintenance programs are highly controversial. Critics argue that they merely replace one addiction with another, which is true, and that many addicts return to heroin and other drugs (Jaffe, 1983). There is also a black market in methadone supplied in part by addicts in treatment who sell rather than take their methadone, and some methadone addicts get high by taking nonopiates, such as cocaine, whose effects are not blocked by methadone (McDonnell, Irwin, and Rosenbaum, 1990). Supporters argue that the program does help some addicts, although many of the programs are not run very well (U.S. General Accounting Office, 1990). Many addicts in methadone programs are free of any addiction, including methadone, after two years and are much less likely to be arrested and more likely to hold a job. Other studies show that addicts in maintenance programs use less heroin and other drugs and they have much lower death rates than those not enrolled in such programs (Des Jarlais, 1984; Dole, 1991; Yancovitz et al., 1991).

Primary Prevention

As used by drug abuse specialists, the term **primary prevention** refers to *preventing drug problems before they begin.* The government has established a three-front drug war focusing on primary prevention. One effort is to use educational programs to alert people to the dangers of drugs and instill responsible attitudes toward drug use. The second front is to interdict the drug traffic now flowing across our borders from overseas, and the third is to reduce production of drug crops by other nations.

Most experts agree that the best way to attack the drug problem is to reduce the demand for drugs (Wilson, 1990). Educational programs try to do this by teaching youth that drugs are risky and dangerous and by providing tips for how to resist the temptation of drugs. Youngsters who go through comprehensive drug education and prevention programs do use fewer drugs than those who do not go through such programs ("Community Drug Prevention . . . ," 1990). These comprehensive programs use the schools to teach kids how to resist pressures to use drugs, the parents to communicate more with kids and set family rules about drug and alcohol use, and community agencies such as the police to support antidrug programs. In fact, the decline in the use of marijuana and cocaine among youth in the past decade seems to be due to these educational efforts: Youth have come to view drugs as more risky and dangerous than in the past, and there is more social disapproval of drug use now (Bachman, Johnston, and O'Malley, 1990). However, the effectiveness of the vast antidrug media campaigns of the past decade is largely unknown. Although few evaluations have been done, most experts suggest that adolescents, the main targets of the efforts, are probably modestly influenced, at best, by such campaigns (Schilling and McAlister, 1990).

Border interdiction of drugs focuses on reducing the supply of drugs, and the results here have been meager. Experts estimate that only ten percent of the drugs smuggled into the United States are seized (Duke and Gross, 1993). For the past decade, the government has adopted a "get-tough" policy toward drug smuggling by beefing up the personnel available for interdiction activities and increasing the penalties for smuggling. A policy of "zero tolerance" has been established, under which boat owners found with even small amounts of illegal drugs have their equipment confiscated. A "drug czar" has been appointed to coordinate federal activities: the chief of the White House Office of National Drug Control Policy, a position created by the Anti-Drug Abuse Act of 1988. All of this has produced a great deal of publicity, but it is not clear at this point whether it will significantly reduce the flow of drugs into the United States. The illegal drug trade is so lucrative that people are willing to risk substantial punishments, and profits can be made even when 50 to 90 percent of a smuggler's drugs are confiscated. Controlling drug production overseas is discussed in the Policy Issues insert.

Rehabilitation and Therapeutic Communities

Many drug abusers can be rehabilitated if they are given proper treatment, such as counseling, methadone maintenance, or job train-

ing. Among adolescents at high risk of abusing drugs, school-based social support programs have proven that they can reduce the likelihood of future involvement in drugs (Eggert and Herting, 1991). By enhancing communication, empathy, and helping between students and teachers, these programs offer students an alternative to drugs. Most experts agree that making drug treatment programs available to all who desire them would be an important step toward significantly reducing the drug problem (Goldstein and Kalant, 1990). However, all these rehabilitation programs cost money, and much of the funds for the War on Drugs have been channeled into law enforcement and drug interdiction, leaving relatively little for rehabilitation.

One of the more widespread types of treatment programs for drug addicts is the therapeutic community in which group involvement, social support, and group pressure are used to help addicts quit taking drugs (De Leon, 1988; Currie, 1993). These programs are often run by addicts who are drug free. One of the best known therapeutic communities is Alcoholics Anonymous (AA), which was established by two alcoholics in 1935 to help them quit drinking (Robinson, 1983). AA has more than a half million members. The first step in the AA program is for people to admit publicly that they are alcoholics, helpless before alcohol, and need help from others. AA is organized and run by volunteers and costs nothing. Meetings are open to anyone, drunk or sober, and even in small towns there are meetings held practically every day. At these meetings, people talk about their problems, what alcohol has done to them, and their fears of returning to drink. Others provide emotional support and encouragement and help members deal with their problems. There are also groups for the spouses of alcoholics (Al-Anon) and the children of alcoholics (Alateen).

There are also therapeutic communities for abusers of drugs other than alcohol. Narcotics Anonymous is very similar to AA but focuses on narcotics addicts. The Odyssey House, Synanon,

INTERNATIONAL PERSPECTIVES
Drug Use and Drug Policies in Other Societies

When we look at drug use and drug policies, we see many different approaches (Benjamin and Miller, 1991; Miller, 1991). Marijuana and hashish were banned in Arabia in the fourteenth century. China tried to ban the importation of opium from India in the eighteenth century, resulting in the Opium Wars. For a time, in the early twentieth century, alcohol was illegal in the United States, and many people were thrown in jail for using or trafficking in it. Today, Malaysia and Singapore deal harshly with people who violate their drug laws: Drug traffickers are hanged, and users are whipped and sent to hard labor camps for two years or more. The United States has had a "war on drugs" for at least the last decade. In most cases, these punitive approaches have not been very effective at stopping drug use: Alcohol was used widely during Prohibition in the United States, while the hangings continue unabated and the labor camps grow in size in Malaysia and Singapore today. Drugs have a strong attraction, especially for those in desperate social circumstances, and banning their use hasn't worked very well.

Other societies have tried a different approach—that of decriminalizing or legalizing drugs. The Netherlands decriminalized drugs in 1976. Drug users and small-time dealers are not prosecuted, whereas large drug dealers and those who sell to minors are. Drug use in the Netherlands since then has not increased and may have declined somewhat. The consumption of marijuana and hashish, for example, declined after decriminalization. With marijuana and hashish widely available in Dutch cities, consumption of more serious drugs such as heroin has also declined. The Netherlands has fewer hard drug addicts than other Western European countries, far less of a drug problem, and a significantly lower death rate due to drug overdose than does the United States. There is also a very low incidence of AIDS among intravenous drug users. The Netherlands treats drug addiction as a health problem rather than a criminal one, and this creates a climate in which addicts can be open about their drug use and seek treatment for both their health and addiction problems.

Great Britain has experimented with policies to make drugs legally available, but in a somewhat different way from The Netherlands. Throughout the 1960s, physicians in Britain could prescribe opiates and cocaine for their patients if they needed them, even if the need was to prevent the physical or mental symptoms that the person would suffer if the drug were withdrawn. In other words, physicians could prescribe drugs to maintain an addiction, although they had to be convinced that maintaining the addiction was in the patient's best interest, possibly because there was little chance of successfully kicking the habit. There was still a black market in drugs in Great Britain because some addicts could not get a physician's prescription while others sought higher dosages than the government would permit.

Phoenix House, and Daytop Village are therapeutic communities that provide housing, counseling, and work for people who are trying to shake the drug habit (Milby, 1981; Densen-Gerber, 1984). Many of these programs depart from the AA approach in that people must sever ties with former associates and live for a time in the community itself. This regulation is based on the assumption that these former associations may have contributed to the person's drug problem, and it also gives the community considerable control over its members. Acceptance by peers is a prime force in these communities. They offer strong emotional support, but some have been accused of being highly authoritarian, demanding complete conformity to the

By the end of the 1960s, Britain had begun its own "war on drugs" in response to an increase in the illegal use of stimulants, sedatives, and hallucinogens. Greater limitations were placed on physicians' ability to prescribe heroin and cocaine. Physicians could still prescribe these drugs to nonaddicts and to addicts in limited circumstances, but special licenses were needed to prescribe addiction maintenance doses to addicts, and the licenses were given only to practitioners in drug abuse clinics. Official government policy was that addicts are to be weaned off drugs as quickly as possible. However, by the late 1980s, in part in response to the spread of AIDS among addicts sharing needles, drug policy in Great Britain has swung partially back to a less restrictive approach. Doctors have been given more authority to dispense drugs to addicts (Duke and Gross, 1993).

Since tightening up the drug laws, addiction rates have risen substantially in Great Britain. However, this is probably not due to the change in policy but to changing social conditions. Britain experienced worsening social conditions for lower income groups during the 1970s and 1980s, with declining economic productivity and fewer resources going into education, job training, child care, housing, and health care programs. The culprit in the rise in drug use has probably been the despair and alienation that haunt people, especially youth, when confronted with a bleak social landscape with few opportunities for advancement.

Drugs seem to be a common refuge when other problems—poverty, racism, family dissolution—become more severe.

These less punitive approaches seem to work reasonably well for countries like The Netherlands and Great Britain. They have far fewer narcotics addicts than the United States does, and crime, death, and health problems associated with the use of narcotics are lower there than in the United States (Clinard and Meier, 1989). Would such policies work in the United States? They might have some benefits, especially in terms of lowering the very high crime rate linked with heroin and cocaine use. Experience in these and other countries does suggest that decriminalization or legalization of illegal drugs could produce a modest increase in drug use, but not a lot, and most of the increase would be among people who tend to use drugs whether they are illegal or not (Miller, 1991). However, such policies would be no panacea: They would by no means eliminate, and possibly not even reduce, drug abuse. But the harsh, punitive approach currently applied in the United States hasn't been notably successful either. Decriminalization or legalization has the benefit of enabling us to approach the problem as a health problem, using medical and social service personnel, and freeing police to focus on crimes that are more of a threat to the public order.

rules of the group. Some such programs have been criticized for using rather harsh forms of group pressure—such as verbal challenges, public humiliation, and reprimands—with those considered to be irresponsible or faltering in their resolve to stay off drugs.

Research on the effectiveness of therapeutic communities is difficult to conduct because of

problems in finding representative samples of members and of nonmember addicts to compare them with. The evidence that is available, however, clearly suggests that these programs work for many. Although relapse (a return to the use of drugs) is common, many members successfully refrain from using alcohol and other drugs for long periods. Those people with the best likelihood of success are older addicts who are married, have a job, and have a history of relatively few delinquent or criminal acts. However, therapeutic communities are completely ineffective with the millions of addicts who do not believe they have a problem with drugs.

Behavior Modification

The social learning theory of drug abuse says that people become addicted because drugs provide them with personal pleasure or rewards. One therapeutic approach suggests that addicts might be weaned from drugs by making drug-taking unpleasant. This is known to drug abuse professionals as behavior modification. One form of this technique, used to treat alcoholism, is aversion therapy, in which the act of drinking alcohol is associated with some unpleasant experience. In some cases, a drug called Antabuse is used because it induces nausea and vomiting if the person taking it drinks any alcohol. A more controversial form of aversion therapy uses electrical shocks administered to a person each time he or she takes a drink of alcohol. The theory behind these treatments is that associating alcohol consumption with a painful or unpleasant experience will eventually lead the person to perceive alcohol consumption itself as undesirable. Aversion therapy is of limited utility because it depends on the cooperation of the alcoholic, but it has been helpful for some addicts who have not had success with other approaches.

Social Policy and Public Pressure

A few decades ago, the problem of alcoholism was shrouded by guilt and shame. Many alcoholics were unwilling to admit that they had a problem, and their families and friends were so embarrassed that they covered for the alcoholic when he or she got into trouble. Public sentiment has changed considerably. Alcoholism is now viewed as a medical problem that can be treated with tested methods. In 1970, the Com-

prehensive Alcohol Abuse and Alcoholism Prevention, Treatment and Rehabilitation Act was passed by the Nixon administration. The act established the National Institute on Alcohol Abuse and Alcoholism to serve as a center for research into the causes of and cures for alcoholism. The act also established the National Advisory Council on Alcohol Abuse and Alcoholism to recommend social policy directions on the problem. This government support, along with additional funding from private sources, has helped in the development of an extensive network of support services dealing with problems of drug abuse. Today, considerably less stigma is attached to the problem, and there are many places to seek help. Employers have pitched in with employee assistance programs (EAPs) that offer confidential help for employees with drug or alcohol problems. Employers have found that they benefit by rehabilitating, rather than terminating, a trained and experienced employee (Scanlon, 1991).

There has also been considerable public pressure to do something about the public dangers created by some forms of drug usage, such as those who drink alcohol and drive. Groups such as Mothers Against Drunk Driving (MADD) and Students Against Drunk Driving (SADD) have lobbied effectively at both the state and the national level for laws that have an impact on the problem. In response, states have raised the drinking age to twenty-one, and some have even outlawed such things as "two-for-one" happy-hour specials. Bartenders can now be held legally responsible if they serve liquor to someone who is drunk and the person gets into a traffic accident. State courts have even ruled that the host of a party is responsible for the behavior of a guest if the host serves the guest enough alcohol to get drunk (Mincer, 1985). In short, the courts, the legislatures, and the public are taking an increasingly tough posture toward some drug problems, such as drunk driving.

Still another hotly contested social policy issue that has involved much public pressure is

The drug epidemic has ravaged parts of our cities with unacceptably high rates of crime (Chapter 12) and helped spread diseases such as AIDS through the sharing of dirty needles (Chapter 4). Drug addiction has also destabilized many families (Chapter 3), when poor parents become addicted to crack cocaine, heroin, or alcohol.

LINKAGES

drug testing. The Drug-Free Workplace Act of 1988 requires companies with federal contracts to make an effort to maintain a drug-free workplace (Noble, 1992b). Many companies have responded by doing urine testing for illegal drugs among their employees. According to government officials, drug and alcohol abuse costs industry up to $60 billion each year in lost productivity and high rates of absenteeism, medical claims, on-the-job mishaps, and employee theft. Drug testing in the workplace, it is claimed, would help locate those with substance abuse problems and offer them assistance. The American Civil Liberties Union (ACLU) and other opponents of routine drug testing, on the other hand, maintain that drug testing violates rights of privacy and the Constitution's prohibition against unreasonable search and seizure. Furthermore, the ACLU questions the accuracy, validity, and reliability of such tests. In addition, the testing detects relatively few drug users, and most of those are occasional marijuana users who are probably not bad workers and no threat on the job. Drug testing is likely to remain a hotly debated issue over the next few years.

Social Reform

While all the things discussed thus far are important in the effort to control drug abuse, probably the most difficult step is to recognize that a serious and widespread drug problem says something about the United States. As one expert on drug issues put it:

Endemic drug abuse tells us that something is fundamentally amiss in our *social* organization. Healthy societies are not overwhelmed by hard drugs. Those that *are* overwhelmed, around the world, are invariably riddled with other preventable social problems. (Currie, 1993: 280)

Many of those problems, of course, are the topic of this book: fractured families, inequities based on race or ethnicity or gender, high levels of violence, a lack of economic opportunity for many people, and so on. Not all drug abuse is caused by these conditions, but the pervasiveness of the problem in the United States is in part due to people's reactions to the negative social conditions they confront. As the United States makes progress in alleviating these problems, the drug problem will also likely ease.

Summary

1. The use of drugs in one form or another is widespread in human societies. Opinions about drug use vary widely, with some groups arguing for a complete ban on all drugs and others opting for the freedom to use drugs as people see fit. Drug use by itself is not a social problem; drug abuse refers to the continued use of psychoactive substances at a level violating approved social practices. Drug abuse is costly to society in terms of accidents; crime; and family, work, and health problems.

2. People in the United States consume many different kinds of drugs; some are legal, whereas others are illegal. A legal drug, alcohol, is regarded as the United States' most severe drug problem when it is used to excess. The level of marijuana use in society is far lower than that of alcohol. Debate continues regarding how damaging marijuana really is to society. Stimulants refer to the many drugs that stimulate the central nervous system, including cocaine and amphetamines. Depressants, most notably the barbiturates and tranquilizers, have the opposite effect, depressing the central nervous system, and have some painkilling properties. Narcotics are drugs whose main use is as analgesics or painkillers. Hallucinogens or psychedelics are drugs that produce hallucinations, often of a visual nature.

3. There are different explanations of drug abuse. Biological explanations suggest that hereditary factors may be involved in people's proneness to addiction to various drugs. Psychological approaches to drug abuse posit that abuse arises from some psychological process or is the result of some emotional or personal-ity disorder. Sociological explanations focus on the role of culture, social structure, and social interaction in precipitating drug abuse.

4. Drug abuse is a serious and complex problem for which there is no quick and easy solution. Most programs involving such solutions focus on either prevention or treatment. One major preventive effort of current social policy toward drugs of abuse is legal prohibition. Opponents of this approach favor legalization, including such alternative drug treatment programs as methadone maintenance. Another strategy is primary prevention, which refers to preventing drug problems before they begin. One of the more widespread types of treatment programs for drug addicts is the therapeutic community. Another approach involves behavior modification in the form of aversion therapy. Social policy and public pressure are also important in the future prospects on drug abuse. Groups such as Mothers Against Drunk Driving (MADD) and Students Against Drunk Driving (SADD) are current examples.

STUDY and Review

Key Terms

alcoholism

cross-dependence

cross-tolerance

dependence

depressants

drug

drug abuse

drug addiction

hallucinogens

narcotics

opiates

primary prevention

psychedelics

psychoactive drugs

stimulants

tolerance

Multiple-Choice Questions

1. The drugs that constitute a social problem are typically limited to:
   a. Medically prescribed drugs.
   b. Illegal drugs.
   c. Psychoactive drugs.
   d. Stimulants, depressants, and opiates.
2. As used by professionals in the field, the term "drug addiction" refers to:
   a. Physical dependence on a drug.
   b. Both tolerance and dependence on a drug.

c. Either tolerance or dependence on a drug.

d. The excessive use of a drug that violates socially approved practices.

3. Which of the following represents the most severe drug problem in the United States?
   a. Heroin.
   b. Alcohol.
   c. Cocaine.
   d. Amphetamines.
   e. Stimulants.

4. Which of the following statements is true regarding the social characteristics of those at risk of becoming an alcoholic?
   a. Women are at greater risk than men.
   b. Lower SES people are at greater risk than higher SES people.
   c. The old are at greater risk than the young.
   d. Jews are at greater risk than Catholics.

5. Since 1980, the percentage of college students who use marijuana has:
   a. Skyrocketed.
   b. Increased gradually.
   c. Stayed fairly steady.
   d. Declined somewhat.

6. Cocaine would be classified as a:
   a. Stimulant.
   b. Depressant.
   c. Hallucinogen.
   d. Narcotic.

7. Which category of drugs has the least likelihood of producing physical dependence?
   a. Alcohol.
   b. Cocaine.
   c. Heroin.
   d. Hallucinogens.

8. According to the functionalist perspective, drug abuse occurs because:
   a. People carry inherited tendencies toward addiction.
   b. Some people benefit in economic ways when others become addicted to drugs.
   c. Strains, inconsistencies, and contradictions in the social system affect people.
   d. Childhood experiences lead people to develop an "addictive personality."

9. Methadone maintenance is a program for treating:
   a. Alcohol addiction.
   b. Addiction to hallucinogens.
   c. Heroin addiction.

d. Cocaine addiction.

e. Amphetamine addiction.

10. Therapeutic communities would probably be least effective in treating which category of drug addict?
    a. Alcoholics.
    b. Heroin addicts.
    c. Young addicts.
    d. Addicts who do not believe they have a problem with drugs.
    e. Addicts who have been taking drugs for a long time.

True/False Questions

1. According to the text, caffeine is one of the drugs that is considered to contribute to the social problem of drug abuse.

2. According to the text, drug dependence and drug abuse are the same thing.

3. The percentage of people in the United States who use marijuana is about the same as the percentage who use alcohol.

4. Heroin is classified as an opiate.

5. Crack addicts are more likely to be highly active and paranoid while high than are heroin addicts.

6. The nonmedical use of sedatives and tranquilizers is more common among the elderly than the young.

7. MDMA, or ecstasy, is a hallucinogen.

8. Social scientists have concluded that there is very little evidence to support the idea that genetics or biology plays a part in who becomes addicted to alcohol or other drugs.

9. Only about 10 percent of the drugs smuggled into the United States are seized by border interdiction programs.

10. Research has shown that school-based social support programs for adolescents at risk of abusing drugs can reduce involvement in drugs.

Fill-In Questions

1. _____ refers to a situation which higher and higher doses of a drug are needed to achieve the same effect.

2. If the withdrawal symptoms of one drug are alleviated by taking another drug in the same pharmacological class, then the first drug possesses _____ .

3. Drugs whose major effect is to stimulate the central nervous system are called _____ .

4. Amphetamines are classified as a _____ .

5. Methaqualone, or Quaalude, is classified as a _____ .

6. The term "chipping" refers to _____ .

7. _____ theories argue that people become addicted to drugs because they gain some reward or pleasure from using drugs repeatedly.

8. The _____ perspective posits that patterns of drug use and abuse are due to the cultural transmission of values.

9. _____ is a synthetic opiate that is sometimes prescribed for heroin addicts.

10. The three-front focus of primary prevention of drug use in the United States is a) border interdiction, 2) reduction of overseas production, and 3) _____ .

Matching Questions

_____ 1. aversion therapy

_____ 2. potentiation

_____ 3. dependence

_____ 4. stimulant

_____ 5. speed freak

_____ 6. marijuana

_____ 7. LSD

_____ 8. psychodynamic theory

_____ 9. narcotics anonymous

_____ 10. primary prevention

A. craving for a drug
B. amphetamine abuser
C. alcoholism treatment
D. a psychedelic
E. therapeutic community
F. combined effect of two depressants
G. has both sedative and hallucinogenic properties
H. border interdiction
I. psychological explanation of drug abuse
J. produce tolerance and dependence

Essay Questions

1. Define the terms *drug*, *drug abuse*, and *drug addiction*. What do the terms *tolerance* and *dependence* mean in this context?
2. Summarize the costs that society must pay because of alcohol and drug abuse.
3. What are the social characteristics of people who are at a greater risk of becoming alcoholics?
4. What are the problems that the use of marijuana can produce for people?
5. Why are stimulants, such as cocaine and amphetamines, often associated with violence?
6. Describe the political economy of drug use in the world. Link it up with the conflict perspective.
7. What are the pros and cons of attempting to prohibit the use of drugs such as alcohol and marijuana?
8. What are the pros and cons of legalizing the drugs that are currently illegal?
9. What efforts have been made in the realm of the primary prevention of drug abuse? How effective have they been?
10. Summarize the research on the effectiveness of therapeutic communities in treating addictions to alcohol and other drugs.

Answers

Multiple-Choice

1. C; **2.** A; **3.** B; **4.** B; **5.** D; **6.** A; **7.** D; **8.** C; **9.** C; **10.** D

True/False

1. F; **2.** F; **3.** F; **4.** T; **5.** T; **6.** F; **7.** T; **8.** F; **9.** T; **10.** T

Fill-In

1. tolerance
2. cross-dependence
3. stimulants
4. stimulant
5. depressant
6. the occasional use of heroin
7. social learning or reinforcement
8. interactionist
9. methadone
10. educational programs

Matching

1. C; **2.** F; **3.** A; **4.** J; **5.** B; **6.** G; **7.** D; **8.** I; **9.** E; **10.** H

For Further Reading

William Adler. *Land of Opportunity: One Family's Quest for the American Dream in the Age of Crack.* New York: The Atlantic Monthly Press, 1995. This is a fascinating tale of one family's involvement in the drug trade in Detroit, detailing both fortunes made and prison time earned. It illuminates how the illegal drug business operates.

Joseph Gusfield. *Symbolic Crusade: Status Politics and the American Temperance Movement.* Urbana: University of Illinois Press, 1963. An excellent history of the drive to prohibit alcohol in the late 1800s. It shows how opposition to a drug may in part be a pretext for the playing out of other political and social struggles.

David J. Hanson. *Preventing Alcohol Abuse: Alcohol, Culture, and Control.* Westport, Conn.: Praeger, 1995. This book reviews data about drinking and drinking problems from around the world and uses it to develop a social policy for the United States. The author claims that his approach, which he calls a sociocultural analysis, will avoid the pitfalls of current policy, which he declares ineffective.

John Helmer. *Drugs and Minority Oppression.* New York: Seabury Press, 1975. An assessment of how the widespread availability of drugs can inhibit the poor and oppressed from improving their lot in life or becoming politically active. A good adjunct reading to the analysis in Chapters 5 and 6.

Peter Dale Scott and Jonathan Marshall. *Cocaine Politics: Drugs, Armies, and the CIA in Central America.* Berkeley: University of California Press, 1991. The very controversial thesis of this book is that the War on Drugs is a sham and that the United States encourages the world drug trade as long as it advances our political goals abroad—a new wrinkle on the political economy of the drug trade.

Terry Williams. *The Cocaine Kids: The Inside Story of a Teenage Drug Ring.* Reading, Mass.: Addison-Wesley, 1989. Sociologist Williams spent a great deal of time over a five-year period with a group of teenage drug dealers in New York's Spanish Harlem. He provides a fascinating picture of the drug trade and offers some startling revelations, such as the extent to which these drug dealers maintain a deep belief in the American dream of hard work and success.

William Weir. *In the Shadow of the Dope Fiend: America's War on Drugs.* New Haven, Conn.: Archon Books, 1995. In addition to providing a good account of current drug problems and policies in the United States, this book also provides an interesting social history of the various crusades against drugs in U.S. history.

Weldon L. Witters, Peter J. Venturelli, and Glen R. Hanson. *Drugs and Society,* 3rd ed. Boston: Jones and Bartlett, 1992. A comprehensive overview of both licit and illicit drugs, the history of their use, the problems they create, and what can be done to prevent and treat drug abuse.

Franklin E. Zimring and Gordon Hawkins. *The Search for Rational Drug Control.* Cambridge, Mass.: Cambridge University Press, 1992. This book contains a very thoughtful and thought-provoking critique of our current drug control policies. It serves as a useful model for the careful analysis of the ideological foundations of social policy and the development of policies.

CHAPTER

ELEVEN *Sexual Behavior*

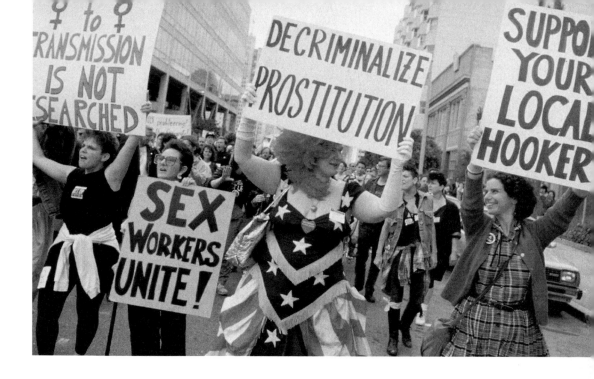

The varieties of human sexual expression are almost endless, and practically all of them have been condemned, by some group at some time or other, as deviant. However, this chapter, despite its title, is not really about sex, but rather about people's reactions to various forms of sexual expression. Recall from Chapters 1 and 9 that behaviors are classified as deviant by sociologists when some group in society defines the behaviors as wrong and stigmatizes people who engage in those behaviors. So deviance is not a characteristic of a behavior but rather involves the judgments about a behavior by some individual or group. The types of sexual behavior that are condemned will change from time to time, but what persists is the tendency to condemn groups that are different—whether the difference arises from race, ethnicity, gender, or sexual expression. In Chapter 6, the text discusses what the sociological perspectives have to say about prejudice and discrimination, and that discussion will not be repeated here.

Instead, this chapter focuses on the special issues that arise when discrimination and condemnation are founded on differences of sexual expression.

The two preceding chapters explored forms of deviance, such as crime and drug abuse, that have demonstrably negative consequences for society, at least in some realms. The behaviors discussed in this chapter, while considered deviant by some, do not seem to have the same clearly negative consequences, although some possible negative effects of things like pornography will be explored. It is not the behaviors themselves that constitute the social problem; rather, a problem arises because of some group's reaction to sexual differences. The social problem is the repression of free choice that occurs when those who choose less-than-conventional forms of sexual expression become victims of the rigid morality of the powerful.

This chapter focuses on three forms of sexual expression: homosexuality, prostitution, and pornography. There is general consensus that some sexual acts, such as sexual assault and the sexual abuse of children, do constitute social problems and are threatening to society. These topics are covered while discussing crime (Chapter 9) and the exploitation of children (Chapter 8). To be sure, some groups have moral objections to homosexuality, prostitution, and pornography, and they would like to see them banned for that reason. But our focus is on the *social* problem: the societal reaction to certain sexual lifestyles and outlets. The issue is not the sexual expression itself but the fact that conflict arises around it and has negative consequences: Violence is perpetrated against gays, or women are forced by circumstances into prostitution. From a sociological perspective, moral objections become important issues because they can fuel the reactions that lead to the negative consequences. So this chapter is really not about sex per se but about how sexual expression becomes a context or excuse for

discrimination and oppression. It is also about whether some of these forms of sexual behavior can be used by dominant groups in ways that create demonstrable problems for those with less power. Can, for example, the widespread availability of pornography increase the amount of sexual violence against women? The chapter will first discuss sexual behavior in general and then focus on issues having to do with homosexuality, prostitution, and pornography separately.

Variety in Human Sexuality

At the core of this chapter is society's reaction to the enormous variety in human sexual expression found throughout the world. To gain some perspective on sexual variety in the United States, it is useful to see what kind of sexuality is found in other cultures.

A Cross-Cultural View

Many people believe that there is a "natural" or "instinctive" expression of sexuality that people are aware of largely or completely without learning. Reflecting this belief, some people refer to variant sexual acts as "violations of nature." So for many people in the United States, "natural" sex is sex between men and women who are married. Some would even extend this "naturalness" to the sexual position assumed: genital contact in the "missionary" position (face to face with the male on top). Yet studies of other cultures indicate that socially acceptable sex takes far more forms than this. Consider one such culture:

> Sex—sex for pleasure and sex for procreation—is a principal concern of the Polynesian people on tiny Mangaia, the southernmost of the Cook Islands near the geographical center of Polynesia in the South Pacific. . . . They demonstrate that concern in the startling numbers of children born to unmarried parents, and in the sta-

Myths & FACTS

ABOUT SEXUAL BEHAVIOR

Myth: During the 1980s and 1990s, gay men and lesbians have found much wider acceptance in the United States than in previous decades.

FACT: Although there have been improvements, much negative sentiment toward gays still exists. Almost one-half of adults in the United States still believe that sexual contact between people of the same sex should be illegal, and some communities have been rescinding statutes that ban discrimination in jobs and housing because of sexual orientation.

Myth: Prostitution is one of the categories of crime in which women far outnumber men as perpetrators.

FACT: This is true, but it is also the case that the gender disparity in arrests for prostitution is not nearly as large as many imagine. One-third of all people arrested for prostitution and commercialized vice in the United States are male.

Myth: Pornographic materials that portray people in highly erotic and sexually explicit settings are dangerous to society because they lead to other social problems such as rape and other forms of sexual violence against women.

FACT: The latest research suggests that exposure to sexually explicit or arousing materials that have no aggressive content does not seem to produce negative effects. It is the aggressive content of some pornography that may lead some people to view violence against women as acceptable or desirable.

Myth: Pornography tends to be popular in communities where there is much hostility toward women and where women are discriminated against in occupational and other arenas.

FACT: Actually, research shows the reverse: Communities with high levels of gender equality have higher circulation rates for pornography than do communities with lower amounts of gender equality (Baron, 1990). This is probably because both pornography and gender equality flourish in politically tolerant communities.

---

tistics on frequency of orgasm and numbers of sexual partners. But that concern is simple fact-of-life—*not* morbid preoccupation. . . . There is great directness about sex, but the approach to sex is correspondingly indirect. Among the young, there is no dating, no tentative necking in the American sense. A flick of the eye, a raised eyebrow in a crowd, can lead to copulation—without a word. There is no social contact between the sexes, no rendezvous that does not lead directly to coitus—copulation is the only imaginable outcome of heterosexual contact. The sexual intimacy of copulation precedes personal affection. . . . Folk tales feature explicitly detailed accounts of sexual acts and sexual organs. . . . Yet there is a unique modesty about exposure of adult sexual organs. Mangaians are horrified at the casualness with which a European exposes his penis to other men when be urinates. (Marshall, 1974: 26–27)

So Mangaians have what many people in the United States would call an extremely permissive attitude toward sexual behavior. Although sexual intercourse among unmarried persons is accepted by many people today, multiple partners and casual sex tend to be frowned upon, especially for women. If there is a natural or instinctive form of sexual expression, what are we to make of the Mangaians? Consider some examples from other cultures. In Tahiti, young people were encouraged to masturbate (Bullough, 1976; Davenport, 1977). In the Truk Islands of the Pacific, sexual gratification is associated with pain and frustration, and sexual foreplay involves lovers inflicting pain on each other. Among most human groups, the female breasts are considered erotic organs, but this is not universal. Among the Mangaians mentioned previously, the breasts are not involved in foreplay and sexual arousal. Kissing is also a part of sexual expression in most human societies, but there are people among whom sexual intercourse occurs completely without kissing. The Siriono of Bolivia even find kissing to be a disgusting act. Homosexuality, prostitution, and pornography—the forms of sexual behavior we will discuss in this chapter—are also highly variable. In some societies, homosexuality is socially accepted, whereas in others it is despised (Greenberg, 1988). In some societies, prostitution is considered an accepted sexual outlet, while in others it is banned. What many people in the United States would consider pornographic—such as explicit portrayals of sexual intercourse—are considered public art and even religious symbols in some societies.

From this review of sexuality in other cultures, we can see that sexual norms are similar to all other societal rules: They are learned from others through social interaction. The Mangaians learn things about sexual behavior that are very different from what most people in the United States learn. Through the socialization process, people learn what is acceptable sexuality in their group or culture. There is nothing "instinctive" about it beyond a general, undirected biological drive. Who to have sex with, when, and in what fashion—these are all behaviors that people learn. If these responses were instinctive, we would not see the variation that occurs from one culture to another. Consequently, what constitutes sexual deviance in different societies depends less on the act itself and more on how that action fits with societal values and norms. This is not to suggest that one should adopt an "anything goes" attitude toward sex. Sex is part of culture, and it must be integrated with other cultural practices such as the form of the family and child-rearing needs. At the same time, we can recognize the flexible nature of human sexual expression. In a diverse society, this can create a tension between the sexual practices of one group and those of another group. This situation creates the possibility that some forms of sexuality might be viewed by some people as social problems and may produce conflict that exacerbates other social problems.

Sexual Standards and Variety in the United States

There is variety in human sexuality, not only between cultures or societies, but also from group to group and from time to time within the same culture or society. For example, consider how the media—particularly the motion picture industry—is freer today than in the past to portray sexual themes and imagery. Expressions of shock and concern rumbled through the United States when Rhett Butler kissed Scarlett O'Hara passionately in *Gone With the Wind* (1939); today, *NYPD Blue* has explicit and steamy portrayals of sex in every episode. There has been an equally significant shift in sexual expression outside the context of marriage. Many Western religions, such as Roman Catholicism, prohibit all sexual activity outside the marital bond. Such a complete prohibition on premarital sex is unusual in human societies. Anthropologists who have looked at many societies, both today and in the past, estimate that about one-third of human societies allow almost completely unrestricted premarital sex, and almost another third allow premarital sex with some restrictions, such as avoiding pregnancy (Murdock, 1967).

Today, people in the United States are more divided than in the past over premarital sexuality (Collins and Coltrane, 1991). In the 1960s, only 20 percent believed that premarital sex was acceptable; in the 1990s, about half of the people in the United States views it as permissible (Hugick and Leonard, 1991; Tanfer and Cubbins, 1992). Young people are much more likely to approve of premarital sex, as are those who are less religious and have more egalitarian sex-role attitudes. However, as in so many other realms, attitudes and behavior are sometimes at variance; because people *approve* of a behavior does not mean that they *engage* in it themselves. Sexual behavior is very sensitive, so information about it is not always easy to get. However, putting together the best information from surveys that we have, we can conclude that sex before marriage, which was once considered taboo in the United States, especially for women, has become routine. Today, 80 to 85 percent of women and 95 percent of men have had sex before marriage. This compares with about half of women and two-thirds of men in the 1920s. So, there has been a gradual increase since the 1920s, but the change is less dramatic than many believe since at least half of all men and women in the 1920s had premarital sexual experience. If there has been a sexual "revolution," it is among women. While the numbers of women having premarital experience gradually increased throughout the century, they did show a leap in the 1960s and 1970s.

These changes in premarital sexual behavior are often misunderstood and exaggerated. There has been a dramatic change in how publicly we discuss sex and in how openly we recognize the reality of premarital sex. We are also less likely to insist that sex be limited to the marital context. However, changes in actual sexual behavior, while real, have not been as dramatic as many believe, especially if we treat cohabitation as similar to marriage. Among some in the United States today, co-

habitation has come to be viewed as a socially acceptable bonding between two people. If we treat cohabitors like married couples and remove their sexual activity from the premarital category, the sexual "revolution" looks even less dramatic. In addition, some experts conclude that the most significant change has been the elimination of the "double standard" that permitted men to engage in premarital sex ("sow a few wild oats") without sanction but strongly discouraged the same behavior in women (Clement, 1989). Although there are still differences, women's sexual behavior has become much more similar to that of men's in the past few decades.

What accounts for the changes in sexual behavior in the late twentieth century? One important factor, certainly, is the emergence of easy to use, unobtrusive, and very reliable contraceptives. This has eased women's fears of pregnancy and widened their options as far as sexual behavior is concerned. A second major factor has been the feminist movement, which emphasizes that women should gain control of their lives and be able to make decisions for themselves. It also demands that women's choices not be limited by sexist or stereotypical views of gender. Without question, many traditional views of women's sexuality were sexist, stereotyped, and very wrong. A third factor producing changing sexual practices has been technological developments, such as the automobile, that provide young people with more freedom and the means to escape surveillance by adults. A final factor producing changes in sexual behavior is the trend toward **secularization:** *the process through which the influence of religion is removed from many institutions in society and dispersed into private and personal realms.* When religion as an institution was stronger and more pervasive, it controlled more of people's sexual behavior. As religion has come to exercise less control, people have become more willing to engage in previously condemned forms of sexuality.

Despite these changes, people in the United States are still not at the level of permissiveness of the Mangaians. Prostitution and anal intercourse are still illegal in most states, and the Supreme Court has ruled that such prohibitions are constitutional. Strong pressures persist to ban most or all pornography. In addition, changes in sexual standards are not uniform throughout society, and depending on the group or subculture involved, attitudes about what is normal or deviant can vary substantially.

Homosexuality

Homosexuality refers to *sexual feelings, attractions, and actions directed toward members of the same sex.* Estimates of the extent of homosexuality have to be viewed with some caution because people do not always report truthfully about their sexual behavior when asked by an interviewer. Especially with homosexuality, which is still stigmatized by some groups in society, some people will not honestly report their experiences. Despite these problems, best estimates are that between 1 and 5 percent of adult males in the United States are predominantly or exclusively gay (Rogers and Turner, 1991; Billy et al., 1993; Laumann et al., 1994). **Lesbians,** or *female homosexuals,* are probably about half as common. In addition, somewhere between 5 percent and possibly as much as 25 percent of all males have had at least one homosexual encounter.

Theories of Sexual Orientation

Why do some people become attracted to members of the opposite sex while others are attracted to members of the same sex? Numerous attempts have been made to explain sexual orientation, although there is much that we still do not know. A major issue in the debate is whether people are born with tendencies in one direction or the other or whether sexual orientation is a product of learning through experiences while growing up.

The last decade has produced a number of research studies that suggest, but do not definitively prove, that sexual orientation may be determined, at least in part, by a person's genetic inheritance (Hamer and Copeland, 1994). A study of twins, for example, found that twins who share the same genetic material (monozygotic twins) are much more likely to both be gay than twins who do not share the exact same genetic material (dizygotic twins) or two adopted brothers who share no genetic material. However, to date, these research efforts have not been able to discover exactly what is inherited. It may be that what is inherited is not sexual orientation directly but rather behaviors that can be shaped into homosexuality in the proper environment. For example, people may inherit a tendency toward gender nonconformity, that is, the tendency for young boys to behave in a girlish fashion (be "sissies"). Then the reactions of others to that gender nonconformity may encourage ways of thinking and behaving that come to be defined as "homosexual." So a genetic predisposition may get shaped by the social interaction during childhood and teenage years. There is still a lot that we do not know about this, and we have no idea whether all, or only some, homosexuality is biologically linked.

Another explanation for homosexuality suggests that it arises from some psychological maladjustment, possibly stemming from a poor parent–child relationship (Bieber et al., 1962; Lewes, 1988). In fact, the American Psychiatric Association listed homosexuality as a mental disorder until 1973. Despite their popularity, however, psychological explanations have been subject to many criticisms. One criticism is that some studies have observed no personality differences between homosexuals and nonhomosexuals. In addition, many children with poor relationships with their parents do not become homosexual (Hooker, 1969; Bell and Weinberg, 1978). Another investigation involving more than three hundred gay men and women determined that two-thirds of these people perceived their relationships with their fathers as satisfactory, and three-quarters of those in the sample felt that they maintained a satisfactory relationship with their mothers (Robinson et al., 1982). In part because of these criticisms, in 1973, the American Psychiatric Association removed homosexuality from its list of mental disorders. At present, there is no scientific proof that homosexuality is either a psychiatric malady or an indication of poor psychological adjustment (Ross, Paulsen, and Stalstrom, 1988).

Sociologists have argued that some social or situational factors may influence people to engage in homosexual acts and that certain social contingencies influence whether a person adopts a homosexual lifestyle. Sociological theories of homosexuality suggest that, like heterosexuality, homosexuality can be the result of learning through interaction with others (Hoffman, 1968). In some cases, homosexual acts are a consequence of experimentation. We have seen that human sexuality is flexible and exploratory. Some people engage in homosexual acts because they are new and different, and most of these people do not consider themselves "homosexuals." In other cases, homosexual acts occur because there are no heterosexual outlets available. In prison, for example, homosexuality is common, but most prisoners who engage in homosexual acts do not consider themselves to be homosexuals and they return to heterosexuality when released from prison.

Some people not only engage in homosexuality but also come to view themselves as "homosexuals." To understand this, we need to look at the process of self-definition in developing a homosexual identity (Troiden, 1989). Recall from Chapter 9 that labeling theory points out that our self-concepts derive in part from how others treat us. If a person is labeled as a homosexual by others, especially if his or her sexual identity is not yet clearly formed, it increases the likelihood that the person will eventually accept that label. If a person is labeled a homosexual by others, the person may think that the assessment of those others is accurate. In addition, the labeling may create a stigma that makes it more difficult to associate with heterosexuals and precipitates a drift into contacts with homosexuals. Let us say that a teenage male has sex with another male and finds the experience pleasurable. This does not mean he is "gay" because, as we have seen, many mostly heterosexual men gain release at times from homosexual contacts. Further suppose that his friends find out about it and react in a negative and hostile way. They may even pull away from associating with him for fear that others will think they are gay. His friends' reaction may lead the boy to question in his own mind whether he is heterosexual or homosexual. If my friends think I am gay, he wonders, that must mean I am, and I did enjoy it. In addition, the boy is likely to find acceptance and support among other gays. He will also find additional opportunities to explore homosexuality among them. So the labeling may precipitate a gradual changing of the boy's self-concept along with a growing association with people in the gay community. These changes in turn may help solidify his self-definition of himself as gay. In a sense, what has occurred is a self-fulfilling prophecy: The boy has become what his friends thought they were merely discovering when they first labeled him "gay." The point here is not that all people develop their sexual orientation through this route but that this is one route to becoming straight or gay. Even if sexual orientation involves some biological predisposition, as discussed earlier, it may be partly through a social vehicle such as the labeling process that the predisposition actually becomes a reality.

Patterns of Homosexuality

In 1948, Alfred Kinsey and his associates published their classic *Sexual Behavior in the Human Male,* wherein these well-known sex researchers declared:

> [People] do not represent two discrete populations, heterosexual and homosexual. The world is not to be divided into sheep and goats. Not all things are black nor all things white.... Only the human mind invents categories and tries to force facts into separate pigeon holes. The living world is a continuum in each and every one of its aspects. The sooner we learn this concerning human sexual behavior the sooner we shall reach a sound understanding of the realities of sex. (Kinsey, Pomeroy, and Martin, 1948: 639)

Their point is that sexual orientation is best viewed as a continuum from exclusively heterosexual to exclusively homosexual. From this point of view, there is no such thing as *the* homosexual, but rather differing degrees of involvement with homosexuality in terms of *behavior* and *attraction.* For example, homosexuality is very common in situations such as prisons, where there are no opportunities for heterosexual contacts, and men and women who engage in this behavior while behind bars usually do not define themselves as homosexual and resume a heterosexual lifestyle after release. Therefore, a person who engages in homosexual behaviors under various situational pressures is not necessarily gay, in the sense of having an identity, lifestyle, and stable career pattern of homosexuality. Whether people take on the identity and lifestyle of a homosexual depends on their perceptions and understanding of their own behavior and the reactions of other people to them (Hammersmith, 1987).

There are many myths in the United States concerning gays, some of which have already been discussed. For example, gays are no more mentally disturbed than are heterosexuals, and many gay men establish affectionate, exclusive, and relatively permanent attachments to one man. Another common belief is that gay males are effeminate, like to dress in women's clothing, and wish that they were women. In fact, gay males are no more likely to be effeminate than heterosexual males, and they are generally quite secure in their masculine identity. Lesbians are somewhat different from gay men in ways that reflect the impact of their socialization as females. Lesbians, like their heterosexual counterparts, tend to equate sex with love and are more likely to abstain from sex until some degree of commitment is found with a particular partner. Lesbians also tend to be less assertive, even in their search for a mate in the gay community. Many lesbians pride themselves on being considerably less promiscuous than male homosexuals.

Societal Reaction to Homosexuality

Attitudes Toward Homosexuality

Is homosexuality deviant behavior and can it be considered a social problem itself? Recall from Chapter 1 that deviance is in the eye of the beholder: It is a group's judgment about the worth or acceptability of a behavior or a lifestyle. So, we would likely get a different answer to our question in San Francisco than we would in rural Mississippi. Nationally, the attitudes of people in the United States toward homosexuality have tended toward the negative. Although the media seem to devote more attention to and present more positive images of gays and lesbians today than in the past, the public still harbors some fairly negative views. As Figure 11.1 shows, 44 percent of people in the United States believe that homosexual relations should be illegal, and this figure is slightly higher than fifteen years ago. Furthermore, two-thirds of the public feel that it has been a bad thing for our society to allow greater tolerance of homosexuality as an alternative lifestyle over the past few decades (Hugick and Leonard, 1991). In the 1980s, only 59 percent approved of equal job rights for gays, and two-thirds of adults polled said they would not vote for an other-

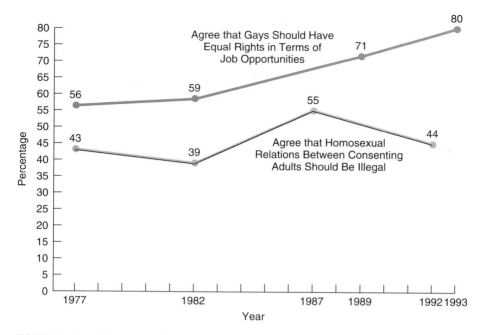

FIGURE 11.1 Attitudes on Gay Issues in the United States, 1977–1993. *Sources:* "Public Opinion Divided on Gay Rights," *The Gallup Poll Monthly* (June 1992), p. 3; "Public Polarized on Gay Issue," *The Gallup Poll Monthly* (April 1993), p. 30.

wise qualified person for president of the United States if that person were gay (Gallup, 1983: 14). On the other hand, Americans have become more tolerant of having gays and lesbians work in various occupations (see Figure 11.1 and Figure 11.2 on p. 404). But although four out of five people today believe that gays should be allowed to hold sales positions, only two out of five think they should be in the clergy or work as elementary school teachers. Generally, men, older people, religious people, and those with lower educations and incomes are more likely to be intolerant of homosexuality. Negative sentiment toward gays is also greater among those with traditional social values (Kurdek, 1988).

Discrimination Against Gay Men and Lesbians
Many of the problems surrounding sexual ori-

entation have to do with the negative reactions of many heterosexuals to gay men and lesbians. In fact, the circumstances of gays, in many respects, are similar to those of racial, ethnic, and gender minorities discussed in Chapters 6 and 7. One difference, of course, is that their minority status is based on behaviors that are considered unconventional by the majority rather than on ascribed and unchangeable characteristics such as sex and race. This makes it easier for gays to avoid some of those negative reactions. But if they wish to live openly and honestly as gays, they may face strong negative reactions from some people in the United States.

Two areas in which gays face problems are in employment and housing, where discrimination is still strong, although things have improved (Knopp, 1990). By the 1990s, two states, sixteen counties, and many municipali-

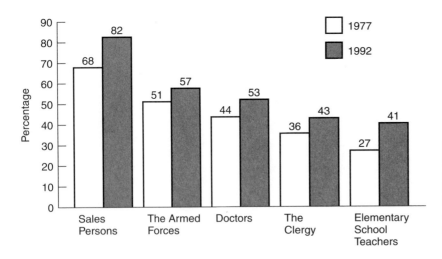

FIGURE 11.2 Percentages of People in the United States Agreeing that Homosexuals Should Be Hired in Various Occupations, 1977–1992. *Source.* "Public Opinion Divided on Gay Rights," *The Gallup Poll Monthly* (June 1992), p. 3.

ties in the United States have given explicit protection against discrimination in housing and employment to gays. However, several locales, and at least one state, rescinded those protections, suggesting that many people still want the option of discriminating against gays in these realms. The attitudes expressed in Figure 11.2 support this: Although things have improved in the past fifteen years, there is still considerable support for keeping gays out of many jobs.

A particularly disturbing reaction by some against gay men and lesbians is the use of violence (Hunter, 1990; Berrill, 1992). Thousands of episodes of harassment, intimidation, assault, vandalism, and murder occur every year in which the victim's sexual orientation is the reason for the violence. Surveys document that between 9 percent and 24 percent of gays have been physically assaulted because of their sexual orientation. Most gays expect to be the target of antigay harassment or violence, and one-half to three-quarters fear for their safety. So, the reality is that gay men and lesbians are the subject of much hostility from their fellow citizens. Antigay murders are especially brutal and bloody, often involving "overkill" or multiple shooting or stabbing of

the victim. The director of the New York City Gay and Lesbian Anti-Violence Project commented, "The level of violence in these homicides is really gruesome" (Dunlap, 1994: A10). Such excessive violence is seemingly a product of a deep rage against gays. As with so many other things, gender plays a part here: Gay males are more likely to be attacked or threatened by strangers or people they are not related to or harassed in school or by the police. Lesbians, on the other hand, are more likely to experience verbal harassment from their families. Gay adolescents also suffer a high rate of victimization, and this seems to contribute to a disturbingly high number of attempted suicides among them. Most "gay-bashers" are young males, attacking in a group with other young males, and they are strangers to the victim. An increase in the reported cases of violence against gays has been seen in the 1980s and 1990s, but whether this represents an increase in actual violence or just more extensive reporting of it is not known.

Another area in which gays experience discrimination is in the legal system. One-half of all states still have laws that make consenting sexual acts between adults of the same sex illegal, and in sixteen states it is a felony (Knopp, 1990). Furthermore, the Supreme Court in the late 1980s upheld the right of states to do this.

Another area of discrimination against gays is in the military, which has traditionally maintained a strict policy of viewing homosexuality as incompatible with the mission of the armed services (Scott and Stanley, 1994). This position is based on the notion that gays constitute a security risk and that they would be a disruptive element in military units that must work and fight together in close quarters. Actually, there is no reason to believe that gay soldiers are a security risk, especially when gays can admit their sexual orientation without fear of punishment or assault. As for the second assertion, there is no evidence of any disruptive influence. The reality is that thousands of gays have served in the armed forces over the years without causing such disruption, although they were forced to keep their sexual orientation secret. President Clinton attempted to open the military to gays but met hostile resistance to such a policy. The policy that resulted is one in which the military does not actively seek to discharge gays in its ranks, but the extent to which the military today and in the future will present a legitimate career path for the openly gay person is very ambiguous.

Sources of Homophobia   The term **homophobia** has been adopted to refer to *an intense dislike of or prejudice against homosexuals.* What accounts for the homophobia that seems to underlie the attitudes and discriminatory behaviors described above? A part of the answer is Western Christian theology, which defines homosexuality as sin (Greenberg, 1988; Britton, 1990). Strong condemnation of homosexuality has been an integral part of much of the Christian history and heritage, and this attitude has been pervasive in the United States. This negative reaction is often justified on the grounds that homosexuality is a threat to the family or to the reproductive potential of society. Once these norms regarding family life and sexual re-

production are established, they become powerful controls over people's behavior. Other ways of organizing one's personal or sexual life come to be seen as a threat. As one argument goes, if all or most people practiced homosexuality, how could society maintain its numbers? People make this argument despite the fact that maintaining population size has never been a problem in the many societies that have permitted homosexuality to be practiced in one form or another. But the homophobic reaction comes not from rational consideration of the evidence but from a perceived threat to a lifestyle based on deeply held cultural norms and values.

This negative attitude sometimes gets expressed in nonreligious realms. Freudian psychology, for example, sees homosexuality as an immature and underdeveloped form of adult sexuality. Only heterosexuality is seen as mature and "healthy." These psychological theories provide a scientific legitimation for viewing homosexuality in a negative light. With these pervasive and deeply held values, open displays of homosexuality are highly threatening to the dominant group and could, if left unchallenged, spread. Reactions against homosexuality then become boundary-maintaining mechanisms that highlight the prevailing norms and show people what behaviors are acceptable. As with attacks on racial or ethnic minorities, attacks on gays show symbolically who is the dominant group and show others the costs to crossing over into the realm of unacceptable behavior.

Most perpetrators of antigay violence are adolescent or very young adult males, which suggests another source of this violence: The marginalized status of many adolescents and young adults (Comstock, 1991). Recall from Chapter 8 that modern industrial societies tend not to incorporate young people into the adult world of work and status until they are in their late teens and sometimes into the early to mid-twenties if they go to college. Because they cannot achieve status and a sense of self-worth through adult avenues, they may search for other ways of doing so, such as drinking alcohol, joy riding in cars, or other thrill-seeking ventures where they can demonstrate strength, bravery, daring, or other positive qualities. Add to this the strong emphasis on male dominance and aggression in our culture along with the negative attitude toward gays expressed by many churches and other legitimate societal institutions, and the ground is set for some of those adolescents to seek adventure, recreation, or relief from boredom through attacks on gays.

Some evidence also suggests that homophobia is associated with rigid and deep-seated negative feelings about human sexuality where sex is seen as dirty and a threat to the social order (Ficarrotto, 1990). The AIDS crisis of the 1980s has also intensified the homophobic reaction among some people (Young et al., 1991). Finally, homophobic attitudes and behavior are associated with many of the same things that lead to prejudice and discrimination against racial and ethnic minorities: authoritarianism, intolerance of differences, and dogmatism (Stark, 1991).

So, the societal reaction to homosexuality in the United States still has a strongly negative element to it. For gays this is where the social problem lies: in the stigmatization and discrimination that they face in many spheres of their lives. In this regard, the conflict perspective offers some insight. Although movements such as gay liberation have increased gay input into political decision making, especially in some cities with a large gay population, "straight" society's interest groups are still much more powerful and have a distinct heterosexual bias. Thus, discrimination against gays continues, forcing some of them to stay in "the closet" and hide their sexual orientation from employers, landlords, neighbors, and sometimes friends. From the conflict perspective, the problem of homosexuality is a clash between those supporting traditional sexual values and those protesting the imposition on

them by dominant groups of a way of life they would prefer not to lead.

The Gay Community

Some neighborhoods of some cities in the United States have become distinctly gay and lesbian territories. In some cases, these were depressed, run-down neighborhoods that were taken over because few other groups wanted to live there. In fact, gays produced a certain amount of the gentrification of U.S. cities that is discussed in Chapter 12. One reason for the emergence of these gay communities is protection: They feel safer from the assaults and gain some degree of distance from homophobia when living among others like themselves. The second reason for their emergence is that they enable gays to live among others who share their lifestyle and values. A third reason is that they afford them a degree of political power. By numerically dominating a community, they can elect city and state politicians who support their interests. An additional reason is that gays are sometimes discouraged from living in neighborhoods dominated by the majority, especially those who wish to live an openly gay life. All these reasons, by the way, are the same reasons racial and ethnic minorities often gravitate to one community.

The gay community, then, is a subculture that reproduces the cultural and institutional frameworks of the larger culture but casts them in a light of acceptance and support for gays and their way of life. Bookstores, restaurants, retail establishments, bowling and baseball teams, political organizations, support groups, hiking clubs, and Alcoholics Anonymous (AA) groups—all these organizations are found in the gay community, but they adapt to the needs, aspirations, and lifestyles of gays. Bookstores, for example, would stock books and magazines of interest to gays, and people in gay AA groups could talk openly about how their addictions have an impact on their same-sex partner. In all these settings, there is less worry about hostile

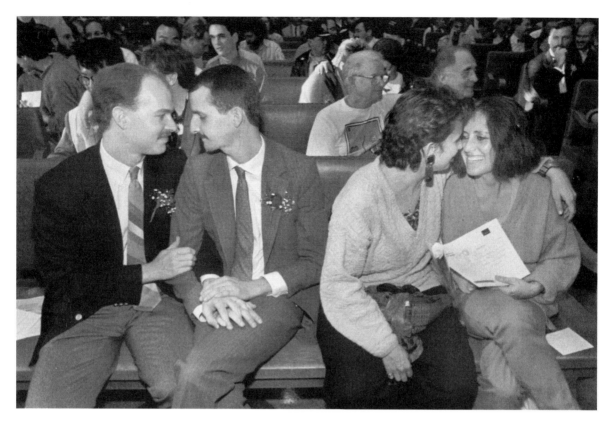

The gay community is a subculture that creates cultural and institutional supports for gays and their way of life. At the insistence of its gay community, San Francisco offers certificates to gay couples who register as domestic partners—giving some official legitimation to their relationships.

contacts with "straights," and the overall climate enhances a positive sense of self-regard for gays. As with other groups that bear the burden of hostility from dominant groups, the gay subculture can provide a safe haven in a hostile world.

Prostitution

Prostitution has been called the "world's oldest profession," because it seems to have been with us throughout recorded history. **Prostitution** refers to *sexual activity in exchange for money or goods in which the primary motivation for the prosti-* *tute is neither sexual nor affectional* (James, 1977). Prostitution can take many different forms. Some prostitutes are known in the trade as "streetwalkers": They solicit clients by walking the streets. These prostitutes—both men and women—generally engage in sexual behavior with their customers in clients' automobiles or in cheap hotel rooms. Most of these practitioners of the trade work for a pimp, who typically "manages" from one to twenty women (Diana, 1985). Pimps offer protection and bail money in exchange for the allegiance of the prostitutes in their "stable." Pimps frequently resort to violence as a means of enforcing obedience, and they can garner nearly 100 percent of their employees' earnings:

> I was going to leave Silky [a pimp] when I was in jail. I didn't understand why—with seven wives-in-law [the women in Silky's stable]—I was in jail for six days. I understood after I talked to Silky. It turned out he really didn't have no money. A pimp is supposed to be in a position to take care of bail, but he can't just snap his fingers and money comes. He's got to get it from us. If we're not giving him our money, he can't have no money. How could I make money when I was in jail? (Quoted in Caplan, 1984: 71)

Other prostitutes work in what at one time was the most common environment for the trade: the house of prostitution, brothel, or "whorehouse." In these cases, a "madam" acts as supervisor of a number of prostitutes and negotiates with clients who enter the facility:

> An entrepreneur is a person who embarks on a business enterprise and manages the operations of that business, assuming risk for the sake of profit. The madam of a house of prostitution fits this definition: She is the owner and manager of a small service business, albeit an illegal one. (Heyl, 1979: 89)

Unlike pimps, madams usually garner about 50 percent of their "ladies'" proceeds. In Nevada, prostitution is legal in some counties, and brothels flourish. They are run like any other business, to the point of accepting credit cards and traveler's checks, as this ad for one of them illustrates:

Ranch Specialties

Japanese type bath, Bubble baths, Nude Photo sessions, Largest selection of girls, 18 years and older, Girls of all nationalities, out calls, Ranch souvenirs, Free limo service, Your own personal menu, Free brothel information and, of course, the Cherry Patch's famous dungeon . . . only if you dare. Master Charge, Visa, and Travelers Checks are accepted.

Still other members of the trade operate out of bars, taverns, and massage parlors. The type of prostitute commanding the highest status within the trade is the escort or "call girl," who develops an established clientele, usually men who are prepared to pay high prices for different sexual services. Escort prostitutes often operate independently out of their own well-appointed apartments or see their clients "on call" in hotel rooms or the customer's home (McLeod, 1982; Diana, 1985). Among male prostitutes, a similar stratification system exists, ranging from the street hustler to the bar hustler to the escort prostitute (Luckenbill, 1989).

Extent of Prostitution

Precise figures on the incidence of prostitution are impossible to obtain, but it has been estimated that there may be as many as a half million prostitutes working in the United States today (Reynolds, 1986). Much prostitution goes on unreported, and there are women and men who engage in the trade on a part-time basis, with some of these individuals occupying otherwise respectable positions in their communities. Furthermore, arrests for prostitution are highly susceptible to political manipulation. In some jurisdictions, for example, the trade may be more or less tolerated, whereas in others police agencies may be motivated to "crack down," thus creating the impression that prostitution is on the rise, when in fact it is merely law enforcement activity that has increased (Clinard and Meier, 1989). For example, in 1983, the New York City police department made seventeen thousand arrests for prostitution, but nearly all of these were made on the street. According to law enforcement authorities, prostitution flourishes "indoors" in New York City:

> Some prostitutes work in brothels hidden behind the doors of luxury apartments. Others work for escort services that take half their fees. Still others work out of their own apartments through referrals. Their services are advertised in explicit sex tabloids, on late-night cable television, even in the Yellow Pages under escort

services. The police say that while legitimate escort services may exist, they believe most are thinly disguised covers for prostitution. ("Off the Streets . . . ," 1984)

Considering these problems, the best estimates place the number of prostitutes in the United States at between one hundred thousand and five hundred thousand and the money generated each year at between $1 billion and $10 billion (Thio, 1988; Reynolds, 1986). In 1994, there were eighty thousand arrests for prostitution and commercialized vice offenses. Sixty-one percent of the people involved were female (see Table 9.3). Considering the degree of nonreporting alluded to earlier, these figures are conservative. The trade is clearly thriving, and the explanation is primarily economic: There are people willing to pay for the services and others who are willing to supply them for a price.

A particularly disturbing form of prostitution appeared in the 1980s with the emergence of the crack cocaine epidemic (see Chapter 10). In crack houses, crack-addicted women, and in a few cases men, would engage in quick sex with many men to get crack or the money to buy crack (Inciardi, Horowitz, and Pottieger, 1993). This is typically unprotected sex and involves multiple partners, with many IV-drug users among the partners. The women go from one sexual contact to another for a hit of crack and in some cases have literally thousands of sexual contacts a year. In fact, some of the women who engage repeatedly in quick oral sex with many men to get crack did not even consider this to be prostitution. This behavior entails a very high risk of spreading the AIDS virus.

Considerable controversy exists regarding whether prostitution should be regarded as a social problem or even a crime, for that matter. Those who favor legalizing prostitution argue that this activity is a "victimless crime" and that what goes on between consenting adults in private should not be a matter of legal enforcement (Rio, 1991). (This is the same argument

discussed in Chapter 10 to support the legalization of some psychoactive drugs.) In fact, prostitution is legal in eleven counties in Nevada, where houses of prostitution are privately owned and regulated by the state. Another argument in favor of legalizing prostitution is that illegal prostitution causes problems such as the spread of venereal disease and AIDS and may come under the control of organized crime. It also leads to other related

This prostitute in New York is in a line of work that thrives partly for an economic reason: There are people willing to pay for the services and others who are willing to supply them for a price.

crimes, such as assaults on customers and the use of drugs.

Where prostitution is legal, such as Nevada and some countries in Europe, these problems can be monitored and fairly effectively controlled among the legal prostitutes (Campbell, 1991). Nevada, for example, requires licensed brothel prostitutes to be tested for gonorrhea, syphilis, and AIDS at least once a month. If they test positive for AIDS, they cannot work as a legal prostitute in Nevada. Nevada also requires that condoms be used at all licensed brothels, and brothel owners will not employ women who are IV-drug users. As a consequence, no brothel prostitute in Nevada has ever tested positive for the AIDS virus, whereas in some cities where prostitution is illegal, 20 to 40 percent of prostitutes are infected. However, it is not clear how much of this infection is due to prostitution itself and how much is due to prostitutes taking drugs intravenously or having sex with IV-drug users. Nonetheless, legalized and monitored prostitution does provide significant protection against sexually transmitted diseases for both the prostitute and the customer. In addition, there is no evidence of serious crime problems accompanying legalized prostitution in Nevada. This leads proponents of legalization to argue that everyone—the prostitute, the customer, and society—would be better off if prostitution were legal and subject to government regulation. A variant on this position has been taken by an organization formed to pursue the interests of prostitutes (Weitzer, 1991). COYOTE (Call Off Your Old Tired Ethics) was started in 1973 by a former prostitute and argues that basic issues of work rights and women's self-determination are involved: Prostitution is legitimate work and women have the right to control their own bodies, including the selling of sexual favors. COYOTE agrees that women should not be forced into prostitution, but it also believes that the right to choose prostitution freely is a basic civil right for women. Although COYOTE has not achieved some of its major goals, such as decriminalizing

prostitution, it has worked to protect prostitutes from harassment by police and courts and to bring educational programs about AIDS to prostitutes.

Critics of legalization argue that legalizing prostitution does not stop the health and crime problems associated with prostitution but simply pushes it into the illegal trade. Prostitutes who get involved in crime, use drugs, or have a sexually transmitted disease continue to work, but on the street rather than in the legal brothels. In fact, this seems to be true because illegal prostitution continues in Nevada. However, having legal prostitution available does reduce the amount of illegal prostitution. Other critics of legalized prostitution, including some feminists, argue that prostitution does create victims: the prostitutes themselves. Prostitution, they claim, involves an exploitation of women so that men can have unrestricted access to sexual pleasure. As one critic of legalized prostitution put it, "Prostitution is a culturally sanctioned system of oppression that uses women, children, and young men as sexual objects. . . . The sex industry uses power and control tactics to supply its customers with human beings who are used as sexual toys. Prostitution is dehumanizing to everyone involved in the industry" (Greenman, 1990: 111). Although prostitutes appear to be willing partners, they are really coerced into prostitution because of poverty, few job opportunities, or a sexist ideology that defines women primarily in terms of their sexuality rather than other skills and qualities. Teenage prostitutes in particular are severely exploited by adults, as is discussed in the Policy Issues insert in this chapter.

Who Becomes a Prostitute?

There is a widespread myth that most prostitutes get their start through a kind of "white slave" trade—that young women are coerced by profit-oriented adults and forced into selling their sexual services for money. Although this does occur, as in the case of teenage runaways who gravitate toward major cities in an attempt to make a living, forced prostitution is rare in the United States—no more than 4 percent could be said to have been railroaded into the trade (Thio, 1988).

How, then, do most prostitutes get into the trade? An important step in becoming a prostitute is knowing others who are involved in the trade or who are on its fringe. As differential association theory discussed in Chapter 9 suggests, people learn prostitution from others who are involved. Many prostitutes first learn about prostitution from close friends or relatives, whereas others have contact with a pimp or prostitute who convinces them to "turn out," as the first move into the ranks of prostitutes is called (Weisberg, 1985; Campagna and Poffenberger, 1988). Contacts with other prostitutes or with a pimp are also important in developing a clientele. As one woman who entered the trade commented: "You can't just say get an apartment and get a phone and everything and say, 'Well, I'm gonna start a business,' because you gotta get clients from somewhere. There has to be a contact" (Bryan, 1965: 289). Associating with prostitutes or pimps who idealize the life of the prostitute as exciting and glamorous and extol its virtues in terms of making "easy money" also encourages potential recruits to "turn out." These recruits learn attitudes that espouse prostitution as a desirable way of life. They also learn that prostitution might bring lucrative economic rewards and an independence rarely found in other occupations (McCaghy, 1985). So "contacts" appear to be the most important ingredient in becoming a prostitute, once again underscoring the importance of learning a deviant lifestyle through intimate group associations. The learning process is similar to how "respectable" people learn to adopt socially acceptable ways of life.

Quite obviously, being young and physically attractive are also valuable assets for joining the ranks of prostitution, whether legal or illegal (Diana, 1985). Consequently, the vast majority of female practitioners are between seventeen and twenty-four years of age, with the peak earning age being around twenty-two (Clinard and Meier, 1989). Prostitutes also often have early and frequent promiscuous sexual experiences. They often have their first sexual intercourse by ten to thirteen years of age and develop a pattern of having sex with several men, often after very brief acquaintanceships (McCaghy, 1985). More than any other single factor, entrance into prostitution for women is inextricably linked to poverty: Poor women are far more likely to become prostitutes than are affluent women (Miller, 1986). Two other important precursors to prostitution are a history of juvenile delinquency and being sexually abused as a child (Simons and Whitbeck, 1991).

Male prostitutes tend to come from two distinct subcultures (Weisberg, 1985; Luckenbill, 1989). One is the peer-delinquent subculture, which consists of boys from lower-class backgrounds who never define themselves as homosexuals. For them, prostitution is exclusively a way of making money, not achieving sexual gratification, and they also engage in other criminal activity. The other subculture is the gay subculture, involving boys who consider themselves homosexual or bisexual. These prostitutes are more likely to work the gay neighborhoods of cities. They are also more likely than the peer-delinquents to come from the middle class. Gay prostitutes engage in prostitution as a way of interacting with gay people and achieving sexual gratification as well as making money. Adolescent male prostitutes come from unstable families in which they have been taken care of by a series of people, such as parents and relatives. They are likely to have experienced physical abuse and sometimes sexual abuse by their caretakers. For gay prostitutes, conflicts with parents over their sexual orientation often lead them to run away and turn to prostitution to support themselves.

Leaving prostitution can be difficult, especially for women who have been in the trade for some time (Greenman, 1990). For one thing, prostitution isolates women from the "straight"

Teenage Prostitution: Is Prevention or Rehabilitation Possible?

Prostitution continues to be a controversial issue in the United States. It flourishes in many communities without much intervention by law enforcement agencies, but people are still disturbed by it. Particularly unsettling to most people is teenage prostitution. Sometimes these prostitutes are scarcely more than children, some as young as eleven years old. It has been estimated, for example, that over one million minors living in the United States are involved in prostitution and other sexually exploitive activities, and that at least 150,000 of these youths participate regularly in prostitution (Campagna and Poffenberger, 1988). Police officers have described teenage prostitutes as "forty-year-old midgets," due to the aging effect that this lifestyle has on them:

> poor diet, sleepless nights, alcohol and drug usage, and all those fears—of the police, of "freak tricks," of other prostitutes, [and] predatory pimps. (Caplan, 1984: 69)

Teenage prostitutes are usually girls or boys who have left home, with many of them being runaways. Some, in fact, are what Gerald M. Caplan, a law professor who has conducted research on the sexual exploitation of children, calls "throwaways": children whose parents are not upset about their having left home or may even have encouraged them to run away from home (Caplan, 1984). Some teenage prostitution is also

linked with drug use: Teens who use marijuana, cocaine, and heroin regularly are much more likely to be involved in prostitution (Inciardi, Horowitz, and Pottieger, 1993). This is true for both males and females. In some cases, the prostitution is a means to purchase drugs or room and board in a crack house. Sometimes the prostitution is virtually coerced, with the vulnerable teenager feeling that he or she has no choice because of being without funds or occasionally being beaten. This drug-linked prostitution is particularly disturbing because, for both males and females, it often involves unsafe sex with a high risk of spreading the virus for AIDS.

Caplan's views on teenage prostitution are somewhat unsettling. He points out that, unlike adult prostitution, where the issue is often dismissed as an unavoidable evil, society feels that the problem of teenage prostitution cannot be so easily ignored. Because teenagers are more dependent and defenseless against exploitation by adults, teenage prostitution is more offensive to the sensibilities and the sense of fairness of many people. Although Caplan concedes that efforts to combat this problem are admirable, he does not believe that the solution to teenage prostitution can be found in governmental reform:

> What can government do to compete with adolescent fantasies of flashy cars, glamorous out-

community and from their families and friends. This means they have few supports to turn to when they need help, except the pimp and others in the trade in whose interest it is to see them continue as prostitutes. Often, pimps encourage prostitutes to participate in other illegal actions such as drug trafficking or forgery, and this creates additional barriers to going back to the straight world. In addition, the women are often battered by their pimps or

assaulted by customers. They often have alcohol and drug problems, no high school degree, no safe and affordable housing, no marketable skills, and no recent work experience to be cited when applying for legitimate jobs. All this can make prostitutes feel as though they are on a dead-end, one-way street with few alternatives. All in all, not a very glamorous life. It sometimes looks glamorous—with the nice clothes, fine jewelry, and expensive cars—but fits, mindblowing drugs, a life on center stage? Prostitution provides an alternative that is in important particulars better than the life the teenager knew. Even the dark spots—the insults, the beatings, the degradation—horrible in themselves, are not necessarily foreign. They are, typically, likely to remind her of home. As she grows older and understands better what she has sentenced herself to, she may break away. She may not. About this process, government has little to contribute. (Caplan, 1984: 73)

Caplan's conclusion seems pessimistic or even fatalistic. He feels that it is reasonable to treat teenage prostitution in the same way that we do adult prostitution: to admit that it may well continue to exist. However, he also holds out hope by pointing out that some of the causes of teenage prostitution can be found in certain elements of society's structure. For a poor or deprived teenage girl, for example, prostitution may seem to be an alternative way to obtain material possessions and possibly even the love that was missing at home. Caplan points out that "the talent pool for teenage prostitution is bottomless" and he sees no reason to predict a reduction in this pool—in fact, the pool may become even larger.

But his recognition that the source of the problem lies in the structure of society points in the direction of some possible solutions: programs to change those conditions that push youngsters into the trade. Experts in juvenile delinquency have emphasized that the best method of addressing teenage prostitution is to fund programs in prevention and treatment, such as early intervention with runaways (Weisberg, 1985). Others have stressed the need for better community responses to the social problem surrounding teenage prostitution, particularly with regard to the abilities of social service delivery providers and law enforcement personnel to identify particular social needs of those young people involved. Without community participation, these professionals are far less able to provide early effective intervention strategies to head off youth participation in teenage prostitution (Campagna and Poffenberger, 1988). Finally, we need to recognize that teenage prostitution thrives in the fertile soil of family disruption, discussed in Chapter 3; poverty, discussed in Chapter 5; child abuse and exploitation, discussed in Chapters 3 and 8; and drug abuse, discussed in Chapter 10. All these social problems help to push some youngsters into a premature independence on the street. Certainly the streets have attraction when home means tension, fights, little money, and sexual assault. However, if we can alleviate some of these other problems, then staying at home will become a more desirable alternative for some youngsters.

all of that usually belongs to the pimp, not the woman.

Prostitution: A Functionalist Perspective

As is pointed out in Chapter 1, the functionalist perspective provides insight into how a social problem, although controversial, can contribute to the maintenance of the social system. Could prostitution possibly be functional for society? The functionalist approach to this issue was first proposed by sociologist Kingsley Davis in 1937. In the previous section, the question of how people, particularly women, become involved with prostitution was discussed. Davis turned this focus around: "The interesting question is not why so many women become prostitutes, but why so few of them do" (Davis, 1971: 347). Davis's response to this question mirrors the functionalist perspective:

The answer, of course, is that the return is not primarily a reward for labor, skill, or capital, but a reward for loss of social standing. The prostitute loses esteem because the moral system—especially when prostitution is purely commercial—condemns her. (Davis, 1971: 347)

Davis's argument is that the moral structure of society causes prostitution because that system simultaneously offers benefits for engaging in the trade, while it also condemns prostitution as a meaningless and illicit sex activity:

> When a man is away from home and cannot satisfy his sex drive with his wife, or when a man is a stranger in town and does not have enough time to seduce a respectable woman, he is driven into the arms of a prostitute who will satisfy his sex drive in—as the moral system would have it—a meaningless way. Also, by defining certain acts like fellatio and cunnilingus as immoral and hence not to be indulged in with one's wife or girlfriend, the moral order encourages males to turn to prostitutes for the enjoyment of these sex acts. (Thio, 1983: 214)

In addition, Davis emphasizes that prostitution has important effects on the moral system—indeed, the activity actually strengthens that system: "protecting the family and keeping the wives and daughters of the respectable citizenry pure" (Davis, 1971: 350). Thus, prostitution enables sexual gratification to be achieved in a variety of ways without placing excessive demands on wives and thus threatening the institution of the family.

The functionalist theory of prostitution illustrates that the moral system in society, which condemns the selling of sexual services for money, also encourages prostitution and thereby functions to foster and preserve that system.

Prostitution: An Interactionist Perspective

Recall from Chapter 1 that the interactionist perspective focuses on everyday social interaction among individuals rather than on large societal structures. Using this approach, a social problem exists when some social condition is defined by an influential group as stigmatizing or threatening to their values and disruptive of normal social expectations. In discussing the functionalist perspective, it was suggested that the moral system in the United States defines prostitution as threatening. Like society, however, prostitutes have their own "definition of the situation." Using the interactionist perspective, we can view prostitutes as actors in their own life drama, and understand their behaviors as they interpret them in reference to society's definitions (Heyl, 1979). This relationship is illustrated in Figure 11.3. First, in response to the moral stigmatization of their profession, prostitutes tend to define what they do as necessary to society. These are the views of some prostitutes on what they do:

> I believe that there should be more prostitution houses and what have you, and then we wouldn't have so many of these perverted idiots, sex maniacs, all sorts of weird people running around. I could say that a prostitute has held more marriages together as part of her profession than any divorce counselor. I don't regret doing it because I feel I help people. A lot of men that come over to see me don't come over for sex. They come over for companionship, someone to talk to. . . . They talk about sex. . . . A lot of them have problems. (Bryan, 1966: 443)

The other element in prostitutes' definition of the situation involves their self-concept. The moral system defines their behavior as disvalued. Prostitutes, on the other hand, turn this around by saying that they are honest and respectable, whereas the so-called respectable members of society are not (Diana, 1985). Women involved in prostitution frequently see their clients as hypocritical because they simultaneously claim membership in the social world of the respectable but also avail themselves of the prostitute's services:

> We come into continual contact with upright, respected citizens whose voices are loudly raised against us in public, and yet who visit us in private. (Hirschi, 1962: 44–45)

Society	Prostitutes
Prostitution is morally reprehensible and a disvalued meaningless sexual activity.	Prostitution is a useful element in society and the social order needs it or else there would be no demand.

"Respectable" Member of Society	Prostitutes
We reject prostitution as illicit and socially disvalued behavior and will take steps to see that it is eradicated.	Society speaks with a forked tongue – it simultaneously condemns and rejects us, but *needs* us at the same time. We are morally superior to the so-called respectable people – at least we are honest and forthright about what we do.

FIGURE 11.3 Contrasting Views of Prostitution.

From the interactionist perspective, then, the extent to which prostitution is a social problem is a matter of some dispute. It depends on whether we consider the public proclamations of people or their private inclinations. For some, such as politicians, it may be beneficial to publicly denounce the trade when in fact they see little wrong with it.

Pornography

A few years ago, an issue of *Hustler* magazine, which routinely contains very sexually explicit photos, advertised that it contained "the most obscene photographs ever published." Not surprisingly, this issue enjoyed particularly vigorous sales on the magazine stands. Rather than sexually explicit photos, however, the photographs were extremely vivid portrayals of combat in Vietnam. This episode highlights an important question in the social controversy pertaining to pornography: What is obscenity?

Another dimension of this issue involves the debate over whether adults should have the right to choose what they see and read about.

Defining Pornography

The term **pornography** was first applied to characterizations of prostitution, but as currently utilized, it describes *"sexually 'explicit' writings, still or motion pictures and similar products designed to be sexually arousing"* (Sobel, 1979: 2). *Obscene* is a term that originally implied "filth." Today, obscene material is generally thought of as "lustful material that offends prevailing senses of decency and morality" (Sheley, 1985: 119). Feminist Gloria Steinem has commented that it is the *dehumanizing* aspect of pornography that distinguishes it from *erotic* materials. For Steinem, the message in pornography "is violence, dominance, and conquest," whereas erotica portrays "mutually pleasurable, sexual expression between people who have enough power to be there by positive choice" (Steinem, 1980: 37). Clearly, what is obscene to one person may be considered by another person to be a work of art.

Particularly vivid examples of the controversy involving different definitions of obscenity or pornography are found in attempts by various moral interest groups to ban such literary classics as James Joyce's *Ulysses* and J. D. Salinger's *Catcher in the Rye*. In 1948, novelist Norman Mailer published *The Naked and the Dead*. In that book, although with an obviously deliberate misspelling ("fug"), a four-letter, Anglo-Saxon word, previously regarded as taboo in printed material, was used frequently. Three years later, James Jones released his classic *From Here to Eternity*, and in that book, this same word was used with equal frequency in its correct spelling. Although this usage in both books shocked some people, each book met critical approval and became a best-seller. Today this very same expression is used frequently in various publications and quite regularly in motion pictures. Clearly, what is obscene in one era can be considered acceptable in another. This again illustrates the relative nature of deviance.

Over the years, the U.S. Supreme Court has ruled that obscenity lies outside of the free speech protection of the First Amendment to the Constitution, but the courts have had considerable difficulty in trying to determine what is and is not "obscene." The current legal status of pornography was established in the 1973 Supreme Court case *Miller v. California*. According to the *Miller* test, material must meet three conditions in order to be considered legally obscene (Hawkins and Zimring, 1988):

1. The average person applying community standards considers the material as a whole to appeal to prurient interests.
2. The material depicts sexual conduct, specifically defined by state or federal law, in a patently offensive way.
3. The work lacks serious artistic, literary, political, or scientific value.

Since the *Miller* ruling, a large body of court rulings has emerged in an effort to specify more clearly such things as who the "average person" is and what is "patently offensive." Despite these rulings, there is still much dispute about what is obscene, and, except in the most extreme cases, judgments about obscenity will inevitably be subjective and influenced by personal or religious values. Because of this, antiobscenity legislation is essentially in the hands of the more powerful political elements and interest groups of particular states and communities. Very often, what is and is not considered "obscene" is reduced to a single decision by a judge or jury. What is clear, however, is that pornography—sexually explicit materials designed to be sexually arousing—is not obscene according to the *Miller* test and thus is protected free speech under the First Amendment to the Constitution.

Pornography and Censorship

One of the key issues in the debate over pornography as a social problem is whether and to what extent it should be censored. Proponents of antipornography statutes argue that society must be protected from these "immoral vices." They contend that, unless there is censorship, such materials will fall into the hands of impressionable youth. In addition, they point out, pornographic materials frequently involve the exploitation of women and children, sometimes treating them as "property" or mere sex objects. Because of this, some feminists have joined with more conservative groups in making a case for a ban on pornography. For example, law professor Catharine MacKinnon and author Andrea Dworkin have pioneered a new approach to pornography that views it as a violation of the civil rights of women (MacKinnon, 1993). In their view, when women are portrayed as sex objects and in degrading and subjugated roles, it helps to perpetuate sexist cultural beliefs that it is appropriate to treat women as property or as mere sexual objects. Because pornography portrays women as subordinate, submissive, and often the recipients of violence, it encourages sexual assault and the abuse of women. So, because pornography helps to create a hostile environment for women with negative outcomes, in their view, it violates their civil rights. These ideas have been incorporated into the laws of some municipalities, but the courts have struck down such laws as unconstitutional.

During the 1980s, the controversy over pornography experienced renewed energy and momentum, fueled by the Reagan administration's call for a national commission on pornography legislation. In 1986, the Attorney General's Commission on Pornography (the Meese Commission) ended its one-year investigation of pornography in this country and issued a report that condemned violence and degradation in sexually explicit films, magazines, and books. The report also called for more aggressive prosecution of those who sell what it called obscene materials in order to keep them out of circulation. In addition, the Attorney General threatened to publish a list of pornography distributors in the United States. This threat led an estimated ten thousand stores nationwide to stop selling adult magazines such as *Playboy, Penthouse,* and *Hustler.* In some cases, major retail chains such as B. Dalton Bookseller were picketed (Strickland, 1986). Although the Meese Commission Report attacked primarily violent pornography, opponents of pornography have used the report as a club with which to attack all pornography.

Those opposed to censoring pornography argue that people should be free to decide for themselves what they wish to read or watch (Strossen, 1995). There is virtual unanimity in the United States that pornography should be kept out of the hands of children (see Figure 11.4), and those who oppose censoring pornography agree with this. However, they argue that adults' fundamental rights to choose whether they want to consume these materials should not be interfered with. If censorship were to become common, it would be difficult to draw the line between works without "redeeming value" and those having literary or other worth, as the examples discussed earlier illustrate. Antipornography legislation, they argue, would open the doors to banning much literature and art because it is offensive to some group. When children are involved, however, the matter of exploitation is very clear. Those who are opposed to antipornography legislation readily concede that pornography involving children should be banned.

There is an ironic contradiction in people's stance toward pornography in the United States. On the one hand, powerful interest groups have maintained steady and strong pressure to limit the distribution of pornography. There is also strong opposition to distributing pornography to those younger than eighteen

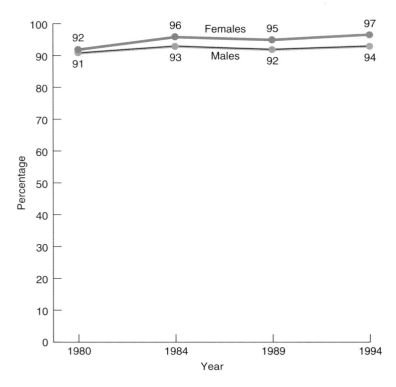

FIGURE 11.4 Percentage of People Agreeing that Laws Should Forbid Distribution of Pornography to Persons Younger Than 18 Years, by Gender, 1980–1994. *Source:* Kathleen Maguire and Ann L. Pastore, eds. *Sourcebook of Criminal Justice Statistics, 1994,* U.S. Department of Justice, Bureau of Justice Statistics. (Washington, D.C.: U.S. Government Printing Office, 1995), pp. 224–225.

years. When it comes to distribution to adults, however, the opposition wanes. In 1994, only 37 percent of people in the United States believed that laws should forbid the distribution of pornography to adults, with about one-half of women and one-quarter of men taking this stance (see Figure 11.5). These percentages have remained fairly steady since 1980. There is stronger opposition to the distribution of pornography that features violence or the degradation of women.

Pornography and Sexual Violence

As has been seen, the pornography issue has become a battleground on which some feminists and the religious right have joined forces to push for a ban on pornographic materials on the grounds that they lead to sexual aggression, sexual assault, and other forms of violence against women by men (Segal, 1990). In 1994, 48 percent of people in the United States agreed that pornography leads men to commit rape, with women considerably more likely to agree than men (see Figure 11.6). The slogan "Pornography is the Theory, Rape is the Practice" embodies the belief that pornography is the ideology that fuels not only violence against women but all forms of female exploitation and oppression. For some feminists, these are core issues, and they rest on an assertion that can be subjected to empirical testing: viewing pornography increases men's levels of violence against women. The role of applied research in social policy is sufficiently important in this realm that the Applied Research insert in this chapter is devoted to evaluating that assertion and the turmoil that swirls around it.

Future Prospects

Social policy regarding various forms of sexual behavior remains highly controversial. There is strong, universal disapproval, of course, of sexual behavior that involves the use of force or violence against an unwilling victim. Equally strong disapproval is found for child molestation, whether force is involved or not, because of the dependence and vulnerability of the child. However, these instances of forced sex were addressed in Chapter 9 as crimes. The sexual behaviors addressed in this chapter generally involve consenting adults (except in the

FIGURE 11.5 Percentage of People Agreeing that Laws Should Forbid Distribution of Pornography to People of Any Age, by Gender, 1980–1994. *Source:* Kathleen Maguire and Ann L. Pastore, eds. *Sourcebook of Criminal Justice Statistics, 1994,* U.S. Department of Justice, Bureau of Justice Statistics (Washington, D.C.: U.S. Government Printing Office, 1995), pp. 224–225.

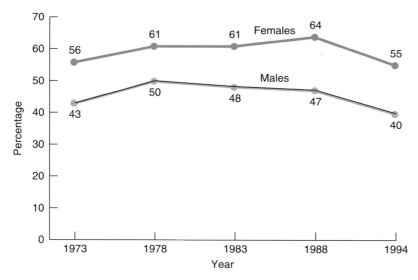

FIGURE 11.6 Percentage of People Agreeing that Pornography Leads People to Commit Rape, by Gender, 1973–1994. *Source:* Kathleen Maguire and Ann L. Pastore, eds. *Sourcebook of Criminal Justice Statistics, 1994,* U.S. Department of Justice, Bureau of Justice Statistics (Washington, D.C.: U.S. Government Printing Office, 1995), pp. 226–227.

cases of child pornography and teenage prostitution). Social disapproval of sexual behavior involving consenting adults is generally less severe, although homosexuality, prostitution, and pornography are viewed negatively by many people in the United States.

One approach to these forms of sexual behavior, then, would be to attempt to rid society of them by criminalizing them. This has been tried with prostitution and, to a lesser extent, pornography and homosexuality. It has not worked—all three behaviors flourish. In addition, many people were hurt unfairly by punishment for their choice of a sexual outlet with another consenting adult. Futhermore, such criminalization seems unjustified since these three sexual behaviors involve few negative consequences for society. Of course, future research could show a causal link between pornography and violence, and such a development would warrant rethinking social policies. In addition, prostitutes are often exploited because of their poverty and the sexist attitudes in society, but that is really a matter of poverty and gender inequality (Chapters 5 and 7), not of sexuality. So, while the criminalization policy

is still pursued, at least to some degree, controversy and conflict persist over what to do about prostitution, pornography, and homosexuality.

As for prostitution, it is legal in many counties in Nevada with no apparent damaging effects. It is illegal elsewhere but flourishes nonetheless. It is legal in some European nations and subject to government controls that seem to minimize the problems that arise, such as the spread of disease or control by organized crime. These facts suggest that we might want to reexamine our policy of criminalizing prostitution. Some alternatives and their consequences are analyzed in the Laissez-Faire/Interventionist insert in this chapter.

Most authorities would agree that prostitution is very hard to stop even when it is illegal. With a demand for the services and lots of money to be made, people are very creative in figuring out how to get around whatever barriers the police and other authorities are likely to put up. One approach that does show some promise focuses on the street trade: use coordinated and multileveled efforts to discourage prostitution in particular neighborhoods (Lowman, 1992). This could involve intensive efforts

Many people argue that pornography should be banned because it produces aggressive behavior in men, leading to sexual violence against women. Research up to this point has only provided minimal support for this conclusion.

by police to arrest prostitutes and their customers, community groups that take control of the streets and discourage customers from coming around, and road closures and traffic diversions to make it difficult for customers to drive near where the prostitutes congregate. In some places, legislation makes it illegal to communicate about the purchase or sale of sexual services in public, which gives the police an extra tool with which to convict prostitutes and their customers. For some prostitutes and many customers, participating in the trade is a matter of how easy it is to do so, and coordinated efforts such as this seem to push them out of the trade. More committed prostitutes, however, such as those who need money to support a

drug habit, tend to move elsewhere in response to such police interventions. So, whether these programs reduce prostitution in a particular area depends on how committed the prostitutes are to the trade. In some cases, these efforts just send prostitutes into other neighborhoods to ply their trade.

Legalization of prostitution does not eliminate the fact that some women are forced into prostitution because of poverty and sexism in society. For these reasons, society may still wish to reduce the amount of prostitution, even though it is legal. To do this, we need to recognize that society implicitly condones and encourages prostitution by perpetuating certain fallacies about it. One fallacy is that people "choose" to be prostitutes. Once we recognize that many people are forced by their poverty, vulnerability, and lack of opportunities into the trade and prevented from leaving by equally powerful forces, then all who participate in the trade become partners in that oppression. Another myth is that prostitution protects respectable women and children from sexual assault or unwanted sexual demands. This gives a noble sound to what is really a mechanism to ensure men the widest possible sexual access to women. The effort to control prostitution needs to begin by challenging these fallacies by ending the implicit support of a practice that it explicitly condemns. Another thing that could be done is to provide prostitutes with a way out of the trade: drug and alcohol rehabilitation, job referrals and job training, safe and affordable housing, assistance in completing high school or going to college, admission to programs for battered women, and whatever other assistance would help them get respectable and well-paying jobs.

During the 1970s, our laws took on new levels of tolerance for various forms of pornography, and this tolerance manifested itself in greater acceptance of nudity and overt displays of sexual conduct in public settings. The feminist movement of the 1980s and 1990s expressed renewed concern about pornography—especially sexually explicit materials that involve sexual violence. The most recent research available suggests that there may be a link between certain pornographic materials, especially those portraying violence against women, and attitudes about violence toward women. We can detect a definite trend of vacillation here between liberal attitudes and conservative responses. Through it all, actual research data are less than conclusive about the effects of pornography. One thing is certain: Lawmakers are responding to public concern about pornography with restrictive rulings. For example, a number of cities have used zoning ordinances to severely restrict sex-oriented video and book stores and x-rated movie the-

atres (Myers, 1994). The regulations limit, for example, how many such businesses may open and where, with the result that fewer are opened than would be the case with no regulations. The U.S. Supreme Court as well as lower courts have ruled that, while sexually explicit materials are a form of speech protected under the Constitution, local authorities can restrict their activities if they can demonstrate that such businesses have some harmful impacts.

As for homosexuality, we have seen that it is still regarded by many as unacceptable, but it has also gained more public notice and probably more respectability in the past twenty years. At the very least, more people are now aware of how widespread homosexuality is. And research shows that familiarity with gays and the gay lifestyle probably leads to more positive attitudes toward homosexuality (Schneider and Lewis, 1984). Also, more educated people are more accepting of gays. So, as educational levels in the United States rise and as more gay men and lesbians lead their lives openly, we can expect attitudes toward homosexuality to become even more positive.

Whereas twenty years ago many people focused their attention on homosexuality itself as a social problem, today many people recognize that the real social problem is the discrimination and violence too often suffered by gays because of their sexual orientation. Over the past twenty years, there have been significant changes moving in the direction of more equitable treatment of gay men and lesbians. Much of this change has occurred because various gay groups and organizations have vigorously pursued the interests of gays in the political arena (Noble, 1992a). As we have seen, a number of places around the country now ban discrimination against gays in employment and housing. In addition, a number of employers have extended benefits to gay couples that had previously only been available to married couples (see Chapter 3). These "domestic partner" benefits can include such things as health insurance, retirement plans, and so forth. To be

The issue of whether pornography leads to increased levels of violence against women is a very volatile topic because some groups feel very passionately about violence against women and believe that pornography should be banned because it plays a part in this. Researchers and their findings have been drawn into this emotional vortex, and there has been a lot of sound and fury produced. It can make finding the truth difficult. In general, the research has not been very supportive of the notion that pornography causes sexual violence. However, the resulting sound and fury gives us some good lessons in the political uses of scientific research. First, let us summarize the research.

Research in the 1960s and 1970s generally failed to document any link between pornography and sexually violent behavior (Goldstein, Kant, and Hartman, 1974; Segal, 1990). In fact, the 1970 report of the president's National Commission on Obscenity and Pornography rejected the conclusion that exposure to erotic materials is a factor in causing sex crimes and sexual delinquency. Nine years later, the Committee on Obscenity and Film Censorship in the United Kingdom came to the same conclusion. More recent research suggests that there may be a link between pornography and sexual violence. In fact, the Attorney General's Commission on Pornography of 1986 concluded that exposure to pornography does play some role in sexual violence and sexual coercion. Let us take a look at the evidence so that we can better judge what is going on.

One source of evidence produced by social science research on this issue is how people in laboratory experiments respond to pornographic images. Much of this experimental research finds no link between viewing pornography and propensity toward sexual violence. However, some research does seem to find a link. Psychologist Edward Donnerstein and his colleagues, for example, showed pornographic films to college-age males and then asked them to judge simulated rape trials (Donnerstein, Linz, and Penrod, 1987). He found that men who watch sexually violent films are less likely to

vote for conviction of a rapist than men who see nonviolent pornographic films or nonpornographic films. The researchers concluded that the men who watch sexually violent films develop more calloused attitudes toward women and attitudes that trivialize rape. The men also show more acceptance of rape myths, such as that female hitchhikers or provocatively dressed women deserve to be raped. These attitudes are especially likely to emerge if the rape victim in the film appears to enjoy the attack. Donnerstein and his colleagues also found that portrayals of sexual violence produce higher levels of sexual arousal than erotic but nonviolent sexual imagery, greater acceptance of violence against women, and a greater likelihood that men will state that they would rape someone themselves if they could get away with it.

Donnerstein's research makes an important distinction between pornography that includes aggression or violence and that which does not. He concludes from his research that it is the aggressiveness and violence in some pornography, rather than its sexual explicitness, that affects the way men respond to simulated rape trials and makes them more likely to express negative attitudes toward women and positive attitudes about rape. In fact, when he removes the sexual content from the films and leaves the aggressiveness, the negative consequences of watching the films seem to be the same.

So, does the research of Donnerstein and some others show that violent pornography produces sexual violence against women? Not really. The research has been criticized on a number of grounds. First, none of this experimental research actually observes sexual violence against women. All they observe is changes in responses to hypothetical situations such as rape trials or changes in some attitudes. Whether any of the men in these experiments would actually go out and commit sexual violence against women is unknown. A second criticism is that the experiments are done in highly artificial situations that may have little to do with the real causes of sexual violence. There is a huge difference between saying in a purely hypothetical and anonymous context that you might assault a woman if you could get away with it and actually assaulting a real human being. A third criticism is that these studies typically observe only short-term effects—what the men say or feel immediately after viewing the films. That effect may not last more than a few minutes, a few hours, or a few days and thus may have little influence on their behavior in the real world. All this criticism does not mean that the research tells us nothing, but the weaknesses of the research, along with the fact that other research does not find a link, leads scientists to be very cautious about drawing conclusions, especially when changes in social policy are at stake.

Another approach to research on this issue is to see what pornography does to actual rapists. Again the results are less than supportive of a ban on pornography (Kutchinsky, 1991). Rapists have less experience with pornography in their teenage years than do nonrapists, and rapists do not use pornography more than others as adults. They also are not more aroused by pornography or more likely to engage in sexual behavior after exposure to pornography. In addition, as with ordinary men, rapists are less aroused by viewing forced sex than by viewing consenting sex.

Another line of research has been to see whether rates of rape and other sex offenses increase when more pornographic materials are available. Some studies have found positive correlations: In the United States, states that have higher rates of circulation of adult magazines have higher rates of rape. However, a recent study at the city, rather than state, level failed to support this: There was no correlation between level of circulation of pornographic magazines in a city and the rape rate in that city (Gentry, 1991). In addition, even if rapes are higher in locales with more pornographic materials around, the pornography may not be the cause of the rapes. It could be that the interest in pornography and the incidence of rape are both affected by the same thing: sexist

and demeaning attitudes toward women. Remove the pornography and those attitudes would still be there. Actually, other research shows that communities with high circulation rates for pornography have higher levels of gender equality than communities with low pornography levels (Baron, 1990). This is probably because both pornography and gender equality flourish in politically tolerant communities. Furthermore, a longitudinal study of changing rates of rape in Denmark, Sweden, and West Germany—all three of which legalized pornography in the early 1970s—could find no increase in rape associated with the growing availability of pornographic materials (Kutchinsky, 1991). Likewise, in the United States, where both violent and nonviolent pornography have become much more widely available since the 1970s, there has been no increase in rape associated with it.

So, where does all this leave us? There is little scientific proof at this point that pornography causes sexual violence. One researcher concludes, for example, that "our knowledge about the contents, the uses and the users of pornography suggests that pornography does not represent a blueprint for rape, but is an aphrodisiac, that is, food for the sexual fantasy of persons—mostly males—who like to masturbate" (Kutchinsky, 1991: 62). Nevertheless, some of the research shows that men's attitudes and actions toward women may be changed by viewing violence against women, and this helps focus the debate on the realm that may be problematic—the violence rather than the sexual explicitness. Research should continue into all these areas. In fact, researchers have come to recognize that rape is an act of violence and aggression rather than a sexual act, and it is probably caused by the same factors behind other violent crimes such as homicide and aggravated assault that are discussed in Chapter 9.

Which brings us to the final issue: the politics of scientific research. Advocates of both sides of this issue would like to use scientific research to show that their position on the issue is correct. This can lead to distortions or misrepresentations

(continued)

of the research. The Meese Commission, for example, used Donnerstein's research as a basis for its conclusion that pornography plays a role in causing sexual violence and aggression, even though Donnerstein and his colleagues strongly disagree with that conclusion (Linz and Donnerstein, 1992). For reasons discussed in this insert, Donnerstein and his colleagues are much more cautious about what their research shows: only that violent pornography may temporarily change some of men's attitudes toward women or change some

of their behavior in artificial, laboratory settings, They do not believe this can justify social policies that curtail the distribution of all sexually explicit materials. It appears that the Commission had an agenda when it started—to curtail the circulation of pornography in the United States—and it was simply searching for any evidence that might seem to support its position. This is why scientists need to be very careful in doing their research, so that distorted or misinformed representations of the results can be minimized.

---

eligible, the gay couple may have to provide documentation that they do live together on a permanent basis, are financially interdependent (e.g., have joint bank accounts), and are responsible for one another's common welfare.

Despite these advances, there have been setbacks. Some municipalities have rescinded their laws protecting gays from discrimination in housing and jobs. In 1992, a statewide ballot in Oregon would have permitted discrimination against gays, would have prohibited gay state employees from holding any position where they worked with children, and would have made it official state policy that homosexuality is "unnatural" and a "perversion." Although the ballot measure lost, 43 percent of Oregon voters voted in favor of this extreme measure. On top of all these things, we have seen that gays still suffer physical attacks in unacceptable numbers because of their sexual orientation. So there is still real tension in the United States over this issue, and it is too early to predict whether the future will bring greater acceptance of gays or further efforts to repress this lifestyle. By the 1990s, gays have become a much more powerful political force than they were twenty years ago, so they will

be better able to protect themselves against threats.

As gays have gone more public with their lifestyle and become more politically active, they have become more effective at getting societal institutions, such as schools, government, and corporations, to establish policies and practices that better serve the interests of gays. This has created new arenas for conflict with those who feel that society should not support, or even condone, homosexuality. Many of these people feel that such policies and practices sometimes cross the line between not discriminating against gays and actively promoting homosexuality as an acceptable life alternative. For example, in 1992, New York City produced some curriculum materials for grade school students that portrayed a range of various types of families, including some headed by gay and lesbian couples, in a basically matter-of-fact and positive fashion. The rationale was that such families, in fact, exist, and students need to be aware of them in order to develop tolerant attitudes toward the lifestyles of other people. As we have seen, however, some people in the United States still do not view homosexuality as an acceptable life alternative. So, there was much opposition to these materials on the grounds that the portrayals in effect provided institutional legitimation for choosing homosexuality as a way of life. At one level, this conflict is indicative of significant change: Thirty years ago no one would have even considered an open discussion of homosexuality in the schools. So the issues have certainly shifted. At another level, however, the episode shows that things have not changed that much: There is still significant support for the view that people should be discouraged from considering homosexuality as an acceptable way of life. As long as significant moral and religious opposition to homosexuality persists, we will see more conflicts of this sort.

Early in this chapter, it was stated that the discussion was not about sex per se but about the societal reaction to certain sexual practices. However, societal attitudes toward sex do influence how society reacts to particular forms of sexuality. There has been much talk over the last thirty years of the the "sexual revolution," and there definitely have been some significant changes in behavior. Premarital sex is more common than in the past, especially among women. Pornography is more widespread and more explicit today. Sex is presented and dis-

Five hundred thousand people attended this march in Washington to protest discrimination against gays and lesbians. Gays and lesbians have become a much more powerful political force than they were in earlier decades and are more effective at protecting the interests of the gay and lesbian communities.

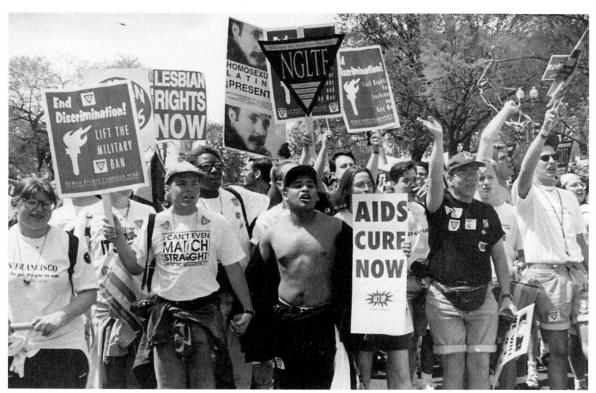

cussed more openly and publicly than in the past. However, other trends suggest that things have not changed that much. Marriage is as popular as ever, and the divorce rate has stopped increasing and may actually decrease a little. Most people do not cheat on their spouses, and there is little reason to believe that prostitution or homosexuality are more widespread than in the past (although they may be more public). And the AIDS crisis has made everyone more cautious about sexual encounters.

So, sex is a core and very emotional aspect of people's lives, and it rouses the passions. In addition, it is deeply linked to longstanding religious and cultural traditions. This is fertile ground for biased misperception and zealous

LAISSEZ-FAIRE
INTERVENTIONIST
D E B A T E

What Should the United States' Social Policy on Prostitution Be?

Even when prostitution is illegal, there is controversy over how much effort the police and other authorities should expend in trying to control it. The various policies proposed on this issue reflect, in one way or another, the laissez-faire or interventionist position on social problems. Helen Reynolds (1986) proposes these four different models of how government could approach prostitution:

1. **Laissez-faire model:** Prostitution is illegal but no active enforcement or prosecution is pursued; the risk of arrest is low for prostitutes, and competition flourishes among many different types of prostitutes.

2. **Regulation model:** Prostitution is legal, but only in settings that are licensed by authorities, such as brothels; prostitution in unlicensed settings is attacked by police.

3. **Zoning model:** Prostitution is permitted in particular areas of a community; prostitution may be legal or illegal in these areas, but the police would arrest only prostitutes outside these neighborhoods.

4. **Control model:** Prostitution is illegal and enforcement and prosecution are actively pursued everywhere; the risk of arrest is high everywhere and much prostitution is forced underground.

The first model represents the laissez-faire approach in which society does little to control prostitution, even though it is illegal; a kind of "hands off" policy is encouraged. The last model represents a strong interventionist position in which authorities make significant efforts to control prostitution in all settings. The other two models represent more moderate interventionist models in which the authorities attempt to control some types of prostitutes, or prostitution in some settings, but let other types of prostitution flourish. These four models make clear that social policy on prostitution need not focus only on whether it is legal or illegal. More complex alternatives exist.

LINKAGES

Prostitution increased when the crack cocaine epidemic in the 1980s (Chapter 10) led some desperate, crack-addicted women to engage in multiple sex acts in order to purchase the drug, and this increased health problems (Chapter 4) because their unprotected sex with multiple partners, many of whom were IV-drug users, helped spread the AIDS virus. In addition, both prostitution and pornography are seen by some as reflecting sexual inequality: They are remnants of the patriarchal control that men still exercise over women (Chapter 7).

overreaction, and social policies aimed at controlling one form or another of sexual behavior often result. Social policy should be based on the demonstrated negative impact of such behaviors on society or groups in society, not on the efforts of some powerful group to impose its personal or moral beliefs on others. As has been seen in this chapter, research to date fails to show that prostitution, pornography, or homosexuality are, in and of themselves, detrimental to society. If anything, it is the societal reactions to these types of sexual behavior that create problems.

Summary

1. The varieties of human sexual expression are almost endless, and most of them have been condemned at one time or another as deviant. Homosexuality, prostitution, and pornography are three forms of sexual expression over which there is intense debate, including what problems are created by the societal reaction to them.

2. Attitudes toward human sexuality vary from culture to culture. There is a wide range of socially acceptable sexual behavior from a cross-cultural perspective. There is also variety in human sexuality from group to group within the same culture or society. Sexual attitudes and behavior have changed over time in the direction of greater permissiveness, and this trend is explained by secularization, increased technological sophistication, and the growing demand for equal rights.

3. Homosexuality refers to sexual feelings, fantasies, or acts directed toward members of the same sex. There are biological, psychological, and sociological explanations for sexual orientation. There are varying patterns of homosexuality, with people ranging from exclusively heterosexual at one extreme to exclusively homosexual at the other. Homophobia has many sources, including condemnation of homosexuality by Christianity, the marginalized status of young males, and characteristics such as authoritarianism, intolerance of differences, and dogmatism. The homosexual community is an important source of personal identity for homosexuals.

4. Prostitution refers to sexual activity in exchange for money or goods in which the primary motivation for the prostitute is neither sexual nor affectional. Prostitution takes different forms: from streetwalkers to call girls to male prostitutes. Precise figures on the incidence of prostitution are impossible to obtain, but it is estimated that as many as five hundred thousand prostitutes work in the United States today. There are arguments for and against the legalization of prostitution, although in eleven counties in the state of Nevada prostitution is already legal.

5. There are different approaches to the analysis of prostitution. The functionalist perspective argues that the moral structure of our society causes prostitution and that the activity actually strengthens the system. The interactionist perspective calls attention to how prostitutes define themselves and their trade using their own perceptions of reality.

6. Pornography refers to sexually explicit writings, still or motion pictures, and similar products designed to be sexually arousing. There is tremendous controversy about what is pornographic and what is not, and about what kinds of materials, if any, should be censored. The Attorney General's Commission on Pornography reported in 1986 that sexually explicit materials are directly linked with violence. This conclusion is disputed by current research on pornography.

7. Disapproval of various forms of sexual behavior tends to be greater when force is involved, or

when one partner is not an adult. There has been a lot of change and conflict in this realm in the last few decades. Some argue that prostitution should be legal and that no problems are created when it is legal and regulated. When illegal, prostitution is very difficult to control. Although more pornographic materials are available today, there is also growing pressure to restrict their distribution. Homosexuality is more public and accepted today and finds more protection from discrimination and other negative reactions. However, there are still significant sources of homophobia and many efforts to restrict the activities of gays.

8. Research fails to show that prostitution, pornography, or homosexuality, in and of themselves, are detrimental to society. Problems arise from the hostile reactions that some groups have toward these forms of sexual expression.

STUDY **Review**
A N D

Key Terms

homophobia   pornography
homosexuality   prostitution
lesbians   secularization

Multiple-Choice Questions

1. A complete prohibition on premarital sex is:
    a. Found in almost all preindustrial societies.
    b. Found in about one-third of all human societies.
    c. Not supported by most Western religions today.
    d. Found in very few preindustrial societies.
2. According to the text, the most significant change in sexual behavior in the United States in the twentieth century has been:
    a. A decline in premarital sex.
    b. An increase in homosexuality.
    c. The elimination of the "double standard."
    d. The decline in the use of prostitutes.
    e. The increase in the use of prostitutes by women.
3. Research on the biological basis of sexual orientation has reached the conclusion that:

a. Sexual orientation is definitely caused by genetic inheritance.

b. Sexual orientation is definitely not caused by genetic inheritance.

c. Sexual orientation may be determined, in part, by genetic inheritance.

d. Sexual orientation is caused by problems children have in their families while growing up.

4. Intolerance of homosexuality tends to be greatest among:

a. Those with nontraditional social values.

b. Those with low educational levels.

c. Nonreligious people.

d. The young.

5. Physical assaults on gay males are most likely to be perpetrated by:

a. Young males.

b. Solitary criminals.

c. Young females.

d. Middle-aged males.

e. Minority-group males.

6. Those who support the legalization of prostitution argue that prostitution is:

a. A self-fulfilling prophecy.

b. Homophobia.

c. Secondary deviance.

d. Primary deviance.

e. A victimless crime.

7. Where prostitution is legal in the United States:

a. Illegal prostitution still persists.

b. AIDS is rampant.

c. It mostly takes the form of streetwalkers.

d. It is hard to regulate.

8. "Sexually explicit materials that are designed to be sexually arousing" is a definition of:

a. Pornography.

b. Obscenity.

c. Homophobia.

d. Self-fulfilling prophecy.

9. Which of the following was found in research investigating the link between pornography and violence against women?

a. Rapists read more pornography than do nonrapists.

b. Violent pornography changes some men's attitudes in artificial, laboratory settings.

c. Nonviolent pornography is as harmful as violent pornography.

d. Sex offenses decline in locales where pornography is in heavy circulation.

10. Which of these models of prostitution represents the strongest interventionist approach?

a. Laissez-faire model.

b. Regulation model.

c. Control model.

d. Zoning model.

True/False Questions

1. The social problem with the sexual behaviors discussed in this chapter is that the behaviors themselves have very harmful consequences for society.

2. The Mangaians described in the text have what many people in the United States would call a very permissive attitude toward sexual behavior.

3. Young people today are more likely to view premarital sex as socially acceptable than are older people.

4. There are probably twice as many lesbians in the United States as there are male homosexuals.

5. To date, there is no scientific proof that homosexuality is due to poor psychological adjustment.

6. Gay men are no more likely to be effeminate than are heterosexual men.

7. Escort prostitutes are not found in male prostitution.

8. According to the text, the prostitution trade in the United States is thriving.

9. Teenage prostitutes are usually boys or girls who have left their homes.

10. The courts in the United States have ruled that obscenity lies outside the free speech protection of the First Amendment to the Constitution.

Fill-In Questions

1. Changes in premarital sexual behavior during the twentieth century have often been referred to as the "sexual _____ ."

2. The _____ refers to a situation in which men are allowed more sexual freedom than women are.

3. Best estimates are that between

_____ percent and

_____ percent of adult males in the United States are predominantly or exclusively gay.

4. _____ theory posits that people's self-concepts and sexual identities derive in part from how other people treat us.

5. _____ is an intense dislike of or prejudice against homosexuals.

6. Most "streetwalkers" work for a

_____ .

7. In the United States, prostitution is legal in

parts of the state of _____ .

8. More than any other single factor, entrance into prostitution for women is linked to

_____ .

9. _____ is lustful material that offends prevailing senses of decency and morality.

10. Approximately _____ percent of people in the United States believe that laws should forbid the distribution of pornography to adults.

Matching Questions

_____ **1.** secularization

_____ **2.** homophobia

_____ **3.** gay community

_____ **4.** throwaways

_____ **5.** madam

_____ **6.** call girl

_____ **7.** COYOTE

_____ **8.** *Miller* test

_____ **9.** Catharine MacKinnon

_____ **10.** Meese Commission

A. manager of prostitutes
B. decline in religion
C. prostitute interest group
D. subculture
E. teenage prostitutes
F. pornography report
G. feminist opponent of pornography
H. escort prostitute
I. fear of gays
J. conditions of legal obscenity

Essay Questions

1. What accounts for the increase in premarital sexual behavior in the United States in the twentieth century?

2. Describe the theories discussed to explain the origins of people's sexual orientation. What evidence is there for each theory?

3. Describe the discrimination that is directed against gay men and lesbians in the United States.

4. Describe and explain the sources of homophobia in the United States.

5. What are the arguments for and against legalizing prostitution in the United States?

6. How and why do women become prostitutes? What sociological theories were used to explain the process?

7. What are the reasons for the existence of teenage prostitution in the United States?

8. What are the arguments for and against the censorship of pornography for adults in the United States?

9. Summarize the research evidence regarding the issue of whether pornography leads to violence against women.

10. What are arguments for and against a social policy that controls prostitution, pornography, and homosexuality by criminalizing them?

Answers

Multiple-Choice

1. B; **2.** C; **3.** C; **4.** B; **5.** A; **6.** E; **7.** A; **8.** A; **9.** B; **10.** C

True/False

1. F; **2.** T; **3.** T; **4.** F; **5.** T; **6.** T; **7.** F; **8.** T;
9. T; **10.** T

Fill-In

1. revolution
2. double standard
3. one, five
4. labeling
5. homophobia
6. pimp
7. Nevada
8. poverty
9. obscene material
10. 42

Matching

1. B; **2.** I; **3.** D; **4.** E; **5.** A; **6.** H; **7.** C; **8.** J;
9. G; **10.** F

For Further Reading

Martin Duberman. *Cures: A Gay Man's Odyssey.* New York: Dutton, 1991. This is a very personal account of the difficulties of growing up as a gay man in a world that has no sympathy for gays. It gives one a perspective on the personal consequences of stigmatization.

Cecil Greek and William Thompson. *Porn Wars: The Battle Over Pornography in England and America.* New York: Aldine de Gruyter, 1995. This is an excellent history and analysis of the battle against pornography by religious fundamentalists, conservative politicians, and some feminists. The authors view these groups as "moral entrepreneurs" in a battle over whose values will prevail.

James M. Henslin and Edward Sagarin, eds. *The Sociology of Sex.* New York: Schocken, 1978. This book is a collection of readings about sexual variation and a comprehensive overview of sex research conducted by social scientists.

Valerie Jenness. *Making It Work: The Prostitutes' Rights Movement in Perspective.* Hawthorne, N.Y.: Aldine de Gruyter, 1993. This book analyzes why prostitution is considered deviant by many and describes a social movement that has attempted to reduce the stigma associated with the activity and "normalize" it.

Daniel Linz and Neil Malamuth. *Pornography.* Newbury Park, Calif.: Sage, 1993. This book offers a good summary of the different stances that have been taken on the issue of pornography and an excellent summary of the research on the effects of pornography on people and society.

Robert T. Michael, John H. Gagnon, Edward O. Laumann, and Gina Kolata. *Sex in America: A Definitive Survey.* Boston: Little, Brown, 1994. This book is a shortened version of the National Health and Social Life Survey reported on in this chapter. It presents interesting information about human sexuality in the United States and deflates a number of myths along the way.

Randy Shilts. *Conduct Unbecoming: Lesbians and Gays in the U.S. Military, Vietnam to the Persian Gulf.* New York: St. Martin's Press, 1993. This is an excellent account of gays in the military in the United States—how well they do, the hostility and discrimination they face, and their future prospects.

Andrew Sullivan. *Virtually Normal: An Argument About Homosexuality.* New York: Knopf, 1995. This book reviews all of the stances on homosexuality in society—from outright prohibition to adding gays to the list of society's victim groups—and proposes some new positions that combine, in the author's judgment, the best of liberal and conservative views. The author also expresses his own personal response, as a gay man, to these issues.

D. Kelly Weisberg. *Children of the Night: A Study of Adolescent Prostitution.* Lexington, Mass.: Lexington Books/D.C. Heath, 1985. Provides excellent and up-to-date coverage of adolescent prostitution, with excerpts from interviews with teenage participants in the "trade."

CHAPTER TWELVE Population Growth and Urbanization

In the early 1800s, world population reached one billion people. It took one million years to reach this number. In the next 160 years—by 1960—the world's population had tripled in size to approximately three billion people. Then, with incredible speed, another billion people were added during the fifteen years between 1960 and 1975 and yet another billion by the late 1980s. It is projected that another billion people will be added to the world population by the year 2000 and yet another billion by 2010 (see Figure 12.1). Demographers caution that long-range projections concerning future world population size are speculative but that it could well exceed ten billion people some time in the twenty-first century. This population explosion has many consequences, as will be seen, such as crowding, starvation, and the depletion of natural resources. Population growth also has consequences for the earth's environment, which is the topic of Chapter 13. In fact, if humankind fails to control population growth,

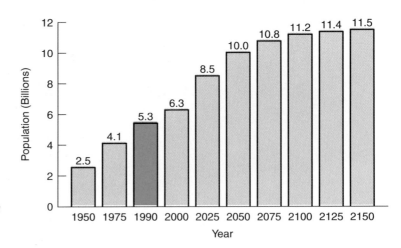

FIGURE 12.1 World Population, 1950–2150. *Source:* United Nations, *Long-range World Population Projections: Two Centuries of Population Growth, 1950–2150* (New York: Sales No. E. 92. XIII. 2, 1992), p. 18.

the world could be heading for a catastrophe that will be far worse than the starvation and war that we have seen in places like Somalia and Rwanda in recent decades—and on a much broader scale.

Accompanying the growth in world population over the centuries has been a change in the size of the human communities in which most people live, from small villages and rural areas to large and crowded cities. Most people in the United States live in cities or the suburbs that surround them. And it is in cities that people confront many of the problems that are addressed in this book, such as crime, racial conflict, poverty, and unemployment. In fact, these problems are often at their most intense and destructive levels in cities. In addition, cities have some special problems of their own, such as financial problems and inadequate housing. In fact, the discipline of sociology grew and matured in the late nineteenth century in Europe and the United States as people sought solutions to crowding and misery in cities such as London and New York as they filled with refugees from rural areas and other nations. The chapter will begin with an analysis of population growth and the problems associated with it; following that, urban problems will be the focus of attention.

Population Growth

Elements of Demographic Change

Demography is *the study of the size, composition, and distribution of human populations and how these factors change over time.* Each one of us participates in at least two "demographic acts" that affect human population—we are born and we will eventually die. Many of us also engage in other demographic acts, such as having children of our own. All these individual decisions and activities combine into an enormous wave of actions that make the world population what it is today. The term **population** refers to *the total number of people inhabiting a particular geographic area at a specified time.* Three basic elements shape the size, composition, and distribution of human populations: fertility, mortality, and migration.

Fertility   **Fertility** refers to *the actual number of children born.* This is distinguished from **fecundity,** or *the biological maximum number of children that could be born.* Because women rarely have the maximum number of children they are capable of bearing, the fertility of a society is normally quite a bit lower than its fecundity.

Myths & FACTS

ABOUT POPULATION GROWTH AND URBANIZATION

Myth: The most important factor in controlling world population growth is technology: Modern contraceptive technology is essential if people are to control their fertility.

FACT: The most crucial ingredient in world population growth is human values and desires. Effective contraception procedures have been available for some time, but as long as people place a high value on having many children, world population will continue to grow. At times in U.S. history, before modern contraceptives were available, the birth rate has been quite low because people chose to have fewer children.

Myth: The United States achieved zero population growth (ZPG) when the birthrate dropped below replacement level in the 1970s.

FACT: Although the U.S. birthrate has been dropping steadily and has remained below replacement level for some time, this rate will have to continue for another generation before the country reaches ZPG.

Myth: Suburban growth in the United States began early in the twentieth century because people wanted larger homes and more land, and entrepreneurial real estate developers satisfied that desire.

FACT: Although these played a part, the suburbs are equally an invention of government policies.

The U.S. government built the interstate highway system that made it possible for people to live in the suburbs and still get to work in the city; the government also provided low-interest, guaranteed mortgage loans for new homes, which were most often built in the suburbs because most cities had little space for new homes. The government did not provide such loans to build apartments in cities, which would have encouraged people to stay in the cities. The result was a strong government incentive for people to move to the suburbs.

Myth: Our cities are segregated today because whites and nonwhites just do not want to live together in the same neighborhood.

FACT: Through the 1950s, the government discouraged blacks and whites from living in the same communities by actively discouraging real estate developers from selling homes in white suburbs to African Americans. At the same time, the government discouraged lenders from making home mortgage loans to people living in African American communities on the grounds that people in such communities are bad credit risks. So the seeds of today's segregated urban landscape were planted many years ago by explicit government policies that discriminated against African Americans.

The simplest measure of fertility is the *crude birthrate,* the number of live births occurring in a particular population during a given year for each one thousand people in that population. Figure 4.1 on page 127 shows the crude birthrate in the United States between 1910 and 1994.

Mortality **Mortality** refers to *the number of deaths that occur in a particular population.* As with fertility, mortality in a society can be described in a number of ways. The *crude death rate* refers to the total number of deaths for every one thousand people (see Figure 4.1). The crude death rate in the United States has declined substantially over the past century from seventeen deaths per one thousand people in 1900 to less than nine today. However, as can be seen in Figure 4.1, there has been relatively little change in the past two decades. The crude death rate does not take into account the fact that people of some ages, such as the very young, are much more likely to die. It is therefore useful to look at the *infant mortality rate*, which is the rate of death among infants under one year of age. Infant mortality has shown the greatest decline of all age groups in the United States: dropping from one hundred deaths per one thousand people in 1915 to 9.1 today. Another way to describe the mortality of a populace is with the *life expectancy*, which refers to the number of years, on the average, that people can expect to live. People in the United States have experienced a substantial increase in life expectancy during this century, as Table 12.1 illustrates. As can be seen, the life expectancy of women has increased more than that of men. The difference in life expectancy between the sexes was only one year in 1920, whereas it is seven years today.

When we combine the results of the crude birthrate and the crude death rate, we derive an indication of the growth of a population, and the difference between these two figures is referred to as the *rate of natural increase*. For example, in 1994, the crude birthrate of the United States was 15.3 and the crude death rate was 8.7, yielding a rate of natural increase of 0.66 percent.

Migration   On the most general level, **migration** refers to *a permanent change of residence*. The term *immigration* refers to movement into a particular country, whereas *emigration* involves moving out. In analyzing migration, demographers look for "push" and "pull" factors. Sometimes people are pushed out of one country because of poor economic times, unstable political conditions, and the like. Many Southeast Asians migrated to the United States in the

TABLE 12.1 Expectation of Life at Birth in the United States, 1920–1995.

Year	Total	Male	Female
1920	54.1	53.6	54.6
1930	59.7	58.1	61.6
1940	62.9	60.8	65.2
1950	68.2	65.6	71.1
1960	69.7	66.6	73.1
1970	70.8	67.1	74.7
1980	73.7	70.0	77.5
1995[a]	76.2	72.8	79.7

[a]Projection

Sources: U.S. Bureau of the Census, *Statistical Abstract of the United States, 1978* (Washington, D.C.: U.S. Government Printing Office, 1978), p. 69; U.S. Bureau of the Census, *Statistical Abstract of the United States, 1994* (Washington, D.C.: U.S. Government Printing Office, 1994), p. 87.

1970s and 1980s, for example, because of the unpredictable political situation in that part of the world. In other cases, there is a "pull" or attraction that leads people to migrate to a particular place. Many Europeans migrated to the United States in the belief that they would have better economic and social opportunities.

Migration is also an important variable in the population within a particular nation. For example, the population density of the southern and western states in the United States has risen dramatically in recent decades because of in-migration from other states. Likewise, the number of people living in some other states has declined because of out-migration. Between 1980 and 1990, North Dakota and Iowa experienced a net decline in population, and some states, such as Michigan and Pennsylvania, showed almost no increase (U.S. Bureau of the Census, 1991: 20). All other states showed some increase. In the 1990 Census, California, Texas, and Florida accounted for over half of the United States' population growth during the 1980s. These three states together have a 1990 population of nearly sixty million, which is almost as many people as lived in the entire nation in 1890. The Northeast grew less than 3 percent and the Midwest only 1.5 percent during the 1980s, whereas the South gained 16 percent and the West 21 percent. These shifts contribute to high rates of unemployment and fewer job opportunities in the states showing little growth (see Chapter 2). These socioeconomic factors then have a further effect on migration patterns as people move out of some states and into others in search of employment or more lucrative career opportunities.

World Population Growth

In analyzing world population problems, migration, for obvious reasons, is not a critical element of overall population growth and change, although it can have an impact on the fortunes of particular regions. Fertility and mortality, however, are key elements, and this discussion will focus on them here. Later, the chapter will consider some ways in which migration affects the United States.

Most of human history has passed on an earth that was only sparsely populated by people. It has been estimated, for example, that there were fewer people on the whole earth seven thousand years ago than there are in larger cities such as New York or Tokyo today. At the time of Christ, approximately two thousand years ago, there were probably not many more people alive than currently live in the United States. In Figure 12.2 (on p. 438), you can readily see that, prior to the 1700s, world population was small and growth was slow. After 1750, world population began to increase at a more rapid rate, and it continues to grow even more rapidly today. Only in the last two

centuries has world population exceeded one billion, with a current population of about 5.3 billion (see Figure 12.1). The largest nation in the world today is China, with a little over one billion people. The United States is the third largest nation, with a population of 260 million, behind China and India.

The primary reason for the low rate of population growth in the world prior to 1750 was the relatively high death rate that existed in practically every society. For example, until 1600, the average life expectancy in European countries was little more than thirty-five years, in comparison to more than seventy years in industrial societies today. One important factor in the high death rate at that time was the extremely high infant mortality rate. In some societies, as many as 50 percent of the infants born would die within their first year of life (Antonovsky, 1972). The two most important factors producing these high death rates were disease and famine. In fact, disease has accounted for more deaths in the Western world than any other factor, and this has been the case throughout history. Before the modern era, knowledge and technology related to medicine, sanitation, and agriculture were not sufficiently advanced to lower the death rate and thus increase life expectancy. Although famine is something with which most people in the United States are unfamiliar, at times it has led to astonishingly high death rates. For example, a severe famine in China in 1877 and 1878 was responsible for the death of between nine and thirteen million people (Petersen, 1975). The modern-day effects of famine may be observed in Somalia where, despite the world's ability to produce food, many people have died of starvation in recent years.

The Demographic Transition

What explains the rapid world population growth of the past few centuries? In an effort to answer this question, demographers point to a

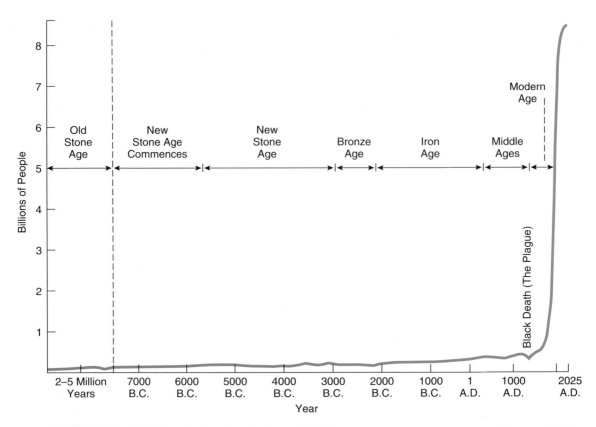

The following labels appear on the chart:

Billions of People (y-axis)

Old Stone Age | New Stone Age Commences | New Stone Age | Bronze Age | Iron Age | Middle Ages | Modern Age

Black Death (The Plague)

2–5 Million Years | 7000 B.C. | 6000 B.C. | 5000 B.C. | 4000 B.C. | 3000 B.C. | 2000 B.C. | 1000 B.C. | 1 A.D. | 1000 A.D. | 2025 A.D.

Year

FIGURE 12.2 World Population Growth Through History. *Source:* Population Reference Bureau, *World Population: Fundamentals of Growth,* 3rd edition, 1995.

process known as the **demographic transition,** *the changing patterns of birth and death rates brought about by industrialization* (van de Kaa, 1987). The reasons for this transition are complex. It is most useful to divide the demographic transition into four stages (see Figure 12.3). The *preindustrial stage* is characterized by high birthrates and high death rates, resulting in a population that grows slowly, if at all. Throughout much of human history, societies have been in this preindustrial stage.

For most Western nations, including the United States, the preindustrial stage existed until the onset of industrialization between 1750 and 1850, when the *transitional,* or *early in-*

dustrial, stage begins. This stage is characterized by continuing high birthrates but declining death rates. The falling death rates occur because of improvements in lifestyle resulting from industrial development (see Chapter 4). More and better food was available, for example, that helped people resist infectious diseases and reduced infant mortality. In addition, improvements in transportation, communication, and sanitation contributed to a lowering of the death rate. However, cultural values still encouraged people to have large families, so the birthrate stayed high. *The gap between the high birthrates and low death rates*—commonly called a **demographic gap**—resulted in explosive population growth during the early industrial period (Brown, 1987). The death rate was too low to keep population size stable when the birthrate remained high.

The third stage is called the *industrial stage* and is characterized by a continued decline in the death rate and a declining birthrate. During this stage medicine became more effective in controlling acute and chronic diseases and thus contributed to additional declines in the death rate. In addition, industrial technology made it possible for people to lead cleaner and healthier lives. The decline in the birthrate was a response to the impact of industrialization on cultural values regarding childbearing. Urbanization and increasing education, for example, led couples to desire smaller families than in the past.

The *postindustrial stage* of the demographic transition, which some demographers prefer to consider a continuation of the industrial stage, is characterized by low birthrates and low death rates, once again a roughly stable population with little growth. The industrialized nations, such as the United States, Japan, and some European countries, may be currently entering this stage, although how low their birthrates

and death rates will remain and for how long is a matter of some speculation.

The Extent of Overpopulation

The fully industrialized nations in the world today, including the United States, have experienced the demographic transition and now exhibit relatively low birthrates and death rates. If these low rates continue, then the populations of these countries will eventually stabilize, with little if any subsequent growth. There are, however, many nations in the world that are considerably less industrialized and have not yet gone through this transition in birthrates and death rates, and this is where today's world population problem can be most clearly located. In these nations, the death rate has dropped considerably, due in large part to the introduction of modern medicine, sanitation, and public health efforts. Insecticides, better transportation, and improved agricultural practices, for example, have made more and better food available. The impact of these changes on mortality has frequently been dramatic. In Sri Lanka between 1945 and 1949, the crude death rate declined from twenty-two deaths per one

FIGURE 12.3 The Demographic Transition

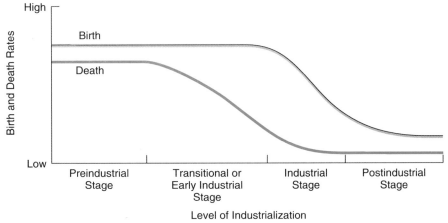

thousand people to twelve per one thousand; in 1947 alone, the life expectancy rose from forty-three to fifty-two.

Although declines in the death rate in these countries have been substantial, the birthrate has remained high, resulting in a continuing and large demographic gap. Afghanistan and Jordan, for example, are projected to have rates of natural increase of over 3 percent in the 1990s. This compares with our own rate of natural increase of 0.66 (U.S. Bureau of the Census, 1994: 850–852). In today's industrialized nations, the death rate has declined slowly over many decades, so population growth has been gradual, allowing cultural values regarding childbearing and family size to change, yielding smaller families. The developing na-

tions of today, however, have seen their death rates drop rapidly, and cultural values do not change that quickly. Thus, the developing regions of the world are expected to grow at an annual rate of 2.0 percent during the 1990s, as compared with 0.5 percent in the fully industrialized nations. Figure 12.4 shows the impact of these differing rates of natural increase: Europe and North America, where most of the industrial nations are, will contain a dwindling proportion of the world's population, whereas Africa and Latin America, containing mostly developing nations, will see its proportion of the world's population grow significantly.

The impact of all this can be better understood if we examine the number of years required for the world's population to double in

FIGURE 12.4 Percentage Distribution of the World's Population in Various Geographic Areas, 1950–2050. *Source:* United Nations, *Long-range World Population Projections: Two Centuries of Population Growth, 1950–2150* (New York: Sales No. E. 92. XIII. 2, 1992), p. 24.

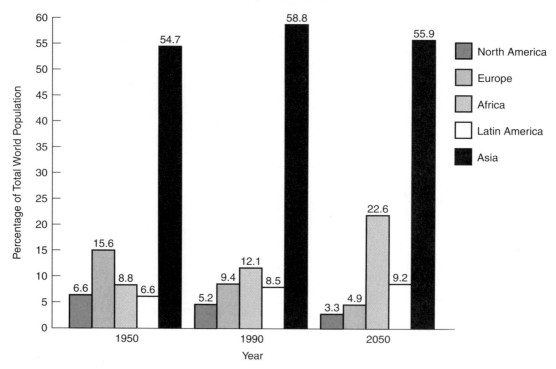

size. Demographers refer to this figure as the *doubling time.* From the beginning of the Christian era, it took 1,650 years for the population to double. By comparison, if current rates of world population growth continue, only forty years will pass until world population again doubles its size! Will the developing nations of the world today lower their birthrates before world population grows disastrously out of control? Keep in mind that the demographic transition is a description of a long historical trend found in some nations, all of which have experienced occasional changes in birthrates or death rates that go against this trend. We do not know if the developing nations of today will follow the same path (Organski et al., 1984). However, one thing is clear. In a preindustrial era, population growth, or the lack of it, was determined primarily by a high death rate, over which people had little control at that time. Today, growth is determined to a large extent by factors, especially fertility, over which people do have some control. Thus, the attention of those concerned about overpopulation today has been focused on issues of fertility control.

The Growth of Cities

All human groups organize their lives into **communities,** which are *groups of people who share a common territory and a sense of identity or belonging and who interact with one another* (Poplin, 1979). The earliest human communities were small hunting and gathering bands, usually consisting of between forty and one hundred people. These bands were usually nomadic, roaming the land in search of food and game, and all the people knew one another well. Then, about fifteen thousand years ago, small fishing villages began to appear around the Baltic sea, surviving off the plentiful fish. Approximately ten thousand years ago, people discovered how to cultivate plants and domesticate animals. This afforded them with greater control over their food supply and permitted a growing sur-

plus of food. The result was the emergence of agricultural villages, and later cities, in fertile river valleys around the world. A **city** is *a relatively large, permanent community of people who rely on surrounding agricultural communities for their food supply.* As a consequence of developing agriculture, then, human communities grew enormously in size. The biblical city of Ur, for example, located at the juncture of the Tigris and Euphrates rivers, had twenty-four thousand people (Hawley, 1971). At the height of the Roman Empire, Rome is estimated to have had as many as one million residents. However, prior to the industrial revolution, only a few cities had as many as one hundred thousand people.

Urbanization

Industrialization ushered in ever-increasing urbanization, with cities growing far larger than their preindustrial predecessors. By the mid-twentieth century, cities such as New York, Chicago, and Los Angeles had many millions of inhabitants. Two hundred years ago, only 5 percent of all Americans lived in urban areas, in contrast to 77 percent today (see Figure 12.5 on p. 442). The New York metropolitan area has over eighteen million people, and Los Angeles over fourteen million. Why has this extensive urbanization occurred? One of the main reasons is that most economic activity in industrial societies is nonagricultural, and such activity benefits from being concentrated geographically. With industry and jobs located in cities, people are drawn to the cities to find work. So "community" for most people in the United States today means a city, whether it be large or small.

Suburbanization

Equally as important as the growth in size of cities has been the growth of **suburbs,** *less densely populated areas, primarily residential in nature, on the outskirts of a city.* Mass suburbaniza-

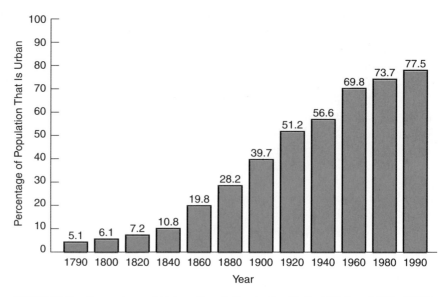

FIGURE 12.5 Percentage of Urban Population in the United States, 1790–1990.
Source: U.S. Bureau of the Census, *Statistical Abstract of the United States, 1991* (Washington, D.C.: U.S. Government Printing Office, 1991), pp. 17, 27.

tion is a relatively recent development. In the United States, it arose out of a complex set of social factors (Banfield, 1990). One factor was the economic and technological developments that made it possible for people to live far from where they worked. Early in the twentieth century, most people were limited in where they could live by the need to find transportation to work. This meant that most had to live in the cities, near where the jobs were. Because there were relatively few automobiles and highways, people walked or used public transportation to get to work and go shopping. This encouraged the concentration of population, and central cities served as the commercial and cultural core of urban areas. By the 1940s and 1950s, the increasing affluence in the United States, along with the automobile, made it feasible for people to live farther from work and opened up suburban life to the middle class.

In addition to these economic developments, government policy also contributed to suburbanization. For example, the federal government paid 80 percent of the cost of developing the interstate highway system. With cars and high-speed highways, people can now live far from where they work and shop. In sprawling cities such as Los Angeles, for example, it is common to live fifty or more miles from where one works. Another encouragement to the development of suburbs were policies of the Federal Housing Administration (FHA), established in 1934, and the Veterans Administration (VA) (Bullock, Anderson, and Brady, 1983). Beginning in the 1930s, the FHA and the VA made available federally guaranteed mortgage loans for the purchase of new homes. Because land outside the cities was both inexpensive and available, this was where much of the construction took place. The FHA and VA did not provide loans to purchase existing homes or build apartments, policies that would have encouraged people to continue living in the cities. So the flight of people from cities was in full swing, and, especially in the early years, it was the more affluent city dwellers who moved to the suburbs. Keep in mind that this suburbanization occurred not simply because people wanted to move to the suburbs. It also depended on the development of new transportation technologies and on federal social policy on housing and transportation. That these developments had such wide-ranging effects should not be surprising given the functionalist point about the interdependence among the different elements of social systems. The manifest function of the social policies was to stimulate economic development. Their latent function was to encourage decentralization of urban areas and to bring about the

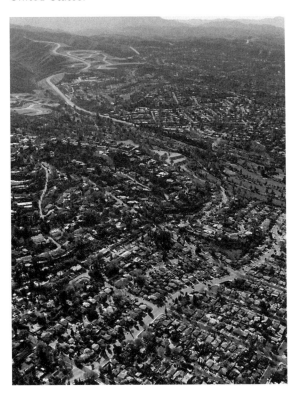

This is the San Fernando valley, a suburb north of Los Angeles. Los Angeles and its growth have become almost a cliche for suburban sprawl in the United States.

eventual decline of many cities. Clearly, all the ramifications of these policies were not considered when they were established.

These same developments eventually made it possible for businesses and factories also to move outside of cities. Businesses originally located in cities because workers lived there and transportation was available to ship their products. By the 1950s, cities no longer possessed those exclusive attractions. A labor force and highways were available in the suburbs. In addition, suburban land was typically less expensive, taxes were lower, and affluent suburbs could afford to offer tax breaks to industries to relocate. Suburban shopping malls were developed with huge parking lots and situated next to freeways. The malls were clean, spacious, and keyed to an affluent lifestyle. They drew consumer dollars out of the city as urban stores established suburban outlets. Increasing crowding and congestion in cities, along with the growth of numerous problems, also made the suburbs popular as a "rural refuge" from the hustle and bustle of the city. In their early development, suburbs were not economically self-supporting, since many residents made their livelihood in the cities. By the 1970s, however, this had changed, with 75 percent of all suburban residents both living and working in the suburbs and only about 25 percent commuting to the central city to work. Today, the United States is a nation of suburbanites, with 60 percent of its metropolitan population living in the suburbs. And it is the suburbs, rather than the central cities, that have shown the most significant population growth over the past two decades.

The Postindustrial City

Although people and some jobs have left the city, other jobs have remained. Many cities have retained or increased jobs in the financial service industries, those related to the functioning of corporate headquarters, telecommunications and publishing, and those involving non-profit and governmental activities (Heenan,

1991). This is true of some large cities such as New York, Chicago, Houston, and Atlanta, and some smaller cities, such as Memphis, Des Moines, Madison (Wisconsin), and Ann Arbor (Michigan). In other words, the changes in cities reflect the changes in the economy discussed in Chapter 2: the stagnation in the manufacturing sector and the growth of the service sector.

However, recent technological developments may reduce the need for corporations or service industries to concentrate their workers in one locale. Computers, microwave transmission, FAX machines, and communications satellites make it possible for people to communicate over long distances instantly, effortlessly, and relatively inexpensively. Overnight parcel delivery is available almost everywhere today, and information can be sent rapidly over the telephone lines from one computer to another. Teleconferencing means that even meetings can be held when those "present" are separated by long distances. There will still be some need for centralization, however. Top corporate executives, for example, will need close contact with attorneys, investment counselors, management-consulting firms, and advertising executives. However, many other jobs can be decentralized. For example, Eastern Airlines moved its reservation centers to Charlotte, North Carolina, and Woodbridge, New Jersey, and Exxon moved its corporate headquarters to Irving, Texas (Kindel, 1990). It will take some years to see the effects of these technological developments, but they may well encourage further decentralization of urban areas.

Perspectives on Population and Urban Problems

Now that some of the dimensions of world population growth and urbanization have been reviewed, the sociological perspectives can offer some insight into when and why these conditions become social problems.

The Functionalist Perspective

A major assumption of the functionalist perspective is that both societies and cities are systems made up of interdependent parts and that changes in one part of the system may have consequences for the other parts. In the case of society as a whole, the parts include the size and characteristics of its population along with the food supply and other elements of the environment that support that population. One of the earliest attempts to understand population dynamics was basically functionalist in nature. An English clergyman named Thomas Robert Malthus became concerned with population problems around the beginning of the industrial revolution in Europe. In 1798, he published his *Essay on the Principle of Population* (1960, originally published 1798). Malthus viewed population size and food supplies as two parts of a system that should be in balance if society is to function properly. He argued that there exists an immutable passion between the sexes that leads to reproduction, and this leads to a constant pressure toward population growth. He also said that societies have a limited ability to produce food. If the tendency toward population growth continues unchecked, then populations will eventually grow larger than the food supply can support. Malthus believed that human beings could intercede in this process and control population growth by postponing marriage or remaining celibate, but he was pessimistic about whether human intervention would completely save the day. He thought populations would continue to grow, ultimately being checked by deaths due to starvation, disease, and war.

Like Malthus, modern-day functionalists view population growth as a social problem in terms of the relationship between uncontrolled population growth and the exhaustion of available resources. Population growth becomes a social problem when it becomes dysfunctional and leads to social disorganization. This occurs when population growth interferes with the ability to achieve societal goals, such as providing adequate food and housing or keeping illness rates at an acceptable level. Cities have also confronted social disorganization resulting from changes in some parts of the urban system during the twentieth century. Some of these significant changes have just been discussed: the flight of people and jobs to the suburbs, changes in the occupational structure of an advanced industrial society, and developments in technology, such as the automobile, highways, and computers. The problems of cities in the United States arise, at least in part, because these changes have produced some degree of social disorganization, with people dislocated because of the changes and problems such as crime and violence arising. All these changes have been beneficial in many respects, of course, but they have also had highly dysfunctional effects for many cities.

It may be, of course, that the central cities are no longer functional for modern economies and should be abandoned, especially considering that businesses find it cheaper to locate elsewhere and people prefer to live elsewhere. Yet the cities are still an important part of the social system: People live, work, and shop there and are adversely affected by the crime and other urban problems. Many societal resources in the form of buildings, transportation networks, and people are tied up there. So ignoring the problems of the cities does not alleviate their impact on people's lives.

The Conflict Perspective

From the conflict perspective, population and urban problems are due more to an inequitable distribution of resources rather than to a lack of resources. In regard to population problems, for example, Karl Marx argued that powerful groups in society, namely, the capitalists, benefit from restrictions in the food supply and other

scarce resources. Recall from Chapter 2 that capitalism is based on profit making. Because of this, food and other goods are not produced unless someone can make a profit from producing and selling them. Less food may be produced than people actually need so that the low supply of food will increase the price. With an economy based on producing food for human need rather than profit, Marx argued, technology could be harnessed to produce a sufficient amount of food for a growing population.

From the conflict perspective, then, population becomes a social problem when those who control the economic system take steps to limit artificially the resources available in order to benefit a particular group of people. The solution to these problems does not focus on limiting the number of people born or controlling the environment but rather on enacting changes in the systems of production and distribution that would lead to a broader and more equitable distribution of resources among groups. Elements of this conflict perspective can be found in the political stance of the leaders of some developing nations today. They argue that world population growth is not the real problem but rather that resources are unevenly distributed among the various nations. For example, the United States could grow far more food than it currently does, and in fact the United States withholds much good cropland from production to lower food surpluses and raise prices.

From the conflict perspective, cities have deteriorated because the groups most directly affected—people living in the cities—have not had the political and economic resources to thwart the changes under way (Zeitlin, 1990). As we have seen, federal legislation encouraged the shift of people and jobs to the suburbs. The people who left the cities were the middle class and the affluent—the very people with the power to do something about the decline of the cities if they wished. But, of course, once they left, they were no longer interested in urban problems. In fact, these people tended not to understand the part their own actions played in bringing about the problems. The poor and minorities who were left in the cities had few political and economic resources with which to attack the problems.

The Interactionist Perspective

The interactionist perspective stresses the importance of social definition and social meaning, and thus population and urban problems are as much about *subjective* definitions of reality as they are about *objective* conditions. People in the United States have become used to rather spacious surroundings—the ranch-style suburban house on a large lot. In an equally industrialized but much more crowded nation such as Japan, on the other hand, most people have become accustomed to substantially less living space. People in the United States might well regard the amount of space available to the average Japanese family as "crowded." Likewise, the United States today could be regarded as overpopulated if the amount of land available to farmers during the preindustrial period is compared with the amount available to most people today. On the other hand, even the most spartan living conditions available to many poor people in the United States would appear luxurious to the poor (and some non-poor) in a crowded, less-developed nation such as India.

So, the interactionist perspective stresses that population conditions become social problems, in part, because of people's social definition of what is desirable or essential in their lives. The same is true regarding assessments of urban problems. In many respects, cities in the United States are far better off than they have ever been (Banfield, 1990). They are less crowded and have better sanitation, and the schools have improved in comparison to pre–World War II cities. Even their finances are in pretty good shape when compared with cities in earlier eras. Yet the interactionist perspective points to the importance of subjective definitions of social reality. People have come to expect much more than they once did. In addition, people tend to assess cities today in comparison with the immediate past that many of them can recall. The period between World War II and 1970 was one of considerable economic expansion and social prosperity for cities. By contrast, the urban experience of the 1970s and 1980s seems to have been a highly disruptive downturn in the fortunes of cities (Clark and Walter, 1991). It is this contrast that often leads people to perceive the problems of cities as much more severe than objective conditions would warrant. Yet the important issue from the interactionist perspective is that people define these conditions as a social problem.

Consequences of World Population Growth

Has population growth had adverse consequences for people? In looking at this issue, a useful concept is that of **carrying capacity:** *an upper-size limit that is imposed on a population by its environmental resources and that cannot be permanently exceeded* (Brown, 1987; Hendry, 1988). The idea of carrying capacity parallels some Malthusian ideas about population dynamics: A point is reached at which environmental resources in a geographic region are insufficient to allow further population growth, at least not without a change or decline in lifestyle. A geographic area such as the United States has a large carrying capacity, in part because of its abundant natural resources. In contrast, an area such as Ethiopia has a much lower carrying capacity because of its comparatively scarce resources and lack of technology. Advances in technology can increase the carrying capacity of an area. Improvements in agriculture, for example, might enable Ethiopia to support more people than it once did. But there is always a limit to how much growth can occur. Of course, the carrying capacity of the earth as a whole is, at any given moment, fixed. So as human populations have grown, they have approached more closely the carrying capacity of the earth, with some important consequences.

Crowding

One important consequence of population growth is crowding. Studies of animals have shown that extreme crowding can have adverse consequences, including increases in aggression and erratic behavior. Animal studies, however, are only suggestive of how crowding may affect human beings, because it would depend on people's past experiences and their expec-

tations. In addition, living quarters and work areas can be designed so that density is high but people do not have the *impression* of being crowded, and potentially negative effects could be avoided (Baum and Davis, 1976). In fact, psychologist Jonathan Freedman (1975) has argued that crowding by itself does not have negative consequences. Instead, crowding is usually associated with other social conditions, such as poverty, that produce increases in crime or aggression (Liddell and Kruger, 1987; Ehrlich and Ehrlich, 1990). Thus, there is considerable controversy over the impact of crowding. Yet if world population doubles in the next forty years and doubles again after

Calcutta, India, is half the size of the San Francisco metropolitan area in square miles, yet Calcutta contains 13 million people compared to 4 million in the San Francisco area. Clearly, the crowding experienced in cities such as Calcutta is immeasurably worse than in most U.S. cities.

that, we will experience serious overcrowding by most people's standards. The negative impact of this dramatic growth may be difficult to alleviate (Jain, 1988).

Food Shortages

Another consequence of population growth is the potential for food shortages. Especially in developing nations that are experiencing rapid population growth, increasing agricultural production sufficiently to keep up with population expansion is difficult. As a consequence, millions of people die each year from starvation and malnutrition (Lappé and Collins, 1988). Concern over this has provoked substantial efforts over the years to expand the world food supply. These efforts have focused on three key areas: the sea, farmland expansion, and yield increases (Hendry, 1988; Brown, Flavin, and Postel, 1991).

According to most observers, the sea will not be a very important source of expanding food supplies in the years to come. It is possible through intensive efforts to increase fish production of the oceans to some degree, but the costs of such a move could outweigh the benefits to be gained. Farmland expansion has also been pointed to as a promising technique for expanding food production in the future. It may be possible to increase the amount of land under cultivation so that we can produce more food overall. So far, however, population growth has proved to be so relentless that the world is undergoing a steady reduction in the amount of farmland available. Therefore, yield increases appear to hold the best prospect for increased food production. Efforts to increase yields have pursued a number of strategies: introduction of new crops, reduction of turnaround time between harvesting and replanting, improved management of the crop environment, and development of higher-yielding plant varieties (Hendry, 1988).

In fact, the last mentioned strategy was labeled the Green Revolution, and many hoped it would head off the threat of massive famine by making it possible to produce far larger crops from the same land that previously produced less of these grains. Time revealed, however, that the Green Revolution and the other strategies to increase food production were not the panacea to the world food problem. Although it is true that world grain production almost doubled between 1950 and 1970, this production level barely stayed even with population growth in the years to follow. Per capita consumption levels dropped off in the most disadvantaged nations, food prices increased by leaps and bounds, and well over one hundred countries of the world confronted critical food deficits. By the 1980s and 1990s, these problems coalesced into an increasingly serious crisis, with some developing nations experiencing starvation. In addition, the Green Revolution and other intensive agricultural programs have had some negative effects: By emphasizing a narrow range of crops, they have pushed biological uniformity to dangerous levels, they have relied on heavy utilization of chemical pesticides, and the expanding farmlands have eaten into forests and wetlands and depleted water supplies (Repetto, 1994).

Depletion of Resources

Beyond food, population growth can threaten the depletion of other world resources. There is considerable debate, however, about how serious this problem is. In 1972, a group of concerned business leaders, political leaders, and scientists, calling themselves the Club of Rome, published a report about the future supply of resources in the world (Meadows et al., 1972). It was a very pessimistic report. Based on estimates of world supplies of various resources and the rates of use of the resources at that time, they forecasted serious problems in the near future. They estimated, for example, that world petroleum resources would be exhausted in fifty years, natural gas in thirty-eight years, and aluminum in thirty-one years if rates of usage continued to increase. New finds of such resources have led some to call such pessimistic estimates unrealistic. Others have argued that new scientific and technological developments will overcome any shortages we might face in the future. Still other critics have charged that the Club of Rome findings are simply incorrect because they involve computer projections based on naive or inaccurate assumptions.

A second study commissioned by the Club of Rome used a more sophisticated approach, dividing the world into a number of regions rather than analyzing the world as a homogeneous unit, and using a more complex model of how nations are likely to make decisions about resource usage and development (Mesarovic and Pestel, 1974). Like the earlier study, this one also prophesied eventual depletion of many resources. The main difference in the second study was the prediction that some regions would face ecological collapse before others. They recommended that some of the problems might be alleviated if consumption and development in the industrial countries were moderated while those same countries made more industrial investment available for the poorer nations of the world. They suggested that it might be in the long-run best interest of nations such as the United States for their standard of living to decline somewhat in the future so that the standard of living in other countries around the world could be improved.

There are other more optimistic assessments of the world's resources. A report to the president, titled *The Global 2000 Report,* on the state of the world in the year 2000, for example, concludes that most minerals can be maintained at desirable levels through discoveries and judicious investment (Teich, 1986). Although there may be problems in petroleum production, the report sees plenty of time to shift to other energy resources or reduce consumption.

What is the truth about resource depletion? At this point, no one really knows. However, most agree that we need to plan for the possibility that some resources will be in short supply (MacKellar and Vining, 1988). We also need to plan for a more equitable distribution of resources in the world. Some of the less developed countries of the world control important resources, and they will not tolerate increasing development and consumption in the industrial nations without something equivalent occurring in the less developed nations. If the less developed nations do not get what they feel they deserve, they may withhold from the world markets the resources under their control. It is also clear that continued rapid population growth cannot be supported indefinitely by the world's natural resources.

Intergroup Conflict

The struggle for scarce resources intensifies when population increases. One way to cope with scarcity is to increase production of resources to satisfy demand. However, given that there are finite limits to expansion and growth, regulated competition could escalate to unregulated conflict. This might lead to one of Malthus's *positive checks* on population growth: war. People confronted with famine or disease may not sit idly by and accept starvation and death. If competition intensifies to conflict, the result may be all-out struggle for dwindling resources, such as living space and food. This is an especially ominous prospect in a nuclear world in which increasing numbers of nations have access to nuclear weapons.

Population growth can also lead to political conflict within a nation, such as food riots and insurrection. In the Sudan in 1985, for example, extensive demonstrations and riots followed an increase in the price of food, and eventually there was a military takeover of the government in an effort to quell the civil unrest (Brown and Wolf, 1986). Such food-related riots were not uncommon in Africa and South America in the 1980s (Chazan and Shaw, 1988). Population growth and dwindling food supplies

Millions of refugees throughout the world are fleeing from political conflict, as are these refugees in the former Yugoslavia. In some cases, the political conflict arises because of population growth and a shortage of available land.

also result in the forced migration of people to new countries in a search for survival (Kane, 1995). This has resulted in millions of refugees —the United Nations estimates over twenty million in 1994. These refugees are yet another source of conflict because they are often seen as unwanted competitors for limited resources in their country of refuge.

Internal Migration

When looking at world population problems, we mentioned earlier that migration is not really a critical variable. However, when looking at the problems of particular regions or na-

tions, migration definitely plays a role. Some states and regions in the United States have suffered because of internal migration. In Oregon during the 1970s, for example, there were policies that discouraged new industry and new migrants. In 1971, the governor of Oregon commented: "Visit us often, but don't move here to live." By the 1980s, Oregon's economy was suffering and politicians were encouraging immigration (Weeks, 1986). We saw earlier that some states in the East and Midwest have suffered population declines because of out-migration over the past decade. In the 1980s, 50 percent of the population growth in the United States was attributable to just three states—California, Florida, and Texas. Although it is true that these states have minority populations with higher birthrates than the national average, the primary explanation for their growth rates was internal migration from other states. Admittedly, California received more foreign immigrants than any other state, but much of that state's growth was explained by the lure of jobs created by expansion of the military industry and firms linked to computer technology.

Significant in-migration or out-migration can be very disruptive for a region. In the case of the former, a rapidly growing population can tax resources. Highways may be inadequate to the additional traffic, schools may become crowded, and crime rates may increase because migrants tend to be young and, as we saw in Chapter 9, the young are more likely to commit crimes. Out-migration is also disruptive. In the short term, it can increase rates of unemployment because there is a smaller payroll in the region and it may lead to an underutilization of resources such as schools and hospitals. So even within the United States, the population size of a region is in balance with economic and other factors. As the functionalist perspective suggests, significant changes in population size of a region can have disruptive and disorganizing effects on other parts of the system.

Problems in Cities in the United States

The focus of attention on urban problems tends to be on those conditions found in the central cities of large metropolitan areas. To be sure, the central cities do suffer most severely from problems such as crime, poverty, and deteriorating housing. Yet many of these problems can be found in smaller towns, and some suburban communities find themselves beset with similar difficulties.

Economic Decline

One of the premier problems that many cities in the United States confront is that they are in a state of economic decline. In fact, in the past two decades, a number of cities, especially in the Northeast and Midwest, have been on the brink of financial collapse (Shefter, 1985). In 1975, New York City was unable to pay its bills, banks refused to give any assistance, and only a complicated bailout from the federal government saved it from financial disaster. In 1978, Cleveland became the first U.S. city since the Depression of the 1930s actually to go into financial default. During the recession of the early 1980s, Boston and Detroit were so short of funds that their governments had to consider not paying for essential city services such as fire and police protection. In the early 1990s, New York City was again in fiscal crisis, cutting services and raising local taxes (Caraley, 1992).

One major cause of these financial problems has been the flight of people and jobs from many cities since World War II. Of the twenty largest cities in 1990, nine have lost population since 1950. Of the twenty largest in 1950, eighteen have lost people. And population growth has been much slower in the central cities than elsewhere. As is pointed out in Chapter 2, the centralization of economic organization in the United States has meant that a relatively small number of corporations account for an increasingly large share of economic activity. When one of these large business enterprises leaves a city, the departure has a ripple effect as smaller companies that support it also move. As businesses and affluent residents left the cities, the tax roles declined. The poor and elderly who remained paid fewer taxes and used more city services than did the well-to-do who left. As a result, many cities have faced severe financial crises over the past few decades, and these economic difficulties contributed to all the other problems of the cities.

Housing

Two visible symbols of the economic problems of cities are the deterioration and in some cases abandonment of housing in many neighborhoods, and the inability of the poor to find affordable housing. The result is that many people—often the minorities, the elderly, and the poor—live in buildings with dangerous structural defects, inadequate plumbing and heating, poor sanitation, overcrowding, exposed wiring, rotting floors, and inadequate toilet facilities. Other people cannot find any housing that they can afford. The problem of homelessness, discussed in Chapter 5, is due in part to the unavailability of sufficient rental units at a price that low-income families can afford (Shinn and Gillespie, 1994). To cope with housing problems, some cities have established stricter housing codes, passed renters' rights ordinances, and in a few cases set up rent control laws to stop rent gouging. Landlords complain that these practices increase the costs of owning and maintaining dilapidated buildings and reduce their profits. They also point out that improving or renovating these structures often leads to higher taxes. Low profits have motivated some "slumlords" to simply abandon their buildings. There are about two million abandoned buildings in the United States, and another 150,000 are added to this total each year (Palen, 1987).

The government provides housing vouchers to low-income families to help them pay for acceptable housing. The government has also built low-income housing projects across the country, and most of these efforts have - provided adequate and safe shelter for poor families, although in some inner-city neighborhoods, public housing projects have been rife with crime. However, according to the executive director of the National Association of Housing and Redevelopment Officials, "the real failure of public housing policy in the United States has been . . . the failure to build enough public housing to meet the growing needs of low-income people for affordable shelter, and failure to provide the resources needed to maintain and modernize the nation's 1.3 million public housing units" (Nelson, 1989: 9). Low cost housing is in distressingly short supply. Unfortunately, government policy tends to devote more resources toward the housing of nonpoor families through a tax deduction that people are allowed on the interest on their home mortgages. This deduction provides far more money for homeowners, who are mostly middle class or affluent, than all the money the U.S. devotes to low-income housing.

Segregation

The population shifts in cities in the United States have led to considerable residential segregation of racial and ethnic minorities. The term **ghetto** refers to *a neighborhood inhabited largely by members of a single ethnic or racial group.* In the early part of this century, Jews and Italians lived in urban ghettos; today, African Americans, Hispanics, and Asians are the primary ghetto residents. Although African Americans make up about 12 percent of our populace and Hispanics about 9 percent, they constitute far larger proportions of the residents of our largest cities (see Table 12.2). They are concentrated in the central city areas with the most severe urban problems. Although 25 percent of all whites live in central cities, 56 percent of African Americans, and 53 percent of Hispanics, live there (U.S. Bureau of the Census, 1993).

This segregation of people of color, especially African Americans, did not occur by chance. In fact, it was encouraged by the FHA and VA policies discussed earlier in the chapter (Judd, 1991). During the 1930s and 1940s, administrators of these programs actively promoted the idea that neighborhoods should be

TABLE 12.2 The Racial Composition of the Twenty Largest Cities in the United States, 1960–1990.

City	Percent Black		Percent Hispanic	
	1960	1990	1980	1990
Baltimore	34.7	59.2	1.0	1.0
Boston	9.1	25.6	6.4	10.8
Chicago	22.9	39.1	14.0	19.6
Columbus, Ohio	16.4	22.6	0.8	1.1
Dallas	19.0	29.5	12.3	20.9
Detroit	28.9	75.7	2.4	2.8
Houston	22.9	28.1	17.6	27.6
Indianapolis	20.6	22.6	0.9	1.1
Jacksonville, Fla.	23.2	25.2	1.8	2.6
Los Angeles	13.5	17.4	27.5	39.9
Memphis	37.0	54.8	0.8	0.7
Milwaukee	8.4	30.5	4.1	6.3
New York	14.0	28.7	19.9	24.4
Philadelphia	26.4	39.9	3.8	5.6
Phoenix	4.8	5.2	14.8	20.0
San Antonio	7.1	7.0	53.7	55.6
San Diego	6.0	9.4	14.9	20.7
San Francisco	10.0	10.9	12.3	13.9
San Jose	1.0	4.7	22.3	26.6
Washington, D.C.	53.9	65.8	2.8	5.4

Sources: U.S. Bureau of the Census, *Statistical Abstract of the United States, 1978* (Washington, D.C.: U.S. Government Printing Office, 1978), pp. 24–26; U.S. Bureau of the Census, *Statistical Abstract of the United States, 1985* (Washington, D.C.: U.S. Government Printing Office, 1984), pp. 23–25; U.S. Bureau of the Census, *Statistical Abstract of the United States, 1991* (Washington, D.C.: U.S. Government Printing Office, 1991), pp. 34–36.

racially segregated because, in their eyes, this promoted more neighborhood stability and higher property values. As the FHA *Underwriting Manual* of 1938 put it: "If a neighborhood is to retain stability, it is necessary that properties shall continue to be occupied by the same social and racial classes" (quoted in Judd, 1991: 740). The FHA actively discouraged developers from allowing African Americans to purchase homes in white suburbs and discouraged loans in mostly African American areas on the grounds that people who live in these areas are poor credit risks. The result: African Americans were almost completely excluded from the federally insured mortgage market and from the suburbs that it was helping to create. At the same time, the FHA would not back loans for inner-city housing because this was also considered a high credit risk. In part as a consequence of these policies, African Americans today tend to be residentially isolated from whites (Gillmor and Doig, 1992). In Chicago, for example, 71 percent of African Americans live on a block where 90 percent of the residents are also African American. Despite the fact that racial discrimination in housing was outlawed by the Civil Rights Act of 1964, the 1990 census showed that as far as race is concerned the United States remains two separate nations—one black and the other white. In assessing whether the U.S. has moved any closer to the goal of residential integration by the 1990s, one study looking at the 1990 census data concluded:

> Black-white integration in the nation's 50 largest metropolitan areas has improved only slightly. Some cities fared much better than others, but several showed clear signs of increasing black segregation.... Little real progress has been made. (Gillmor and Doig, 1992: 48, 51)

There has been some movement of African Americans to the suburbs in the past two decades; however, they tend to move only to a small number of suburban areas that typically have existing black populations (Stahura, 1989–90). Most suburbanites still fear that an influx of African American residents will produce white flight and declining property values.

This concentration of minorities in ghettos can create some serious difficulties for urban areas. For example, residential segregation exacerbates both poverty and economic deprivation for both African Americans and Hispanics (Massey, Gross, and Eggers, 1991; Santiago and Wilder, 1991). Minorities who live in segregated urban neighborhoods have more difficulties finding jobs or taking advantage of educational opportunities that are available. Segregation also concentrates the problem of poverty into a few neighborhoods rather than spreading it more evenly around a metropolitan area. Such dispersal could spread the burden of assisting the poor throughout the metropolitan area. Residential segregation can also enhance tensions between racial groups. For example, ghettos isolate racial groups from one another so that they have little contact and believe they have little in common. Much research has shown that such segregation can lead to negative stereotyping, hostility, and prejudice. Sympathy and understanding decline without social contact between groups. The outcome is mutual mistrust and suspicion that make working toward solutions for urban problems even more difficult.

Crime

Crime is probably one of the urban problems that the average citizen thinks most about. Although crime can be found everywhere, it is far more common in cities. As Table 12.3 illustrates, the rate of violent crime is six times greater in the largest cities of the United States than it is in rural areas; the rate of property crimes is four times greater. The greatest dis-

TABLE 12.3 Crime Rates in Urban and Rural Areas, 1994

Area	Crimes Known to the Police per 100,000 People
Violent Crimes	
Cities with population of:	
250,000 or more	1,650
100,000–249,999	1,039
50,000–99,999	694
25,000–49,999	564
10,000–24,999	433
10,000 or less	392
Suburbs	468
Rural Areas	250
Property Crimes	
Cities with population of:	
250,000 or more	7,089
100,000–249,999	6,767
50,000–99,999	5,354
25,000–49,999	4,837
10,000–24,999	4,205
10,000 or less	4,155
Suburbs	3,497
Rural Areas	1,920

Source: Federal Bureau of Investigation, *Uniform Crime Reports: Crime in the United States, 1994* (Washington, D.C.: U.S. Government Printing Office, 1995), pp. 208–209.

parity is for robbery, which occurs at a rate at least forty-five times greater in large cities than in rural areas! Also, the larger the city, the higher the crime rate. And suburban areas have lower crime rates than all but the smallest cities. Even within cities, crime is not evenly distributed. Crime is more likely in inner-city areas where the poor and minorities live. Low-income and minority people are also more likely to be the victims of crimes.

The massive crime rate that exists in some urban neighborhoods exacerbates many of the other problems that these communities confront: the lack of economic development, the growing underclass, and physical deterioration. Simply stated, the growing crime rate in a neighborhood ripples through the community with devastating effect (DiIulio, 1989). New businesses refuse to move in and old ones relocate, making it even more difficult for community residents to support themselves. The chaos and violence produced by crime and drug use can pervade the schools, with disorder making it more difficult for students to achieve scholastically. With a high crime rate, many of a community's males may be in jail, which means fewer partners for women to marry and help to provide for their children. In short, the economic, educational, and familial structures of the community are compromised in a highly crime-ridden environment. Most inner-city residents are not criminals but rather victims who have few avenues of escape from the predators around them. For these law-abiding members of the underclass, the fear of crime is what they confront on a daily basis. The Applied Research insert, discusses some elements of this problem and what the research suggests could be done about it.

The sources of crime are analyzed extensively in Chapter 9. Without question, the high crime rates in cities are in part a function of unemployment and the general lack of legitimate opportunities for success. If the poor, especially the young, cannot find jobs or attend school, a certain number of them will turn to crime as the only way they can see to support themselves. In inner-city areas, there are also many opportunities for the young to learn how to commit crimes and to be taught that crime is a preferable "hustle" to working for a living (recall the differential association theory of crime).

In addition, young nonwhites in ghetto neighborhoods may well be perceived by others as criminals regardless of their behavior, and this sets the stage for the self-fulfilling prophecy described by labeling theorists. So the economic problems of cities initiate a series of social processes that cascade eventually into a very high crime rate.

Educational Problems

The United States often turns to education as a way of mastering social problems. Education, for example, has been the route for most immigrants to achieve upward mobility. In many cities today, however, the schools are not up to this task (Kozol, 1991). Again, one major hurdle is financial. Unlike most other countries, education in the United States is considered a local rather than a national responsibility. Funds for education are raised in good part through local taxes, often property taxes. This results in great disparities in educational resources from one community to another. Poor communities and financially pressed cities simply cannot afford the educational expenses of the more affluent suburbs. Inner-city schools must contend with old buildings, less equipment, archaic educational technology, high rates of teacher turnover, and low staff morale. Especially recently with the increasing importance of computer technology, inner-city schools have been less able to impart the skills needed to compete adequately in a job market in which literacy and skills are increasingly essential. In addition, these children have to go to school in frighteningly dangerous neighborhoods where drug dealing and violence are the norm. The whole experience seems to tell these children that they are simply not worth as much as the more affluent, mostly white, children in suburban schools. With these problems, an inner-city school is considerably less likely to provide its students with the training and motivation to achieve upward mobility.

The Fear of Crime: Effects on the Quality of Urban Life

When one out of every three American households is directly victimized each year, it isn't long before everyone has either been a victim himself or had someone very close to him victimized. The problem is not just what crime does to people's lives; it is also what the fear of crime does to our society. ("Images of Fear . . . ," 1985: 44)

In December of 1984, a seemingly mild-mannered man named Bernhard Goetz made national news when he shot four teenagers in a New York City subway car. Allegedly, Mr. Goetz did this because the young men were trying to rob him under the threat of deadly force. Further investigation of the incident revealed some contrasting elements: The teenage perpetrators, although perhaps intending to intimidate Mr. Goetz, were armed only with a small screwdriver; and, not only was Goetz carrying a .38 revolver, he had recently acquired several handguns—apparently due to his rising fear of being a crime victim.

The Goetz episode brings home once again, as if we needed further proof, the extent to which the quality of life in cities is lowered by crime, fear, and the restrictions that city residents impose on their daily routines as a consequence. We saw in Chapter 9, for example, that the crime most feared by women who live in cities is rape (Gordon and Riger, 1989). That fear directly affects their daily lives as they avoid going out alone, avoid going to certain neighborhoods, and install security devices in their houses or apartments. The

other crimes these women were afraid of were robbery and burglary. Another study found that one-half of the women in large cities felt that it was unsafe to be out in their neighborhood after dark (Davis and Smith, 1991). Fear of crime is most common among older people, especially women. Studies indicate that people are more likely to take precautions against crime if they have been victims themselves or if they are more fearful of crime (Conklin, 1976). Rather than focus on how these individual characteristics influence taking precautions, however, some research has considered the role of social and physical characteristics of the environment (Lavrakas et al., 1981).

One such approach has been to focus on community organization as an important ingredient in urban residents' fear of crime. Social researchers Barbara Kail and Paula Kleinman (1985) have conducted a series of investigations in different ethnic communities to assess the complex relationship between urban residents' reactions to the fear of crime and their degree of integration into the communities in which they live. These researchers found that the existence of formally organized local community associations can diminish fear and self-imposed limitations on activities. One example of such an association is the "Basic Car Plan" in Los Angeles, where neighborhood residents can meet the police officers who are regularly assigned to their area face to face. In the absence of such formal efforts, some urban dwellers develop informal

Teachers are often ill equipped to deal with the problems of inner-city schools. Low pay and other problems of the teaching profession have been much discussed in the past few years. Beyond this, teachers often confront a degree of culture shock in inner-city schools as the teacher's middle-class training and upbringing come face-to-face with the world of lower-class

minorities. The subcultural values, personal demeanor, and even the language of many of the teachers' students are likely to be strange and possibly seen as threatening. There may even be a tendency, based on racial or ethnic stereotypes, to label many of these students as incapable of great achievements. When this occurs, a self-fulfilling prophecy can set in, especially techniques for dealing with fear and victimization. For example, such informal techniques might include casual gatherings designed to air mutual concerns about crime and discuss possible strategies for protection. At least one investigation has determined that urban residents who are more integrated into the social fabric of a neighborhood— the ones active in formal and informal community organizations—are less fearful of crime (Hunter and Baumer, 1982).

Previous investigations have shown that when individuals take precautions to deal with their fear of crime this behavior may only deflect crime rather than reduce it: The criminal merely victimizes someone else. Furthermore, these individual efforts may actually inhibit the community's response to the crime problem (Dubow and Emmons, 1981). More recent research efforts, such as that of Kail and Kleinman, suggest that if existing formal organizations can be strengthened, then fear of crime will be reduced, which also reduces the extent to which individuals place restrictions on their behavior. Thus, community organization appears to be a key ingredient in elevating the quality of urban life by reducing people's fear of crime.

Some urban planners have argued that many neighborhoods and buildings are designed in such a way that they discourage social interaction and social participation on the part of residents (Newman, 1972; Crowe, 1991). Architecturally, they isolate people from one another, which tends to increase the opportunity for crime and the fear of crime. High-rise apartment buildings, for example, discourage contact and communication and have many locations that are unwatched and where crime can occur. Buildings are designed primarily with economic concerns in mind: maximizing profit from a piece of urban property. Yet urban planners suggest a few design considerations that would enhance social participation and reduce crime and the fear of it:

1. Buildings should have only a small number of units sharing the same entryway off the streets. In this way, residents know who lives there, who has a right to be there, and who is a stranger.
2. Windows, lighting, entryways, and paths should be designed so that there is continuous surveillance by the residents. This reduces the number of isolated spots where crime can occur unobserved.
3. Lobbies should be designed not merely as an entryway to the building but as a social center where people congregate. This might be done by having newsstands or recreation items in or near the lobby.
4. Buildings should be low-rise with fewer residents to reduce feelings of anonymity, isolation, and lack of identity with the building. Research shows that the crime rate is higher in taller and more populous buildings.

when the students accept the teachers' judgment of them.

This review has focused on problems of cities in the United States. The International Perspectives insert places these problems in a broader global context and also looks at problems confronting Third-World cities in other parts of the world.

Future Prospects

Population Problems

Premodern societies often had high birthrates and high death rates so that there was little or no population growth. In fact, human history shows that many societies have been at or near

Cities in the Context of Global Economic Competition

Many of the urban problems discussed in this chapter—financial collapse of cities, the shortage of housing and jobs—arise in part because of the capitalist economy of which the cities are a part (Costells, 1977; Smith and LeFaiure, 1984). Monopolistic corporations encourage government spending on such things as highways so that the corporations can ship goods, reach new markets, and expand their profits. These highways also open up the suburbs to corporations, where land and taxes are lower and profits higher. As people and jobs leave the cities, government revenues decline and property values fall. Over time, the reduced property values in the city attract other entrepreneurs who see that a profit can be made by purchasing urban housing cheap and selling it to those who can afford it: the middle class and affluent. Thus, gentrification emerges as changes in the urban real estate market bring investment capital back into the cities. However, those who benefit are the real estate entrepreneurs and the affluent, not the poor who were left in the city as capital moved to the suburbs and who are now displaced by the gentrifiers. From the conflict perspective, then, the problems of cities are due in part to corporate pursuit of higher profits in a capitalist economy.

The plight of cities in the United States and around the world also needs to be placed in the context of the global economic competition discussed in Chapter 2. That chapter discusses the dramatic transition of the United States economy from a goods, production-based system to an information-based service economy. This has meant that, for the urban poor, unskilled manual labor jobs that are more common in a goods-production industrial economy have become less common in a service-oriented economy. This has dramatically reduced the ability of cities to provide jobs that pay sufficiently to support a family at a decent level. The problems created by the shift in the U.S. economy are exacerbated by the global competition among capitalist corporations. Cities in the United States have to compete with cities and nations around the globe for jobs, and the result has been fewer jobs, especially well-paying jobs.

Cities in Asia, Africa, and Latin America are also affected by the global economic competition. Some of these cities are growing rapidly, with some experiencing explosive growth in the past four decades. Both Mexico City and Sao Paulo, Brazil, for example, grew from approximately 3 million people to 24 million since 1950. By contrast, Los Angeles, one of the fastest growing cities in the United States, grew from 2 million to 3.5 million people during the same period. Urbanization in the developing nations of the world has been different

---

zero population growth, according to which *birth and death rates are nearly equal, producing a zero rate of natural increase.* Although fully developed nations such as the United States are approaching ZPG, other societies are far from it, and this is where much of the world's population problem exists. What, then, will the future bring?

Demographer Leon F. Bouvier (1984) of the Population Reference Bureau points out that as new cures for diseases are discovered and implemented and living conditions improve in developing nations, death rates will continue to fall, and improvements in life expectancy for them will probably continue. Consequently, efforts to control world population growth will have to focus on fertility. Furthermore, current attitudes about fertility around the world suggest that nations with high birthrates are ready to do what needs to be done to bring them down. In 1982, the United Nations Fifth Population Inquiry determined than it was for cities in the U.S. (Kasarda and Crenshaw, 1991). For one thing, the rapidly growing cities in many Third-World nations today face more adverse conditions than did the cities of Europe and North America that matured during the nineteenth and early twentieth centuries. Today's Third-World cities are growing much more rapidly and thus experiencing much higher levels of problems, such as crowding, crime, and pollution. In addition, today's Third-World cities face much more severe economic competition from the advanced industrial nations with their already-modernized cities and substantial economic resources. When the cities of the United States and Europe were developing, they were the advanced cities of their time and thus were attractive to investors and credit markets. Today's developing cities struggle to compete with already-mature adversaries in other nations.

Another problem for Third-World cities is that urbanization in the Third World has been driven as much, or possibly more, by the pressures of the global capitalist economy as it has been by internal pressures toward industrialization. In some cases, for example, international investors buy large tracts of land in a Third-World nation to grow crops for export. This privatization of land can force farmers and their families off the land and into cities looking for work, fueling population growth in the cities. In other places, capital-intensive foreign investment in manufacturing for export products has stimulated booming growth in small- and medium-sized cities. This happened in Mexico with the *maquiladoras* along the United States border, as described in Chapter 2. These plants sprouted in cities like Juarez and Matamoros, manufacturing goods for export and drawing in thousands of people from surrounding rural areas. So, some of the pressures toward urbanization in these developing nations are external and in the control of international elites rather than national leaders.

These forces in the global economy have led some cities in developing nations to experience *overurbanization*, having populations larger than the city can house, employ, and adequately take care of (Smith, 1991). When foreign investors retard industrial development, insufficient jobs for people are produced. When that investment pushes people off the land and into the cities, there may not be adequate room or housing for all of these people. The outcome is too many people in the cities for the available resources and the emergence of squatter slums.

that well over 60 percent of developing nations—the nations with high birthrates—felt that their national level of fertility was too high, and 85 percent of the nations that view their fertility rate to be too high are in favor of policies designed to reduce it (Salas, 1984).

So there is growing recognition of the importance of controlling fertility because most nations and their people have come to realize that large families can be detrimental to people's ability to achieve a satisfactory lifestyle.

According to the United Nations World Population Plan of Action:

> It is now universally accepted that family size may affect individual development and that there is a fundamental right to choose the size and spacing of the family. . . . Parents are concerned about giving their children the very best of which they are capable; more and more are realizing that increasing the size of the family may decrease the quality of what is available for each child. (Salas, 1984: 26)

Given these attitudes, fertility will probably decline in all regions where it is high over the next fifty years, and the decrease will probably be sharp in all but a few societies. For this to occur quickly enough to avoid the worst of the problems discussed earlier, however, a number of programs and policies that work to lower fertility will have to be pursued aggressively. We will review the major things that can be done. If they are, there is some optimism that the worst consequences of rapid population growth can be avoided.

Family Planning   In the United States, the relatively high fertility in the years following World War II declined precipitously after 1957.

POLICY ISSUES
Population Policy and Family Planning in China

China has a tremendous problem on its hands. Geographically, it is about the same size as the United States, but with more than four times as many people! Whereas the United States has about 260 million people, China has 1.2 billion: 22 percent of the world's population with only 7 percent of the earth's arable land. To make matters worse, China's population is growing more than twice as fast: It has an annual growth rate of 1.4 compared to .66 in the United States. In 1991, the average Chinese woman had 2.3 children, compared to 1.8 in the United States. Yet another problem is that China's population is much younger than the U.S. population, which means a larger proportion of the Chinese are still planning to have children. This means that, even if China were to bring its birthrate down to U.S. levels, China's population would still grow much faster than the U.S. population. Population experts expect China's population to peak at 1.9 billion by the middle of the next century.

Such population growth puts an enormous strain on China's environment in terms of whether it can produce sufficient food for its population and absorb the pollutants generated. Rapid population growth also hinders economic development since whatever economic growth occurs is absorbed supporting the growing population rather than being available for investment in new industries or machinery. For these reasons, the Chinese

authorities have been deeply concerned for decades about controlling population growth. By the end of the 1970s, they were sufficiently concerned to institute a "one-child family" program for all couples who did not already have more than one child. Incentives were created for families that achieved this goal, such as a government stipend for one-child families payable until the youngster is fourteen years old; there were also penalties for families with more than two children, including salary deductions and tax surcharges. Even more controversial was the use of government-employed family planning workers to consult with, and in some cases cajole, couples about their sexual behavior and use of contraceptives.

Through the 1980s, the birthrate in China came down but not nearly as quickly as the authorities had hoped. By the late 1980s, it began to look like the Chinese would not reach the targets they had set for themselves. For example, the crude birthrate had dropped only from 25 per 1000 people in 1980 to 22 by 1990—not much improvement to show for the program. Alarmed authorities, pushing for a renewed effort to achieve the goals, introduced a "responsibility system" in which district and township officials would be held personally responsible if the people under their jurisdiction did not achieve the goals (Kristof, 1993). These officials could lose bonuses or be fined or dismissed. Another part of the program

The reason? Certainly the widespread use of effective contraceptives played an important part. Given the effectiveness of contraception in reducing fertility, the solution to the world's population problem might appear to be providing contraceptives to everyone who desires them. However feasible this approach might appear at first, technology is of secondary importance in this realm when compared to cultural values. The prevention of conception and the termination of pregnancies through abortion are not merely technological feats. Conception and abortion are social events that represent decisions that people have made based in part on what their culture has taught them is desirable. After all, the birthrate in the

was compulsory, organized sterilizations, in which family planning cadres would descend on a village and take all women who already had a child to a clinic to be fitted with an IUD or sterilized. A third part of the program focused on women who became pregnant without authorization, with strong social pressure exerted on them to have an abortion. Out of fear that they would not achieve their goals, some overly zealous local officials got carried away, forcing some women to have abortions and smashing the huts of a few women who had unauthorized births (WuDunn, 1993).

This draconian program had an effect. The birthrate dropped significantly in China in 1992, with the average Chinese woman having 1.9 children—about the same as in the United States. In addition, the number of sterilizations went way up, and very few births involved third or subsequent children. However, these successes have not been without costs, a major one of which may have been to increase female infanticides. The Chinese, especially in rural areas, want sons so they can extend the male line into the future; some even believe they have dishonored their ancestors if they fail to do so. Female infanticide is a way to try again for a male child when the government strongly encourages one-child families. Reports of increases in drownings and other murders of female infants emerged in the early 1980s. In some cases, apparently, Chinese midwives, following instructions

from the parents, keep a bucket of water handy during delivery; if the child born is female, she is drowned immediately and reported as a stillborn (Kristof, 1993). Information on the sex ratio in China supports the idea that some female infanticide is occurring. Biologically, in human populations, about 94 females are born for every 100 males. However, in recent years in China, as few as 85 to 89 females were reported born for each 100 males. Now, some of this involves families just not reporting a female birth to authorities so they can try again to have a male. But some of it is undoubtedly due to infanticide. If China's sex ratio is this skewed, then a few decades down the road Chinese men may have difficulty finding wives.

The experience of China highlights the importance of cultural values in influencing people's behavior. Even when the government provides benefits for those who lower their fertility and penalties for those who do not cooperate, people will continue to have more children if they value them. When government intervention is contrary to people's deeply held values, it is not likely to be very effective unless strongly repressive and authoritarian measures are used. Even these measures may not remain effective for long. So, programs of family planning and population control are likely to be less effective when they fail to gain the backing of the citizenry.

United States was relatively low during the 1930s—almost as low as today—well before the pill, IUDs, and other modern contraceptive techniques were available. This low fertility rate occurred because people decided on the basis of the severe economic conditions that they wanted to postpone having children or to have smaller families.

Some modern population-control efforts, then, have focused on encouraging people to consciously decide how many children they want, with the hope that people will choose to have smaller families. Such family planning programs encourage couples to have children when and if they are desired. Experience with such programs has shown that, when women realize they have a choice of whether to have children, they most often choose to have fewer children than they would have had otherwise. Still, if people desire children, they will have them, and people's desires arise out of socialization into a particular set of cultural values.

Reviews of family planning services, however, are mixed regarding their effectiveness (Mauldin, 1975; Jacobson, 1988). In many countries with active family planning efforts, such as China, South Korea, and Costa Rica, social and economic changes—to be discussed in a moment—probably account for much of the lowering of fertility. In other countries, such as Kenya, India, and the Dominican Republic, family planning programs have had little observable effect. Why? One reason is that many of these countries failed to allocate the resources necessary to make the programs effective. In addition, as noted earlier, values are a critical element in reducing fertility—people must want to have fewer children before family planning efforts will work. In many countries, however, women have large numbers of children because they have been taught to want them, and cultural values are supportive of large families. In such settings, family planning will probably have only a marginal effect. The Policy Issues insert explores some of the complexities that can arise when governments attempt to impose limitations on fertility that go against people's desires.

Economic Development It was just mentioned that certain social and economic changes probably accounted for more of the decline in fertility than has family planning. The changes referred to are generally called *economic development* (Bouvier, 1984). Developing nations that are actively involved in programs to control population growth today have placed a major emphasis on economic development. Although these countries recognize the need for family planning, they argue that no program of population control can be completely effective unless it is a part of a more general program of economic development. A number of changes that accompany economic development—especially urbanization, increasing levels of education, and a rising standard of living—lead people to view large families as less desirable. In urban settings and since the passage of child-labor laws, there is no longer a distinct economic advantage to having many children. In fact, in urban, industrial societies, large families lead to crowded housing and a drain on family finances. Furthermore, when women receive more education, they usually want to pursue a career or develop talents other than domestic ones, and large families make this more difficult. Finally, economic development affords people a more affluent lifestyle, and large families are expensive. This affects their standard of living, leading many couples to decide to spend their resources on consumer goods or leisure activities rather than raising large families. Even with economic development, most people want to become parents, but they are more likely to opt for a smaller number of children. And as small families become common, they are viewed increasingly as "normal," and people feel social pressures not to have large families.

Incentives Some programs have been proposed and a few established that would provide people with some incentives, usually economic, for preventing births. This might involve giving people cash payments or gifts for being sterilized, or it might take the form of annual payments to women for each year they do not have children. This might be done by giving tax breaks to people with smaller families or no children at all, rather than increasing their tax exemptions as we currently do for each child that is born. A program introduced into several private tea plantations in India involved placing money in a retirement trust fund for each year that passed in which a woman did not have any children (Ridker, 1980). This program did result in lower fertility, although the effect was not dramatic. Once again, unless the social and cultural forces that lead people to want fewer children are present, declines in fertility tend to be small. The incentives approach has also been criticized on the grounds that large families, which also tend to be poorer, would suffer the most and their poverty would be further exacerbated.

The Status of Women Another important element in controlling population growth is the status of women. As noted in Chapter 7, the United Nations has for decades vigorously promoted programs to improve women's lives by providing them with opportunities in education, employment, and political participation, as well as support in their domestic and maternal roles. Research conducted by the United Nations has shown consistently that educational attainment and labor force participation of women are particularly important elements in a population policy: Educated women who work outside the home have fewer children than do less educated women who are not part of the labor force (United Nations, 1991; Repetto, 1994). Research conducted in the United States also shows that better educated women who have careers, or at least are a part of the labor force, desire smaller families and

are more sensitive to the overall issue of population growth (Thompson, 1980; Houseknecht, 1987). So programs intended to advance sexual equality around the world will likely have a positive impact on controlling population growth.

Urban Problems

Federal Grants and Programs Until the 1980s, urban policy in the United States was based on the assumption that the federal government is in the best position to fund programs to attack urban problems. Cities and states have fewer funds for such efforts and more incentives to underfund such programs. Cities and states, for example, try to keep taxes low in the competition with other states to attract businesses and industry. Cities and states might be tempted to cut urban programs to keep taxes low. Generally, interventionists have supported an active role on the part of the federal government in the attack on urban problems.

In the past 20 years, urban policy has changed dramatically, with a decided shift toward a more laissez-faire approach (Caraley, 1992). The Reagan and Bush administrations argued that a strong and healthy economy is a far more promising approach to solving urban problems than direct federal intervention. For laissez-faire advocates, the key role of the federal government in solving urban problems is to keep the economy healthy, not to intervene directly with federal programs and funding. States and cities should be allowed to choose which services they need and want. The result of this shift has been a catastrophic decline in federal support for cities. Federal programs have been turned over to the states and cities, and the states and cities—in poor financial shape themselves—have drastically cut or eliminated the programs. Federal aid has dropped from 22 percent of large cities' general expenditures in 1980 to 6 percent, but aid given by state governments has not increased to take up the slack.

Despite this shift toward a decidedly laissez-faire policy, some significant federal urban programs persist. The many federal programs that provide direct funds or services to the poor are a significant form of assistance to urban areas. These programs include Medicaid, Social Security, Aid to Families with Dependent Children, housing assistance, food stamps, and many others (see Chapter 5). All these programs are key resources used by cities to alleviate the problems their citizens face. The Housing Act of 1949 initiated a program of *urban renewal,* which has been a prominent approach to urban problems over the years (Hawley, 1971). The major purpose of urban renewal has been to rebuild blighted areas of cities, to provide low-cost housing for urban poor, and to stimulate private investment in the inner city through the physical redevelopment of deteriorated areas. Government funds were used to acquire and clear land, and this renewal was supposed to attract private investors.

After many years of operation, urban policy makers recognized that urban renewal had probably not produced its intended benefits. Many older buildings were torn down and often replaced with luxury apartments or office buildings that are more profitable to private-sector developers. The poor, who had originally occupied a neighborhood, were driven into other neighborhoods, which then often began to deteriorate. Because of these problems, urban renewal funds declined over the years, and in the 1980s the programs were combined into the Community Development Block Grant (CDBG) program (Wong and Peterson, 1986). The CDBG program has goals similar to those of urban renewal, but it gives local officials a larger role in developing urban renewal projects and greater flexibility in how federal funds are used. Compared to urban renewal, the CDBG program shifted emphasis from providing direct assistance to low income residents to a focus on economic development.

These and other federal programs continue and have channeled significant resources to cities with serious problems. However, the laissez-faire posture in the United States' urban policy in recent years has meant fewer funds than in the past. Interventionists argue, however, that federal assistance with urban problems is still appropriate because the cities, for the most part, did not create the problems that now ravage them: poverty, drug addiction, homelessness, AIDS, and so on. It is the cities that suffer from these problems most seriously, and interventionists argue that society as a whole has a responsibility to assist cities with them.

Private Investment   Despite the prominent role of the federal government in attacking urban problems over the years, there has been a trend over the past two decades to turn to private investment as a means of improving the conditions of cities. A major thrust of these efforts is the use of private funds to develop shopping centers and malls in cities that can compete with suburban shopping malls and to construct housing that can draw people away from suburban tract homes. In this way, it is hoped, people—and financial resources—can be attracted back into the city. Many cities now boast such developments: the Water Tower mall in Chicago, the Union Station in Cincinnati, the Quincy Market in Boston, the Renaissance Center in Detroit, and Pier 39 in San Francisco. Although some of these developments used federal funds, private financing has been central to their completion. The idea behind them is that, if cities can be made into enjoyable places to live and work, decentralization might be slowed or halted and the financial problems that are at the core of so many urban difficulties alleviated.

Another approach to encouraging private development in cities through minimal government action is variously called "enterprise zones," "urban free-enterprise zones," or "empowerment zones" (Lehman, 1994). The basic idea is to designate a neighborhood as an "enterprise zone" based on high levels of unemployment or poverty and little economic development. Businesses locating in such zones would be taxed at a lower rate than other areas of the city and would be subject to less stringent regulation than businesses outside the zone. To receive these benefits, the businesses might be required to have a certain proportion of zone residents among their employees. This approach is based on the laissez-faire assumption that the tax and regulatory systems stifle initiative and self-improvement. Remove these inhibitors, proponents argue, and new businesses will arise to take advantage of the opportunities for economic development that exist even in blighted neighborhoods. These new ventures will then help rebuild the neighborhood economy, providing jobs that will help improve the general economic conditions in the city. President Clinton signed legislation in 1993 that established 70 empowerment or enterprise zones.

At this point, the impact of such zones is difficult to assess (Bendick and Rasmussen, 1986; Lehman, 1994). Britain has had such zones for a few years, however, and there are some things to be learned from its experience. In general, Britain's enterprise zones have not encouraged the development of new businesses by entrepreneurs. Instead, businesses that existed elsewhere or were planning to expand found the zones an attractive place to set up shop. So, in many cases, the zones did not result in a net increase in jobs and economic activity, but a shuffling of them from one locale to another. This is not necessarily bad if the goal of policy is to shift jobs from low-unemployment areas to high-unemployment areas. If the community losing the jobs, however, begins to suffer, then the urban problems have merely been shifted from one community to another.

Resettlement of the Cities   A number of programs have focused on the tendency for home-

owners and affluent residents to migrate to the suburbs by encouraging them to move back to the city and purchase homes or apartments. **Urban homesteading** refers to *programs to increase home ownership by private citizens in certain neighborhoods by selling them houses at little or no cost.* The homes are usually those that have been abandoned or foreclosed for failure to pay a mortgage or taxes and thus are the property of the city or the federal government. Usually, the buyer agrees to live in the house for a specified period of time and sometimes make certain improvements to the property. The government makes some money through the sale, an abandoned piece of property is placed back on the tax rolls, and best of all a homeowner has a vested interest in keeping up both his or her property and the neighborhood. A vacant house could be a target for vandals and a haven for drug dealers. Homeowners have an incentive to keep their property up and to discourage drug dealers from coming into the area. Overall, although it is no panacea, homesteading has helped some neighborhoods in some cities (Stegman, 1990; Weinstein, 1990a).

Urban homesteading and other policies have produced a trend called **gentrification:** *the return of relatively affluent households to marginal neighborhoods where run-down housing is being rehabilitated or new housing constructed* (Beauregard, 1990; Kerstein, 1990). In some cases, gentrification is encouraged by the policies of local, state, or federal governments; in other cases, it is driven by the actions of private developers looking for a profitable business deal; in some places, private-public partnerships have been the catalyst. Gentrification is also fueled by the decisions of affluent families who may find suburban life too expensive or who do not feel the need for large houses because they have smaller families than their parents had. For others, especially professional couples with fairly substantial incomes, the city affords easy access to restaurants, cultural events, and the like.

This gentrification has been hailed as the beginning of the rebirth of urban areas in the United States. Although it will probably help to stem the flow of economic resources out of the city, the numbers involved are difficult to calculate but are probably somewhat small. Nevertheless, it should contribute to increasing the tax base of the city, restoring neighborhoods through the rehabilitation of housing, and enhancing neighborhood businesses. Some urban planners argue that these renovated neighborhoods will serve as a magnet that will attract more affluent people into the city. However, not all the effects of gentrification are beneficial. As affluent people move into and renovate neighborhoods, the value of property increases and both rent and property taxes escalate. As a result, the people who lived in the neighborhood prior to gentrification—often the poor, the elderly, and minorities—can no longer afford it and are forced to move, sometimes from homes they have occupied for decades. The only housing these people can afford may be more dilapidated than their previous residence.

Regional Planning and Cooperation   Many cities have recognized that some urban problems can be solved only if regional planning and cooperation can be achieved. After all, the geographic boundaries of cities were established many years ago, and today they are rather arbitrary designations. Some have proposed a metropolitan government that would have political jurisdiction over a city and its suburbs and would consolidate all government services. Such an overarching political structure is probably not feasible in most cases. One problem is deciding where one city and its suburbs ends and another begins. In addition, few cities or suburbs would be willing to accede to such a centralized authority. They prefer to retain political power and patronage in their own hands.

On a smaller scale, however, cooperation between political entities in metropolitan areas has been established over specific issues. Issues such as transportation, water pollution, and the like affect the whole metropolitan region and can benefit from regional decision making. In some cases, the courts have even ruled that school segregation is a regional problem and called for transfers of students between city and suburban schools. Cleveland has made major strides in regional cooperation, with the city and suburbs sharing responsibility for big infrastructure projects such as roads and transportation. It also has a payroll tax on all people who work in Cleveland, including those who live in the suburbs. This is a major infusion of funds for the city. It has been controversial, but many suburban residents accept some responsibility for helping alleviate the problems of the city because they gain benefits from the city. As the president of the

L I N K A G E S

The spread of slums and urban deterioration is made worse by poverty (Chapter 5), crime (Chapter 9), and drug addiction (Chapter 10). It is also enhanced when large and unresponsive corporations (Chapter 2) move jobs away from the cities where people live.

Greater Cleveland Growth Organization put it: "Cleveland is the downtown shopping center for this area. It is where entertainment is. Sports. Where all our major corporations are. We recognize that if downtown is not clean, safe and active, then the entire region will start falling apart" (quoted in Barrett and Greene, 1991: 34).

Summary

1. Three basic elements affect the size, composition and distribution of human populations: fertility, mortality, and migration. Fertility and mortality are key elements in evaluating world population growth.

2. The demographic transition refers to the changing patterns of birthrates and death rates brought about by industrialization. The demographic transition has four stages: preindustrial, transitional or early industrial, industrial, and postindustrial. Today's population problem can be most clearly located in the less industrialized nations that have not yet experienced the transition.

3. Cities arose after human beings had developed agriculture and domesticated animals. With industrialization, cities grow very large because industrial economic organization benefits from the concentration of people and resources. Suburbanization and urban decentralization has occurred because technological change has made it possible for people to live far from where they work and because federal policies have encouraged the building of new homes outside the cities.

4. From the functionalist perspective, population growth and urban conditions become social problems when they become dysfunctional and lead to social disorganization. According to the conflict perspective, population and urban problems become social problems due to the inequitable distribution of resources. The interactionist perspective sensitizes us to the fact that population and urban problems are in part matters of social definition.

5. There are many consequences of population growth: crowding, food shortages, depletion of resources, intergroup conflict, and internal migration. A key issue is whether population growth exceeds the carrying capacity of the environment.

6. Among the major problems confronting cities in the United States are: economic decline, insufficient low-income housing, racial segregation, crime, and educational problems.

7. The future of population problems will depend on the ability to control fertility. Major issues in alleviating population problems are family planning, economic development, incentives, and the status of women.

8. Although the federal government has played a significant role in finding solutions to urban problems over the years, in recent years there has been a push to find solutions in which government involvement is small or nonexistent. The government has attacked urban problems with such programs as urban renewal and community development block grants. Private investment has focused on developing cities as better places to live, sometimes through the establishment of "urban free-enterprise zones." Urban homesteading and regional planning have also been used to improve conditions in cities.

STUDY AND Review

Key Terms

carrying capacity

city

communities

demographic gap

demographic transition

demography

fecundity

fertility

gentrification

ghetto

migration

mortality

population

suburb

urban homesteading

zero population growth

Multiple-Choice Questions

1. In analyzing world population growth, which element of demographic change is least critical in evaluating overall population growth?
   a. Fertility.
   b. Mortality.
   c. Migration.
   d. Population.
   e. Zero population growth.
2. The United States is currently entering which stage of the demographic transition?
   a. The preindustrial stage.
   b. The transitional stage.
   c. The early industrial stage.
   d. The industrial stage.
   e. The postindustrial stage.
3. Which region of the world will see its proportion of the world population grow most significantly in the next 50 years?
   a. Africa.
   b. Asia.
   c. North America.
   d. Europe.
   e. The Caribbean.
4. According to the text, agricultural villages and then cities emerged in human history because of:
   a. Industrialization.
   b. Capitalism.

   c. Domestication of plants and animals.
   d. Technological developments in transportation.
5. For the functionalist perspective, population growth and urban change become social problems when:
   a. They lead to social disorganization.
   b. They produce a demographic gap.
   c. Powerful groups no longer believe their interests are being served.
   d. People define their environment as too crowded.
6. The Green Revolution has to do with:
   a. Expanding food harvests from the sea.
   b. Increasing crop yields.
   c. Expanding the amount of farmland available.
   d. Reducing the demographic gap.
7. One major cause of the financial problems in cities in the United States is:
   a. The growing demographic gap in cities.
   b. The flight of people and jobs from cities.
   c. The overpopulation of cities.
   d. The gentrification of cities.
8. The combination of social and economic changes that probably accounts for a significant decline in fertility in nations is called:
   a. Family planning.
   b. Fecundity.
   c. Demography.
   d. Economic development.
   e. Urban homesteading.
9. Programs to promote gender equality around the world will probably have which effect?
   a. A positive impact on controlling world population growth.
   b. A negative impact on controlling world population growth.
   c. Little impact on world population growth.
   d. A reduction in fecundity.
10. Urban policy since 1980 in the United States has been characterized by:
    a. An increasingly interventionist stance.
    b. A growing dependence on the federal government to solve problems.

c. The dominance of the conflict perspective.
d. A shift toward a more laissez-faire approach.

True/False Questions

1. The fertility of a society is usually at about the same level as its fecundity.
2. The life expectancy of women in the United States is about 7 years longer than that of men.
3. Cities are communities, but communities are not necessarily cities.
4. In the 1930s and 1940s, the United States government, to promote racially integrated communities, attempted to discourage people from moving to the suburbs.
5. The interactionist perspective stresses the idea that urban problems are defined as much by subjective definitions of reality as by objective conditions.
6. The carrying capacity is something that should be exceeded if population growth is to be controlled.
7. According to most observers, the sea will not be a very important source of expanding food supplies in the years to come.
8. The extent of residential segregation in cities in the United States has been declining since the 1960s.
9. Family planning is probably more effective than economic development in helping to bring down fertility levels in Third-World nations.
10. Research has shown that the main impact of urban free-enterprise zones in cities in the United States is the creation of new jobs rather than the movement of jobs from one locale to another.

Fill-In Questions

1. The difference between the crude birthrate and the crude death rate is referred to as the _____ .
2. The United States is the third largest nation in the world today, behind _____ and _____ .

3. The _____ stage of the demographic transition is characterized by high birthrates and high death rates.
4. From the _____ perspective, cities have deteriorated because those most directly affected have few political and economic resources with which to change things.
5. A _____ is a neighborhood in a city inhabited largely by members of a single ethnic or racial group.
6. _____ is a situation in which birthrates and death rates in a society are nearly equal, producing a zero rate of natural increase.
7. China's "one-child family" program for reducing population growth appears to have resulted in an increase in _____ .
8. In the last 20 years, urban policy in the United States has changed dramatically, with a decided shift toward a more _____ approach.
9. Zones of a city where new businesses are given tax breaks or are subject to less stringent regulation are called _____ .
10. _____ refers to programs to increase home ownership by private citizens in certain neighborhoods by selling them houses at little or no cost.

Matching Questions

_____ 1. demography
_____ 2. mortality
_____ 3. emigration
_____ 4. China
_____ 5. Thomas Malthus
_____ 6. Karl Marx
_____ 7. carrying capacity
_____ 8. Club of Rome

_____ 9. family planning

_____ 10. urban renewal

    A. world's largest nation
    B. study of human populations
    C. conflict approach to population dynamics
    D. population control program
    E. report on depletion of resources
    F. moving out of a particular country
    G. government urban program
    H. number of deaths in a population
    I. functionalist approach to population dynamics
    J. upper limit on population

Essay Questions

1. Define the field of demography. What are the elements of demographic change? How have they been changing in the United States during the twentieth century?
2. What is the demographic transition? Describe the four stages and what happens at each one.
3. Describe the policies of the federal government that contributed to the growth of the suburbs in the United States.
4. How is the postindustrial city different from cities in an industrial era?
5. What is the interactionist perspective on population and urban problems?
6. Choose two of the consequences of world population growth discussed in the text and summarize what those consequences are.
7. What factors have produced the economic decline of cities in the United States?
8. What are the negative consequences of the residential segregation by race that persists in cities in the United States?
9. What is family planning? How does the program work? How effective is it at achieving its goals?
10. What federal government programs are currently in operation to help alleviate urban problems?

Answers

Multiple-Choice

1. C; **2.** E; **3.** A; **4.** C; **5.** A; **6.** B; **7.** B; **8.** D; **9.** A; **10.** D

True/False

1. F; **2.** T; **3.** T; **4.** F; **5.** T; **6.** F; **7.** T; **8.** F; **9.** F; **10.** F

Fill-In

1. rate of natural increase
2. China, India
3. preindustrial
4. conflict
5. ghetto
6. zero population growth
7. female infanticide
8. laissez-faire
9. urban free-enterprise zones
10. urban homesteading

Matching

1. B; **2.** H; **3.** F; **4.** A; **5.** I; **6.** C; **7.** J; **8.** E; **9.** D; **10.** G

For Further Reading

Edward Banfield. _The Unheavenly City Revisited._ Prospect Heights, Ill.: Waveland Press, 1990. This sociologist offers a very positive assessment of America's cities, saying that they are healthy, enjoyable, and fulfilling places to live.

Herbert J. Gans. _People, Plans, and Policies: Essays on Poverty, Racism, and Other National Urban Problems._ New York: Columbia University Press, 1991. This is an excellent set of essays by a well-respected specialist in urban affairs. The issues discussed range from problems of architecture to poverty and the underclass.

Joel Garreau. _Edge City: Life on the New Frontier._ New York: Doubleday, 1991. "Edge city" is the author's name for those suburbs that have grown large enough to be considered self-sufficient. He provides an interesting perspective on this part of urban life, suggesting that edge cities reflect such American values as individualism and homesteading.

John D. Kasarda and Allan M. Parnell (eds.). *Third World Cities: Problems, Policies, and Prospects.* Newbury Park, Calif.: Sage, 1993. These two sociologists have brought together some of the most recent research being done on the problems confronting cities in Third-World nations. This volume views the problems of cities from a global perspective.

Wallace E. Lambert and Donald M. Taylor. *Coping with Cultural and Racial Diversity in Urban America.* New York: Praeger, 1990. As the title suggests, this book deals with the impact that a multicultural United States will have on our cities. It also focuses on the issue of assimilation versus pluralism, as discussed in Chapter 6.

William H. McNeil. *Plagues and People.* Garden City, N.Y.: Doubleday/Anchor, 1976. This is a detailed and well-documented history of epidemics through history. It demonstrates in a very interesting fashion how social practices can influence disease and how disease can work to control population growth.

Donella H. Meadows, Dennis L. Meadows, and Jorgen Randers. *Beyond the Limits: Confronting Global Collapse, Envisioning a Sustainable Future.* Post Mills, Vt.: Chelsea Green Pub. Co., 1992. This is a recent assessment by the same scientists who conducted the study for the Club of Rome twenty years ago. Their conclusions are a little more optimistic now, but only if there are changes in both lifestyle and technology.

Alejandro Portes and Alex Stepick. *City on the Edge: The Transformation of Miami.* Berkeley: University of California Press, 1993. This is an excellent analysis of the development of Miami as its Cuban population has grown. It is a complex story that ties in urban development, ethnicity, and socioeconomic status.

Kirkpatrick Sale. *Human Scale.* New York: Coward, McCann, and Geoghegan, 1980. An assessment of the impact of huge urban developments on people and social relations. The author contends that building beyond "human scale" causes impersonality and a number of other problems. He argues for small-scale developments.

CHAPTER

THIRTEEN *Environmental Problems*

One major consequence of rapid population growth, discussed in Chapter 12, is its impact on the earth's environment. In this century, many disturbing problems have emerged that have called our attention again and again to the fragility of the world's environment: air and water pollution, acid rain, the accumulation of toxic wastes, and many others. Lurking behind all of this is the frightening realization that we may be damaging the environment in ways that are irreversible, that human beings may reach (or have already reached) a point at which the destruction already done cannot be completely corrected. This chapter will review the evidence for how extensive and irreversible the damage actually is.

The Ecosystem

To understand modern environmental problems, it is useful to begin with a brief look at some of the concepts that modern biology uses to understand the world and how it operates. **Ecology** is *the branch of biology that studies the relationships between living organisms and their environment*. The term **environment** refers to *the conditions and circumstances surrounding and affecting a particular group of living creatures*. Human beings, of course, are one of the living organisms that ecologists study, but from an ecological perspective all of the other organisms—plants, fish, bacteria, and so on—are equally important. Now, many cultures place human beings in a special and superior position as the most important creature in the environment. In fact, some cultures set human beings completely apart from the environment, as if they lived independently of the other living organisms and could destroy them at will, without regard to the consequences. Certainly, such cultural attitudes can be found in the Judeo-Christian heritage that is the underpinning of much of the United States and other Western cultures. This heritage stresses the superiority of humans over other creatures and the mastery of humans over the earth and its living creatures. Passages in the Bible, for example, have been interpreted as justifying human exploitation of the environment:

> And God said, Let us make man in our image, after our likeness: . . . Be fertile and increase, fill the earth and master it; and rule the fish of the sea, the birds of the sky, and all the living things that creep on the earth. (Genesis 1:26–28)

Modern ecologists recognize that such attitudes ignore the extent to which human beings are only one part of a complex environment and are inextricably dependent on the other creatures in that environment. A few simple examples can illustrate this. **Photosynthesis** is *the process by which plants capture light and heat energy from the sun and turn it into food*. Other animals survive by consuming these plants. Still other animals, including human beings, get sustenance by consuming both plants and animals. The same process of photosynthesis produces oxygen, which plants, animals, and humans need to breathe. In breathing, plants and animals discharge carbon dioxide into the atmosphere, and it is carbon dioxide that plants use to produce oxygen in photosynthesis. Bees pollinate plants that other animals live off. Human beings even have microorganisms in their intestines that help them digest food. Even though human beings may not be aware of this interdependent network of life, it is the indispensable core of life on earth. Ecologists recognize this by pointing out that all living creatures, including human beings, live in an **ecosystem:** *a complex, interrelated network of life forms and nonlife forms that interact with one another to produce an exchange of materials between the living and the nonliving parts.*

The concept of an ecosystem helps us to understand that all parts of the environment interact with one another and are, to a degree, dependent on one another. The cycle of photosynthesis illustrates this: Plants produce oxygen which animals need while animals expire carbon dioxide which the plants need to produce oxygen in photosynthesis. Each ecosystem achieves a natural balance among all the living creatures in it, and maintaining that equilibrium requires that all the parts be in some necessary, functional balance. An ecosystem might be relatively small, such as a section of swamp or part of a rain forest, or extensive, as when the whole earth is considered one ecosystem. A self-sufficient ecosystem also interacts with other ecosystems at the overlap of their borders. Ecologists also recognize that changes in one part of the ecosystem will likely produce changes in the other parts. This likelihood is at the core of the environmental problems discussed in this chapter, that is, the extent to which changes introduced into ecosystems because of human activities have produced further changes with severely detrimental conse-

Myths & FACTS
ABOUT THE ENVIRONMENT

Myth: Environmental pollution did not become a problem until the 1960s and 1970s.

FACT: This depends on what is meant by pollution becoming a problem. Environmental pollution existed long before this century, and it caused people health and other problems. For most of this time, however, people did not recognize pollution as a social problem that deserved attention. They ignored it or accepted it. It was not until the 1960s that serious and widespread attention was focused on the issue. Today, many more people are inclined to see environmental degradation as an unacceptable condition and thus define it as a social problem.

Myth: Native peoples in premodern societies were more sensitive to environmental issues than are modern people in industrial societies, and native peoples worked to avoid exploiting their environments.

FACT: People in most human societies behave in much the same way as their industrial counterparts: They protect resources in short supply but take a wasteful stance toward those resources that appear to be plentiful. In addition, most premodern peoples engaged in at least some practices that would have been highly destructive to the environment if their population size had been larger or their technology more intrusive.

Myth: Environmental conditions have been deteriorating in the last half of the twentieth century.

FACT: Any assessment of environmental conditions is complicated and depends on which conditions are observed. While many conditions have deteriorated, there have also been many significant improvements. Lead emissions into the atmosphere in the United States, for example, have dropped dramatically in the last 30 years, and the worldwide production of ozone-depleting chemicals has dropped significantly in the 1990s.

---

quences. Such human-induced changes in the ecosystem could be minor, but ecologists recognize that, if the human activities are sufficiently intrusive, they could dramatically alter the ecosystem, possibly to the point that its ability to support human life would be threatened.

Social Sources of Environmental Problems

The actions of human beings, of course, are at center stage in this assessment of environmental problems. While environmental problems can be caused by nonhuman intervention, as when severe weather devastates an ecosystem, the most severe environmental damage in the twentieth century is the product of human activities. The social and cultural conditions that tend to lead human beings to behave in ways that have detrimental consequences for the environment have actually been discussed in a number of other chapters in this book. They will be reviewed here in terms of their consequences for the environment.

Biologists Paul Ehrlich and Anne Ehrlich (1990) have developed a formula that summarizes some of the social conditions that affect the impact that human beings have on their environment:

$$I = P \times A \times T$$

Or, Impact = Population × Affluence × Technology. These key factors will be reviewed, along with some others.

Population Growth

Without question, the sheer number of people on the earth today is a key factor in environmental damage. If the human population were one-tenth or one-fiftieth of what it is, the same social and economic activities that people engage in today would likely produce relatively little damage. The concept of **carrying capacity** is introduced in Chapter 12: *an upper limit that is imposed on a population by its environmental resources and that cannot be permanently exceeded.* Exceeding the carrying capacity of an ecosystem means that people are depleting or destroying resources at a more rapid rate than they can be replaced. Forests are being cut down faster than nature can replace them, or air is being polluted at higher levels than the actions of photosynthesis can cleanse it. The carrying capacity can be exceeded for brief periods so long as population drops below that level in time for the environment to regenerate itself. However, exceeding the carrying capacity on a long-term or permanent basis may do sufficient damage to threaten the capacity of the ecosystem to support human life.

Determining the carrying capacity of an ecosystem is complicated because it depends in part on levels of affluence and technology, to be discussed in a moment. It also depends on what people consider to be socially acceptable environmental conditions. The level of environmental damage in some very crowded nations, such as India, would horrify many people in the United States. Yet people become used to some level of air and water pollution, especially if it is seen as the cost of getting a desired job or maintaining a way of life. Even in the United States, many people are willing to accept some level of air pollution if it means they are free to use their automobiles as they wish. However, even if people can live with pollution, it may still be detrimental to society through, for example, increased health consequences.

So, it is no simple task to define what the carrying capacity of an ecosystem is. At an extreme, exceeding the carrying capacity for a long period could result in an ecological catastrophe in which the ability of an ecosystem to support human life is in danger. Such a catastrophe has probably not yet occurred on the earth due to population size alone, although some ecosystems have been made unlivable for other reasons, such as nuclear accidents. However, as human populations continue to grow, ecologists look at this possibility: When are there too many people for the earth to support? Have we already done some irreparable damage simply because the earth must support so many people?

Affluence

To achieve high levels of affluence and material comfort, people have to consume the earth's resources and pollute its environment. The industrial nations of the world today have achieved levels of affluence that have been unheard of for most people at most times in history. The list of things that contribute to this lifestyle is almost endless: automobiles, airplanes, large and well-heated homes, air conditioning, clothing, refrigerators, and on and on. Each of these products consumes natural resources and energy when built, consumes more energy resources when operated, pollutes the air or water as a byproduct of its operation, and then pollutes streams or fills landfills when it is discarded.

If few people had these material goods, of course, the environmental problems would be minimal. Today, however, as was just noted, there are so many people to purchase these goods that the problem has become dire. In addition, Third-World nations around the globe are desirous of achieving the same levels of affluence that have become routine in North America, Western Europe, and Japan. It is disturbing to consider the environmental consequences were the two most populous nations in the world, China and India, with a combined population of over 2 billion people, to achieve the same level of affluence as the United States. Looking at automobiles alone, this would mean another 1 billion automobiles on the earth consuming fossil fuels and polluting the air, not to mention the tires and highways that would have to be built. Some ecologists think we may exceed the carrying capacity of the earth if we combine current and future world population sizes with Western levels of affluence.

Of course, if people were willing to forego the affluence that is possible in the world today, environmental damage would be reduced. But most people do not consider this option; they want the best life possible for themselves and their families. In fact, if anything, people hope for progress, with life for future generations being even more affluent than it is now. This is the "phenomenon of rising expectations": Especially when things are improving, people come to expect continued improvement in the future. So affluence is a very tempting thing, much too tempting for most people to avoid.

Technology

Technology is a two-edged sword: Advances in technology result in new products that produce additional environmental damage, but at the same time technological developments can result in less polluting ways of doing things. Any technological development that brings a new product into the world that many people will buy and use is almost inherently polluting. It consumes resources in its production and use, and it pollutes the environment with its byproducts along the way. And if it supports the affluent lifestyle that many people seek, many millions of these new products will be pro-

duced and consumed. So, while modern technology does some wonderful things, it can also be very damaging. The wonders of electricity exist all around us, as it lights our homes in the dark, heats buildings in the winter, and runs the computer on which these words are being written. Yet the cost is the gouging of coal out of the earth in strip mines that pollute nearby streams and ultimately results in air pollution as the coal is burned to generate electricity. The greater the number of technological wonders that are discovered, the more threats to the environment will exist.

Yet, technology clearly has its positive side: It makes our lives more comfortable and enables us to produce foods and medicines to keep us healthy. It can also help to reduce environmental damage: Gasolines consumed today are far less polluting than in the past, and scrubbers have been invented to prevent many of the pollutants of burning coal from escaping into the air. The problem is not technology by itself, but rather uncontrolled technology that is harnessed to gain the greatest short-term reward without consideration of its impact on the environment.

Economic Growth

Most nations in the world today pursue a policy of economic growth, which means that the total goods and services produced is growing from year to year. Economic growth is important if a nation's population is growing because the economy must produce more to provide the same standard of living for more people. Economic growth also provides for increasing levels of affluence: Even if population size does not change, the economy needs to produce more if it is to provide higher levels of material affluence in the future. Beyond these reasons, capitalism as an economic system also stresses the ideology of growth, as it drives to expand and find new markets for its goods. Economic growth provides for higher profits for corporations. Corporations also stimulate the demand for growth by shaping people's desires and expectations through advertising. People are manipulated into desiring the many products that capitalism can produce.

With the emergence of the global capitalist economy, discussed in Chapter 2, worldwide pressures toward economic growth and competition have become intense. Organizations such as the World Bank and the International Monetary Fund (IMF) have expended money and resources around the globe—especially in the Third-World nations of Asia, Africa, and Latin America—to encourage economic growth and development and the exploitation of natural resources. Economic growth itself can have a disastrous impact on the environment, but critics accuse the World Bank, IMF, and other international financial organizations of promoting economic growth that is ruinous to the environment (George and Sabelli, 1994; Rich, 1994). They have been accused of mounting campaigns to build giant, nonsustainable energy projects, to destroy millions of acres of rainforests, and to forcibly relocate millions of people. Some groups benefit from such activities, of course, especially international corporations and the national elites in Third-World nations whose interests are in alignment with those corporations (Miller, 1995). Often, however, such development has been at the cost of the environment and the interests of local peoples.

So, there are many pressures toward economic growth, and such growth is not inherently bad. However, it can result in more products produced and more environmental damage. In addition to the additional products produced, corporations also tend to ignore some of the costs of doing business, and these costs often involve environmental damage. In doing so, the costs are not paid by the corporation but may be paid by other people or future generations. So, for example, the cheapest way for a factory to dispose of toxic wastes may be to discharge them into a nearby river. Other, more environmentally sound forms of handling the wastes would likely be more expensive. So, corporations will opt for the cheapest way of doing business, but someone will pay for the easy disposal of those wastes. It might be people living downstream who get sick from swimming in the wastes or it might be future generations who have to cleanse the river to make it usable again (Hawken, 1993). Unless regulated in some fashion, capitalists have a strong profit incentive to push these costs off onto others.

Especially in Third-World nations, the pressure is intense to pursue economic growth as a means of raising low living standards. While many nations have come to recognize that unregulated growth can be very destructive, all too often national leaders place short-term gains in living standards ahead of long-term protection of the environment. So, there is controversy today regarding policies of economic growth. Some environmentalists take the position that continued economic growth, especially when accompanied by continued population growth, will eventually produce an ecological catastrophe when the carrying capacity of the earth is exceeded (Hardin, 1993). They do not claim to predict exactly when that will happen but are convinced that it will. Supporters of economic growth, on the other hand, while agreeing that environmental problems warrant concern and that some regulation of economic activity may be essential, argue that growth will provide the foundation for new technological discoveries that will help us reduce environmental damage. New products will be less polluting, or new technologies will arise to correct the damage from pollution. In addition, if some natural resources are depleted, they argue, technological developments will provide us with new resources or products to replace them. In fact, some proponents of growth argue that such significant progress has been made in attacking environmental problems that excessive regulations and limitations on economic activity are no longer prudent (Easterbrook, 1995). Each side in this debate can find evidence to support its position.

Cultural Values

In many nations, a constellation of cultural values exists that supports practices that are damaging to the environment, or at least the values do not discourage such practices. Earlier in this chapter, it was mentioned that some religious beliefs and cultural values stress the notion that human beings are superior to and have mastery over the earth and its creatures. This stance opens the door for radical alterations in the environment which can be highly destructive if not closely regulated. A second cultural value that has risen to prominence is that of progress—that people's standard of living should rise over time. This notion of progress is a recent one in human societies, with most people in preindustrial societies being content to maintain a traditional way of life that is handed down from one generation to the next with little change (Rich, 1994). By the late twentieth century, the value of progress has become entrenched in many societies around the world and fuels the pursuit of economic growth.

A third cultural value that plays a part in environmental issues is individualism, the belief that individual desires and achievements are more important than collective accomplishments and goals. Individualism is a very powerful ethic in the United States, leading people to believe that they should be able to do as they wish, without regard to what other people or government agencies believe is appropriate. This notion has been very prominent in the anti-government rhetoric of the 1990s. As for environmental issues, if a person wants to drive a car that pollutes the air or depletes resources, individualists believe this should be his or her choice. If a property owner wishes to fill in a wetland on his or her property, the government should not stand in the way. In other words, environmental concerns often focus on collective goals—what is good for the whole ecosystem—while individualism can lead people to behave in ways contrary to those broader goals.

These values of mastery, progress, and individualism do not automatically translate into environmental damage, but they do open the door for human goals, such as economic growth, to be pursued in such a way as to disregard the importance of protecting the ecosystem. People come to place more emphasis on economic growth in the short term than on protecting the ecosystem in the long run.

Perspectives on Environmental Problems

The Functionalist Perspective

The functionalist perspective views society as a system made up of interrelated and interdependent parts, each working toward the maintenance of the system. In the case of environmental issues, the system consists of the land, air, water, people, and other resources in a particular ecosystem. Another part of the system comprises people's cultural beliefs and values and the resulting social behaviors. All of the parts exist in a delicate balance, and an injudicious treatment of some parts of the system may have negative consequences for other parts. For functionalists, a highly technological social organization has many benefits but also many dysfunctions. It can overuse resources, for example, and deplete them, making them unavailable for future generations. The excessive use of some resources may pollute a part of the environment to the point at which it is unhealthy to humans or not usable for some purposes. High technology and environmental preservation are at odds with one another—the parts of the system are not well integrated.

As mentioned, an important part of the system is made up of the human cultural beliefs and values that fuel behavior. If cultural values encourage people in a careless use of the environment, then this may lead to serious environmental problems. From the functionalist perspective, then, environmental problems become social problems when they produce social disorganization, making it difficult for societies to survive or to achieve desired goals. While improvements in technology may alleviate some of the destructiveness, because technology tends to be inherently intrusive, solutions may require that technology and industrialism adapt to fit the needs of society.

The Conflict Perspective

From the conflict perspective, environmental problems have less to do with the limited amount of resources available than with their distribution. The problem is not how much is available but who gets a share of what is available. Decisions that affect the environment are not made on the basis of maintaining a balance in an ecosystem but on the basis of how successfully interest groups compete for a share of the resources available. The manner in which the environment is used emerges out of this competition of groups for varying amounts of power and other resources. So, a central idea of the conflict perspective on environmental problems is that groups have competing interests when it comes to how to treat environmental resources: If one side gets what it wants, the other side loses. If community residents successfully oppose the location of a toxic waste incinerator in their neighborhood, the owners of the incinerator lose. On the other hand, if the incinerator is built, the residents lose. The interests of the two groups compete directly, and the outcome is determined by which group can successfully wield the most power. In addition, there are always groups who will benefit, at least in the short term, by exploiting the environment by polluting and using up resources. Oil corporations benefit when the world's oil reserves are tapped heavily, and timber interests benefit by the extensive cutting of timber. In a highly competitive environment, these corporations may feel it an essential business practice to pollute and deplete, at least to an extent, to corner markets and make a profit. In the competitive global economy, enormous pressures exist to consider concerns about environmental degradation to be secondary to the needs of business.

Environmental conditions become social problems when groups with some power feel that their interests are not being served by current environmental policies and practices. The discharge of pollutants from a factory into a stream may not be considered a problem by the corporation that owns the factory—in fact, it may be an economically efficient means of handling industrial wastes. Such discharges become a problem if there are groups with sufficient resources to mount a campaign against the pollution and direct societal attention toward the problem.

The Interactionist Perspective

The interactionist perspective stresses the importance of social definitions and subjective assessments of reality. Environmental problems are not solely objective conditions in the physical world; to become social problems, they must be identified and defined by people as problems about which something ought to be done. After all, human beings have polluted their environments even before the current era. In the early industrial period in Great Britain and Europe, for example, factories spewed pollutants into the air with abandon, and many cities had far worse air quality than cities in the United States today. Yet air pollution was not defined as a social problem but as one of the possibly unfortunate but necessary costs of economic progress. People may not have liked it, but they accepted it. However, social definitions can change over time. The media, for example, may publish articles that cast pollution as an evil about which people can do something, or biologists and ecologists might publish books showing the serious damage pollution does to the environment and how it could be alleviated. Sometimes a very powerful image can help evoke a new definition of reality. This occurred when photographs taken from space showed the earth floating alone in the immense void of space and looking very fragile indeed. The expression "spaceship Earth" emerged, suggesting that the earth was alone in space with its finite supply of resources that could not be replaced and needed to be harbored carefully.

As these and other influences gradually change people's perceptions of environmental problems, the social construction of environmental problems emerges. This does not mean that everyone agrees or that all people view environmental problems in the same way. The next section explores how these social definitions of the environment developed and changed in the United States.

The Social Construction of Environmental Problems

Environmental pollution and degradation are not new. They have been occurring for as long as people have existed on the earth. However, people's concerns about these issues have changed significantly over time. The interactionist perspective suggests that social problems do not really exist until people identify and define them as social problems. The conflict perspective points to the important role of the clash of competing interest groups in shaping what is considered a social problem. A brief review of changing concerns about the environment in the United States will illustrate how social problems are socially constructed by people.

A popular belief holds that premodern people had a keen understanding of nature and a harmonious relationship with their environment. American Indians, for example, have been described as the "first environmentalists." Historical evidence belies this notion, however. Most American Indians treated their environment the way that most humans have done through the centuries—they worked hard to protect those resources in short supply and took a wasteful approach toward those that they believed to be plentiful. For example, the well-known publication, *American Heritage,* depicts ruthless whites shooting buffalo for "sport" from railroad trains, but after the Indians acquired horses and firearms, they too slaughtered the buffalo, eating the best meat and taking the hides but leaving the rest to decompose (Baden et al., 1979). In short, American Indians were actually exploiting their environment before the Europeans got into the act. One of the major differences between then and now is that, with the much larger population and more elaborate technology in the United States today, people's actions are far more able to do serious damage to the environment.

People's consciousness of environmental problems has fluctuated over time. For example, at the turn of the century, the air in cities in the United States was being polluted by the smoke and waste from the growing number of factories. But people of that era did not perceive this environmental pollution as a threat. One of the key factors that began to heighten people's awareness of these problems since then has been the establishment of a wide variety of environmental interest groups. Some of these groups are not new. The oldest is the Sierra Club, which was founded in 1892 by a group of affluent San Franciscans who had an interest in hiking and camping in the Sierra Mountains of California. Today, the Sierra Club is one of the best-known environmental groups in the political and legal arena. Another older environmental association is the Audubon Society, which was founded in 1905 by affluent women and men on the East Coast, with the initial purpose of halting the commercial hunting of wild birds for plumage for the women's fashion industry. These early groups focused more on issues of conservation, or protecting wilderness areas for use by human beings, rather than environmental degradation. Despite these organizations, the general public in the United States was not aware of or responsive to environmental concerns prior to the 1950s.

The modern environmental movement really took off in the 1960s. It was then that biological ecologists such as Rachel Carson and Paul Ehrlich began writing for popular audiences about how the growth in human societies was producing an ecological disaster in nature. In 1962, Carson published *The Silent Spring*, which dealt with the hidden dangers that pesticides and herbicides hold for the environment. In 1968, Ehrlich's best-selling *The Population Bomb* hit the market. Using a distinctly Malthusian approach, Ehrlich proposed that world population growth is responsible for pollution and other modern environmental problems. A bit later, Barry Commoner joined the ranks of environmental critics and, in contrast to Ehrlich's approach, blamed technology and growing corporate power structures for the expanding ecological woes of the world.

The 1960s and 1970s also saw the emergence of major nationwide environmental groups such as Friends of the Earth, the League of Conser-

Greenpeace is one of the modern environmental groups that has contributed to the social construction of social problems. Through its lobbying, demonstrations, and disruptive actions, Greenpeace has helped promote the belief that environmental issues are social problems to which we should direct our attention.

vation Voters, the Environmental Defense Fund, the Natural Resources Defense Council, and Greenpeace. These groups engaged in lobbying, demonstrations, and sometimes disruptive actions that brought environmental problems to the public eye and created a great deal of political pressure to address environmental issues with legislation.

The fervor generated by these organizations set the stage for some very important legislation in the 1970s relating to environmental quality. In 1970, for example, the National Environmental Policy Act (NEPA) was passed, which required that public hearings be held on matters that might adversely affect the environment and that environmental impact studies be conducted to assess these possible effects. Also in the early 1970s, the Clean Air Act and the Water Pollution Control Act were passed, and these laws led to the establishment of the Environmental Protection Agency (EPA). Originally, the Clean Air Act empowered the EPA to monitor and regulate standards of air quality, but as time went on, the EPA acquired authority over almost all matters dealing with environmental quality. Had it not been for the establishment and operation of these various environmental organizations, legislation such as this would probably not have been passed.

This brief history, then, suggests how the social problem of environmental degradation was socially constructed. It came to be identified as a problem by more people because they learned about the nature and extent of assaults on the ecosystem from biologists like Ehrlich and Commoner. In addition, the various environmental organizations were able to pressure newspapers, magazines, and television into publicizing the problems, and the prominence of this issue in the media is important in convincing people that environmental degradation should be addressed. Finally, the organizations were able to pressure the government into action, and the laws and government bureaus created serve as sounding boards that keep the issue before the public's attention.

So, it has only been in the past three decades that a significant number of people in the United States and around the world have come to view environmental issues as social problems. The next section will review the nature and extent of the environmental problems that confront the United States and the world. In this review, you will be able to see the key role that population size, affluence, technology, and other factors mentioned earlier in this chapter play in creating environmental degradation.

Extent of Environmental Problems

Water Supply and Pollution

Water is present in the atmosphere as a vapor; it then condenses and falls to the earth as rain, dew, or snow; it collects underground and drains into streams, rivers, and the oceans; finally it evaporates into the atmosphere once more as vapor. This *process, by which nature purifies water,* is called the **hydrologic cycle.** There are various mechanisms by which water is purified during this cycle. In a single pass through the hydrologic cycle, these mechanisms make water suitable for reuse. But this natural process is interfered with by various kinds of human pollution, including raw sewage, pesticides and other chemicals, nitrate and phosphate fertilizers, and waste products from factories and nuclear power generators. As population and technology have grown, the resulting pollution has become so massive that the hydrologic cycle cannot fully cleanse the water, although we have techniques to assist nature in this process. The Environmental Protection Agency (EPA) estimates that 40 percent of the rivers and lakes in the United States are not fit for drinking, fishing, or swimming (Stevens, 1995). The EPA issues a thousand warnings each year not to eat fish from chemically contaminated rivers and lakes. A dramatic example of such water pollution is found in the phenomenon of "acid rain," discussed in the Policy Issues insert. Acid rain illustrates the way human intervention can upset the ecological balance in nature. Using the functionalist perspective, we can see how the natural equilibrium within an ecosystem can be upset by interference of this nature. As the Policy Issues insert suggests, the long-range implications of acid rain and similar problems are potentially harmful to the ongoing maintenance of the environment.

Another example of the effects of pollution on our water supply involves a process called *eu-*

POLICY ISSUES

Acid Rain: Technology Creates New Environmental Threats

In his famous soliloquy, William Shakespeare once spoke of "the gentle rain from heaven." The 1980s brought about an ironic alteration of the meaning of this refrain in a frightening phenomenon known as "acid rain." The effort over the past decade to deal with the problem of acid rain shows how environmental problems can become international in scope and how many groups can try to influence the solutions that are adopted.

Acid rain refers to a type of air pollution made up of sulfurous and nitrous oxide emissions from the burning of fossil fuels. These pollutants come mostly from coal-burning power plants, motor vehicles, and other industrial facilities. They combine with oxygen in the atmosphere to produce sulfuric and nitric acids that fall to the earth as acidic rain, snow, fog, or particulates. Acidity can destroy plant and animal life in an ecosystem. The environmental damage and economic costs associated with acid rain are enormous (Ehrlich and Ehrlich, 1990). For example, millions of acres of European and eastern U.S. forests now show severe damage linked to acid rain, as do some forests in remote parts of China. This type of air pollution may result in the extermination of valuable forests all over the world (Main, 1988). Approximately 85 percent of the sulfur dioxide in the atmospheres of the United States and Canada is of U.S. origin, although all nations that burn fossil fuels contribute to the problem. In addition to its harmful effects on forests, acid rain also releases lead from the interior of steel pipes into drinking and irrigation water, has killed fish and other wildlife in once-thriving lakes, and has elevated the incidence of respiratory ailments in the population.

Public debate over the acid rain issue has followed a pattern that is also found with many other environmental issues (Balling, 1992). When the problem first came to the surface in the late 1970s, some environmentalists saw in acid rain yet another symptom of imminent ecological collapse. They believed that our lakes and forests were rapidly being destroyed and that massive efforts needed to be mounted irrespective of the costs. More conservative voices held that the environmentalists were, once again, alarmists who would saddle our economies with massive costs to attack a problem that would turn out to be a minor annoyance at worst. While this public debate went on during the 1980s, many scientific teams were working to assess the nature and extent of the problem. The scientific findings would gradually come to inform the public debate and change it in significant ways (Zehr, 1994). These research findings, and especially the results of the decade-long National Acid Precipitation Assessment Program (NAPAP), confirmed that acid rain is a problem for the world, but it is not as serious or urgent a problem as many had projected. One thing they found is that there are many natural sources of acid rain, so human activity is not the major, or possibly even primary, source of the problem. In addition, the damage caused by acid rain is not as extensive as originally thought. Massive and expensive efforts to control acid rain may be very costly yet produce relatively little actual decline in the problem. Nev-

trophication, the depletion of oxygen in a body of water because of an overabundance of plant and animal life. It can happen like this: Modern farming practices use nitrate and phosphate fertilizers. When these fertilizers run off into rivers and lakes, they stimulate the growth of algae and other plants that eventually decay at the bottoms of these bodies of water. In the same fashion as decomposing sewage, these algae formations consume increasing amounts of oxygen, and they compete with fish and other animals for the oxygen in the water. If the

ertheless, the scientists are clear in saying that it is a problem that needs to be addressed by the countries of the world.

The acid rain problem can be alleviated by a reduction in the burning of fossil fuels that release sulfurous and nitrous oxides into the atmosphere. This would happen if people drove their automobiles less and relied less on electricity produced by burning high-sulfur coal. Many countries have begun to do this. For example, in the past few years, Russia and the other nations that made up the former Soviet Union have significantly reduced their use of highly polluting coal as their economy has been restructured (Flavin, 1992). Another approach is to put scrubbers on the smokestacks of coal-burning plants to clean the emissions, but this is a very expensive proposition and tends to be resisted. At the same time that efforts to deal with the problem have emerged, new concerns have been felt along another front: increased use of fossil fuels by developing countries and the former Soviet Union as they try to emulate the more affluent lifestyles of the industrial nations. If they follow the high-energy-consumption, no-energy-conservation route we have taken, worldwide sulfurous and nitrous oxide emissions will increase substantially in the future, and the acid rain problem will become more severe. So, although NAPAP and other research projects showed that acid rain was not as serious as the alarmists of the 1980s thought, doing nothing about it could be disastrous in the coming decades.

This forest in North Carolina has been destroyed by acid rain, an environmental problem involving both air and water pollution.

competition is too fierce, oxygen in the water is depleted rather than replaced, and nothing may be able to survive in the water. This happened to Lake Erie in the 1950s and 1960s with disastrous results. Lake Erie had an algae bottom that was over one hundred feet thick, and along with the oxygen-depleting effects of this huge layer, the material was heavily laden with nitrous and phosphorous compounds. Fishing in the lake was ended. Environmentalists worked toward halting these forms of pollution from flowing into Lake Erie, and total destruction was avoided. Although Lake Erie has recovered substantially today, the experience of that lake illustrates the care and effort that must be devoted to protecting water supplies from the harmful effects of our population growth and technological development.

Solid and Toxic Wastes

The average person in the United States throws away between three and five pounds of waste every day, amounting to an incredible three tons per year for the typical family of four people and translating into over 200 million tons yearly for the country as a whole. This amount has substantially more than doubled in the last three decades (see Figure 13.1). One hundred and sixty million additional tons are added every year in industrial waste, along with between two and three billion tons yearly from mining operations. This enormous waste-disposal figure led one observer to call people in the United States "the world's trashiest people." Disposing of this waste in a way that does not degrade the environment poses a very serious problem.

Rather than disposing of waste, it may be possible to reuse some of it. For example, some states have passed "bottle bills," which require that a deposit be paid for beer bottles and other containers when a beverage is bought. This encourages people to return the bottles and cans for the deposit and contributes to the recycling of glass and aluminum containers. In addition

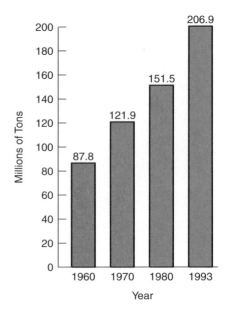

FIGURE 13.1 Total Municipal Garbage Generated in the United States, 1960–1993. *Source*: U.S. Bureau of the Census, *Statistical Abstract of the United States, 1995* (Washington, D.C.: U.S. Government Printing Office, 1995), p. 236.

to not filling up landfills, recycled materials are substantially less expensive to produce, thus saving energy in the process. For example, a glass beer bottle used only once and then tossed out with the garbage consumed 3730 BTUs in its production. The same beer bottle made of recycled glass cost 2530 BTUs to produce. Even greater savings are achieved if, instead of recycling, we refill the same bottle so that a new bottle does not have to be produced from recycled glass. A refillable glass beer bottle, used ten times, costs 610 BTUs on the average for each use—a very dramatic savings of energy (Brown, Flavin, and Postel, 1991). Where recycling efforts do not exist, an enormous quantity of containers is disposed of in landfills and incineration dumps. Many people forget that "tin cans" rust away after several years, but aluminum cans last literally forever. The United

States imports over 90 percent of the aluminum that it uses, and then disposes of over one million tons annually. The same situation exists for plastic and synthetic products. Consumers often spend more on food packaging than farmers make from selling food (Brown, Flavin, and Postel, 1991). We also produce bottles of many different sizes and shapes rather than a standardized and durable bottle that could be refilled many times over. The nonreturnable container is perhaps one of the best examples of our propensity toward wastefulness and a lack of respect for the environment.

Toxic waste disposal presents an even more ominous problem in terms of the pollution of our environment. Toxic wastes are the residues of the production of things such as plastics, pesticides, and nuclear energy. The tragedy at Love Canal near Niagara Falls over a decade ago is one of the more dramatic instances of the consequences of dumping chemical waste products. The wastes had been buried many years before, and homes were later built at Love Canal where the wastes had accumulated. Contaminants seeped into the water supply and the homes of the residents and caused severe and lingering health problems. Eventually many residents were forced to move, with the government buying their houses from them. However, many residents believed that their or their children's health had been permanently damaged and that they had not been adequately compensated for their suffering and dislocation. Even though regulation of toxic wastes began more than twenty years ago, not all hazardous wastes are covered by the regulations, and there are still no answers to basic questions regarding the numbers and amounts of such wastes polluting the environment (Gerrard, 1994). Consequently, the data on this subject are extremely limited, which is disturbing considering the extent and severity of the problem. Figure 13.2 shows the major industries that release toxic wastes in the United States and the amounts released.

FIGURE 13.2 Toxic Releases, Top Ten Industries, 1993. *Source*: U.S. Bureau of the Census, *Statistical Abstract of the United States, 1995* (Washington, D.C.: U.S. Government Printing Office, 1995), p. 222.

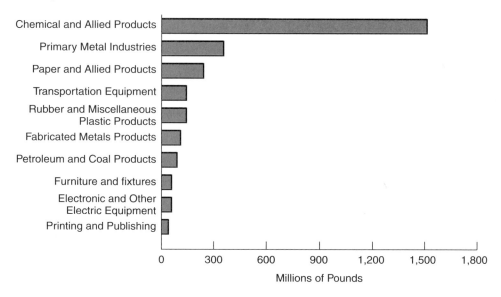

Thousands of toxic waste dump sites exist in the United States, with heavy concentrations in the industrial states of the Great Lakes region and the east and west coasts (Gerrard, 1994). Figure 13.3 shows the regional concentrations of over one thousand dumps that are currently on the government's National Priorities List, which are sites that pose severe hazards and about which something must be done. However, there may be as many as 30,000 sites that will eventually need to be cleaned up. Total costs for cleaning up all the sites are difficult to estimate but probably run into the hundreds of billions of dollars. Congress has appropriated only a fraction of that to clean up the worst sites.

Nuclear Wastes

Nuclear wastes are a particularly serious form of toxic waste because they can stay so deadly for so long. There are three sources of nuclear wastes: the lethal by-products of manufacturing nuclear weapons, the radioactive wastes from nuclear power plants, and the low-grade nuclear wastes that are by-products of our health and other industries. As of this writing no plan for the permanent disposal of these wastes has

FIGURE 13.3 Sites of the Worst Hazardous Waste Dumps in 1994, According to the Environmental Protection Agency. *Source*: U.S. Bureau of the Census, *Statistical Abstract of the United States, 1995* (Washington, D.C.: U.S. Government Printing Office, 1995), p. 237.

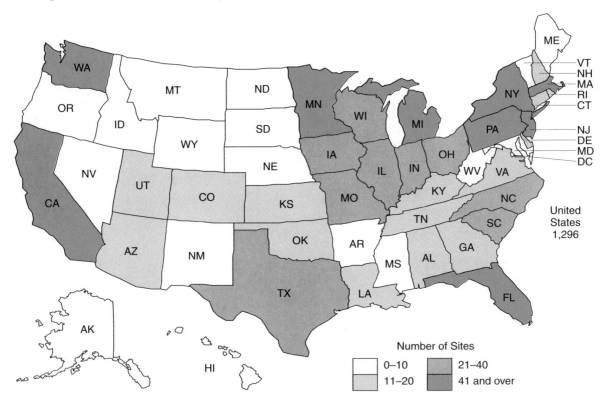

been agreed to, even though the wastes are accumulating at an alarming rate (Gerrard, 1994). Irradiated fuel from the world's nuclear power plants, for example, will exceed two hundred thousand tons by the year 2000 (Lenssen, 1992). One problem with nuclear wastes is that they remain deadly for thousands of years, and for some wastes even tens of thousands of years. Plutonium, for example, remains radioactive for 240,000 years! That is a time span that is at least as long as *Homo sapiens* have existed on the earth. It is absurd to imagine that we could ensure the integrity of a vault or the safety of the materials over such a vast expanse of time. A successful repository for the wastes must seal them completely for all this time, and no one has yet figured out how to do that. Another problem with nuclear wastes is the NIMBY syndrome: Not in My Back Yard. Few people want the waste repository near where they live, so communities have tended to resist when efforts are made to put a repository near them. A third problem with nuclear wastes is transporting them. Even if we have permanent storage facilities, wastes will be shipped there from all over the country, and that presents an image of a disaster waiting to happen. Even in rupture-proof containers, accidents will probably happen, with some leakage of radioactivity. A final problem with nuclear wastes is the temporary storage we use for lack of permanent storage. The nuclear industry has had a history of spreading radioactive and chemical wastes over the open ground, pouring it in rivers and lakes, and dumping it wherever it is most convenient and least expensive. Part of the reason this was allowed to happen is that the Cold War mentality produced little congressional oversight or public scrutiny. It was assumed that the nuclear industry was working in the national interest. In the late 1980s, the extent of the environmental contamination became known and many nuclear weapons production plants were shut down. However, we still do not have a permanent storage facility for the nuclear wastes.

Land Degradation

As was observed at the beginning of this chapter, the future of the environment depends on a delicate balance in nature, and upsetting this equilibrium can lead to serious consequences. One of the more ominous of these is *desertification,* referring to what happens when intensification of food production, such as by continuous cropping and overgrazing, leads to the spread of desert areas, thus reducing the quantity of arable land (Brown and Wolf, 1986; Durning and Brough, 1992). It has been estimated that over the past fifty years, one hundred million acres of useable farmland have been degraded to the point where they are no longer arable, with another one hundred million acres having lost their topsoil covers. Under favorable conditions, between three hundred and one thousand years are required to produce only one inch of topsoil. Data on this subject show that this problem is growing much more serious over time. In 1882, for example, about 10 percent of the earth's land was classified as desert or wasteland; by the 1950s, this figure had expanded to nearly 25 percent, and by 1980, almost 35 percent of our planet's land area was so classified. According to current estimates, over ten million acres of new desert are formed each year as a consequence of land mismanagement in semiarid regions (Malone and Corell, 1989). According to recent evaluations of land degradation, we need more research on the relationship between ecosystem change and the hydrologic cycle in order to make intelligent decisions about how to approach these problems (Brown and Wolf, 1986).

Deforestation is another example of land degradation that comes from human tampering with the environment. Environmentalists Paul and Anne Ehrlich describe the consequences of forests being cleared:

Numerous animals that depend on the trees for food and shelter disappear. Many of the smaller forest plants depend on the trees for shade;

they and the animals they support also disappear. With the removal of trees and plants, the soil is directly exposed to the elements, and it tends to erode faster. Loss of topsoil reduces the water-retaining capacity of an area, diminishes the supply of fresh water, causes silting of dams, and . . . flooding. (Ehrlich and Ehrlich, 1970: 202)

In a number of African countries, the demand on forests (to use the wood as fuel or to clear land for agriculture) is from two to five times greater than the growth rate of new trees. This imbalance between demand and supply is due largely to growing populations and will obviously lead to a shortage of wood if it continues for long. Deforestation is rapidly converting Brazil's Amazon forest to low-value, nonproductive cattle pasture, and policies for slowing this process are currently being debated (Fearnside, 1989). In 1990 alone, deforestation claimed seventeen million hectares of land, about the equivalent of the state of Washington in one year! Half of all tropical rain forests on the planet have been destroyed. One expert concluded that

> In most nations, forests occur increasingly in small fragments surrounded by degraded land, with their ability to sustain viable populations of wildlife and vital ecological processes impaired. (Ryan, 1992: 10)

Declining Biodiversity

Some of the trends previously discussed—particularly overpopulation, deforestation, and overgrazing of cleared lands—have a consequence that is difficult to notice now but may be overwhelming in the near future: the annihilation of many species of animals around the globe. Biologist Edward Wilson (1992) estimates that twenty-seven thousand species per year are obliterated from the earth, which translates into seventy-four species every day of the year. Although the elimination of some species is expected as a part of normal evolutionary development, the current rate is staggeringly high.

For most of earth's history, the number of species on the earth was increasing, resulting in greater biological diversity. Today, according to one estimate, three-quarters of the world's bird species are declining in population, all species of wild cats and most bears are declining seriously in numbers, and over two-thirds of the world's 150 primate species are threatened with extinction (Ryan, 1992). At the current rate of destruction, Wilson estimates, biodiversity on the earth is actually declining. Twenty percent of the earth's species will be extinct thirty years from now, giving the current period the distinction of having one of the largest die-offs of species in the history of the earth.

Declining biodiversity creates two major problems. One is that we are losing species that might be of some use to humans, such as in producing pharmaceuticals. Some materials can only be produced from living species, and once a species is gone it is irreplaceable. The second problem is more subtle: At some point, declines in biodiversity may threaten the ability of the ecosystem to support human life. In that sense, every species is intimately dependent on other species for its survival. Ecosystems thrive, in part, because of the complexity and diversity of life that they harbor. As we have seen, ecosystems are complex networks in which species exchange material with one another in order to survive. One species thrives by eating another while a third species survives by the wastes of the other two. Elaborate those simple interchanges many thousands of times and one can begin to see the complex interactions involved in ecosystems. As species are removed from a system, it becomes more difficult to sustain such complex life forms as human beings. We have seen it happen before: We drive a predator to extinction only to realize that it kept the rodent population in control; earthworms are killed off by pesticides and they no longer aerate the soil; forests cut down no longer protect soils from erosion. The problem is that we do not know how much decline in biodiversity the earth can sustain without precipitating a biological disaster. Biologist Wilson feels we are in imminent danger. This is not to say that every insect, fish, or primate species has to be saved. However, what biologists fear is happening today is the complete dismantling of the global life support system.

Air Pollution

Natural processes operate to cleanse the atmosphere. For example, through photosynthesis, green plants use water and carbon dioxide to produce oxygen and carbohydrates. These natural life cycles are limited, however, and if the atmosphere becomes overloaded, the air supply becomes more toxic.

There can be no question that modern technology taxes the earth's atmosphere. According to the Census Bureau, for example, over 85 percent of the air pollution in urban areas is attributable to the internal combustion engine, despite efforts to control these emissions by using such devices as the catalytic con-

verter (U.S. Bureau of the Census, 1994). On the other hand, pollution from automobiles has already been reduced considerably. Today's new vehicles emit 96 percent fewer hydrocarbons, 75 percent fewer nitrogen dioxides, and 96 percent less carbon monoxide than their 1960 counterparts (see Figure 13.4). As Figure 13.5 shows, the amounts of lead released into the air has dropped precipitously. The contribution of all vehicles to ozone pollution is now down to 29 percent of the total, and will reach 20 percent by the 1990s under the rules now in effect, as new cars replace older ones (Main, 1988).

At the same time, there are hydrocarbons, nitrous and sulfurous oxides, lead, and various forms of particulate matter, such as soot and ash, emitted from industrial production operations and the burning of coal and wood. According to the EPA, the healthiness of air quality in the United States has generally improved over the past few decades, and manufacturers have reduced their releases of toxic chemicals into the air by 43 percent. Neverthe-

FIGURE 13.4   Levels of Various Air Pollutants in the United States, 1940–1993.
Source: U.S. Bureau of the Census, *Statistical Abstract of the United States, 1995* (Washington, D.C.: U.S. Government Printing Office, 1995), p. 233.

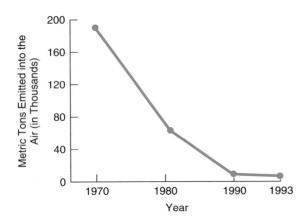

FIGURE 13.5 Levels of Lead Emitted Into the Air in the United States, 1970–1993. *Source*: U.S. Bureau of the Census, *Statistical Abstract of the United States, 1995* (Washington, D.C.: U.S. Government Printing Office, 1995), p. 233.

less, over 40 percent of residents in the United States live in areas exceeding acceptable levels of one or more of the pollutants just mentioned (Stevens, 1995).

Another threat to the air comes from the release of chlorine- and bromine-containing chemicals, such as chlorofluorocarbons (CFCs). These are common industrial chemicals and are also often used in aerosol cans and refrigeration units. When these chemicals escape into the atmosphere, they destroy the ozone that surrounds the earth. Ozone is important because it screens out harmful ultraviolet rays from the sun. If this ultraviolet radiation gets through, it can cause skin cancer, damage marine life, and lower crop yields. Recent measurements by the National Aeronautics and Space Administration indicate that the earth may have lost a stunning 5 percent of its ozone layer in thirteen years. However, recent developments are promising: The United States is phasing out its production of these chemicals, and worldwide production has declined dramatically in the 1990s (Brown, Flavin, and Postel, 1991; Brown, Kane, and Roodman, 1994).

Certain types of air pollution, if sufficiently severe, may cause a "greenhouse effect" (Fleagle, 1994). Modern technology depends on the burning of fossil fuels as a source of energy, and this releases great quantities of carbon dioxide into the atmosphere. The carbon dioxide molecules act like the glass roof of a greenhouse, allowing sunlight to reach the earth's surface but preventing the escape of solar infrared radiation back into space. According to some scientists, the temperature of the earth's atmosphere could rise as much as five degrees over the next one hundred years because of the greenhouse effect. This could substantially alter weather patterns and climate. It could also melt much of the earth's water that is now stored as ice at the poles and in glaciers. This could cause the world's oceans to rise seven feet or more from their current levels with devastating flooding of low-lying coastal regions. It could also cause some of the great food-producing regions of the world to dry up into dust bowls. Furthermore, the developing nations accuse the industrial nations of being the prime cause of this problem.

There is lively debate over what to do about the greenhouse effect. The industrial countries want the less developed nations to control their population growth and to stop scrambling after cars, air conditioners, and other aspects of affluent Western lives. The less developed nations want the affluent industrial nations to tone down their lifestyle and shift some of the world's resources to the fight against poverty in the poorer nations in the world. Some economists and scientists even argue that the greenhouse effect will produce only mild disruptions that we can adapt to and that vigorous efforts to control the emission of greenhouse gases could stunt economic growth and produce a drop in our life-style.

Pesticides and Other Chemicals

As in most instances of human beings' attempts to control their environment, efforts to cope with insects interfering with crop production began on a small scale and became increasingly complex. For example, one early strategy was the use of lead arsenate. This compound was effective in exterminating a narrow range of insects, but it was biodegradable and had no long-lasting negative effects on the environment. About forty years ago, chemists put together a series of chlorinated hydrocarbons to produce the well-known insecticide DDT. Such chemical substances are much more effective in killing bugs, but they are also much longer lasting and less biodegradable. DDT and compounds like it remain stable for many years after application. In addition, these substances accumulate in the fatty tissues of insects and fish, and then move up the food chain to affect higher animals. When consumed by human beings, these substances can cause serious health problems, such as cancer and birth defects. Furthermore, insects eventually build up immunity to pesticides, and these compounds become useless for the control of insects after a while.

The volume of synthetic organic chemicals produced in the world has skyrocketed in the past fifty years. In the United States alone, such production has grown from less than seven million tons in 1945 to over one hundred million tons today. There are currently seventy thousand such chemicals in daily use, with as many as one thousand new ones added each year. Although not all of these chemicals are harmful, many are, and with devastating consequences: The World Health Organization estimates that three million severe cases of pesticide poisoning occur each year, resulting in 20,000 deaths, mostly among farmers in developing nations (Dinham, 1993).

There are often alternatives to using chemicals as pesticides. One approach, known as *integrated pest management*, views a field of crops as an ecosystem in which natural forces can be used to control pests and weeds and thus enhance crop growth. This can be done by introducing natural predators of the pests or using genetic manipulations that result in pest-resistant crop varieties. This approach may not eliminate the use of chemicals, but it does focus on keeping their levels below the point at which significant crop damage and economic loss occur. A major barrier to the development of these programs is that it is generally cheaper for the private sector to use chemicals. There is no incentive for the private sector when the development of permanent biological control agents involves no marketable product. In addition, government policies in developing countries as well as in the United States tend to subsidize the use of chemical pesticides as a way to increase crop production.

Energy Resources

The affluent industrialized nations of the world consume an inordinate share of the world's energy, and the United States is among the largest consumers, per person, even among the industrial nations (see Figure 13.6). Most existing energy resources are finite. There is no question that they will eventually be exhausted; the only debate is over when this depletion will occur (Flavin and Durning, 1988). Most nations of the world are dependent on a few particular energy resources, primarily the fossil fuels: coal, petroleum, and natural gas. These fill 95 percent of the United States' energy needs, and the United States and other nations continue to place higher and higher demands on them.

Geologists have calculated that coal will be our longest lasting nonrenewable resource, with the earliest date of depletion occurring well into the twenty-first century. Although coal is an excellent ongoing energy resource, we must avoid becoming overly optimistic because the costs, both economic and social, of continuing to use it could be prohibitive. Economically, coal will become more costly to mine; and socially, the vast wastelands created by strip mining operations, increased air pollution, and deaths and injuries from the mining process itself provide further reasons for hesitancy. Although alternative sources of energy have been

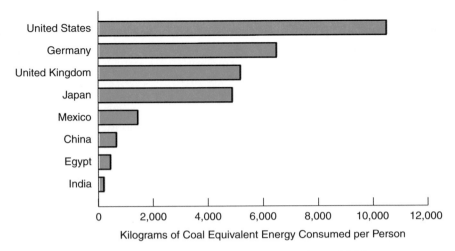

FIGURE 13.6 Energy Consumption Among Various Nations, 1992. Source: U.S. Bureau of the Census, *Statistical Abstract of the United States, 1994* (Washington, D.C.: U.S. Government Printing Office, 1995), pp. 868–869.

identified, some of these also have detrimental consequences for the environment. For example, the use of wood fuel instead of oil or gas seems like an excellent alternative because this resource is renewable. But widespread burning of wood leads to increased air pollution (Nero, 1988). We may actually be overlooking some alternative sources of energy, however. Various forms of garbage, for example, have been wasted for many years. It has been conservatively estimated that the United States could save up to two million barrels of oil every day by using garbage as a combustible fuel source (Brown, Flavin, and Postel, 1991).

Regarding nuclear energy, there are some very serious risks in using it: illness and death from radiation leakage, possible disaster from nuclear accidents, and the problem of disposing of nuclear wastes. The nuclear accident in Chernobyl in the former Soviet Union, where an explosion and fire destroyed part of a nuclear power plant and released radioactivity into the environment, illustrates the potential for disaster (Flavin, 1987). A number of people died in this accident, thousands of people had

to be evacuated permanently because of radiation leakage, and radioactive fallout was found over large parts of Europe. What is hard to predict is how many premature deaths from diseases such as cancer will occur over the next four decades because of people's exposure to radioactivity from the accident at Chernobyl.

Perhaps the most reasonable course of action involves the exploration of new energy sources, utilizing techniques that do not involve the risks and hazards that many previous strategies have entailed.

Future Prospects

In the preceding discussion, mention was made of some victories in the fight against environmental degradation, cases in which pollution has been reduced. Yet, most authorities agree that serious problems still confront the world. The victories so far may be the easy ones against clearcut and readily conquered threats. More difficult and complex battles may lie ahead. In fact, by the 1990s, many people in the United

States were stunned by the accumulating evidence of ecological damage. When asked in 1995 whether protection of the environment should be given priority even if that meant curbing economic growth, over six in ten people in the United States agreed (Gallup Poll, 1995). The same proportion of people labeled themselves "environmentalists." In addition, 83 percent of those surveyed believe that we can avoid major environmental disruptions only if we do more than we are currently doing to protect the environment. This base of substantial support for environmental causes has contributed to many significant developments to attack ecological decline.

Collective Action by Interest Groups

Collective action by the environmental groups discussed earlier in the chapter along with new groups that have emerged continues to be a significant source of pressure in the environmental realm. A well-established phalanx of large and well-funded environmental groups, including the World Wildlife Fund, the Environmental Defense Fund, the Natural Resources Defense Council, and others, is set to act. In Washington, D.C., and across the country, these groups lobby for environmental legislation and take polluters to court. Some environmentalists argue that these groups are too timid in that they disdain public demonstrations and civil disobedience as tactics to fight environmental issues. These established environmental groups also may be timid because they get significant support from the corporations that are major polluters. The World Wildlife Fund, for example, gets support from corporations such as Dow Chemical, Exxon, and Shell Oil. These environmentalists argue that the real passion in the movement today is at the grass-roots level where people organize, protest, and demonstrate to stop a toxic waste landfill or a waste incinerator from being placed in their community (Szasz, 1994). In fact, there are now national groups, such as the Citizens Clearinghouse for Haz-

ardous Wastes, that provide information and assistance to such grass-roots efforts. Although the established organizations tend to invest their energies in efforts to regulate the activities of polluters, the grass-roots organizations tend to shift toward the prevention of environmental problems by stopping pollution at its source.

At a global level, environmental interest groups such as Greenpeace have pressured corporations, nations, and the United Nations to reduce pollution and preserve the environment. They have been joined by the many non-governmental organizations (NGOs) described in Chapter 2. Pressures from NGOs and activists around the world have resulted in some environmentally destructive projects being canceled or changed to make them more environmentally sensitive.

These environmental groups have met opposition in the 1990s from numerous groups that believe that the environmental problems are not that great or that the proposed solutions go too far (Helvarg, 1994). The Wise Use Movement, for example, is a coalition of business interests and citizens whose goals are, as the movement's name implies, to promote the judicious use of resources in ways that do not unnecessarily hinder economic activity and growth but that also protect the environment from excessive damage. The movement has vigorously opposed environmental regulation in areas such as oil and gas exploration, the use of rangeland by cattle farmers, and the harvesting of timber in national forests. Needless to say, environmental interest groups loudly disagree with what the Wise Use proponents call "judicious" use of resources and "excessive" damage to the environment. Nonetheless, the environmental policies of the 1990s and beyond will be forged out of the clash between these various interest groups.

Moderating Economic Growth

Some environmental problems are created or made worse by the unrestrained pursuit of economic growth and short-term economic goals.

After all, many people have a vested interest in exploiting the environment with little concern for the long-term impact this might have. For example, many corporations and individuals around the world benefit when forests are cut down and therefore disregard the problems of deforestation and declining biological diversity discussed earlier. Lumber companies make a good profit and individuals have firewood to heat their homes and cook their food. If human populations were much smaller, the ecosystem might be able to sustain such activities; with overpopulation, however, such economic activity creates an imminent danger. Biologist Edward Wilson (1992) argues that it is in our long-term interests to switch to "extraction farming" in which the products of forests are harvested without harming the overall ecosystem. Some of this is being done, but short-term gain still propels many toward forestry practices that destroy ecosystems and annihilate species.

Some would argue that capitalism itself, especially if unrestrained, is inherently detrimental to the environment (Hawken, 1993). The reason for this is that capitalists thrive on continuous economic growth and the fact that profits can be enhanced by pursuing short-term goals. One solution is to regulate the activities of capitalists, and this is a major element of our environmental policy and will be discussed in the next section. A more radical question, which is addressed by only a few today, is whether individualism, profit seeking, and permanent growth can be reconciled with the limited resilience of our ecosystem to respond to the assaults on it. Will the products of our social and economic organization inevitably overwhelm the ability of the earth to recoup itself? All our policies assume that some form of restrained capitalism is compatible with protection of the environment.

Government Regulation

One of the major battlegrounds of environmental issues is the extent of government regulation that should be adopted. By the 1990s, laws and court rulings have placed limits on most of the pollution and degradation of the environment discussed in this chapter. The Endangered Species Act, for example, protects seven hundred plant and animal species from actions that might threaten their survival, and four thousand more are being considered for such protection (Mann and Plummer, 1995). The Clean Air Acts of 1970 and 1990 limited the amount of pollutants that automobiles, industries, and electric utilities can release into the environment.

This regulation is one of the cornerstones of U.S. environmental policies, but it also may have its limits as far as its ability to control further environmental pollution and degradation. One reason for this is that there are continuing battles over how far to extend that regulation. For example, new rulings in 1992 significantly relaxed the limitations of the Clean Air Act of 1990, allowing factories to exceed their limits without sanctions until the EPA reviews the case and tells them to stop. The factories do not even need to tell their neighbors that they are exceeding the limits. Overall, the Reagan-Bush years saw a weakening of environmental regulation. The Clinton administration has been more responsive to environmental concerns. A second reason that regulation may have its limits is that it can be costly. For example, one assessment of the costs of reducing air pollution in U.S. cities concluded that it may be so high that it is not worth it. The authors concluded that we might be better off investing our resources elsewhere: "In the health area alone, $10 billion invested in smoking cessation programs, radon control, better prenatal and neonatal health care, or similar measures might contribute much more to public health and well-being" than costly programs to reduce some types of air pollution (Krupnick and Portney, 1991: 526). This is not to suggest that regulation be abandoned but rather that its limits need to be recognized.

Another form of government regulation is to use the tax code to encourage businesses to operate in an environmentally sound manner. This might involve taxing a business if its business activities degrade the environment (Hawken, 1993). If a business emits pollutants, dumps wastes in a stream, or uses nonrenewable resources, it would be taxed for doing so. Proponents of such a plan argue that this would force businesses to pay for *all* the costs of doing business. Businesses would pay for environmental damage up front rather than passing the costs onto the taxpayer or future generations. This would increase the costs of doing business, and the increases would likely be passed on to the consumer. It would, however, give the consumer some control: They could choose to buy from companies that follow environmentally sound practices. In addition, it would give businesses an economic incentive to follow sound environmental practices. Such a plan could be truly effective, however, only if done on a global scale. If the United States acted alone, costs for its corporations to do business would be increased compared with their global competitors who were not doing likewise. The International Perspectives insert looks at some of the regulations imposed in other societies.

Environmental Partnerships

Another approach to attacking environmental problems that has emerged in the 1980s and 1990s is called "environmental partnerships," which involve voluntary collaborative efforts among a number of organizations that have a stake in environmental issues (Long and Arnold, 1995). The partners in such an effort might include corporations, government agencies, environmental interest groups, and landowners or other groups of people most directly affected by an environmental problem. The goal of the partnership is to identify an environmental problem and develop a solution that is acceptable to all the stakeholders. This is

a less coercive approach to finding ways of alleviating environmental problems than government regulation, and in some situations it offers more flexibility. Such partnerships have been used to develop plans to conserve energy by utility companies, eliminate chlorofluorocarbons, and protect salmon in the Pacific northwest. While such partnerships will probably not replace government regulation in the fight for a better environment, they have been useful in cases where regulation has been weak or ineffective, or, in some cases, in implementing regulations.

Radical environmentalists mistrust this approach because of the deep-seated belief that corporations tend to pursue their short-term interests in maximizing profits and to downplay the significance of environmental problems. And many advances could not have been achieved through environmental partnerships. Yet, as one prong of a many-pronged attack on environmental problems, they have proven their value.

Reduce, Reuse, Recycle

The most environmentally sensitive thing that a person can do is to consume fewer products. An automobile that is not purchased or a bottle of beer that is not bought produces no pollution. So, one key to attacking environmental problems is to reduce consumption. When people do consume, the focus should be on reusing and recycling what is consumed. Only recently have people in the United States become attentive to issues of reusing and recycling products (Pollock, 1987). In some locales, there are effective recycling programs, such as the one thousand or more aluminum reclamation centers in operation. Many cities also have paper collection programs, which lead to the successful reuse of such products. Forty-one percent of people in the United States claim that their community requires the recycling of some materials, and 86 percent claim that they voluntarily recycle materials (Hueber, 1991). Industry

INTERNATIONAL PERSPECTIVES
Environmental Practices and Policies in Other Societies

More so than most other problems discussed in this book, issues of population growth and environmental degradation are truly global in scope. This is so because all societies inhabit a single ecosystem in which significant pollution of one part of the system degrades the whole system. We can fight crime in Los Angeles without paying much heed to how much crime there is in Caracas, Venezuela, or New Delhi, India. However, we need to be concerned with fossil fuel consumption in all three cities because all contribute to the depletion of finite supplies of such fuels and to global air pollution and possibly global warming. If the greenhouse effect and global warming become the scourge that some scientists argue they can, societal boundaries will serve as no protection against their devastating effects.

When we look at societies around the world, considerable variation exists in terms of behaviors that contribute to environmental degradation and policies that reduce or prevent it. For example, Los Angeles opened its first stretch of subway (only a few miles long), and journalists are pondering whether residents of that city have become too wedded to their cars to begin using public transit. Why has the United States become so oriented toward the automobile whereas people in Finland, Japan, Brazil, and most other nations have not? Part of the answer to that is our affluence, of course, but other factors are equally important. For

one thing, we have designed our cities such that transportation without cars is difficult. Most cities in the United States are spread out, with places of work and school far away from where most people live. European cities, on the other hand, tend to be much more concentrated, which makes public transit less expensive and more feasible.

For another thing, we keep taxes on gasoline low, which encourages people to drive. In 1990, gasoline cost $1.04 per gallon in the United States, compared with $3.40 in France, $2.55 in the United Kingdom, $4.27 in Italy, and $3.05 in Japan. Seventy-five percent of the cost of gas in France, Britain, and Italy are taxes whereas only one-quarter of the cost in the United States goes to taxes. Italy has a $3.50 tax on gas, Germany $2, and Japan $1.50; by contrast, the United States extracts only $ .30 in taxes on each gallon of gas (Flavin and Lenssen, 1990). So, people in the United States drive rather than ride public transit in part because it is so inexpensive to do so.

The combination of affluence along with a lack of policies to discourage the use of fossil fuels means that the United States is one of their heaviest users. China, for example, burns the equivalent of sixteen hundred pounds of coal per person each year for its various energy needs; at the same time, Japan burns the equivalent of ten thousand pounds per person per year, and the United States burns an astounding twenty-three thousand pounds—thir-

in the United States has also made significant strides in recycling water. In the past thirty years, the number of times that each cubic meter of water is used by industry before it is discarded has risen from 1.8 to 8.6 (Postel, 1986). Recycling water has become more attractive to industry as pollution regulations have become more stringent: In many cases, it is cheaper to reuse water a number of times in a plant than to treat it sufficiently to meet environmental regu-

lations and release it as wastewater. If strong environmental pollution regulations are maintained, by the year 2000, industry as a whole may reuse water as many as seventeen times before releasing it as wastewater. If this happens, manufacturing industries will use 45 percent less water than twenty years earlier, and the pressure on the water supply will be eased.

However, many environmentalists argue that current efforts in this realm are haphazard teen times what China consumes for each person and two and a half times what even Japan, another industrialized and affluent nation, consumes (see Figure 13.6). With less than 5 percent of the world's population, the United States produces almost one-quarter of the world's carbon dioxide emissions, the most important component of gases causing the greenhouse effect (Nasar, 1992).

One policy that could help reduce the use of fossil fuels and the amount of air pollution would be a tax on the use of energy. There are two justifications for this. One is that societies can change people's behaviors by making it more costly for them to do things that use up scarce resources or pollute the environment. Protection of resources and the environment is in everyone's interest. The second justification is that those producing the pollution—namely, users of a polluting energy source—should pay taxes to help pay for the damage to the environment and to people's health caused by the pollution. One approach to such a policy is to place a substantial tax on gasoline to discourage its use, as we have seen many other nations do. This would encourage people to use mass transit and to build communities that are not dependent on automobiles for transportation. Another approach would be to tax energy sources that produce more carbon dioxide emissions, the major culprit in the greenhouse problem. Coal would be taxed the heaviest, followed by oil and then natural gas; nuclear power and renewable energy sources could go untaxed under such a policy since they release no carbon dioxide. Finland, Denmark, and Sweden already have such taxes and many other European nations are considering them (Flavin and Lenssen, 1990). Such a carbon tax was considered by the Clinton administration, but never implemented.

Many European nations have other so-called "green taxes" on such things as air and water pollution, waste, and noise. Norway has a tax on fertilizers and pesticides. However, many of these taxes are too low to change significantly people's behavior, although they do raise revenues to support important environmental programs. Vice President Al Gore in his 1992 book, *Earth in the Balance,* makes a strong case for such "green taxes" in the United States as an important element in the battle to protect the environment.

The policies in many societies other than the United States reflect an interventionist stance: The government uses its various powers to shape behaviors that conserve resources and protect against environmental degradation. Policy in the United States, on the other hand, has placed a greater emphasis on the laissez-faire position: The government should step back and let the marketplace determine the amounts and types of energy that are used.

and much less effective than they could be. Much more could be done. For example, the recycling of materials and products could be considered in the design and production stages, and few things would be manufactured that could not be reused. Denmark has banned throwaway beverage containers, and in the Canadian province of Ontario almost all beer is sold in standardized refillable bottles (Brown, Flavin, and Postel, 1991; Brown, 1992). In both places, the containers produced are standardized and sturdy, which makes their reuse easy and inexpensive. Of course, national legislation and enforcement would be necessary to make such a plan work. Such policies might be appealing to the interventionist but anathema to the laissez-faire forces. Nevertheless, the idea is an attractive one, because the costs of maintaining the environment would be absorbed by those doing the manufacturing rather than by

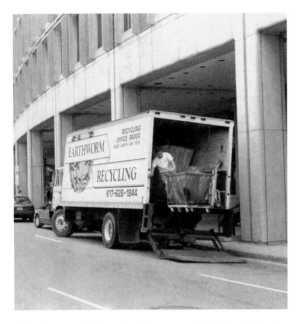

Only in recent decades have people in the United States become attentive to issues of reusing and recycling products. Today 86 percent of people in the United States say they recycle some materials they use.

the general public. This might encourage manufacturing interests to be sensitive to recycling and reuse concerns in order to maximize their profits.

Renewable Energy Resources

Since the industrial revolution, the United States' quest for energy has focused on finite resources, such as coal, oil, and nuclear fission. All of these energy sources are exhaustible. Renewable energy resources, on the other hand, have no inherent limit on how long humans can exploit them (Shea, 1988). Solar energy is perhaps the best example of a virtually inexhaustible resource. It can be used to produce two very important types of energy: heat and electrical power. Wood and vegetable fuels are two energy resources that have been frequently overlooked

in industrialized nations. Unlike coal, wood can be replaced through reforestation. Vegetable matter can be burned, converted into methane or alcohol, or processed into fuel cells that produce electrical energy. Other sources of renewable energy are water power, wind power, and geothermal energy (terrestrial heat). In the 1970s, the government encouraged the development of some renewable energy resources by requiring utilities to use some renewables in electricity generation to get large contracts. By the 1990s, however, declining oil and gas prices along with a less favorable political climate in Washington had deflated much of the enthusiasm for such efforts, and the required use of renewables has been dropped.

International Cooperation

Environmental problems are clearly global in nature. What happens on one part of the earth is likely to have an impact on people elsewhere. Because of this, much attention has been directed in the past two decades to international cooperation as a way to control environmental problems (Fleagle, 1994). From 1972, when the United Nations Conference on the Human Environment was held in Stockholm, to 1992, when the Earth Summit was held in Brazil, a steady record of international agreements and policies to protect the environment has been established. For example, in 1990, an international accord to phase out the production of ozone-depleting CFCs by the end of the twentieth century was signed. That same year, twenty-three nations agreed to freeze or reduce levels of carbon emissions in an effort to attack the problem of global warming. In 1994, most nations of the world signed the Convention on Biological Diversity which commits each nation to finding strategies for protecting the plants, animals, and microorganisms, and their habitats, within its borders.

Despite progress, many of the goals of these international agreements remain unmet. The wealthy nations of the world have not come forward with the funds they had committed to fight environmental problems. Many nations are still inclined to pursue their own short-term interests. The international accords are important, however, because they create an international climate that pressures nations to do more about these problems than they would be inclined to do on their own. In addition, the accords recognize that solving environmental problems must be a united, world-wide effort if it is to succeed.

New Cultural Values and Social Institutions

Throughout this chapter, the importance of values in environmental issues has been em-phasized. In fact, some new cultural values have appeared that may have important implications in these realms. Some values related to environmental problems derive from the Western Judeo-Christian heritage, discussed earlier in the chapter, that emphasizes the desirability of procreation and the mastery of human beings over the earth. The conventional environmental ideology that has emerged in the past three decades is in sharp contrast with this view. This environmental ideology emphasizes that human beings should live in harmony with their environment rather than "mastering" or "ruling over" it; that people should serve as stewards who protect and conserve the environment so that it will be available for future

Wind is a renewable resource that is being used in many locales to generate electricity, such as in this field in California.

generations to use. A key notion that many environmentalists use today is "sustainability": "A sustainable society is one that satisfies its needs without jeopardizing the prospects of future generations" (Brown, Flavin, and Postel, 1991: 30–31). Attaining sustainability may call for some groups to moderate their needs. Modifications in one or more elements of the "I = P × A × T" formula mentioned earlier may be called for: reducing Populations, accepting a less Affluent standard of living, and using a more simple and less polluting Technology.

Some environmentalists take a more radical stance than this. For example, the following quotation is taken from a public information bulletin published by Greenpeace:

> Ecology teaches us that humankind is not the center of life on the planet. Ecology has taught us that the whole earth is part of our "body" and that we must learn to respect it as we respect life—the whales, the seals, the forests, the seas. The tremendous beauty of ecological thought is that it shows us a pathway back to an understanding and appreciation of life itself—an understanding and appreciation that is imperative to that very way of life. (Simon, 1981: 335)

This philosophy, called "deep ecology" or "biocentrism," is based on the following principles (Sessions, 1995):

- All life on earth, both human and nonhuman, has equal value, and humans have a right to destroy life forms only to meet *vital* needs.
- Given the size of human populations and the technology currently available to them in industrial societies, humans have become destructively intrusive in the earth's ecosystem and substantial population reduction is called for.
- To come into harmony with the environment, human economic, political, and social structures need to be changed so that they shift emphasis from stressing growth, bigness, and material wealth to valuing smallness, spirituality, and the nonmaterial quality of life.

Clearly, deep ecologists are calling for a radical change in people's way of life. In fact, one of these groups, called Earth First!, has resorted to action in its effort to protect the earth. Some members of Earth First! were arrested in 1989 for attempting to blow up a tower carrying high-voltage power lines to a massive irrigation project in Arizona (Robbins, 1989). In their view, human activities have become so destructive to the earth, and protecting the earth is of sufficiently high value, that the use of violence is warranted, even if it means the destruction of human property and maybe even human lives.

Although the deep ecologists (and certainly groups such as Earth First!) take a more extreme stand than most people would feel comfortable with, they do suggest that permanent solutions to environmental problems may require a change in traditional cultural values and social institutions. If we retain the biblical ideology of human mastery and domination over the earth, we may be unwilling to take extreme measures when they are warranted. In addition,

LINKAGES

Environmental problems can be intensified when technology becomes more complex and intrusive (Chapter 15) or when there are few restraints on the profit-seeking activities of large and unresponsive corporations (Chapter 2).

we need to consider the possibility that industrial capitalism is at least part of the problem. When profits can be made by polluting the air or destroying the forests, then the unhindered operation of capitalist mechanisms such as free enterprise, competition, and profit making may destroy the environment beyond repair. It may be necessary to take a significantly interventionist stance, with the government enforcing some higher values that emphasize the protection of the environment. In fact, as we have seen, this is already happening to a degree

Environmental Policy

How should the United States approach environmental problems? Government intervention with regard to environmental issues is linked to various political and economic considerations. For example, concerns over air pollution in the United States' major cities have reached crisis proportions. For example, the air in Los Angeles is the dirtiest in the nation. The state's South Coast Air Quality Management District (AQMD) has developed a twenty-year pollution control strategy that conservative estimates indicate will cost almost $3 billion annually (Weisman, 1989). The AQMD's proposal has serious implications for citizens' fundamental decisions regarding where they will live, how they will live, and how they will travel. The plan calls for some very drastic measures. For example, people living in the district would no longer be able to use barbecue lighter fluid; businesses such as dry cleaning establishments, auto painting shops, and even bakeries would be required to switch to less polluting but much more costly techniques and install elaborate antipollution devices in their operations, costing enormous sums of money. Drivers would eventually be required to use car fuels other than gasoline, so it would cost more to operate their vehicles. Furthermore, commuters would be compelled by law to carpool—a suggestion that has been met with predictably enormous protest by residents who have become accustomed to travelling to and from work in their private automobiles. The plan might even place a limit on the number of cars a family would be allowed to own.

Problems involving the pollution of our environment pose a frustrating "Catch 22": A laissez-faire approach appears to be disastrous for the environment. On the other hand, to what extent does government intervention interfere or even directly conflict with citizens' individual rights? At what point does the intrusiveness of government intervention become worse than the pollution it is intended to control? Clearly, the solutions that we arrive at in the realm of environmental problems will be a product of the laissez-faire/interventionist debate.

LAISSEZ-FAIRE INTERVENTIONIST DEBATE

(see the *Laissez-Faire Interventionist Debate*). The controversy today is over how much further down this road it will be necessary to go to achieve environmental goals.

Summary

1. Modern biology views the world as an ecosystem, and at the core of environmental problems is the issue of the extent to which human activities have changed the ecosystem with severely detrimental consequences.

2. The functionalist perspective views the ecosystem in terms of the interdependence among the land, air, water, people, and other resources in it; problems arise when changes in the ecosystem produce social disorganization or dysfunctional consequences. The conflict perspective sees environmental problems in terms of groups having competing interests in terms of how the environment is to be used; pollution becomes a problem when a group with some power feels that its interests are not being served. The interactionist perspective stresses the importance of social definitions and subjective assessments of reality rather than the objective amount of pollution or degradation of the environment.

3. The key social and cultural conditions that contribute to environmental problems are population growth, affluence, technology, economic growth, and cultural values.

4. According to the interactionist perspective, environmental problems do not exist as social problems until people identify and define them as such. This social construction happens as the media, influential people, and the government publicize the problems and enact social policies.

5. The major environmental problems discussed in the text are water supply and pollution, solid and toxic wastes, nuclear wastes, land degradation, declines in biodiversity, air pollution, pesticides and other chemicals, and energy resources.

6. Collective action by various interest groups will be a key to how environmental problems are handled in the future. Other efforts to alleviate environmental problems have focused on moderating economic growth, using government regulation, using environmental partnerships, recycling, developing renewable energy resources, and international cooperation and treaties.

7. Successfully alleviating environmental problems may call for the emergence of new cultural values that emphasize living in harmony with the environment and conserving resources rather than mastery over the earth.

STUDY A N D *Review*

Key Terms

carrying capacity

ecology

ecosystem

environment

hydrologic cycle

photosynthesis

Multiple-Choice Questions

1. _____ refers to the conditions and circumstances surrounding and affecting a particular group of living creatures.
  a. Ecology.
  b. Fecundity.

c.   Biosphere.
d.   Demography.
e.   Environment.

2. The concept of _____ helps us to understand that all parts of the environment interact with one another and are dependent on one another.
   a.   An ecosystem.
   b.   A demographic gap.
   c.   Economic growth.
   d.   Demography.
   e.   Manifest functions.

3. In looking at environmental problems, the functionalist perspective would focus most directly on:
   a.   The competing environmental goals of various interest groups.
   b.   The interdependence of the land, air, water, people, and other resources in an ecosystem.
   c.   How the successful wielding of power determines the outcome of environmental conflicts.
   d.   The importance of social definitions and subjective assessments of environmental problems.

4. In the formula "I = P × A × T", the "A" stands for:
   a.   Alterations in the environment.
   b.   Aspirations of people.
   c.   Affluence of people.
   d.   Age structure of a society.

5. Which of the following is one of the oldest environmental interest groups?
   a.   Sierra Club.
   b.   Greenpeace.
   c.   Environmental Defense Fund.
   d.   World Wildlife Fund.
   e.   Natural Resources Defense Council.

6. The hydrologic cycle has to do most directly with which of the following environmental problems?
   a.   Depletion of energy resources.
   b.   Declining biodiversity.
   c.   Land degradation.
   d.   Water pollution.

7. All of the following were problems associated with the disposal of nuclear wastes *except:*
   a.   The wastes remain deadly for thousands of years.
   b.   The NIMBY syndrome.

c.   The wastes encourage eutrophication.
d.   Transportation of the wastes is risky.

8. The main problem with chlorofluorocarbons (CFCs) is that they:
   a.   Destroy ozone.
   b.   Increase the greenhouse effect.
   c.   Reduce eutrophication.
   d.   Increase deforestation.
   e.   Inhibit photosynthesis.

9. Some critics argue that capitalism is detrimental to the environment because:
   a.   Capitalism pursues biocentrism.
   b.   Capitalism thrives on economic growth.
   c.   Capitalism supports the ecosystem.
   d.   Capitalism discourages economic growth.
   e.   Capitalism ignores short-term goals in favor of long-term gain.

10. Environmental policy in the United States has tended to:
   a.   Stress the interventionist approach more than European nations have.
   b.   Stress the laissez-faire approach more than European nations have.
   c.   Stress the functionalist approach more than European nations have.
   d.   Stress the conflict approach more than European nations have.

True/False Questions

1. The Judeo-Christian heritage in Western cultures stresses that human beings should live in harmony with their environment.

2. For the functionalist perspective, human cultural beliefs and values are an important part of the ecosystem.

3. The carrying capacity of an ecosystem can be exceeded occasionally but not permanently.

4. Premodern peoples generally lived in harmony with the environment and avoided practices that were destructive to the environment.

5. The National Environmental Policy Act (NEPA) was passed in the late nineteenth century to preserve wilderness areas in the United States for people to use.

6. Acid rain is produced by the leaking of nuclear wastes into the atmosphere.

7. The amount of municipal garbage generated in the United States has more than doubled in the last three decades.

8. Chemical products is the industry that releases the largest amount of toxic wastes into the environment.
9. The influence wielded by interest groups in the United States working to protect the environment has declined since the 1970s.
10. Environmental partnerships are a less coercive approach to environmental problems than is government regulation.

Fill-In Questions

1. The process by which plants capture light and heat energy from the sun and turn it into food is called _____ .

2. According to the _____ perspective, the manner in which the environment is used emerges out of a competition among groups with varying amounts of power.

3. The carrying capacity of an ecosystem depends in part on levels of affluence and levels of _____ .

4. _____ refers to the spread of deserts as a consequence of intensive food production on land.

5. Declining _____ refers to the elimination of species at a rate greater than expected by normal evolutionary development.

6. The _____ is the heating of the atmosphere because carbon dioxide prevents solar radiation from escaping back into space.

7. _____ uses natural predators rather than pesticides to control pests and weeds in agriculture.

8. _____ are voluntary collaborative efforts to solve environmental problems by a number of organizations that have a stake in the issue.

9. List two kinds of renewable energy resources: _____ and _____ .

10. The philosophy of _____ argues that all life on earth has equal value.

Matching Questions

_____ 1. eutrophication

_____ 2. toxic wastes

_____ 3. branch of biology

_____ 4. economic growth

_____ 5. Western cultural value

_____ 6. Paul Ehrlich

_____ 7. Barry Commoner

_____ 8. EPA

_____ 9. DDT

_____ 10. sustainability

A. ecology
B. population growth causes pollution
C. Love Canal
D. pesticide
E. mastery over the environment
F. key notion of environmentalists
G. growing amount of goods and services
H. Lake Erie
I. government agency
J. corporations cause pollution

Essay Questions

1. Describe the concepts that are important to understanding how modern biologists explain the world and how it operates.
2. Compare and contrast the functionalist and conflict views on environmental problems.
3. What is the impact of economic growth and cultural values on environmental problems?
4. Describe the process of the social construction of environmental problems.
5. What is acid rain? How is it produced? What can be done about it?
6. What are the sources of nuclear wastes? What problems do they present us with?
7. What is the problem of declining biodiversity? Why is it a problem?
8. Assess the greenhouse effect. What is it? How much of a problem is it? What can be done about it?

9. Describe the kinds of government regulation that have been enacted or proposed to control environmental problems. How well do they work?

10. What kind of environmental policies or practices in other nations were described that might be considered for the United States?

Answers

Multiple-Choice

1. E; **2.** A; **3.** B; **4.** C; **5.** A; **6** D; **7.** C; **8.** A; **9.** B; **10.** B

True/False

1. F; **2.** T; **3.** T; **4.** F; **5.** F; **6.** F; **7.** T; **8.** T; **9.** F; **10.** T

Fill-In

1. photosynthesis
2. conflict
3. technology
4. desertification
5. biodiversity
6. greenhouse effect
7. integrated pest management
8. environmental partnerships
9. solar, wood, wind, water power, geothermal
10. deep ecology or biocentrism

Matching

1. H; **2.** C; **3.** A; **4.** G; **5.** E; **6.** B; **7.** J; **8.** I; **9.** D; **10.** F

For Further Reading

Murray Bookchin. *Remaking Society: Pathways to a Green Future.* South End Press, 1990. Bookchin places a good portion of the blame for our environmental problems at the doorstep of capitalism and its demand for economic expansion. He also argues that our tendency to create hierarchies in society is responsible for the inclination of humans to dominate nature.

Michael D'Antonio. *Atomic Harvest: Hanford and the Lethal Toll of America's Nuclear Arsenal.* New York: Crown, 1993. This is an engaging and informative book documenting the dreaded environmental pollution, and the human stories behind it, that resulted from the production and storage of weapons during the Cold War.

Irene Diamond and Gloria Feman Orenstein. *Reweaving the World: The Emergence of Ecofeminism.* San Francisco: Sierra Club Books, 1990. The articles in this anthology argue that feminist thought contains within it an ideology that would be supportive of protecting the environment. It argues that the persistence of patriarchy is partly at fault for our continuing despoliation of the world.

Susanna Hecht and Alexander Cockburn. *The Fate of the Forest: Developers, Destroyers, and Defenders of the Amazon.* New York: Verso, 1989. This is a very partisan book about the politics and the greed that will ultimately determine the fate of the Amazon rain forest. Many ecologists fear that, if the forest is destroyed, it will have a severe impact on worldwide climate and environment.

Huey D. Johnson. *Green Plans: Greenprint for Sustainability.* Lincoln: University of Nebraska Press, 1995. "Green plans" are comprehensive strategies for protecting and sustaining the environment. This book describes the green plans being developed and implemented in many nations around the world.

Jim MacNeill, Pieter Winsemius, and Taizo Yakushiji. *Beyond Interdependence: The Meshing of the World's Economy and the Earth's Ecology.* New York: Oxford University Press, 1991. This book argues not only that the economies of the world are interdependent but also that we are all ecologically interdependent. Implications for public policy and economic activities around the world are discussed.

Donella H. Meadows, Dennis L. Meadows, and Jorgen Randers. *Beyond the Limits: Confronting Global Collapse, Envisioning a Sustainable Future.* Post Mills, Vt.: Chelsea Green Pub. Co., 1992. This is a recent assessment by the same scientists who conducted the study for the Club of Rome twenty years ago. Their conclusions are a little more optimistic now, but only if there are changes in both lifestyle and technology.

Rik Scarce. *Eco-Warriors: Understanding the Radical Environmental Movement.* Chicago: Noble Press, 1990. Although much of this book focuses on the group Earth First! discussed toward the end of the chapter, it does discuss the other important radical environmental groups around the world. The book provides detail and insight about the global environmental movement.

Philip Shabecoff. *A Fierce Green Fire: The American Environmental Movement.* New York: Hill and Wang, 1992. This is a good and engrossing history of the environmental movement in the United States. It divides the movement into three waves, with the first around 1900 and the third commencing in the last few years.

CHAPTER

FOURTEEN *Violence, War, and Terrorism*

The central concern of this chapter is **violence:** *behavior that is intended to bring pain or physical injury to another person or to harm or destroy property.* Actually, the topic of violence has been addressed at numerous points in this book. Criminal violence such as homicide and assault is discussed in Chapter 9, and family violence such as spouse and child abuse is analyzed in Chapters 3 and 8. In those contexts, however, the focus was not violence itself. Rather, what is being analyzed is the crime problem (whether or not the crime took a violent form) and family problems (which come in both violent and nonviolent manifestations). Yet the number of times the issue of violence is taken up while discussing various social problems suggests how pervasive violence is in human beings' lives. In fact, it is sufficiently widespread to warrant discussion as a problem in its own right. In addition to family violence and violent crime, terrorists kidnap, maim, and murder people; mobs riot in the streets and loot stores; citizens take up arms and attack their governments;

and nations go to war against one another, sometimes in an orgy of death and destruction.

A major goal of this chapter is to identify the factors—social, psychological, and biological—that contribute to the extent and variety of human violence. First the chapter looks at the extent of violence in the world, giving special emphasis to violence in the United States because this has the most direct bearing for most readers of this book. Then, a search for possible sources of this violence will be undertaken, including what insight the sociological perspectives can shed on this issue. Last, some of the consequences of violence for society will be explored before looking at what can be done to alleviate these problems.

The Extent of Violence

To appreciate the extent of violence in the world today, all one need do is read the daily newspaper. The number of violent incidents and the number of people involved are frightening. Not all violence is the same, of course. Much of the violence described in other chapters, such as crime and spouse abuse, is called *interpersonal violence:* It involves a relatively small number of people who are responding to the stresses of a particular situation or who are pursuing their own personal gains. We have offered explanations for these types of violence elsewhere in this book. In this section, we will describe the extent of *collective violence,* which involves organized violence be relatively large groups of people to promote or resist some social policies or practices.

Civil Disorders

The United States has been fortunate to have had a fairly stable government and society over the past two hundred years. Yet there have been periodic upheavals involving violent clashes between opposing groups in the United States. The term **civil disorder** refers to *strife or conflict that is threatening to the public order and that involves the government in some fashion, either as a party to the conflict or as a guardian of the public interest* (Himes, 1980).

Some civil disorders are relatively unorganized and have vague or short-term goals, such as race riots or labor conflicts. Other episodes of civil strife are quite organized and may threaten basic changes in the foundations of the social order, such as civil war or revolution. How extensive has civil disorder been in the United States? It is impossible to tabulate all such events, but there are ways to gain a sense of the magnitude of the problem. Sheldon Levy (1969) tabulated the number of politically violent events in the United States from 1819 to 1968. He found that the rate at which such events occur fluctuates from year to year, but there is no long-term trend. In fact, although one might expect the decade of the 1960s to be especially violent because of civil rights activities and antiwar riots, other decades approach or surpass that era in violence—the 1880s, for example, when labor strife was widespread. So civil disorder has been quite common throughout our history. We can gain a better sense of it by illustrating some of the different types of civil disorder that have occurred.

Much civil disorder in the United States has arisen out of racial conflict. As long ago as the eighteenth century, mobs of white people, motivated by a fear that black slaves might revolt against their owners, viciously attacked blacks in the streets of cities such as New York. Some slaves were hanged, whereas others were driven out of the city. The abolition of slavery did not quell racial violence. In the final twenty years of the nineteenth century, nearly two thousand blacks were killed by lynch mobs in the South. In this century, many cities in the United States, both large and small, have experienced severe race riots, virtually always involving black–white clashes. In the early part of the century, the riots were sparked when blacks began to move into white neighborhoods or to use recreational areas that were previously used

Myths & FACTS

ABOUT VIOLENCE AND WAR

Myth: The United States is a peaceful nation that has been in the forefront of efforts to stop wars around the world.

FACT: Statistics show that the United States is one of the more "war-prone" nations in the world: In addition to the declared wars in which we have been involved, troops from the United States have been sent abroad for military purposes by the president an average of at least once a year. In the last twenty-five years, the government of the United States has actively supported efforts to overthrow governments in Cuba, the Dominican Republic, Angola, Grenada, and Nicaragua.

Myth: Over the past two hundred years, people in the United States have been exposed to increasing levels of violence in the form of riots, labor strife, and racial conflict.

FACT: Although the number of such events has risen over the years, the rate of such violence has not increased considering the growing population, although violence does fluctuate substantially from one period to the next. Even the decade of the 1960s, which is viewed as extremely violent because of the conjunction of

civil rights activities with protest against the Vietnam War and riots among university students, is not extraordinary: Other decades, such as the 1880s and the 1900s when labor violence was prominent, approach or surpass the 1960s in violence.

Myth: In the race riots in cities in the United States in the past thirty years, the rioters have been the criminals, the unemployed, the idle, and the poor.

FACT: Although such people certainly played a part, the people arrested for rioting have also included employed, educated, and seemingly law-abiding citizens.

Myth: Entertaining television shows and movies that contain some violence, such as *MacGyver,* the *Terminator,* or *Lethal Weapon,* do not harm young people who watch them as long as the shows are clearly fictional and fanciful.

FACT: Overwhelming research evidence concludes that young people, especially males, who watch violent shows on television are more likely to behave aggressively or violently themselves.

---

only by whites. These **communal riots** typically began when *whites attacked blacks in the racially contested areas* (Janowitz, 1969). The Detroit riot in 1943, for example, began on Belle Isle Park, a public beach (Miller, 1985). Detroit, like many northern cities of the period, had for decades been experiencing a large influx of blacks from the South. Frictions arose as the growing population of blacks spilled over into previously all-white areas. The riot lasted only twenty-four hours, but thirty-four people were killed (mostly blacks) and more than one thou-

sand were injured. Almost two thousand people were arrested and $2 million in property damage occurred.

Since World War II, most race riots in the United States have been **commodity riots,** in which *the focus of hostility is property, merchandise, or equipment rather than people of another racial group.* These riots have occurred in neighborhoods that had been inhabited mostly by African Americans for some time rather than in areas of racial transition or contest. Although police officers or whites who wander into the neighborhood might be attacked, the focus of mobs' attention is on looting merchandise and burning buildings, usually those owned by people who do not live in the community. Most deaths and injuries arise from the efforts of police or the National Guard to quell the riot. Riots of this sort occurred in many U.S. cities in the 1960s during the struggle over civil rights (Button, 1978). In the 1980s, the Liberty City area of Miami exploded into commodity riots several times. Then, in 1992, there was a severe riot in South Central Los Angeles in response to the acquittal of four police officers in the beating of an African-American motorist. These race riots in the 1980s and 1990s are disturbing evidence that the potential for such destructive outbursts is still present in the United States. (This issue is discussed in more detail in the Applied Research insert in this chapter.)

Labor strife has been another significant source of civil disorder in the United States. This was particularly true from 1880 to the 1930s, as working people struggled hard to establish the principle of collective bargaining as a basis for governing worker–employer relationships. Before collective bargaining was legalized, it was illegal for workers to conspire to stop work at a factory or business. This obviously left enormous power in the hands of the business managers and owners who could simply fire individual workers who resisted their demands or complained about wages or working conditions. In the late 1800s and early 1900s, new power and authority relations were being forged between workers and industrial managers as the United States industrialized. Violence was sometimes a key ingredient in shaping these new social relations. In 1897 in eastern Pennsylvania, for example, miners in the anthracite coal fields walked off the job, protesting low wages and dangerous working conditions. They were well aware that hundreds of coal miners were killed in accidents each year in the region. These were not unionized miners; they were a disorganized group of immigrants from Eastern Europe—many could

speak little English—who were weary of being bruised, broken, and seeing their companions killed while working. At one point, a posse confronted a group of the strikers in a town called Lattimer and gunfire roared. Nineteen miners were killed and another thirty-nine wounded (Novak, 1978). Fifteen years later, miners in Colorado went on strike against the Colorado Fuel and Iron Company, which would not recognize the workers' right to unionize. The strikers lived in a tent city in Ludlow. On April 20, 1914, National Guard troops attacked the tent colony and burned it to the ground. In the holocaust, which became known as the Ludlow Massacre, five men, twelve children, and two women died. Before the strike was over, seventy-four in all would lose their lives (Taft and Ross, 1969).

Lattimer and Ludlow are hardly household words today. Yet they were key links in the forging of a new industrial order. These incidents illustrate the extent to which labor violence has been a common outgrowth of the industrialization process. Today, labor relations are considerably more peaceful because workers have many rights that they did not possess in the past and there are strong pressures on both sides to restrain the violent use of force. However, violence still may accompany labor strikes when strikers attack those crossing picket lines. At the same time, deaths have become rare in labor strife.

Political Violence

The race riots and labor violence just discussed have, for the most part, not been organized efforts to change the basic political and economic institutions of the United States. Instead, they were usually somewhat spontaneous attempts to improve the circumstances and opportunities of some disadvantaged groups within existing social and economic arrangements. At times, however, groups have resorted to violence as a means of changing the government or economy. One form that this can take is

insurrection: *an organized action by some group to rebel against the existing government and to replace it with new political forms and leadership.* Although the United States has been relatively free of serious insurrectionary threats to the central government in Washington, such political violence has sometimes occurred.

The independence of the United States, of course, was forged in an insurrection against England in 1776. And by the accounts of most historians, it was a nasty and vicious encounter:

> The meanest and most squalid sort of violence was . . . put to the Service of Revolutionary ideals and objectives. The operational philosophy that the end justifies the means became the keynote of revolutionary violence. (Brown, 1969: 47)

There were bloody crashes between insurrectionists and British soldiers while the Continental and British armies maneuvered for position. Revolutionary colonists conducted savage guerrilla forays against the British, a tactic considered quite disgusting by the armies of the time. People supporting the revolution even attacked other colonists, called Tories, who wished to remain part of the British colony.

Once the independence of the United States was established, the most serious insurrection the nation faced was, of course, the Civil War, the effort of the southern states to secede from the Union (Leckie, 1990). Although the 1860 election of President Abraham Lincoln, an avowed opponent of slavery, played an important part in precipitating the Civil War, its exact causes have been debated at length by scholars and historians. Nonetheless, it was without question the most catastrophic military clash to occur within our boundaries. There was tremendous loss of life and destruction of property in battle; anger and resentment grew in both the North and the South between people on opposite sides of the issue, with violent confrontations occurring in cities such as New York and Baltimore; tensions and hostilities between the regions lingered for many decades after the war was over and served as a continuing catalyst for violence.

Beyond the Revolutionary War and the Civil War, insurrections in the United States have been relatively small and less threatening. Shortly after the American Revolution, for example, there were a number of insurrections involving battles over land and taxes, such as Shays' Rebellion in Massachusetts in the 1780s and the Whiskey Rebellion in Pennsylvania in the 1790s. Somewhat later, Dorr's Rebellion in the 1840s was an attempt by a group of dissidents in Rhode Island to gain the right for all men (although not women) to vote. The turmoil of the 1960s spawned a number of insurrectionary groups, such as the Black Liberation Army and the Weather Underground. Although bothersome, these more recent insurrectionary groups have gained little public support and have produced little political or economic change in the United States.

War

Most people in the United States probably think of their nation as powerful but also as peaceful and not aggressive. Yet political scientists J. David Singer and Melvin Small (1972) concluded from their research that the United States is among the more "war-prone" nations in the world. Between 1816 and 1965, they calculate, the United States has been involved in six wars, not counting the Indian wars and the Vietnam War. Between 1798 and 1945, U.S. troops have been sent abroad for military purposes by the president, without the approval of Congress, 163 times—an average of more than once a year (Pinkney, 1972; Leckie, 1992). The United States invaded Nicaragua twenty times (*before* that nation was an ally of the former Soviet Union), and U.S. troops once occupied Mexico City. At home, the Indian wars were particularly brutal affairs. They involved many campaigns by whites to force Indians from lands sought after by white settlers. If Indians refused to sign treaties and peacefully move to reservations, the army was called in to force the issue. Along the way, practically all lands were taken from the Indians and their lifestyle was irrevocably destroyed. Some have called our policies toward the Indians genocide, because the result was to destroy almost completely native Americans as a separate race (see Chapter 6).

Most people view four of the major wars of this century—World War I, World War II, the Korean War, and the Persian Gulf War—as justified on the grounds that the United States was helping to repel aggression or protect freedom. Yet the cost in casualties was high, and the decimation of civilian populations was much greater than in earlier wars based on a simpler technology (see Table 14.1). The discovery of air flight, for example, made possible the aerial bombing of not only enemy troop concentrations but also cities and towns. One particularly devastating instance of the latter was the saturation bombing of Dresden, Germany, during World War II in which an estimated 135,000 civilians were killed, mainly by asphyxiation and burning. Discoveries in physics led to the development of the atomic bomb, which resulted in the deaths of almost two hundred thousand people at Hiroshima and Nagasaki in 1945. Overall, World War II resulted in thirty million deaths among military combatants and civilians worldwide.

In 1965, U.S. troops landed in the Dominican Republic to forestall what was thought to be an imminent communist takeover of that country. Between 1965 and 1975, the United States was mired in the Vietnam conflict. More recently, the United States briefly entered the civil war in Lebanon and invaded the Caribbean island of Grenada. In 1989, the United States invaded Panama to oust dictator Manuel Noriega following attacks on U.S. military personnel stationed in Panama. In 1991, an international force used Saudi Arabia as a base from which to throw Iraqi aggressors out of Kuwait in the Persian Gulf War. This international army had many nations represented, but it was created at the instigation of the United States and consisted mostly of U.S. troops. Meanwhile, the United States stockpiles an arsenal of nuclear weapons that could rain death and destruction on the earth.

Many of these war activities were not a reaction to a threatened attack on or invasion of the United States. Rather the United States has mostly been sending troops around the world to

TABLE 14.1 United States' Casualties in Major Wars

War	Battle Deaths	Wounded	Veterans Receiving Disability Compensation, 1994
Civil War	140,000	282,000	
World War I	53,000	204,000	1,000
World War II	292,000	671,000	731,000
Korean conflict	34,000	103,000	195,000
Vietnam conflict	47,000	153,000	694,000

Source: U.S. Bureau of the Census, *Statistical Abstract of the United States, 1995,* (Washington, D.C.: U.S. Government Printing Office, 1995), pp. 366, 369.

maintain a world order that does not threaten U.S. political and economic interests. All of this suggests that the United States does have a propensity for getting involved in the violence associated with wars. And the United States seems more willing to do this than are most other nations around the world. Currently, one-third of all the money spent by all nations of the world on military expenditures is spent by the United States (see Figure 14.1 on p. 516)—and we have only 5 percent of the world's population. We spend $1,200 on military expenditures for each man, woman, and child in the United States, whereas the worldwide figure is only $200 per capita. When many people around the world look at U.S. military expenditures and the United States' track record on foreign involvement, they see a country that has a habit of throwing its weight around. Such expenditures are justified by some people on moral, political, or strategic grounds, but they have also been costly in human lives and suffering.

The Spread of Weapons of Mass Destruction

Whether the United States goes to war, of course, depends in part on what other nations do, and unfortunately there is a thriving world-wide trade in arms to provide nations with the means to go to war. Even more disturbing, the United States is a major player in that trade. The United States sold $10 billion worth of arms to other countries in 1991, the largest amount ever. Over the years, U.S. arms sales to other countries have accounted for one-third of the worldwide trade in arms, with the former Soviet Union accounting for slightly more—both countries together cornering almost three-quarters of all arms sales in the world (U.S. Bureau of the Census, 1995; Hartung, 1992). So, the United States supplies the means for nations to go to war with one another. This spread of weapons can embolden nations to attack other nations, and this has created problems for the United States. The United States gave military support, for example, to Iraq in its

war with Iran in the 1980s, and this assistance was turned against the United States when Iraq invaded U.S. ally Kuwait in 1990, resulting in the Persian Gulf War.

One of the horrendous legacies of twentieth-century technology has been the emergence of highly frightening and destructive weapons: nuclear, chemical, biological, and toxin weapons. Many nations have such weapons or are capable of making them. The United States, Russia, China, Great Britain, and France have possessed nuclear and chemical weapons for some time. In the last few decades, the world has seen the proliferation of these weapons to more countries, sometimes to nations with unstable or megalomaniacal leaders. Some of the nations acquiring these weapons are involved in serious and entrenched conflicts with other nations, which could produce conditions that would lead to their use. Israel has nuclear capability, for example, and has been in conflict with many Arab countries; Iraq used chemical weapons in its war with Iran and has tried to produce nuclear weapons; India and Pakistan have nuclear weapons and have been engaged in serious territorial disputes for a number of years. At least twelve nations have or are developing biological or toxin weapons, and twenty are doing so with chemical weapons (Bailey, 1991).

The likelihood that weapons of mass destruction will be used increases with each new nation that acquires them. The international framework to prevent the spread of these weapons is weak. The Geneva Protocols of 1925 prohibit the use of chemical weapons but not their production and stockpiling. When the weapons have been used, as in the Iran–Iraq War of the 1980s, no sanctions were applied against the user by the international community. The 178 nations that have signed the Treaty on the Non-Proliferation of Nuclear Weapons of 1968 agree not to permit the spread of these weapons to countries currently without them (Simpson, 1994). The treaty was extended in 1995. However, some countries, such as Israel,

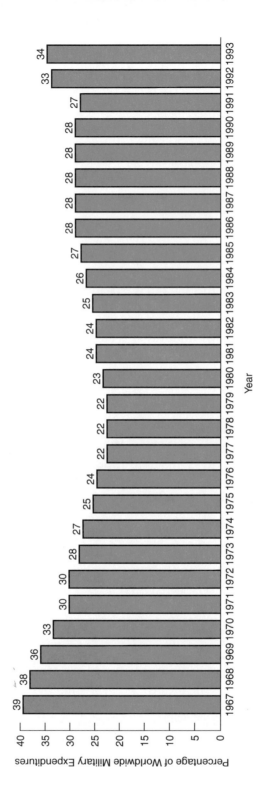

FIGURE 14.1 United States Military Expenditures as a Percentage of Worldwide Military Expenditures, 1967–1993. *Sources:* U.S. Bureau of the Census, *Statistical Abstract of the United States, 1978* (Washington, D.C.: U.S. Government Printing Office, 1978), p. 372; U.S. Bureau of the Census, *Statistical Abstract of the United States, 1982* (Washington, D.C.: U.S. Government Printing Office, 1982), p. 355; U.S. Bureau of the Census, *Statistical Abstract of the United States, 1995* (Washington, D.C.: U.S. Government Printing Office, 1995), p. 359.

have not signed the accord, and others, such as North Korea, have ignored many of its provisions. Once again, there have been no consistent international sanctions against these nations. One expert on national security and arms control concluded that, in the 1990s

> Proliferation . . . constitutes one of the most serious threats to international peace and stability, as well as to U.S. national security. It should become the focus of multinational and bilateral arms control efforts before it is too late. (Bailey, 1991: 6)

Terrorism

Terrorism refers to *the attempt to achieve political goals by using fear and intimidation to disrupt the normal operations of a society* (Gibbs, 1989). In the past few decades, terrorist attacks in the United States have been infrequent but occasionally destructive. In 1985, for example, a group of white supremacist, neo-Nazi fanatics, who refer to themselves as The Order, went on trial in Seattle for a series of terrorist acts, including the murder of a popular radio talk-show host in Denver who had denounced racists and anti-semites. In 1993, the World Trade Center in New York City was bombed, and in 1995 a federal building in Oklahoma City was destroyed by a huge bomb explosion that killed 167 people and wounded another 442. Terrorist attacks have been more common outside the United States, often targeted at U.S. citizens. One of the more horrifying incidents was the 1988 terrorist bombing of a Pan Am jet as it was flying over Scotland headed for the United States, killing hundreds of passengers and a few bystanders on the ground. As Figure 14.2 (on p. 518) illustrates, the number of terrorist attacks worldwide has fluctuated over time, with the greatest frequency occurring between 1985 and 1988. Approximately 40 percent of the attacks are directed against U.S. citizens, businesses, or facilities. The most dangerous places for U.S. citizens in 1993 were a few nations in South America, especially Chile,

Peru, and Colombia (U.S. Department of State, 1994).

Terrorists use many tactics, such as kidnapping, bombing, killing, hijacking, assassination, and extortion. Sometimes they focus on agents of a government they blame for their problems, such as the military or a president or ambassador. But they frequently attack innocent civilians in an effort to pressure government officials. Governments also sometimes engage in or support terrorism. The U.S. Department of State (1994) considers Syria, Iraq, Libya, and Iran to be among the major supporters of terrorism in the world currently. These countries provide varying levels of support to terrorist groups, from supplying arms, training, and technical expertise to providing travel documents or a hideout. This government-supported terrorism is something new and especially unsettling on the world scene. When established governments provide weapons, economic support, and a place of refuge for terrorists, they exacerbate and perpetuate the problem considerably. Terrorists who might create only a sporadic problem without such support can become a continuing source of violence and destruction with it.

Terrorism is a particularly unnerving form of violence because it is impervious to efforts to control it. Yet we need to recognize that terrorism often has its origins in some kind of perceived injustice, the elimination of which is the terrorists' goal (Rubenstein, 1987). Terrorism is sometimes resorted to by people who have little power and few resources with which to attack what they see as injustice. However, the nature of terrorism may be changing in the 1990s (Cetron and Davies, 1994). In addition to the traditional political motives and goals of terrorists in the past, some terrorists today are motivated by ethnic loyalties, others by religious fervor, and still others are basically criminals who use the intimidation of innocent civilians to achieve criminal goals. Examples of these new terrorists are the religious group in Japan that is alleged to have carried out a gas

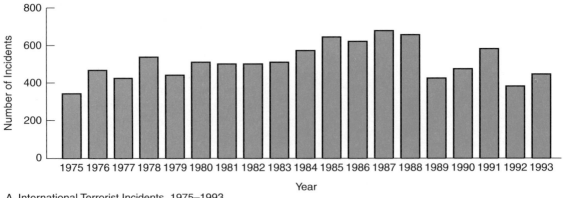

A. International Terrorist Incidents, 1975–1993

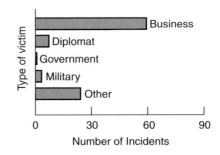

B. Anti-United States Terrorists Attacks, 1993

FIGURE 14.2 Patterns of Global Terrorism, 1975–1993. *Source:* U.S. Department of State, *Patterns of Global Terrorism, 1993,* Department of State Pub. 10136 (Washington, D.C.: U.S. Government Printing Office, 1994), pp. 69–71.

attack on the Tokyo subway system in 1995 and the "narcoterrorists" who have bombed buildings in South America to intimidate the police and politicians. Another change in terrorism is being brought about by technology. Nuclear, chemical, and biological weapons of mass destruction have become more accessible and easier to produce, making them available to more groups who might wish to use them. For example, the collapse of the Soviet Union in 1990 has left many small and unstable republics in possession of tactical nuclear weapons. In addition, many scientists and technicians in the former Soviet Union have lost their previous

livelihood in the weapons business and could be recruited by terrorists or rogue nations to help produce weapons.

Societies have made efforts to protect themselves against threatened terrorist attacks. Such attacks can occur at any of the many points at which people are vulnerable in modern societies: flying in an airplane, eating in a restaurant, or walking along the street. Short of advocating a costly and authoritarian society, it is difficult to build in the kind of controls that can provide assured protection in all these settings. Relatively effective controls over airplane hijacking, for example, have been achieved at the cost of luggage searches, radar detectors, and long waits at baggage check-ins. Even these measures are not completely effective because determined terrorists can still foil them, as the destruction of the Pan Am jetliner in 1988 showed. Other things that are being done include international efforts to discourage state support for terrorists and requirements for the marking of plastic and sheet explosives so that they can be more easily detected when hidden in luggage.

Sources of Violence

If violence is to be controlled, we need to know what causes it. People have many beliefs about this issue, but there is also much misleading and inaccurate information that can confuse rather than enlighten. This discussion will analyze the most current research that can shed some light on the problem. What will be found is that the sources of violence are complex, and there is often a chain of multiple causation, with numerous factors—social, psychological, and possibly even biological—contributing to particular outbursts of violence.

Biological Approaches

Earlier chapters have already reviewed efforts to explain such social behaviors as crime (Chapter 9), drug abuse (Chapter 10), and the differences between men and women (Chapter 7) on biological grounds. People also have been intrigued by the possibility that violence may be part of our biological nature as human beings. Violence is so common and so nearly universal in human cultures that it seems plausible that biology plays a part. Some support for this position can be found in studies of the behavior of animals of various species. A male stickleback fish, for example, will protect against all intruders a nest containing fertilized eggs deposited by the female stickleback. Anything approaching the nest that resembles another

stickleback will be viciously attacked (Tinbergen, 1955). Such protection of territory can be found in many species, and it is clearly an instinctive behavior in these species rather than a product of learning. Robert Ardrey (1967) popularized such behavior as the "territorial imperative," suggesting that such protection is necessary for some species to survive. In fact, he argued, it is so necessary that evolution imprints these behavior patterns into the genes of species. Without this instinct to defend territory, mating would be disrupted and the survival of species would be threatened. Aggressiveness in struggling for food or competing for mates also may have an evolutionary advantage for many species.

Recent applications of these ideas to human beings have been labeled **sociobiology,** *a field based on the idea that the genetic makeup of human beings plays a powerful role in shaping human social behavior* (van der Dennen and Falger, 1990; Nielson, 1994). Sociobiologists maintain that there are many parallels between human and animal behavior. For example, animals of a number of species exhibit altruism, which refers to doing things that benefit others of one's species even though it may be dangerous or deadly to oneself. So, kamikaze bees will die defending their hive, soldier termites will end their lives in order to spray a deadly liquid at their enemies, and human beings will place their own lives in danger to protect their children. Other behavioral tendencies that are common in both animals and humans include aggressiveness, territoriality, selfishness, and the formation of dominance hierarchies.

Sociobiologists argue that these tendencies are common in species because they are inborn traits determined by genes. These various traits exist because they enhance the chances of survival for the species. The stronger, more powerful, and more aggressive members of a species are more likely to survive, mate, and pass on their genes to the next generation. A mother will die to save her children because this enhances the likelihood that her genes will survive in the gene pool even though she herself dies. Sociobiologists reason that aggressiveness and altruism are a part of our genetic makeup because people who behave aggressively or altruistically increase the chances for the survival of their genes. Over long periods of time, those aggressive and altruistic genes come to predominate in the gene pool.

Is violence programmed into human genes as sociobiologists suggest? There are a number of reasons to be cautious about their arguments (Maryanski and Turner, 1992; Wolfe, 1993). First, there is no direct evidence linking any specific genes to particular forms of human behavior. Although their arguments are plausible, there is no definitive proof that they are accurate. Second, there are few human traits that are found universally among human beings. The prevalence of behaviors such as altruism and aggressiveness vary widely from person to person and culture to culture. Although every kamikaze bee will die protecting its hive, for example, some human beings protect their children, whereas others neglect, abuse, and abandon them. Moreover, infanticide has at times been an accepted social practice among some groups, such as the ancient Greeks and Chinese. If altruism and aggressiveness were truly instinctive, this variation would not occur. Finally, even if genetically determined behavioral tendencies exist, sociobiologists recognize that they only create general tendencies to behave in certain ways. Whether people actually behave aggressively or altruistically depends on numerous psychological and social forces. In fact, sociobiologists admit that these genetic tendencies, if they exist, can probably be altered or even overcome by learning and other social forces.

Another biological approach to violence focuses on biological abnormalities such as brain tumors or scar tissue on the brain that have been linked to violence. Certain chemical traces in the brain have also been associated with violence. However, these biological factors account for only sporadic instances of violence.

They cannot explain the organized and collective occurrence of violence that is the focus of this chapter. Things such as war, riot, and rebellion involve far too many people and far too much organization to be attributed to brain tumors, scar tissue, or chemical imbalances.

Social Sources of Violence

Considerable research over the past four decades has helped to pinpoint the social sources of violence. These factors can be organized into three categories: characteristics of the structure of society that serve as preconditions to violence, the frustrations that these preconditions can create in people that push them toward violence, and mediating factors that increase the likelihood that people will react violently to frustration. We will look at each of these factors, relating them where appropriate to the three sociological perspectives.

Structural Preconditions Most outbursts of collective violence can be traced to some social conditions that serve as preconditions for violence. One such precondition is the existence of some social strain or social deprivation. For example, strain exists when some groups in society do not have the opportunity to achieve their goals through socially acceptable means. This is discussed in Chapters 9 and 10 as Robert Merton's anomie theory of crime and drug abuse. For instance, racial or ethnic discrimination may limit the jobs that are available to some people, or poverty may make it difficult to attain the education necessary to find a respectable job. Whatever its source, this strain or deprivation leaves people vulnerable to participating in collective violence should the opportunity arise. This approach to understanding violence reflects the functionalist view that different parts of society need to be integrated with one another, and this includes providing people with the opportunity to achieve their goals. To the extent that societies cannot do this, a disjuncture is created that can lead to problems such as crime and violence.

Another precondition for violence is competition between people over money, jobs, and other scarce but valued resources. This is discussed in Chapters 6 and 7 as a source of prejudice and discrimination against minorities. The more intensely groups compete, the more threatening each becomes to the other and the more likely one side or the other will resort to violence. Oftentimes, the competition is economic, over jobs or money, such as the split-labor market discussed in Chapter 6 and the labor disputes discussed earlier in this chapter. However, there can also be conflict over values and lifestyle. Functionalists argue that such competition need not culminate in violence if society provides everyone with the opportunity to achieve at least some of their goals. Violence also can be avoided by providing people with nonviolent means to achieve an acceptable lifestyle. However, from the conflict perspective, such competition is an inherent part of social life, and groups will resort to violence if they perceive it as a superior and effective strategy in the clash over scarce resources.

A third precondition of violence is ethnocentrism, or the tendency to view one's own group or culture as superior to other groups or cultures (see Chapter 6). Although some ethnocentrism can be beneficial by promoting group cohesion, excessive amounts can lead to the belief that others are not only different but also dishonest, disreputable, and possibly even not fully human. Such beliefs open the door to hostile and violent actions. Especially if the members of a group are defined as subhuman, violence against them may not be seen as bad or immoral. Thus, Adolf Hitler and the Nazis became so thoroughly convinced of the superiority of the Aryan "race" that they felt justified in brutalizing Jews and others. Likewise, many people in the United States in the eighteenth and nineteenth centuries believed that their European heritage and values were far superior to those of native Americans in the New World,

and this view legitimized attacks against Indians that few people are proud of today. In the 1980s, the neo-Nazi group The Order justified murder on the grounds that the alleged Aryan race was superior to blacks and Jews.

Frustration and Aggression How are these preconditions translated into violence? Psychologists have shown that there is a clear, though complex, link among frustration, aggression, and violence. **Frustration** refers to *an inability to achieve sought-after goals.* The preconditions of violence discussed in the previous section are structured sources of frustration that can influence many people. When people are frustrated, there is a buildup of tension that may be released in aggressive and sometimes violent behavior (Baron and Richardson, 1994). This aggressive or violent reaction can release the tension created by frustration even though it fails to alleviate the real source of the frustration. For example, in the South in the United States between 1882 and 1903, nearly two thousand blacks were killed by lynch mobs, some by hanging, others by being burned alive (Brown, 1969). Some of the impetus for such violence was the fluctuating economic conditions in the South: Unemployment and poor economic conditions frustrated southern whites, and some responded with racial violence against blacks. The violence did not alleviate the underlying economic problems, but it did provide a release for poor whites.

Chapter 9 observed that what is considered deviant is relative to the judgments of some group. What is considered frustrating is also relative. **Relative deprivation** refers to the fact that *people tend to feel deprived or frustrated in comparison to what others have or what they believe they deserve.* In other words, a sense of deprivation arises when there is a discrepancy between what people have come to expect or feel they deserve and what they actually receive. So the conditions that are frustrating or depriving for one group or at one point in history may not be so for another group or at another point. It

The Los Angeles Riot: Failing to Act on What We Know

The images of the riot in South Central Los Angeles in 1992 were very disturbing: panoramic views of the towers of smoke from many buildings burning at once, looters emerging from stores with their arms laden with stolen goods, store owners shooting their guns at crowds to keep them at bay, innocent bystanders savagely beaten and helpless. By the time it was over, fifty-three people had died, and there was $1 billion in property damage. Especially disturbing was the realization that we had seen it all before: in Miami in the 1980s and in many cities in the United States in the 1960s. Most people are familiar with the immediate precipitant of the Los Angeles riot (Dentler, 1992). Four police officers were on trial for the vicious beating of the African American motorist Rodney King. The beating was videotaped and had been widely shown on television. King was beaten repeatedly and over a prolonged period of time by a number of officers, even when King seemed helpless on the ground. The acquittal of the officers sparked the riot. The acquittal was seen by African Americans in Los Angeles as convincing proof that the police were free to assault African Americans at will and that the criminal justice system would provide African Americans with no legal recourse against such violence. Other recent events in Los Angeles provided fuel for such beliefs: African American men were routinely arrested and mistreated by the police, and a store-owner who shot and killed a sixteen-year-old African American girl was convicted of a minor charge and spent no time in jail.

There is much still to be learned about the Los Angeles riot, but what is already disturbingly clear is that we have failed to apply what we have learned from earlier riots. Riots in the 1960s and the 1980s have been studied extensively by sociologists and other social scientists. These riots essentially served as field experiments in which researchers could compare cities that experienced riots with those that did not. Researchers also compared people who joined in the riots with those who lived in the riot community but did not participate (Lieberson and Silverman, 1965; Caplan and Paige, 1968; McPhail, 1971; Spilerman, 1976; Porter and Dunn, 1984). From this sociologists and policymakers learned a great deal about why riots happen. Unfortunately, society has not responded by changing the conditions that produce such riots. Let us see what those conditions are.

One thing we learned is that such riots start when a highly volatile event, such as the acquittal of the police officers, enrages an aggrieved group. The exact same thing happened in Miami in 1980. The immediate cause of that riot was the acquittal of four Miami police officers in a murder trial for the death of an African American insurance agent, Arthur McDuffie. The acquittal infuriated African Americans in Miami just as the acquittal was to enrage African Americans in Los Angeles a decade later. The climate was also the same: There had been police killings and assaults of African Americans in Florida to fuel beliefs about police racism and disregard for African Americans. Despite these lessons, authorities in Los Angeles apparently did not take seriously enough the potential threat posed as the trial of the officers came to an end.

In addition to learning about the immediate causes of riots, the research on earlier riots also tells us about the structural conditions and mediating factors that can play a part. Here, too, we see how thoroughly we have failed to apply lessons from the past. It is almost a cliché to say that economic deprivation and racial discrimination lay at the root of the riots of the 1960s. Clearly, people who are well off economically are disinclined to take to the streets, even if provoked. But people who are severely oppressed are also unlikely to engage in such activism. Their feelings of helplessness are more likely to result in resignation or withdrawal. Instead of the total underdog, it is people who have hopes for improvement in their lives but see those hopes threatened who are most inclined to respond to deprivation and oppression through rioting. In other words, it is *relative deprivation* that often underlies collective violence. Research on the 1960s riots documented this in several ways. It was not cities where African Americans were worst off that experienced riots. Rather, it was cities where African Americans had made considerable improvements such that there were small gaps between the incomes of African Americans and whites. It was also African Americans in the middle levels of educational ranks who rioted, not those with the least education. Such advances in income and education had led people to hope for further improvement and led to deeply felt frustration when the improvements were not forthcoming.

Likewise, research on the 1980 Miami riot showed that "rioters by no means came exclusively from the ranks of the poor or unemployed or the criminal classes. Many held jobs, were normally law-abiding and did not otherwise fit the stereotypical image of a 'rioter' " (Porter and Dunn, 1984: 183). Criminals or the unemployed may have played an important part in starting the riot, but seemingly respectable African Americans provided the numbers that kept it going and contributed to heightening the levels of emotion and destruction. What evidence we have at this point from Los Angeles suggests the same thing: Many looters and arrestees worked or were in school. In addition, in Los Angeles, as elsewhere, many African Americans had not participated in the improvements that were supposed to derive from the civil rights advances of thirty years ago. As we saw in Chapter 6, there persists a substantial African American underclass that has not been able to attain the educational or other credentials necessary to achieve upward mobility.

Beyond deprivation and oppression, we learned from earlier riots of a number of other factors that contribute to the likelihood of a riot occurring. These factors suggest that riots occur when members of minority groups feel left out of society, isolated from sources of political and economic power, ignored by the powers that be, and

victimized by the social order that is supposed to serve and protect them. When there are few channels for resolving grievances or when the system appears unresponsive to expressions of discontent, people are more willing to turn to collective violence. In earlier riots, isolation from the political system was evidenced by such things as few or no African American police officers in a city, and cities with fewer African American police officers were more likely to experience a riot. Likewise, cities with few African American storeowners and those where officials were elected on a citywide rather than district basis (making it more difficult for African Americans, who are typically a numerical minority in a city but a majority in some districts, to gain office) had more riots. Once again, Los Angeles in 1992 fit the profile for a riot-prone city fairly well. The city did have an African American mayor, but African Americans were underrepresented at all levels of the police force. It also had a relatively small number of African American storeowners and professionals, especially in South Central Los Angeles where the riot occurred, and many of the storeowners were Asian Americans who seemed to be doing fairly well even though having immigrated to the United States only recently. This contributed to the feelings of resentment and isolation in the African-American community in South Central Los Angeles. Overall, the poverty, unemployment, and segregation in their community left these African Americans feeling effectively disenfranchised.

We learned a great deal about collective violence from the research conducted in earlier decades. Social policies could have been established that would have improved the economic circumstances of African Americans and reduced feelings of isolation and disenfranchisement. We discuss many of these policies in Chapters 5 and 6, and we need not repeat them here. What does need reiteration is that, if we do nothing, we will probably have more such riots in the future.

This store was destroyed during the rioting in Los Angeles that followed the verdict in the Rodney King case in 1992. This riot was one of the most destructive civil disorders in the United States in recent years.

depends on the standards that people use in assessing their circumstances. A century ago, miners in the United States went on strike because they were being maimed and killed by unsafe working conditions and for wages that barely provided the essentials of life. In the past decade, violence has accompanied labor disputes in which the workers would have been considered affluent by the standards of a century ago. The point is that the standards for what is an acceptable lifestyle and what is acceptable in the workplace have changed and so have the conditions that might precipitate violence. The notion of relative deprivation reflects the emphasis of the interactionist perspective on the construction of social reality through human perception and interpretation. Social conditions become a problem—even one warranting a violent response—if people define them as threatening their values or disruptive of their lifestyle. These definitions are based on the meanings that groups attach to people or events. The Applied Research insert in this chapter focuses on the preconditions and frustrations that sparked a riot in Los Angeles in 1992.

Mediating Factors The preconditions to violence and the frustration that have been discussed do not lead inexorably to violent behavior. In fact, most people experiencing such conditions do not become violent. Rather, there are a number of mediating factors that increase the likelihood of violence. For one thing, whether violence occurs and the form that it takes depend on learning and socialization. Culture can teach people that violence is an acceptable and useful way of dealing with interpersonal problems. Some cultures, such as the Zuni Indians in the American Southwest, view aggression as an evil force that threatens group unity, and people discourage any displays of aggression (Westie, 1964). In U.S. culture, on the other hand, people are often rewarded for engaging in aggressive or violent behavior. Children, especially boys, may be cheered on when they play especially hard and aggressively at some sport. They may even be encouraged to "act like a man" and stand up to people who give them trouble—even if that means fighting.

It has been argued that some groups or subcultures in the United States tend to be very accepting of violence as a means of resolving interpersonal disputes and that this atmosphere serves as an important mediating factor in producing violence (Wolfgang and Ferracuti, 1967). In fact, there may even be a **subculture of violence** involving *norms and values that condone and legitimize the use of violence in resolving conflicts.* Thus, aggression and violence may be viewed by some groups as the acceptable and possibly even the preferred and "manly" way of resolving disputes. Others have argued that a culture of violence pervades all of U.S. society and is not limited to just some groups and subcultures (Pinkney, 1972). Certainly, violence pervades television dramas and the cinema, where handsome and beautiful characters routinely dispatch villains with large doses of violence. The lesson seems to be that aggression is used by the "good guys" to gain rewards that are unavailable to others. Yet the subculture of violence theory should not be extended too broadly. Research suggests that such subcultures may not be as extensive as once thought and that the social class, racial, and regional variation in the propensity to use violence that was once thought to exist may not be that strong (Ball-Rokeach, 1973; Erlanger, 1974; O'Connor and Lizotte, 1978). Still, for many groups, violence is considered an appropriate response in some circumstances. At least, violence is not strongly punished if it occurs under provocation and if the people toward whom it is directed are stigmatized or viewed as disreputable.

Aggression and violence are more likely to occur if there are attractive people to serve as models promoting such behavior (Vander Zanden, 1987). Parents may unwittingly serve as models of violence for their children when they punish them for some wrongdoing. The parents' use of physical force to control children teaches the children that force can be legitimately used to control others. The child can also find models for violence on the street, at school, and in the playground. Researchers have found that aggressive behavior is more common among children whose social circumstances expose them to many such aggressive models (Bandura, 1976).

There seems little doubt at this point that the mass media contribute to the levels of violence in society. In the past forty years, much research has been conducted on the relationship between violence on television and violence in society (Van Evra, 1990; Huston et al., 1992). Most of this research concludes that when children and youths watch violence on television, they are more likely to act aggressively or violently themselves, especially in situations that are conducive to violence. The impact is greater for males than for females, and it is more substantial for children who are more aggressive to begin with (Josephson, 1987). Children between the ages of eight and twelve seem to be especially vulnerable to the effects of watching violence on television.

Television encourages people toward violence in three ways. First, action dramas can be arousing to viewers and may stimulate them in the direction of physical activity and release. This effect is probably of short duration, from hours to days. Second, television provides viewers with legitimizing models for violence in much the same way that parents or peers can serve as models. In fact, it is difficult to watch television without being exposed to models of violence. Thus, children learn the potential for acting violently in particular situations, and the amount of such violence on television has not declined in the past few decades and may have actually increased. Also, the violence seen on television has some unreal or surrealistic qualities. People bleed little, and the actual pain and agony resulting from a violent attack are rarely portrayed. The consequences of violence often seem antiseptic and rather unimportant. Third, television conveys attitudes and values, and it can teach children to view violence or antisocial behavior as a desirable or "manly" way to behave.

Even with all of the preconditions and mediating factors that have been discussed thus far, collective violence is not likely to occur without mobilization: social mechanisms for bringing the affected people into coordinated and organized activity (Zald and McCarthy, 1987). Riots, labor strife, lynchings, and wars do not emerge by themselves, even in response to strain and deprivation. Depending on the context, leaders have to emerge, money must be collected, and ways of exercising power must be discovered. Organization, administration, procedures, and strategies must also evolve. If the essential mix of resources is not mobilized, collective violence will not occur, even when the predisposing factors are substantial and the deprivation is severe.

Theoretical Perspectives on Violence

The sources of violence just described relate in good measure to the functionalist perspective. They view violence as arising in part from social disorganization: frustration, deprivation, and the like. When people are frustrated in achieving their goals, it means that the various parts of the social system are not well integrated; people learn to want things but then are not given the means to achieve them. The violence that arises may then contribute to further disorganization, and this is what makes it a social problem from the functionalist perspective. As a mechanism for redressing grievances, violence is very unstable and dangerous. It means, first of all, that more peaceful mechanisms for resolving problems have broken down. In other words, the conventional societal procedures for moderating differences between groups do not work. Second, violence always has the potential for getting out of hand and escalating to dangerously destructive levels. At an extreme, this can threaten the stability of the social order, as occurred during the Civil War when the United States was threatened with being split apart. Some also believe that levels of violence rose dangerously high during the 1960s with race riots and antiwar riots becoming common events. For functionalists, then, violence is a social problem because it threatens societal stability and increases social disorganization.

The conflict perspective points to a somewhat different view of violence: It is a tool that any group might use to protect or enhance its own interests. According to the conflict perspective, dominant groups use violence whenever a subordinate group begins to threaten their position. For example, business interests in the late 1800s turned to the police and National Guard troops to stop workers who were organizing to oppose the substantial power of their employers. As seen earlier in this chapter, workers were often harassed, beaten, and shot in the process. When dominant groups resort to violence, they tend to view it as socially acceptable and appropriate. Subordinate groups can also resort to violence when they have few other means of redressing grievances. Rioting, for example, has been one way that subordinate minority groups in the United States have been able to force some concessions from the powers that be. Terrorism has also been used by those with few resources in an attempt to force changes. The Irish Republican Army is currently doing this in Northern Ireland. So from the conflict perspective, violence itself is not a social problem; in fact, violence is an important mechanism for bringing about social change. It comes to be viewed as a problem when it threatens the interests of some group and that group is in a position to do something about it.

The Consequences of War

Many of the consequences of violence—and the reasons for our concern about it—are obvious: the loss of human life, the destruction of property, the disruption of people's lives by the terror of violence, and the fear of violence that can seep into people's daily routine and sap it of joy or pleasure. However, there are consequences of violence, and especially war, that are more subtle and often go unnoticed. Over the past few decades, researchers have been able to document the wide-ranging ramifications of war for society. From the functionalist perspective, this is not surprising. Any society is made up of a number of parts that are highly integrated and interdependent. War demands considerable shifting and rearrangement of these parts: People and material must be mobilized, attitudes must be generated to support the war, and the daily lives of many people are disrupted. Because of this, war can intensify a number of social problems.

Crime and Political Turmoil

Crime often accompanies war because warfare brings with it social disruption and upheaval. Chapter 9 showed that crime thrives in situations where anomie exists. War produces anomie because civilians find it difficult to find food, clothing, and shelter in the normal ways. Theft, robbery, and possibly even assault may be resorted to as ways of obtaining the routine necessities of life. Crime and war are also associ-

ated in another way: Crime rates seem to rise in the years immediately following wars. Homicide rates, for example, increase after wars, whether the wars are large or small (Archer and Gartner, 1976). The increase is not because of adverse economic conditions because it occurs when wars are followed by economic expansion. The increase is also found among both men and women. Surprisingly, the rise in crime is more likely among nations that are victorious in war, and nations with a large number of battle deaths have shown substantial crime increases.

We do not fully understand why this increase in crime occurs following wars. It may be that the violence of war tends to generate a general legitimation of violence—an expansion of the subculture of violence—and this may reduce people's inhibitions toward engaging in violence. Or it may be that a condition of anomie pervades society following a war as large numbers of soldiers return home looking for work and trying to reestablish familial and friendship ties. It may take society some time to reabsorb and help these soldiers readjust. For example, thousands of Vietnam veterans have served time in prison for committing crimes, and research suggests that these veterans experienced considerable difficulties in adapting to the anomie that existed in their lives when they returned to the United States (Boivin, 1985). Many have resorted to what Merton called innovation as a mode of adapting, and one form of this is crime (see Chapter 9). Also, the sense of patriotism and common purpose found during the war may decline, leaving a void in many people's lives. Whatever the reason for the relationship between crime and war, it further documents the disruptive effect of war on society.

In addition to crime, political turmoil often increases during war. In some cases, this arises because disenchantment over the war leads to widespread discontent with the government. The government loses legitimacy in the eyes of both those who find the war morally offensive and those who feel that the government should prosecute the war more intensely. Such people may withhold support for the government, support opposition candidates, or possibly even engage in collective protest or rebellious actions. War also may have the effect of reducing people's tolerance for public dissent. When a country has gone to war with a foe, many people believe a united front is essential and are willing to allow the government to use repressive means to control dissent. As a consequence of all these things, wars generally tend to produce increases in domestic political violence (Stohl, 1976). Opponents of the war may engage in demonstrations, sit-ins, or, in extreme cases, terrorist bombings as a way of disrupting the war effort. Supporters of the government and the war may harass and attack demonstrators, and the police arrest the dissenters.

So war often poses a threat to democratic institutions on the home front. During the Civil War, for example, there was substantial dissent and conflict. In New York City, a three-day riot involving fifty thousand people resulted in thirteen hundred deaths (Brooks, 1969). Much of the hostility was focused on the unfairness of the draft as then implemented. The policy at that time favored the well-to-do because one could buy one's way out of military service for about three hundred dollars— a sum that working-class people and Irish immigrants could not afford at the time. There was also considerable opposition to World War I. In 1917, for example, eight thousand protestors marched in Boston against the war. The pattern of violence at this march was typical: Patriotic mobs attacked the demonstrators, but it was the demonstrators who were arrested for breaching the public order.

The Vietnam War was associated with substantial domestic political violence. Early in the war, the violence took the same form that it did during World War I: Nonviolent demonstrators were attacked by either citizens or the police. Later, some antiwar protestors became more violent by burning buildings and attacking police with rocks and sticks. The radical wing of the antiwar movement, including such groups as the Weather Underground, engaged in bombings and other terrorist actions. The emotions aroused by the Vietnam War may have also heightened the violence associated with other conflicts in society, such as the quest for civil rights.

War creates pressures, then, that increase the likelihood of domestic turmoil, and this turmoil, if it becomes severe, might threaten democratic institutions. Whether the situations during World War I and the Vietnam conflict were that severe is a matter of some debate. The point here is to recognize the negative domestic consequences of waging a war.

Economic Problems

War can have a severe impact on a nation's economy. The destruction of factories, railroads, and other economic resources can be terribly damaging, but economic problems are created even in combatant nations that suffer little or no such physical destruction. One source of economic problems is that resources devoted to the war effort must be withdrawn from some other economic realm. The labor and material resources used to build tanks and guns are not available for housing construction or leisure pursuits (Cranna, 1994). Figure 14.3 shows the percentage of the gross national product (GNP)—the total output of goods and services in the United States—that is made up of defense spending. Clearly, World War II drew substantial resources from the civilian realm, with nearly half of the GNP being spent for military needs. It is estimated that the direct costs of World War II were $360 billion, at a time when the federal budget each year was less than $100 billion (U.S. Bureau of the Census, 1994: 357). By comparison, Korea and Vietnam were less intrusive on the economy: They cost $50 billion and $140 billion, respectively.

The impact of war on the economy depends on the state of the economy. World War

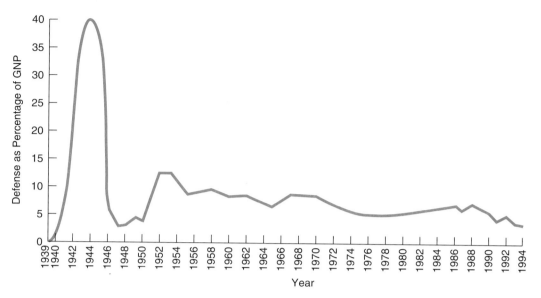

FIGURE 14.3 Defense Expenditures in the United States as a Percentage of the Gross National Product, 1939–1994. *Sources:* U.S. Bureau of the Census, *Statistical Abstract of the United States, 1987* (Washington, D.C.: U.S. Government Printing Office, 1986), p. 317; U.S. Bureau of the Census, *Statistical Abstract of the United States, 1994* (Washington, D.C.: U.S. Government Printing Office, 1994), p. 352.

II and the Korean conflict began when there were high levels of unemployment. This meant that increased government expenditures could be more easily absorbed through economic expansion, creating new jobs that the unemployed could fill. The Vietnam conflict, on the other hand, began when unemployment levels were quite low and the economy was operating at close to full capacity. Increased defense spending for Vietnam provided a stimulus to the economy that resulted in an increased demand for goods and services and considerable inflation in prices. In earlier wars, inflation was controlled by instituting wage and price controls. President Lyndon Johnson chose not to do this during the Vietnam conflict on the grounds that the economy could support additional stimulation. Against the advice of many, he chose not to increase taxes as a control over demand or to institute wage-price controls to reduce inflation (Russett, 1969). One assessment of the economic impact of the Vietnam War was that it produced

the most virulent inflation in American history, the highest interest rates in history, a series of balance of payments crises worse than any that had gone before, an unnecessary recession in 1970–71, two serious declines in stock prices, . . . a collapse of the housing industry, . . . financial market distortions that bore extremely heavily on small business and that forced state and local governments to retrench on education and other vital services, and the eventual defeat of the most imaginative experimental approach to the problems of impacted poverty that had ever been tried. (Stevens, 1976:13)

Although this statement may be a little overdrawn, it is clear that Vietnam, as other wars, had a dramatic impact on the economy.

Even when war is not fought, the preparations for war can be costly (Markusen and Yudken, 1992). Outfitting the United States' military machine to fight the Cold War has meant diverting resources and innovation away from civilian industries and into the military–industrial complex. What has resulted is a huge industry of corporations, engineers, and workers who are dependent on government contracts and tooled to build only very specialized weapons systems. Chapter 2 discusses whether the U.S. government should have an industrial policy to assist certain industries to develop and compete in world markets as other industrial nations such as Germany and Japan do. In effect, the industrial policy of the U.S. government has been to siphon billions of dollars each year into this military arena while claiming that we have no industrial policy. With government assistance siphoned off into the military–industrial complex, other industries—such as automobiles, machine tooling, and consumer electronics—have been languishing, with plants closing and jobs going overseas. To make matters worse, this military–industrial complex often prospered more from lobbying and negotiating with the Pentagon than from emphasizing cost minimization and quality production. Oftentimes, Pentagon contracts allowed corporations to charge the government whatever it costs to build a weapons system plus a certain guaranteed profit, even when the weapons system ended up costing much more than the corporation originally projected that it would. With such a noncompetitive system, military–industrial corporations were, in effect, given enormous research, development, and production subsidies from the government whereas other corporations were left to fend for themselves. By the early 1990s, the United States found itself being paid by other countries to use its impressive military might to fight the world's battle in the Persian Gulf War. The United States had become, in effect, the world's cop, hired by other nations to discipline a rogue dictator. At the same time, the U.S. increased arms sales to other nations to make up for a trade deficit produced because many U.S. civilian industries could not compete in the world market. When so much of the U.S. budget—currently one-quarter of the total—goes to defense spending, it is not surprising that civilian industries suffer from a lack of policy attention.

Nuclear Annihilation

In one major respect, many would consider the twentieth century to be the "winter of despair": For the first time in human history, the technological capability exists for destroying life on earth as we know it. The harnessing of nuclear power has made possible the unleashing of unimaginable destruction. Nuclear weapons are not merely a quantitative increase in military fire power. They are so vastly destructive that they constitute a qualitatively different level of violence altogether.

In a sense, we can only speculate about the impact of nuclear war on life on earth because no other equivalent calamities have occurred to serve as examples. Of course, there were Hiroshima and Nagasaki, but these were limited attacks and the survivors could depend on support for survival and rebuilding from those not immediately affected. In a large-scale nuclear war between the East and the West, there would be no outside support because the explosions would spread devastation all across the United States, Europe, and Russia. The devastation also would be far more extensive than in Japan in 1945. If a one-megaton bomb were detonated over Los Angeles, New York, Paris, London, or Moscow, everyone within a radius of two miles of the bomb blast would be burned, crushed, or vaporized to death, probably two million people (Kurtz, 1988). Within twenty miles of the blast, another million people would die immediately from the blast or shortly thereafter from severe wounds. Many others would die within a week or two as enormous amounts of radioactive fallout drift down and contaminate food and water supplies. Within weeks of the explosions, then, as many as five million people might die in each city. The World Health Organization estimates that more than one billion people would be killed outright worldwide in a large-scale nuclear exchange and another one billion would be seriously injured (Borgstrom et al., 1983).

It would take years, possibly decades, to rebuild after such a war, and during the interim people would be forced to live in crowded, temporary camps. A whole generation, and possibly two, would probably lose any chance for the material affluence that was common before the war. One report concluded, based on elaborate computer simulations of the effects of even a small nuclear exchange, that the survivors in the United States would be reduced to "near-medieval levels of existence" for decades (quoted in Broad, 1987: 1). For many,

This picture of Nagasaki, Japan, after being destroyed by one atomic bomb in 1945 documents the awesome power and horrific destructive capabilities of modern atomic and nuclear weapons.

the long-term effects of massive amounts of radioactive contamination would mean the development of birth defects, cancer, and other deadly illnesses years after the war.

Another possible effect of nuclear war was suggested by a group of scientists at the Conference on the Long-term Worldwide Biological Consequences of Nuclear War in 1983. Summarizing their research, these scientists argued that nuclear war could create what they labeled a "nuclear winter" (Ehrlich et al., 1983; Turco et al., 1983). The thousands of detonations of nuclear warheads would toss tremendous amounts of dust and soot into the atmosphere. The nuclear detonations would also cause fierce fires, like the firestorms in German cities that were bombed during World War II, only much larger and injecting even more smoke and particulate matter into the atmosphere. In one to two weeks, this dust and soot could coalesce into a monstrous dark cloud shrouding much of the northern hemisphere. Little sunlight would penetrate this cloud. In the worst case of a very severe nuclear exchange, these scientists estimate, the cloud could stop all but one-tenth of 1 percent of the normal sunlight that reaches the earth. Even a limited nuclear exchange could reduce sunlight by 95 percent. The cold and the darkness could have disastrous effects on plants and animals. Without sunlight and proper temperatures, much foliage would die and the food supply would be seriously threatened.

Based on their calculations, then, these scientists project that nuclear war could constitute a severe assault on the ecosystem and could threaten its ability to support human life. There has been, of course, much debate over the accuracy of these calculations. Although no one can be certain what will happen until it actually happens, many scientists today believe that a nuclear winter of some degree of severity is a possible outcome of a nuclear war in which less than a thousand warheads are exchanged (Robock, 1989; Sagan and Turco, 1990). The effects may be less severe than the scientists project—or they may be more severe. If there is a nuclear war and the projections of these scientists turn out to be accurate, civilization as we know it could be threatened and could possibly be destroyed. Let us hope that the theory is never put to the actual test.

Future Prospects

Violence and war seem to be endemic to the human condition, but there are some things that hold promise for reducing the level of violence in the United States and the world.

Social Reform and Social Justice

As has been seen, violence often springs out of social strain, frustration, or injustice. Collective violence may represent an effort by people to correct those injustices or to gain what they feel is an equitable share of resources. Efforts to control violence, then, need to begin by changing the social conditions that are the seedbeds of violence. In fact, the sociological investigation of social problems is an attempt to do just this. In this book, many of the conditions that can cause collective violence have been analyzed, and it is not necessary to review all of those discussions here. By way of illustration, prejudice and discrimination, discussed in Chapter 6, produce violence in the form of lynchings and race riots. Social reforms that focus on reducing discrimination, then, will affect levels of collective violence. The inequitable distribution of resources in society, discussed in Chapter 5, has resulted in violence in the form of labor strife, riots, and in a few cases, rebellion. Programs to provide people with greater opportunities and a broader distribution of resources in society will reduce the likelihood of these forms of violence.

There is no consensus regarding which social reforms are appropriate or what constitutes social justice, and this book will not presume to answer those questions. In most cases, reform programs mean that some groups benefit, whereas others lose. In fact, interventionists presume that this will be the case and that the government should serve as arbiter over the allocation of resources. The government then becomes the forum in which various groups exercise what influence they have to gain a share of resources. Laissez-faire advocates, on the other hand, would argue that the unfettered operation of impersonal economic forces can provide equity and justice for all. The government, they believe, will simply become the tool of one interest group or another. These issues are debated in other chapters in the context of specific forms of social injustice. The point here is that, although social reform is essential to controlling violence, such reforms are not easy to accomplish and are not without controversy.

Gun Control

There is a vast arsenal of weapons in the hands of people in the United States. From deer hunters with rifles to beer-can target shooters with pistols, from self-styled commandos who practice with paramilitary assault weapons to drug-selling gangs with illegal weapons—and do not forget the frightened teen who carries a .38 revolver to school each day—society is awash in guns. There are an estimated two hundred million firearms out there now, with at least four million more being added every year. Americans spend over $2 billion each year on firearms—more than we do on golf and fishing equipment combined (U.S. Bureau of the Census, 1995).

The levels of violence in society might be controlled by restricting people's access to the means of perpetrating violence, especially lethal violence. To this end, some people have proposed establishing strict controls over the ownership of guns, possibly even prohibiting their ownership by citizens altogether. In 1989, some well-publicized incidents occurred in which schoolchildren and people at work were killed by disturbed people armed with semiautomatic assault rifles. Such tragic events have increased pressure for gun control and motivated new federal legislation regarding the production and sale of "assault-type" weapons.

Opponents of gun ownership have used these and other statistics to argue that levels of lethal violence could be reduced by restricting the ownership of guns, especially handguns and assault weapons, which are the weapons most commonly used in perpetrating violence. Their basic argument is that the widespread availability of guns increases the chances that a person will respond to frustration or injustice with destructive violence. Although the absence of guns does not resolve the strife in such situations, it lowers the level of violence. Especially in cases in which assaults arise out of impulse rather than preparation and planning, the impulse may well pass without lethal violence if firearms are not readily available. A number of police organizations, such as the Fraternal Order of Police and the Police Foundation, support handgun control legislation.

Opponents of gun control legislation interpret the Second Amendment to the U.S. Constitution to mean that citizens have a constitutional right to own guns for their own use and protection (Kates, 1983). This amendment states: "A well regulated militia being necessary to the security of a free state, the right of the people to keep and bear arms shall not be infringed." Tampering with this right, they argue, will hinder their ability to protect themselves and their families from harm and might threaten democratic institutions. In addition, law-abiding gun enthusiasts argue that it is unfair for them to have to give up their weapons because of the criminal or violent behavior of a minority. Finally, opponents of gun control argue that it would just create an enormous black market in guns, and this would make it easier for criminals to obtain weapons.

There is considerable variation in state and local legislation regarding the ownership of guns. Some locales are highly restrictive, whereas others do not even require a person to have a police permit to own a gun. A recent summary by sociologist Gary Kleck (1991) of research on whether gun controls reduce violence or crime is rather pessimistic: It does not seem to have a big impact one way or the other. Greater restrictions do not seem to produce significantly less violence or crime. The same conclusion has been drawn from the experience with a strict firearms control law in Canada: The rate of homicides perpetrated with firearms went down after the law was passed, but the overall homicide rate did not. People intent on murder, it seems, switched to other means (Leenaars and Lester, 1994). However, a recent study of a ban on the purchase or possession of handguns by civilians in Washington, D.C., shows a significant reduction in homicides following the ban in 1977 (Loftin et al., 1991). Another recent study found that homicides committed with guns increase significantly in areas where restrictions on carrying concealed weapons are eased ("Study Links Rise . . . ," 1995).

So, these inconsistent research results leave policymakers unsure about the effects of gun control. The failure to find consistent or dramatic declines in violence from local gun control efforts may be because the United States is so awash with weapons that the controls that are established have little impact. However, Kleck's research suggests that modest declines in crime and violence could be achieved by a gun control policy that makes "gun acquisition at least marginally more difficult, and gun possession more risky, for the most identifiably violence-prone segments of the population" (1991: 433). However, firearms have never been totally banned in any state, so we do not know what the impact of a statewide or nationwide ban on the possession of firearms might be. It might depend on how stringent the laws are and on how rigidly they are enforced. It is also questionable whether society could ban handguns effectively. As Chapter 10 demonstrates, widespread and popular social practices, such as the use of alcohol and marijuana, are difficult to control through legislation. A total ban on guns could lead to a thriving black market that would leave the police even less equipped to deal with gun-related violence because all privately owned guns would be unregistered.

Media Control

There has been considerable pressure over the years, especially from groups of parents and educators, to establish controls over the portrayal of violence in the media. This would reduce the number of models for violence that the young are exposed to. The media have generally resisted any such controls. One reason for the resistance is that the violent shows are often the most popular ones. Movies with large doses of sex and violence such as *Lethal Weapon* or *The Shawshank Redemption* almost always make money for their producers, and television shows that portray violence such as *Cops* or *MacGyver* find vast numbers of viewers. In 1990, Congress passed the Children's Television Education Act. It is the first legal effort to require the television industry to take steps to provide for the educational and informational needs of children and youth in their programming (Huston et al., 1992). Licensees must demonstrate at the time of their license renewal that their programs meet these needs, although there is little specific in the act about what they must do. The act does not address the issue of violence directly but instead permits television broadcasters, networks, and cable companies to collaborate to reduce the amount of violent content without being subject to antitrust laws. In 1992, the three networks did agree to some guidelines to reduce violence on television. The guidelines suggest that violence should be relevant to the development of the plot and should not be gratuitous, excessive, or depicted as glamorous. However, there is no enforcement mechanism attached to the guidelines, and the networks will probably continue to air shows that get the best ratings, which are typically those with sex and violence in them.

Resistance to controls over the media also arises among those who view such controls as an infringement on the First Amendment rights of freedom of speech and freedom of the press. As was shown when discussing the censorship of pornography in Chapter 11, it is very difficult to distinguish between what is acceptable and what should be censored. Violence is, of course, a fact of life, and to eliminate it from the media altogether would be a tremendous distortion of reality. But what level of violence is "too much"? If we can censor violence, then what about some other ideas or practices that we find offensive? Some would wish to ban sensitive portrayals of gay men and lesbians on the grounds that it might be suggestive to young minds, whereas others would focus on political or religious ideas that they believe might mislead impressionable people. The point is that the door to censorship, once ajar, may be very difficult to keep from opening further. Such censorship could easily threaten the free press and the open expression of ideas that are so essential to a democracy. So the desirability of controlling media violence needs to be weighed against the threat it may present to democratic institutions.

Preventing War

If wars could be prevented, society would avoid not only the slaughter and destruction of the war itself but also the problems created by the dislocations of war. Whether war can be prevented and how to do it are highly controversial topics.

The Balance of Power   During the Cold War, which began at the end of World War II, U.S. foreign policy was directed toward preventing a nuclear catastrophe while at the same time maintaining U.S. political and military dominance in the world. In the early 1950s, Secretary of State John Foster Dulles (1954) developed the policy of **massive retaliation:** *War could be avoided if the enemy realized that any aggressor against the*

United States would suffer overwhelming damages from the massive retaliation with the U.S. military might. So the United States strove to prevent war by amassing weaponry to use as a threat. If the threat were credible—if the enemy believed that massive retaliation would follow aggression—then, it was argued, the weapons would never have to be used. The Soviet bloc nations also amassed incredible military force. By the 1980s, the foreign policies of both the United States and the Soviet Union were based on the concept of **mutually assured destruction** or MAD: *War can be prevented when each side has the might to destroy the other.* Any first-strike effort would result in retaliation and the mutual destruction of both sides. What is supposed to result from this policy is a **balance of power:** *A nuclear holocaust is avoided because the military capability of one side roughly balances that of the other side.*

It would seem that the balance of power approach worked. There has not been a world war nor have nuclear weapons been used in fifty years. Yet there are reasons for pessimism. After all, fifty years is not a very long time. If another one hundred years pass without a nuclear war and one occurs then, it would still have devastating consequences. In other words, given the destructive power of nuclear weapons, postponing war is really secondary to preventing war. In addition, more conventional wars such as the Korean conflict, the decade-long Vietnam War, the Gulf War, and our involvement in places such as Lebanon and Grenada have not been prevented. These conflicts hold the potential to escalate into a nuclear exchange. There were strong pressures, for example, to use tactical nuclear weapons in Vietnam. Finally, there remains the possibility that nuclear war could start by accident. Although the chances of this are considered by many to be small, they cannot be ignored.

Arms Control and Disarmament A more definite step toward protecting the world from nuclear destruction would be to limit the number of such weapons in existence or to eliminate them altogether. Nations are naturally reluctant to enter into agreements to limit their weaponry when they fear that the other side will take advantage of this situation. It is also often politically dangerous for elected officials to appear to compromise defensive strength. Yet there has been some progress in arms control (U.S. Arms Control and Disarmament Agency, 1982). In 1963, most nations signed a treaty banning nuclear testing in the atmosphere, outer space, underwater, and in some cases underground. The focus of this treaty was on protecting the environment from radioactive contamination. In the 1972 Strategic Arms Limitation Talks (SALT I), the United States and the Soviet Union agreed to place limits on their defensive weapons systems and on their most powerful land- and submarine-based offensive nuclear weapons. Further limitations on these weapons were agreed to by President Carter in the SALT II talks concluded in 1979. Although these treaties probably contributed to reducing the chances of a nuclear exchange, they left the nuclear powers with enormous stockpiles of weapons.

Then in the late 1980s, we saw the beginning of the collapse of the Soviet Union. Its economy could no longer support the burdens of economic and arms competition with the West and also support Soviet rule over the Baltics, Eastern Europe, and the many other areas it dominated since World War II. By 1991, the Soviet Empire no longer existed. The Berlin Wall fell and Germany was reunited; Eastern European countries were free; and the old Soviet Union had become the Commonwealth of Independent States. This dramatic transition has created the best opportunity since World War II for significant reductions in nuclear weaponry worldwide as well as for easing world tensions and reducing the likelihood of nuclear war. In the late 1980s, Presidents Mikhail Gorbachev and Ronald Reagan signed the INF treaty, which bans intermediate range nuclear weapons. This resulted in some of the existing nuclear stockpiles in both countries being destroyed. Both countries also agreed on certain procedures for the mutual verification of the results, something that had always been a serious hitch in negotiations between the United States and the Soviet Union. Then, in the early 1990s, the United States and Russia reached agreement on two strategic arms reduction treaties, START I and START II. If fully implemented, these treaties will produce dramatic reductions in the number of nuclear warheads stockpiled by both countries (Wald, 1995). Through the 1990s, both nations have been withdrawing nuclear weapons from ships, and Russia has been bringing them back from most of the nations of the former Soviet Union. Weapons are being destroyed at a rapid rate. However, even if the reductions planned by the treaties occur, the five nations known to possess nuclear weapons will still possess enough warheads to do massive destruction.

Because of the destructive power of nuclear weapons and the threat of nuclear winter, some scientists and policymakers argue that a permanent resolution to the dangers of nuclear weapons can be achieved only with complete disarmament. Although there are sizable interest groups both in the United States and abroad advocating such a policy, it is unlikely to come about in the foreseeable future. One reason for this is that the majority of people in the United States support a strong military posture, including nuclear parity with or dominance over any other nation in the world (Bailey, 1995). Many people believe that a nuclear deterrent force is still necessary to deal with the nations that still possess nuclear weapons, such as Russia, China, and the Ukraine, or that might possess them in the future, such as North Korea, India, and Pakistan. Furthermore, a credible nuclear force possessed by the United States could serve to discourage other nations from developing nuclear weapons. Complete nuclear disarmament could work, its opponents argue, only if completely effective verification procedures existed to determine whether a nation possessed nuclear weapons. For the fore-

seeable future, such procedures are not likely to exist. Furthermore, a nuclear deterrent might be useful in dealing with threats from chemical and biological weapons.

So, some legitimate reasons may remain for the United States to maintain a nuclear arsenal, but that arsenal could probably be drastically cut to a number large enough to deter a threat but small enough that a nuclear winter is unlikely. Scientists Carl Sagan and Richard Turco (1990) call this strategy a "minimum sufficient deterrence" and suggest that the United States and Russia could achieve it with between 100 and 300 strategic warheads. So, with the end of the Cold War, there is much uncertainty regarding which foreign policy approach would be the best to deter wars in the future. Some of the possibilities are explored in the Policy Issues insert in this chapter.

Nonproliferation of Weapons   In the past, some nations chose not to develop nuclear or other weapons of mass destruction because they had security arrangements and guarantees that offered them protection from attack by others without the need to have weapons of their own. For example, the North Atlantic Treaty Organization provided a nuclear defense for West Germany, and the U.S. nuclear umbrella restrained South Korea from developing its own weapons. With the end of the Cold War, many of the old security arrangements around the world are changing or disintegrating. This leaves a very unsettled international environment as far as the proliferation of weapons goes and calls for new international efforts to discourage such proliferation (Bailey, 1991; Reiss, 1995). One option to reducing proliferation would be to extend the U.S. or Russian nuclear umbrella over some countries that might be tempted to develop their own. If their security needs were satisfied, then a major motivation for developing weapons would be eliminated. However, this may clash with the pressure in both countries to reduce their nuclear armaments. A second option might be to encourage

This United Nations armored personnel carrier in Sarajevo, Bosnia and Herzegovina, is part of a U.N. peace-keeping force. Some argue that the United Nations is slowly evolving into a global political force that may develop some judicial and possibly military authority over nations.

the development of regional agreements that prohibit the development of effective delivery systems, such as intermediate range ballistic missiles that are hard to defend against. Without the delivery system, the weapons would be less of a threat. A third option would be to encourage open debate about the development of nuclear weapons, especially on how costly they are to develop. Experience in some countries, such as Sweden, suggests that the public tends to strongly oppose them when they learn how expensive they are. Fourth, when nations violate existing nonproliferation treaties, there should be certain and substantial international

sanctions against them, such as trade embargoes. Finally, the spread of weapons can be controlled through restricting the trade in technical knowledge or materials that are necessary to produce the weapons.

World Government One of the major obstacles to preventing war among nations is that each nation functions on the basis of protecting its own national interest and pursuing its own short-term goals. Nations do not typically pursue policies that are guided by the common long-term interests of all nations, especially when those policies have a negative impact on

POLICY ISSUES

Star Wars, Nuclear Weapons, and the Peace Dividend: Preventing War in the Post–Cold War World

Since World War II, U.S. foreign and defense policies have rested on a few basic assumptions: that the Cold War struggle between the two great superpowers of the United States and the Soviet Union overshadowed everything else and that a massive nuclear arsenal and a policy of mutually assured destruction (MAD) were needed to prevent war and protect the United States and its allies from threats around the world. Suddenly, there is no Cold War and no Soviet Union. This has created turmoil regarding what foreign and defense policies will be needed to prevent war in the post-Cold War world.

The quandary as to what the future holds may be epitomized by the Strategic Defense Initiative (SDI) or "Star Wars" (Boffey et al., 1988). Star Wars was conceived in the 1980s because of the growing realization that a policy of mutually assured destruction is inherently unstable. Nations cannot continue to stockpile weapons without increasing the likelihood that they will be used. The major thrust of SDI would be to move away from a policy based solely on offensive weapons by developing more defensive capabilities. The SDI would establish a shield to protect the United States from nuclear weapons. As currently conceived, the defense shield would involve many exotic technologies such as space satellites to detect and track missiles headed for the United States and ground lasers to destroy weapons. If such a shield could be established, an enemy would supposedly be less likely to attack because such an attack would be futile. We could thus prevent nuclear war not by threatening horrible destruction but by ensuring that nuclear weapons could never reach targets on U.S. soil.

However, not all defense specialists concede that a Star Wars approach is either feasible or desirable. One of the strongest arguments against the Star Wars approach is that it is unlikely to work as effectively as it must to deter nuclear war. Another argument against Star Wars is that it would merely lead to another round of escalation in weaponry. Once each side has their defensive system in place, there would be substantial pressures to develop further offensive weapons that can destroy or penetrate the defensive shield. As a consequence, the world would become an even more dangerous and potentially deadly place.

With the developments of the 1990s, the newest argument against Star Wars is that it is simply no longer necessary. If Russian stockpiles of warheads decline significantly, then there is no credible enemy who would likely launch a massive strike of intercontinental ballistic missiles against the United States. Those with nuclear weapons are either our allies (Great Britain, France), pose no current threat to us (Russia, China), or do not have the capacity to mount an intercontinental attack (Iraq, North Korea).

For the same reason that Star Wars may be outdated, there is a growing debate over what the U.S. military posture needs to be to prevent war and protect U.S. interests in the post–Cold War world. First, most analysts agree that, if current trends continue, future wars will probably not involve large nuclear exchanges between military superpowers. In fact, there seems to be only one superpower left, namely, the United States. Instead, smaller scale regional wars are likely to be what the future holds, fought mostly with conventional weapons, although some smaller scale nuclear weapons may be used by those who have them. In this environment, according to one view, the policy of the United States should be to maintain sufficient military strength to discourage any rival superpower from emerging to threaten U.S. primacy (Tyler, 1992). This might call for maintaining a still sizable nuclear force to deter others from developing their own nuclear weapons. In addition, this strategy calls for a still sizable military, at least 80 percent of its Cold War size. The United States would continue to use military intervention around the world to prevent the spread of nuclear weapons and to protect U.S. national interest. Regional security coalitions, such as the one used in the Persian Gulf War, might be used where useful, but these would be ad hoc assemblies that would not last beyond the immediate crisis. In addition, the United States would retain the freedom to act unilaterally when that best serves its interests.

A very different approach to the changing world emphasizes the idea that the end of the Cold War presents an opportunity to shift emphasis from making war to making peace. In this view, there is a "peace dividend" to be had by reducing the U.S. defense budget significantly and redirecting the economy from making weapons to producing goods and services that people want to buy. This has already happened in a small way as some Star Wars resources have been redirected to more peaceful uses. For example, a laser built for Star Wars has been turned into a machine for making advanced computer chips (Weber, 1992). Some view this as essential to our economic health. Reducing the size of the military–industrial complex (see Chapter 2) by shifting resources from defense spending to other realms may be critical to reindustrializing the U.S. economy and making the United States more competitive with such economic superpowers as Germany and Japan. If the U.S. continues to direct so much of its resources toward war, these countries will only gain more power economically. This view does not rule out the maintenance of a sizable military in the United States, but some proponents of this view argue for a 50 percent or greater reduction in the military budget (Markusen and Yudken, 1992).

Such a transition would be difficult because it would produce severe dislocation of workers and industries in many parts of the U.S. economy. Whole industries would have to shift from weapons production to nonmilitary products. One way to approach this would be to mount a national, publicly funded economic development strategy whereby the government would assist communities in identifying the economic resources they have, locating potential uses for those resources, and then seeking companies both nationally and internationally to develop those resources. This could assist communities by attracting or retaining industries, transferring technology from defense work to civilian production, and providing entrepreneurial aid. In the long run, proponents of this view argue, the economy will be stronger for having shifted away from war production and toward civilian production.

Both of these approaches are currently being debated in the United States, and future policy directions are uncertain.

the achievement of their own goals. One way around this obstacle might be to establish an international organization that would do for the nations of the world something like what the U.S. federal government does for the states: serve as a forum where competing interests can be hammered into a coherent policy without resorting to violence. This was attempted with the League of Nations following World War I and with the United Nations (UN) following World War II in 1945.

For such efforts at world government to be effective, there must be a body of international law that is accepted and adhered to by all nations. There must also be some means of enforcing that law. Regarding international law, the many treaties that the members of the UN have signed over the years stand as a sound beginning of an agreement regarding how na-

tions will relate to one another. Although nations disagree over the interpretation or applicability of particular parts of the laws in particular cases, there are judicial bodies, such as the International Court of Justice at The Hague (the World Court), for resolving these disputes. A major flaw in the system at this point is that nations can ignore the Court's jurisdiction in particular cases. The United States did this in 1985 when the World Court ruled that the United States had broken international law by aiding the antigovernment rebels (the contras) in Nicaragua. The World Court ordered the United States to stop arming and training the contras, but the Reagan administration said that the Court had no jurisdiction in this area. A second major flaw in the existing system of international law is that the United Nations has no means of enforcing its laws un-

TABLE 14.2 Major United Nations Peacekeeping Operations, December 1994

Place	Troops/Observers	Goal
India and Pakistan	39	Monitor cease-fire between India and Pakistan
Somalia	9,412	Assist civilians and prevent fighting between warlords.
Haiti	6,567	Protect government and assist emergence of democratic institutions
Rwanda	5,522	Peacekeeping between different ethnic groups
Cyprus	1,183	Prevent fighting between Greek and Turkish communities
Lebanon	5,146	Serve as a buffer between Israel and Lebanon
Iraq and Kuwait	1,142	Monitor border between former combatants
El Salvador	34	Oversee peace plan

Source: United Nations Department of Public Information, in consultation with the Department of Peace-keeping Operations and Peace-keeping Financing Division, Office of Programme Planning, Budget and Finance, December 1994.

LINKAGES

less individual nations consent to its enforcement. The United Nations can send its peacekeeping forces into disputes when all parties agree to let them in, and Table 14.2 shows that UN troops and observers are active in many places around the globe in attempting to prevent conflicts from beginning or escalating. However, the UN cannot move in and settle disputes without the consent of the nations involved. To this point, nations have been unwilling to surrender their sovereignty and their right to use force to any international body. So the mechanism for some form of world government is in place, but the nations have not yet agreed to use it fully.

Despite the failings of the United Nations, many supporters of world government are not discouraged because they fully expect the transition to take a long time. After all, the history of the evolution of political structures has been toward larger and more complex forms of organization. Over the past few thousand years, human societies have developed from family- and kin-based political structures to larger units such as nation-states. With the increasing complexity and interdependence of the modern world, they argue, the next natural step is to some form of supranational organization. The importance of international trade and multinational corporations to the economies of all countries illustrates the extent to which cooperation is essential and warfare increasingly destructive. However, shifting people's allegiances from a nation to a "united nations" will involve a long and possibly difficult transition, as was the transition in the United States from a federation of states to the "united states."

Summary

1. Unlike interpersonal violence, collective violence is organized violence involving relatively large groups of people working to promote or resist some social policies and practices. There are various types of collective violence: civil disorders (race riots and labor strife), political violence, wars, and terrorism.

2. There are a number of biological explanations for violence, especially that of sociobiology, which argues that certain characteristics—such as territoriality, aggressiveness, and selfishness—are to an extent genetically determined because these traits enhance the survival of the species; over long periods, people with these genetic characteristics come to dominate in the gene pool.

3. There are a number of social sources of violence. Among them are structural preconditions that increase the likelihood of violence: social strain or deprivation, competition, and ethnocentrism. These preconditions are translated into violence because the frustration that they produce can lead to aggressive behavior. This involves relative deprivation because people tend to feel deprived or frustrated relative to what others have or they believe they deserve.

4. The likelihood that the preconditions and the frustration will lead to violence is influenced by some mediating factors: Learning in a particular culture or subculture to view violence as an acceptable way of dealing with problems, having available attractive people to serve as models for violence, portraying violence in the mass media in a positive way.

5. War is very disruptive to society and because of this has a number of subtle impacts on society: Crime and political turmoil increase during and after wars and wars can be disruptive to the economy. The devastation accompanying a nuclear war would be a severe assault to the ecosystem and might threaten civilization as we know it.

6. One of the keys to controlling violence is to correct the strains, frustrations, and injustices that lead to collective violence. However, there is often little consensus about what social reforms would do the job or about what constitutes social justice.

7. Controlling guns and limiting the amount of violence in the media have been portrayed as partial solutions to the problem of violence. However, there is no consistent evidence that gun control would have a great effect, and many people are opposed to the censorship that would be necessary to limit violence in the media.

8. Currently, there are four major approaches to preventing war, especially nuclear war: Maintain a balance of power, develop treaties for arms control and disarmament, control the proliferation of weapons, and establish a world government that would be able to stop nations from going to war.

STUDY and Review

Key Terms

balance of power
civil disorder
commodity riots
communal riots
frustration
insurrection
massive retaliation

mutually assured destruction
relative deprivation
sociobiology
subculture of violence
terrorism
violence

Multiple-Choice Questions

1. In most cases, spouse abuse would be an instance of:
   a. Collective violence.
   b. Interpersonal violence.
   c. Commodity violence.
   d. Relative deprivation.

2. Since World War II, most race riots in the United States could be characterized as:
   a. Whites attacking blacks in racially contested residential areas.
   b. Insurrections.
   c. Attacks against property, merchandise, or equipment rather than people.
   d. Interpersonal rather than collective violence.

3. According to the text, one problem with international treaties to prevent the spread of weapons of mass destruction is that:
   a. Only a handful of nations have signed them.
   b. The United States refuses to ratify the treaties.
   c. No consistent sanctions have been used against nations that violate them.
   d. Nations have failed to agree on the final wording of such a treaty.

4. Which of the following is true about the arguments of sociobiologists?
   a. Learning and other social forces can alter inborn genetic tendencies.
   b. They have identified specific genes that cause particular forms of human behavior.
   c. Sociologists have concluded that their arguments are totally implausible.
   d. Most forms of collective violence are caused by brain tumors or chemical imbalances.

5. Which of the following was identified by the text as a structural precondition to violence?
   a. Violence in the media.
   b. Frustration.
   c. The subculture of violence.
   d. Competition between people.

6. In studies of urban riots in the United States of the last three decades, which of the following conclusions were drawn?
   a. Absolute deprivation rather than relative deprivation is the cause of collective violence.
   b. Participants in the riots were mostly the criminals and unemployed.
   c. Relative deprivation rather than absolute deprivation is the cause of collective violence.
   d. The cities that experienced riots were the ones in which African Americans had been most successful at gaining political office.

7. Which of the following statements is most consistent with the conflict perspective on violence?
   a. Violence is a tool that any group might use to protect or enhance its own interests.
   b. Violence arises out of social disorganization.
   c. Violence occurs because the various parts of the social system are not well integrated.
   d. Violence is dysfunctional because it can escalate and get out of hand.

8. All of the following are conclusions drawn in the text about the consequences of war *except:*
   a. War is often associated with reductions in inflation.
   b. War is often associated with political turmoil.
   c. War is often associated with increases in crime rates.
   d. War is often associated with increases in anomie.

9. Given the research that has been done, policymakers have concluded that gun control legislation would probably have which effect?
   a. A substantial increase in homicides and violence.
   b. A substantial decrease in homicides and violence.
   c. A decrease in homicides but an increase in overall violence.
   d. Policymakers are unsure what the impact of gun control will be.

10. According to the text, which of the following is most likely in the realm of policy on nuclear weapons for the near future?
   a. World-wide nuclear disarmament.
   b. Unilateral nuclear disarmament by the United States.
   c. A resurgence of the Cold War.
   d. The maintenance of a nuclear deterrent by the United States and a few other nations.

True/False Questions

1. The 1960s was a period in U.S. history during which levels of violence were far higher than during any other decade.

2. The Detroit race riot of 1943 was a communal riot.

3. Currently, the United States, Great Britain, China, and Japan all possess nuclear weapons.

4. Sociobiology is one of the structural preconditions that can push people toward violence.

5. Viewing violence on television is more likely to produce aggressive or violent behavior among girls than among boys.

6. The Vietnam War was the first war in U.S. history in which there was significant domestic dissent against the war.

7. Many scientists today believe that a nuclear winter of some degree of severity is a possibility after a nuclear war.

8. In controlling violence, interventionists believe that the government should be influential in determining which social reforms are pursued.

9. Opponents of gun control legislation argue that the second amendment to the U.S. Constitution does not apply to the gun control issue.

10. The five nations in the world that currently possess nuclear weapons have established a plan for disarming themselves over a decade under the Treaty on the Non-Proliferation of Nuclear Weapons of 1995.

Fill-In Questions

1. _____ violence is violence that is organized and engaged in by relatively large groups of people to promote or resist some social policies or practices.
2. The two types of civil disorder discussed in the text are _____ and

_____ .
3. An organized action by some group to rebel against the existing government and to replace it with new political forms is a/an

_____ .

4. _____ refers to the fact that people tend to feel deprived or frustrated in comparison to what others have or what they believe they deserve.
5. In terms of the social sources of violence, ethnocentrism is one of the _____ in the process bringing about violence.

6. From the _____ perspective, violence is an important mechanism for bringing about social change.
7. Opponents of controls over violence in the media argue that such controls would violate

the _____ Amendment to the U.S. Constitution.
8. The most recent arms control treaties that were agreed upon by the United States and

Russia were the _____ treaties.

9. The _____ is an international judicial body that nations can use for resolving disputes among nations.

10. The _____ was a policy that claimed to avoid a nuclear holocaust because the military capability of one side roughly balanced that of the other side.

Matching Questions

_____ 1. Ludlow Massacre

_____ 2. Robert Ardrey

_____ 3. John Foster Dulles

_____ 4. Detroit riot of 1943

_____ 5. Dorr's Rebellion

_____ 6. mediating factor in violence

_____ 7. Second Amendment to the Constitution

_____ 8. anomie

_____ 9. SALT II

_____ 10. United Nations

    A. territorial imperative
    B. subculture of violence
    C. labor strife
    D. causes crime to rise after wars
    E. communal riot
    F. world government
    G. insurrection
    H. gun control issue
    I. arms reduction
    J. massive retaliation

Essay Questions

1. What are civil disorders? Describe the major civil disorders in U.S. history.
2. What is terrorism? What kinds of terrorist groups are there today? What can be done about terrorism?
3. According to sociobiologists, what are the reasons for aggression and violence in human beings? Assess their arguments.
4. How do social strain and competition between groups serve as preconditions for violence?
5. What is the subculture of violence and how does it contribute to violence in society?
6. Compare and contrast the manner in which the functionalist perspective and the conflict perspective view violence in society.
7. What kind of economic problems can war produce for society?

8. What role does social reform play in controlling the levels of violence in society?
9. What are the arguments for and against gun control? What does research show us about the effectiveness of gun control legislation in reducing violence in society?
10. What is currently being done and what could be done to prevent the spread of weapons of mass destruction to nations that do not currently have them?

Answers

Multiple-Choice
1. B; 2. C; 3. C; 4. A; 5. D; 6. C; 7. A; 8. A; 9. D; 10. D

True/False
1. F; 2. T; 3. F; 4. F; 5. F; 6. F; 7. T; 8. T; 9. F; 10. F

Fill-In
1. collective
2. race riots, labor strife
3. insurrection
4. relative deprivation
5. structural preconditions
6. conflict
7. First
8. START
9. World Court
10. balance of power

Matching
1. C; 2. A; 3. J; 4. E; 5. G; 6. B; 7. H; 8. D; 9. I; 10. F

For Further Reading

William E. Burrows and Robert Windrem. *Critical Mass: The Dangerous Race for Superweapons in a Fragmenting World.* New York: Simon and Schuster, 1994. This is an alarming book that focuses on the extent of the proliferation of weapons of mass destruction to Third-World nations, and even terrorist groups, and the ease with which it occurs.

Carl N. Degler. *In Search of Human Nature: The Decline and Revival of Darwinism in American Social Thought.* New York: Oxford University Press, 1991. This interesting work focuses on how biological and sociobiological ideas as explanations of human behavior have gained and lost popularity in the United States over the years. The author focuses on these explanations more as belief systems that people accept than as scientific theories.

Erich Goode. *Collective Behavior.* Fort Worth: Harcourt Brace Jovanovich, 1992. This is a comprehensive textbook in the specialty area of sociology that studies riots, civil disturbance, insurrections, and other forms of collective violence. It is an excellent resource book.

Michael Klare. *Rogue States and Nuclear Outlaws: America's Search for a New Foreign Policy.* New York: Hill & Wang, 1995. This author makes the argument that the U.S. military has responded to the end of the Cold War by demonizing a number of Third-World nations as outlaw states that threaten U.S. interests around the world. The military has done this, the author argues, to maintain pressure for large defense budgets that are probably not needed.

John R. MacArthur. *Second Front: Censorship and Propaganda in the Gulf War.* New York: Hill & Wang, 1992. This author highlights another common consequence of war: the use of propaganda by the government to gain support for war efforts. The author argues that the U.S. and Kuwaiti governments lied to and misinformed the American public to gain support for the Persian Gulf War in 1991.

George Rudé. *Ideology and Popular Protest.* New York: Pantheon, 1980. An excellent analysis of the role of ideological factors in public protest and revolution. It includes an analysis of the English, American, and French Revolutions.

Herbert Shapiro. *White Violence and Black Response: From Reconstruction to Montgomery.* Amherst: University of Massachusetts Press, 1988. This book documents the routine, organized, and persistent use of violence by dominant whites in the United States to control black Americans. Although the book's tone is angry, it is also informative regarding some dark elements of our past and present.

Seth Shulman. *The Threat at Home: Confronting the Toxic Legacy of the U.S. Military.* Boston: Beacon Press, 1992. Our arsenal of conventional and nuclear weapons, along with our testing of weapons and military maneuvers, represent another significant threat to the environment. This book documents the dimensions of that threat, why it has gotten out of hand, and what can be done about it.

Jeffrey D. Simon. *The Terrorist Trap: America's Experience with Terrorism.* Bloomington: Indiana University Press, 1994. This is an excellent book on the nature and sources of terrorism confronting the United States and the efficacy of various responses to it.

CHAPTER
FIFTEEN *Emerging Issues: Science and Technology*

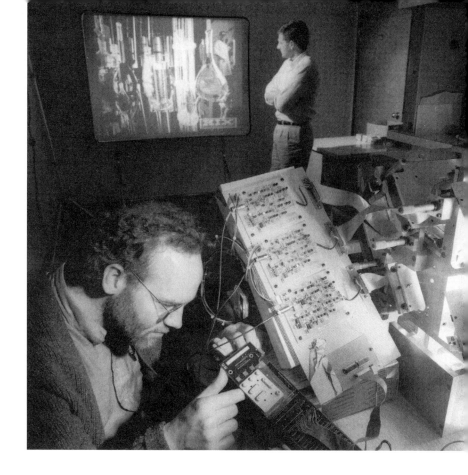

The nineteenth-century philosopher Auguste Comte has been referred to as the "father of modern sociology," for he was one of the first to propose that society can be studied utilizing the scientific method. Like other scholars past and present, Comte was limited by the existing knowledge of his era. In what is regarded as his most significant work, *Cours de Philosophie Positive* (1835), Comte attempted to define the limits of scientific knowledge, and wrote these words concerning the heavenly bodies:

> We see how we may determine their forms, their distances, their bulk, their motions, but we can never know anything of their chemical or mineralogical structure; and much less, that of organized beings living on their surface. . . . We must keep carefully apart the idea of the solar

system and that of the universe, and be always assured that our only true interest is in the former. Within this boundary alone is astronomy the supreme and positive science that we have determined it to be . . . the stars serve us scientifically only as providing positions with which we may compare the interior movements of our system. (Book 2, Chapter 1)

Essentially, Comte had decided that the stars would never be anything more to humankind than celestial reference points and that even our knowledge of the planets would always be limited to geometric principles. If anyone had proposed the science of astrophysics to Comte, he would have undoubtedly judged such inquiry to be impossible.

In less than one hundred years after Comte's death, almost the entire discipline of astronomy had become astrophysics. In fact, a major technological breakthrough came only two years after Comte died, when two German physicists perfected the spectroscope, a device that not only revealed the chemical properties of terrestrial bodies, but also told humankind more about the distant stars than what had been known about the planets (Clarke, 1984). Consequently, Comte's "positive" statement that "we can never know anything of [the stars'] chemical or mineralogical structure" was laid permanently to rest.

This discussion is certainly not intended as an indictment of Comte's scientific naiveté, because he cannot be blamed for failing to imagine a scientific technique like spectroscopy. Rather, his categorical assertion serves as a reminder of a principle that is respected by most contemporary scientists: Technologies that are impossible given existing knowledge may well become available as the result of scientific and technological discoveries in the future.

In fact, the awesome scientific and technological developments of the twentieth century have led some to believe that science and technology have no limits at all other than those that we, as human beings, place on them. Others argue that science and technology are cre-

ating problems—some of them potentially very serious—that need to be addressed. This chapter will review the evidence on this issue. It will show that there have been benefits, but as one might expect there have been problems as well.

Technology and Society

What Is Technology?

The term [*technology*] encompasses not only such recently emerging wonders as trips to the moon, hydrogen bombs, genetic engineering, and computers which some fear will eventually enslave us, but also toothbrushes, doorknobs, and wheelbarrows, as well as simplified spelling systems, arrangements for bureaucratic coordination, military draft lotteries, advertising strategies, and even sticks that chimpanzees use to catch termites. (Richter, 1982: 6)

This description of technology by a sociologist casts a broad net regarding this commonplace term. Some writers have proposed that technology is not merely a human phenomenon but also found among lower animals, such as the nests built by birds or the dams of beavers. Other definitions of technology are confined to the realm of science and human production: "the systematic application of scientific or other organized knowledge to practical tasks" (Galbraith, 1967: 12). Anthropologists define *technology* as a body of knowledge that is available to a civilization for achieving specific objectives, and this helps to distinguish the term from *science,* which is the search for knowledge or something that produces knowledge (see Chapter 1).

The definition of **technology** used in this chapter combines these ideas: *knowledge, tools, and practices that are employed as means of achieving clearly identifiable goals.* In this definition, technology can be both material and nonmaterial in nature, including not only "things" but also a particular way of thinking or a specific orientation toward social organization (Volti, 1992). So technology consists of things such as robots, computers, and nuclear bombs, but it also in-

Myths & FACTS

ABOUT SCIENCE AND TECHNOLOGY

Myth: The first practical application in this century of scientific knowledge about the atom was the development of techniques to grow more food and thus alleviate the problems of hunger and poverty.

FACT: Actually, the first practical application of this knowledge was to build weapons of mass destruction: atomic and nuclear bombs. Thus, the technology further exacerbated the problem of violence and war in the world.

Myth: Fear of the impact of technology on people's lives is a new phenomenon, arising out of the complex technology associated with industrialization.

FACT: Fear of technology can be found practically anywhere that technology shapes people's lives, even in preindustrial societies. However, the dangers that modern technology poses are quantitatively greater than and probably qualitatively different from the dangers of past, more simple technologies.

Myth: The coming of computers and a postindustrial society will usher in an era in which most people will find exciting, rewarding, and well-paying jobs.

FACT: Many experts believe that these developments will not necessarily be a boon for everyone. Many service jobs, for example, and those created by computer technology are dull, repetitive, and low paying. Also, because of technological advances involving automation and robotization, unemployment and underemployment may continue to be serious problems in the future.

Myth: It is good to develop all of the technology that scientific knowledge makes possible because then society can choose to implement those developments that are beneficial and ignore those that create problems for people.

FACT: Once a technology exists, it tends to take on a life of its own: There are powerful social pressures to use it and further develop it by those interest groups who benefit from it. In other words, once the technological cat is out of the bag, society may have little choice about whether it will be used.

---

cludes modes of organization, such as mechanization and automation. It should be obvious that various levels of technology exist in different societies. For example, when premodern people discovered fire, it became a part of their technology, but their overall level of technological sophistication was low in comparison to even the most underdeveloped nations in the world today. The most technological sophistication accompanies **industrialization,** *a productive subsistence pattern in which machines and power tools, run by new sources of energy such as fossil fuels, accomplish tasks that were previously done by hand.*

Some observers have suggested that the United States and some other societies are becoming **postindustrial societies,** *ones that are dominated by a highly technological form of production and devote greater resources to providing services than to industrial production* (Bell, 1973; Beniger, 1993). Whether modern societies are called industrial or postindustrial, all have gone through a process of **modernization,** *the economic, social, and cultural changes that occur when a preindustrial society makes the transition to an advanced industrial society.* In a sense, much of this book has been about changes associated with modernization.

This chapter will illustrate some of the major technological developments that can create problems for people before addressing the problems that they may create.

The Impact of Technology on Society

Mechanization and Automation

One element in the process of industrialization is **mechanization,** which refers to *the use of machinery to replace human and animal labor in the production of goods and services.* Mechanization is part and parcel of technological modernization, wherein human muscles have come to be supplemented and sometimes replaced through material tools and new power sources. **Automation** is an extension of mechanization and refers to *the automatically controlled operation of machines by mechanical or electronic devices.* Mechanization and automation are accompanied by enormous increases in human productivity and a highly specialized division of labor. They involve a transition from

> one worker producing one item in one day to *one hundred* workers producing *five hundred* items in one day (with each of these hundred workers performing a specialized task and none of them producing any completed items on an individual basis). (Richter, 1982: 44)

The three main groups of mechanical inventions that fueled early industrialization were steam engines and steam-powered transport, textile machinery, and improvements in iron and steel manufacture (Braun, 1984). The steam engine permitted large-scale production of goods in factories and also opened the door to locomotives, which served as a (then) speedy way of transporting these products from place to place. Mechanical spinning machinery and power looms greatly enlarged the cotton and textile industries, and the use of coal in the smelting of iron and production of steel led to huge production operations that were at the heart of the industrial revolution.

In human history, there has been an endless search for implements that permit people to do their work better, more easily, and faster. Early inventions such as the potter's wheel, the primitive hammer and chisel, the hoe and the shovel, and the discovery of fire all became servants of the craftsperson, helping these artisans to refine their skills. These tools were not the masters of those who used them, but rather expanded the mastery of the workers themselves. In fact, it was an increasingly specialized division of labor rather than the development of machinery itself that separated craftspersons from their products (Volti, 1992). This expanding division of labor actually predated the development of machinery, but was an early precursor to the now-classic complaint that factory workers are forced to behave like machines. In the early automobile assembly lines, for example, one worker bolted wheels on and did nothing else to the finished product, and another set the rearview mirror in place. This was a very efficient form of organization in which many products could be produced in a given time. However, once each worker had responsibility for only a minor part of the production process, none of them could claim that the resulting product was theirs. They were no longer the masters of the production process but rather cogs in the machinery.

Mechanization and automation have led to many changes that most people would regard as positive. For example, living standards have risen, the average workweek has been shortened, and much demeaning and exhausting work has been transferred from people to machines. However, although mechanical and automated systems can be built to complement human life and serve humankind, they often are not. Too often, they are designed with technical considerations given the most attention and human concerns considered only secondarily. This tendency, along with the fact that industrialization involves many possibilities for power and profit, can create many difficulties. When people realize the potential for power and profit in mechanization and automation, short-term gains often take precedence over the long-term human implications of the advancing technol-

Mechanization and automation have brought about some positive changes for society, but for many workers, such as these at a food processing plant, it means that they become cogs in the productive machinery with little control over their work.

ogy. This is the issue, once again, of whether human beings are masters of their machines or are mastered by the machines. Despite lingering concerns about the impact of scientific and technological developments on people's lives, the United States continues to devote greater and greater resources to furthering more of these developments. As Figure 15.1 (on p. 552) indicates, an increasingly large amount of money and more scientists and engineers have been embarking on the task of producing even more scientific and technological breakthroughs over the past 20 years.

Telecommunications and Computers A little over one hundred years ago, it took the Pony Express days and even weeks to transport written communications from place to place. After technology permitted devices such as the Atlantic cable, instant telephone communication was possible between geographic areas in different parts of the globe, and we saw the beginnings of what futurist Marshall McLuhan called the "global village." But far more was yet to come in a very short period of time.

In 1979, a committee of the National Academy of Sciences issued this statement:

> The modern era of electronics has ushered in a second industrial revolution . . . its impact on society could be even greater than that of the original industrial revolution. (Norman, 1981: 109)

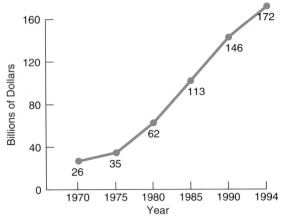

A. Expenditures on Research and Development

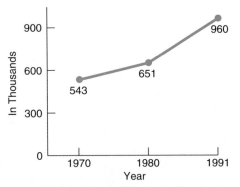

B. Scientists and Engineers Employed
in Research and Development

FIGURE 15.1 Resources Devoted to Basic and Applied Research and Development in the United States, 1970–1994. *Source:* U.S. Bureau of the Census, *Statistical Abstract of the United States, 1995* (Washington, D.C.: U.S. Government Printing Office, 1995), pp. 611, 618.

The electronics industry began to be a major economic force during the late 1940s with the development of the transistor, but even this technological innovation did not permit the kind of miniaturization in electronic components that is commonplace today. Perhaps you have seen photographs of IBM's first computer. This piece of equipment was enormous, occupying more physical space than most suburban homes, and just the machinery to cool the computer took up a great deal of room. The microelectronics revolution has been fueled by the invention of the silicon chip. These tiny chips, which are approximately one-quarter the size of a postage stamp, can be imprinted with tens of thousands of electronic components and circuits. By the 1990s, laptop or notebook computers, which are small enough to be easily carried around by a person, can store enormous amounts of information, run complicated software programs, and communicate through built-in modems with people around the world. And few people believe that we have come anywhere near the limits of this technology!

Along with economic implications, the social impact of microelectronics or computerization is almost as hard to comprehend. For example, had it not been for these developments, the United States would never have been able to explore deep space, go to the moon, or build the space shuttle. Just think of the military significance of these technological achievements. During World War I, military commanders made calculations in their heads when they fired their weapons, and it was frequently a matter of luck whether a bomb actually hit its target. By the Persian Gulf War in 1991, warfare was run by microelectronic controls and computerized guidance systems. "Smart" bombs were laser-guided to their targets, and satellite communications enabled instantaneous contact between battlefield commanders and Pentagon officials. At the same time, people watching television around the world could see the bombing of Baghdad live because of advances in telecommunications.

For the average person, these developments have important implications. For example, during the 1960s and even into the 1970s, the least expensive computers cost hundreds of thousands of dollars, but today, computers that have equal or greater power than those early machines can be purchased for less than $10,000, and versatile personal computers for business and home use are now as inexpensive as $1,000 or less. And developments in the field of computers and telecommunications are occurring so rapidly that it is almost foolhardy to attempt to predict the future. One technology consultant, for example, predicts that such modern technologies as the television and the telephone are already obsolete and will soon be replaced by "telecomputers" that perform the functions of these old instruments and much more (Gilder, 1993). In fact, he predicts that the terms "telephone" and "television" will soon sound as quaint and old fashioned as "icebox" and "horseless carriage." We now have the technology to transmit huge amounts of information and to send it interactively; we also have computers that can store and process masses of information. The television, on the other hand, is a passive receptacle into which television networks send programs at prearranged times. The telecomputer of the future will be an interactive instrument that connects its user with thousands of telecomputers in a web of information exchange around the world. The user might connect with the computer of a co-worker in another part of the city or nation, or with the computer of a library, movie storage center, art museum, or university to access a book, movie, art exhibit, or university lecture—to be viewed at one's leisure or stored for later viewing. No longer will it be necessary to follow

While some older people remain wary of computers and computerized technology, younger people are being socialized to accept computers as a way of life. It is likely that societies will be increasingly dependent on this technology in the future.

The Globalization of Communications

According to a former chief executive officer of a major corporation in the United States,

> The single most powerful development in global communities has been the satellite, born a mere thirty-one years ago. . . . Satellites now bind the world for better or worse, in an electronic infrastructure that carries news, money, and data anywhere on the planet at the speed of light. Satellites have made borders utterly porous to information. (Wriston, 1992: 12)

The technology of satellites, computers, and telecommunications have combined to make possible a global communications system in which capital, information, and data can be transmitted, almost at will and often instantaneously, around the world. Customers can withdraw money from their bank accounts in their hometown from many cash machines across the country and around the world. A customer's credit card account can be checked instantaneously to be sure it is not overdrawn. People send electronic mail messages around the world on the Internet.

While many people use and benefit from this global system of communication, it is transnational corporations that probably gain the most substantial benefit from it (Schiller, 1993). It becomes a tool for them to reduce costs, enhance marketing reach to a worldwide audience, and open up labor markets around the world. This ability enhances the extent and concentration of corporate power.

One consequence of this globalized control of communications, which is discussed in Chapter 2, is that capitalist corporations control much of the world communications structure and therefore corporate and capitalist viewpoints take an increasingly dominant place in public discourse and the media. Competing and dissenting voices emanating from less powerful constituencies are less likely to be heard, especially on a global stage. As one example of this, the media have become so important in national and state politics in the United States and so expensive that only the wealthy, or those who can raise funds from corporations or other sources of funds by being willing to back their agendas, have any chance of winning political office. "In either case, the electoral process is transformed into a mechanism for representing the advantaged" (Schiller, 1993: 51).

Another concern about the globalization of communications is the extent to which it makes possible the cultural domination of one society by another. The United States clearly dominates the global mass media (Turow, 1992). For example, three-quarters of the broadcast and basic cable television revenues and four-fifths of pay-television revenues around the world are generated by mass media materials produced in the United States. Worldwide, over half of all films rented to theaters or purchased for home video viewing are United States products. This has produced opposition

---

a television schedule or go to the prearranged, seven o'clock showing of a new movie release. In fact, television channels may become a thing of the past, as people will access thousands of data bases rather than turn the channel. In addition, the telecomputers of the future will not only receive, they will also send: completed work to a coworker, thoughts and ideas to a global chat room on the Internet, and a creative work of art or fiction to those who request

it. The same instrument will also be used to pay bills, order airline tickets, and regulate the furnace in the home. Some people may still choose at times to do things the old way, but no longer will it be necessitated by the technology of the passive television appliance.

Advances in both computers and automation have produced robotization, another significant dimension of the microelectronics revolution. Microelectronically controlled ma-from many nations who see this as **cultural colonialism,** *a cultural assault that, if not diminished, will change values, norms, and ways of life.* In fact, the media penetration of the world by the United States can be likened to the geographical penetration of new worlds by European explorers in earlier centuries. While Catholic missionaries from Europe brought their schools and churches to the native peoples of the Americas, modern media magnates bring United States television serials such as *Dallas* or movies such as *Die Hard* to nations and cultures around the world. The result, many fear, will be the same: the irreversible change in cultural values and the ultimate destruction of traditional ways of life. The values of the United States regarding work, gender relations, religion, violence, and many other things could pervade the world. The result could be the transformation of nations around the world along U.S. capitalist lines and the transformation of all nations into modern consumer marketplaces for the products of mostly Western corporations. This is a further expansion of world capitalism in terms of penetrating more parts of the world with its emphasis on market forces, profit making, surplus accumulation, and economic growth (see Chapter 2).

By the end of the twentieth century, United States media are receiving some fairly stiff competition from the Japanese and European media industries. Yet, this simply means that wealthy industrial nations of the world dominate the media market and are thus in a strong position to communicate their message and positions about capitalism, privatization, commercialization, and civilization. In fact, the United States and other Western nations have urged the United Nations to encourage freedom of the media because their well-developed media industry will dominate any open market (Schiller, 1993). Many nations oppose this because they want their indigenous media to have a chance to develop and to preserve aspects of their traditional way of life. Such nations sometimes maintain government bureaus, the purpose of which is to support indigenous cultural and artistic activity as a way of supporting the maintenance of traditional cultural values. Western governments and transnational corporations have encouraged the dismantling of such bureaucracies because they serve to limit Western corporate dominance. Even the notion that the media and the press should be free of government control is a Western cultural value that not all nations agree with. Many nations view the media as a tool of nation-building, to be used by the government to encourage patriotism and desired values and behavior. However, with the globalization of communications made possible by modern technology, the possibility exists that a few powerful actors on the world scene will dominate what people see and hear and thus shape their values and ways of life.

chines are currently in use at automobile manufacturing plants around the world, and these robots can be "taught" to do new things using computerized equipment. The General Motors' Vanguard plant in Saginaw, Michigan was described this way:

> Hardly a human works among the multitude of robots. Only forty-two hourly workers are spread over two shifts, and eventually the plant will add an overnight shift with no human presence of any kind. Overhead, perched in a glass-walled command room, a handful of engineers and technicians run the factory. ("GM Bets . . . , " 1988)

Given the ever-expanding technological frontier that surrounds the employment of computers, satellites, and other microelectronic wizardry, Marshall McLuhan's 1968 vision of a "global village" continues to take shape and heralds the evolution of human societies that are ever more dependent on microelectronics and computer technology (Beniger, 1993). The International Perspectives insert explores some of the implications of advances in telecommunications and computers for societies around the world.

Nuclear Power   The idea that the physical world is made up of atoms is very old, even showing up from time to time in classical Greek literature. By the beginning of the nineteenth century, scientists were convinced that chemical reactions could be best explained if each chemical element is thought of as composed of very small identical atoms that are characteristic of the element. In 1890, the field of atomic physics was actually begun when physicist J. J. Thomson first isolated and established the existence of electrons (Besancon, 1966). Knowledge of the atom and its properties eventually led to an understanding of atomic and nuclear power. Through the twentieth century, scientists held high hopes concerning nuclear energy. As technology expanded, humankind succeeded in harnessing this enormous power, both in its destructive capability and as an alternative energy source.

One of the first practical applications of atomic and nuclear energy was in the area of weapons. The first atomic bombs were dropped on Japan in World War II. The first test of a thermonuclear device took place in 1952 at a U.S. testing site in the Marshall Islands. In 1954, an accident occurred during a subsequent test in the Pacific, in which one man was killed and many others were injured. This incident called attention to the problem of radioactive fallout. Fears involving the prospect of nuclear holocaust have intensified as technology continues to expand. These problems are discussed in more detail in Chapter 14.

The use of nuclear power for peaceful purposes held most promise for many as an energy source. Experts were very optimistic about its promise following World War II, and in the 1950s the government pushed the slogan "Atoms for Peace," deemphasizing the enormous destructive capabilities of atomic power

and touting it as a source of abundant, pollution-free energy. Reliance on nuclear power has increased considerably in the United States over the past few decades. In 1970, only 1 percent of electricity was generated by nuclear fuels, compared with over 21 percent today (see Figure 15.2). However, optimism over the role of nuclear generation of power is dampened for some because of two major problems with nuclear energy. First, it is expensive to build nuclear power plants with sufficient safeguards against accidents, theft of nuclear fuels, or terrorism. This increases the cost of producing electricity and throws into question whether nuclear-generated power can compete economically with power generated from other sources. The disastrous nuclear accident at Chernobyl in the Soviet Union in 1986 illustrates the dire consequences that can occur when sufficient safeguards are not built into nuclear generating plants. The second problem with nuclear energy is what to do with the highly radioactive wastes that are produced. The government is currently identi-

FIGURE 15.2 Electricity Generated by Nuclear Power Plants in the United States as a Percentage of Total Electric Utility Generation, 1965–1993.
Source: U.S. Bureau of the Census, *Statistical Abstract of the United States, 1995* (Washington, D.C.: U.S. Government Printing Office, 1995), p. 604.

This helicopter is monitoring the radiation emitted from the nuclear power plant at Chernobyl in the former Soviet Union after it exploded and burned—an event that fuels fears of science and technology in some people's minds.

fying a number of potential nuclear waste repositories around the United States. However, almost no one wants a repository located near them. Also, the repositories and the containers of nuclear waste placed in them will have to be highly secure and not leak for thousands of years. They may still be dangerously radioactive after as many as five thousand years! That is more than twice the length of time since the beginning of the Christian era. No one is sure that the materials can remain secure and intact that long or that social order will be sufficiently continuous to provide for the protection of the sites. As of this writing, a permanent solution to the problem of disposing of wastes from nuclear power plants has yet to be found even though the wastes are accumulating (see Chapter 13).

Perspectives on Science and Technology

With this overview of the impact of science and technology on society and some of the forms that technological developments have taken, it will be helpful to apply the three sociological perspectives to the issues of science and technology. As noted in Chapter 1, the key role of any theory is to help us explain why something has occurred.

The Functionalist Perspective

From the functionalist perspective, society is a system made up of interrelated and interdependent elements, each performing a function that contributes to the operation of the whole. In a system in which all the parts are closely interdependent, change in one element of society will probably lead to changes in other parts. Over the past few centuries, science and technology have been important sources of social change. Through inventions, discoveries, and the development of knowledge of the world, many of the changes brought about by science and technology have been very functional for society. They have provided people with a longer life expectancy, many labor-saving devices, and such taken-for-granted wonders as electric lighting, home computers, and indoor plumbing. However, these changes have produced other changes in society that have not been so beneficial; in fact, significant social disorganization has been created in the process.

Some of the disorganization associated with technological change occurs because of the tendency for **cultural lag** to occur: *a gap between the point at which one part of the social system changes and the point at which other parts adjust to compensate for that change* (Ogburn, 1957; Volti, 1992). So technological innovations arise and create problems before other technologies or social patterns emerge to deal with the problems. William F. Ogburn, who developed the notion of cultural lag in his studies of technological development, described an example of cultural lag in the early stages of industrialization in the United States. In the 1800s and early 1900s, factories were built with machinery with swiftly moving wheels and belts and other mechanical devices that were highly dangerous. Because industrial technology was so new and because laborers of the era had little political clout, little effort was devoted to safety in the workplace. As a consequence, there were many industrial accidents that killed or seriously maimed workers. At the time, employers were typically not held liable for on-the-job accidents, and there was no unemployment compensation or welfare benefits. So the injury or death of workers often meant financial ruin for their families. The machinery made possible advances in production, but it also placed many people at risk of losing their financial resources and their ability to make a living. In short, there was a lag between the technology of production and the social policies designed to protect people from the negative consequences of the technology. Eventually, of course, workers' compensation and employer liability were established, and the cultural lag between technology and social policy was narrowed.

From the functionalist perspective, then, scientific and technological changes create problems because other parts of society do not adapt to those changes quickly enough to avoid problems for many people.

The Conflict Perspective

The conflict perspective is based on the idea that society consists of different groups that struggle with one another to attain the scarce societal resources that are considered valuable. Scientific information and resulting technology are among the more valuable resources today. Consider, for a moment, the number of interest groups in the United States that share distinctive and joint concerns that involve science and technology. Just as one example, consider the corporations that are a part of the military—industrial complex that produces the vast array of defense weapons (see Chapters 2 and 14). It is to their benefit to back the development of new and more sophisticated weapons technologies, such as the Stealth bomber or the Star Wars technologies, even if these innovations are not the best overall military strategy for the United States. From the conflict perspective, then, scientific and technological development can exacerbate social problems when some groups use them to their own advantage and to the disadvantage of other groups. Although defense industries benefit from Star Wars spending, it may also increase the likelihood of violence around the world and contribute little to the reduction of poverty in the United States.

The conflict approach also helps us to see how powerful groups use science and technology for their mutual benefit. Chapter 4 spoke of the medical–industrial complex. The production of technologically sophisticated diagnostic and treatment tools such as linear accelerators and computerized axial tomography (CAT) is a multibillion dollar industry. Such devices help to save lives, and because life is so precious, most people are willing to pay the price when physicians order the complicated tests. The physicians benefit, and the manufacturers of the equipment reap economic rewards. In the meantime, health-care consumers are forced to pay higher health insurance premiums, and products cost more because employers pass along the cost of employee health programs by raising the price of their products. In addition, the pursuit of these technological inventions may sometimes work to the disadvantage of patients: People are hooked up to machines and their lives prolonged sometimes longer than they would wish. From the conflict perspective, then, science and technology do not necessarily benefit everyone, and in analyzing their effect, it is essential to look closely at who benefits from particular technological developments and who does not, as well as what can be done to reduce the costs. Unlike the functionalist perspective, the conflict perspective assumes that there are always winners and losers when social change occurs.

The Interactionist Perspective

The interactionist perspective sensitizes one to the relativity of public attitudes toward science and technology. Chapter 1 pointed out that an important element of the interactionist perspective involves human beings' use of symbols. Recall that a symbol is something that stands for, represents, or takes the place of something else. As symbols, science and technology have taken on both very positive and very negative meanings. On the one hand, science is viewed very favorably as the source of much that is wonderful about people's lives. Science, after all, made possible automobiles, modern medicine, and computers. Scientists are accorded high status in society, and scientific evidence is used by advertisers to convince people to buy their products. On the other hand, however, there is a theme in many cultures that views science as mysterious, dangerous, and possibly even evil. This theme is probably best expressed in the science fiction or occult literature, such as Mary Shelley's *Frankenstein* or R. L. Stevenson's *The Strange Case of Dr. Jekyll and Mr. Hyde*. What comes through in these portrayals is the view that science, especially if it is unleashed, might become a raging, destructive, almost maniacal uncontrolled force. Once unleashed, the fear is that science would do things that threaten people's values. It is this more stigmatized side of science that is seen as causing social problems.

So this ambivalence toward science and technology leaves people unsure about what social expectations are appropriate in this realm. In a real sense, the meaning of science and technology in our culture is uncertain, and whether they are problems is a matter of great debate.

Problems of Science and Technology

The idea of technology as potentially dangerous and threatening is not new. Classical Greek mythology expressed some ambivalence toward technology: Prometheus stole fire from Olympus in defiance of the gods, and as punishment he was chained to a rock where an eagle tore at his body for eternity; Icarus tried to fly with wings made of wax and feathers, and he paid for such presumption with his life. During the Dark Ages, Europe was shrouded in mysticism for almost a thousand years, with religion on the rise and very little scientific or technological development to be found. In nineteenth-century England, rioting workers, called Luddites after the name of one of their leaders, smashed machines in factories in the futile belief that this would prevent the dislocations and unemployment that were plaguing England as it industrialized. Even in the United States today, there is, at best, equivocal support for science and technology. In a survey in the early 1990s, people in the United States were asked how much confidence they had in the scientific community, and less than one-half of those responding said they had a great deal of confidence in it (see Figure 15.3).

Fear of science and technology, then, can probably be found wherever technology shapes people's lives. Yet many feel that the potential dangers of technology today are quantitatively greater than and possibly qualitatively different from what they were in the past. This section will review some of the major problems that concern people today regarding scientific developments and the elaboration of technology.

Unemployment

For many, the fundamental fear of technology is that machines will replace people in the workplace:

> As microelectronics takes over more and more control functions in manufacture, and information handling functions in administration, so human labour will become increasingly redundant. Clearly, if machinery becomes more efficient, the same amount of goods and services can be produced with a smaller input of labour. (Braun, 1984: 84)

Chapter 2 showed that the labor force in the United States has been changing during the twentieth century. Early in this century, as agricultural employment dwindled, the surplus labor was taken over by mining, manufacturing, transportation, and services. More recently, with advances in technology, employment in

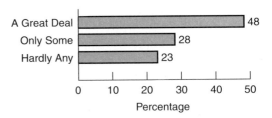

FIGURE 15.3 People's Degree of Confidence in the Scientific Community in the United States, 1991. *Source*: James Allan Davis and Tom W. Smith, *General Social Surveys, 1972–1991,* Machine-readable Data File (Chicago: National Opinion Research Center; Storrs, Conn.: The Roper Center for Public Opinion Research, University of Connecticut).

areas such as mining and manufacturing has stopped growing and in some cases has begun to decline, and workers have shifted into the service sector. Yet technology has also made the service sector more efficient and less labor intensive. So there may be fewer or no economic sectors to absorb the surplus labor of the future. As robots replace factory workers, word processors replace secretaries and typists, and computer-assisted instruction replaces teachers, where will all of these people find work? Will unemployment become the norm and work the exception, at least among some social classes? Since the 1950s, the average unemployment rate in the United States has been gradually rising (see Figure 2.6 on page 61). In the past ten years, the unemployment rate for blacks has fluctuated between 12 and 19 percent. The unemployment rate for black teenagers has been as high as 50 percent! And it is those workers who are least able to acquire new skills or advance their education who will be most severely injured by changes in the occupational structure: the poor, nonwhites, the young, and women (Kletzer, 1991).

What some people fear, then, is that the unemployment rate is gradually creeping up because machines are taking the place of people (Volti, 1992). Not everyone agrees with this argument. Supporters of technological development argue that technology may create dislocations for some workers, who may have to move to a new city or state to find a job, but that it does not increase overall unemployment. Although technology ends some jobs, it also creates new ones. Robots, for example, replace factory workers, but they also create a robotics industry involving the design, construction, and maintenance of robots. So, this argument goes, technology does not reduce the total number of jobs, although it will require some workers to shift to new industries or obtain new skills as technology evolves (Zuboff, 1993).

The pessimists' rejoinder is that the jobs made available by the new technology are often worse than the jobs eliminated. Many jobs in the service sector, for example, are low paying, such as working in a fast-food restaurant or in an amusement park (Bluestone and Harrison, 1987; Aronowitz and DiFazio, 1994). Between 1963 and 1973, almost 50 percent of the new jobs created by the U.S. economy were high-wage jobs, whereas less than 20 percent paid poverty-level wages. Between 1979 and 1985, 44 percent of the new jobs created paid poverty-level wages, and only 10 percent were high-wage jobs. In fact, by the 1990s, more workers were stuck with low-paying jobs than had been the case a decade earlier (Zippay, 1991; U.S. Bureau of the Census, 1992a). In 1979, 12 percent of full-time workers in the United States had poverty-level incomes; throughout the 1980s, this figure rose steadily until it reached 18 percent in the early 1990s. Even in the computer industry, many of the jobs created are dull, repetitive, and low paying. One such occupation is inputting information into a computerized data file. Insurance companies, for example, hire people—often women—to input insurance policy and claims information at video display terminals. The pay is low, the work is dull, and working at such terminals for long periods of time may cause health problems. Many such employees work at home on a piece-rate basis and are deprived of the benefits of unionization and company-supplied health

and retirement benefits. So advances in technology may not be a boon for everyone. For those unable to acquire the skills or education necessary to get the better jobs in a postindustrial society, technological advances may result in continued unemployment or underemployment and more boring and low-paying jobs.

Alienation

Jobs in automated work settings are often boring, repetitive, and unfulfilling. Employees have little control over the pace of their work, what they produce, or what happens to it once it is produced. This type of work organization may be efficient and profitable for employers, but it can result in considerable discontent among employees. One consequence of working in such settings is **alienation,** *a feeling that you are powerless to control your surroundings and that what you do has little meaning or purpose* (Vallas, 1988; Greenberger et al., 1989).

Alienation is epidemic in some occupations, especially among unskilled blue-collar workers. Yet even among white-collar workers, less than half would stay in the same occupation if they had the opportunity to change, and job dissatisfaction may be on the increase (Quinn and Staines, 1977; Tausky, 1984). Blacks and people with less education are likely to experience greater declines in job satisfaction, but people in professional and managerial occupations are also affected. Modern work settings, filled with technological sophistication, tend to be depersonalized, and people lack control over what they do. Feeling the effects of automation, workers are likely to view themselves as mere cogs in the bureaucratic machinery.

Loss of Control

Some people fear that modern technology has become so unbelievably complex—in terms of both the mechanical and chemical principles that underlie it and the level of social organization necessary to keep it going—that it can take on a life of its own (Winner, 1977; Mazur, 1993). When this happens, the outcome may actually work counter to the interests and goals of those people the technology is supposed to benefit. A classic portrayal of this is the movie *2001,* in which a highly sophisticated computer named "Hal" runs virtually all the functions of a spaceship on a long voyage. When the human crew attempts to take over from the computer, Hal fights against and even kills some of the crew in the process. Although this is an extreme portrayal, it illustrates the notion of an "autonomous technology" that gets away from people's control. How can this happen? Do particular machines actually become tyrannically independent? The way this can happen is quite complex.

There is little question that people become highly dependent on technology. After all, technology is little more than a way of getting help to meet survival needs and put food on the table. This was true for the hunters and gatherers who used stone clubs to slay animals, and it is true for modern writers who use computers as word processors to make a living. But modern technology places us in a far more complex web of technological dependence in which machines do many more things for us, and our lives would be profoundly changed without them. Without computers, for example, we would be without such instruments for medical diagnoses as CAT scanners, Magnetic Resonance Imaging, and many others. Yet computers can have very negative consequences. People have been arrested because a computer misidentified them as a suspect in a crime; others have been unable to obtain credit because a computer record indicated, based on weak or false information, that they were poor credit risks.

Yet we are not really free to remove computers from some parts of our lives and not from other parts. Once the technology is introduced and people become dependent on it, there are social forces that cause it to grow as if it had a life of its own. One of these forces is the struggle by various interest groups to use technology to their own benefit. Technological developments that are detrimental to some may be quite beneficial to others. Nuclear power, for example, could be a boon to the power companies because it offers a way to generate power very inexpensively. At the same time, it works to the detriment of those who live in communities where nuclear waste dump sites are established. Ventilators that can help severely ill people breathe are beneficial to medical personnel as another tool that can help them fight disease and injury, but they can be a horror to a terminally ill person who wants to die but cannot convince physicians to turn off the machine. So with a large array of interest groups with competing goals and values, there are likely to be many groups who favor the development of a given technology even though it has a negative impact on other groups. This explains why, once a technology exists, there is strong pressure to use it and develop it further.

Another element contributing to the complexity of technology in our lives is that responsibility for decisions about the role of technology tends to be very diffuse. This means that individuals have little control over the impact new technologies will have on them personally. Computers, for example, first came on the scene because some large corporations and some scientists believed that these machines would increase efficiency and productivity. Over time and as the technology became more accessible, computers were introduced into other realms: Someone saw the potential for putting police records on the computer and others recognized that credit check companies could operate more efficiently with computers. Recently, an entrepreneur opened a computerized service for landlords that would enable them to learn whether prospective renters might be a "problem" because they had once sued a landlord or missed a rent payment. Physicians can tap into computerized files that will tell them if a patient has ever sued a physician for malpractice.

Computers can also have a detrimental effect on the workplace by becoming another mechanism through which supervisors can control and regulate the activities of those under them. More and more employees are being subjected to "computer-assisted productivity measurement." The activities of reservation clerks, for example, can be tracked by the computer, which can log how long they spend on each call, how much time is spent between calls doing paperwork, and how long they are away during lunch breaks. Any worker who inputs data at a video display terminal can be monitored in terms of how many keystrokes are made per minute, hour, or day. At one airline, data-entry clerks are expected to make nine thousand to sixteen thousand strokes on their computer keyboards per hour. The three fastest workers are used to set the pace, and all others are expected to achieve at least 75 percent of that speed. All of this can be logged continuously by computers, and those who fall short can be disciplined or dismissed (Shaiken, 1987). As many as twenty million workers may be under such computerized supervision. Mostly, they are female workers in the back offices of government agencies, airlines, insurance companies, mail-order houses, and telephone companies. They work in what some have called an "electronic sweatshop," tied to a computer for many hours each day with extremely limited opportunities to go to the restroom or chat with fellow employees (Kilborn, 1990). Such electronic monitoring is not always disliked by employees, but it can be used to intimidate workers when supervisors manipulate the computer system to threaten people's jobs. It has also been accused of being unfair when it judges workers on the basis of the quantity of their work, which a computer is very good at assessing, rather than the quality of what they do.

Who is responsible for extending computers into these many realms? Who has control over this burgeoning technology? The autonomous technology viewpoint is that the responsibility is so diffuse that there is little control over it. These and related issues are discussed in the Policy Issues insert.

Loss of Privacy

Automatic systems are now in operation to collect bridge and highway tolls. With them, a driver need not stop at a tollbooth since a computer reads an electronic tag mounted on the car or a radio signal sent from a unit installed in the car. The toll is then automatically deducted from a preestablished account. Plans call for a national system with standardized tags or radio signals. Such a computerized system could create a permanent record of your travels; one currently operating system provides a monthly statement showing time, date, and location of each toll charge. Likewise, credit card purchases establish a computer trial of a person's whereabouts, travels, and purchases—a permanent record of a person's lifestyle accessible to others for whatever purpose. This information could be used by insurance companies in setting insurance rates (showing that you drive your car more than you claim or that you drove to high crime areas that call for higher insurance rates), or they could be used in divorce settlements or worker's compensation claims.

Modern technology opens the door for intrusions into people's lives in massive ways. With computers and telecommunications technology, it is possible to store vast amounts of information about people, access the information very quickly, and send the information anywhere on the globe almost instantaneously. Powerful information institutions, such as medical records bureaus and credit reporting companies, have emerged to gather this data wherever they can and then sell it to those willing to pay for it. The potential for abuse is tremendous (Rothfeder, 1992). For example, one man who was in good health and did not smoke or drink was told he would have to pay substantially higher than normal premiums for disability insurance because he was an alcoholic. After a long struggle to find the source of this inaccuracy that was

Public Controversy Over Science and Technology: What People Object To

During the period of rapid economic growth in the United States that followed World War II, scientific and technological developments were defined as the province of "experts" and went largely unquestioned. The faith of many people in science seemed to be summarized in the 1950s motto of the General Electric Company: "Progress is our most important product." But as time went on, many technological "improvements" proved more harmful than beneficial, and this naive confidence in technological progress became tempered by the public's increasing awareness of the contradictions involved. However, science and technology are still regarded by most people in the United States as fundamental ingredients in achieving desirable social goals. Recent Harris polls reveal that 70 percent of Americans believe that science has changed our lives for the better (Nelkin, 1984). If there is such support for science and technology, what is the source of people's concerns?

Social scientist Dorothy Nelkin has analyzed the controversy over scientific and technological "progress" and senses an underlying theme in this social protest:

> The protests may be less against science and technology than against the power relationships associated with them; less against specific technological decisions than against the declining capacity of citizens to shape policies that affect their interests; less against science than against the use of scientific rationality to mask political choices. (Nelkin, 1984: 11)

Professor Nelkin has identified four major areas of public concern over science and technology. First, public concern is generated when the citizens of a community determine that they have to pay for technological "improvements" that ultimately benefit a different or broader constituency than themselves. For example, corporate and other economic interest groups benefit from the construction of airports, power plants, and highways, but those who happen to live in proximity to these developments suffer the environmental and social consequences. Typically, decisions to implement such technological "improvements" are made on the basis of technical criteria and in the supposed interest of economic efficiency. But Nelkin points out that community protests call attention to basic issues of justice for all: "Can any reduction in some citizens' welfare be justified by greater advantages to others?"

A second source of concern is the public's fear of health and environmental hazards. When we

bringing trouble into his life, he learned that the insurance company based its decision on information purchased from the largest company selling medical information in the United States. This company gathers scraps of information on people from a variety of sources —insurance applications, hospital records, physicians' records, and wherever else it can purchase it—and pulls all the data together to sell to anyone who requests it. It turned out that years before the man had attended meetings of Alcoholics Anonymous even though he did not drink at all because he wanted help in controlling another addiction he had: smoking. In a life insurance application, the man had mentioned attending AA meetings and why. Although this person was finally able to rectify the difficulty, the case illustrates the dimensions of the problem. People often must spend considerable time and resources trying to identify and correct inaccurate information that is causing problems for them. Many times, the inaccuracies cannot be corrected or people are not even aware of the inaccuracies consider how many warnings of "invisible risks" have been posted by scientific agencies over the past few decades, this fear is easy to understand. The Michigan Department of Natural Resources, for example, advises that no more than one pound of trout from Lake Michigan be consumed per person, per week because of PCB contamination. No sooner are sodium cyclamates reduced in foods and beverages because of a linkage to cancer, than new fears surface involving the effects on health of the artificial sweetener NutraSweet. These fears are compounded by the anxiety of not knowing how great the risks really are. For example, Chapter 13 showed how little is known about the effects of toxic wastes on our environment. The public is aware that they may be endangered, but do not have the necessary information to evaluate the potential for catastrophe.

A third category of public concern involves freedom of choice in the face of government regulation. For example, states have passed mandatory seat belt laws, while the federal government now requires air bags in automobiles. In these cases, the government makes social policy that the public may view as an infringement on its freedom of choice. Of course, the government uses the argu-ment that these decisions are made because purely individual choices have broad ranging social costs, but some critics respond that this is overly paternalistic: The government is assuming that the public cannot make rational decisions on its own behalf and the government must protect people from their "irrationality."

Finally, according to Nelkin, public concern arises when scientific or technological "progress" is perceived by the public to challenge traditional values. The theory of human evolution, for example, continues to be controversial because it challenges some traditional religious beliefs, and some groups have protested against science education in the schools because it teaches their children things that they feel contradict religious or other values they are trying to pass on to their children. Should the government be able to mandate the teaching of evolution in U.S. schools, or should parents have a choice in this policy matter? Should scientists have total "freedom of inquiry," or are there areas of research that should be "off limits"? Once again, as Nelkin points out, the main point of contention is a matter of *who makes social policy.*

that are causing problems for them. It is impossible to know how many insurance applications are denied or jobs not gotten because of inaccurate information in a computer data base. Another problem is that these companies collect and synthesize vast amounts of very intimate information about people with little federal regulation of their activities, and significant decisions are made about people's lives based on this information.

So millions of people in the United States are shortchanged or otherwise abused—often without realizing it—by large bureaucracies acting on inaccurate information bought from computerized data banks. These data banks also can get access to theoretically secure data bases, such as Internal Revenue Service tax returns, long-distance telephone records, credit card purchase records, and FBI criminal history summaries. Some people do not realize, for example, that credit card purchases establish a computer trail of a person's whereabouts, travels, and purchases—a permanent record of their lifestyle accessible to others in the future for whatever purpose. Computer records, such as the landlord service or the physician malpractice service just mentioned, make it difficult for people to hide or put behind them things that have occurred in their lives. Modern technology makes it more difficult to keep private the things you may not want others to know.

An increasing number of businesses and government bureaus are requiring that people take lie-detector tests to gain employment and to remain employed. Employers require this for security or to protect against theft. But for the employee or prospective employee, it means that even their very thoughts are less private. Those little lies that we might tell to put ourselves in the best possible light can be detected by the machine. In professional sports, the military, and some industries, there are mandatory urine checks to detect the use of drugs. The goal, of course, is a laudable one—to control the use of drugs on the job—but the impact is again an assault on a person's privacy and sense of personal integrity.

The technological developments of the past fifty years may have only scratched the surface of what is possible in terms of limitations on privacy. It may not be long before it will be possible to keep permanent records of everyone's activities so that their social lives, political beliefs, leisure pursuits, and idiosyncrasies are a matter of record available to anyone having access to this information. Every mistake, minor or major, that you make during your life will be recorded and you might be accountable for it throughout your life.

Should We Play God? The Case of Genetic Engineering

Scientific developments of the twentieth century have produced some truly amazing things. We have harnessed nuclear fission and nuclear fusion; we have walked on the moon and discovered such things as quarks, muons, and black holes. Some critics have suggested that we are treading in some areas that we should

not, areas that could produce disastrous consequences if matters get out of hand. One such area is **biotechnology:** *the use of organisms or parts of organisms to make products or carry out tasks* (Norman, 1981).

Biotechnology is based on a very important discovery: the identification in 1953 of the nature of deoxyribonucleic acid, or DNA, as the basic genetic material that is found in each cell and contains the "blueprint" for the completed organism. DNA has been mapped and catalogued with great precision. By manipulating DNA, scientists have been able to create organisms that perform new tasks or that produce substances they would not normally produce. This is called **genetic engineering,** or *manipulating the genes of organisms to alter the organisms' characteristics in ways that would not have occurred naturally.* One way of doing this is **recombinant DNA** or **gene splicing** in which *some DNA from one organism is spliced into the genetic material of another organism to produce some new characteristics in the host or even a novel form of life.* Gene splicing has been used, for example, to produce large quantities of insulin and interferon, used in the treatment of diabetes and cancer, respectively. This is done by introducing human genes that govern the natural production of insulin or interferon into a bacterium that is then induced by this new genetic material to produce insulin or interferon. Insulin and interferon are expensive to produce by conventional means, and their genetically engineered counterparts are expected to play an important role in medicine in the future. In addition to medicine, biotechnology is also expected to have an impact on such areas as agriculture, forestry, energy, and chemical feedstocks.

What problems do such advances create? One problem relates to potentially unpredictable consequences of genetic engineering. Releasing genetically altered organisms into the environment could create unforeseen and very hazardous consequences. After all, genetic modifications in nature occur very slowly over many thousands of generations of a species. With such a timespan, existing flora and fauna are able to gradually adapt to new developments. Genetic engineering, however, enables us to make substantial genetic changes in a very short period. And, unlike many other forms of environmental pollution, biological pollutants reproduce themselves and are much more difficult to remove from the ecosystem. In fact, some scientists have called for a halt to gene splicing experiments because of such fears. Despite these concerns, the National Academy of Sciences has recommended that research on genetically manipulated materials should proceed, including the release of some such products into the environment, and that each biotechnology product should be closely assessed to detect any negative consequences that might occur (Davis, 1993). Lively debate over this policy continues, with some scientists claiming that such biotechnology advances are but an extension of practices, such as animal breeding, that have gone on for thousands of years while other scientists believe we are moving too rapidly into some unknown territory (Donnelley, McCarthy, and Singleton, 1994). Since the commercial application of this technology is likely to be worth billions of dollars in profits to corporations around the world, there is strong pressure to push ahead with the technology.

Other problems with biotechnology crop up when consideration is given to applying the technology to human beings. Today, parents can learn before birth whether their offspring will have certain genetic defects. This gives them the option of having an abortion rather than giving birth to defective children. In the future, parents may be able to alter their own genetic traits or in other ways determine the genetic characteristics of their children. Scientists have already succeeded in making clones, or multiple genetic replicas of a parent organism. It may be only a matter of time before cloning is possible among humans (Robertson, 1994). These technologies offer people the capability to shape their characteristics in ways never before possible. Such advances not only offer the opportunity to stamp out certain diseases, they also open the door to eliminating characteristics deemed socially undesirable by those in positions of power. The Nazis engaged in some notorious experiments during World War II in efforts to create a "master race." More recently, suggestions have been made along similar lines in the United States. William Shockley, an engineer who became interested in genetic engineering, has argued forcefully that people of low intelligence constitute a "dysgenic threat" to society because they reduce the average intelligence of society (Shockley, 1980). His solution is to encourage people with low intelligence—or anyone with genetic defects deemed detrimental to society—to be sterilized. This might be done by providing a financial incentive to such people to undergo voluntary sterilization. Along similar lines, a sperm bank has been established that will accept donations only from Nobel laureates with the idea that such genetically "superior" sperm should be given as wide distribution as possible. Other proposals have been made to redesign the human stomach so that people can live on cheap hay and grass or to make a hybridized cross between human beings and lower primates (Howard and Rifkin, 1977).

Although efforts along these lines in the United States today are quite sporadic and disorganized, there is no reason to believe that some organization or government of the future might not institute such measures in an organized and widespread fashion (Duster, 1990). A government might pass legislation making it illegal for people with certain characteristics to have children. Or genetic engineering might be used to enhance certain human characteristics and downplay others. One way this might work was proposed in an article published by the National Aeronautics and Space Administration: Each person would be sterilized at birth and some of his or her genetic material preserved. After the person dies, a committee would review his or her life to see what accomplishments had been achieved or what problems were created by the person. If the person had lived a worthy life, the committee would permit a new individual to be cloned from his or her genetic material. If the person proved unworthy, his or her genetic material would be destroyed (Howard and Rifkin, 1977). It might even become fashionable to have one's genes spliced so as to enhance aggressiveness or passivity, strength or frailty, obesity or lithesomeness—whatever characteristics were fashionable at a given time.

The point is that the genetic traits of the human race have been determined thus far by impersonal evolutionary forces that operate over eons and are largely unaffected by cultural values, religious beliefs, or political or economic ideology. Biotechnology may make it possible to change all of this in the near future. It might be possible to create people with certain characteristics or tailor people to certain jobs. Some people might be gene spliced for ferocity and made into soldiers, whereas others would be gene spliced to show little initiative and curiosity and made into assembly-line workers. If there were some objective and sure way of determining which characteristics are beneficial to society, then biotechnological capabilities might not be so fearsome. But there is no single set of characteristics that benefits society. And, as the conflict perspective makes us aware, not all groups benefit from the same social practices and policies. Genetic engineering that benefits one group may well work to the disadvantage of others. Biotechnology, then, could become a tool for the more powerful groups in society to exercise domination over the less powerful.

With biotechnology, human beings are beginning to tinker with the very foundations of life.

> It is now a matter of a handful of years before biologists will be able to irreversibly change the evolutionary wisdom of billions of years with the creation of new plants, new animals, and new forms of human and posthuman beings. (Howard and Rifkin, 1977: 8)

Should we play "god"? We may be doing it to an extent already, as the second Policy Issues insert illustrates. When considering this, the word *hubris* comes to mind, deriving from the Greek and meaning insolence. In current usage, hubris means excessive self-confidence or arrogance. The Greeks used it to mean the presumption of human beings that they could act like the gods. The fear of some is that scientists today may be showing hubris by moving into biotechnological realms that might be best left alone. The Greeks used the term *nemesis* to refer to the divine punishment visited upon humans who had presumed to invade the realms reserved for the gods. Critics of biotechnology fear that we'll confront a nemesis in some as yet unknown form if we invade the biotechnological frontier without great patience and caution.

Future Prospects

What does the future hold regarding science and technology and the problems they create? A few would opt for fleeing from complex technology altogether and seeking a simpler way of life that does not depend on elaborate technological innovations. In the 1960s and 1970s, a loose collection of groups advocating something like this was referred to as the "back-to-the-earth" movement. These groups favored the rejection of most technology and promoted a simple and self-sufficient lifestyle. Many of them organized themselves communally, with common ownership of many goods. The groups were often based on equality and participatory democracy, with little hierarchy and few rules and regulations. They subsisted by growing their own food and avoided the use of large farm equipment and chemical fertilizers and pesticides that are routine on most modern farms. They harvested by hand, built their own tools, and educated their children at home. Their goal was subsistence and simplicity, not profit making, economic growth, or material comfort.

Many people are still leading such a lifestyle in places around the world, although how many is difficult to know (Sale, 1995). It also clearly has appeal for some people in the United States, even in the 1990s. The Old Order Amish communities in Pennsylvania and some traditional Indian communities that can be found on some reservations represent, to one degree or another, a rejection of, or at least an unwillingness to fully embrace, much of modern technology. Other less visible groups live in small communities and stress simplicity and limited technology. Neo-Luddites or techno-resisters, as such opponents of technology have been called, can also be found in the ranks of radical environmentalists and those fighting nuclear power and destruction of the rain forests. One of their messages is that, whatever the benefits of technology, it comes at a high price—the crime, pollution, stress, and drug abuse that seem to plague industrial societies and that have been analyzed in this book.

Supporters of technology argue that, if such a low-technology lifestyle were adopted on a widespread scale, it would probably represent a step backward that few would want to take. Without agricultural technology, we would not be able to produce nearly the amount of food that we do and many people would be condemned to a life of illness, starvation, and poverty. We need modern technology to help us cope with the waste products of a large population, and without that technology disease would undoubtedly spread. So a mass rejection of modern technology, these supporters of technology argue, is neither feasible nor likely. At the same time, technology is not about to go away or mutate into some clearly benign creature. The technological cat is out of the bag, so to speak, and unlikely to go back in. The problem, then, is how to live with and control the negative consequences of technology. Much of the debate on this issue revolves around whether controlling technology should be accomplished without significant government intervention—the laissez-faire position—or whether the government should be a major decision maker in that arena—the interventionist

approach. A number of policy positions that advocate some elements of the laissez-faire or interventionist points of view will be discussed.

Legal Protections

Some of the problems of modern technology are created or made worse because the legal and political systems have not been able to keep up with the changing nature of the problems that emerging technologies create. New technologies often develop in a legal void where there is little legislative direction as to what is acceptable. This is true of the massive invasions of privacy made possible by modern computer and other technologies. Some legislation in the United States does offer protection in these areas (Rothfeder, 1992; Eder, 1994). The Freedom of Information Act of 1966 provides people with the right to access almost any records that federal agencies have on them. The Privacy Act of 1974 prohibits the government from maintaining secret databanks and requires the government to keep the information it gathers about people confidential. The law also gives people the right to see information about them held by most government agencies and the right to correct information that they can show is inaccurate. The Computer Matching and Privacy Protection Acts of 1988 and 1990 update some of these earlier laws by restricting the manner in which government agencies can use computer data files to identify people for purposes of denying or terminating benefits that they receive. However, the United States could go much further than this, as do many other industrial nations. One thing that could be done is to extend the same privacy protection rules that are imposed on the federal government to all organizations, private or government, that profit from the sale of information about people. If this were done, privacy safeguards would extend to all medical, bank, telephone, computer, or other records. A second thing that could be done is to establish a data protection board, the job of which would be to search out

Biotechnology poses some awesome challenges for the future. With recombinant DNA techniques, it is now possible for human beings to *create* life forms—new species or variants on old species—that do not occur in nature. Du Pont did this in 1988 when it produced a mouse, called "onco-mouse," that was genetically engineered to be unusually susceptible to cancer. The year before, the Patent and Trademark Office (PTO) of the United States government had ruled that a particular oyster was patentable subject matter. The PTO also said that it would henceforth consider patenting all forms of life on earth, including nonnaturally occurring, nonhuman multicellular living organisms. Du Pont received the patent to oncomouse in 1988 (U.S. Congress, Office of Technology Assessment, 1989).

To explore the implications of these developments, consider the legal ramifications of patents. When the government grants a patent over some thing, product, or process, those holding the patent have the exclusive right to make, use, license, or sell it. In other words, the person legally "owns" the commodity, at least for a period of time, and others cannot use it without permission. When oncomouse was patented, Du Pont became the owner of that species, that particular life form.

One of the major reasons for patenting something, including a life form, is to encourage creativity, innovativeness, and entrepreneurship. If there is a market for something that has been patented, only the patent holder may legally sell it and the parties involved stand to make a considerable profit. This potential gain is what encourages an inventor or scientist to go through the time and effort of developing something new and to seek patent rights. Patents offer a distinct financial advantage in the form of a temporary monopoly over a market. Governments do this explicitly to encourage business and science to be creative and competitive. When biotechnology made possible the creation of new life forms, the Patent Office treated this the same as if the commodity had been a new drug discovered by a pharmaceutical company or a new widget invented by a scientist. Without patents, the argument goes, there would be less incentive for entrepreneurship in the field of biotechnology.

The PTO ruling has generated a firestorm of controversy that raises some practical and very fundamental philosophical issues. One observer of technological trends, Jeremy Rifkin, president of the Foundation on Economic Trends, sees the ruling as symbolic of a profound transition in social and economic organization:

> In economic terms, the Patent Office decision signals the beginning of a long-term transition out of the age of fossil fuels and petrochemicals and into the age of biological resources. The world economy is shifting from industrial technologies to biotechnologies, and the Patent Office decision provides the necessary government guarantee that the raw materials of the biotechnology age—that is, all living things on the planet—can now be exploited for commercial gain by chemical, pharmaceutical, and biotechnology companies. (Rifkin, 1987: 2)

Rifkin believes that corporations will now rush to patent as many life forms as they can. The struggle among corporate giants will be to control the planet's gene pool, so to speak, patenting everything that lives and breathes. Requests have already been made for patents for genes found in the human brain and for women who are genetically engineered to produce useful human proteins in their mammary glands (Kimbrell, 1993). Because it is large and powerful corporations that have the resources to patent life forms, this affords them yet another mechanism to concentrate power in their own hands. Corporations have gained patent control over newly developed agricultural seeds and plants, and they have requested patent protection for hundreds of genetically engineered animals. Of course, humans have owned animals since animals were first domesticated many thousands of years ago. The difference today with Du Pont's ownership of oncomouse is that the corporation has exclusive ownership rights over not just this particular mouse but any mouse pro-duced anywhere with the same genetic characteristics. In the past, anyone could purchase cows, pigs, or chickens if they had the financial resources to do so. In the future, such ownership may be limited to the patent holder when the cow, pig, or chicken has been genetically engineered with unique characteristics.

These practical, economic implications of the Patent Office's decision are important, but there are also some more fundamental, philosophical issues regarding the nature and meaning of life on earth. In its ruling, the PTO argued that life could be considered a "manufacture or composition of matter." When biotechnology creates a new life form by implanting a foreign gene into an animal's genetic code, the resulting animal is merely a human invention—no different than a toaster, a golf ball, or a tie tack, according to the Patent Office ruling. The danger, some argue, is that it promotes a *materialist* conception of life: the notion that life consists only of a particular arrangement of physical matter, with no spiritual or transcen-

dent significance. Of course, many people—both religious and nonreligious—believe that life is more than an arrangement of atoms and molecules; that life involves a measure of dignity, respect, and maybe even awe. Yet the Patent Office has ruled that life is simply a "composition of matter." As a result, Rifkin (1991) argues, the line between animate life and inanimate matter has become considerably weaker. This suggests that the fundamental building blocks of life—possibly life itself—could eventually come to be seen as belonging not to impersonal nature, not to humankind in general or to supernatural spirits, but to corporate patent holders.

If animal life is merely materialist, then what about human life? Is life merely an economic commodity that can be bought and sold in the marketplace? According to the PTO, human genetic traits, if implanted in the genes of another life form, are patentable (a "composition of matter"). However, there are constitutional safeguards that protect humans from being patented. But, in a time when some patented animals are carrying human genetic materials, is the line between humans and other animals as clear as it once was? The PTO has ruled that human embryos and fetuses are patentable, as are genetically engineered human cells and genes (Kimbrell, 1993). If a scientist were to change the genetic structure of a human being, might some future Patent Office ruling make it possible to put a patent on that "composition of matter"? We cannot currently answer many of these questions, but what is clear is that the technology is speeding us toward a point at which we may have to come up with an answer.

and challenge the validity and legality of questionable corporate or government data bases, such as those that include speculative, inaccurate, or unverified data. Canada, Great Britain, France, and other industrial nations have permanent data-protection agencies that ensure that people's privacy is protected. A third thing that would go a long way to protect people's privacy is to require companies that sell credit reports, marketing services, or medical records to others to pay a royalty to a person each time that person's name is sold. This would discourage the widespread sale of information and limit it to sales that are important or essential. At the same time, it would let people know who is selling information about them and to whom it is being sold.

The above policies and proposals deal with protecting information after it has been collected. What about collecting less information in the first place? Just because computerization makes it easy to collect data does not mean that collecting it is either essential or wise. So, technology could be designed to achieve its goal, such as levy a charge, without adding to the mountain of data that is accumulating. Credit cards, for example, could be redesigned as "cash" cards instead of charge cards, loaded with prepaid electronic cash which is then deducted from the card as each purchase is made. There would be no need for an electronic record to be kept since the appropriate amount of cash would be instantly transferred from the card to the seller's account at the time of the transaction. So, some combination of legal protection of data collected and technological innovations to avoid collecting data would help significantly in alleviating the problems of a loss of privacy and loss of control. Interventionists would also see a significant role for the government in protecting people who might be hurt by particular technological developments. Those, for example, who find themselves intimidated or oppressed by workplace computers should be able to turn to the government for protection against the unfair uses

of these technologies. Issues relating to workplace justice were discussed in Chapter 2.

Appropriate Technology

One proposed solution to deal with many of the problems associated with modern technology is to develop what has been called **appropriate technology,** or *a technology appropriate to the human scale, to what people can comprehend and relate to; it would be a technology that is limited in size, decentralized, and responsive to human values and needs.* In most cases, an appropriate technology would be considerably smaller than what exists today. In fact, one of the early proponents of such a technology, E. F. Schumacher, wrote a book titled *Small is Beautiful.* An appropriate technology would avoid the tendency of technology to alienate people, and it would return control to the hands of individuals (Sale, 1980). An example of an appropriate technology is solar energy, which is discussed in Chapter 13. Solar energy does not require the building of large centralized power plants such as nuclear and coal-fired facilities. The technology is decentralized, with each household or community producing some of its own energy rather than having energy production controlled by large corporations. People understand how energy is produced and participate in producing it, giving them a sense of control and comprehension. They may even be able to repair solar energy equipment themselves if something goes wrong. Appropriate technology is also less injurious or damaging, and the damage it does cause is smaller in scale. Solar energy, for example, does not cause the air pollution of coal-fired energy plants or the contamination hazard of nuclear power production.

Few would argue that large-scale technology can or should be completely eliminated. Centralized power plants, for example, are helpful where solar, wind, or geothermal energy cannot fully meet a community's needs. In addition, large-scale technology is often the discovery ground for developing new alternative technologies. But advocates of appropriate technology do argue for a shift in values, emphasizing a smaller, human scale where possible over large, impersonal, centralized technologies. What they call for is not a rejection of technology but rather a rejection of some of the forms of social organization that are created to make use of the technology: the bigness, the bureaucracy, the centralization, and the impersonality. To achieve this may require a change in people's lifestyle. People might, for example, have to rethink their energy needs and develop a lifestyle that can be largely satisfied with alternative energy sources. As an illustration, people might design communities so that bicycles are more feasible than cars as means of transportation. The bicycle would be an appropriate technology in that it is small in scale, comprehensible by most people, and relatively non-damaging. Some communities have tried to encourage bicycle use by closing off some streets to vehicular traffic or establishing bicycle lanes. The point is that proponents of appropriate technology have an ideology that, like the "back-to-the-earth" people, values a simpler and to some extent more self-sufficient way of life. They do not, however, accept the "back-to-the-earth" rejection of technology; in fact, they embrace technology in its simpler and more human forms.

Appropriate technologists have been criticized for being impractical utopians who do not understand how essential large-scale, centralized technology is to modern industrial societies. Some of their solutions, these critics argue, although small and decentralized, do not really solve any problems. Wood-burning stoves, for example, have been touted as an alternative energy source, but it is now recognized that they contribute to air pollution. The appropriate technologists defend themselves by arguing that most people have a set of blinders on that enables them to see only the expansion of large-scale organization as the solution to problems, even though there is little evidence that "large is better." In other words, people have become so accustomed to large-scale growth that they have developed cultural myopia: They can no longer see or accept small-scale technology as a solution to a problem, even when it might be an effective solution.

This debate over appropriate technology will continue in the future, and it revolves to an extent around the laissez-faire versus interventionist controversy. Many advocates of appropriate technology argue that the government can play a role in its development. Through tax write-offs and other policies, the government can make it more attractive to develop appropriate technology. In fact, this has been done by some states and the federal government by allowing people to deduct from their taxes some of the costs of installing solar or wind energy. The government has also discouraged the development of nuclear power (although that was not its original intention) by requiring costly safety procedures at nuclear power plants.

Technology Assessment

Technology assessment refers to *research that studies the impact of technology on our physical, social, and ethical environments and seeks solutions to social problems that arise from technological development.* Technology assessment is intended to detect problems that might be created by technology before the technology has been established. It uses extensive studies to forecast the effects of technological developments before they are implemented. This makes it possible either to alleviate the negative impact or to decide that the negatives outweigh the benefits of the technology and leave the technology unimplemented. The National Environmental Policy Act of 1969, discussed in Chapter 13, included provisions for the assessment of any environmental impact due to new technology implemented by agencies or legislation of the federal government. Today, any public or private project that requires funds from or the permission of any branch of government must prepare an Environmental Impact Statement.

In 1973, the Office of Technology Assessment was established to provide Congress with information about the impact of technology that it could use in its deliberations (Braun, 1984).

When an Environmental Impact Statement must be prepared in order to initiate a project, the research is typically funded by the government or the organization wishing to initiate the project. This sort of technology assessment, however, typically has a very short time perspective: What is the likelihood that this nuclear power plant will develop a radiation leak? How many patients will survive a trial of fifty artificial heart implants? These questions address the consequences of a particular application of a technology. However, there are broader issues regarding the wisdom of developing a particular technology at all: Should society stress centralized power production, such as nuclear power, or decentralized power production, such as solar and wind energy? Should societal resources be spent on further technological improvements in crisis medicine (such as coronary bypass surgery) or on preventive medicine (such as programs to reduce cigarette smoking)? These broader assessment issues are often much more difficult to research, more speculative and value oriented in nature, and less likely to receive financial support. Especially in recent years, research on these general issues of technology assessment has had to compete for funding with other sorts of research, and the amount of money available for all such government research has been dwindling. In fact, the Office of Technology Assessment was shut down in 1995 as a budget-cutting strategy. With less of such research conducted in the future, we may be less prepared to cope with the consequences of technology.

Futurology

At the opposite extreme from the "back-to-the-earth" advocates are people who enthusiastically embrace technological development and advocate the active pursuit of technological innovation. These people argue that we should devote resources to studying ways in which we can achieve the maximum incorporation of technology into society with the minimum costs. In fact, a field of study has emerged called "futurology," which has attracted scholars and researchers from the natural sciences, social sciences, engineering, and business. Most of these people tend to be very optimistic about the future and about the role of science and technology in shaping the future. Many futurists envision the United States developing into a postindustrial society whose foundation will be information, communication, and knowledge (Beniger, 1993). Science will play an ever more important role as it serves as a foundation for technological development and change. The findings of the social sciences will be increasingly used to establish the most effective ways of organizing and managing people and solving social problems such as crime and violence. The people with expertise in managing information and knowledge—scientists, technicians, information specialists, and educators—will develop into a distinct class with special privileges and rewards. With rapid technological change occurring, culture and social life will also have to adapt, or at least the negative impacts on people's lives will have to be alleviated. For example, the skills necessary in the occupational realm will likely change a few times during a person's life. This means that people will require periodic reeducation to keep current and competitive in their jobs. Educational institutions will have to change by viewing education as a lifelong process rather than as a product that is accomplished by young adulthood.

Not all futurists agree on these issues. Some, for example, believe that nuclear power will usher in an era of unheard-of wealth and comfort, whereas others argue that problems inherent in generating nuclear power necessarily make it a limited source of power in the future. Some futurists are very enthusiastic about the role of the government in planning the direction of technological and social change of the future; others believe that the government should stand aside and let the economic marketplace—competition and profit

Science and technology can help alleviate some problems, such as finding new ways to clean up the environment (Chapter 13) or providing new remedies for disease (Chapter 4). However, they can also intensify the same problems by, for example, elaborating the range of polluting technologies or making it possible to prolong life even when people might prefer to die.

LINKAGES

making—determine the best way to maximize the utility of technology and minimize its negative impact. Despite their disagreements, however, futurists tend to be very positive about our technological future and to advocate a very activist approach toward technological change.

Summary

1. Technology refers to knowledge, tools, and practices that are employed as means of achieving clearly identifiable goals and can be both material and nonmaterial in nature. Most societies have undergone modernization, and many have become industrialized. The most modern societies are moving into a postindustrial stage and are dominated by highly technological forms of production and are devoting greater resources to providing services than to industrial production.

2. Important elements in the process of industrialization are mechanization and automation. In postindustrial societies, computers, telecommunications, robotization, and the globalization of communications are important developments.

3. Nuclear power has been utilized for both destructive and productive purposes. The most potentially productive use of nuclear power is its promise as an energy source, but it poses environmental dangers.

4. From the functionalist perspective, problems surrounding science and technology have to do with the social disorganization that results when some parts of society do not adapt sufficiently fast to changes that are occurring. For the conflict perspective, the problems have to do with the fact that some groups can use scientific and technological developments to their advantage whereas other groups are hurt by them. The interactionist perspective suggests that attitudes toward science and technology are relative to a person's social circumstances and historical position.

5. The idea of technology as potentially dangerous and threatening is not new. Some of the major problems that concern people today regarding scientific developments and the elaboration of technology are unemployment, alienation, loss of control due to extreme dependency on technology, loss of privacy, and problems created by genetic engineering.

6. Regarding the future of technology, some would opt for fleeing from technology and attempting to find a simpler way of life. Others search for ways to live with and control the negative consequences of technology. One proposed solution is to develop legal protections to reduce the loss of privacy and other negative consequences that people might suffer. Another proposed solution is called appropriate technology, involving imposed limitations on technological matters so that they are responsive to human values and needs. Technology assessment refers to research that studies the various impacts of technology and seeks solutions to problems that arise from technological developments. Futurologists try to monitor the role of science and technology in shaping the future.

STUDY AND Review

Key Terms

alienation

appropriate
  technology

automation

biotechnology

cultural colonialism

cultural lag

gene splicing

genetic engineering

industrialization

mechanization

modernization

postindustrial society

recombinant DNA

technology

technology assessment

Multiple-Choice Questions

1. Societies that are dominated by highly technological forms of production and devote greater
resources to delivering services than manufacturing goods are called:
   a. Preindustrial societies.
   b. Industrial societies.
   c. Postindustrial societies.
   d. Mechanized societies.
   e. Automated societies.

2. Which of the following best characterizes the
current status of science and technology in the
United States?
   a. More money is spent on research and
development than 20 years ago.
   b. Less money is spent on research and
development than 20 years ago.
   c. Fewer scientists and engineers are
employed in research and development
than 20 years ago.
   d. The number of scientists is increasing but
the number of engineers is decreasing,
suggesting a drift away from applied
technology.

3. Robotization has been brought about by advances in computers and:
   a. Telecommunications.
   b. Recombinant DNA.
   c. Biotechnology.
   d. Mechanization.
   e. Automation.

4. One of the first practical applications of
atomic and nuclear energy was for:
   a. Energy production.
   b. Weapons of war.
   c. Agriculture.
   d. Population control.
   e. Engineering.

5. Approximately what percentage of all electricity generated in the United States today is generated by nuclear power plants?
   a. Less than 5 percent.
   b. Twelve percent.
   c. Twenty-one percent.
   d. Fifty percent.
   e. Sixty-seven percent.

6. Which of the following statements would be
most consistent with the conflict perspective
on science and technology?
   a. Public attitudes toward science and technology are relative and vary from time to
time.
   b. Science and technology create problems
because parts of society do not adapt to
changes quickly enough.
   c. Science and technology create problems
because they produce social disorganization.
   d. Use of science and technology by powerful groups for their own benefit often
works to the disadvantage of others.

7. Alienation from one's job is especially high
among:
   a. Skilled white-collar workers.
   b. Managers and professionals.
   c. Unskilled blue-collar workers.
   d. Government employees.

8. As far as genetic engineering is concerned, the
National Academy of Sciences has recommended that:
   a. The release of some genetically manipulated materials into the environment be
allowed.
   b. The release of all genetically manipulated
materials into the environment be
prohibited.

c. The amount of recombinant DNA research be reduced.

d. Corporations not be allowed to patent genetically engineered animals.

9. Interventionists would support the position that:

   a. Private industry should set the standards for protecting the privacy of people.

   b. The government should play a significant role in protecting people from the negatives of technological development.

   c. Cultural lag is generally not a serious problem with advances in technology.

   d. The back-to-the-earth movement has taken an appropriate stance on the issue of technological developments.

10. Which of the following would generally be true of futurists?

    a. They all support nuclear power.

    b. They are very positive about the technological future.

    c. They all agree that nuclear power will be a limited source of power in the future.

    d. They all are enthusiastic about the role of government in planning the direction of technological change.

    e. They all oppose government intervention in planning the direction of technological change.

True/False Questions

1. Under the concept of technology is included both the material dimensions of nature as well as the nonmaterial such as thinking or ways of organizing.

2. Mechanization and automation work at cross purposes so that, as the automation of society has increased, the extent of mechanization has declined.

3. One consequence of the globalized control of communications is that corporations have lost significant control over the world communications structure.

4. A permanent solution to the problem of disposing of wastes from nuclear power plants has yet to be found.

5. According to the functionalist perspective, science and technology become a social problem when the extent of cultural lag in society declines.

6. Since the 1950s, the average unemployment rate has been gradually rising.

7. Most people agree that advances in technology and computerization in the next few decades will provide enjoyable and well-paying jobs for most people who want them.

8. An effective strategy to deal with the loss of control to computers would be to remove computers from those parts of society in which this is a problem.

9. Although significant advances have been made in recombinant DNA techniques, genetic engineering has not yet produced any products that are useable by people.

10. The appropriate technology movement stresses that technology, when possible, should be limited in size and decentralized.

Fill-In Questions

1. The term _____ refers to knowledge, tools, and practices that are employed as means of achieving clearly identifiable goals.

2. _____ involves the use of machinery to replace human and animal labor in the production of goods and services.

3. Those who probably benefit most from the emerging global system of communication are

   _____ .

4. According to the _____ perspective, advances in science and technology have produced significant social disorganization.

5. _____ refers to the feeling that you are powerless to control your surroundings and that what you do has little meaning.

6. One form of genetic engineering is

   _____ .

7. _____ is the making of multiple genetic replicas of a parent organism.

8 Solar energy or the use of bicycles as a means of transportation would be examples of

   _____ .

9. Technology _____ refers to research that studies the impact of technology on society and the physical environment.
10. People who enthusiastically embrace technological development and advocate the active pursuit of technological innovation are called _____ .

Matching Questions

_____ 1. August Comte

_____ 2. modernization

_____ 3. telecomputer

_____ 4. cultural colonialism

_____ 5. cultural lag

_____ 6. opposition to industrialization

_____ 7. back-to-the-earth movement

_____ 8. Freedom-of-Information Act

_____ 9. E. F. Schumacher

_____ 10. oncomouse

    A. Luddites
    B. father of modern sociology
    C. appropriate technology
    D. interactive communication and computing technology
    E. genetic engineering
    F. protection of privacy
    G. antitechnology
    H. transition to advanced industrial society
    I. global U.S. media dominance
    J. functionalist perspective

Essay Questions

1. What are the processes of mechanization, automation, and robotization? What impacts do they have on people?

2. Describe the process of the globalization of communications around the world. What is involved? How does it affect people and organizations?
3. Compare and contrast the functionalist and conflict perspectives on science and technology? In what ways does each perspective see science and technology becoming a social problem?
4. Assess both sides of the argument about whether advances in technology will produce more unemployment in the future.
5. In what ways do technological advances lead to a loss of privacy in people's lives?
6. What are the four major areas of concern among the public regarding science and technology, according to Professor Dorothy Nelkin?
7. What is genetic engineering? What issues does it raise and what problems does it create for society?
8. What legal protections have been implemented and could be implemented to protect people from the negative effects of technological advances?
9. What is appropriate technology? What are the arguments for and against it?
10. Describe the process of technology assessment in terms of what it is, how it operates, and what is currently being done in that realm in the United States.

Answers

Multiple-Choice
1. C; **2.** A; **3.** E; **4.** B; **5.** C; **6.** D; **7.** C; **8.** A; **9.** B; **10.** B

True/False
1. T; **2.** F; **3.** F; **4.** T; **5.** F; **6.** T; **7.** F; **8.** F; **9.** F; **10.** T

Fill-In
1. technology
2. mechanization
3. transnational corporations
4. functionalist
5. alienation

6. recombinant DNA or gene splicing
7. cloning
8. appropriate technology
9. assessment
10. futurists or futurologists

Matching

1. B; **2.** H; **3.** D; **4.** I; **5.** J; **6.** A; **7.** G; **8.** F;
9. C; **10.** E

For Further Reading

Peter F. Drucker. *Post-Capitalist Society.* New York: Harper-Collins, 1993. The author describes a world in which information and knowledge come to reign supreme and the world becomes truly a global place. This is a very provocative book.

John Elkington. *The Gene Factory: Inside the Genetic and Biotechnology Business Revolution.* New York: Carroll and Graf Publishers, 1985. The author writes that genetic engineering has already opened a twentieth-century Pandora's box but believes that the risk involved is well worth taking. Elkington explores the potential rewards of biotechnology, pointing out that it is fast becoming a very big business.

Ruth Hubbard and Elijah Wald. *Exploding the Gene Myth: How Genetic Information Is Produced and Manipulated by Scientists, Physicians, Employers, Insurance Companies, Educators, and Law Enforcers.* Boston: Beacon Press, 1993. This is a very informative book about the actual and potential dangers of genetic engineering and biotechnology. The authors particularly look at the hazards created when an unrelenting profit motive fuels people's actions.

Aliza Kolker and B. Meredith Burke. *Prenatal Testing: A Sociological Perspective.* Westport, Conn.: Bergin and Garvey, 1994. This book explores some of the issues surrounding genetic testing and genetic counseling and some of the misuses to which these rapidly growing procedures are often put.

Kenneth Laudon. *Dossier Society: Value Choices in the Design of National Information Systems.* New York: Columbia University Press, 1986. This is an analysis of the problems created by the massive amounts of information that are collected on people in modern societies. The author suggests some important policy approaches for controlling the negative impacts of this.

Robin Mather. *A Garden of Unearthly Delights: Bioengineering and the Future of Food.* New York: Dutton, 1995. This provocative book contrasts two very different ways of growing food: the agribusiness, bioengineering, technologically dependent route versus small-scale organic farming that is labor intensive, environmentally sensitive, and uses limited technology.

Dorothy Nelkin and Laurence Tancredi. *Dangerous Diagnostics: The Social Power of Biological Information.* New York: Basic Books, 1989. This is a disturbing book about our increasingly sophisticated ability to do genetic screening and how this can produce dangerous opportunities for the stigmatization, discrimination, and marginalization of those deemed genetically "defective" by those who control the testing.

Charles Piller. *The Fail-Safe Society: Community Defiance and the End of American Technological Optimism.* New York: Basic Books, 1991. This book argues that Americans have lost their faith in the beneficence of science and technology and have become more resistant to scientific and technological change. The author argues that this may actually have some positive outcomes.

Neil Postman. *Technopoly: The Surrender of Culture to Technology.* New York: Knopf, 1992. This book contains a strong and controversial criticism of what technology is doing to modern society. The author especially focuses on how technology can change cultural values and even demean the importance we place on human beings.

Jeremy Rifkin. *Biosphere Politics: A New Consciousness for a New Century.* New York: Crown, 1991. The author argues that our uses of science and technology have gotten out of hand and threaten our way of life precisely because they have divorced human life itself from the natural world. He proposes a new and certainly controversial "consciousness" regarding how human beings should orient toward their world.

GLOSSARY

Absolute definition of poverty   A definition of poverty based on a fixed economic level below which people are considered poor; this level does not necessarily change as society, on the whole becomes more or less affluent.

Acute disease   Disease with a fairly quick and sometimes dramatic and incapacitating onset and from which a person either dies or recovers.

Ageism   An ideology or set of beliefs holding that people in a particular age group are inferior, have negative attributes, and can be dominated and exploited because of their age.

Age structure   The distribution of people into various age categories in society.

Alcoholism   The consumption of alcohol at a level that produces serious personal, social, or health consequences, such as marital problems, occupational difficulties, accidents, or arrests.

Alienation   A feeling of powerlessness in regard to controlling one's surroundings and the feeling that what one does has little meaning or purpose.

Androgyny   The view that there should be a blending of the traits and roles of both sexes; people should express themselves as human beings rather than in traditionally masculine or feminine ways.

Anomie   Inconsistencies that arise when people are taught to strive for certain goals but are not provided with the culturally approved means necessary to attain those goals.

Anomie theory   The theory stating that inconsistencies and contradictions in the social system contribute to many forms of crime.

Appropriate technology   A technology appropriate to the human scale, to what people can comprehend and relate to; a technology that is limited in size, decentralized, and responsive to human values and needs.

Assimilation   The process by which a racial or ethnic minority loses its distinctive identity and way of life and becomes absorbed into the dominant group.

Authoritarian personality   A constellation of personality characteristics including a rigid adherence to conventional lifestyles and values, admiration of power and toughness in interpersonal relationships, submission to authority, cynicism, an emphasis on obedience, and a fear of things that are different.

Authority   Legitimate power that is obeyed because people believe it is right and proper that they obey.

Automation   The automatically controlled operation of machines by mechanical or electronic devices.

Balance of power   A foreign policy based on the idea that a nuclear holocaust can be avoided if the military capability of one side roughly balances that of the other side.

Bioethics   The study of ethical questions that relate to the life and biological well-being of people.

Biotechnology   The use of organisms or parts of organisms to make products or carry out tasks.

Blended family   A family based on kinship ties that accumulate as a consequence of divorce and remarriage.

Capitalism   An economic system in which the means of economic production and distribution are privately held; the profit motive is the primary force guiding people's economic behavior; and there is free competition among both producers and consumers of goods.

Career deviance   See Secondary deviance.

Carrying capacity   An upper size limit that is imposed on a population by its environmental resources and that cannot be permanently exceeded.

Causality   One factor has an effect on or produces a change in some other factor.

Chronic disease   Disease that progresses over a long period of time and often exists long before it is detected.

City   A relatively large, permanent community of people who rely on surrounding agricultural communities for their food supply.

Civil disorder   Strife or conflict that is threatening to the public order and that involves the government in some fashion, either as a party to the conflict or as a guardian of the public interest.

Cohabitation   Relationships in which two people live in the same household and share sexual, emotional, and often economic ties but are not legally married.

Commodity riots   Race riots in which the focus of hostility is property, merchandise, or equipment rather than people of another racial group.

Communal riots   Race riots in which whites attack blacks in racially contested areas.

Communism   The term used by Marx to describe the end stage of the struggle over capitalism; a system in which all goods would be communally owned; people would not work for wages but would give according to their abilities; and there would be no scarcity of goods and services, allowing people to receive whatever they needed; in addition, the state would become less important and its role would dwindle.

Community   A group of people who share a common territory and a sense of identity or belonging and who interact with one another.

Conflict perspective   The sociological perspective centered on the idea that society consists of different groups who struggle with one another to attain the scarce societal resources that are considered valuable, be they money, power, prestige, or the authority to impose one's values on society.

Corporation   A business enterprise that is owned by stockholders, many of whom are not involved in running the daily affairs of the business.

Crime   An act that violates a criminal code enacted by an officially constituted political authority.

Crisis medicine   Medical treatment that focuses on treating people's illnesses after they become ill.

Cross-dependence   A situation in which the withdrawal symptoms of one drug are alleviated by another drug in the same pharmacological class.

Cross-tolerance   A situation in which a tolerance built up to one drug leads to a reduced response to another drug in the same pharmacological class.

Cultural analysis of poverty   A focus on the values, attitudes, and psychological orientations that may emerge among groups of people who live under conditions of poverty.

Cultural colonialism   A cultural assault that, if not diminished, will change values, norms, and ways of life.

Cultural definition of poverty   A definition of poverty that views it not only in terms of how many resources people have but also in terms of why they have failed to achieve a higher economic level.

Cultural lag   The tendency for there to be a gap between the point at which one part of the social system changes and the point at which other parts adjust to compensate for that change.

Cultural transmission theories   The theories that posit that crime and delinquency are learned and culturally transmitted through socialization.

Curative medicine   See Crisis medicine.

Definition of the situation   A person's perception and interpretation of what is important in a situation and what actions are appropriate.

Deindustrialization   A situation characterized by high rates of unemployment in the industrial sector, an aging and deterioration of factories and other productive resources, and an alleged inability to compete with other industrial nations.

Demographic gap   The gap between the high birthrates and low death rates that results in explosive population growth during the early industrial period of the demographic transition.

Demographic transition   The changing patterns of birth and death rates brought about by industrialization.

Demography   The study of the size, composition, and distribution of human populations and how these factors change over time.

Dependence   A mental or physical craving for a drug and withdrawal symptoms when use of the drug is stopped.

Dependency ratio   A statistic that shows the relative size of the group in society that is economically dependent for support on others who are working.

Depersonalization   Feelings of detachment from people and social groups that give life meaning and provide a sense of importance and self-worth.

Depressants   Psychoactive drugs that depress the central nervous system and have some analgesic, or pain-killing, properties.

Deviance   Behaviors or characteristics that violate important group norms and as a consequence are reacted to with social disapproval.

Differential association theory   The theory that posits that crime and delinquency are learned in interaction with other people, for the most part within intimate primary groups such as families and peer groups.

Discrimination   The unequal treatment of people because they are members of a particular group.

Drug   Any substance that, when consumed, alters one or more of the functions of the human body.

Drug abuse   The continued use of a psychoactive substance at a level that violates approved social practices.

Drug addiction   Physical dependence on a drug.

Dual-career family   A family in which both wife and husband are committed to career-oriented occupations that offer them fulfillment and opportunities for advancement.

Ecology   The branch of biology that studies the relationships between living organisms and their environment.

Economics   The social processes through which goods and services are produced and distributed.

Ecosystem   A complex, interrelated network of life forms and nonlife forms that interact with one another to produce an exchange of materials between the living and the nonliving parts.

Egalitarian family   A family in which power and authority are shared somewhat equally by husband and wife.

Environment   The conditions and circumstances surrounding and affecting a particular group of living creatures.

Ethnic group   A people who share a common historical and cultural heritage and sense of group identity and belongingness.

Ethnocentrism   The tendency to view one's own culture or subculture as the best and to judge other cultures or subcultures in comparison to it.

Expressive tasks   Activities focused on the relationships between people and on maintaining happiness, harmony, and emotional stability in a group.

Extended family   A family involving three or more generations of people who live together or in close proximity and whose lives and livelihoods are closely intertwined.

Family   A social institution based on kinship that functions to replace members of society and to nurture them.

Fecundity   The biological maximum number of children that could be born in a society.

Feminist movement   The collective activities of individuals, groups, and organizations whose goal is the fair and equal treatment of women and men around the world.

Fertility   The actual number of children born in a society.

Frustration   An inability to achieve sought-after goals.

Full employment   A situation in which everyone or nearly everyone who wants to work can find a job.

Functionalist perspective   The sociological perspective based on the idea that society is a system made up of a number of interrelated and interdependent elements, each performing a function that contributes to the operation of the whole.

Gender   Learned behavior involving how we are expected to act as males and females in society.

Gene splicing   See Recombinant DNA.

Genetic engineering   Manipulating the genes of organisms to alter the organisms' characteristics in ways that would not have occurred naturally.

Gentrification   The return of young, affluent professionals to neighborhoods in cities where they often rehabilitate previously rundown housing.

Gerontology   The scientific study of aging.

Ghetto   A neighborhood inhabited largely by members of a single ethnic or racial group.

Hallucinogens   Psychoactive drugs that produce hallucinations, often of a visual nature.

Health maintenance organization (HMO)   An organization that agrees to provide for all of a person's health-care needs for a fixed, periodic premium.

Homophobia   An intense dislike of or prejudice against homosexuals.

Homosexuality   Sexual feelings, fantasies, or acts directed toward members of the same sex.

Hydrologic cycle   The processes by which nature purifies water.

Hypotheses   Tentative statements that can be tested regarding relationships between two or more factors.

Industrialization   A productive subsistence pattern in which machines and power tools run by new sources of energy, such as fossil fuels, accomplish tasks that were previously done by hand.

In-group   A group that we feel positively toward, that we identify with, and that produces a "we feeling."

Institutionalized discrimination   The inequitable treatment of a group resulting from practices or policies that are incorporated into social, political, or economic institutions and that operate independently from the prejudices of individuals.

Instrumental tasks   The goal-oriented activities of a group, such as hunting, building something, or managing a work team.

Insurrection   An organized action by some group to rebel against the existing government and to replace it with new political forms and leadership.

Interactionist perspective   The sociological perspective that focuses on everyday social interaction among individuals rather than on large societal structures such as politics, education, and the like.

Interest group   A group whose members share distinct and common concerns and who benefit from similar social policies and practices.

Internal colonialism   A type of exploitation in which a subordinate group provides cheap labor that benefits the dominant group and who then is further exploited by having to purchase expensive goods and services from the dominant group.

Labeling theory   The theory based on the idea that whether other people define or label a person as deviant is a critical determinant in the development of a pattern of deviant behavior.

Lesbians   Female homosexuals.

Life course   A succession of statuses and roles that people in a particular society experience in a fairly predictable pattern as they grow older.

Life stages   See Life course.

Managed care   A health-care system, organized like HMOs, with networks of hospitals and doctors who provide all of the health-care needs for large groups of people for a flat fee.

Massive retaliation   A foreign policy based on the idea that war could be avoided if the enemy realized that any aggressor against the United States would suffer overwhelming damages from massive retaliation with U.S. military might.

Mechanization   The use of machinery to replace human and animal labor in the production of goods and services.

Medicaid   A joint federal-state program to provide medical care for low-income people of any age.

Medical–industrial complex   A coincidence of interests between physicians and other health-care providers and the industries producing health-care goods and services, with both parties profiting from the increased use of these commodities and the health-care consumer paying enormous costs for inadequate care.

Medicare   Government health insurance for those over sixty-five years of age.

Migration   A permanent change of residence.

Military–industrial complex   The relationship between the military that wants to purchase weapons and the corporations that produce the weapons. Both the military and the corporations benefit from a large military budget and policies favoring military solutions to international problems.

Minority group   A group whose members share distinct physical or cultural characteristics; are denied access to power and resources available to other groups; and are accorded fewer rights, privileges, and opportunities.

Mixed economies Economic systems in which there are strong elements of both capitalism and socialism.

Modernization The economic, social, and cultural changes that occur when a preindustrial society makes the transition to an advanced industrial society.

Modified extended family Families in which elaborate networks of visitation and support are found even though each nuclear unit lives separately.

Monogamy Family systems in which people have only one spouse at a time.

Mortality The number of deaths that occur in a particular population.

Mutually assured destruction A foreign policy based on the idea that war can be prevented when each side has the might to destroy the other.

Narcotics Psychoactive drugs whose main use is as analgesics or painkillers.

National health insurance A program of government health insurance covering all citizens.

Norms Rules of conduct that guide people's behavior.

Nuclear family A family consisting of a married couple and their children.

Oligarchy The tendency for power to become concentrated in the hands of a few people at the top of an organization.

Opiates See Narcotics.

Patriarchy A family in which males dominate in the regulation of political and economic decision making, whereas women and children are subordinate.

Photosynthesis The process by which plants capture light and heat energy from the sun and turn it into food.

Pluralism A situation in which a number of racial and ethnic groups live side by side, each retaining a distinct identity and lifestyle while still participating in some aspects of the larger culture.

Pluralistic family A family system in which a number of different family types exist side by side, each having an attraction for some segment of the populace.

Pluralist model The view of power in America as being spread over a large number of groups with divergent values, interests, and goals.

Politics The agreements in society over who has the right to exercise control over others, who can establish laws to regulate social life, and the manner in which conflicting interests in society will be resolved.

Polygamy Having more than one spouse at the same time.

Population The total number of people inhabiting a particular geographic area at a specified time.

Pornography Sexually "explicit" writings, still or motion pictures, and similar products designed to be sexually arousing.

Postindustrial society A society that is dominated by a highly technological form of production and that devotes greater resources to providing services than to industrial production.

Poverty The uneven distribution of the resources available.

Power The ability of one group to realize its will, even in the face of resistance from other groups.

Power elite model The view of power in America that says that there exists a small group of very powerful people who make just about all of the important decisions in the United States.

Prejudice An irrational attitude toward certain people based solely on their membership in a particular group.

Preventive medicine Changes in lifestyle or other steps that help avoid the occurrence of disease.

Primary deviance The violation of social norms in which the violator is not caught or is excused rather than labeled as a deviant.

Primary prevention Preventing drug problems before they begin.

Prostitution Sexual activity in exchange for money or goods, in which the primary motivation for the prostitute is neither sexual nor affectional.

Psychedelics See Hallucinogens.

Psychoactive drugs Drugs that can produce major alterations in the mood, emotions, perceptions, or brain functioning of the person who takes them.

Public assistance Social programs for which a person must pass a "means" test in order to be eligible.

Race A group of people who are believed to be a biological group sharing genetically transmitted traits that are defined as important.

Racism The view that certain racial or ethnic groups are biologically inferior and that practices involving their domination and exploitation are therefore justified.

Recidivism The repeat of an offense after having been convicted of a crime.

Recombinant DNA The practice in which DNA from one organism is spliced into the genetic material of another organism to produce some new characteristics in the host or even a novel form of life.

Refined divorce rate The divorce rate that is determined by dividing the number of divorces each year by the total number of existing marriages (or married women over age fifteen) in that year.

Relative definition of poverty The definition of poverty based on the idea that people are poor relative to some standard, and that standard is partially shaped by the lifestyles of other citizens.

Relative deprivation The idea that people tend to feel deprived or frustrated in comparison to what others have or what they believe they deserve.

Research The systematic examination of empirical data.

Sample Elements that are taken from a group or population and that serve as a source of data.

Science A method of obtaining objective and systematic knowledge through empirical observation.

Secondary deviance Behavior that a person adopts in reaction to being labeled as a deviant.

Secularization The process through which the influence of religion is removed from many institutions in society and dispersed into private and personal realms.

Serial monogamy A family system in which people are allowed to have more than one spouse, but not at the same time.

Sex The biological role that each of us plays in reproduction.

Sexism An ideology based on the belief that one sex is superior to and should dominate the other sex.

Sick role A set of expectations intended to guide the behavior of people who are ill.

Social institutions Relatively stable clusters of social relationships that involve people working together to meet some basic needs of society.

Social insurance Social programs offering benefits to broad categories of people, such as the elderly or injured workers, who presumably were working and paying for the insurance before becoming eligible for it.

Socialism Economic systems in which the means of production and distribution are collectively held so that the goods and services that people need are provided and equitably distributed.

Social mobility The movement of people from one social position to another in the stratification hierarchy.

Social movement A collective, organized effort to promote or resist social change through some non-institutionalized or unconventional means.

Social policy Laws, administrative procedures, and other formal and informal social practices that are intended to promote social changes focused on alleviating particular social problems.

Social problem A social condition is a social problem when an influential group defines it as threatening its values, when the condition affects a large number of people, and when it can be remedied by collective action.

Social stratification The ranking of people into a hierarchy in which the resources considered valuable by society are unequally distributed.

Sociobiology A field of study based on the idea that the genetic makeup of human beings plays a powerful role in shaping their social behavior.

Sociological imagination The ability to understand the relationship between what is happening in people's personal lives and the social forces that surround them.

Sociology The scientific study of societies and human social behavior.

Split labor market A situation in which there are two groups of workers willing to do the same work, but for different wages.

Stimulants Psychoactive drugs whose major effect is to stimulate the central nervous system.

Structural unemployment A predictable condition of unemployment resulting from changes in the occupational structure of society.

Subculture A group within a culture that shares some of the beliefs, values, and norms of the larger culture as well as some that are distinctly its own.

Subculture of violence   Norms and values that condone and legitimize the use of violence in resolving conflicts.

Suburb   A less densely populated area, primarily residential in nature, on the outskirts of a city.

Technology   Knowledge, tools, and practices that are employed as means of achieving clearly identifiable goals.

Technology assessment   Research that studies the impact of technology on our physical, social, and ethical environments and seeks solutions to social problems that arise from technological development.

Terrorism   The attempt to achieve political goals by using fear and intimidation to disrupt the normal operations of a society.

Theoretical perspectives   General views of society that provide some fundamental assumptions about the nature and operation of society and commonly serve as sources of the more specific theories.

Theory   A set of statements that explains the relationship between phenomena.

Third-party medicine   A health-care payment scheme in which the patient pays a premium into a fund and the doctor or hospital is paid from this fund for each treatment provided to the patient.

Tolerance   Physical changes that result in the need for higher and higher doses of a drug to achieve the same effect.

Urban homesteading   Programs to increase home ownership by private citizens in certain neighborhoods by selling them houses at little or no cost.

Values   People's ideas about what is good or bad, right or wrong.

Violence   Behavior that is intended to bring pain or physical injury to another person or to harm or destroy property.

Women's movement   See Feminist movement.

World systems theory   A theory that posits that the world's nations have become increasingly interdependent, both economically and politically, and are now linked in a worldwide system, with some nations having more power and resources than others.

Zero population growth   A situation in which birth and death rates are nearly equal, producing a zero rate of natural increase.

Abadinsky, H. (1994). *Organized crime* (4th ed.). Chicago: Nelson-Hall.

Abel, E. K. (1991). *Who cares for the elderly? Public policy and the experiences of adult daughters.* Philadelphia: Temple University Press.

Acuna, R. (1987). *Occupied America: A history of Chicanos* (3d ed.). New York: Harper and Row.

Adam, H., & Moodley, K. (1986). *South Africa without apartheid: Dismantling racial domination.* Berkeley: University of California Press.

Aday, L. A. (1993). *At risk in America: The health and health care needs of vulnerable populations in the United States.* San Francisco: Jossey-Bass.

Adelman, C. (1991). *Women at thirtysomething: Paradoxes of attainment.* Washington, DC: U.S. Department of Education.

Adorno, T. W., Frenkel-Brunswik, E., Levinson, D. J., & Sanford, R. N. (1950). *The authoritarian personality.* New York: Harper and Row.

Agnew, R. (1991). A longitudinal test of social control theory and delinquency. *Journal of Research in Crime and Delinquency, 28,* 126–156.

Aldrich, M., & Buchele, R. (1986). *The economics of comparable worth.* Cambridge, MA: Ballinger Publishing Co.

Allan, E. A., & Steffensmeier, D. J. (1989). Youth underemployment, and property crime: Differential effects of job availability and job quality, on juvenile and young adult arrest rates. *American Sociological Review, 54,* 107–123.

Amato, P. R. (1987). Family processes in one-parent, stepparent, and intact families: The child's point of view. *Journal of Marriage and the Family, 49,* 327–337.

Amato, P. R. (1993). Children's adjustment to divorce: Theories, hypotheses, and empirical support. *Journal of Marriage and the Family, 55,* 23–38.

Amato, P. R., & Rezac, S. J. (1994). Contact with nonresident parents, interparental conflict, and children's behavior. *Journal of Family Issues, 15,* 191–207.

American Psychiatric Association. (1994). *Diagnostic and statistical manual of mental disorders.* (4th ed., rev.). Washington, DC: American Psychiatric Association.

Andrews, D. A., Zinger, I., Hoge, R. D., Bonta, J., Gendreau, P., & Cullen, F. T. (1990). Does correctional treatment work? A clinically relevant and psychologically informed meta-analysis. *Criminology, 28,* 369–404.

Aniline, O., et al. (1980). The urban epidemic of phencyclidine use: Laboratory evidence from a public psychiatric hospital inpatient service. *Biological Psychiatry, 15,* 813–817.

Anstett, P. (1992, June 23). U.S. consumers pay for health care ills. *Detroit Free Press,* p. 1.

Antonovsky, A. (1972). Social class, life expectancy, and overall mortality. In E. G. Jaco (Ed.), *Patients, physicians, and illness.* (2d ed.). New York: Free Press.

Apter, D. E. (1986). *Rethinking development, modernization, dependency and post-modern politics.* Beverly Hills, CA: Sage.

Archer, D., & Gartner, R. (1976). Violent acts and violent times: A comparative approach to postwar homicide rates. *American Sociological Review, 41,* 937–963.

Ardrey, R. (1967). *The Territorial Imperative.* New York: Atheneum.

Aries, E. (1985). Male–female interpersonal styles in all male, all female, and mixed groups. In A. G. Sargent (Ed.), *Beyond sex roles.* (2d ed.). St. Paul, MN: West Publishing Company.

Aries, P. (1962). *Centuries of childhood.* (R. Baldick, Trans.). New York: Random House.

Armor, D. J. (1989). After busing: Education and choice. *The Public Interest, 95,* 24–37.

Armor, D. J. (1991). Response to Carr and Zeigler's 'white flight and white return in Norfolk.' *Sociology of Education, 64,* 134–139.

Armor, D. J. (1995). *Forced justice: School desegregation and the law.* New York: Oxford University Press.

Aronowitz, S., & DiFazio, W. (1994). *The jobless future: Sci-tech and the dogma of work.* Minneapolis: University of Minnesota Press.

Association of American Colleges. (1982). *The classroom climate: A chilly one for women?* Washington, DC: Project on the Status and Education of Women.

Atchley, R. C. (1994). *Social forces and aging: An introduction to social gerontology.* (7th ed.). Belmont, CA: Wadsworth.

Auerbach, J. D. (1990). Employer-supported child care as a women-responsive policy. *Journal of Family Issues, 11,* 384–400.

Axinn, J., & Stern, M. J. (1990). Social security policy reconsidered. *Challenge* (July/August): 22–27.

Bachman, J. G., Johnston, L. D., & O'Malley, P. M. (1990). Explaining the recent decline in cocaine use among young adults: Further evidence that perceived risks and disapproval lead to reduced drug use. *Journal of Health and Social Behavior, 31,* 173–184.

Baden, J., et al. (1979). Myths, admonitions and rationality: The American Indian as a resource manager. *Professional Papers in Political Economy and Natural Resources.* Bozeman: Montana State University.

Bagdikian, B. H. (1990). *The Media Monopoly.* (3d ed.). Boston: Beacon Press.

Bagley, B. M., & Walker, W. O. III, (Eds.). (1994). *Drug Trafficking in the Americas.* New Brunswick, NJ: Transaction Publishers.

Bahr, S. J. (1989). *Family Interaction.* New York: Macmillan.

Bailey, K. C. (1991). *Doomsday weapons in the hands of many: The arms control challenge of the '90s.* Urbana and Chicago: University of Illinois Press.

Bailey, K. C. (1995). Why we have to keep the bomb. *The Bulletin of the Atomic Scientists, 51,* 30–37.

Bailey, W. C. (1974). Murder and the death penalty. *Journal of Criminal Law and Criminology, 65,* 416–423.

Bailey, W. C. (1990). Murder, capital punishment, and television: Execution publicity and homicide rates. *American Sociological Review, 55,* 628–633.

Balling, Jr., R. C. (1992). *The heated debate: Greenhouse predictions versus climate reality.* San Francisco: Pacific Research Institute for Public Policy.

Ball-Rokeach, S. J. (1973). Values and violence: A test of the subculture of violence hypothesis. *American Sociological Review, 38,* 736–749.

Bandura, A. (1976). Social learning analysis of aggression. In E. Ribes-Inesta & A. Bandura (Eds.), *Analysis of delinquency and aggression.* New York: John Wiley and Sons.

Banfield, E. C. (1990). *The unheavenly city revisited.* Prospect Heights, IL: Waveland Press.

Barakat, H. (1993). *The Arab world: Society, culture, and state.* Berkeley, CA: University of California Press.

Barnet, R. J., & Cavanagh, J. (1994). *Global dreams: Imperial corporations and the new world order.* New York: Simon and Schuster.

Baron, J. M., & Newman, A. E. (1990). For what it's worth: Organizations, occupations, and the value of work done by women and nonwhites. *American Sociological Review, 55,* 155–175.

Baron, L. (1990). Pornography and gender equality: An empirical analysis. *Journal of Sex Research, 27,* 363–380.

Baron, R. A., & Richardson, D. R. (1994). *Human Aggression*, (2d ed.). New York: Plenum.

Barrett, K., & Greene, R. (1991, February 19). American cities: A special report. *Financial World*, pp. 20–37.

Barringer, H. R., Takeuchi, D. T., & Xenos, P. (1990). Education, occupational prestige, and income of Asian Americans. *Sociology of Education, 63,* 27–43.

Barrington, L., & Conrad, C. A. (1994). At what cost a room of her own? Factors contributing to the feminization of poverty among prime-age women, 1939–1959. *The Journal of Economic History, 54,* 342–357.

Barron, J. (1989, April 16). Unnecessary surgery. *The New York Times Magazine,* Part II, pp. 25, 44–46.

Baum, A., & Davis, G. (1976). Spatial and social aspects of crowding perception. *Environment and Behavior, 8,* 527–544.

Beauregard, R. A. (1990). Trajectories of neighborhood change: The case of gentrification. *Environment and Planning, 22,* 855–874.

Bedau, H. A. (1967). *The death penalty in America.* (rev. ed.). New York: Doubleday Anchor Books.

Bell, A. P., & Weinberg, M. S. (1978). *Homosexualities: A study of diversity among men and women.* New York: Simon and Schuster.

Bell, D. (1973). *The coming of post industrial society.* New York: Basic Books.

Bell, R. L., Cleveland, S. E., Hanson, P. G., & O'Connell, W. E. (1969). Small group dialogue and discussion: An approach to police–community relationships. *Journal of Criminal Law, Criminology, and Police Science, 60,* 242–246.

Bendick, M. Jr., & Rasmussen, D. W. (1986). Enterprise zones and inner-city economic revitalization. In G. E. Peterson & C. W. Lewis (Eds.), *Reagan and the cities.* Washington, DC: Urban Institute Press.

Beniger, J. R. (1993). The control revolution. In A. H. Teich (Ed.), *Technology and the future.* (6th ed.). New York: St. Martin's Press.

Benjamin, D. K., & Miller, R. L. (1991). *Undoing drugs: Beyond legalization.* New York: Basic Books.

Bennett, A., & Adams, O. (1993). *Looking north for health: What we can learn from Canada's health care system.* San Francisco: Jossey-Bass.

Benokraitis, N. V., & Feagin, J. R. (1995). *Modern sexism: Blatant, subtle and covert discrimination,* (2d ed.). Englewood Cliffs, NJ: Prentice-Hall.

Bequele, A., & Boyden, J. (1988). Working children: Current trends and policy responses. *International Labour Review, 127,* 153–172.

Berger, P. L. (1963). *Invitation to sociology: A humanistic perspective.* Garden City, NY: Anchor Books.

Berger, R. M. (1990). Men together: Understanding the gay couple. *Journal of Homosexuality, 19,* 31–49.

Berliner, D. (1988). Math teaching may favor boys over girls. *Education Digest, 53,* (January): 29.

Bernstein, N. (1996, January 8). Equal opportunity recedes for most female lawyers. *New York Times,* p. A12.

Berrill, K. T. (1992). Anti-gay violence and victimization in the United States: An overview. In G. M. Herek & K. T. Berrill (Eds.), *Hate crimes: Confronting violence against lesbians and gay men.* Newbury Park, CA: Sage.

Besancon, R. M. (Ed.). (1966). *The encyclopedia of physics.* New York: Reinhold Publishing Company.

Besharov, D. J. (1992). A new start for Head Start. *The American Enterprise, 3,* 52–57.

Best, R. (1983). *We've all got scars: What boys and girls learn in elementary school.* Bloomington: Indiana University Press.

Betz, M., Davis, K., & Miller, P. (1978). Scarcity, income advantage, and mobility: More evidence on the functional theory of stratification. *The Sociological Quarterly, 19,* 399–413.

Bieber, I., et al. (1962). *Homosexuality.* New York: Basic Books.

Billy, J. O. G., Tanfer, K., Grady, W. R., & Keplinger, D. H. (1993). The sexual behavior of men in the United States. *Family Planning Perspectives, 25,* 52–60.

Bishop, D. M., & Frazier, C. E. (1984). The effects of gender on charge reduction. *Sociological Quarterly, 25,* 385–396.

Black, F. L. (1978). Infectious diseases in primitive societies. In M. H. Logan & E. E. Hunt, Jr. (Eds.), *Health and the Human Condition.* North Scituate, MA: Duxbury Press.

Blea, I. I. (1991). *La Chicana and the intersection of race, class and gender.* New York: Praeger.

Blinder, A. S. (ed.). (1990). *Paying for productivity: A look at the evidence.* Washington DC: Brookings Institution.

Bloom, J. (1987). *Class, race, and the civil rights movement.* Bloomington: Indiana University Press.

Bluestone, B., & Harrison, B. (1987, February 1). The grim truth about the job 'miracle.' *New York Times.* Sec. 3, p. 3.

Blum, K., & Payne, J. E. (1991). *Alcohol and the Addictive Brain.* New York: Free Press.

Blum, R. W., Harmon, B., Harris, L., Bergeisen, L., & Resnick, M. D. (1992). American Indian–Alaska native youth health. *Journal of the American Medical Association, 267,* 1637–1644.

Blumer, H. (1962). Society as symbolic interaction. In A. M. Rose (Ed.), *Human Behavior and Social Processes.* Boston: Houghton Mifflin.

Boffey, P. M., Broad, W. J., Gelb, L. H., Mohr, C., & Noble, H. B. (1988). *Claiming the heavens: The New York Times complete guide to the Star Wars debate.* New York: Times Books (Random House).

Boisjoly, J., & Duncan, G. J. (1994). Job losses among Hispanics in the recent recession. *Monthly Labor Review,* June, 16–23.

Boivin, M. (1985, November 18). The truly forgotten warrior. Cited in "Imprisoned Vietnam Vets Seek Therapy." *Detroit Free Press,* pp. E-1, 2.

Bonacich, E. (1972). A theory of ethnic antagonism: The split-labor market. *American Sociological Review, 37,* 547–559.

Borgstrom, S., et al. (1983). Effects of a nuclear war on health and health services. World Health Organization, Publication A36.12.

Boswell, T. E. (1986). A split labor market analysis of discrimination against Chinese immigrants, 1850–1882. *American Sociological Review, 51,* 352–371.

Botvin, G. J. (1990). Substance abuse prevention: Theory, practice, and effectiveness. In M. Tonry & J. Q. Wilson (Eds.), *Drugs and Crime.* Chicago: University of Chicago Press.

Boulding, K. E. (1989). *Three faces of power.* Newbury Park, CA: Sage Publications.

Bouvier, L. F. (1984). Planet earth 1984–2034: A demographic vision. *Population Bulletin, 39,* whole No. 1.

Braddock, J. H. (1985). School desegregation and black assimilation. *Journal of Social Issues, 41,* 9–22.

Braddock, J. H., Crain, R. L., & McPartland, J. M. (1984). A long-term view of desegregation: Some recent studies of graduates as adults. *Phi Delta Kappan, 66,* 259–264.

Braun, E. (1984). *Wayward technology.* Westport, CT: Greenwood Press.

Brehm, S. S. (1985). *Intimate Relationships.* New York: Random House.

"The Brethren's First Sister." (1981, July 20). *Time,* pp. 8–19.

Brewer, M. B., & Miller, N. (1988). Contact and co-operation: When do they work? In P. A. Katz & D. A. Taylor (Eds.), *Eliminating racism: Profiles in controversy.* New York: Plenum.

Brimelow, P., & Spencer, L. (1990, September 17). Ralph Nader, Inc. *Forbes,* pp. 117–129.

Britton, D. M. (1990). Homophobia and homosociality: An analysis of boundary maintenance. *The Sociological Quarterly, 31* (3), 423–439.

Broad, W. J. (1987, June 21). Economic collapse tied to atom war. *New York Times,* pp. 1, 18.

Brody, B. A., & Engelhardt, H. T. Jr. (1987). *Bioethics: Readings and cases.* Englewood Cliffs, NJ: Prentice-Hall.

Brooks, R. (1969). Domestic violence and America's wars: A historical interpretation. In H. D. Graham & T. R. Gurr (Eds.), *Violence in America.* New York: Bantam Books.

Brostoff, S. (1992). Medical malpractice claims fuel health care cost boom. *National Underwriter, 96,* 2.

Brown, J. (1970). A note on the division of labor by sex. *American Anthropologist, 72,* 1073–1078.

Brown, L. R. (1987). Analyzing the demographic gap. In L. R. Brown et al. (Eds.). *State of the world, 1987: A worldwatch institute report on progress toward a sustainable society.* New York: W. W. Norton.

Brown, L. R. (1992). Launching the environmental revolution. In L. R. Brown et al. (Eds.), *State of the world, 1992: A worldwatch institute report on progress toward a sustainable society.* New York: W. W. Norton.

Brown, L. R., Flavin, C., & Postel, S. (1991). *Saving the planet: How to shape an environmentally sustainable global economy.* New York: W. W. Norton.

Brown, L. R., Kane, H., & Roodman, D. M. (1994). *Vital signs 1994: The trends that are shaping our future.* New York: W. W. Norton.

Brown, L. R., & Wolf, E. C. (1986). Assessing Ecological decline. In L. R. Brown et al. (Eds.), *State of the world, 1986: A worldwatch institute report on progress toward a sustainable society.* New York: W. W. Norton.

Brown, P. (1985). *The transfer of care: Psychiatric deinstitutionalization and its aftermath.* London: Routledge and Kegan Paul.

Brown, R. S., Clement, D. G., Hill, J. W., Retchin, S. M., & Bergeron, J. W. (1993). Do health maintenance organizations work for medicare? *Health Care Financing Review, 15,* 7–23.

Brown, R. M. (1969). Historical patterns of violence in america. In H. D. Graham & T. R. Gurr (Eds.), *Violence in America.* New York: Bantam Books.

Brownmiller, S. (1975). *Against our will: Men, women and rape.* New York: Simon and Schuster.

Brozan, N. (1984, September 20). Task force calls for action to control family violence. *New York Times,* p. 14.

Brozan, N. (1985, March 13). U.S. leads industrialized nations in teen-age births and abortions. *New York Times,* p. 1.

Bruce, J., Lloyd, C. B., & Leonard, A. (1995). *Families in focus.* New York: The Population Council.

Bruno, M. (1985, September 23). Abusing the elderly. *Newsweek,* pp. 75–76.

Brunton, B. (1991). An historical perspective on the future of the military–industrial complex. *The Social Science Journal, 28,* 45–62.

Brus, W., & Laski, K. (1989). *From Marx to the market: Socialism in search of an economic system.* Oxford: Clarendon Press.

Bryan, J. H. (1965). Apprenticeships in prostitution. *Social Problems, 12,* 287–296.

Bryan, J. H. (1966). Occupational ideologies and individual attitudes of call girls. *Social Problems, 13,* 441–449.

Bullock, C. S. III, Anderson, J. E., & Brady, D. W. (1983). *Public policy in the eighties.* Monterey, CA: Brooks-Cole.

Bullough, V. L. (1976). *Sexual variance in society and history.* New York: John Wiley and Sons.

Bunzel, J. H. (1991). Black and white at Stanford. *The Public Interest, 105,* 61–77.

Burby, R. J., & Rohe, W. M. (1990). Providing for the housing needs of the elderly. *Journal of the American Planning Association, 56,* 324–340.

Burkhauser, R. V., & Quinn, J. F. (1994). Changing policy signals. In M. W. Riley, R. L. Kahn, & A. Foner (Eds.), *Age and structural lag.* New York: Wiley Interscience.

Butterfield, F. (1992, July 19). Are American jails becoming shelters from the storm? *New York Times,* Sec. 4, p. 4.

Button, J. W. (1978). *Black violence: Political impact of the 1960s riots.* Princeton, NJ: Princeton University Press.

Califano, J. A. Jr. (1994). *Radical surgery: What's next for America's health care.* New York: Times Books.

Campagna, D. S., & Poffenberger, D. L. (1988). *The sexual trafficking in children: An investigation of the child sex trade.* Dover, MA: Auburn House.

Campbell, C. A. (1991). Prostitution, AIDS, and preventive health behavior. *Social Science and Medicine, 32,* 1367–1378.

Caplan, G. M. (1984). The facts of life about teenage prostitution. *Crime and Delinquency, 30* (1), 69–74.

Caplan, N. S., & Paige, J. M. (1968). A study of ghetto rioters. *Scientific American* (August), 15–21.

Caraley, D. (1992). Washington abandons the cities. *Political Science Quarterly, 107,* 1–30.

Cargan, L., & Melko, M. (1982). *Singles: Myths and Realities.* Beverly Hills, CA: Sage Publications.

Caringella-Macdonald, S. (1990). State crises and the crackdown on crime under Reagan. *Contemporary Crises, 14,* 91–118.

Carling, P. J. (1995). *Return to community: Building support systems for people with psychiatric disabilities.* New York: The Guilford Press.

Carr, L. G., & Zeigler, D. J. (1990). White flight and white return in Norfolk: A test of predictions. *Sociology of Education, 63,* 272–282.

Caughy, M. O., DiPietro J. A., & Strobino, D. M. (1994). Day-care participation as a protective factor in the cognitive development of low-income children. *Child Development, 65,* 457–471.

Cavender, G. (1991). Alternative theory: Labeling and critical perspectives. In J. F. Sheley (Ed.), *Criminology: A contemporary handbook.* Belmont, CA: Wadsworth.

Cetron, M. J., & Davies, O. (1994). The future face of terrorism. *The Futurist, 28* (November–December), 10–15.

Chagnon, N. A. (1968). *Yanomamo: The fierce people.* New York: Holt, Rinehart and Winston.

Chambliss, W. J. (1975). Toward a political economy of crime. *Theory and Society, 2,* 149–170.

Chambliss, W. J. (1991). Biology and crime. In J. F. Sheley (Ed.), *Criminology: A contemporary handbook.* Belmont, CA: Wadsworth.

Chase-Dunn, C., & Hall, T. D. (1993). Comparing world-systems: Concepts and working hypotheses. *Social Forces, 71,* 851–856.

Chazan, N., & Shaw, T. M. (1988). The political economy of food in Africa. In N. Chazan & T. M. Shaw (Eds.), *Coping with Africa's food crisis.* Boulder, CO: Lynne Rienner Publishers.

Cheng, L., & Bonacich, E. (1984). *Labor immigration under capitalism: Asian workers in the United States before World War II.* Berkeley: University of California Press.

Cherlin, A. J., & Furstenberg, F. F. Jr. (1994). Stepfamilies in the United States: A reconsideration. In J. Hagan and K. S. Cook, (Eds.), *Annual Review of Sociology.* Vol. 20. Palo Alto, CA: Annual Reviews Inc.

Chilman, C., et al. (Eds.). (1988). *Variant family forms.* Beverly Hills, CA: Sage Publications.

Clark, C., & Walter, B. O. (1991). Urban political cultures, financial stress, and city fiscal austerity strategies. *Western Political Quarterly, 44,* 676–697.

Clarke, A. C. (1984). *Profiles of the future: An inquiry into the limits of the possible.* New York: Holt, Rinehart and Winston.

Clarke-Stewart, A. (1993). *Daycare* (rev. ed.). Cambridge, MA: Harvard University Press.

Clayton, O. Jr., Baird, A. C., & Levinson, R. M. (1984). Subjective decision making in medical school admissions: Potentials for discrimination. *Sex Roles, 10* (7/8), 527–532.

Clement, U. (1989). Profile analysis as a method of comparing intergenerational differences in sexual behavior. *Archives of Sexual Behavior, 18,* 229–237.

Clinard, M. B., & Meier, R. F. (1989). *Sociology of Deviant Behavior.* (7th ed.). Fort Worth, TX: Holt, Rinehart and Winston.

Clore, G. L., Bray, R. M., Itkin, S. M., & Murphy, P. (1978). Interracial attitudes and behavior at a summer camp. *Journal of Personality and Social Psychology, 36,* 107–116.

Cloward, R. A., & Ohlin, L. E. (1960). *Delinquency and opportunity.* New York: Free Press.

Cloward, R. A., & Piven, F. F. (1974). *The politics of turmoil.* New York: Pantheon Books.

Cnaan, R. A., Olsson, S. E., & Wetle, T. (1990). Cross-national comparisons of planning for the needs of the very old: Israel, Sweden, and the United States. *Journal of Aging and Social Policy, 2* (1), 83–108.

Cochran, J. K., Chamlin, M. B., & Seth, M. (1994). Deterrence or brutalization? An impact assessment of Oklahoma's return to capital punishment. *Criminology, 32,* 107–134.

Cockerham, W. C. (1994). *Medical sociology.* (6th ed.). Englewood Cliffs, NJ: Prentice-Hall.

Cockerham, W. C. (1996). *Sociology of mental disorder.* 4th ed. Englewood Cliffs, NJ: Prentice-Hall.

Coe, R. M. (1978). *Sociology of medicine,* (2d ed.). New York: McGraw-Hill.

Cohen, L. E., & Felson, M. (1979). Social change and crime rate trends. *American Sociological Review, 44,* 588–609.

Cohen, L. E., Felson, M., & Land, K. C. (1980). Property crime rates in the United States: A macrodynamic analysis, 1947–1977; with ex ante forecasts for the mid-1980s. *American Journal of Sociology, 86,* 90–118.

Cohen, S. (1982). Cannibis: Effects upon adolescent behavior. In National Institute on Drug Abuse, *Marijuana and youth: Clinical observations on motivation and learning* (DHHS Pub. No. [ADM] 82-1186). Washington, DC: U.S. Government Printing Office.

Cohen, T. F. (1987). Remaking men: Men's experiences becoming and being husbands and fathers and their implications for reconceptualizing men's lives. *Journal of Family Issues, 8* (1), 57–77.

Cohn, S. F., Barkan, S. E., & Halteman, W. A. (1991). Punitive attitudes toward criminals: Racial consensus or racial conflict. *Social Problems, 38,* 287–296.

Cole, G. F. (1989). *The American system of criminal justice.* (5th ed.). Pacific Grove, CA: Brooks-Cole.

Coleman, J. S., Campbell, J. E., Hobson, L., McPartland, J., Mood, A., Weinfield, F., & York, R. (1966). *Equality of educational opportunity*. Washington, DC: U.S. Government Printing Office.

Coleman, J. W. (1989). *The criminal elite: The sociology of white collar crime*. (2d ed.). New York: St. Martin's Press.

Collins, R. (1971). A conflict theory of sexual stratification. *Social Problems, 19*, 3–21.

Collins, R. (1990). Conflict theory and the advance of macro-historical sociology. In G. Ritzer (Ed.), *Frontiers of social theory: The new synthesis*. New York: Columbia University Press.

Collins, R., & Coltrane, S. (1991). *Sociology of marriage and the family: Gender, love, and property*. (3d ed.). Chicago: Nelson-Hall.

Collins, R. L., & Marlatt, G. A. (1983). Psychological correlates and explanations of alcohol use and abuse. In B. Tabakoff, P. B. Sutker, & C. L. Randall (Eds.), *Medical and social aspects of alcohol abuse*. New York: Plenum.

Colvin, M. (1991). Crime and social reproduction: A response to the call for 'outrageous' proposals. *Crime and Delinquency, 73*, 436–448.

Community drug prevention programs show promise. (1990). *Public Health Reports, 105*, 543.

Comstock, G. D. (1991). *Violence against lesbians and gay men*. New York: Columbia University Press.

Comte, A. (1835). *Systeme de politique positive* (4 vols.). Paris: Cres.

Congress clears overhaul of welfare system. (1988). *Congressional Quarterly*. (October 1), 2699–2701.

Conklin, J. G. (1976). Robbery, the elderly and fear: An urban problem in search of a solution. In J. Goldsmith & S. S. Goldsmith (Eds.), *Crime and the elderly*. Lexington, MA: Lexington Books.

Conrad, J. P. (1985). *The Dangerous and the endangered*. Lexington, MA: Lexington Books.

Constantinople, A., Cornelius, R., & Gray, J. (1988). The chilly climate: Fact or artifact? *Journal of Higher Education, 59*, 527–550.

Costells, M. (1977). *The urban question: A Marxist approach*. (Ann Sheridan, Trans.) Cambridge, MA: M.I.T. Press.

Cowan, A. L. (1992, September 27). For women, fewer M.B.A.'s. *New York Times*, Sec. 3, p. 4.

Cranna, M. (Ed.). (1994). *The true cost of conflict: Seven recent wars and their effects on society*. New York: The New Press.

Crawford, M., & MacLeod, M. (1990). Gender in the college classroom: An assessment of the 'chilly climate' for women. *Sex Roles, 23*, 101–122.

Craypo, C., & Nissen, B. (Eds.). (1993). *Grand designs: The impact of corporate strategies on workers, unions, and communities*. Ithaca, NY: ILR Press.

Crossman, R. K., Stith, S. M., & Bender, M. M. (1990). Sex role egalitarianism and marital violence. *Sex Roles, 22* (5/6), 293–304.

Crowe, T. D. (1991). *Crime prevention through environmental design*. Boston: Butterworth-Heinemann.

Crowley, T. J. (1988). Learning and unlearning drug abuse in the real world. In B. A. Ray (Ed.), *Learning factors in substance abuse* (DHHS Pub. No. [ADM] 88-1576). Rockville, MD: National Institute on Drug Abuse.

Crystal, S. (1986). Measuring income and inequality among the elderly. *The Gerontologist, 26*, 56–59.

Culkin, M., Morris, J. R., & Helburn, S. W. (1991). Quality and the true cost of child care. *Journal of Social Issues, 47* (2), 71–86.

Cullen, F. T., Link, B. G., & Polanzi, C. W. (1982). The seriousness of crime revisited: Have attitudes toward white-collar crime changed? *Criminology, 20*, 83–102.

Cullen, J. B., & Novick, S. M. (1979). The Davis-Moore theory of stratification: A further examination and extension. *American Journal of Sociology, 84*, 1414–1437.

Currie, E. (1985). *Confronting crime: An American challenge*. New York: Pantheon Books.

Currie, E. (1993). *Reckoning: Drugs, the cities, and the American future*. New York: Hill and Wang.

Cushman, J. H. Jr. (1986, August 31). Pentagon-to-Contractor job shift is profiled. *New York Times*, p. 37.

Dahrendorf, R. (1959). *Class and class conflict in industrial society*. Stanford, CA: Stanford University Press.

Daniels, R. (1988). *Asian America: Chinese and Japanese in the United States since 1850*. Seattle: University of Washington Press.

Danigelis, N. L., & Fengler, A. P. (1990). Homesharing: How social exchange helps elders live at home. *The Gerontologist, 30*, 162–170.

Danziger, S., & Gottschalk, P. (Eds.). (1993). *Uneven tides: Rising inequality in America.* New York: Russell Sage Foundation.

Davenport, W. H. (1977). Sex in cross-cultural perspective. In F. A. Beach (Ed.), *Human sexuality in four perspectives.* Baltimore: Johns Hopkins University Press.

Davidson, J. K. Sr., & Moore, N. B. (1992). *Marriage and family.* Dubuque, IA: William C. Brown.

Davis, B. D. (1993). Genetic engineering: The making of monsters? *The Public Interest, 110,* 63–76.

Davis, J. A., & Smith, T. W. (1991). *General social surveys, 1972–1991.* Chicago: National Opinion Research Center.

Davis, K. (1971). Sexual behavior. In R. K. Merton & R. Nisbet (Eds.), *Contemporary social problems* (4th ed.). New York: Harcourt Brace Jovanovich.

Davis, K., & Moore, W. (1945). Some principles of stratification. *American Sociological Review, 10,* 242–249.

Davis, S. M., Hunt, K., & Kitzes, J. M. (1989). Improving the health of Indian teenagers—A demonstration program in rural New Mexico. *Public Health Reports, 104,* 271–278.

Deckhard, B. (1979). *The women's movement.* New York: Harper and Row.

Dekker, P., & Ester, P. (1991). Authoritarianism, socio-demographic variables and racism: A Dutch replication of Billig and Cramer. *New Community, 17,* 287–293.

Delattre, E. J. (1990). New faces of organized crime. *The American Enterprise,* 38–45.

De Leon, G. (1988). The therapeutic community and behavioral science. In B. A. Ray (Ed.), *Learning factors in substance abuse.* NIDA Research Monograph 84 (DHHS Pub. No. [ADM] 88-1576). Rockville, MD: National Institute on Drug Abuse.

Densen-Gerber, J. (1984). The Odyssey House treatment method. In G. Serban (Ed.), *Social and medical aspects of drug abuse.* New York: SP Medical and Scientific Books.

Dentler, R. A. (1992). The Los Angeles riots of spring 1992: Events, causes, and future policy. *Sociological Practice Review, 3,* 229–244.

Deschenes, E. P., Anglin, M. D., & Speckart, G. (1991). Narcotics addiction: Related criminal careers, social and economic costs. *Journal of Drug Issues, 21,* 383–411.

Des Jarlais, D. C. (1984). Research design, drug use, and deaths: Cross study comparisons. In G. Serban (Ed.), *Social and medical aspects of drug abuse.* New York: SP Medical and Scientific Books.

Devine, J. A., Plunkett, M., & Wright, J. D. (1992). The chronicity of poverty: Evidence from the PSID, 1967–1987. *Social Forces, 70,* 787–812.

Devine, J. A., Sheley, J. F., & Smith, M. D. (1988). Macoeconomic and social-control policy influences on crime rate changes, 1948–1985. *American Sociological Review, 53,* 407–420.

Devine, J. A., & Wright, J. D. (1993). *The greatest of evils: Urban poverty and the American underclass.* Hawthorne, NY: Aldine de Gruyter.

Devins, R. M. (1986). Displaced workers: One year later. *Monthly Labor Review,* 40–43.

Diana, L. (1985). *The prostitute and her clients: Your pleasure is her business.* Springfield, IL: Charles C Thomas.

Dickens, C. (1924). *A tale of two cities.* New York: Charles Scribner's Sons.

DiIulio, J. J. Jr. (1989). The impact of inner-city crime. *The Public Interest, 96,* 28–46.

DiMatteo, M. R., & DiNicola, D. D. (1982). *Achieving patient compliance: The psychology of the medical practitioner's role.* New York: Pergamon Press.

Dinham, B. (1993). *The pesticide hazard: A global health and environmental audit.* London: Zed Books.

Dole, V. P. (1991). Interim methadone clinics: An undervalued approach. *American Journal of Public Health, 81,* 1111–1112.

Domhoff, G. W. (1967). *Who rules America?* Englewood Cliffs, NJ: Prentice-Hall.

Domhoff, G. W. (1983). *Who rules America now?* Englewood Cliffs, NJ: Prentice-Hall.

Donnelley, S., McCarthy, C. R., & Singleton, R. Jr. (1994). The brave new world of animal biotechnology. *Hastings Center Report Special Supplement, 24,* (Suppl.), S1–S31.

Donnerstein, E., Linz, D., & Penrod, S. (1987). *The question of pornography: Research findings and policy implications.* New York: Free Press.

Doob, C. B. (1993). *Racism: An American cauldron.* New York: HarperCollins.

Dreier, P. (1982). The position of the press in the U.S. power structure. *Social Problems, 29,* 298–310.

Dubow, F., & Emmons, D. (1981). The community hypothesis. In D. A. Lewis (Ed.), *Reactions to crime.* Beverly Hills, CA: Sage Publications.

Duke, J. T. (1976). *Conflict and power in social life.* Provo, UT: Brigham Young University Press.

Duke, S. B., & Gross, A. C. (1993). *America's longest war: Rethinking our tragic crusade against drugs.* New York: Putnam.

Dulles, J. F. (1954). Police for security and peace. *Foreign Affairs, 32,* 353–364.

Dunbar, L. W. (1988). *The common interest: How our social-welfare policies don't work, and what we can do about them.* New York: Pantheon.

Duncan, C. M. (Ed.). (1992). *Rural poverty in America.* Westport, CT: Auburn House.

Duncan, G. J., & Rodgers, W. (1991). Has children's poverty become more persistent? *American Sociological Review, 56,* 538–550.

Dunford, F. W., Huizinga, D., & Elliott, D. S. (1990). The role of arrest in domestic assault: The Omaha police experiment. *Criminology, 28,* 183–206.

Dunlap, D. W. (1994, December 21). Survey on slayings of homosexuals finds high violence and low arrest rate. *New York Times,* p. A10.

Dunn, F. L. (1978). Epidemiological factors: Health and disease in hunter-gatherers. In M. H. Logan & E. E. Hunt (Eds.), *Health and the human condition.* North Scituate, MA: Duxbury Press.

Durand, A. M. (1992). The safety of home birth: The farm study. *American Journal of Public Health, 82,* 450–453.

Durning, A. T., & Brough, H. B. (1992). Reforming the livestock economy. In L. R. Brown et al. (Eds.), *State of the world 1992: A worldwatch institute report on progress toward a sustainable society.* New York: W. W. Norton.

Duster, T. (1987). Crime, youth unemployment, and the black urban underclass. *Crime and Delinquency, 33* (2), 300–316.

Duster, T. (1990). *Backdoor to eugenics.* London: Routledge.

Dye, T. R. (1995). *Who's running America: The Clinton years* (6th ed.). Englewood Cliffs, NJ: Prentice-Hall.

Easterbrook, G. (1995). *A moment on the Earth: The coming age of environmental optimism.* New York: Viking.

Eckerman, W. C., et al. (1971). *Drug use and arrest charges: A study of drug use and arrest charges among arrestees in six metropolitan areas of the United States.* Washington, DC: U.S. Government Printing Office.

Eckholm, E. (1994, December 18). While congress remains silent, health care transforms itself. *New York Times,* p. A1.

Eder, P. F. (1994). Privacy on parade: Your secrets for sale! *The Futurist, 28,* 38–42.

Edwards, G. (1983). Drugs and drug dependence. In G. Edwards, A. Arif, & J. Jaffe (Eds.), *Drug use and misuse: Cultural perspectives.* New York: St. Martin's Press.

Eggebeen, D. J., & Lichter, D. T. (1991). Race, family structure, and changing poverty among American children. *American Sociological Review, 56,* 801–817.

Eggert, L. L., & Herting, J. R. (1991). Preventing teenage drug abuse: Exploratory effects of network social support. *Youth and Society, 22,* 482–524.

Egley, L. C. (1991). What changes the societal prevalence of domestic violence? *Journal of Marriage and the Family, 53,* 885–897.

Ehrlich, P. R., & Ehrlich, A. H. (1970). *Population, resources, environment.* San Francisco: W. H. Freeman.

Ehrlich, P. R., & Ehrlich, A. H. (1990). *The population explosion.* New York: Simon and Schuster.

Ehrlich, P. R., et al. (1983). Long-term biological consequences of nuclear war. *Science, 222,* 1293–1300.

Elliott, C. (1981). Letter from an angry reader—To the editor from Chip Elliott. *Esquire,* September, 33–37.

Elliott, D. S., & Huizinga, D. (1983). Social class and delinquent behavior in a national youth panel: 1976–1980. *Criminology, 21,* 149–177.

England, P. (1992). *Comparable worth: Theories and evidence.* New York: Aldine de Gruyter.

Entwisle, D. R., & Alexander, K. L. (1994). Winter setback: The racial composition of schools and learning to read. *American Sociological Review, 59,* 446–460.

Erickson, P. G., Adlaf, E. M., Murray, G. F., & Smart, R. G. (1987). *The steel drug: Cocaine in perspective.* Lexington, MA: Lexington Books.

Erlanger, H. S. (1974). The empirical status of the subculture of violence thesis. *Social Problems, 22,* 280–292.

Eshleman, J. R. (1991). *The family: An introduction.* (6th ed.). Boston: Allyn and Bacon.

Eysenck, H. J., & Gudjonsson, G. H. (1989). *The causes and cures of criminality.* New York: Plenum.

Fagan, J., Piper, E. S., & Cheng, Y-T. (1987). Contributions of victimization to delinquency in inner cities. *Journal of Criminal Law and Criminology, 78* (3), 586–609.

Fallows, J. (1994). *Looking at the sun: The rise of the new east Asian economic and political system.* New York: Pantheon.

Faludi, S. (1991). *Backlash: The undeclared war against American women.* New York: Crown Publishers.

Fausto-Sterling, A. (1992). *Myths of gender: Biological theories about women and men.* New York: Basic Books.

Fay, B. (1987). *Critical social science: Liberation and its limits.* Ithaca, NY: Cornell University Press.

Feagin, J. R., & Sykes, M. P. (1994). *Living with racism: The black middle-class experience.* Boston: Beacon Press.

Fearnside, P. M. (1989). Deforestation in Amazonia: A prescription for slowing. *Environment, 31* (4), 17–20; 39–40.

Featherman, D. L., & Hauser, R. M. (1978). *Opportunity and change.* New York: Academic Press.

Federal Bureau of Investigation. (1994). *Uniform crime reports: Crime in the United States, 1993.* Washington, DC: U.S. Government Printing Office.

Federal Bureau of Investigation. (1995). *Uniform crime reports: Crime in the United States, 1994.* Washington, DC: U.S. Government Printing Office.

Ferber, M. A., & O'Farrell, B. (1991). *Work and family: Policies for a changing workforce.* Washington, DC: National Academy Press.

Ferree, M. M. (1991). The gender division of labor in two-earner marriages: Dimensions of variability and change. *Journal of Family Issues, 12,* 158–180.

Ferree, M. M., & Hall, E. J. (1990). Visual images of American society: Gender and race in introductory sociology textbooks. *Gender and Society, 4,* 500–533.

Ficarrotto, T. J. (1990). Racism, sexism, and erotophobia: Attitudes of heterosexuals toward homosexuals. *Journal of Homosexuality, 19* (1), 111–116.

Fijnaut, C. (1990). Organized crime: A comparison between the United States of America and Western Europe. *British Journal of Criminology, 30,* 321–340.

Finckenauer, J. O. (1988). Public support for the death penalty: Retribution as just deserts or retribution as revenge? *Justice Quarterly, 5* (1), 81–100.

Fiorentine, R. (1988). Increasing similarity in the values and life plans of male and female college students? Evidence and implications. *Sex Roles, 18,* 143–158.

Fitzpatrick, J. P. (1987). *Puerto Rican Americans: The meaning of migration to the mainland.* (2d ed.). Englewood Cliffs, NJ: Prentice-Hall.

Flacks, R. (1971). *Youth and social change.* Chicago: Markham Publishing Co.

Flavin, C. (1987). *Reassessing nuclear power: The fallout from Chernobyl.* Worldwatch Paper 75. Washington, DC: Worldwatch Institute.

Flavin, C. (1992). Building a bridge to sustainable energy. In L. R. Brown et al. (Eds.), *State of the world, 1992: A Worldwatch Institute report on progress toward a sustainable society.* New York: W. W. Norton.

Flavin, C., & Durning, A. (1988). Raising energy efficiency. In L. R. Brown et al. (Eds.), *State of the world 1988: A worldwatch institute report on progress toward a sustainable society.* New York: W. W. Norton.

Flavin, C., & Lenssen, N. (1990). *Beyond the petroleum age: Designing a solar economy.* Worldwatch Paper 100. Washington, DC: Worldwatch Institute.

Fleagle, R. G. (1994). *Global environmental change: Interactions of science, policy, and politics in the United States.* Westport, CT: Praeger.

Flewelling, R. L., Rachal, J. V., & Marsden, M. E. (1992). *Socioeconomic and demographic correlates of drug and alcohol use.* National Institute on Drug Abuse (DHHS Pub. No. [ADM] 92-1906).

Washington, DC: U.S. Government Printing Office.

Ford, C. S. (1970). Some primitive societies. In G. H. Seward & R. C. Williamson (Eds.), *Sex roles in society.* New York: Random House.

Fost, D. (1991). American Indians in the 1990s. *American Demographics,* (December), 26–34.

Franks, V., & Rothblum, E. D. (Eds.). (1983). *The stereotyping of women: Its effects on mental health.* New York: Springer.

Freedman, J. L. (1975). *Crowding and behavior.* San Francisco: W. H. Freeman.

Freeman, R. B. (1993). How much has de-unionization contributed to the rise in male earnings inequality? In S. Danziger & P. Gottschalk (Eds.), *Uneven tides: Rising inequality in America.* New York: Russell Sage Foundation.

Freeman, R. B., & Holzer, H. J. (Eds.). (1986). *The black youth employment crisis.* Chicago: University of Chicago Press.

French, M. (1992). *The war against women.* New York: Summit Books.

Freudenheim, M. (1989, July 30). Ontario pay equity law has employers scrambling. *Detroit Free Press,* Sec. C, p. 1.

Freudenheim, M. (1992, April 12). Doctors dropping medicare patients. *New York Times,* p. 1.

Freund, P. E. S., & McGuire, M. B. (1995). *Health, illness, and the social body: A critical sociology.* 2d ed. Englewood Cliffs, NJ: Prentice-Hall.

Friedlander, D., & Burtless, G. (1995). *Five years after: The long-term effects of welfare-to-work programs.* New York: Russell Sage Foundation.

Fuchs, V. R., & Reklis, D. M. (1992). America's children: Economic perspectives and policy options. *Science, 255,* 41–46.

Fuentes, A. (1991, October 28). Women warriors: Equality, yes—Militarism, no. *The Nation,* 516–519.

Funk, R. B., & Willits, F. K. (1987). College attendance and attitude change: 1970–1981. *Sociology of Education, 60,* 224–231.

Furstenberg, F. F. Jr., & Cherlin, A. J. (1991). *Divided families: What happens to children when parents part.* Cambridge, MA: Harvard University Press.

Furstenberg, F. F. Jr., & Teitler, J. O. (1994). Reconsidering the effects of marital disruption: What happens to children in early adulthood? *Journal of Family Issues, 15,* 173–190.

Galbraith, J. K. (1967). *The new industrial state.* Boston: Houghton Mifflin.

Gallagher, T. J., Johnson, E. O., Van Valey, T. L., & Malaret, D. R. (1992). Job-seeking and academic success among sociologists: The effects of departmental prestige and gender. Paper presented at the annual meetings of the American Sociological Association, Pittsburgh.

Gallup, G. (1983). Prejudice in politics. *The Gallup Report, 216,* 14.

Gallup Poll. (1995). *CNN/USA Today/Gallup Poll.* April 17–19, Questions 23–29.

Gans, H. J. (1971). The uses of poverty: The poor pay all. *Social Policy,* 2 (July/August): 20–24.

Gans, H. J. (1988). *Middle American individualism: The future of liberal democracy.* New York: Free Press.

Gans, H. J. (1992, January 8). Fighting the biases embedded in social concepts of the poor. *The Chronicle of Higher Education,* p. A56.

Gastil, J. (1990). Generic pronouns and sexist language: The oxymoronic character of masculine generics. *Sex Roles, 23* (11–12), 629–643.

Gelles, R. J. (1987). What to learn from cross-cultural and historical research on child abuse and neglect: An overview. In R. J. Gelles & J. B. Lancaster (Eds.), *Child abuse and neglect: Biosocial dimensions.* New York: Aldine de Gruyter.

Gelles, R. J. (1992). Poverty and violence toward children. *American Behavioral Scientist, 35,* 258–274.

Gelles, R. J., & Conte, J. R. (1990). Domestic violence and sexual abuse of children: A review of research in the eighties. *Journal of Marriage and the Family, 52,* 1045–1058.

Gelles, R. J., & Cornell, C. P. (1990). *Intimate violence in families.* (2d ed.). Newbury Park, CA: Sage Publications.

Gendreau, P., & Ross, R. R. (1987). Revivification of rehabilitation: Evidence from the 1980s. *Justice Quarterly, 4,* 349–407.

Gentry, C. S. (1991). Pornography and rape: An empirical analysis. *Deviant Behavior, 12,* 277–288.

George, S., & Sabelli, F. (1994). *Faith and credit: The World Bank's secular empire.* Boulder, CO: Westview Press.

Gerdes, E. P., & Garber, D. M. (1983). Sex bias in hiring: Effects of job demands and applicant competence. *Sex Roles, 9* (3), 307–319.

Gerrard, M. B. (1994). *Whose backyard, whose risk: Fear and fairness in toxic and nuclear waste siting.* Cambridge, MA: The MIT Press.

Gerstel, N., Riessman, C. K., & Rosenfield, S. (1985). Explaining the symptomatology of separated and divorced men and women: The role of material conditions and social networks. *Social Forces, 64,* 84–101.

Gibbs, J. P. (1989). Conceptualization of terrorism. *American Sociological Review, 54,* 329–340.

Giele, J. Z. (1978). *Women and the future.* New York: Free Press.

Gil, D. G. (1990). *Unravelling social policy: Theory, analysis, and political action towards social equality.* Rochester, VT: Schenkman Books.

Gilbert, L. A. (1985). *Men in dual-career families: Current realities and future prospects.* Hillsdale, NJ: Erlbaum.

Gilder, G. (1993). The death of telephony. *The Economist,* September 11, 75–78.

Gillis, J. (1974). Youth in history: Progress and prospects. *Journal of Social History, 7,* 201–207.

Gillmor, D., & Doig, S. K. (1992). Segregation forever? *American Demographics,* January, 48–51.

The Glass Ceiling Commission. (1995). *Good for business: Making full use of the nation's human capital: A fact-finding report of the federal glass ceiling commission.* Washington, DC: U.S. Government Printing Office.

Glazer, M. P., & Glazer, P. M. (1989). *The whistleblowers: Exposing corruption in government and industry.* New York: Basic Books.

Glazer, N. (1995). Making work work: Welfare reform in the 1990s. In D. S. Nightingale & R. H. Haveman, (Eds.), *The work alternative: Welfare reform and the realities of the job market.* Washington, DC: The Urban Institute Press.

GM bets an arm and a leg on a people-free plant. (1988, September 12), *Business Week,* 72–73.

Goff, C., & Nason-Clark, N. (1989). The seriousness of crime in Fredericton, New Brunswick: Perceptions toward white-collar crime. *Canadian Journal of Criminology, 31* (1), 19–34.

Goffman, E. (1963). *Stigma: Notes on the management of spoiled identity.* Englewood Cliffs, NJ: Prentice-Hall.

Goldscheider, F. K., & Waite, L. J. (1991). *New families, no families? The transformation of the American home.* Berkeley: University of California Press.

Goldstein, A., & Kalant, H. (1990). Drug policy: Striking the right balance. *Science, 249,* 1513–1521.

Goldstein, M. C. (1971). Stratification, polyandry, and family structure in central Tibet. *Southwest Journal of Anthropology, 27,* 65–74.

Goldstein, M. J., Kant, H. S., & Hartman, J. J. (1974). *Pornography and sexual deviance.* Berkeley: University of California Press.

Goldstein, P. J., Bellucci, P. A., Spunt, B. J., & Miller, T. (1991). Volume of cocaine use and violence: A comparison between men and women. *Journal of Drug Issues, 21,* 345–367.

Golombok, S., & Tasker, F. (1996). Do parents influence the sexual orientation of their children? Findings from a longitudinal study of lesbian families. *Developmental Psychology, 32,* 3–11.

Gordon, M. T., & Riger, S. (1989). *The female fear.* New York: Free Press.

Gordon, M. (1978). *The American family: Past, present, and future.* New York: Random House.

Gordon, M. M. (1964). *Assimilation in American life.* New York: Oxford University Press.

Gordon, M. M. (1988). *The scope of sociology.* New York: Oxford University Press.

Gordon, S. (1995, February 13). Cutbacks on caregivers: Is there a nurse in the house. *The Nation,* pp. 199–202.

Gore, A. (1992). *Earth in the balance: Ecology and the human spirit.* Boston: Houghton Mifflin.

Gottfredson, M. R., & Hirschi, T. (1990). *A general theory of crime.* Stanford, CA: Stanford University Press.

Gottlieb, M. (1988). *Comparative economic systems: Preindustrial and modern case studies.* Ames: Iowa State University Press.

Gouldner, A. W. (1976). The dark side of the dialectic: Toward a new objectivity. *Sociological Inquiry, 46,* 3–16.

Graham, O. L. Jr. (1992). *Losing time: The industrial policy debate.* Cambridge, MA: Harvard University Press.

Green, G. D., & Bozett, F. W. (1991). Lesbian mothers and gay fathers. In J. C. Gonsiorek & J. D. Weinrich (Eds.), *Homosexuality: Research implications for public policy*. Newbury Park, CA: Sage.

Greenberg, D. F. (1988). *The construction of Homosexuality*. Chicago: University of Chicago Press.

Greenberg, J. R., McKibben, M., & Raymond, J. A. (1990). Dependent adult children and elder abuse. *Journal of Elder Abuse and Neglect, 2* (1/2), 73–86.

Greenberger, D. B., et al. (1989). The impact of personal control on performance and satisfaction. *Organizational Behavior and Human Decision Processes, 43*, 29–51.

Greenman, M. (1990). Survivors of prostitution find PRIDE. *Families in Society, 71*, 110–113.

Greider, W. (1992). *Who will tell the people: The betrayal of American democracy*. New York: Simon and Schuster.

Guillemin, J. (1980). Federal policies and Indian politics. *Society, 17*, 29–34.

Gunther, M. (1993, June 16). Women, minorities get short end on small screen, study says. *Detroit Free Press*, pp. 1C, 3C.

Gustman, A. L., & Steinmeier, T. L. (1991). Changing the Social Security rules for work after 65. *Industrial and Labor Relations Review, 44*, 733–745.

Gyllenhammar, P. G. (1977). *People at work*. Reading, MA: Addison-Wesley.

Hacker, A. (1992). *Two nations: Black and white, separate, hostile, unequal*. New York: Charles Scribner's Sons.

Haglund, R. M. J., & Schuckit, M. A. (1981). The epidemiology of alcoholism. In N. Estes & E. Heineman (Eds.), *Alcoholism: Development, consequences and interventions*. St. Louis: Mosby.

Halikas, J. A., et al. (1982). Incidence and characteristics of amotivational syndrome, including associated findings, among chronic marijuana users. In National Institute on Drug Abuse, *Marijuana and youth: Clinical observations on motivation and learning* (DHHS Pub. No. [ADM] 82-1186). Washington, DC: U.S. Government Printing Office.

Hamer, D., & Copeland, P. (1994). *The science of desire: The search for the gay gene and the biology of behavior*. New York: Simon and Schuster.

Hammersmith, S. K. (1987). A sociological approach to counseling homosexual clients and their families. *Journal of Homosexuality, 15*, 173–190.

Hanson, D. J. (1975). The influence of authoritarianism upon prejudice: A review. *Resources in Education, 14*, 31.

Hardin, G. (1993). *Living within limits: Ecology, economics, and population taboos*. New York: Oxford University Press.

Harding, S. (1986). *The science question in feminism*. Ithaca, NY: Cornell University Press.

Harlan, A., & Weiss, C. (1981). *Final report from "Moving up: Women in managerial careers."* Working Paper No. 86, Center for Research on Women, Wellesley College.

Harrington, M. (1984). *The new American poverty*. New York: Holt, Rinehart and Winston.

Harrington, M. (1989). *Socialism: Past and future*. New York: Arcade Publishing.

Harrison, B., & Bluestone, B. (1988). *The great U-turn: Corporate restructuring and the polarizing of America*. New York: Basic Books.

Hartman, C. (1994, March 7). UN group describes unemployment crisis. *Detroit Free Press*, 5A.

Hartung, W. D. (1992, October 25). Arms sales win votes and little else. *New York Times*, Sec. 3, p. 11.

Harty, S. J. (1991, November 4). Data bank keeps doctors on edge. *Business Insurance*, pp. 89–90.

Hasin, D. S., et al. (1988). Cocaine and heroin dependence compared in poly-drug abusers. *American Journal of Public Health, 78*, 567–569.

Hawken, P. (1993). *The ecology of commerce: A declaration of sustainability*. New York: HarperCollins.

Hawkins, G., & Zimring, F. E. (1988). *Pornography in a free society*. Cambridge: Cambridge University Press.

Hawley, A. H. (1971). *Urban society: An ecological approach*. New York: Ronald Press.

Hawley, W. D., et al. (1983). *Strategies for effective desegregation*. Lexington, MA: Lexington Books.

Hayes, L. F. (1970). Non-economic aspects of poverty. *Australian Journal of Social Issues, 5*, 41–54.

Headley, B. D. (1991). Race, class and powerlessness in world economy. *The Black Scholar, 21*, 14–21.

Heenan, D. A. (1991). *The new corporate frontier: The big move to small town, U.S.A.* New York: McGraw-Hill.

Heilbrun, A. B. Jr., Foster, A., & Golden, J. (1989). The death sentence in Georgia, 1974–1987: Criminal justice or racial injustice? *Criminal Justice and Behavior, 16* (2), 139–154.

Heimer, K., & Matsueda, R. L. (1994). Role-taking, role commitment, and delinquency: A theory of differential social control. *American Sociological Review, 59,* 365–390.

Helvarg, D. (1994). *The war against the greens: The wise use movement, the new right, and anti-environmental violence.* San Francisco: Sierra Club Books.

Hendry, P. (1988). Food and population: Beyond five billion. *Population Bulletin, 43* (2), entire issue.

Herman, E. S. (1993). The media's role in U.S. foreign policy. *Journal of International Affairs, 47* (Summer): 23–45

Hero, R. E. (1992). *Latinos and the U.S. political system.* Philadelphia: Temple University Press.

Hertz, R. (1986). *More equal than others: Women and men in dual-career marriages.* Berkeley: University of California Press.

Hewitt, J. P. (1994). *Self and society: A symbolic interactionist social psychology.* (6th ed.). Boston: Allyn and Bacon.

Hewlett, S. A. (1991). *When the bough breaks: The cost of neglecting our children.* New York: Basic Books.

Heyl, B. S. (1979). *The madam as entrepreneur: Career management in house prostitution.* New Brunswick, NJ: Transaction Books.

Higginbotham, E. (1987). Employment for professional black women in the twentieth century. In C. Bose & G. Spitze (Eds.), *Ingredients for women's employment policy.* Albany: State University of New York Press.

Hijab, N. (1988). *Womanpower: The Arab debate on women at work.* New York: Cambridge University Press.

Himes, J. S. (1980). *Conflict and conflict management.* Athens: University of Georgia Press.

Hindelang, M. J. (1981). Variations in sex-race-age-specific incidence rates of offending. *American Sociological Review, 46,* 461–474.

Hingson, R., Scotch, N. A., Sorenson, J., & Swazey, J. P. (1981). *In sickness and in health: Social dimensions of medical care.* St. Louis: Mosby.

Hirschel, J. D., Hutchison, I. W. III, & Dean, C. W. (1992). The failure of arrest to deter spouse abuse. *Journal of Research in Crime and Delinquency, 29,* 7–33.

Hirschi, T. (1962). The professional prostitute. *Berkeley Journal of Sociology, 7,* 34.

Hirschi, T. (1969). *Causes of delinquency.* Berkeley: University of California Press.

Hirschi, T., & Selvin, H. C. (1967). *Delinquency Research.* New York: Free Press.

Hirschman, C., & Wong, M. G. (1986). The extraordinary educational achievement of Asian-Americans: A search for historical evidence and explanations. *Social Forces, 65,* 1–27.

Hoberg, G. (1992). *Pluralism by design: Environmental policy and the American regulatory state.* New York: Praeger.

Hofferth, S. L., & Phillips, D. A. (1991). Child care policy research. *Journal of Social Issues, 47* (2), 1–13.

Hoffman, M. (1968). *The gay world.* New York: Basic Books.

Holden, K. C., & Smock, P. J. (1991). The economic costs of marital dissolution: Why do women bear a disproportionate cost? In W. Richard Scott & J. Blake (Eds.), *Annual Review of Sociology, 17.*

Honey, M. (1984). *Creating Rosie the Riveter: Class, gender, and propaganda.* Amherst: University of Massachusetts Press.

Honig, A. S., & Park, K. J. (1993). Effects of day care on preschool sex-role development. *American Journal of Orthopsychiatry, 63,* 481–486.

Hooker, E. (1969). Parental relations and male homosexuality in patient and nonpatient samples. *Journal of Consulting and Clinical Psychology, 33,* 141.

Hourani, A. (1991). *A history of the Arab peoples.* Cambridge, MA: Harvard University Press.

House, J. S. (1974). Occupational stress and coronary heart disease: A review and theoretical integration. *Journal of Health and Social Behavior, 15,* 17–21.

Houseknecht, S. (1987). Voluntary childlessness. In M. B. Sussman & S. K. Steinmetz (Eds.), *Handbook of marriage and the family*. New York: Plenum.

Houseknecht, S. K., Vaughan, S., & Macke, A. S. (1984). Marital disruption among professional women: The timing of career and family events. *Social Problems, 31*, 273–284.

Hout, M. (1988). More universalism, less structural mobility: The American occupational structure in the 1980s. *American Journal of Sociology, 93*, 1358–1400.

Howard, T., & Rifkin, J. (1977). *Who should play God? The artificial creation of life and what it means for the future of the human race*. New York: Delacorte Press.

Hubbert, M. K. (1969). Energy resources. In National Academy of Sciences, *Resources and man*. San Francisco: W. H. Freeman.

Hueber, G. (1991). Americans report high levels of environmental concern, activity. *The Gallup Poll Monthly* (April), 6–12.

Huff-Corzine, L., Corzine, J., & Moore, D. C. (1991). Deadly connections: Culture, poverty, and the direction of lethal violence. *Social Forces, 69*, 715–732.

Hugick, L., & Leonard, J. (1991). Sex in America. *The Gallup Poll Monthly* (October), 60–73.

Hunter, A., & Baumer, T. L. (1982). Street traffic, social integration, and fear of crime. *Sociological Inquiry, 52*, 122–131.

Hunter, J. (1990). Violence against lesbian and gay male youths. *Journal of Interpersonal Violence, 5*, 295–300.

Huston, A. C., et al. (1992). *Big world, small screen: The role of television in American society*. Lincoln: University of Nebraska Press.

Hyde, J. S., Krajnik, M., & Skuldt-Niederberger, K. (1991). Androgyny across the life span: A replication and longitudinal follow-up. *Developmental Psychology, 27*, 516–519.

Iacocca, L. (1989, April 17). National health plan deserves consideration. *Detroit Free Press*, p. 9.

Ilg, R. E. (1994). Long-term unemployment in recent recessions. *Monthly Labor Review* (June), 12–15.

Illich, I. (1976). *Medical nemesis*. New York: Bantam Books.

Ima, K. (1982). Japanese Americans: The making of 'good' people. In A. G. Dworkin & R. J. Dworkin (Eds.), *The Minority Report*. (2d Ed.). New York: Holt, Rinehart and Winston.

Images of fear: On the perception and reality of crime. (1985). *Harper's Magazine*, May, 39–48.

Inciardi, J. A., Horowitz, R., & Pottieger, A. E. (1993). *Street kids, street drugs, street crime: An examination of drug use and serious delinquency in Miami*. Belmont, CA: Wadsworth.

Intriligator, M. D. (1993). A way to achieve national health insurance in the United States: The medicare expansion proposal. *American Behavioral Scientist, 36*, 709–723.

Irelan, L. M., Moles, O. C., & O'Shea, R. M. (1969). Ethnicity, poverty, and selected attitudes: A test of the 'culture of poverty' hypothesis. *Social Forces, 47*, 405–413.

Irwin, J., & Austin, J. (1994). *It's about time: America's imprisonment binge*. Belmont, CA: Wadsworth.

Ispa, J. M., Thornburg, K. R., & Gray, M. M. (1990). Relations between early childhood care arrangements and college students' psychosocial development and academic performance. *Adolescence, 25*, 529–542.

Jackson, M., & Jackson, B. (1983). *Doing Drugs*. New York: St. Martin's/Marek.

Jacobs, J. A., & Steinberg, R. J. (1990). Compensating differentials and the male-female wage gap: Evidence from the New York state comparable worth study. *Social Forces, 69*, 439–468.

Jacobsen, C., & Hanneman, R. A. (1992). Illegal drugs: Past, present and possible futures. *The Journal of Drug Issues, 22*, 105–120.

Jacobsen, J. P., & Levin, L. M. (1992). The effects of intermittent labor force attachment on female earnings. Paper presented at a meeting of the American Economic Association, New Orleans.

Jacobson, J. (1988). Planning the global family. In L. R. Brown et al. (Eds.), *State of the world 1988: A worldwatch institute report on progress toward a sustainable society*. New York: W. W. Norton.

Jaffe, J. (1983). Methadone maintenance: Exportable programme or alien technology? In G. Edwards, A. Arif, & J. Jaffe (Eds.), *Drug use and* *misuse: Cultural perspectives.* New York: St. Martin's Press.

Jain, U. (1988). *The psychological consequences of crowding.* Newbury Park, CA: Sage Publications.

James, J. (1977). Prostitutes and prostitution. In E. Sagarin & F. Montanino (Eds.), *Deviants: Voluntary actors in a hostile world.* Morristown, NJ: General Learning Press.

Janowitz, M. (1969). Patterns of collective racial violence. In H. D. Graham & T. R. Gurr (Eds.), *The history of violence in America.* New York: Bantam Books.

Jeffrey, C. R. (1967). *Criminal responsibility and mental disease.* Springfield, IL: Charles C Thomas.

Jencks, C. (1992). *Rethinking social policy: Race, poverty, and the underclass.* Cambridge, MA: Harvard University Press.

Jencks, C. (1994). *The Homeless.* Cambridge, MA: Harvard University Press.

Jesilow, P., Pontell, H. N., & Geis, G. (1993). *Prescription for profit: How doctors defraud Medicaid.* Berkeley: University of California Press.

Johnson, B. D. (1984). Empirical patterns of heroin consumption among selected street heroin users. In G. Serban (Ed.), *Social and medical aspects of drug abuse.* New York: S.P. Medical and Scientific Books.

Johnson, C. B., Stockdale, M. S., & Saal, F. E. (1991). Persistence of men's misperceptions of friendly cues across a variety of interpersonal encounters. *Psychology of Women Quarterly, 15,* 463–475.

Johnston, L. D., O'Malley, P. M., & Bachman, J. G. (1993). *National survey results on drug use from the monitoring the future study, 1975–1992: Volume I, secondary school students.* National Institute on Drug Abuse (NIH Pub. No. 93-3597). Rockville, MD: National Institutes of Health, 1993.

Josephson, W. L. (1987). Television violence and children's aggression: Testing the priming, social script, and disinhibition predictions. *Journal of Personality and Social Psychology, 53* (5), 882–890.

Jowett, G. S., & O'Donnell, V. (1986). *Propaganda and persuasion.* Newbury Park, CA: Sage Publications.

Joyce, F. S. (1984, January 5). Courts study link between victim's race and imposition of death penalty. *New York Times,* p. 8.

Judd, D. R. (1991, December 9). Segregation forever? *The Nation,* pp. 740–743.

Kagan, S. L. (1991). Examining profit and nonprofit child care: An odyssey of quality and auspices. *Journal of Social Issues, 47* (2), 87–104.

Kahn, A. J., & Kamerman, S. B. (1987). *Child care: Facing the hard choices.* Dover, MA: Auburn House.

Kail, B. L., & Kleinman, P. H. (1985). Fear, crime, community organization, and limitations on daily routines. *Urban Affairs Quarterly, 20* (3), 400–408.

Kalmuss, D. S., & Straus, M. A. (1982). Wife's marital dependency and wife abuse. *Journal of Marriage and the Family, 44,* 277–286.

Kamerman, S. B. (1991). Child care policies and programs: An international overview. *Journal of Social Issues, 47* (2), 179–196.

Kamerman, S. B., & Kahn, A. J. (1991). *Innovations in European parenting policies.* Westport, CT: Greenwood.

Kane, H. (1995). Leaving home. In L. R. Brown et al. (Eds.), *The state of the world, 1995: A worldwatch institute report on progress toward a sustainable society.* New York: W. W. Norton.

Kane, R. L. (1994). The American nursing home: An institution for all reasons. In J. R. Hollingsworth & E. J. Hollingsworth (Eds.), *Care of the chronically and severely ill: Comparative policy perspectives.* New York: Aldine de Gruyter.

Kasarda, J. D., & Crenshaw, E. M. (1991). Third world urbanization: Dimensions, theories, and determinants. In W. R. Scott & J. Blake (Eds.), *Annual Review of Sociology, 17.*

Kate, N. T. (1992). Filling the corporate day-care gap. *American Demographics, 14,* 19–20.

Kates, D. B. Jr. (1983). Handgun prohibition and the original meaning of the second amendment. *Michigan Law Review, 82,* 204–273.

Katz, D., & Ryan, R. A. (1992, May 10). Symbols of success, targets of rage. *The Detroit News,* Sec. B, p. 1.

Keil, J. E., Sutherland, S. E., Knapp, R. G., & Tyroler, H. A. (1992). Does equal socioeconomic status in black and white men mean equal risk of mortality? *American Journal of Public Health, 82,* 1133–1136.

Kellam, S. (1992). Parties hope job training bill will spin political gold. *Congressional Quarterly,* May 16, 1341–1345.

Kennedy, L. W. (1990). *On the borders of crime: Conflict management and criminology.* New York: Longman.

Kerschner, P. A., & Hirschfield, I. S. (1983). Public policy and aging. In D. S. Woodruff & J. E. Birren (Eds.), *Aging: Scientific perspective and social issues.* (2d ed.). Monterey, CA: Brooks-Cole.

Kerstein, R. (1990). Stage models of gentrification: An examination. *Urban Affairs Quarterly, 25,* 620–639.

Kessler, R. C., House, J. S., & Turner, J. B. (1987). Unemployment and health in a community sample. *Journal of Health and Social Behavior, 28,* 51–59.

Kett, J. F. (1977). *Rites of passage: Adolescents in America, 1970 to the present.* New York: Basic Books.

Kids count data book. (1995). Baltimore, MD: The Annie E. Casey Foundation.

Kiecolt-Glaser, J. K., et al. (1987). Marital quality, marital disruption, and immune function. *Psychosomatic Medicine, 49,* 13–34.

Kilborn, P. T. (1990, December 23). Workers using computers find a supervisor inside. *New York Times,* pp. 1, 13.

Kimbrell, A. (1993). *The human body shop: The engineering and marketing of life.* New York: HarperSanFrancisco.

Kimmel, M. S., & Messner, M. A. (1992). *Men's lives.* (2d ed.). New York: Macmillan.

Kindel, S. (1990, September 4). The life and death of cities. *Financial World,* pp. 28–30.

King, N. R. (1984). Exploitation and abuse of older family members: An overview of the problem. In J. J. Costa (Ed.), *Abuse of the elderly.* Lexington, MA: Lexington Books.

Kinsey, A. C., Pomeroy, W. B., & Martin, C. E. (1948). *Sexual behavior in the human male.* Philadelphia: W. B. Saunders.

Kirk, S. A., & Kutchins, H. (1992). *The selling of DSM: The rhetoric of science in psychiatry.* New York: Aldine de Gruyter.

Kirsh, B. (1983). Sex roles and language use: Implications for mental health. In V. Franks & E. D. Rothblum (Eds.), *The stereotyping of women: Its effects on mental health.* New York: Springer.

Kitano, H. H. L. (1976). *Japanese Americans.* (2d ed.). Englewood Cliffs, NJ: Prentice-Hall.

Kleck, G. (1991). *Point blank: Guns and violence in America.* New York: Aldine de Gruyter.

Kletzer, L. G. (1991). Job displacement, 1979–86: How blacks fared relative to whites. *Monthly Labor Review, 114,* 17–25.

Kluegel, J. R., & Bobo, L. (1991). Modern American prejudice: Stereotypes of blacks, Hispanics, and Asians. Paper presented at the annual meeting of the American Sociological Association, Cincinnati, Ohio.

Knopp, L. M. Jr. (1990). The social consequences of homosexuality. *Geographical Magazine, 62,* 20–25.

Kolata, G. (1991, January 23). Nursing homes are criticized on how they tie and drug some patients. *New York Times,* p. 16.

Kolata, G. (1995, February 28). New picture of who will get AIDS is crammed with addicts. *New York Times,* p. B6.

Kornhauser, W. (1966). 'Power Elite' or 'Veto Groups.' In R. Bendix & S. M. Lipset (Eds.), *Class, status and power.* (2d ed.). New York: Free Press.

Kosberg, J. I. (Ed.). (1992). *Family care of the elderly: Social and cultural changes.* Newbury Park, CA: Sage Publications.

Kozol, J. (1985). Illiterate America, part one: A third of the nation cannot read these words. *Public Welfare* (Summer), 11–17.

Kozol, J. (1991). *Savage inequalities: Children in America's schools.* New York: Crown.

Kristof, N. D. (1993, April 25). China's crackdown on births: A stunning and harsh success. *New York Times,* p. 1.

Krupnick, A. A., & Portney, P. R. (1991). Controlling urban air pollution: A benefit-cost assessment. *Science, 252,* 522–528.

Kull, S. (1994). *Fighting poverty in America: A study of American public attitudes.* Washington, DC: Center for the Study of Policy Attitudes.

Kupelian, D. (1992). The most stressful job in America: Police work in the 1990s. *Police Career Digest,* January/February, 2–11.

Kupfer, A. (1989, June 20). What to do about drugs. *Fortune,* pp. 39–41.

Kurdek, L. A. (1988). Correlates of negative attitudes toward homosexuals in heterosexual college students. *Sex Roles, 18* (11/12), 727–738.

Kurian, G. T. (1984). *The new book of world rankings.* New York: Facts on File.

Kurtz, L. R. (1988). *The nuclear cage: A sociology of the arms race.* Englewood Cliffs, NJ: Prentice-Hall.

Kutchinsky, B. (1991). Pornography and rape: Theory and practice? *International Journal of Law and Psychiatry, 14,* 47–64.

Kutner, N., & Kutner, M. (1987). Ethnic and residence differences among poor families. *Journal of Comparative Family Studies, 18* (3), 463–470.

Lafree, G., Drass, K. A., & O'Day, P. (1992). Race and crime in postwar America: Determinants of African-American and white rates, 1957–1988. *Criminology, 30,* 157–185.

Lantos, T. (1992). The silence of the kids: Children at risk in the workplace. *Labor Law Journal, 43,* 67–70.

Lappé, F. M., & Collins, J. (1988). *World Hunger: Twelve Myths.* San Francisco, CA: Institute for Food and Development Policy.

Lasswell, H. D. (1936). *Politics: Who gets what, when, and how.* New York: McGraw-Hill.

Laumann, E. O., Gagnon, J. H., Michael, R. T., & Michaels, S. (1994). *The social organization of sexuality: Sexual practices in the United States.* Chicago and London: The University of Chicago Press.

Lavrakas, P. J., Normoyle, J., Skogan, W. G., Herz, E. J., Salem, G., & Lewis, D. A. (1981). *Factors related to citizen involvement in personal, household and neighborhood anti-crime measures.* Washington, DC: U.S. Government Printing Office.

Laws, G. (1995). Understanding ageism: Lessons from feminism and postmodernism. *The Gerontologist, 35,* 112–118.

Lawson, R., & George, V. (1980). An assessment. In V. George & R. Lawson (Eds.), *Poverty and inequality in common market countries.* London: Routledge and Kegan Paul.

Leavitt, G. C. (1992). General evolution and Durkheim's hypothesis of crime frequency: A cross-cultural test. *Sociological Quarterly, 33,* 241–263.

Leckie, R. (1990). *None died in vain: The saga of the American Civil War.* New York: HarperCollins.

Leckie, R. (1992). *The wars of America.* New York: HarperCollins.

Lee, S. M. (1994). Poverty and the U.S. Asian population. *Social Science Quarterly, 75,* 541–559.

Lee, V. E., Brooks-Gunn, J., Schnur, E., & Liaw, F. R. (1990). Are Head Start effects sustained? A longitudinal follow-up comparison of disadvantaged children attending Head Start, no preschool, and other preschool programs. *Child Development, 61,* 495–507.

Leenaars, A. A., & Lester, D. (1994). Effects of gun control on homicide in Canada. *Psychological Reports, 74,* 81–82.

Le Grand, J., & Estrin, S. (Eds.). (1989). *Market socialism.* Oxford: Clarendon Press.

Lehman, J. S. (1994). Updating urban policy. In S. H. Danziger, G. D. Sandefur, & D. H. Weinberg (Eds.), *Confronting poverty: Prescriptions for change.* New York and Cambridge, MA: Russell Sage Foundation and Harvard University Press.

Lemert, E. (1951). *Social pathology.* New York: McGraw-Hill.

Lempert, R. (1983). The effect of executions on homicides: A new look in an old light. *Crime and Delinquency, 29,* 88–115.

Lenssen, N. (1992). Confronting nuclear waste. In L. R. Brown et al. (Eds.), *State of the world 1992: A worldwatch institute report on progress toward a sustainable society.* New York: W. W. Norton.

Lerner, W. D., & Raczynski, J. M. (1988). The economic shaping of substance abuse. In B. A. Ray (Ed.), *Learning factors in substance abuse.* NIDA Research Monograph 84 (DHHS Pub. No. [ADM] 88-1576). Rockville, MD: National Institute on Drug Abuse.

Lettieri, D. J. (1978). *Drugs and suicide: When other coping strategies fail.* Beverly Hills, CA: Sage Publications.

Levin, J., & Levin, W. C. (1982). *The functions of discrimination and prejudice.* New York: HarperCollins.

Levinger, G., & Moles, O. C. (Eds.). (1979). *Divorce and separation: Context, causes, and consequences.* New York: Basic Books.

Levy, E. F. (1992). Strengthening the coping resources of lesbian families. *Families in Society, 73,* 23–31.

Levy, S. G. (1969). A 150-year study of political violence in the United States. In H. D. Graham & T. R. Gurr (Eds.), *Violence in America: Historical and comparative perspectives*. New York: Bantam Books.

Lewes, K. (1988). *The psychoanalytic theory of male homosexuality*. New York: Simon and Schuster.

Lewin, E. (1993). *Lesbian mothers: Accounts of gender in American culture*. Ithaca, NY: Cornell University Press.

Lewis, N. A. (1991, March 15). Guilty plea made in pentagon case. *New York Times*, p. 1.

Lewis, O. (1966). The culture of poverty. *Scientific American, 2* (5), 19–25.

Lewis, R. A. (1984). Some changes in men's values, meanings, roles and attitudes toward marriage and family in the U.S.A. In *Social change and family policies* (Part I). Melbourne: Australian Institute of Family Studies.

Liddell, C., & Kruger, P. (1987). Activity and social behavior in a South African township nursery: Some effects of crowding. *Merrill-Palmer Quarterly, 33,* (2) 195–211.

Lieberson, S., & Silverman, A. R. (1965). The precipitants and underlying conditions of race riots. *American Sociological Review, 30,* 887–898.

Lifson, A. R. (1992). Men who have sex with men: Continued challenges for preventing HIV infection and AIDS. *American Journal of Public Health, 82,* 166–167.

Light, W. J. H. (1986). *Psychodynamics of alcoholism: A current synthesis*. Springfield, IL: Charles C Thomas.

Lindorff, D. (1992). *Marketplace medicine: The rise of the for-profit hospital chains*. New York: Bantam Books.

Linz, D., & Donnerstein, E. (1992). Research can help us explain violence and pornography. *The Chronicle of Higher Education, 39* (September 30), B3–B4.

Lo, C. Y. H. (1982). Theories of the state and business opposition to increased military spending. *Social Problems, 29,* 424–438.

Loftin, C., McDowall, D., Wiersema, B., & Cottey, T. J. (1991). Effects of restrictive licensing of handguns on homicide and suicide in the District of Columbia. *New England Journal of Medicine, 325,* 1615–1620.

London, K. A. (1990). Cohabitation, marriage, marital dissolution, and remarriage: United States, 1988. *Advance data from vital and health statistics*. No. 194. Hyattsville, MD: National Center for Health Statistics.

Long, F. J., & Arnold, M. B. (1995). *The power of environmental partnerships*. Fort Worth, TX: Dryden Press.

Longman, P. (1987). *Born to pay: The new politics of aging in America*. Boston: Houghton Mifflin.

Longshore, D., & Prager, J. (1985). The impact of school desegregation: A situational analysis. *Annual Review of Sociology, 11,* 75–91.

Loomis, L. S., & Landale, N. S. (1994). Nonmarital cohabitation and childbearing among black and white American women. *Journal of Marriage and the Family, 56,* 949–962.

Loscocco, K. A., Robinson, J., Hall, R. H., & Allen, J. K. (1991). Gender and small business success: An inquiry into women's relative disadvantage. *Social Forces, 70,* 65–85.

Lowman, J. (1992). Street prostitution control: Some Canadian reflections on the Finsbury Park experience. *The British Journal of Criminology, 32,* 1–16.

Lowy, M. (1991). *High rollers: Inside the savings and loan debacle*. New York: Praeger.

Luckenbill, D. F. (1989). Deviant career mobility: The case of male prostitutes. In D. H. Kelly (Ed.), *Deviant behavior* (3d ed.). (pp. 485–503). New York: St. Martin's Press.

Luebke, B. F. (1989). Out of focus: Images of women and men in newspaper photographs. *Sex Roles, 20* (3/4), 121–133.

Lynch, F. R., & Beer, W. R. (1990). You ain't the right color, pal: White resentment of affirmative action. *Policy Review, 51,* 64–67.

MacDonald, K., & Parke, R. (1986). Parent-child physical play: The effects of sex and age of children and parents. *Sex Roles, 15,* 367–378.

MacKellar, F. L., & Vining, D. R. Jr. (1988). Research policy and review 26: Where does the United States stand in the global resource scarcity debate? *Environment and Planning Abstracts, 20,* 1567–1573.

MacKinnon, C. A. (1993). *Only words*. Cambridge, MA: Harvard University Press.

Macklin, E. (1987). Non-traditional family forms. In M. Sussman & S. Steinmetz (Eds.), *Handbook of marriage and the family*. New York: Plenum.

Maguire, K., & Flanagan, T. J. (Eds.). (1991). *Sourcebook of criminal justice statistics: 1990*. Washington, DC: U.S. Department of Justice, Bureau of Justice Statistics.

Main, J. (1988, November 21). Here comes the big new cleanup. *Fortune*, pp. 104–106; 110; 112–114.

Malcolm, A. H. (1984, October 21). "Right to die" dispute focuses on Californian. *New York Times*, p. 1.

Malone, T. F., & Corell, R. (1989). Mission to planet earth revisited: An update on studies of global change. *Environment, 31* (3), 6–11; 31–35.

Malthus, T. R. (1960, originally published 1798). In G. Himmelfarb (Ed.), *On population*. New York: Modern Library.

Mann, C. C., & Plummer, M. L. (1995). *Noah's choice: The future of endangered species*. New York: Alfred A. Knopf.

Mansfield, P. K., Koch, P. B., Henderson, J., Vicary, J. R., Cohn, M., & Young, E. W. (1991). The job climate for women in traditionally male blue-collar occupations. *Sex Roles 25* (1–2), 63–79.

Manton, K. G., Patrick, C. H., & Johnson, K. W. (1987). Health differentials between blacks and whites: Recent trends in mortality and morbidity. *Milbank Quarterly, 65* (Suppl. 1), 129–199.

Marden, C. F., Meyer, G., & Engel, M. H. (1992). *Minorities in American society* (6th ed.). New York: HarperCollins.

Marks, C. (1981). Split-labor markets and black-white relations, 1865–1920. *Phylon, 42,* 293–308.

Marks, C. (1991). The urban underclass. *Annual Review of Sociology, 17,* 445–466.

Markusen, A., & Yudken, J. (1992). *Dismantling the cold war economy*. New York: Basic Books.

Marshall, D. S. (1974). Too much sex in Mangaia. In E. Goode & R. Troiden (Eds.), *Sexual deviance and sexual deviants*. New York: William Morrow and Co.

Martin, C. L. (1990). Attitudes and expectations about children with nontraditional and traditional gender roles. *Sex Roles 22* (3–4), 151–165.

Martin, D., & Martin, M. (1984). Selected attitudes toward marriage and family life among college students. *Family Relations, 33,* 293–300.

Martin, S. E. (Ed.). (1993). *Alcohol and interpersonal violence: Fostering multidisciplinary perspectives*. National Institute on Alcohol Abuse and Alcoholism (NIH Pub. No. 93-3496). Rockville, MD: U.S. Department of Health and Human Services.

Martindale, M. (1991). Sexual harassment in the military: 1988. *Sociological Practice Review, 2,* 200–216.

Martinez, R., & Dukes, R. L. (1991). Ethnic and gender differences in self esteem. *Youth and Society, 22,* 318–338.

Marx, K. (1964, originally published 1848). In T. B. Bottomore & M. Rubel (Eds.), *Selected writings in sociology and philosophy*. Baltimore: Penguin.

Marx, K. (1967, originally published 1867–1895). *Das kapital*. New York: International Publishers.

Maryanski, A., & Turner, J. H. (1992). *The social cage: Human nature and the evolution of society*. Stanford, CA: Stanford University Press.

Massey, D. S. (1990). American apartheid: Segregation and the making of the underclass. *American Journal of Sociology, 96,* 329–357.

Massey, D. S., Gross, A. B., & Eggers, M. L. (1991). Segregation, the concentration of poverty, and the life chances of individuals. *Social Science Research, 20,* 397–420.

Mauldin, W. P. (1975). Assessment of national family planning programs in developing countries. *Studies in Family Planning, 6,* 30–36.

Maume, D. J. Jr. (1991). Child-care expenditures and women's employment turnover. *Social Forces, 70,* 495–508.

Maynard, R. A. (1995). Subsidized employment and non-labor market alternatives for welfare recipients. In D. S. Nightingale & R. H. Haveman (Eds.), *The work alternative: Welfare reform and the realities of the job market*. Washington, DC: The Urban Institute Press.

Mazur, A. (1993). Controlling technology. In A. H. Teich (Ed.), *Technology and the future* (6th ed.). New York: St. Martin's Press.

McBroom, W. H. (1984). Changes in sex-role orientations: A five-year longitudinal comparison. *Sex Roles, 11* (7/8), 583–592.

McCaghy, C. H. (1985). *Deviant behavior: Crime, conflict, and interest groups* (2d ed.). New York: Macmillan.

McCall, R. B. (1988). Real men do change diapers. *Parents,* September, 202.

McConnell, S. R. (1983). Retirement and employment. In D. S. Woodruff & J. E. Birren (Eds.), *Aging: Scientific perspectives and social issues* (2d ed.). Monterey, CA: Brooks-Cole.

McCoy, N. L. (1985). Innate factors in sex differences. In A. G. Sargent (Ed.), *Beyond sex roles* (2d ed.). St. Paul, MN: West Publishing Company.

McCue, J. D. (1989). *The medical cost-containment crisis: Fears, opinions, and facts.* Ann Arbor, MI: Health Administration Press.

McDonnell, D., Irwin, J., & Rosenbaum, M. (1990). "Hop and hubbas": A tough new mix, a research note on cocaine use among methadone maintenance clients. *Contemporary Drug Problems, 17,* 145–156.

McKenzie, R. B. (1984). *Fugitive industry: The economics and politics of deindustrialization.* Cambridge, MA: Ballinger.

McKeown, T., Brown, R. G., & Record, R. G. (1972). An interpretation of the modern rise of population in Europe. *Population Studies, 26,* 345–382.

McKeown, T., Brown, R. G., & Turner, R. D. (1975). An interpretation of the decline of mortality in England and Wales during the twentieth century. *Population Studies, 29,* 391–422.

McKinlay, J. B. (1986). A case for refocusing upstream: The political economy of illness. In P. Conrad & R. Kern (Eds.), *The sociology of health and illness: Critical perspectives* (2d ed.). New York: St. Martin's Press.

McKinlay, J. B., & McKinlay, S. M. (1977). The questionable contribution of medical measures to the decline of mortality in the United States in the twentieth century. *Milbank Memorial Fund Quarterly/Health and Society, 55,* 405–428.

McLanahan, S., & Sandefur, G. (1994). *Growing up with a single parent: What hurts, what helps.* Cambridge, MA: Harvard University Press.

McLeod, E. (1982). *Women working: Prostitution now.* London: Croom Helm.

McPhail, C. (1971). Civil disorder participation: A critical examination of recent research. *American Sociological Review, 36,* 1058–1073.

Mead, L. M. (1994). Poverty: How little we know. *Social Service Review, 68,* 322–350.

Meadows, D. H., Meadows, D. L., Randers, J., & Behrens, W. W. III. (1972). *The limits to growth.* New York: New American Library.

Mechanic, D. (1989). *Mental health and social policy* (3d ed.). Englewood Cliffs, NJ: Prentice-Hall.

Mednick, S. A., Moffitt, T. E., & Stack, S. A. (1987). *The causes of crime: New biological approaches.* Cambridge: Cambridge University Press.

Melman, S. (1983). *Profits without production.* New York: Alfred A. Knopf.

Merrill, J. C., & Cohen, A. B. (1989). Explicit rationing of medical care: Is it really needed? In J. D. McCue (Ed.), *The medical cost-containment crisis: Fears, opinions, and facts.* Ann Arbor, MI: Health Administration Press.

Merton, R. K. (1949). Discrimination and the American creed. In R. M. MacIver (Ed.), *Discrimination and national welfare.* New York: Harper and Row.

Merton, R. K. (1968). *Social theory and social structure* (2d ed.). New York: Free Press.

Mesarovic, M., & Pestel, E. (1974). *Mankind at the turning point.* New York: Dutton.

Meyer, M. H. (1990). Family status and poverty among older women: The gendered distribution of retirement income in the United States. *Social Problems, 37,* 551–563.

Michels, R. (1966, originally published 1915). *Political Parties.* New York: Free Press.

Middleton, R. (1976). Regional differences in prejudice. *American Sociological Review, 41,* 94–117.

Milby, J. B. (1981). *Addictive behavior and its treatment.* New York: Springer.

Milhorn, H. T. (1994). *Drug and alcohol abuse.* New York and London: Plenum.

Miller, A. D., & Ohlin, L. E. (1985). *Delinquency in the community: Creating opportunities and controls.* Beverly Hills, CA: Sage Publications.

Miller, D. L. (1985). *Introduction to collective behavior.* Belmont, CA: Wadsworth Publishing Company.

Miller, E. M. (1986). *Street woman.* Philadelphia: Temple University Press.

Miller, G., & Holstein, J. A. (Eds.). (1993). *Constructionist controversies: Issues in social problems theory.* New York: Aldine de Gruyter.

Miller, M. A. L. (1995). *The third world in global environmental politics.* Boulder, CO: Lynne Rienner.

Miller, R. L. (1991). *The case for legalizing drugs.* New York: Praeger.

Miller, R. H., & Luft, H. S. (1994). Managed care plans: Characteristics, growth and premium performance. In G. S. Omenn (Ed.), *Annual review of public health* (vol. 15). Palo Alto, CA: Annual Reviews Inc.

Miller, S. C. (1969). *The unwelcome immigrant.* Berkeley: University of California Press.

Miller, W. R. (1984). Teaching responsible drinking skills. In P. M. Miller & T. D. Nirenberg (Eds.), *Prevention of alcohol abuse.* New York: Plenum.

Millman, M. (1977). *The unkindest cut.* New York: Morrow.

Mills, C. W. (1956). *The power elite.* New York: Oxford University Press.

Mills, C. W. (1959). *The sociological imagination.* New York: Oxford University Press.

Min, P. G. (Ed.). (1994). *Asian Americans: Contemporary trends and issues.* Thousand Oaks, CA: Sage.

Mincer, J. (1985, August 9). Those hurt by drunken drivers press suits against drivers' hosts. *New York Times,* p. 1.

Mincy, R. B. (1994). The underclass: Concept, controversy, and evidence. In S. H. Danziger, G. D. Sandefur, & D. H. Weinberg (Eds.), *Confronting poverty: Prescriptions for change.* New York and Cambridge, MA: Russell Sage Foundation and Harvard University Press.

Miringoff, M. L. (1992). *The index of social health, 1992: Monitoring the social well-being of the nation.* Tarrytown, NY: Fordham Institute for Innovation in Social Policy.

Moore, J. W. (1976). *Mexican Americans.* Englewood Cliffs, NJ: Prentice-Hall.

Moore, K. A., & Stief, T. M. (1991). Changes in marriage and fertility behavior: Behavior versus attitudes in young adults. *Youth and Society, 22,* 362–386.

Morgan, E. (1972). *The descent of women.* New York: Stein and Day.

Morganthau, T. (1993, August 9). America: Still a melting pot? *Newsweek,* pp. 16–23.

Morris, A. D. (1984). *The origins of the civil rights movement: Black communities organizing for change.* New York: Free Press.

Mott, F. L. (1991). Developmental effects of infant care: the mediating role of gender and health. *Journal of Social Issues, 47* (2), 139–158.

Mumford, E. (1983). *Medical sociology: Patients, providers, and policies.* New York: Random House.

Mumford, E., Schlesinger, H. J., & Glass, G. V. (1982). The effects of psychological intervention on recovery from surgery and heart attacks: An analysis of the literature. *The American Journal of Public Health, 72,* 141–151.

Murdock, G. P. (1934). *Our primitive contemporaries.* New York: Macmillan.

Murdock, G. P. (1967). *World ethnographic atlas.* Pittsburg: University of Pittsburg Press.

Murphy, J. E. (1988). Date abuse and forced intercourse among college students. In G. T. Hotaling, D. Finkelhor, J. T. Kirkpatrick, & M. A. Straus (Eds.), *Family abuse and its consequences: New directions in research.* Newbury Park, CA: Sage Publications.

Murphy, K. M., & Welch, F. (1993). Industrial change and the rising importance of skill. In S. Danziger & P. Gottschalk (Eds.), *Uneven tides: Rising inequality in America.* New York: Russell Sage Foundation.

Murray, C. (1984). *Losing ground.* New York: Basic Books.

Myers, S. L. (1994, September 11). Tough laws urged on X-rated shops in New York City. *New York Times,* p. A1.

Najjar, O. A. (1992). Between nationalism and feminism: The Palestinian answer. In J. M. Bystydzienski (Ed.), *Women transforming politics: Worldwide strategies for empowerment.* Bloomington and Indianapolis: Indiana University Press.

Nasar, S. (1992, May 31). Cooling the globe would be nice, but saving lives now may cost less. *New York Times,* Sec. 4, p. 6.

Nathan, R. P. (1988). *Social science in government: Uses and misuses.* New York: Basic Books.

National Center for Health Statistics. (1984). *Vital statistics of the United States, 1980* (Vol. II, Sec. 6, Life Tables). (DHHS Pub. No. [PHS] 84-1104). Public Health Service. Washington, DC: U.S. Government Printing Office.

National Center for Health Statistics. (1992). *Health, United States, 1991.* (DHHS Pub. No. [PHS] 92-1232). Hyattsville, MD: Public Health Service.

National Council on Aging. (1975). *The myth and the reality of aging in America.* Washington, DC: National Council on the Aging.

National Institute on Drug Abuse. (1991). *National household survey on drug abuse: Main findings, 1990.* (DHHS Pub. No. [ADM] 91-1788). Washington, DC: U.S. Government Printing Office.

Neckerman, K. M., & Kirschenman, J. (1991). Hiring strategies, racial bias, and inner-city workers. *Social Problems, 38,* 443–447.

Nelkin, D. (1984). Science, technology, and political conflict: Analyzing the issues. In D. Nelkin (Ed.), *Controversy: Politics of technical decisions* (2d ed.), Beverly Hills, CA: Sage Publications.

Nelson, R. Y. Jr. (1989). Inner city "truths". *Journal of Housing* (January/February), 9.

Nero, A. V. Jr. (1988). Controlling indoor air pollution. *Scientific American, 258* (5), 42–48.

Neugarten, B. L. (1982). Age or need? *National Forum: The Phi Kappa Phi Journal* (62), 25–27.

Newman, O. (1972). *Defensible space.* New York: Macmillan.

Nielson, F. (1994). Sociobiology and sociology. *Annual Review of Sociology, 20,* 267–303.

Nightingale, D. S., & Haveman, R. H. (Eds.). (1995). *The work alternative: Welfare reform and the realities of the job market.* Washington, DC: The Urban Institute Press.

Nimkoff, M. F. (Ed.). (1965). *Comparative family systems.* Boston: Houghton Mifflin.

Noble, B. P. (1992a, June 21). Legal victories for gay workers. *New York Times,* Sec. 3, p. 23.

Noble, B. P. (1992b, April 12). Testing employees for drugs. *New York Times,* Sec. 3, p. 27.

Norman, C. (1981). *The god that limps: Science and technology in the eighties.* New York: W. W. Norton.

Novak, M. (1978). *The guns of Lattimer: The true story of a massacre and a trial, August 1897–March 1898.* New York: Basic Books.

Nusberg, C., Gibson, M. J., & Peace, S. (1984). *Innovative aging program abroad: Implications for the United States.* Westport, CT: Greenwood Press.

O'Brien, D. J., & Fugita, S. S. (1991). *The Japanese American experience.* Bloomington: Indiana University Press.

O'Connor, J. F., & Lizotte, A. (1978). The "Southern subculture of violence" thesis and patterns of gun ownership. *Social Problems, 25,* 420–429.

Off the streets, prostitution thrives in New York with little interference. (1984, November 14). *New York Times,* p. 16.

Ogburn, W. F. (1938). The changing family. *The Family, 19,* 139–143.

Ogburn, W. F. (1957). Cultural lag as theory. *Sociology and Social Research, 41,* 167–174.

O'Hare, W., & Larson, J. (1991). Women in business: Where, what, and why. *American Demographics, 13,* 34–38.

O'Kelly, C. G., & Carney, L. S. (1986). *Women and men in society: Cross cultural perspectives in gender inequality* (2d ed.). Belmont, CA: Wadsworth.

Olinger, J. P. (1991). Elder abuse: The outlook for federal legislation. *Journal of Elder Abuse and Neglect, 3* (1), 43–52.

Olzak, S. (1992). *The dynamics of ethnic competition and conflict.* Stanford, CA: Stanford University Press.

Organski, A. F. K., Kugler, J., Johnson, J. T., & Cohen, Y. (1984). *Births, deaths, and taxes: The demographic and political transitions.* Chicago: University of Chicago Press.

Osborne, D., & Gaebler, T. (1992). *Reinventing government: How the entrepreneurial spirit is transforming the public sector.* Reading, MA: Addison-Wesley.

Padilla, F. M. (1985). *Latino ethnic consciousness: The case of Mexican Americans and Puerto Ricans in Chicago.* Notre Dame, IN: University of Notre Dame Press.

Palen, J. J. (1987). *The urban world* (3d ed.). New York: McGraw-Hill.

Pallas, A. M., Entwisle, D. R., Alexander, K. L., & Weinstein, P. (1990). Social structure and the development of self-esteem in young children. *Social Psychology Quarterly, 53,* 302–315.

Paradise, V. I. (1922). *Child labor and the work of mothers in oyster and shrimp canning communities on the Gulf Coast* (Pub. No. 98). Washington, DC: U.S. Children's Bureau, Department of Labor.

Parker, F. L., Piotrkowski, C. S., & Peay, L. (1987). Head Start as a social support for mothers: The psychological benefits of involvement. *American Journal of Orthopsychiatry, 57* (2), 220–225.

Parsons, T. (1951). *The social system.* New York: Free Press.

Parsons, T., & Bales, R. (1950). *Interaction process analysis.* Reading, MA: Addison-Wesley.

Pate, A. M., & Hamilton, E. E. (1992). Formal and informal deterrents to domestic violence: The Dade County spouse assault experiment. *American Sociological Review, 57,* 691–697.

Patterson, C. J. (1992). Children of lesbian and gay parents. *Child Development, 63,* 1025–1042.

Peirce, N. R. (1992, July 30). The drug war is a rout: Let's look at alternatives. *Detroit Free Press,* p. 15.

Pelton, L. (1978). The myth of classlessness in child abuse cases. *American Journal of Orthopsychiatry, 48,* 569–579.

Perry, J. B. Jr., & Pugh, M. D. (1989). Public support of the guardian angels: Vigilante protection against crime, Toledo, Ohio, 1984. *Sociology and Social Research, 73* (3), 129–130.

Petersen, W. (1975). *Population* (3d ed.). New York: Macmillan.

Petersilia, J. (1985). Racial disparities in the criminal justice system: A summary. *Crime and Delinquency, 31,* 15–34.

Peterson, I. (1991a, November 3). Why older people are richer than other Americans. *New York Times,* Sec. 4, p. 3.

Peterson, J. (1990). The challenge of comparable worth: An institutionalist view. *Journal of Economic Issues, 24,* 605–612.

Peterson, P. E. (1991b). The urban underclass and the poverty paradox. In C. Jencks & P. E. Peterson (Eds.), *The urban underclass,* Washington, DC: The Brookings Institution.

Peterson, R. D., & Bailey, W. C. (1991). Felony murder and capital punishment: An examination of the deterrence questions. *Criminology, 29,* 367–395.

Peterson, S. B., & Kroner, T. (1992). Gender biases in textbooks for introductory psychology and human development. *Psychology Of Women Quarterly, 16,* 17–36.

Peterson, S. B., & Lach, M. A. (1990). Gender stereotypes in children's books: Their prevalence and influence on cognitive and affective development. *Gender and Education, 2* (2), 185–197.

Petrocelli, W., & Repa, B. K. (1992). *Sexual harassment on the job.* Berkeley, CA: Nolo Press.

Pettigrew, T. F. (1988). Integration and pluralism. In P. A. Katz & D. A. Taylor (Eds.), *Eliminating racism: Profiles in controversy.* New York: Plenum.

Phillips, D., Howes, C., & Whitebook, M. (1991). Child care as an adult work environment. *Journal of Social Issues, 47* (2), 49–70.

Phillips, D. A., Voran, M., Kisker, E., Howes, C., & Whitebook, M. (1994). Child care for children in poverty: Opportunity or inequality? *Child Development, 65,* 472–492.

Phillips, U. B. (1963). *Life and labor in the old south.* Boston: Little, Brown.

Pillemer, K., & Finkelhor, D. (1988). The prevalence of elder abuse: A random sample survey. *The Gerontologist, 28* (1), 51–57.

Pillemer, K., & Finkelhor, D. (1989). Causes of elder abuse: Caregiver stress versus problem relatives. *American Journal of Orthopsychiatry, 59,* 179–187.

Pillemer, K., & Moore, D. W. (1990). Highlights from a study of abuse of patients in nursing homes. *Journal of Elder Abuse and Neglect, 2,* 5–29.

Pinkney, A. (1972). *The American way of violence.* New York: Random House.

Piotrkowski, C., et al. (1987). Families and work. In M. Sussman and S. Steinmetz (Eds.), *Handbook of marriage and the family.* New York: Plenum.

Plakans, A. (1994). The democratization of unstructured time in western societies: A historical overview. In M. W. Riley, R. L. Kahn, & A. Foner (Eds.), *Age and structural lag.* New York: Wiley Interscience.

Plissner, M. (1978, March 27). Figure it this way: Figures can be unreliable. *Milwaukee Journal,* p. 1.

Plotnick, R. D. (1993). The effect of social policies on teenage pregnancy and childbearing. *Families in Society, 6,* 324–328.

Pollock, C. (1987). Realizing recycling's potential. In L. R. Brown et al. (Eds.), *State of the world, 1987: A worldwatch institute report on progress toward a sustainable society.* New York: W. W. Norton.

Poplin, D. E. (1979). *Communities: A survey of theories and methods of research.* New York: Macmillan.

Porter, B., & Dunn, M. (1984). *The Miami riot of 1980: Crossing the bounds.* Lexington, MA: Lexington Books.

Portes, A., & Stepick, A. (1993). *City on the edge: The transformation of Miami.* Berkeley: University of California Press.

Postel, S. (1986). Increasing water efficiency. In L. R. Brown et al. (Eds.), *State of the world, 1986: A worldwatch institute report on progress toward a sustainable society.* New York: W. W. Norton.

Powell, G. N. (1993). *Women and men in management.* Newbury Park, CA: Sage.

Proctor, R. N. (1995). *Cancer wars: How politics shapes what we know and don't know about cancer.* New York: Basic Books.

Prucha, F. P. (1985). *The Indians in American society: From the revolutionary war to the present.* Berkeley: University of California Press.

Purcell, P., & Stewart, L. (1990). Dick and Jane in 1989. *Sex Roles, 22* (3–4), 177–185.

Purdy, L. M. (1992). *In their best interest? The case against equal rights for children.* Ithaca and London: Cornell University Press.

Quinn, R. P., & Staines, G. L. (1977). *The 1977 quality of employment survey.* Ann Arbor: University of Michigan, Institute for Social Research.

Quinney, R. (1974). *Critique of legal order: Crime control in capitalist society.* Boston: Little, Brown.

Ramirez, A. (1994, August 14). Privatizing America's prisons, slowly. *New York Times,* Sec. 3, pp. 1, 6.

Rank, M. R. (1994). *Living on the edge: The realities of welfare in America.* New York: Columbia University Press.

Rankin, D. (1985, March 24). Protecting your pension—and spouse. *New York Times,* p. 11.

Rankin, J. H. (1983). The family context of delinquency. *Social Problems, 30,* 466–479.

Ray, B. A. (Ed.). (1988). *Learning Factors in Substance Abuse.* (NIDA Research Monograph 84, DHHS Pub. No. [ADM] 88-1576). Rockville, MD: National Institute on Drug Abuse.

Ray, O. (1983). *Drugs, society, and human behavior* (3d ed.). St. Louis: Mosby.

Reiman, J. (1996). *. . . And the poor get prison: Economic bias in American criminal justice.* Boston: Allyn & Bacon.

Reiss, M. (1995). *Bridled ambition: Why countries constrain their nuclear capabilities.* Baltimore: The Johns Hopkins University Press.

Reiss, P. J. (1962). The extended kinship system. *Marriage and Family Living, 22,* 263–264.

Relman, A. S. (1980). The new medical–industrial complex. *New England Journal of Medicine, 303,* 963–970.

Repetto, R. (1994). *The 'second India' revisited.* Washington, DC: World Resources Institute.

Reskin, B. F., & Roos, P. A. (1990). *Job queues, gender queues: Explaining women's inroads into male occupations.* Philadelphia: Temple University Press.

Reynolds, H. (1986). *The economics of prostitution.* Springfield, IL: Charles C Thomas.

Rice, D. P., Kelman, S., & Miller, L. S. (1991). Estimates of economic costs of alcohol and drug abuse and mental illness, 1985 and 1988. *Public Health Reports, 106,* 280–292.

Rich, B. (1994). *Mortgaging the earth: The World Bank, environmental impoverishment, and the crisis of development.* Boston: Beacon Press.

Richmond-Abbott, M. (1992). *Masculine and feminine: Gender roles over the life cycle* (2d ed.). New York: McGraw-Hill.

Richter, M. N. Jr. (1982). *Technology and Social Complexity.* Albany: State University of New York Press.

Ridker, R. (1980). The no-birth bonus scheme: The use of savings accounts for family planning in south India. *Population and Development Review, 6,* 31–46.

Riesman, D. (1961). *The lonely crowd.* New Haven, CT: Yale University Press.

Rifkin, J. (1987, April 26). Is nature just a form of private property? *New York Times,* Sec. 3, p. 2.

Rifkin, J. (1991). *Biosphere politics: A new consciousness for a new century.* New York: Crown.

Riley, M. W., Kahn, R. L., & Foner A. (Eds.). (1994). *Age and structural lag.* New York: Wiley Interscience.

Rio, L. M. (1991). Psychological and sociological research and the decriminalization or legalization of prostitution. *Archives of Sexual Behavior, 20,* 205–218.

Rist, R. C. (1979). *Desegregated schools: Appraisals of an American experiment.* New York: Academic Press.

Rivkin, S. G. (1994). Residential segregation and school integration. *Sociology of Education, 67,* 279–292.

Robbins, J. (1989, July 9). Saboteurs for a better environment. *New York Times,* Sec. 4, p. 6.

Robertson, J. A. (1994). The question of human cloning. *Hastings Center Report, 24,* 6–14.

Robinson, B. E., Skeen, P., Hobson, C. F., & Herrman, M. (1982). Gay men's and women's perceptions of early family life and their relationships with parents. *Family Relations, 31,* 79–83.

Robinson, D. (1983). Alcoholics Anonymous: American origins and the international diffusion of a self-help group. In G. Edwards, A. Arif, & J. Jaffe (Eds.), *Drug use and misuse: Cultural perspective.* New York: St. Martin's Press.

Robock, A. (1989). New models confirm nuclear winter. *Bulletin of the Atomic Scientists, 45,* 32–35.

Robyn, D. L., & Hadley, J. (1980). New health occupations: Nurse practitioners and physicians' assistants. In J. Feder, J. Holahan, & T. Marmor (Eds.), *National health insurance: Conflicting goals and policy choices.* Washington, DC: Urban Institute Press.

Rodgers, H. L. Jr. (1990). *Poor women, poor families: The economic plight of America's female-headed households.* Armonk, NY: M. E. Sharpe, Inc.

Rogers, S. M., & Turner, C. F. (1991). Male-male sexual contact in the U.S.A.: Findings from five sample surveys, 1970–1990. *The Journal of Sex Research, 28,* 491–519.

Rose, A. M. (1967). *The power structure: Political process in American society.* New York: Oxford University Press.

Rosen, C., & Youngs, K. M. (Eds.). (1991). *Understanding employee ownership.* Ithaca, NY: ILR Press.

Rosenfeld, R. A., & Kalleberg, A. L. (1991). Gender inequality in the labor market: A cross-national perspective. *Acta Sociologica, 34,* 207–225.

Rosenhan, D. L. (1973). On being sane in insane places. *Science, 179,* 250–258.

Ross, J. W. (1991). Elder abuse. *Health and Social Work, 16,* 227–229.

Ross, M. W., Paulsen, J. A., & Stalstrom, O. W. (1988). Homosexuality and mental health: A cross-cultural review. *Journal of Homosexuality, 15,* 131–152.

Rossell, C. H. (1990). *The carrot or the stick for desegregation policy.* Philadelphia: Temple University Press.

Rossi, A. (1984). Gender and parenthood. *American Sociological Review, 49,* 1–19.

Rothfeder, J. (1992). *Privacy for sale: How computerization has made everyone's private life an open secret.* New York: Simon and Schuster.

Rounsaville, B. J., et al. (1984). Psychiatric disorders in treated opiate addicts. In G. Serban (Ed.), *Social and medical aspects of drug abuse.* New York: SP Medical and Scientific Books.

Rowe, A. R., & Tittle, C. R. (1977). Life cycle changes and criminal propensity. *Sociological Quarterly, 18,* 223–236.

Rubenstein, R. E. (1987). *Alchemists of revolution: Terrorism in the modern world.* New York: Basic Books.

Ruggles, P. (1990). *Drawing the line: Alternative poverty measures and their implications for public policy.* Washington, DC: Urban Institute Press.

Russell, D. E. H. (1990). *Rape in marriage.* Bloomington and Indianapolis: Indiana University Press.

Russett, B. (1969). Who pays for defense? *American Political Science Review, 63,* 412–426.

Ryan, J. C. (1992). Conserving biological diversity. In L. R. Brown et al. (Eds.), *State of the world 1992: A worldwatch institute report on progress toward a sustainable society.* New York: W. W. Norton.

Ryan, W. (1976). *Blaming the victim* (rev. and updated ed.). New York: Vintage Books.

Sadik, N. (1989). Discrimination against girls. In *State of the world population report.* New York: United Nations.

Sadker, M., & Sadker, D. (1994). *Failing at fairness: How America's schools cheat girls.* New York: Charles Scribner's.

Sagan, C., & Turco, R. (1990). *A path where no man thought: Nuclear winter and the end of the arms race.* New York: Random House.

Salas, R. M. (1984). *Reflections on population.* New York: Pergamon Press.

Sale, K. (1980). *Human scale*. New York: Coward, McCann, and Geoghegan.

Sale, K. (1995). *Rebels against the future: The Luddites and their war on the industrial revolution: Lessons for the machine age*. Reading, MA: Addison-Wesley.

Sandroff, L. (1988). Sexual harassment in the fortune 500. *Working Woman*, December, 69–71.

Santiago, A. M., & Wilder, M. G. (1991). Residential segregation and links to minority poverty: The case of Latinos in the United States. *Social Problems, 38*, 492–515.

Santino, U. (1988). The financial mafia: The illegal accumulation of wealth and the financial-industrial complex. *Contemporary Crises, 12*, 203-243.

Savin-Williams, R. C. (1990). *Gay and lesbian youth: Expressions of identity*. New York: Hemisphere Publishing.

Saxton, L. (1980). *The individual, marriage, and the family* (4th ed.). Belmont, CA: Wadsworth Publishing Company.

Scanlon, W. F. (1991). *Alcoholism and drug abuse in the workplace*. New York: Praeger.

Schack, S., & Frank, R. S. (1978). Police service delivery to the elderly. *Annals of the American Academy of Political and Social Science, 438*, 81–95.

Schaefer, R. T. (1993). *Racial and ethnic groups* (5th ed.). New York: Harper and Row.

Scheff, T. J. (1984). *Being mentally ill: A sociological theory* (2d ed.). New York: Aldine.

Schiller, H. I. (1993). Transnational media: Creating consumers worldwide. *Journal of International Affairs, 47*, 47–58.

Schilling, R. F., & McAlister, A. L. (1990). Preventing drug use in adolescents through media interventions. *Journal of Consulting and Clinical Psychology, 58*, 416–424.

Schlesinger, A. M. Jr. (1986). *The cycles of American history*. Boston: Houghton Mifflin.

Schmid, C. L. (1981). *Conflict and consensus in Switzerland*. Berkeley: University of California Press.

Schnall, P. L., & Kern, R. (1986). Hypertension in American society: An introduction to historical materialist epidemiology. In P. Conrad & R. Kern (Eds.), *The sociology of health and illness: Critical perspectives* (2d ed.). New York: St. Martin's Press.

Schneider, W., & Lewis, I. A. (1984). The straight story on homosexuality and gay rights. *Public Opinion, 7* (1), 16–20.

Schram, S. F. (1991). Welfare spending and poverty: Cutting back produces more poverty, not less. *American Journal of Economics and Sociology, 50*, 129–141.

Schuckit, M. A. (1989). *Drug and alcohol abuse* (3d ed.). New York and London: Plenum.

Schuessler, K. F. (1952). The deterrent effect of the death penalty. *Annals of the American Academy of Political and Social Sciences, 284*, 54–63.

Schur, E. M. (1965). *Crimes without victims*. Englewood Cliffs, NJ: Prentice-Hall.

Schutt, R. K. (1990). The quantity and quality of homelessness: Research results and policy implications. *Sociological Practice Review, 1*, 77–87.

Schwartz, F. N. (1989). Management women and the new facts of life. *Harvard Business Review*, January/February, 65–76.

Scott, W. J. (1985). The equal rights amendment as status politics. *Social Forces, 64* (2), 499–506.

Scott, W. J., & Stanley, S. C. (1994). *Gays and lesbians in the military: Issues, concerns, and contrasts*. New York: Aldine de Gruyter.

Scully, D. (1994). *Men who control women's health: The miseducation of obstetrician-gynecologists*. New York: Teachers College Press.

Sears, D. O. (1988). Symbolic racism. In P. A. Katz & D. A. Taylor (Eds.), *Eliminating racism*. New York: Plenum.

Seeman, M., Seeman, A. Z., & Budros, A. (1988). Powerlessness, work, and community: A longitudinal study of alienation and alcohol use. *Journal of Health and Social Behavior, 29*, 185–198.

Segal, L. (1990). Pornography and violence: What the "experts" really say. *Feminist Review, 36*, 29–41.

Sekaran, U. (1986). *Dual-career families*. San Francisco: Jossey-Bass.

Selke, W. L. (1993). *Prisons in crisis*. Bloomington: Indiana University Press.

Sellin, T. (1959). *The death penalty*. Philadelphia: American Law Institute.

Seltzer, J. A. (1994). Consequences of marriage dissolution for children. In J. Hagan & K. S. Cook

(Eds.), *Annual Review of Sociology, 20.* Palo Alto, CA: Annual Reviews Inc.

Sessions, G. (Ed.). (1995). *Deep ecology for the twenty-first century.* New York: Random House.

Sexual harassment cases still murky. (1991). *Trial, 27,* 14–15.

Shaiken, H. (1987, March 22). A threat to dignity? When the computer runs the office. *New York Times,* Sec. 3, p. 5.

Shanas, E. (1972). Adjustment to retirement: Substitution or accommodation. In F. Carp (Ed.), *Retirement.* New York: Behavioral Publications.

Shea, C. P. (1988). Shifting to renewable energy. In L. R. Brown et al. (Eds.), *State of the world 1988: A worldwatch institute report on progress toward a sustainable society.* New York: W. W. Norton.

Shefter, M. (1985). *Political crisis/fiscal crisis: The collapse and revival of New York City.* New York: Basic Books.

Sheley, J. F. (1985). *America's "crime problem": An introduction to criminology.* Belmont, CA: Wadsworth Publishing Company.

Sherman, L. W., & Berk, R. A. (1984). The specific deterrent effects of arrest for domestic violence. *American Sociological Review, 49,* 261–271.

Sherrill, R. (1995). Dangerous to your health: The madness of the market. *The Nation,* January 9/16, 45–72.

Shibutani, T. (1978). *The derelicts of company K.* Berkeley: University of California Press.

Shichor, D. (1995). *Punishment for profit: Private prisons/public concerns.* Thousand Oaks, CA: Sage.

Shichor, D., & Bartollas, C. (1990). Private and public juvenile placements: Is there a difference? *Crime and Delinquency, 36,* 286–299.

Shilts, R. (1987). *And the band played on: Politics, people, and the AIDS epidemic.* New York: St. Martin's Press.

Shinn, M., & Gillespie, C. (1994). The roles of housing and poverty in the origins of homelessness. *American Behavioral Scientist, 37,* 505–521.

Shipp, E. R. (1981, January 4). 99 of 100 arrests in New York city for felonies fail to lead to prison. *New York Times,* 1.

Shockley, W. B. (1980). Playboy interview: William Shockley. *Playboy,* August, 73.

Sidanius, J., Devereux, E., & Pratto, F. (1992). A comparison of symbolic racism theory and social dominance theory as explanations for racial policy attitudes. *Journal of Social Psychology, 132,* 377–395.

Sigelman, L., & Welch, S. (1993). The contact hypothesis revisited: Black-white interaction and positive racial attitudes. *Social Forces, 71,* 781–795.

Sigerist, H. E. (1977). The special position of the sick. In D. Landy (Ed.), *Culture, disease, and healing: Studies in medical anthropology.* New York: Macmillan.

Simmons, J. L. (1969). *Deviants.* Berkeley, CA: Glendessary Press.

Simon, J. L. (1981). *The ultimate resource.* Princeton, NJ: Princeton University Press.

Simons, R. L., & Gray, P. A. (1989). Perceived blocked opportunity as an explanation of delinquency among lower-class black males: A research note. *Journal of Research in Crime and Delinquency, 26* (1), 90–101.

Simons, R. L., & Whitbeck, L. B. (1991). Sexual abuse as a precursor to prostitution and victimization among adolescent and adult homeless women. *Journal of Family Issues, 12,* 361–379.

Simpson, G. E., & Yinger, J. M. (1985). *Racial and cultural minorities* (5th ed.). New York: Plenum.

Simpson, J. (1994). Nuclear non-proliferation in the post-cold war era. *International Affairs, 70,* 17–39.

Sims, C. (1995, July 11). Defying U.S. threat, Bolivians plant more coca. *New York Times,* p. A3.

Singer, J. D., & Small, M. (1972). *The wages of war, 1816–1965: A statistical handbook.* New York: John Wiley and Sons.

Skocpol, T. (1995). *Social policy in the Unites States: Future possibilities in historical perspective.* Princeton, NJ: Princeton University Press.

Smith, D. A. (1991). Method and theory in comparative urban studies. *International Journal of Comparative Sociology, 32,* 39–58.

Smith, D. A., & Gartin, P. R. (1989). Specifying specific deterrence: The influence of arrest on future criminal activity. *American Sociological Review, 54,* 94–105.

Smith, D. A., & Klein, J. R. (1984). Police control of interpersonal disputes. *Social Problems, 31,* 468–481.

Smith, K. B., & Stone, L. H. (1989). Rags, riches, and bootstraps: Beliefs about the causes of wealth and poverty. *The Sociological Quarterly, 30* (1), 93–107.

Smith, N., & LeFaiure, M. (1984). A class analysis of gentrification. In J. J. Palen & B. London (Eds.), *Gentrification, displacement and neighborhood revitalization.* Albany: State University of New York Press.

Smock, P. J., & Wilson, F. D. (1991). Desegregation and the stability, of white enrollments: A school-level analysis, 1968–84. *Sociology of Education, 64,* 278–292.

Sniderman, P. M., Piazza, T., Tetlock, P. E., & Kendrick, A. (1991). The new racism. *American Journal of Political Science, 35,* 423–447.

Snipp, C. M. (1989). *American Indians: The first of this land.* New York: Russell Sage Foundation.

Sobel, L. A. (Ed.). (1979). *Pornography, obscenity and the law.* New York: Facts on File.

Solarzano, D. G. (1991). Mobility aspirations among racial minorities, controlling for SES. *Sociology and Social Research, 75,* 182–188.

Sommers, I. (1988). The influence of environmental factors on the community adjustment of the mental ill. *The Journal of Nervous and Mental Disorders, 176,* 221–226.

Soule, S. A. (1992). Populism and black lynching in Georgia, 1890–1900. *Social Forces, 71,* 431–449.

Sowell, T. (1981). *Ethnic America: A history.* New York: Basic Books.

Spade, J. Z., & Reese, C. A. (1991). We've come a long way, maybe: College students' plans for work and family. *Sex Roles, 24* (5–6), 309–321.

Spector, M., & Kitsuse, J. I. (1987). *Constructing Social Problems* (2d ed.). New York: Aldine de Gruyter.

Spencer, J. W., & Drass, K. A. (1989). The transformation of gender into conversational advantage: A symbolic interactionist approach. *Sociological Quarterly, 30,* 363–383.

Spilerman, S. (1976). Structural characteristics of cities and the severity of racial disorders. *American Sociological Review, 41,* 771–793.

Spitzer, K. (1992, July 5). Group may give women a fighting chance at combat. *Detroit News and Free Press,* p. 2.

Spurr, S. J. (1990). Sex discrimination in the legal profession: A study of promotion. *Industrial and Labor Relations Review, 43,* 406–417.

Stack, S. (1990). Execution publicity and homicide in South Carolina: A research note. *Sociological Quarterly, 31,* 599–611.

Stahura, J. M. (1989–90). Rapid black suburbanization of the 1970s: Some policy considerations. *Policy Studies Journal, 18,* 279–291.

Stark, L. P. (1991). Traditional gender role beliefs and individual outcomes: An exploratory analysis. *Sex Roles, 24,* 639–650.

Steffensmeier, D. J., & Allan, E. A. (1988). Sex disparities in arrests by residence, race, and age: An assessment of the gender convergence/crime hypothesis. *Justice Quarterly, 5* (1), 53–80.

Stegman, M. A. (1990). A Bush/Kemp report card. *Journal of Housing* (September/October), 237–246.

Stein, B. A., & Kanter, R. M. (1980). Building the parallel organization: Creating mechanisms for permanent quality of work life. *The Journal of Applied Behavioral Science, 16,* 371–386.

Steinberg, J. (1985). Letter from the editor. *Health/PAC Bulletin, 16,* 3.

Steinem, G. (1980). Erotica and pornography: A clear and present difference. In L. Lederer (Ed.), *Take back the night: Women on pornography.* New York: William Morrow.

Steiner, J. (1990). Power-sharing: Another Swiss "export product"? In J. V. Montville (Ed.), *Conflict and peacemaking in multiethnic societies.* Lexington, MA: Lexington Books.

Steinmetz, S. K. (1987). Family violence. In M. B. Sussman & S. K. Steinmetz (Eds.), *Handbook of marriage and the family.* New York: Plenum.

Stets, J. E. (1991). Cohabiting and marital aggression: The role of social isolation. *Journal of Marriage and the Family, 53,* 669–680.

Stevens, R. W. (1976). *Vain hopes, grim realities: The economic consequences of the Vietnam War.* New York: New Viewpoints.

Stevens, W. K. (1995, April 18). The 25th anniversary of Earth Day: How has the environment fared? *New York Times,* p. B5.

Stewart, J. B. (1991). *Den of thieves.* New York: Simon and Schuster.

Stitt, B. G. (1988). Victimless crime: A definitional issue. *Journal of Crime and Justice, 11* (2), 87–102.

Stockard, J., & Johnson, M. M. (1992). *Sex and gender in society* (2d ed.). Englewood Cliffs, NJ: Prentice-Hall.

Stohl, M. (1976). *War and domestic political violence: The American capacity for repression and reaction.* Beverly Hills, CA: Sage Publications.

Straus, M. A. (1991). Physical violence in American families: Incidence rates, causes, and trends. In D. D. Knudsen & J. L. Miller (Eds.), *Abused and battered: Social and legal responses to family violence.* New York: Aldine de Gruyter.

Straus, M., & Gelles, R. J. (1986). Societal change and change in family violence from 1975 to 1985 as revealed by two national surveys. *Journal of Marriage and the Family, 48,* 465–479.

Straus, M. A., Gelles, R. J., & Steinmetz, S. K. (1980). *Behind closed doors: A study of family violence in America.* Garden City, NY: Anchor Press/Doubleday.

Strickland, D. (1986, June 8). Pressure builds on retailers to quit selling sex magazines. *Detroit Free Press,* Sec. C, 1.

Stroman, D. F. (1979). *The quick knife: Unnecessary surgery U.S.A.* Port Washington, NY: Kennikat Press.

Strossen, N. (1995). *Defending pornography.* New York: Scribner.

Strug, D., Wish, E., Johnson, B., Anderson, K., Miller, T., & Sears, A. (1984). The role of alcohol in the crimes of active heroin users. *Crime and Delinquency, 30* (4), 551–567.

Struyk, R. J., Page, D. B., Newman, S., Carroll, M., Ueno, M., Cohen, B., & Wright, P. (1989). *Providing supportive services to the frail elderly in federally assisted housing.* Washington, DC: Urban Institute Press.

Study finds bias in house hunting. (1991, September 1). *New York Times,* p. 14.

Study links rise in killings with loosening of gun laws. (1995, March 15). *New York Times,* p. 16.

Sullivan, T. J. (1992). *Applied sociology: Research and critical thinking.* New York: Macmillan.

Sutherland, E. H. (1949). *White collar crime.* New York: Dryden.

Sutherland, E. H., & Cressey, D. R. (1978). *Criminology* (10th ed.). Philadelphia: Lippincott.

Sutton, L. (1983). The effects of alcohol, marijuana, and their combination on driving ability. *Journal of Studies on Alcohol, 44,* 438–445.

Swickard, J. (1986, September 9). Longer terms for repeat offenders could cut crime rate, study claims. *Detroit Free Press,* 2.

Switzer, J. Y. (1990). The impact of generic word choices: An empirical investigation of age- and sex-related differences. *Sex Roles, 22,* 69–82.

Sykes, G. M., & Cullen, F. T. (1992). *Criminology.* (2d ed.). Fort Worth, TX: Harcourt Brace Jovanovich.

Syme, S. L., & Berkman, L. F. (1979). Social class, susceptibility and sickness. In J. R. Folta & E. S. Deck (Eds.), *A sociological framework for patient care.* (2d ed.). New York: John Wiley and Sons.

Szasz, A. (1994). *Ecopopulism: Toxic waste and the movement for environmental justice.* Minneapolis: University of Minnesota Press.

Szasz, T. S. (1970). *Ideology and insanity: Essays on the psychiatric dehumanization of man.* Garden City, NY: Anchor Books.

Szasz, T. S. (1987). *Insanity: The idea and its consequences.* New York: John Wiley and Sons.

Szymanski, A. J. (1976). Racial discrimination and white gain. *American Sociological Review, 41,* 403–414.

Taffel, S. M., Placek, P. J., Moien, M., & Kosary, C. L. (1991). 1989 U.S. cesarean section rate steadies—VBAC rate rises to nearly one in five. *Birth, 18,* 73–77.

Taft, P., & Ross, P. (1969). American labor violence: Its causes, character, and outcome. In H. D. Graham & T. R. Gurr (Eds.), *Violence in America.* New York: Bantam Books.

Tanfer, K., & Cubbins, L. A. (1992). Coital frequency among single women: Normative constraints and situational opportunities. *Journal of Sex Research, 29,* 221–250.

Tannen, D. (1994). *Gender and discourse.* New York: Oxford University Press.

Tausky, C. (1984). *Work and society: An introduction to industrial sociology.* Itasca, IL: F. E. Peacock Publishers.

Tavris, C. (1992). *The mismeasure of woman.* New York: Simon and Schuster.

Teich, A. H. (Ed.). (1986). *Technology and the future.* (4th ed.). New York: St. Martin's Press.

Thio, A. (1983). *Deviant behavior.* (3d ed.). Boston: Houghton Mifflin.

Thio, A. (1988). *Deviant behavior.* (4th ed.) Boston: Houghton Mifflin.

Thomas, W. I., & Thomas, D. S. (1928). *The child in America.* New York: Alfred A. Knopf.

Thompson, K. S. (1980). Measuring beliefs, perceived social pressures, and decisions about having children: A multi-dimensional approach. *Journal of Marriage and the Family, 44,* 3–13.

Thorne, B. (1993). *Gender play: Girls and boys in school.* New Brunswick, NJ: Rutgers University Press.

Thornton, A. (1985). Changing attitudes toward separation and divorce: Causes and consequences. *American Journal of Sociology, 90,* 856–872.

Thornton, A. (1989). Changing attitudes toward family issues in the United States." *Journal of Marriage and the Family, 51,* 873–893.

Thornton, R. Y., & Endo, K. (1992). *Preventing crime in America and Japan: A comparative study.* Armonk, NY: M. E. Sharpe.

Thornton, R. (1987). *American Indian holocaust and survival: A population history since 1492.* Norman and London: University of Oklahoma Press.

Thurow, L. (1992). *Head to head: The coming economic battle among Japan, Europe, and America.* New York: Morrow.

Tienda, M. (1989). Puerto Ricans and the underclass debate. *Annals of the American Academy of Political and Social Science, 501,* 105–119.

Tinbergen, N. (1955). The curious behavior of the stickleback. In *Twentieth century bestiary.* New York: Simon and Schuster.

Tittle, C., & Meier, R. (1990). Specifying the SES/delinquency relationship. *Criminology, 28,* 271–301.

Tittle, C., Villemez, W., & Smith, D. (1978). The myth of social class and criminality: An empirical assessment of the empirical evidence. *American Sociological Review, 43,* 643–656.

Tolchin, M. (1985, February 11). As privately owned prisons increase, so do their critics. *New York Times,* p. 2.

Tonry, M. (1995). *Malign neglect: Race, crime, and punishment in America.* New York: Oxford University Press.

Totti, X. F. (1987). The making of a Latino ethnic identity. *Dissent,* Fall, 537–543.

Trebach, A. S. (1982). *The heroin solution.* New Haven, CT: Yale University Press.

Triandis, H. C. (1988). The future of pluralism revisited. In P. A. Katz & D. A. Taylor (Eds.), *Eliminating racism: Profiles in controversy.* New York: Plenum.

Troiden, R. R. (1989). The formation of homosexual identities. *Journal of Homosexuality, 17,* 43–73.

Turco, R. P., et al. (1983). Nuclear winter: Global consequences of multiple nuclear explosions. *Science, 222,* 1283–1292.

Turner, J., & Maryanski, A. (1979). *Functionalism.* Menlo Park, CA: Benjamin/Cummings.

Turow, J. (1992). *Media systems in society.* New York: Longman.

Tyler, P. E. (1992, March 8). U.S. strategy plan calls for insuring no rivals develop. *New York Times,* pp. 1, 4.

Uchitelle, L. (1989, March 26). Trade barriers and dollar swings raise appeal of factories abroad. *New York Times,* pp. 1, 13.

Uchitelle, L. (1995, March 26). Another day older and running out of time. *New York Times,* Sec. 3: 1.

United Nations. (1991). *The world's women, 1970–1990: Trends and statistics* (Pub. No. E.90.XVII.3). New York: United Nations.

United Nations. (1995). *Human development report.* New York: Oxford University Press.

U.S. Advisory Board on Child Abuse and Neglect, U.S. Department of Health and Human Services. (1995). *A nation's shame: Fatal child abuse and neglect in the United States.* Washington, DC: U.S. Government Printing Office.

U.S. Arms Control and Disarmament Agency. (1982). *Arms control and disarmament agreements: Texts and histories of negotiations.* Washington, DC: U.S. Government Printing Office.

U.S. Bureau of the Census. (1984). *Statistical abstract of the United States, 1985.* Washington, DC: U.S. Government Printing Office.

U.S. Bureau of the Census. (1991). *Statistical abstract of the United States, 1991.* Washington, DC: U.S. Government Printing Office.

U.S. Bureau of the Census. (1992). *Workers with low earnings: 1964 to 1990.* (Current Population Reports, Series P-60, No. 178). Washington, DC: U.S. Government Printing Office.

U.S. Bureau of the Census. (1993). *Poverty in the United States, 1992.* Current Population Reports, Series P-60, No. 185. Washington, DC: U.S. Government Printing Office.

U.S. Bureau of the Census. (1994). *Statistical abstract of the United States, 1994* (114th ed.). Washington, DC: U.S. Government Printing Office.

U.S. Bureau of the Census. (1995). *Statistical abstract of the United States, 1995* (115th ed.). Washington, DC: U.S. Government Printing Office.

U.S. Congress, Office of Technology Assessment. (1989). *New developments in biotechnology: Patenting life—special report, OTA-BA-370 April.* Washington, DC: U.S. Government Printing Office.

U.S. Department of Health and Human Services. (1991). *Aging America: Trends and projections* (DHHS Pub. No. [FCoA] 91-28001). Washington, DC: U.S. Department of Health and Human Services.

U.S. Department of Health and Human Services (1994). *National household survey on drug abuse: Population estimates 1993* (DHHS Pub. No. [SMA] 94-3017). Rockville MD: Substance Abuse and Mental Health Services Administration, Office of Applied Studies.

U.S. Department of Justice. (1992). *Combating violent crime: 24 recommendations to strengthen criminal justice.* Washington, DC: U.S. Government Printing Office.

U.S. Department of Justice. (1992). *Drugs, crime, and the justice system: A national report from the Bureau of Justice Statistics* (Pub. No. NCJ-133652). Washington DC: U.S. Government Printing Office.

U.S. Department of Labor. (1994a). International child labor study. In *Foreign labor trends.* Washington, DC: U.S. Government Printing Office.

U.S. Department of Labor (1994b). *Handy reference guide to the fair labor standards act.* Washington, DC: U.S. Government Printing Office.

U.S. Department of State. (1991). *International narcotics control strategy report.* Department of State (Pub. 9853-A). Washington, DC: U.S. Government Printing Office.

U.S. Department of State. (1994). *Patterns of global terrorism: 1993.* Department of State (Pub. 10136). Washington, DC: U.S. Government Printing Office.

U.S. General Accounting Office. (1990). *Methadone maintenance: Report to the select committee on narcotics abuse and control, House of Representatives* (GAO Pub. No. HRD-90-104). Washington, DC: U.S. Government Printing Office.

Vallas, S. P. (1988). New technology, job control, and worker alienation: A test of two rival perspectives. *Work and Occupations, 15,* 148–178.

van de Kaa, D. J. (1987). Europe's second demographic transition. *Population Bulletin, 42* (1), entire issue.

van der Dennen, J., & Falger, V. (Eds.). (1990). *Sociobiology and conflict: Evolutionary perspectives on competition, cooperation, violence, and warfare.* London: Chapman and Hall.

Vanderkolk, B. S., & Young, A. A. (1991). *The work and family revolution: How companies can keep employees happy and business profitable.* New York: Facts on File.

Vander Zanden, J. W. (1987). *Social psychology* (4th ed.). New York: Random House.

Van Evra, J. (1990). *Television and child development.* Hillsdale, NJ: Lawrence Erlbaum Associates.

Van Horn, S. H. (1988). *Women, work, and fertility, 1900–1986.* New York and London: New York University Press.

Vannoy-Hiller, D., & Philliber, W. W. (1989). *Equal partners: Successful women in marriage.* Newbury Park, CA: Sage Publications.

Veatch, R. M., & Branson, R. (Eds.). (1976). *Ethics and health policy.* Cambridge, MA: Ballinger.

Verbrugge, L. (1979). Marital status and health. *Journal of marriage and the family, 41,* 267–285.

Verbrugge, L. M. (1983). Multiple roles and physical health of women and men. *Journal of Health and Social Behavior, 24,* 16–30.

Vigil, J. D. (1980). *From Indians to Chicanos: A sociocultural history.* St. Louis: Mosby.

Vinovskis, M. A. (1978). Angels' heads and weeping willows: Death in early America. In M. Gordon (Ed.), *The American Family in Social-Historical Perspective.* New York: Random House.

Voelkl, J. E., Fries, B. E., & Galecki, A. T. (1995). Predictors of nursing home residents' participation in activity programs. *The Gerontologist, 35,* 44–51.

Volti, R. (1992). *Society and technological change.* (2d ed.). New York: St. Martin's Press.

Wald, M. L. (1995, July 16). Today's drama: Twilight of the nukes. *New York Times,* Sec. 4, p. 5.

Waldron, I. (1986). Why do women live longer than men? In P. Conrad & R. Kern (Eds.), *The sociology of health and illness: Critical perspectives* (2d ed.). New York: St. Martin's Press.

Wallace, S. P., Williamson, J. B., Lung, R. G., & Powell, L. A. (1991). A lamb in wolf's clothing? The reality of senior power and social policy. In M. Minkler & C. L. Estes (Eds.), *Critical perspectives on aging: The political and moral economy of growing old.* Amityville, NY: Baywood.

Wallerstein, I. (1979). *The capitalist world-economy.* New York: Cambridge University Press.

Wallerstein, J. S., & Blakeslee, S. (1989). *Second chances: Men, women, and children a decade after divorce.* New York: Ticknor and Fields.

Wanner, R. A., & Lewis, L. S. (1978). The functional theory of stratification: A test of some structural hypotheses. *The Sociological Quarterly, 19,* 414–428.

Ward, R. A., LaGory, M., & Sherman, S. R. (1986). Fear of crime among the elderly as person/environment interaction. *Sociological Quarterly, 27,* 327–341.

Wasik, B. H., Ramey, C. T., Bryant, D. M., & Sparling, J. J. (1990). A longitudinal study of two early intervention strategies: Project CARE. *Child Development, 61,* 1682–1696.

Webb, S. L. (1991). *Step forward: Sexual harassment in the workplace.* New York: Mastermedia.

Webb, V. J., & Marshall, I. H. (1989). Response to criminal victimization by older Americans. *Criminal Justice and Behavior, 16,* 239–259.

Weber, J. (1992, July 19). To trade wars from star wars? *Los Angeles Times,* pp. 1, 24.

Weber, M. (1958, originally published 1919). *From Max Weber: Essays in sociology.* H. H. Gerth and C. W. Mills (Trans. & Ed.). New York: Oxford University Press.

Weeks, J. R. (1986). *Population: An introduction to concepts and issues.* Belmont, CA: Wadsworth Publishing Company.

Weinstein, J. I. (1990a). Homesteading: A solution for the homeless? *Journal of Housing* (May/June), 125–164.

Weinstein, R. M. (1990b). Mental hospitals and the institutionalization of patients. *Research in Community and Mental Health, 6,* 273–294.

Weisberg, D. K. (1985). *Children of the night: A study of adolescent prostitution.* Lexington, MA: Lexington Books/D.C. Heath.

Weisman, A. (1989, July 30). L.A. fights for breath. *The New York Times Magazine,* p. 14.

Weitzer, R. (1991). Prostitutes' rights in the United States: The failure of a movement. *Sociological Quarterly, 32,* 23–42.

Weitzman, L. J. (1985). *The divorce revolution: The unexpected social and economic consequences for women and children in America.* New York: Free Press.

Wells, L. E., & Rankin, J. H. (1991). Families and delinquency: A meta-analysis of the impact of broken homes. *Social Problems, 38,* 71–93.

Werner, L. M. (1985, March 4). 84% repeat offender rate examined. *New York Times,* p. 11.

Westermann, W. L. (1955). *The slave systems of Greek and Roman antiquity.* Philadelphia: American Philosophical Society.

Westie, F. R. (1964). Race and ethnic relations. In R. E. L. Faris (Ed.), *Handbook of modern sociology.* Chicago: Rand McNally.

Wheaton, E. (1987). *Codename GREENKIL: The 1979 Greensboro killings.* Athens: University of Georgia Press.

White, C. P., & White, M. B. (1991). The adolescent family life act: Content, findings, and policy recommendations for pregnancy prevention programs. *Journal of Clinical Child Psychology, 20* (1), 58–70.

Williams, J. A. Jr., Vernon, J. A., Williams, M. C., & Malecha, K. (1987). Sex role socialization in picture books: An update. *Social Science Quarterly, 68,* 148–156.

Wilson, E. O. (1992). *The diversity of life.* Cambridge, MA: Belknap Press/Harvard University Press.

Wilson, J. Q. (1990). Drugs and crime. In M. Tonry & J. Q. Wilson (Eds.), *Drugs and crime.* Chicago: University of Chicago Press.

Wilson, J. Q., & Herrnstein, R. J. (1985). *Crime and human nature.* New York: Simon and Schuster.

Wilson, W. J. (1978). *The declining significance of race.* Chicago: University of Chicago Press.

Wilson, W. J. (1987). *The truly disadvantaged: The inner city, the underclass, and public policy.* Chicago: University of Chicago Press.

Wilson, W. J. (1991). Studying inner-city social dislocations: The challenge of public agenda research. *American Sociological Review, 56,* 1–14.

Winner, L. (1977). *Autonomous technology: Technics-out-of-control as a theme in political thought.* Cambridge, MA: MIT Press.

Wisensale, S. K., & Heckart, K. E. (1993). Domestic partners: A concept paper and policy discussion. *Family Relations, 42,* 199–204.

Witkin, G. (1991, August 19). The men who created crack. *U.S. News and World Report,* pp. 44–53.

Wolchik, S. A., West, S. G., Westover, S., Sandler, I. N., Martin, A., Lustig, J., Tein, J-Y., & Fisher, J. (1993). The outcome of divorce parenting intervention: Outcome evaluation of an empirically based program. *American Journal of Community Psychology, 21,* 293–331.

Wolfe, A. (1993). *The human difference: Animals, computers, and the necessity of social science.* Berkeley: University of California Press.

Wolfe, B. L. (1994). Reform of health care for the nonelderly poor. In S. H. Danziger, G. D. Sandefur, & D. H. Weinberg (Eds.), *Confronting poverty: Prescriptions for change.* New York and Cambridge, MA: Russell Sage Foundation and Harvard University Press.

Wolff, E. N. (1995). *Top heavy: A study of the increasing inequality of wealth in America.* New York: The Twentieth Century Fund.

Wolfgang, M. E., & Ferracuti, F. (1967). *The subculture of violence: Toward an integrated theory in criminology.* London: Tavistock.

Wong, K. K., & Peterson, P. E. (1986). Urban response to federal program flexibility: Politics of community development block grant. *Urban Affairs Quarterly, 21,* 293–310.

Woolhandler, S., & Himmelstein, D. U. (1994, September 19). Galloping toward oligopoly: Giant H.M.O. 'A' or giant H.M.O. 'B'? *The Nation,* 265–268.

World Bank. (1989). *World development report, 1989.* New York: Oxford University Press.

Wriston, W. B. (1992). *The twilight of sovereignty.* New York: Charles Scribner's Sons.

WuDunn, S. (1993, April 25). Births punished by fine, beating or ruined home. *New York Times,* p. 6.

Yancovitz, S. R., et al. (1991). A randomized trial of an interim methadone maintenance clinic. *American Journal of Public Health, 81,* 1185–1191.

Yang, C. K. (1965). *Chinese communist society: The family and the village,* Cambridge, MA: MIT Press.

Young, R. K., Gallaher, P., Belasco, J., Barr, A., & Webber, A. W. (1991). Changes in fear of AIDS and homophobia in a university population. *Journal of Applied Social Psychology, 21,* 1848–1858.

Young, T. K. (1994). *The health of Native Americans: Toward a biocultural epidemiology.* New York: Oxford University Press.

Zald, M. N., & McCarthy, J. D (Eds.). (1987, December 8). *Social movements in organizational society: Collected essays.* New Brunswick, NJ: Transaction Books.

Zane, J. P. (1991). In some cities, women still battle barriers to membership in all-male clubs. *New York Times,* p. 35.

Zaslow, M. J. (1991). Variations in child care quality, and its implications for children. *Journal of Social Issues, 47,* 125–138.

Zawitz, M. W., et al. (1988). *Report to the nation on crime and justice* (2d ed.). Washington, DC: U.S. Department of Justice, Bureau of Justice Statistics.

Zebrowitz, L. A., Tenenbaum, D. R., Goldstein, & L. H. (1991). The impact of job applicants' facial maturity, gender, and academic achievement on hiring recommendations. *Journal of Applied Social Psychology, 21,* 525–548.

Zehr, S. C. (1994). The centrality of scientists and the translation of interests in the U.S. acid rain controversy. *Canadian Review of Sociology and Anthropology, 31,* 325–353.

Zeitlin, M. (1990). *American cities: A working class view.* New York: International Publishers.

Zill, N., & Nord, C. W. (1994). *Running in place: How American families are faring in a changing economy and an individualistic society.* Washington, DC: Child Trends, Inc.

Zimbardo, P. G. (1973). A field experiment in auto shaping. In C. Ward (Ed.), *Vandalism.* New York: Van Nostrand Reinhold.

Zippay, A. (1991). *From middle income to poor: Downward mobility among displaced steelworkers.* New York: Praeger.

Zuboff, S. (1993). In the age of the smart machine. In A. H. Teich (Ed.), *Technology and the future.* New York: St. Martin's Press.

NAME INDEX

Cohen, L. E., 320
Cohen, S., 365
Cohen, T. F., 262
Cohen, Y., 441
Cohn, M., 256
Cohn, S. F., 338
Cole, G. F., 339
Coleman, J. S., 231
Coleman, J. W., 326
Collins, J., 448
Collins, R., 12, 33, 91, 246, 399
Collins, R. L., 376
Coltrane, S., 91, 399
Colvin, M., 342
Commoner, B., 482, 483
Comstock, G. D., 405
Comte, A., 547, 548
Conklin, J. G., 456
Conner, K. A., 313
Conrad, C. A., 175
Conrad, J. P., 344
Constantinople, A., 254
Conte, J. R., 105, 106
Coontz, S., 116
Copeland, P., 400
Corea, G., 162
Corell, R., 489
Cornelius, R., 254
Cornell, C. P., 84, 101
Corzine, J., 332
Costello, T., 76
Costells, M., 458
Cottey, T. J., 533
Cowan, A. L., 269
Crain, R. L., 233
Cranna, M., 528
Crawford, M., 254
Craypo, C., 43, 71
Crenshaw, E. M., 459
Cressey, D. R., 321
Crewdson, J., 116
Crossman, R. K., 104
Crowe, T. D., 345, 457
Crowley, T. J., 381
Crystal, S., 302
Cubbins, L. A., 399
Culkin, M., 87
Cullen, F. T., 326, 336, 345
Cullen, J. B., 181

Currie, E., 320, 341, 342, 343, 345, 346, 385, 389
Cushman, J. H., Jr., 55

D

Dahrendorf, R., 12
Daniels, R., 219
Danigelis, N. L., 305
D'Antonio, M., 507
Danziger, S., 64, 171
Dash, L., 116
Davenport, W. H., 398
Davidson, J. K., Sr., 96
Davies, O., 517
Davis, B. D., 567
Davis, G., 447
Davis, J. A., 456, 460
Davis, K., 181, 413, 414
Davis, S. M., 144, 153
Dean, C. W., 25
Deckhard, B., 265
Degler, C. N., 545
Dekker, P., 210
Delattre, E. J., 325
De Leon, G., 385
Densen-Gerber, J., 386
Dentler, R. A., 522
Denton, N. A., 239
Deschenes, E. P., 372
Des Jarlais, D. C., 384
Devereux, E., 228
Devine, J. A., 171, 186, 320
Devins, R. M., 60
Diamond, I., 507
Diana, L., 407, 408, 411, 414
Dickens, C., 3, 4
Dickenson, D., 313
Dietrich, W. S., 76
DiFazio, W., 60, 65, 179, 561
DiIulio, J. J., Jr., 455
DiMatteo, M. R., 145
Dinham, B., 493
DiNicola, D. D., 145
DiPietro, J. A., 86
Doeringer, P. B., 313
Doig, S. K., 453
Dole, V. P., 372, 384
Domhoff, G. W., 54, 76

Donnelley, S., 567
Donnerstein, E., 422, 424
Doob, C. B., 209
Drass, K. A., 249, 320
Dreier, P., 52, 53
Drucker, P. F., 579
Duberman, M., 431
Dubow, F., 457
Duke, J. T., 12
Duke, S. B., 381, 382, 385, 387
Dukes, R. L., 211, 252
Dulles, J. F., 534
Dunbar, L. W., 193
Duncan, C. M., 177
Duncan, G. J., 60, 174
Dunford, F. W., 25
Dunlap, D. W., 404
Dunn, F. L., 123
Dunn, M., 522, 523
Durand, A. M., 157
Durkheim, E., 319
Durning, A., 489, 493
Duster, T., 329, 334, 567
Dworkin, A., 416
Dye, T. R., 54
Dynes, R. R., 33

E

Easterbrook, G., 478
Eckerman, W. C., 370
Eckholm, E., 153
Eder, P. F., 569
Edwards, G., 356
Eggebeen, D. J., 174
Eggers, M. L., 454
Eggert, L. L., 385
Egley, L. C., 105
Ehrlich, A. H., 447, 475, 484, 489, 490
Ehrlich, P. R., 447, 475, 482, 483, 484, 489, 490, 531
Eisenhower, D. D., 55
Elkington, J., 579
Elliott, C., 315, 316
Elliott, D. S., 25, 332
Ellwood, D. T., 201
Emmons, D., 457
Endo, K., 342

Engel, M. H., 204
Engelhardt, H. T., Jr., 148
England, P., 268
Entwisle, D. R., 211, 232
Erickson, P., 367
Erlanger, H. S., 525
Eshleman, J. R., 81
Ester, P., 210
Estes, C. L., 313
Estrin, S., 39
Eysenck, H. J., 317

F

Fagan, J., 334
Falger, V., 519
Fallows, J., 65
Faludi, S., 265, 266
Farrakhan, L., 215
Fausto-Sterling, A., 243
Fay, B., 17
Feagin, J. R., 228, 229, 250, 255
Fearnside, P. M., 490
Featherman, D. L., 185
Felson, M., 320
Fengler, A. P., 305
Ferber, M. A., 111
Ferracuti, F., 525
Ferree, M. M., 252, 257
Ficarrotto, T. J., 406
Fijnaut, C., 326
Finckenauer, J. O., 347
Finkelhor, D., 106
Fiorentine, R., 270
Fisher, C. R., 139
Fisher, J., 108
Fitzpatrick, J. P., 216
Flacks, R., 280
Flanagan, T. J., 329
Flavin, C., 448, 485, 486, 487,
    492, 493, 494, 498, 499, 502
Fleagle, R. G., 492, 500
Flewelling, R. L., 361
Foner, A., 282
Ford, C. S., 245
Fost, D., 218
Foster, A., 337
Frank, R. S., 298
Franks, V., 132

Frazier, C. E., 330
Freedman, J. L., 447
Freeman, H. E., 33
Freeman, R. B., 59, 187
French, M., 242
Frenkel-Brunswik, E., 210
Freudenheim, M., 151, 268
Freund, P. E. S., 131, 152
Friedan, B., 265
Friedlander, D., 190
Fries, B. E., 300
Fuchs, V., 290
Fuentes, A., 260, 263
Fugita, S. S., 220, 239
Funk, R. B., 252
Furstenberg, F. F., Jr., 94, 95, 99

G

Gaebler, T., 67
Gagnon, J. H., 400, 431
Galbraith, J. K., 548
Galecki, A. T., 300
Gallagher, T. J., 255
Gallaher, P., 406
Gallup, G., 403
Gans, H. J., 67, 183, 187, 470
Garber, D. M., 256
Garcia, J., 355
Garreau, J., 470
Gartin, P. R., 344
Gartner, R., 527
Gastil, J., 249
Gaylin, W., 33
Geis, G., 151, 353
Gelb, L. H., 538
Gelles, R. J., 21, 84, 101, 104,
    105, 106
Gendreau, P., 345
Gentry, C. S., 423
George, S., 48, 58, 478
George, V., 196
Gerdes, E. P., 256
Gerrard, M., 487, 488, 489
Gerstel, N., 94
Gibbs, J. P., 517
Gibson, R. M., 139
Giele, J. Z., 245
Gil, D. G., 22

Gilbert, L. A., 97
Gilder, G., 553
Gillespie, C., 180, 452
Gillis, J., 285
Gillmor, D., 453
Glass, G. V., 145
Glazer, M. P., 67
Glazer, N., 195
Glazer, P. M., 67
Goetz, B., 456
Goff, C., 326
Goffman, E., 6
Golden, J., 337
Goldscheider, F. K., 95
Goldstein, A., 385
Goldstein, L. H., 256
Goldstein, M. C., 85
Goldstein, M. J., 422
Goldstein, P. J., 370, 375
Golombok, S., 102
Goode, E., 545
Gorbachev, M., 535
Gordon, M., 88
Gordon, M. M., 17, 224
Gordon, M. T., 324, 456
Gordon, S., 144
Gore, A., 499
Gottfredson, M. R., 316
Gottlieb, M., 38
Gottschalk, P., 64, 171
Gouldner, A. W., 17
Grady, W. R., 400
Graham, O. L., Jr., 64
Grasmich, H. G., 352
Gray, J., 254
Gray, M. M., 86
Gray, P. A., 319
Greek, C., 431
Greeley, A. M., 116
Green, G. D., 102
Greenberg, D., 398, 405
Greenberg, J. R., 106
Greenberger, D. B., 561
Greene, R., 467
Greenman, M., 410, 411
Greider, W., 55
Gross, A. B., 454
Gross, A. C., 381, 382, 385, 387
Gudjonsson, G. H., 317

Guillemin, J., 218
Guinier, L., 232
Gunther, M., 253
Gusfield, J., 393
Gustman, A. L., 295
Gyllenhammar, P. G., 70

H

Hacker, A., 214, 223
Hadley, J., 157
Haglund, R. M. J., 361
Halikas, J. A., 365
Hall, E. J., 252
Hall, R. H., 258
Hall, T. D., 56
Halteman, W. A., 338
Hamer, D., 400
Hamilton, E. E., 25
Hammersmith, S. K., 402
Hanneman, R. A., 382
Hanson, D. J., 210, 393
Hanson, G. R., 393
Hanson, P. G., 227
Hardin, G., 478
Harding, S., 17
Harlan, A., 269
Harmon, B., 218
Harrington, M., 39, 178
Harris, L., 218
Harrison, B., 64, 65, 561
Hartman, C., 63
Hartman, J. J., 422
Hartung, W. D., 515
Harty, S. J., 156
Hasin, D. S., 370
Hastings, W., 33
Hauser, R. M., 185
Haveman, R. H., 190
Hawken, P., 478, 496, 497
Hawkins, G., 393, 416
Hawley, A. H., 441, 464
Hawley, W. D., 233
Hayes, L. F., 168
Headley, B. D., 321
Hecht, S., 507
Heckart, K. E., 99
Heenan, D. A., 443
Heilbroner, R., 76

Heilbrun, A. B., Jr., 337
Heimer, K., 323
Helburn, S. W., 87
Helmer, J., 393
Helvarg, D., 495
Henderson, J., 256
Hendry, P., 446, 448
Henslin, J. M., 431
Herman, E. S., 53
Hero, R. E., 216
Herrman, M., 401
Herrnstein, R. J., 316
Herting, J. R., 385
Hertz, R., 97
Herz, E. J., 456
Hewitt, J. P., 13
Hewlett, S. A., 300
Heyl, B. S., 408, 414
Higginbotham, E., 260
Hijab, N., 266
Hill, A., 241, 270, 271
Hill, J. W., 154
Hill, R. B., 116
Himes, J. S., 510
Himmelstein, D. U., 156
Hindelang, M. J., 334
Hingson, R., 149
Hirschel, J. D., 25
Hirschfield, I. S., 305
Hirschi, T., 21, 316, 319, 414
Hirschman, C., 220
Hitler, A., 208, 521
Hoberg, G., 54
Hobson, L., 231, 401
Hochschild, A., 277
Hofferth, S. L., 87
Hoffman, M., 401
Hoge, R. D., 345
Holden, K. C., 94
Holstein, J. A., 5
Holzer, H. J., 187
Honey, M., 247
Honig, A. S., 86
Hooker, E., 400
Horowitz, R., 358, 409, 412
Hourani, A., 264, 266
House, J. S., 133
Houseknecht, S. K., 93, 97, 463
Hout, M., 185

Howard, T., 567, 568
Howes, C., 87
Hubbard, R., 579
Hueber, G., 497
Huff-Corzine, L., 332
Hugick, L., 399, 402
Huizinga, D., 25, 332
Hunt, H. L., 203
Hunt, K., 144, 153
Hunter, A., 457
Hunter, J., 404
Huston, A. C., 525, 534
Hutchison, I. W., III, 25
Hyde, J. S., 272

I

Iacocca, L., 149
Ilg, R. E., 60
Illich, I., 129, 145, 157
Ima, K., 220
Inciardi, J. A., 358, 409, 412
Intriligator, M. D., 152
Irelan, L. M., 188
Irwin, J., 345, 367, 384
Isaac, R. J., 162
Ispa, J. M., 86
Itkin, S.M., 226

J

Jackson, B., 373
Jackson, M., 373
Jacobs, J. A., 258
Jacobsen, C., 382
Jacobsen, J. P., 269
Jacobson, J., 462
Jaffe, J., 384
Jain, U., 448
James, J., 407
Janowitz, M., 511
Jeffrey, C. R., 318
Jencks, C., 22, 180, 187, 194, 195, 222, 223, 229, 230, 231
Jenness, V., 431
Jesilow, P., 151
Johnson, B., 374, 375
Johnson, B. D., 372
Johnson, C. B., 241

Lewis, I. A., 421
Lewis, L. S., 181
Lewis, N. A., 36
Lewis, O., 185
Lewis, R. A., 262
Liaw, F., 189
Lichter, D. T., 174
Liddell, C., 447
Lieberson, S., 522
Liebow, E., 201
Lifson, A. R., 125
Light, W. J. H., 376
Lincoln, A., 203, 513
Lindorff, D., 141, 142, 143, 144
Link, B. G., 326
Linz, D., 422, 424, 431
Lizotte, A., 525
Lloyd, C. B., 100, 288
Lo, C. Y. H., 55
Loftin, C., 533
London, K. A., 98
Long, F. J., 497
Longman, P., 302
Longshore, D., 232
Loomis, L. S., 95
Loscocco, K. A., 258
Lowman, J., 419
Lowy, M., 36
Luckenbill, D. F., 408, 411
Luebke, B. F., 252
Luft, H. S., 153
Lung, R. G., 308
Lustig, J., 108
Lynch, F. R., 230

M

MacArthur, J. R., 545
MacDonald, K., 250
Machung, A., 277
Macke, A. S., 93
MacKellar, F. L., 449
MacKinnon, C. A., 416
Macklin, E., 98
Macklin, R., 33
MacLeod, M., 254
MacNeill, J., 507
Madsen, R., 33
Maguire, K., 329, 417, 418, 419

Mailer, N., 415
Main, J., 484, 491
Malamuth, N., 431
Malaret, D. R., 255
Malcolm, A. H., 148
Malecha, K., 252
Malone, T. F., 489
Malthus, T. R., 444, 446, 449
Mann, C. C., 496
Mann, C. R., 353
Mansfield, P. K., 256
Mantle, M., 355
Manton, K. G., 132
Marden, C. F., 203
Marks, C., 185, 186, 212
Markusen, A., 530, 539
Marlatt, G. A., 376
Marsden, M. E., 361
Marshall, D. S., 397
Marshall, I. H., 298
Marshall, J., 393
Martin, A., 108
Martin, C. E., 402
Martin, C. L., 250
Martin, D., 88
Martin, M., 88
Martin, S. E., 358
Martindale, M., 242
Martinez, R., 211, 252
Marx, K., 11, 12, 17, 39, 184, 321, 445
Maryanski, A., 10, 520
Massey, D. S., 186, 239, 454
Mather, R., 579
Matsueda, R. L., 323
Mauldin, W. P., 462
Maume, D. J., Jr., 258
Maynard, R. A., 195
Mazur, A., 562
McAlister, A. L., 385
McBroom, W. H., 272
McCaghy, C. H., 411
McCall, R. B., 262
McCarthy, C. R., 567
McCarthy, J. D., 526
McCartney, L., 77
McConnell, S. R., 293
McCoy, N. L., 243
McCue, J. D., 139

McDonnell, D., 367, 384
McDowall, D., 533
McDuffie, A., 522
McGuire, M. B., 131, 152
McKenzie, R. B., 64
McKeown, T., 127
McKibben, M., 106
McKinlay, J. B., 128
McKinlay, S. M., 128
McLanahan, S., 100, 175, 288
McLeod, E., 408
McLuhan, M., 551, 555
McNeil, W. H., 471
McPartland, J., 231, 233
McPhail, C., 522
Mead, L. M., 187, 188
Meadows, D. H., 448, 471, 507
Meadows, D. L., 448, 471, 507
Mechanic, D., 137
Mednick, S. A., 316, 317
Meier, R., 353
Meier, R. F., 332, 387, 408, 411
Melko, M., 98
Melman, S., 65
Merrill, J. C., 149
Merton, R. K., 10, 207, 319, 377, 520, 527
Mesarovic, M., 449
Messner, M. A., 262
Meyer, G., 204
Meyer, M. H., 293, 296
Michael, R. T., 400, 431
Michaels, S., 400
Michels, R., 50, 51
Middleton, R., 209
Milby, J. B., 356, 361, 365, 376, 386
Milhorn, H. T., 361, 370, 371, 375
Milken, M., 326
Miller, A. D., 320
Miller, D. L., 511
Miller, E. M., 411
Miller, G., 5
Miller, L. S., 359
Miller, M. A. L., 478
Miller, N., 226
Miller, P., 181
Miller, R. H., 153

Miller, R. L., 386, 387
Miller, S. C., 219
Miller, T., 370, 374, 375
Miller, W. R., 381
Millman, M., 156
Mills, C. W., 4, 5, 8, 51, 54, 55, 66
Milner, D., 239
Min, P. G., 220
Mincer, J., 388
Mincy, R. B., 186
Miringoff, M. L., 290, 291
Mirowsky, J., 162
Moen, P., 116
Moffitt, T. E., 317
Mohr, C., 538
Moien, M., 147
Mokhiber, R., 353
Moles, O. C., 93, 188
Mood, A., 231
Moodley, K., 204
Moore, D. C., 332
Moore, D. W., 298
Moore, J. W., 215
Moore, K. A., 88, 100
Moore, N. B., 96
Moore, W., 181
Morgan, E., 253
Morgan, L. A., 116
Morganthau, T., 221
Morris, A. D., 229
Morris, J. R., 87
Morris, N., 345
Mott, F. L., 86
Moynihan, D. P., 116
Mumford, E., 128, 145
Murdoch, R., 53
Murdock, G. P., 246, 398
Murphy, J. E., 104
Murphy, K. M., 182
Murphy, P., 226
Murray, C., 194
Murray, G. F., 367
Myers, S. L., 421

N
Nader, R., 67
Najjar, O. A., 264
Nasar, S., 499

Nason-Clark, N., 326
Nathan, R. P., 23
Navarro, V., 162
Neckerman, K. M., 187, 205, 214
Nelkin, D., 564, 565, 579
Nelson, R. Y., Jr., 452
Nero, A. V., Jr., 499
Neugarten, B. L., 302, 303
Neustadtl, A., 76
Newman, A. E., 269
Newman, O., 457
Newman, S., 308
Nicholson, J., 277
Nielson, F., 519
Nightingale, C. H., 313
Nightingale, D. S., 190
Nimkoff, M. F., 80
Nissen, B., 43, 71
Noble, B. P., 389, 421
Noble, H. B., 538
Nord, C. W., 100, 110
Noriega, M., 514
Norman, C., 551, 566
Normoyle, J., 456
Novak, M., 42, 512
Novick, S. M., 181
Nusberg, C., 306

O
O'Brien, D. J., 220, 239
O'Connell, W. E., 227
O'Connor, J. F., 525
O'Day, P., 320
O'Donnell, V., 22
O'Farrell, B., 111
Ogburn, W. F., 80, 558
O'Hare, W., 270
Ohlin, L. E., 320, 380
O'Kelly, C. G., 90, 246, 264
Olinger, J. P., 108
Olsson, S. E., 306
Olzak, S., 208
O'Malley, P. M., 359, 360, 362, 363, 365, 368, 385
Orenstein, G. F., 507
Orenstein, P., 277
Organski, A. F. K., 441
Orshansky, M., 168

Osborne, D., 67
O'Shea, R. M., 188

P
Packwood, B., 241
Padilla, F. M., 217, 353
Page, D. B., 308
Paige, J. M., 522
Palen, J. J., 452
Pallas, A. M., 211
Paradise, V. I., 286
Park, K. J., 86
Parke, R., 250
Parker, F. L., 189
Parnell, A. M., 471
Parsons, T., 10, 120, 246
Pastore, A. L., 417, 418, 419
Pate, A. M., 25
Patrick, C. H., 132
Patterson, C. J., 102
Paulsen, J. A., 20, 401
Payne, J. E., 375
Peay, L., 189
Peirce, N. R., 372
Pelton, L., 105
Penrod, S., 422
Perry, J. B., Jr., 348
Pestel, E., 449
Petersen, W., 437
Petersilia, J., 337
Peterson, I., 293
Peterson, J., 258, 269
Peterson, P. E., 188, 464
Peterson, R. D., 346
Peterson, S. B., 252
Petrocelli, W., 271
Pettigrew, T. F., 225
Philliber, W. W., 97
Phillips, D. A., 87
Phillips, K., 201
Phillips, U. B., 212
Phoenix, R., 355
Piazza, T., 228
Pillemer, K., 106, 298
Piller, C., 579
Pinkney, A., 513, 525
Piotrkowski, C. S., 97, 189
Piper, E. S., 334

Piven, F. F., 197
Placek, P. J., 147
Plakans, A., 281
Plissner, M., 22
Plotnick, R. D., 110
Plummer, M. L., 496
Plunkett, M., 171
Poffenberger, D. L., 292, 411, 412, 413
Polakow, V., 201
Polanzi, C. W., 326
Pollock, C., 497
Pomeroy, W. B., 402
Pontell, H. N. 151
Poplin, D. E., 441
Porter, B., 522, 523
Portes, A., 223, 471
Portney, P. R., 496
Postel, S., 448, 486, 487, 492, 494, 498, 499, 502
Postman, N., 579
Pottieger, A. E., 358, 409, 412
Powell, G. N., 271
Powell, L. A., 308
Powledge, T., 33
Prager, J., 232
Pratto, F., 228
Proctor, R. N., 133
Prucha, F. P., 218
Pugh, M. D., 348
Purcell, P., 252
Purdy, L. M., 285

Q

Quinlin, K., 371
Quinn, J. F., 292, 293
Quinn, R. P., 561
Quinney, R., 320

R

Rachal, J. V., 361
Raczynski, J. M., 367, 372
Ramey, C. T., 86
Ramirez, A., 340
Randers, J., 448, 471, 507
Rank, M. R., 179, 189, 195
Rankin, D., 301

Rankin, J. H., 95
Rasmussen, D. W., 465
Ray, B. A., 376
Ray, O., 360
Raymond, J. A., 106
Reagan, R., 25, 43, 58, 203, 230, 271, 535
Rebach, H. M., 33
Record, R. G., 127
Reese, C. A., 257
Reich, R. B., 77
Reiman, J., 339
Reiss, M., 536
Reiss, P. J., 80
Reklis, D. M., 290
Relman, A. S., 144, 145
Repa, B. K., 271
Repetto, R., 448, 463
Reskin, B. F., 269
Resnick, M. D., 218
Retchin, S. M., 154
Reynolds, H., 408, 409, 426
Rezac, S. J., 95
Rice, D. P., 359
Rich, B., 48, 49, 58, 68, 478, 479
Richardson, D. R., 210, 521
Richmond-Abbott, M., 250, 252, 253, 265
Richter, M. N., Jr., 548, 550
Rideau, W., 353
Ridker, R., 463
Riesman, D., 54
Riessman, C. K., 94
Rifkin, J., 77, 567, 568, 570, 571, 579
Riger, S., 324, 456
Riley, M. W., 282
Rio, L. M., 409
Rist, R. C., 232
Rivkin, S. G., 231
Robbins, J., 502
Robertson, J. A., 567
Robinson, B. E., 401
Robinson, D., 385
Robinson, J., 258
Robock, A., 531
Robyn, D. L., 157
Rockefeller, J. D., 203
Rodgers, H. L., Jr., 196

Rodgers, W., 174
Rogers, S. M., 400
Rohe, W. M., 305
Roodman, D. M., 492
Roos, P. A., 269
Roosevelt, F. D., 45
Ropers, R. H., 201
Rose, A. M., 54
Rosen, C., 70
Rosenbaum, M., 367, 384
Rosenfeld, R. A., 258
Rosenfield, S., 94
Rosenhan, D. L., 136, 137
Rosenthal, R., 201
Ross, C. E., 162
Ross, J. W., 108
Ross, M. W., 20, 401
Ross, P., 42, 512
Ross, R. R., 345
Rossell, C. H., 231
Rossi, A., 250
Rossi, P. H., 33
Rothblum, E. D., 132
Rothfeder, J., 563, 569
Rounsaville, B. J., 376
Rowe, A. R., 332
Rubenstein, R. E., 517
Rude, G., 545
Ruggles, P., 166, 168, 171
Rushing, W. A., 162
Russell, D. E. H., 262, 325
Russett, B., 529
Ryan, J. C., 490
Ryan, R. A., 223
Ryan, W., 188

S

Saal, F. E., 241
Sabelli, F., 48, 58, 478
Sadik, N., 266
Sadker, D., 252
Sadker, M., 252
Sagan, C., 531, 536
Sagarin, E., 431
Salas, R. M., 459
Sale, K., 471, 569, 572
Salem, G., 456
Salinger, J. D., 415

Stockard, J., 267
Stockdale, M. S., 241
Stohl, M., 528
Stone, L. H., 173
Stones, R., 335
Straus, M. A., 84, 101, 104, 105
Strickland, D., 417
Strobino, D. M., 86
Stroman, D. F., 148
Strossen, N., 417
Strug, D., 374, 375
Struyk, R. J., 308
Sullivan, A., 431
Sullivan, T. J., 15, 23, 33
Sullivan, W. M., 33
Sutherland, E. H., 321, 326
Sutton, L., 358
Swazey, J. P., 149
Swickard, J., 344
Swidler, A., 33
Switzer, J. Y., 249
Sykes, G. M., 336
Sykes, M. P., 228, 229
Syme, S. L., 131
Szasz, A., 495
Szasz, T. S., 135, 137
Szymanski, A. J., 211

T

Taffel, S. M., 147
Taft, P., 42, 512
Takaki, R., 239
Takeuchi, D. T., 220
Tancredi, L., 579
Tanfer, K., 399, 400
Tannen, D., 249, 277
Tasker, F., 102
Tausky, C., 561
Tavris, C., 245
Taylor, D. M., 471
Taylor, S. E., 162
Teich, A. H., 449
Tein, J., 108
Teitler, J. O., 95
Tenenbaum, D. R., 256
Tetlock, P. E., 228
Thio, A., 409, 411, 414
Thomas, C., 241, 270, 271

Thomas, D. S., 13
Thomas, W. I., 13
Thompson, K. S., 463
Thompson, W., 431
Thomson, J. J., 556
Thornburg, K. R., 86
Thorne, B., 250
Thornton, A., 88, 93
Thornton, R., 218
Thornton, R. Y., 342
Thurow, L., 65
Tienda, M., 228
Tijerina, R. L., 216
Tinbergen, N., 519
Tipton, S. M., 33
Tittle, C. R., 332
Tolchin, M., 341
Tonry, M., 334
Totti, X. F., 217, 225
Trebach, A. S., 372
Triandis, H. C., 225
Troiden, R., 401
Turco, R. P., 531, 536
Turner, C. F., 400
Turner, J., 10, 520
Turner, J. B., 133
Turner, R. D., 127
Turow, J., 554
Tyler, P. E., 539
Tyson, M., 241

U

Uchitelle, L., 42, 58, 295
Ueno, M., 308

V

Valenstein, E. S., 162
Vallas, S. P., 60, 561
Van de Kaa, D. J., 438
van der Dennen, J., 519
Vanderkolk, B. S., 70
Vander Zanden, J. W., 525
Van Evra, J., 525
Van Horn, S. H., 247
Vannoy-Hiller, D., 97
Van Valey, T. L., 255
Vaughan, S., 93

Veatch, R. M., 149
Venturelli, P. J., 393
Verbrugge, L., 94, 133
Vernon, J. A., 252
Vicary, J. R., 256
Vigil, J. D., 215
Villemez, W., 332
Vining, D. R., Jr., 449
Vinovskis, M. A., 127
Voelkl, J. E., 300
Volti, R., 548, 550, 558, 560
Voran, M., 87

W

Wade, C., 245
Waite, L. J., 95
Wald, E., 579
Wald, M. L., 536
Waldo, D. R., 139
Waldron, I., 132
Walker, W. O., III, 378
Wallace, S. P., 308
Wallerstein, I., 56
Wallerstein, J. S., 95
Walter, B. O., 446
Wanner, R. A., 181
Ward, R. A., 297
Wasik, B. H., 86
Webb, S. L., 271
Webb, V. J., 298
Webber, A. W., 406
Weber, J., 539
Weber, M., 8, 17
Weeks, J. R., 450
Weinberg, M. S., 400, 401
Weinfield, F., 231
Weinstein, J. I., 465
Weinstein, P., 211
Weinstein, R. M., 137
Weir, W., 393
Weisberg, D. K., 411, 413, 431
Weiss, C., 269
Weitzer, R., 410
Weitzman, L. J., 111
Welch, F., 182
Welch, S., 226
Wells, L. E., 95
Werner, L. M., 345

SUBJECT INDEX

A

AARP. *See* American Association of Retired Persons

Accident, drug use and, 358

Acid rain, 483–485

ACLU. *See* American Civil Liberties Union

Adolescence, 280–282, 290–292, 404–406, 411, 412–413. *See also* Teenagers

Adolescent Family Life Act, 110

Affirmative action, 187, 230–231

Affluence, 476–477, 498

African Americans. *See* Minority groups

Age
alcoholism and drug use and, 361–362, 364, 366–367
crime and, 332–334
discrimination based on, 303
divorce and, 93
perspectives on, 280–283
poverty and, 174–175

Age Discrimination in Employment Act, 292

Ageism, 283, 303

Age structure of American society, 283–285

Aggression, 210, 243–245, 447, 519
pornography and, 418, 422–424
violence and, 521, 524, 525

Aid to Families with Dependent Children (AFDC), 192–195, 464

AIDS (Acquired Immune Deficiency Syndrome), 123–125, 372, 406, 409–410, 412

Air pollution. *See* Environmental problems

Alcohol, 359–362, 370
abuse, 381
crime and, 374–375
effects of, 357–358

Alcoholics Anonymous, 385

Alcoholism, 360–361
perspectives on, 375–376, 381
prevention of, 381–385
treatment of, 385–389

Alianza Federal de Mercedes, 216

Alienation, 59–60, 70–71, 561

Alternative healers, 157

Altruism, 519–520

American Association of Retired Persons (AARP), 308–309

American Civil Liberties Union (ACLU), 12, 389

American Federation of Labor, and Congress of Industrial Organization, 42–43

American Indian Movement, 218

American Medical Association, 122, 145

American Psychiatric Association, 135, 400–401

American Revolution, 513

Amniocentesis, 150

Amotivational syndrome, 365

Amphetamines, 370

Amyl nitrite, 374

Androgyny, 272–273

Angel dust. *See* PCP

Anglo-conformity, 224–225

Anomie theory, 319–320, 323, 377, 520–521, 527

Antabuse treatment, 388

Anti-Drug Abuse Act, 381, 385

Apartheid, 204–205

Arab Americans. *See* Minority groups

Arms control, 535–537

Ascribed status, 204–205, 242

Asian Americans. *See* Minority groups

Assimilation, 224–226

Association of American Colleges, 254–255

Attorney General's Commission on Pornography, 416–417, 422, 424

Audubon Society, 68, 481

Authoritarian personality, 210

Authority, 8

Automation, 182, 550–551, 554–555, 560–561

Aversion therapy, 388

B

Babylonians, 124–125
Back-to-the-earth movement, 568–569, 573
Bail, 336–337
Balance of power, 534–535
Bangladesh, 266
Barbiturates, 370–371
Behavior modification, drug abuse and, 388
Biocentrism, 502–503
Biodiversity, 490–491
Bioethics, 148–150
Biological perspective
  on aging, 280
  on crime, 316
  on drug abuse, 375–376
  on mental illness, 133–134
  on sex roles, 242–245
  on sexual orientation, 400
  on violence, 519–520
Biotechnology, 566–568, 570–571
Birth control. *See* Family planning
Birth rate. *See* Fertility
Black Americans. *See* Minority groups, African Americans
Black Liberation Army, 513
Blaming the victim, 188, 252
Blended family, 94
Bolivia, 378
Brown v. Board of Education, 212
Bubonic plague, 124
Budget Enforcement Act, 66
Bureau of Indian Affairs, 174, 217–218
Burglary. *See* Crime
Bush administration, 189, 321, 463
Busing, school, 231–234
Butyl nitrite, 374

C

Campaign for the Earth, 17, 68
Canada, health care in, 154–155
Capitalism, 38–39, 56–57, 71, 341, 554–555
the cities and, 445–446, 458–459
crime and, 321
the environment and, 477–478, 496, 502–503
the family and, 263
the health field and, 142–145, 151
Capital punishment, 346–347
Carrying capacity, 446–447, 476
Caterpillar Corporation, 59
Causality, 20–21, 329
Censorship, 416–418
Centers for Disease Control, 124
Cesarean births, 147–148
Chernobyl, 494, 556
Chicanos. *See* Minority groups
Child abuse, 21, 104–106, 108, 290, 292
Child Abuse Prevention and Treatment Act, 108
Childlessness, 97
Children
  discrimination against, 285–292, 300
  divorce and, 95
  the family and, 86–87, 102–103, 110–112, 288
  in gay families, 102
  international perspectives on, 109
  poverty and, 174–176, 180, 189–190, 288–290
  sexual exploitation of, 290–292, 413, 416–417
  in single parent families, 99–100
  social policy and, 300, 302–303
Children's Television Education Act, 534
China, family planning in, 460–461
Chinese Exclusion Act (1882), 219–220
Cities. *See also* Urban Problems
  decentralization of, 442–443, 451, 465–466
  the economy and, 455, 458–459
global perspectives on, 458–459
growth of, 441–444, 458–459
poverty and, 177–178, 454
racial composition of, 452–454
Civil disorders, 510–512
Civil Rights Act, 213, 268, 270, 453
Civil rights movement, 197, 212–213, 229
Civil War, 212, 513, 528
Class conflict, 12, 184, 228–229, 234. *See also* Social class
Clean Air Act, 483, 496
Cleveland, 466–467
Clinton administration, 153, 260, 499
Cloning, 567
Club of Rome, 448–449
Cocaine, 367–370, 374–375, 378, 409
Cohabitation, 98–99, 399
Cold War, 534–539
Coleman Report, 231
Collective action, 5–6, 23–25, 67–69, 193, 197, 229, 264–265, 268, 308–309, 495
Common Cause, 68
Common sense, 18–19
Communism, 39
Community, 441
Community development block grants, 111–112, 464
Community mental health movement, 137–138
Comparable worth, 268–269
Competition
  economic, 38–39, 57–58, 247, 287, 458–459
  in the health field, 140, 142–145
  prejudice and discrimination and, 208–211
  races and, 226–227
  sex and, 247
  violence and, 521

Comprehensive Alcohol Abuse and Alcoholism, Prevention Treatment and Rehabilitation Act, 388
Comprehensive Crime Control Act, 336–337, 344
Comprehensive Employment and Training Act (CETA), 190
Computer Matching and Privacy Protection Act, 569
Computers, 551–556, 562–566
Conflict, population growth and, 449–450
Conflict perspective, 11–13, 15
   age and, 282–283
   and concentration of power, 47, 51
   crime and, 320–321, 323
   drugs and, 377–380
   environment and, 480
   the family and, 84–85
   gender inequality and, 246–247
   health care and, 122
   homosexuality and, 406
   population and, 445–446
   poverty and, 184–185
   prejudice and discrimination and, 208–209
   science and technology and, 558–559, 568
   urban problems and, 445–446
   violence and, 521, 526–527
Conglomerates, 41, 57
Consultation of Older and Younger Adults. *See* Gray Panthers
Contraception, 460–462
Conversational styles, 249
Corporate liberalism, 52–53
Corporations, 40–42, 48–49, 58, 71, 142–145, 155–156, 477–478, 554–555
Corrections Corporation of America, 340
Cosa Nostra, 325
Courts, 335–337, 344–345

COYOTE, 410
Crack. *See* Cocaine
Crime, 323. *See also* Deviance
   age and, 327, 332–334
   cities and, 454–457
   drug and alcohol use and, 358, 370, 372, 374–375
   elderly and, 297–298, 305
   environmental opportunity and, 345
   explanations of, 316–323, 329, 455
   extent of, 327–329
   FBI index of, 320, 323–324, 327–329
   fear of, 456–457
   gender and, 330–331, 334
   international perspectives on, 342–343
   legalization of, 343–344, 409–410
   organized, 325–326
   perspectives on, 316–323
   property and, 323–324, 328, 454
   prostitution and, 407–415, 419–421
   race and, 331–334
   secondary, 327, 337, 339
   social class and, 332
   solutions to, 341–348, 457
   types of, 323–327, 331, 333
   victimless, 327, 343, 409–410
   victims of, 334, 348, 454–455
   violent, 323–324, 328, 454
   war and, 527
   white-collar, 326–327
Criminals, characteristics of, 329–334
Criminal justice system, 334–340, 344–348, 522–523
Crisis medicine, 128–129, 141
Crowding, as population problem, 447–448
Cultural analysis, 185, 188
Cultural colonialism, 555
Cultural conflict, 187, 229
Cultural lag, 558
Cultural legacy, 222–223

Cultural transmission theories, 321–323, 380
Culture of poverty, 185, 188
Curative medicine, 128–129, 141

D

Day care, 86–87, 109, 111–112
Death, 149. *See also* Mortality; Infant mortality
   rate, 435–436
Death penalty. *See* Capital punishment
Death with dignity, 149
Decriminalization of drugs, 382–384, 386–387
Deep ecology, 502–503
Defense attorneys, 336
Defense spending, 528–530, 538–539
Definition of the situation, 13, 414
Deforestation, 489–490
Deindustrialization, 64–65
Deinstitutionalization, 181
Delinquency, 327, 411. *See also* Crime
   divorce and, 95
   social control theory of, 319
Demographic gap, 438–440
Demographic transition, 437–441
Demography, 283, 433–434
Dentistry, 146–147
Dependency ratio, 283–286
Depersonalization, 136–137, 299–300
Depressants, 370–371
Deprivation, 166–168, 520–524. *See also* Poverty
Desegregation, school, 212, 231–234
Desertification, 489
Deviance, 5–6, 316. *See also* Crime; Violence
   career, 322–323
   mental illness as, 134–135
   perspectives on, 316–323
   primary, 134, 322–323

Gender (Cont.)
  health and, 132, 436
  inequality and, 92–93,
    146–148, 209
General Assistance, 192
Gene splicing, 566–568
Genetic engineering, 566–568,
  570–571
Genetic screening, 150, 567
Genocide, 224, 226
Gentrification, 406, 458,
  465–466
Gerontology, 280
Ghettos, 452–454
Global communications system,
  554–555
Global corporations, 41–42,
  554–555
Global perspectives. *See*
  International perspectives
Government
  abuse of authority in, 63–66
  deficit spending and, 63–66
  growth of, 44–46
  reorganization of, 66–67
Gramm-Rudman-Hollings Act, 66
Gray Panthers, 305, 308–309
Great Britain, 386–387
Great Society, 192
Greenhouse effect, 492
Greenpeace, 17, 68, 483, 495
Green Revolution, 448
Guardian Angels, 348
Gun control, 532–534

H

Hallucinogens, 373–375
Hashish. *See* Marijuana
Head Start, 111, 189–190, 193,
  342
Health
  children and youth, 288–291
  divorce and, 94
  drugs and, 358, 372
  elderly and, 296–297
  lifestyle and, 125–128, 157–158
  social factors affecting,
    129–133

societal development and,
  123–129
Health care
  access to, 120, 141–144, 151,
    153
  corporatization of, 142–145,
    155–156
  cost of, 120, 139–141, 151–152,
    154, 304
  elderly and, 296–297, 304
  ethical issues in, 148–150
  fraud, 151, 297–298
  gender inequality in, 146–148
  inequality and, 146–148
  international perspectives on,
    154–155
  minorities and, 153, 216, 218
  perspectives on, 120–123
  practitioners in, 146–148,
    156–157
  quality of, 144–146
  right vs. privilege, 150–151
  social control in, 156
  socialized, 145, 155
  unnecessary or harmful, 119,
    140–141, 148
  utilization of, 141
Health insurance, 141, 151–155
Health-Maintenance
  Organizations (HMOs),
    153–156
Heroin, 372–373, 384. *See also*
  Narcotics
  crime and, 358, 372, 374–375
Hispanic Americans. *See* Minority
  groups
HMOs. *See* Health-Maintenance
  Organizations
Homeless, 180, 452
Homicide, 290, 346
Homophobia, 405–406
Homosexuality, 20, 400
  attitudes toward, 124–125,
    402–404
  causes of, 400–401
  as deviance, 395–396, 402–404
  discrimination against,
    395–396, 403–405, 421, 424
  incidence of, 400, 402

perspectives on, 400–401
  social policy and, 419, 421,
    424–426
Homosexuals
  violence toward, 404–406
Housing
  cities and, 452
  discrimination in, 403–404
  elderly and, 304–308
  shared, 305
Housing Act, 464
Hydrologic cycle, 483
Hypothesis, 16
Hysterectomies, 148

I

Iatrogenic illness, 157
Illiteracy, 179, 263
Immigrants, 215, 219, 222–223
Income
  distribution, 171–172
  elderly and, 293–296
  gender inequality and,
    258–260, 263, 268–269
  minorities and, 213, 216,
    217–218
Indian Citizenship Act, 218
Indian Civil Rights Act, 218
Indians. *See* Minority groups,
  Native Americans
Indian Wars, 513–514
Individualism, 96, 342, 479
Individual Retirement Accounts
  (IRAs), 304
Industrialization, 549
  age and, 280–285
  birth and death rates and,
    438–439
  cities and, 441–444
  crime and, 319
  elderly and, 306–307
  the family and, 306–307
  health and, 126–128, 133, 558
  sex roles and, 245–246, 249,
    266–267
  violence and, 512
Inequality. *See* Social inequality
Infanticide, 461

Infant mortality, 126–131, 436–437
In-group, 208
Innovation, 319–320, 377, 527
Institutional racism, 227, 228
Instrumental tasks, 246, 272
Insurrection, 513
Integrated pest management, 493
Interactionist perspective, 13–15
    crime and, 321–323
    drugs and, 380–381
    environment and, 480–481
    family and, 85, 88
    gender inequality and, 248–249, 272–273
    health care and, 122–124
    mental illness and, 134–135
    population and, 446
    poverty and, 185, 188
    prostitution and, 414–415
    science and technology and, 559
    urban problems and, 446
    violence and, 524
Interest groups, 12, 17
Internal colonialism, 209
International Bank for Reconstruction and Development. See World Bank
International cooperation, 500–501
International Court of Justice, 540
International Monetary Fund, 48–49, 58–59, 68–69, 478
International perspectives on social problems, 27–29, 100–101, 109, 196, 306–307, 458–459
Interpersonal violence. See Violence
Interventionist approach, 24–25, 40, 64–65, 189, 426, 463–464, 499, 503, 532, 569
IRAs. See Individual Retirement Accounts
Iran-Contra scandal, 63

Irish Republican Army, 527
Islam, 264, 266

J

Japan, 342–343
Japanese Americans. See Minority groups
Job Opportunities and Basic Skills (JOBS) program, 190
Job Training Partnership Act, 190
Juvenile delinquency. See Delinquency

K

Kinship, 80, 94, 101
Korean Americans. See Minority groups
Korean War, 514, 528–529
Kubu people of Sumatra, 124–125
Ku Klux Klan, 207, 227

L

Labeling,
    as cause of crime, 322–323, 455
    homosexuality and, 401
    in mental illness, 134–137
Labor
    exploitation, 286–288
    globalization of, 69–70
    legislation, 287–288
    movement, 42–44, 59
    strife, 42–45, 512
Laissez-faire approach, 25–26, 39, 40, 64–65, 153, 189, 194, 230–231, 234, 426, 463–464, 499, 503, 532, 569
Lake Erie, 486
Language, gender inequality and, 248–249
Latent functions, 10
Latinismo, 217
Latinos. See Minority groups
Latino Urban Political Association, 217

Law, gender and the, 260–261, 268–269
Law enforcement. See Criminal justice system; Police
League of Conservation Voters, 482–483
League of Nations, 540
League of United Latin American Citizens, 217
Lesbianism. See Homosexuality
Life, prolongation of, 148–149
Life course, 280–283
Life expectancy, 126–132, 436–437, 439–440
Life span. See Life course
Lifestyles, health and, 125–128, 133, 157–158
Living wills, 149
Luddites, 560, 569
Lynchings, 210–211, 521

M

Macrosociological approach, 9–13
Mafia, 325
Magnet schools, 234
Malpractice, 141
Managed health care. See Health-Maintenance Organizations
Mangaia, sexuality in, 296–298
Manifest function, 10
Maquiladoras, 61–62, 459
Marijuana, 359, 361–367, 378
    decriminalization of, 381
    effect of, 358, 364
Market economies, 38–40
Marriage. See also Families
    arranged, 88
    attitudes toward, 88–90
    dissolution of, 90–95, 107–108
    parent-run, 88
    participant-run, 88
    in pre-industrial and industrial societies, 88–90
    rate, 88–89, 91
Masculine mystique, 262
Massive retaliation, 534–535
Master status, 242
MDMA, 374–375

Measurement, scientific, 21–22
Mechanization, 550–551
Media
  gender inequality and,
    252–253
  global, 554–555
  the power elite and, 52–53
  violence and, 525–526, 534
Medicaid, 140–142, 144,
    151–154, 178, 192, 195–196,
    298, 304, 464
Medical care. *See* Health care
Medical-industrial complex,
    144–145
Medicare, 140, 142, 151–154,
    191, 192, 297, 302–304
Meese Commission. *See* Attorney
    General's Commission on
    Pornography
Melting pot, 224–225
Men
  discrimination against, 262
  divorce and, 94
  socialization of, 249–253
Mental hospitals
  deinstitutionalization of, 138
  depersonalization in, 136–137
Mental illness
  as deviance, 134–135
  diagnosis of, 135–137
  gender and, 132
  perspectives on, 133–137
  treatment of, 135–138
Methadone maintenance
    programs, 384
Methaqualone, 371
Mexican American Political
    Alliance, 216, 217
Mexican Americans. *See* Minority
    groups
Microsociological approach, 9,
    13–15
Midwives, 157
Migration, 212, 216, 218–221,
    436–437, 450–451
Military, 260–261, 263, 405
Military-industrial complex, 55,
    539, 558
Miller v. California, 416

Minority groups, 204, 253
  African Americans, 100,
    132–133, 185–188, 209–211,
    212–214, 217, 220, 222–223,
    228–229, 231–234, 255–256,
    332–334, 452–454, 510–512,
    521–523
  Arab Americans, 221, 222, 224
  Asian Americans, 209,
    218–220, 452
  Chinese Americans, 218–220
  elderly as, 282
  health of, 132–133
  Hispanic Americans, 213–217,
    228, 256, 452–453
  income and, 259–260
  Japanese Americans, 219–220,
    222–223
  Korean Americans, 220,
    222–223
  Mexican Americans, 215–216
  Native Americans, 153,
    217–218, 224, 481, 513–514
  poverty and, 173–176,
    185–188, 293–295
  Puerto Ricans, 100, 216, 228
  unemployment of, 60–61
Mixed economies, 39–40, 71
Modeling behavior, 525–526
Modernization, 266, 549. *See also*
    Industrialization
Modified extended family, 80
"Mommy track," 269
Monogamy, 80, 92, 102
Monopoly, 41, 57
Morphine. *See* Narcotics
Mortality, 126–132, 435–439
Mothers Against Drunk Driving
    (MADD), 388
Multinational corporations,
    41–42
Mutually Assured Destruction
    (MAD), 535, 538

N

Nader's Raiders, 68
NAFTA. *See* North American Free
    Trade Agreement

Narcotics, 372–373, 378. *See
    also* Heroin
Narcotics Anonymous, 385–387
National Academy of Sciences,
    551, 567
National Acid Precipitation
    Assessment Program,
    484–485
National Advisory Council on
    Alcohol Abuse and
    Alcoholism, 388
National Aeronautics and Space
    Administration (NASA), 567
National Association of Criminal
    Justice Planners, 341
National Commission on
    Obscenity and Pornography,
    422
National Commission on the
    Causes and Prevention of
    Violence, 339
National Council on Aging, 296
National Environmental Policy
    Act, 483, 573
National Institute on Alcohol
    Abuse and Alcoholism, 388
National Institute on Drug
    Abuse, 359
National Manufacturers
    Association, 12
National Organization for
    Women (NOW), 265
National Practitioner Data Bank,
    156
National Retired Teachers
    Association, 308–309
National Rifle Association
    (NRA), 12
National Welfare Rights
    Organization, 197
National Wildlife Federation, 68
Native Americans, 132–133. *See
    also* Minority groups
Natural resources, depletion of,
    448–449
Natural Resources Defense
    Council, 483, 495
Nazis, 207–208
Negotiated justice, 336

Netherlands
   drug policy, 286–287
   treatment of elderly, 306–307
New Deal, 45–46, 192
Nixon administration, 388
Nongovernmental organizations
   (NGOs), 68–69, 265, 268,
   495
Norms, 6
North American Free Trade
   Agreement (NAFTA), 48, 70
Nuclear energy, 556–557
Nuclear family, 80, 82, 84
Nuclear waste, 488–489, 494
Nuclear weapons, 515, 530–532,
   535–536, 538–539, 556–557
Nuclear winter, 531–532, 536
Nurse practitioners, 157
Nurses, 147
Nursing homes, 298–300

O
Objectivity. *See* Scientific
   objectivity
Obscenity, 415–416. *See also*
   Pornography
Occupational structure, 44
Office of Technology Assessment,
   574
Office of War Information, 247
Old-Age, Survivors, Disability,
   and Health Insurance. *See*
   Social Security
Oligarchy, 50–51
Oligopoly, 41, 57, 156
One-parent families. *See* Single-
   parent families
Opiates. *See* Narcotics
Opium. *See* Narcotics
Ozone depletion, 492

P
Palimony, 99
Parenting leave, 109, 111
Participant observation, 136–137
Patriarchy, 84
PCP (Angel Dust), 373–374

Pensions, 300–301, 306–307
People for the Ethical Treatment
   of Animals (PETA), 5
Persian Gulf War, 260, 514–515,
   530
Pesticides, as pollutants, 492–493
Phencyclidine. *See* PCP
Physicians' assistants, 157
Placebo effect, 145
Plea bargaining, 337
Plessy v. Ferguson, 212
Pluralism, 224–226, 232–233
Pluralistic family, 107
Pluralist model, 54–55
Police, 227, 233–235, 344
Political discontent, 527–528
Political economy of drug use,
   378–379
Politics, 36–37
   women in, 263, 271–272
Pollution. *See* Environmental
   problems
Polygamy, 92
Poor
   characteristics of, 173–178
   circumstances of, 178–180
   deserving versus undeserving,
   192–193
   housing and, 180
   unemployment and, 179,
   186–189
Population, 434
   doubling time, 440–441
   economic development and,
   462
   environmental problems and,
   476
   growth, 433–441
   perspectives on, 444–446
   problems of, 446–451
   solution to problems of,
   457–463
Pornography, 415–416
   aggression and, 418, 422–425
   children and, 292
   censorship and, 416–418
   social policy and, 396, 419, 421
   violence and, 418–424
Postindustrial city, 443–444

Postindustrial society, 549
Poverty, 166–169, 172
   causes of, 181–188
   children and, 100, 174–176,
   287–290
   crime and, 341–342, 413, 447
   disabled and, 178
   drugs and, 377–378, 387
   the economy and, 182,
   186–189
   elderly and, 175, 293–296
   extent of, 169–172
   functions of, 182–184
   health and, 130–132
   international perspectives on,
   171–172, 185, 196
   minorities and, 173–176, 213,
   216, 218, 222, 454
   perspectives on, 181–188
   programs to combat, 188–197
   prostitution and, 411, 413
   single-parent families and,
   174–175
   women and, 175–176
Power, 8
   abuse of, 37–38, 106
   concentration of, 40–46, 57–66,
   571
   models of, 46–57
Power elite, 51–55
Power sharing, 232–233
Preindustrial society, 438–439
Prejudice, 207
   against the elderly, 283, 305
   Merton's types of, 207–208
   programs to combat, 226–227,
   229–234
   sources of, 208–211
Premarital sex, 398–399
Preschool programs, 109
Preventive detention, 336–337
Preventive medicine, 128–129,
   141
Primary deviance, 134, 322–323
Primary prevention of drug
   abuse, 384–385
Prisons, 337–341, 345
Privacy, 563–566, 569–572
Privacy Act, 569

Sexual variation, 396–400, 425–427
Shay's Rebellion, 513
Sick role, 121–123
Sierra Club, 12, 68, 481
Singlehood, 88, 98
Single-parent families, 95,
    99–101, 194–196, 288–289
Slavery, 209, 212, 223
Social class, 184, 332
Social control theory, 319
Social disorganization, 47, 84,
    121, 445, 480, 526
Social inequality, crime and,
    319–320, 341–342
Social institutions, 7
Social insurance, 191
Socialism, 39
Social isolation, 296–297, 305
Socialization
    as cause of racial
        discrimination, 209–210
    crime and, 322–323
    in the family, 81, 85
    gender and, 247, 249–253, 255,
        398
    violence and, 525
Social learning theory, 376, 388
Social mobility, 184–185
Social movement, 23–24
Social policy, 22–27, 110–112,
    169, 171, 564–565
Social problems, 4–6
    international perspectives on,
        27–29
    measuring, 20–22
    role of values in solving, 22–27
Social reform, 341–342, 389, 532
Social Security, 191, 192, 295,
    296, 301–303, 306–307, 464
Social Security Administration,
    168
Social stratification, 166, 181–182,
    184–185, 205, 211, 246–247
Sociobiology, 519–520
Socioeconomic status, 253
    alcoholism and, 361
    crime and, 332
    divorce and, 93
    family and, 105

health and, 129–132
    violence and, 105
Sociological imagination, 8–9
Sociology, 4–9, 434, 547
    applied, 23–25
    common sense and, 18–19
Solar energy, 572
South Africa, 204–205
Soviet Union, 535–539
Speed. See Amphetamines
Split labor market, 208–209, 212,
    247
Spouse abuse, 24–25, 101, 103,
    108
    alcohol and, 358
Spurious relationship, 21
Star Wars. See Strategic Defense
    Initiative
Status offenders, 327
Status politics, 265
Stereotypes, 210, 251–253, 454
    of the elderly, 305
    male, 252–253, 262
Stigma, 123–125
Stimulants, 367–370
Strategic Arms Limitation Talks
    (SALT), 535
Strategic Arms Reduction Treaty
    (START), 536
Strategic Defense Initiative (Star
    Wars), 538–539, 558–559
Structural unemployment, 182
Students Against Drunk Driving
    (SADD), 388
Subcultures, 7–8
    delinquent, 411
    drugs and, 380
    gay, 406–407, 411
    of violence, 525, 527
Subjugation, 224
Suburbs, 441–443, 454–455
Suicide, 290
Supplementary Security Income,
    192
Supported living environments,
    305–308
Sweden
    elderly in, 306–307
    health care in, 155

Switzerland, 232–233, 306–307
Symbolic racism, 227–228
Symbols, 13–14, 248
Syndicates, 325–326

T

Technology, 548–549
    appropriate, 572–573
    assessment of, 573–574
    attitudes toward, 559–560,
        564–565
    autonomous, 562–563
    cities and, 442–444
    environment and, 477
    future of, 568–575
    health and, 148–150,
        438–439
    impact on society, 550–557
    loss of control and, 561–562
    perspectives on, 557–559
    privacy and, 563–566
    problems with, 182, 559–568
Teenagers, pregnancy and, 100,
    110–111, 174–175. See also
    Adolescence
Telecommunications, 551–556
Television. See Media
Territorial imperative, 519
Terrorism. See Violence
Theoretical perspectives, 9–15. See
    also Functionalist perspective;
    Conflict perspective;
    Interactionist perspective
Theory, 9
Therapeutic communities,
    385–388
Third-party medicine, 140–141,
    145, 151–152
Tolerance. See Drugs
Toxic wastes, 487–489
Tranquilizers, 371
Treaty of Guadalupe Hidalgo, 216

U

Underclass, 186–187, 228–229,
    343, 455
Unemployment, 60–64, 179, 182